EDP: CONTROLS AND AUDITING

EDP: CONTROLS AND AUDITING

Fourth Edition

W. THOMAS PORTER
Touche Ross & Co.

WILLIAM E. PERRY
William E. Perry Enterprises, Inc.

 Kent Publishing Company

A Division of Wadsworth, Inc., Boston, Massachusetts

Senior Editor: John B. McHugh
Production Editor: Marianne L'Abbate
Interior and Cover Designer: Carol Rose
Production Coordinator: Linda Siegrist
Cover Photo: Edith G. Haun/Stock, Boston

Kent Publishing Company
A Division of Wadsworth, Inc.

Printed in the United States of America

3   4   5   6   7   8   9   —   88   87   86

Library of Congress Cataloging in Publication Data

Porter, W. Thomas.
  EDP: controls and auditing.

  Bibliography: p.
  Includes index.
  1. Electronic data processing departments—Auditing.
I. Perry, William E.   II. Title.   III. Title: EDP:
controls and auditing.
HF5548.35.P67   1984   657′.45′02854   83–25540
ISBN 0–534–03062–9

PREFACE

We have incorporated material to make the audit process described in the fourth edition of this book consistent with that recommended by the American Institute of Certified Public Accountants. We added a chapter on audit and control of computer crime (Chapter 14); expanded the material on controls; incorporated the concept of risk in Chapter 4, and then expanded and explained the relationship of the auditor and risk; and added a chapter giving the CPA examination questions on EDP auditing for the past several years. In addition, end-of-chapter problems and cases were added and revised as deemed appropriate.

Chapter 1 is an examination of the auditing function and the impact of EDP on the auditor's role. In Chapter 2, we discuss information systems design to provide perspective to auditors in designing and evaluating computerized controls. We describe flowcharting conventions and techniques for audit purposes in Chapter 3.

Standards recently introduced by the American Institute of Certified Public Accountants, the greater reliance on computer systems, and the Foreign Corrupt Practices Act have significantly emphasized the importance of controls in organizations. We introduce this concept in Chapter 4 with a discussion on risks in a computerized business environment. The chapter explains the relationship between risk and control, and the means by which control can reduce risk. Chapter 5 expands the concepts of control and relates it to an automated business environment. Chapter 6 deals with organizational controls, documentation, and operating practices. In Chapter 7 we discuss how application controls are designed, and in Chapter 8 we discuss processing controls as they relate to input, computer updating, and output phases of processing applications.

While the entire book is directed toward the evaluation of controls and data in an automated application, the EDP audit process is described in detail in Chapter 9. The evaluation of internal control in EDP systems—with a review of organizational aspects and operating practices, and a detailed review of accounting applications in EDP systems—is described. The testing of EDP systems, both with and without the use of the computer, is also discussed. In Chapter 10 we examine the development and use of computer audit programs for performing auditing tasks, with the inclusion of the use of audit software packages. The case studies presented in Chapters 9, 10, and 15 support the theoretical framework of the book and guide the practitioner in the methods of using the computer in auditing.

In Chapter 11, we discuss the problems and peculiarities of auditing client records that are produced by outside service centers. The audit approach is discussed to evaluate both the service center processing systems and the accounting files. Chapter 12 is a discussion of the control requirements and problems confronting the auditor who is involved in auditing applications using on-line data base systems. In Chapter 13, we talk about the advanced audit techniques for EDP applications and when these techniques should be utilized.

Chapter 14 is designed to address the new and increasing problem of computer crime, and to help the auditor understand the techniques being used to defraud and abuse computer systems. How to counter those strategies with computer crime audit techniques is presented. Chapter 16 presents new questions on EDP auditing from the CPA exam. Previous chapters have included some of the older CPA questions. With the increasing emphasis on EDP auditing, however, this chapter will help the CPA candidate prepare for EDP auditing related topics. The appendixes include a documentation standards manual, an EDP control questionnaire used to evaluate EDP systems, a case study used to test data in testing batch EDP systems, a list of audit software packages, a case study on the use of test data in on-line systems, a glossary, and a bibliography.

Although this book is written primarily from the viewpoint of the auditor, much of the material is equally valid for use by data processing people. Systems designers will likely be interested in the chapters on controls and on the use of the computer in auditing, which will enable them to acquire an understanding and appreciation of the auditor's role in evaluating EDP systems. This book is designed primarily for persons who have a basic knowledge of electronic data processing and auditing concepts and techniques.

Most of the case studies that are presented have been used in colleges and universities throughout the country—many of them have been used in continuing education programs for audit and data processing professionals conducted by the authors over the past twenty years. All case studies have been selected for their interest and educational value. They can be used as foundations for class discussion rather than as illustrations of either correct or incorrect handling of audit problems—there are no right answers! The educational value of these studies is derived from the practice that the student or practitioner receives in analyzing audit problems in EDP situations.

The authors would like to extend appreciation to the following reviewers for their helpful evaluations and suggestions: Stephen D. Harlan, Jr., Peat, Marwick, Mitchell & Co.; Robert Dickens, Duke University; John Myers, Indiana University; Donald R. Wood, William C. Mair, and Kent Yarnall, all of Touche Ross & Co. Much of the material that has been added to the fourth edition has been developed by or under the auspices of federal agencies, particularly the National Bureau of Standards. The authors are appreciative of the excellent work fostered by the National Bureau of Standards, and are pleased to incorporate that work in this edition.

W. Thomas Porter
William E. Perry

CONTENTS

Chapter 3   Defining and Flowcharting Systems   51

Chapter 4   Risks in a Computerized Business Environment   97

Chapter 5 Controls in an EDP Environment 125

Chapter 6 General Controls 149

Chapter 7   Application Control Design   201

Chapter 8   Application Control Review   227

Chapter 9   EDP Audit Process   273

Chapter 10   Evaluation of Records Produced by EDP Systems   331

Chapter 11   Auditing Records Produced by Service Centers   359

EDP: CONTROLS AND AUDITING

EDP AUDIT PROCESS*

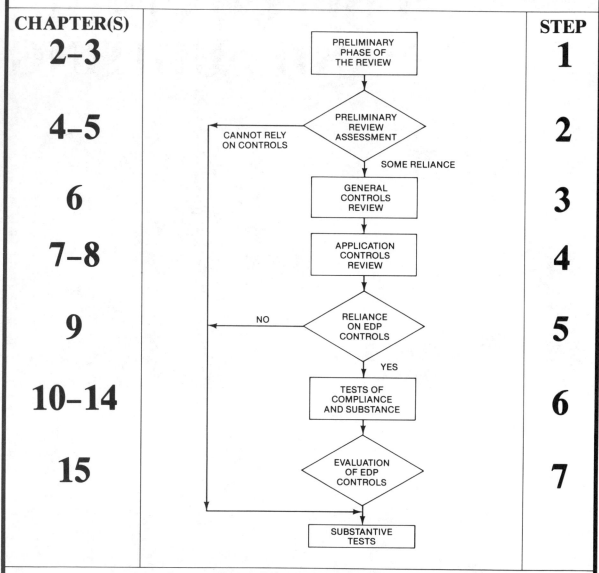

CHAPTER(S)

2–3

4–5

6

7–8

9

10–14

15

STEP

1

2

3

4

5

6

7

PRELIMINARY
PHASE OF
THE REVIEW

PRELIMINARY
REVIEW
ASSESSMENT

CANNOT RELY
ON CONTROLS

SOME RELIANCE

GENERAL
CONTROLS
REVIEW

APPLICATION
CONTROLS
REVIEW

RELIANCE
ON EDP
CONTROLS

NO

YES

TESTS OF
COMPLIANCE
AND SUBSTANCE

EVALUATION
OF EDP
CONTROLS

SUBSTANTIVE
TESTS

* Diagram is adapted from The Auditor's Study and Evaluation of Internal Control in EDP
Systems, *pages 21–24. Copyright © 1977 by the American Institute of Certified Public Accountants,
Inc. (See Figure 9.1 for a full explanation of the steps.)*

EDP ATTRIBUTES AND AUDITING

Electronic data processing (EDP) represents one of the major technological advances in business in the last fifteen to twenty years. EDP systems can handle a large number of varied tasks, from processing a simple payroll to simulating the effect of alternative decisions on all operations of a business. Top management, formerly conservative in the use of EDP, has begun to realize the tremendous potential of the computer in promoting operational efficiency and effective decision making. Currently, EDP is being boldly applied to management control and strategic planning functions.

In addition, computers are making an increasing impact on consumers and households. Electronic Funds Transfer Systems (EFTS) are enabling people to do their banking and pay their bills in grocery stores, parking lots, and by telephones in their homes. Instantaneously, checks can be cashed, bill and loan payments made, and deposits or withdrawals completed. We truly are beginning to enter into what some have called the cashless society.

The Computerized Business Environment

The computer has been labeled the dominant advance of the twentieth century. Fully utilized, the computer can dramatically change the way an organization conducts business. For example, the commercial airline industry completely revamped its reservation procedures. Banks have installed computers at teller work stations and use computer-directed automatic cash-dispensing terminals.

Department stores replenish their stock on the basis of sales recorded on point-of-sale cash registers.

The impact of the computer on a business organization varies, depending on how that computer is used. In some organizations the impact is minimal. In other organizations business transaction processing stops when the computer goes down.

Successful business operations have learned to minimize the impact of business risks. Each new venture a business undertakes has associated with it new or increased risks. The organization must identify and control those risks.

When a computer is introduced into a business organization, new or increased risks are also introduced. For example, in a computer processing environment the same error may be reproduced thousands of times in one day because of the consistency and speed of computer processing. Thus, one of the new risks introduced by a computer is that of repetition of errors.

Because of these new and increased risks, new methods of audit and control must be introduced. The objectives of control do not change when a computer is introduced, but the methods must. For example, the control objective of processing accurate data is the same in both a manual and a computerized environment. However, in a computerized environment controls must be installed to reduce the risk of the repetition of error in order to ensure that the data produced are accurate. These changes in control and processing methods result in new methods of audit. Auditors use special software designed for their use in conducting audits of computerized applications. This is software needed to extract data from computer files.

The auditor must learn new skills to work effectively in a computerized business environment. These new skills are in three broad areas: first, an understanding of computer concepts and systems design; second, an ability to identify the new and increased risks and know what controls are effective in lessening those risks; and third, a knowledge of how to use the computer to audit the computer. These are the new skills needed to review computer technology.

Impetus for New Audit Methods

Auditors often ignored the computer during the 1960s, auditing around the computer. Auditors found there was normally sufficient evidence to audit effectively without direct involvement in assessing the controls within the computer systems. Most organizations had redundant controls external to the computer application that provided auditors with sufficient assurance that the systems were functioning correctly.

As computer systems became more integrated and complex, the amount and frequency of noncomputer evidence decreased. Auditors found an increasing need to extract data from computer applications. Unable to get at computer data with existing audit methods, they needed new methods. The major public accounting firms developed software for auditors to fulfill this need. This software permitted auditors to obtain computer data independently of the data processing personnel.

Some of the earliest efforts in computer control and audit came from the Canadian Institute of Chartered Accountants. In 1970 they published a manual outlining the types of controls needed in a computerized business environment. This Computer Control Guidelines manual was followed in 1975 by a companion Computer Audit Guidelines manual. The audit manual explained how to assess the adequacy of computer controls.

The American Institute of Certified Public Accountants issued an auditing standard in 1974 requiring CPAs to evaluate computers during their audit. This Statement on Auditing Standard No. 3 stated:[1]

> Section 320.33 of SAS No. 1 discusses methods of data processing as follows: Since the definition and related basic concepts of accounting control are expressed in terms of objectives, they are independent of the method of data processing used; consequently, they apply equally to manual, mechanical, and electronic data processing systems. However, the organization and procedures required to accomplish those objectives may be influenced by the method of data processing used.
>
> Because the method of data processing used may influence the organization and procedures employed by an entity to accomplish the objectives of accounting control, it may also influence the procedures employed by an auditor in his study and evaluation of accounting control to determine the nature, timing, and extent of audit procedures to be applied in his examination of financial statements.
>
> A data processing system may be wholly manual or may include a combination of manual activities, mechanical activities, and electronic data processing (EDP) activities. EDP applications vary considerably, from routine applications that process a small payroll to complex, integrated applications that process accounting, production, marketing, and administrative information simultaneously. In some data processing systems, accounting control procedures are performed by people in one or more departments. In EDP systems, many or even most of these control procedures may be performed by the EDP process itself. When EDP is used in significant accounting applications, the auditor should consider the EDP activity in his study and evaluation of accounting control. This is true whether the use of EDP in accounting applications is limited or extensive and whether the EDP facilities are operated under the direction of the author's client or third party.
>
> The first general auditing standard is as follows: "The examination is to be performed by a person or persons having adequate technical training and proficiency as an auditor." If a client uses EDP in its accounting system, whether the application is simple or complex, the auditor needs to understand the entire system sufficiently to enable him to identify and evaluate its essential accounting control features. Situa-

[1] SAS No. 3, pages 1–2. Copyright © 1974 by the American Institute of Certified Public Accountants, Inc. 1211 Avenue of the Americas, New York, N.Y. 10036.

tions involving the more complex EDP applications ordinarily will require that the auditor apply specialized expertise in EDP in the performance of the necessary audit procedures.

The Institute of Internal Auditors launched a major study on control and audit in a computerized business environment. This $500,000 study funded by the International Business Machine Corporation concluded that organizations had spent too little effort on control. This widely circulated report recommended that the most fruitful use of audit time in a computerized environment is involvement in systems under development.

In 1972, the United States Government Accounting Office (GAO) issued the pamphlet "Standards for Audit of Governmental Organizations, Programs, Activities & Functions" (the Yellow Book). This publication discussed how the role of the auditor has changed to meet an increasing demand for information in a far more complex society that expects more services from governmental units at all levels. Providing such information in an economic, efficient, and effective manner has been facilitated by the emergence of the electronic digital computer—though it is certainly true that mastering the use of this computer has initially complicated the auditor's job.

With the computer becoming more complex through the development of sophisticated multiprogramming capacity, coupled with telecommunication links and a wide variety of new input and output devices, another dimension has been added to the role of the auditor. In order for him or her to fulfill professional responsibilities, the auditor must now be able to perform a wide variety of tasks which, until recently, did not exist or were not considered within the auditor's scope.

For example, when manual systems were audited, a wide variety of approaches were generally available and the most appropriate would be selected for the given circumstances. If there were control weaknesses, corrective changes were easily formulated and suggested. However, it is now possible to produce a data processing system with such poor controls that neither the auditor nor the manager can rely on the system's integrity. For this reason, audit review during the design and development process of an automated system has become crucial if management is to be provided needed assurance that auditable and properly controlled systems are being produced.

Moreover, once systems are placed in operation, the auditor must continue to review both general controls and application controls. Such reviews are to ensure that systems support management policy and produce reliable results. For a system already in operation when an audit is scheduled, the auditor needs to determine whether the system's objectives are being met.

For these reasons, the GAO mandated in the 1981 revision of their audit standards that auditors participate in systems development. This influential arm of the legislative branch of government stated in their standards, in the list on the next page, that the auditors shall

- Review general controls in data processing systems to determine whether (a) the controls have been designed according to management direction and known legal requirements and (b) the controls are operating effectively to provide reliability of, and security over, the data being processed

- Review application controls of installed data processing applications upon which the auditor is relying to assess their reliability in processing data in a timely, accurate, and complete manner.

In addition to reviewing general and application controls, the auditor should, as we have mentioned, have a role in the design and development of new data processing systems or applications and significant modifications thereto. Compliance with this objective may not always be feasible because audit organizations may not have the resources or staff skills to review the design and development of these systems. However, such review should be an auditing goal.

The transition from mechanical data processing to automatic data processing produces the need to revise traditional audit approaches. The complexity and scope of such systems requires that the auditor give greater attention both to the system that processes data and the actual data. If the system is reasonably secure and adequately controlled, the auditor can rely on the data processed and reported.

In 1977, Congress passed the Foreign Corrupt Practices Act. Appended to this act is a requirement that corporations covered under the Securities and Exchange Act of 1934 must maintain adequate systems of internal accounting control. This has caused many organizations to conduct in-depth studies regarding the adequacy of controls in their computerized applications (see Chapter 5 for a discussion of this statute).

It is only natural to expect that with increased dependence on the computer, there will be more regulations and procedures governing the use of the computer. The United States Controller of the Currency believed that there were enough differences in control and audit in computerized banking applications that the controller has issued several procedures dealing specifically with the computer. In addition, the late Senator Ribicoff introduced legislation into Congress dealing with computer crime. This, coupled with the many privacy laws that apply to computer systems, continues to accelerate the need for new methods for assessing the adequacy of controls in computerized applications.

Auditing and Auditors

Broadly speaking, *auditing* is undertaken to increase the reliability of information where reliability may be defined as congruence between the messages transmitted and the realities being described. Auditing may take place beneficially whenever a review of information by a party other than the preparer increases the probability that the information accurately reflects what it purports to reflect. Although this objective relates auditing to information, it by no means limits its scope to financial information or even more restrictively to financial statements. In some cases it is conceivable that perhaps the information to be audited may be not an explicit statement, but an implicit representation by a management, such that controls are adequate.

Given the objective of increasing the reliability of information, the following definition of auditing is suggested:

> Auditing is the examination of information by a third party other than the preparer or the user with the intent of establishing its reliability and the reporting of the results of this examination with the expectation of increasing the usefulness of the information to the user.[2]

Within the framework of this definition, many types of information may be audited by different types of auditors. For example, *external* auditors, or CPAs, are usually involved in rendering opinions on financial statements of business enterprises. More recently they have also been requested by management, regulatory agencies, and creditors to furnish reports on the evaluation of internal control and to assist management in the development of current-value information to show the effects of inflation on historical-cost-based financial statements. Possibly, in the future, they may be asked to render opinions on forecasts included in published annual reports.

Internal auditors typically are involved in independently appraising accounting, financial, and operating activities within an organization as a basis for serving management. Such an activity is looked upon as a managerial control function and involves the measurement and evaluation of the effectiveness of controls in the organization.

Auditors in the state and federal *government* are involved in a variety of audit examinations including income tax examinations, the evaluation of the use of governmental funds by governmental agencies and organizations contracted by the government, and the evaluation of the effectiveness of management in governmental agencies in discharging their agency responsibilities.

No matter what the objectives of the various auditors might be, the analysis of systems and data processing activities used to generate accounting, financial, and operating information is required. In many organizations that are audited, the accounting and financial systems have been computerized. The major *objective* of this book, then, is to examine the auditing process in computerized environments and to show how EDP equipment provides a powerful tool to the auditor for making his or her auditing procedures more effective and for providing increased service to clients.

The determination of whether or not to have an internal audit staff is a top

---

[2] *W. Thomas Porter, Jr., and John C. Burton,* Auditing: A Conceptual Approach, *p. 5, Wadsworth, Belmont, Calif., 1971.*

management decision. However, more and more large organizations have an internal audit staff. Internal auditors normally report to a member of organizational management. A few internal audit departments, especially in the banking and insurance industries, report directly to the audit committee of the board of directors. In many other organizations, internal auditors have a dual reporting responsibility: the audit committee of the board and the finance director.

External and internal auditors normally work together to achieve overall audit objectives. In 1975 the American Institute of CPAs approved Statement on Auditing Standard No. 9, which recognized that CPAs rely on the work of internal auditors in the performance of their work. However, because of the wide range of activities conducted by internal auditors, CPAs make a determination of reliance on internal auditors client by client.

Internal auditors are normally heavily involved in the audit of operations, while external auditors devote more time to the financial statements. While both must evaluate the impact of the computer, the internal auditor normally gets more involved in the internal operation of the computer application than does the public accountant. This is emphasized by the GAO standard requiring governmental internal auditors to become involved in the system development process.

A recent study by The Institute of Internal Auditors showed that approximately one-fourth of their membership are CPAs. Thus, a large number of CPAs are establishing a career path within internal audit.

Internal auditors continue to upgrade their work through professional associations. The Institute of Internal Auditors has a Certified Internal Auditor program (CIA designation), the Bank Administration Institute has a certification program for bank auditors (CBA designation), and the EDP Auditors Association has a certification for EDP auditors (CISA designation).

Impact of EDP on Auditing and Control

Auditors should be concerned about computerized systems because these systems have a major impact on the ways by which an organization conducts its business. Computerized systems are not merely new means to process paper work. Frequently, the system of internal controls must be restructured because of the characteristics of a computer system. This has resulted in a series of control gaps, causing new risk exposures for organizations using computers. Three major concerns for the auditor are

1. Changes that occur in the environment of the auditor and in the data processing systems when a computer is used.

2. Opportunities that the computer affords for performing auditing tasks more effectively and efficiently.

3. Increased possibilities for theft, extortion, and espionage—crime by computer—as a result of a computerized environment.[3]

Environmental Changes

When a computer is used to process accounting and financial data, the auditor needs to *understand* the concepts and terminology of data processing and control in order to *communicate* with EDP personnel about computerized activities and systems. The auditor has her or his own audit language and specialized set of terms. Typically, she or he interacts with financial management and accounting technicians who understand auditing language and terminology. In an EDP system, the auditor must interact with EDP management and computer technicians who have their own set of terms. The need to understand EDP concepts is fundamental to the proper review and evaluation of computerized processing and the use of computers in auditing.

Another change in the auditor's environment is the *complexity* of computerized systems. Technical developments in both the "hardware" and "software" of EDP systems have increased the operating performance and decreased the operating costs of computer-based systems. As a result, more and more organizations have successfully automated basic administrative and accounting functions such as payroll, accounts receivable, and accounts payable. They have adopted more complex management control systems such as forecasting, profit planning, and production scheduling and are contemplating the development of sophisticated models to plan and control overall activities more effectively.

The auditor's environment is also changed by the fact that computers are being used increasingly by all types of organizations, large and small. The advent of time-sharing systems and service centers has made the use of computers economically and technically feasible for very small companies.

Change in the auditor's environment is also brought about by automation, namely, its effect on *organization structure* and responsibilities and particularly on the functions concerned with data processing. Electronic data processing enables many processing steps to be concentrated into one department, thus eliminating the traditional internal control made available by the separation of duties in the recording process. In electronic systems, concentration also has another meaning: the collection in one place of traditional accounting data along with operating data. There is an unmistakable trend toward combining all logically related elements of data processing into a single integrated system, or *data base*. Consider the many different steps involved in the typical processing of a customer's order: credit analysis, production scheduling, inventory control, billing, sales analysis, accounts receivable, and perhaps commission

---

[3] *See Donn Parker,* Crime by Computer. *Scribner's, New York, 1976 and also W. Thomas Porter, "Computer Raped by Telephone . . . and Other Futuristic Felonies,"* The New York Times Magazine, *September 8, 1974.*

payroll. In manual and punched-card systems, the processing of a customer's order is accomplished through a series of separate and distinct steps, each carried out by different individuals who frequently are located in different departments. By use of electronic equipment, most of these functions can be concentrated in one department, the data processing center.

Processing Changes   In an EDP system, major changes occur in the processing of accounting and financial transactions. Computerized applications have resulted in changes in the *audit trail,* which consists of the documents, journals, ledgers, and work sheets that enable an auditor to trace an original transaction forward to a summarized total or a summarized total backward to an original transaction. The use of computers has brought about several changes in the audit trail. First, developments in data collection equipment, communication facilities, and random-access memories enable companies to eliminate or reduce source documents ordinarily used in manual or mechanized systems.

Second, more data are maintained in *machine-readable files* such as magnetic tapes or disks, which eliminate or reduce the need for certain historical records and registers. In non-EDP systems, the auditor becomes accustomed to ledger records with accumulated historical data and detailed journals; in these systems, such records and journals are important for operations. In an EDP system, however, there are several significant variations from the traditional records normally accessible to the auditor. The records maintained on magnetic tape and magnetic disk (machine-readable) files require special arrangements to access them; that is, they are not readable in their natural state. The journal is not a part of the mainstream of processing, nor is it a natural byproduct. It takes a specific action at a recognizable cost to create such transaction registers. Also, the journal diminishes in importance if significant items for reporting are produced on an exception basis, as they may be in an EDP system. Also, in EDP systems it is relatively inefficient to carry much previous activity in current files. In *random-access files,* previous status is usually displaced by new data; in *sequential files,* intermediate processing results are not usually retained.

Another processing change brought about by the computer is the inclusion of significant processing controls in the computer programs themselves, thereby shifting the review (editing) of the transactions processed from people to the computer. Edit routines include *program checks* to determine the validity and completeness of input transactions and the reasonableness of these transactions as they flow through the system.

Finally, processing is changed by the *integration* of accounting data with operational data in the machine-readable files of a company. For example, normally an automated inventory file will include not only data on quantity available, unit cost, and unit price (accounting data), but also operating data such as forecasted demand for the item of inventory, economic order quantity, reorder point, and vendor data used in inventory replenishment decisions. Systems designers might integrate data in perpetual accounting records with data found in accounts payable files and purchasing records. Obviously, such an integration is designed to remove the redundancy of data in corporate files and minimize the number of files necessary to store and produce data required by the multiplicity of users of the corporate information system. Integrated systems, or data bases, have been made possible by the development of data collection equipment, communication facilities, random-action storage devices, advanced software techniques, and time-sharing hardware.

The Increase of Computerized Crime

Because computers are taking over the processing in the environments where white-collar crimes have occurred in the past, it is not too surprising that over 400 computer crime cases have been reported. The $2 billion Equity Funding Corporation fraud is one of these cases. It started in 1964 on a manual basis, then adopted use of computers. By 1973, computers at Equity Funding were heavily involved in the creation and processing of over 64,000 phony insurance policies.

Interesting glimpses into some of the recorded cases during the seventies reveal these stories:

An engineering student was arrested on charges of stealing some $1 million worth of supplies from Pacific Telephone & Telegraph Co. over a 2-year period. The student combined his technical ability with a set of system instructions found in the company's trash cans to learn how to use the company's computerized ordering system. He used a speedy touch-tone telephone to place the orders with an authorized entry code he found in the discarded system manual. Using this code to get into the computerized system, he was able to vary his orders as to point of origin and point of delivery in order to stay just below the telephone company's sales loss allowance for each location—information also gleaned from the discarded manual. After only 40 days in jail, he went into the consulting business to advise clients on how to prevent computer rip-offs.

Encyclopedia Britannica accused three computer operators on the night shift of copying nearly 3 million names from a computer file containing the company's "most valued" customer list. The employees were accused of selling the list to a direct mail advertiser. Brittannica claimed the list was worth $3 million and sued the employees for $4 million.

An employee of a national time-sharing system penetrated the files of a competitor's system to extract a proprietary program valued at $25,000. This case caused worldwide publicity, including 3-in. headlines in the Paris *Herald Tribune:* "Computer Raped by Telephone." It was the first case in which a warrant was issued to search the memory of a computer for evidence. The programmer was convicted and given a suspended sentence for theft of a trade secret even though a witness in a related civil suit revealed that it was common for programmers in both of the companies involved to access the other's computer in an unauthorized manner.

The chief teller at the Union Dime Savings Bank in New York City was charged with stealing more than $1.5 million. Apparently the teller was able to transfer "electronic money" from legitimate accounts in computer files to fraudulent accounts and then withdraw real money. He also was able to "redeposit" the "electronic money" at quarterly interest payment times in order to briefly make all the account balances correct.

A clerk at Morgan Guaranty Trust Co. in New York was convicted of embezzling $33,000. The embezzlement was performed with the aid of an accomplice who received dividend checks sent to him by the bank's computer. The computer was instructed to issue dividend checks in the names of former shareholders who had sold their stock in companies for which Morgan Guaranty acted as transfer agent. After the issuance of the checks, the computer was instructed to erase all record of issuing the dividend checks.

In addition to the increasing number of computer crimes, increased losses per incident of abuse are also evident. A bank embezzlement study showed that monetary losses associated with computers were ten times greater than non-computerized bank embezzlement. Because of this vulnerability to computerized crime, control features must be instituted by management of organizations using computers.

Categories of Computers

The term *computer* has traditionally meant a machine that has the ability to process data stored in its memory. However, using this definition, we find there are millions of computers—because typewriters, television sets, and automobiles all have microprocessors that meet this general definition. Therefore, from an audit perspective we must know which pieces of equipment pose a concern to auditors. For example, a typewriter that can hold data in storage and move it within storage poses little challenge to the auditor. On the other hand, a computer that controls inventory is of major concern to the auditor.

Computers of concern to the auditor tend to fall into three general categories. It is best to look at these categories independently of the type of equipment involved. For example, a hand-held computer may or may not be of concern to the auditor. The real concern is the use of the computer and not the specific piece of hardware.

We can divide computers into the following three categories (see Figure 1.1):

1. Computers that process corporate requirements. These are computers whose systems deal with the interaction of two or more departments within an organization. This type of processing is normally performed by a large-scale mainframe computer or, as it is sometimes referred to, a *maxicomputer*. An example would be the IBM 3033. These are very large machines—in price (normally over $50,000), size, and speed.

2. Computers that process departmental requirements. These machines are normally dedicated to the work of a single department. Although they may be under the control of a single individual, they are normally processing the work of a single department, such as the credit department. This type of processing tends to be performed by what is called a *minicomputer*. An example would be an IBM System/32 or 34. Also in

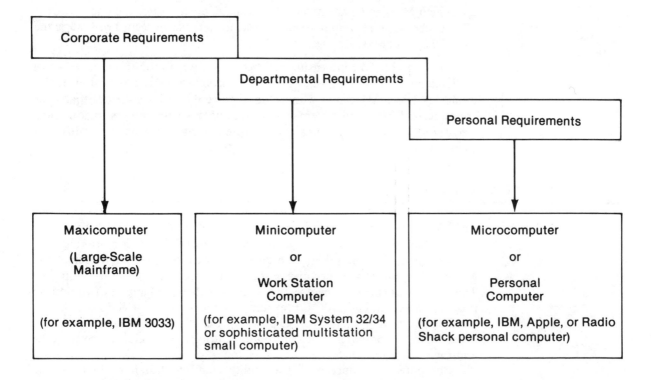

Figure 1.1 Categories of Computers

this category are sophisticated multistation small computers. These work stations replace many of the files and processes used by individuals.

3. Computers for personal requirements of an individual, the *microcomputer*. The computer in this instance is used as an extension of an individual's mind to help him or her perform tasks that were previously performed manually. Examples of computers of this type would be the Apple, Radio Shack, or the IBM personal computer. There is a tremendous growth of this type of computer. Many predict that the personal computer will be as common in business as the telephone.

Much of this book deals with the large-scale mainframe computers. This is because the majority of accounting systems are still processed on the large centralized computers. On the other hand, there is a rapid decentralization of processing, as the smaller computers become more prevalent. Note that most of the audit processes applicable to the large-scale mainframe are also applicable to the minicomputer. The major difference is that the larger computer installations permit a segregation of functions that is frequently not possible in the smaller computer. Thus, in the smaller installation the auditor may have to rely more on compensating controls, such as independently maintained control totals. Let us explore some of the attributes of the mini- and microcomputers.

Microcomputers Microcomputer is a term applied to a computer used by a single individual. It is also frequently called a *personal computer*. On the other hand, the power built into some of today's microcomputers exceeds the capacity of the large-scale mainframe computers of fifteen years ago. Generally, the user of the microcomputer does not write software for the machine.

Here are some types of uses that individuals make of personal computers:

- Financial record keeping and analysis—general ledger packages in a variety of analytical software packages for evaluating financial information are available. The best known is the VISICALC software. Many people believe that it is the financial software that has accounted for the rapid growth of the microcomputers.

- Word processing—the composition of letters, reports, lists, etc. is greatly facilitated on the microcomputer. Tasks that were complex manually become easy on the small computers.

- List processing—existing lists, addresses, telephone directories, etc. can be easily updated and accessed on the small computers.

- News and financial services—users of microcomputers can subscribe to an ever-growing list of news services. These provide such information as stock reports, technological news, general news, etc. These types of services can be expected to expand, enabling the microcomputer user to have access to huge amounts of information.

* Industry packages—many software systems are written for the small business person. For example, packages for dentists, motel managers, farmers, etc. are readily available to help with some of the specialized processing of that industry.

The microcomputers are growing larger, and the mainframe computers are getting cheaper at the lower end. Therefore, the distinction between the maxi, mini, and micro is disappearing. Industry experts believe that there will be two basic types of computers in the future: one will be the large central computer; and the other, the work station attached to that computer. Work stations will be the sophisticated microcomputers tied into networks or other computer capacity for assistance when needed. While there will still be room for the small independent computer, the auditor's concern will be concentrated more on the work station.

Minicomputers

Minicomputer is a term applied to a computer larger than a microcomputer but smaller than a large-scale mainframe computer. It is a relative term: it does not mean "little" because today's mini is bigger than the largest computer of twenty years ago. A minicomputer is normally found in a user's environment processing a limited number of applications. Many minis are obtained to process single applications. However, the capabilities of many minis are greater than those of the large computers of the early 1970s. The smaller minicomputers are frequently referred to as microcomputers.

The auditor's concern about the mini is that it may not be subject to the same controls as larger computers in the same organization. For example, one individual may have complete control over programming, operating, and controlling applications, which in a larger operation would be segregated among many people. Therefore, the auditor needs to view control differently, and use different audit procedures. For example, the auditor might do more substantive testing in a minicomputer environment.

In the next few subsections (up to the main heading on page 18, "Requirements and Opportunities for Auditors," we shall be looking at a description by Price Waterhouse & Co. of what the minicomputers are and how one must deal with them in auditing.

Major Characteristics of Minicomputer Installations.[4] A minicomputer installation may range from small, special purpose computers that process only one application through powerful systems comparable with larger systems. Rather than attempt to define a minicomputer, the important aspect, from the auditor's viewpoint, is the

---

[4] Accounting Controls in a Minicomputer Installation *(c) 1979. Price Waterhouse, New York, N.Y. Reprinted by permission.*

control environment. The control considerations discussed in this guide would be applicable to computer installations with the following characteristics:

- Staff and location of computer—usually operated by a small staff, often located within a user department, and the location normally lacks physical security

- Programs—many minicomputer installations use application systems supplied by manufacturers or software houses

- Processing mode—usually interactive data entry and/or on-line file updates where the majority of input is entered from an on-line terminal device and data may be edited, verified, and balanced on entry; the majority of input is entered by user department staff on terminal devices in user areas; and the majority of data files are accessible for inquiry and direct update

Control Problems to Consider in Minicomputer Installations. In the minicomputer installation just described, the most significant potential internal accounting control weakness is the lack of an adequate segregation of duties between those who initiate transactions, those who record these transactions and those responsible for the custody of the company's assets. This potential weakness may be compounded by the lack of controls in the operating systems and application programs which could help monitor systems usage, help assure data integrity and accuracy, and help protect data files. Simply turning on the system and using a terminal may place the complete records and systems of the company at one's fingertips with no record of systems usage. A knowledgeable user may be able to modify, delete or copy data or programs with readily accessible computer programs.

Although there are other potential internal accounting control weaknesses in the minicomputer installations, most are derived from this lack of segregation of duties and lack of computerized controls. The auditor should keep in mind, however, that the control objectives remain the same for any computer installation. In reviewing a minicomputer installation, the auditor should be alert to compensating controls within either the manual of computerized areas of the application that might offset apparent weaknesses. In addition, he should be conscious of the cost of any control recommended versus the benefit to be derived.

The various control objectives and techniques are discussed under the following headings:

- Organizational
- Operations and processing
- Systems development and modification
- Documentation

ORGANIZATIONAL CONTROLS. The main control objective of organizational controls is to limit the concentration of functions within the EDP department. In the larger installations this is accomplished by segregation of programming, operations and data control (control group) within the EDP department. This segregation is possible because of the number of people involved. Often with a minicomputer installation, the systems analysis, design and programming, maintenance of system software, and operations are concentrated in one or two persons. In addition, data is often entered directly by users from terminal devices located in the user department.

This environment is similar to the one-person bookkeeping department where control could be established by proper supervision and the separation of initiating transactions from the recordkeeping and the custody of assets. This is an important control sometimes overlooked in a minicomputer installation. A simple example might be a situation where checks are prepared by the minicomputer but users control unused checks and the signing of the checks. Such after-processing approval by an appropriate official is an effective control in many instances in a small installation.

The implementation of the controls discussed below will help offset the control weaknesses caused by the lack of segregation of duties.

OPERATION AND PROCESSING CONTROLS. The main objectives of operations and processing controls are:

- To ensure that only complete, accurate and authorized data is processed
- To prevent or detect accidental errors or fraudulent manipulation of data
- To ensure the adequacy of the management or audit trail
- To provide security against accidental destruction of records and to ensure continuous operations

CONTROLS OVER SYSTEMS DEVELOPMENT AND MODIFICATIONS. The objectives of these controls are to ensure that effective systems are developed and that systems and programs are properly maintained. The procedures should not vary greatly from those for larger computer installations. Standards should be defined for design, programming and testing procedures, and user approval should be required at all stages of development.

Two particular points to consider with minicomputer installations are purchased software and modifications to existing programs.

DOCUMENTATION. Documentation is important in all EDP installations but because of the relatively few employees involved in minicomputer installations, it becomes even more important. Consideration should be given to assigning responsibility to an officer outside the computer area for assuming that adequate documentation exists. The client may not be knowledgeable about data processing standards and documentation and may wish to consider calling on outside parties such as its auditors to review the standards periodically and ascertain that the documentation meets these standards.

Requirements and Opportunities for Auditors

Changes that occur in the environment of the auditor and in data processing systems as a result of using computers provide significant opportunities for the auditor. The concentration of data processing establishes the need for the auditor's evaluation of *organizational control* over the data processing department to make sure that there is a segregation of data processing functions to safeguard assets and to effectively utilize the resources, human and machine, allocated to the EDP activity.

Because of the complexity of EDP systems, *documentation and operating practices* need to be developed and standardized, which gives an opportunity for the auditor to determine if such standards exist and if they are used effectively. The attribute of computerized control in *processing* of accounting and financial data provides the auditor with an opportunity to evaluate the client's use of program controls and to determine the existence and effectiveness of such controls in the system. Because more data are in machine-readable files, the auditor has a great opportunity to use the computer in performing auditing tasks. The high speed of the computer allows the auditor to process or reprocess a complete file of transactions in less time than it would take to test a very small sample manually. Because of the *integration* of accounting and operational data in machine-readable files and integrated data bases, the auditor may be able to perform procedures that he or she may have wanted to perform in the past but would have found exceedingly lengthy or even impossible.

In summary, electronic data processing has made a significant impact on data processing. Many attributes of an EDP system affect the auditor and the work he or she performs. The changed audit trail and the computer's speed, accuracy, and edit abilities require the auditor to examine traditional auditing procedures and adopt procedures that are most efficient and effective for electronic systems. The concentration of processing in EDP systems and the complexity of such systems require the auditor to be familiar with the planning, programming, and necessary documentation of EDP activities. An understanding of electronic data processing and the types of controls in electronic systems is important for the auditor's evaluation of internal control and for the use of computers in auditing.

Summary

People are inconsistent. The one thing that the auditor can count on about people is that they may not perform the same task twice in the same manner. Industrial psychologists tell us that there are patterns to this inconsistency. For example, error rates seem to peak immediately before lunch and at the start of a holiday weekend.

Control and audit concepts are designed around this inconsistency. We attempt to control inconsistency in several ways: by segregation of functions, so that two people perform parts of a task and then compare results; by having one individual review the work of another; and by developing batch controls to ensure the integrity of the detailed records. Auditing takes samples of the work to measure the degree of consistency or inconsistency.

As systems become computerized, inconsistency changes to consistency. Right or wrong, computers will produce the same results, given the same set of circumstances, time and time again. The one thing you can depend on a computer to do is to be consistent. This is why it is possible for the computer to produce 10,000 bad payroll checks in an hour, or issue $50 million of duplicate welfare checks. Once instructed, the computer will do exactly what it is instructed to do.

Many of the old control and audit principles were built to deal with the fact that people are inconsistent and may be untrustworthy. The computer, being a machine and processing consistently, needs *new* control methods and new audit practices. The methods used in manual systems are generally not effective in automated systems.

Since the introduction of the computer in many organizations, sufficient hard-copy evidence has been produced by the computerized applications to permit auditing around the computer. But currently, much of that evidence is disappearing again. For example, if Richard Grove owed you $100 and he paid you by check, that check would provide evidence of the existence of the transaction. Should you take Grove to court for nonpayment, his presentation of the evidence—the check—would eliminate any questions regarding the outcome of the case. On the other hand, if Grove withdrew money from his account with a banking automatic teller machine, the only evidence of the occurrence of that transaction would be the recording on an electronic surface that someone inserted a card and pushed some buttons at a terminal. In a court case, the evidence Grove would exhibit would be a disk pack or reel of tape. It is much easier to challenge the legitimacy of a few bits arranged electronically on computer media than that of a signed, endorsed, and processed physical bank check.

Auditors attempting to apply many of the existing audit practices to computer systems will find they are not effective. For example, computer systems tend to make few mistakes; but when these errors occur they tend to be large. Given this type of processing environment, the auditor using sampling may never find the cause of the problem. The computer system may process the results correctly 364 days a year, and on the 365th day make a multimillion dollar error. So, the auditor would have concluded through sampling that there

Difference Between Financial and EDP Auditing

The characteristics of manual systems are inconsistency of the people doing the processing and a concern over the integrity of people. The characteristics of computer processing are consistency of processing and reliance on electronic evidence. Because of these characteristics, auditing of manual systems concentrates on the evaluation of the evidence produced by the system, while the computer audit must concentrate on the adequacy of controls because the electronic evidence is no better than the controls that protect it.

were no problems, while there was, in fact, a problem and it was in the system of internal controls.

Because of the changes in processing attributable to the computer (i.e., consistency of processing and greater reliance on electronic evidence), the emphasis in computer auditing shifts from a data audit to an audit of the system of internal controls. This means that the EDP auditor will spend a much larger percentage of the audit time in learning the system and evaluating the controls than would a financial auditor in the audit of a manual system. Financial auditing traditionally has concentrated on analysis of the evidence; EDP auditing concentrates much more on the evaluation of internal controls.

Problems

1. How has EDP affected the working environment of each of these auditors?
   (a) External auditor
   (b) Internal auditor
   (c) Government auditor

2. What role can an internal auditor play in the systems development efforts of a company?

3. Explain the ways by which improvements could be made in the working relationships between an internal audit department and an EDP department.

4. How has the potential for crime and embezzlement changed (increased or decreased) with the use of computers in organizations?

5. List the specific opportunities for increased service that each of the auditors listed below can provide for clients contemplating the use of or currently using the computer for accounting and financial processing:
   (a) External auditor
   (b) Internal auditor
   (c) Government auditor

6. Table 1.1 on page 22 is a record layout of the inventory record in a client's magnetic tape inventory file, updated periodically for inventory transactions. Describe
   (a) How the operating and accounting data have been integrated into the record and how each of the data fields in the record is used for accounting and operating purposes.
   (b) How an auditor could use the data in the records for auditing purposes.

7. On the subject of audit trails, explain
   (a) What is an audit trail?
   (b) Do audit-trail requirements for the auditor differ from those of management and, if so, how?
   (c) How have EDP systems changed the audit trail?

Table 1.1
Tape-Record Format

FIELD NUMBERS	DESCRIPTIONS	POSITIONS
1	Region code	1–2
2	Buyer	4
3	Stock number (first three numbers designate produce line)	5–16
4	Warehouse stored	17
5	EOQ (Economic Order Quantity)	22–24
6	MOP (Minimum Order Point)	25
7	Lead Time	26–27
8	Unit of issue (ea.)	28–29
9	Date (Julian)* of last issue	30–33
10	Quantity on order	39–43
11	Back order	44–48
12	Unit cost (xxx.xx)	50–55
13	Date order due in	55–60
14	On hand quantity	62–67
15	Unit selling price (xxx.xx)	68–72
16	Contingency (buffer stock)	72–73
17	Demand forecast	74–79

*Under the Julian dating system, January 1 is day number 001; February 1 is day number 032, and so on.

8. For the following material, comment on (a) its validity and (b) implications for auditors.

EDP systems can be characterized best from a control standpoint as system control in contrast to individual control. In manual processing of accounting information, each individual involved in the processing flow exercises a certain amount of control as documents pass through the various stages of the accounting process. Some people exercise control by reviewing source documents for invalid transaction codes, unreasonable amounts, arithmetic errors, and other improper data. Others compare totals of individual items to independently derived control totals.

In manual systems, then, internal control is largely achieved by individual review and crosscheck. In an EDP system, however, control is system oriented rather than people oriented because transactions are either entered into the processing flow in machine-readable form or converted to machine-readable form early in the processing system. The transactions are then processed without human intervention under the control of computer progams. These programs, internally stored in computer memory, constitute the systems; and much of the control is embodied in them in the form of programmed checks.

Such a transfer of activities that were previously performed by many people to one "person" is not a surrender of internal control. In fact, the kind of control attributed to separation and specialization of clerical functions is strengthened in electronic systems because of the computer's uniformity in the execution of policies and procedures and the difficulty of making changes in the detailed and complex program instructions.

9. The microcomputer (i.e., personal computer) is being purchased in large quantities by businesses. What is the major use of the personal computer in business?

10. An individual is performing an analysis of the financial statements using VISICALC. What type of computer should the individual use and why?

11. What is the major difference between financial and EDP auditing?

EDP AUDIT PROCESS*

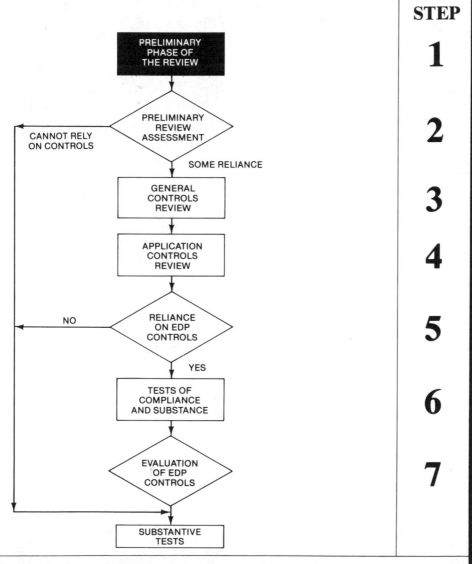

STEP

1

2

3

4

5

6

7

* *Diagram is adapted from* The Auditor's Study and Evaluation of Internal Control in EDP Systems, *pages 21–24. Copyright © 1977 by the American Institute of Certified Public Accountants, Inc. (See Figure 9.1 for a full explanation of the steps.)*

OBTAINING AND USING INFORMATION

(1) Preliminary Phase of the Review

Purpose: To yield an understanding of the accounting system, including both EDP and non-EDP segments:

- Flow of transactions and significance of output.
- Extent to which EDP is used in significant accounting applications.
- Basic structure of accounting control, including both EDP and user controls.

Methods: Inquiry and discussion; observation; review of documentation; tracing of transactions; control questionnaires and checklists.

OBJECTIVE

The preliminary review of an EDP audit involves understanding electronic evidence. This chapter discusses information in a computerized business environment.

Executives, administrators, systems analysts, accountants, production specialists, and others in every type of organization are asking, "What is the computer doing to help me do my job?" The answer hinges on how well information is managed as an organizational resource. The information cycle begins when management recognizes a need for information. It continues through the evaluation processes even though management's immediate need for information may have been satisfied.

Information is a costly resource that must be managed as other resources are managed such as cash, inventories, personnel, and facilities. The reason for this is that good information is *the essential* ingredient in decision making. In government and industry, the need for improved information systems has become critical because of the steady growth in the size and complexity of organizations and programs. The full impact of the computer and the influence it has on the organization is not obvious. However, that influence is substantial and becomes even more so as the use of computers increases.

Need for Information

In the second half of this twentieth century we have seen intensive task specialization; a growth in the number of employees, or clients serviced; increasing diversification of operational functions; a proliferation of organizational components; and geographical expansion in the scope of operations. Ideally, then, a contemporary organization may be characterized as a vast maze of interconnected and interdependent elements, all organized and operating to achieve a common objective or related objectives—whether this objective be to produce a product, defend the nation against attack, or serve the needs of the public.

As enterprises grow in size and complexity, and as they attempt to adapt to rapidly changing environments—missiles, competitors, or the population explosion—military commanders, business managers, and government administrators must receive, process, and use large volumes of information rapidly.

In their efforts to survive and adapt in a world of rapid and incessant change, many organizations are making greater use of the new *information technology* exemplified by, but not limited to, the electronic digital computer. Unfortunately, the use of a new dynamic technology to overcome crises generates its own unique problems. These problems include creating an efficient process for the development of systems employing the new technology and dealing with the effects of the new development process on management and operations.

Therefore, we are concerned about *information* as distinct from *data*. In this context a *datum is a fact in isolation* while *information is an aggregate of facts so organized or a datum so utilized as to communicate an idea or reveal a condition.* Thus, information is meaningful data, whereas data alone have no particular meaning or significance.

For our purposes, information is the result of relating random data to some specified purpose or objective. From this point of view, *data processing* is a set of activities that transforms data into information. This distinction between data and information should be stressed. We will focus attention upon the uses of data rather than upon the data processing tools per se. This is why we say that information is a costly resource that must be managed similarly to the way organizations manage cash, inventories, personnel, facilities, and other resources. Our concern is the efficient and effective management of that particular resource.

Information Management

Staff members generate the information needed to run any organization. The organization then owns the information and management has the responsibility to use that information for the success of the enterprise. The greater the success, the more the assets accumulate. And then more attention is given to making sure the assets are used in the best interests of the organization.

Information is an asset, and it accumulates. Also, if not properly managed, it has a proliferation factor of its own. Since the advent of the computer, the accumulation of information has accelerated, and companies race to know the most in order to be number one. Some organizations have been less successful than others because they did not give enough attention to information management.

Problems are created by people who do not know what information is needed or for how long. As a result, they want to retain all material as long as the organization is in operation. Government inquiries and rules have compounded the problem of information reserves. However, positive results can be achieved if careful attention is given to information as an asset. *Information management* is the term that refers to the proper use of an organization's information.

At the beginning of the information flow, from *generation* to *final disposition,* one must decide what should be documented (recorded) as evidence of operations and what should be received as communications from outside the organization. One needs to know these things: What information is needed? In what form? For how many people? And further along, there will be other questions: How long should the information be retained? How secured? Can it be readily retrieved? Finding answers to such questions may be challenge enough, but one still must not overlook the audit, legal, and tax requirements. And, before final disposition of information, there's the historical aspect for future generations. Altogether, these are the reasons for an organization to record or document information about its life. However, many organizations seem to concentrate on the financial facts of operating for a profit without realizing that insufficient attention to information management may be inhibiting the growth of their operations.

Let us look at a situation involving undocumented information and see if we can draw a parallel for the philosophy of handling documented information. For instance, a verbal communication represents undocumented information—such as a good reputation, or goodwill—transmitted by word of mouth. And, conversely, when verbal communications are negative, an organization often tries to correct its image. When the organization has done little to create either impression, it is generally wisest to stay neutral—there is no documented proof to back up either contention. When an organization has documented information, it can still remain neutral. By careful management of information in the regular course of business, an organization will have sufficient evidence to present as proof of its good intentions and its performance ability. Legitimate organizations should have no fear that such information may be used against them.

What we are talking about is an information management (I.M.) program that will get the correct information to the right people as quickly and efficiently as possible. The decision makers, properly informed, can set the right course for an organization's continued success. Of course, tomorrow's operations will not be the same as today's; judgment of tomorrow's operations cannot be made on the basis of yesterday's information. Current information is needed to make decisions for today and tomorrow. Management must decide how long to retain each kind of information and set retention guidelines for others.

Since information came to be considered a science (I.S.) a few decades ago, we have come to use information much more efficiently. With the help of the computer and data processing techniques, information becomes available in the desired form more quickly than ever before.

How does the information get processed? The right people must be given the opportunity to apply their knowledge to a particular situation within a specific organization. Though no two circumstances will be the same, the same basic principles can be applied and similar equipment can be used. An information manager is needed to oversee such programs. To cope with innovations and the constantly changing demands of the program, this person must be adaptive, possess a high level of authority in the organization, be trained in the various techniques of information control, and be aware of the latest systems available for doing the best job possible. Also, this person must know the audit, legal, and tax requirements involved with furnishing information.

Few organizations develop a complete and sound information management program and even fewer select an information manager. In large organizations, the information manager is supported by a team of professionals who work to get the program established and functioning.

Now, let's take a look at the contribution that information management makes in the effective operations of an organization.

Generation of Information

When information is generated, one must consider these questions: Who needs what? In what form? How many copies? How often? When answers to these questions are difficult to determine, it is worthwhile to start with the best guides available and make adjustments on the basis of accumulated experience. Copiers can be an asset or a liability in this situation. With classified information, it is very important to control copying. The information manager must know who wants the classified information and for what purposes.

Unless there is some control over copying activities, unnecessary copies and use of the copier for noncompany items can become costly copying problems. One copy routed to several interested people can reduce the number of distributed copies. Control over copies may deny a luxury to those who like to have their own copy of every piece of information whether they ever use it or not. A survey can quickly ascertain who really needs a copy for further reference. Another way to keep distribution copies to a minimum is to put one copy in a central file where several people have access to it.

Abuses may exist in the area of procedures. Several functions in an organization have reason to prepare outlines of standard practices. In handling personnel, one must be instructed how to hire, train, care for health and safety on the job, and finally retire people. In handling finances, one must be instructed in how to pay for materials, for people's services, and taxes as well as how to collect funds for the organization. In manufacturing one must be taught how to purchase materials, turn them into product, package them for sale, and distribute the end product. Administratively, there are many rules and guidelines to be followed. Each responsible area must prepare the master information and have it approved. Then, each department must have copies made, collated, packaged, and distributed to each person who uses that information. This goes on continually because of the need to keep procedures up to date. Consider the kind of savings obtainable if an organization were to forbid each unit to issue procedures separately. An information manager could effect important savings by establishing standard publishing techniques using common equipment, similar systems, and trained personnel. Procedures must be generated and advancements might include the use of micrographics to reduce the high cost of mailing copies of procedures to the far-flung operating areas of a large, complex organization.

Receipt of Information

When information is received from outside the organization, one must ask questions like these: Who has the right to open which packages or envelopes? What are the best ways of quickly distributing received information so it gets to the persons who need to know in the most secure and efficient manner? Should sender be promptly notified that certain information is not needed or is not acceptable in existing form? Should receptionists make additional copies to distribute to the others who should be made aware of the information? Should copies be made for others who may be helpful in preparing answers to questions or problems raised in the received documents? Probably the screening and distribution of information can be best handled by authorized persons who are trained to decide which material should go to whom.

Use of Information

Once information has been distributed to the persons who need it, there is little that can be done about controlling it until it can be brought back into the overall system. One method is to have the information management team review all purchases for information storage units. This review may reveal buildup areas in which volume might be reduced rather than storage units added. Careful and thorough dissemination of an information management policy may encourage users of information to retain it only as needed and then move it along to the storage area for inactive records.

Another way to control copies of documents until they can be transferred to a records center is the use of central files. Usually, a trained person is put in charge of this high-reference area that operates much like a library. A central file enables management to know where information is, who is responsible for quick retrieval of it, and that there is a followup system to rely upon so that information won't go astray once it is loaned out. In some cases, the master copy is not loaned but a duplicate copy is sent to the requester to avoid the risk of loss or delay in retrieving the master.

There are times when some important document is known to exist somewhere within the organization and many hours are spent searching through individual files. This can be very costly, particularly when the time of high-salaried personnel is involved. A properly managed central file will substantially reduce the risk of losing documents or, at least, let the searchers know that the information no longer exists, thus avoiding a long, fruitless search.

Data Versus Information

A large percentage of data processing resources are expended to store data and to make them readily available. It is efficient processing of those *data* that provides managers with valuable *information*.

First, let's analyze data in a computerized environment. Then, we will discuss how the data are used in the operation of an organization. Most computer data are coded, and must be decoded before they are useable information.

Let us examine the hierarchy of data in a computerized environment. The five levels are these:

1. Characters (may also be called by different computer vendors a *word* or *byte*)—a representation of one alphanumeric character. In some computers this represents two decimal digits or a number.

2. Data element (frequently called a *field*)—an element of data within a record that is an item of information. For example: name, account number, amount.

3. Record—a set of related data elements (or fields) grouped together by a common bond.

4. File—a set of related records grouped together by a common bond.

5. Data base—an integrated file containing multiple record types that may be accessed in a nonsequential manner.

To better illustrate this hierarchy, consider the records concerned with how we spend money.

Our personal expenditure data base would include our checking account, all our cash receipts, income tax returns, payroll deduction stubs, invoices, letters ordering merchandise, order forms, plus catalogs and so forth that we use to decide which items to buy. This data base contains a variety of information related to spending our money.

If we begin to sort this data, we find we can categorize it by functions. Accountants do this because it is difficult to comprehend a data base as a whole. From an accounting viewpoint, files are much more logical than separate items or than the whole. For example, we have a file of checks, we have a file of cash receipts, we have a file of catalogs and other sources of supply for which we expend our monies, and so on. We call these *files* because they are collections of similar data.

As we continue to move down our hierarchy of data, the levels become more familiar. Files comprise the records that are kept together because of a common use. For example, a check file is a file of all the checks we have issued. The cash receipts file is a file of receipts for merchandise we have bought with cash. Individually these receipts or checks are records. A record is a series of data elements grouped together by a common function. In the case of a check, the common bond is that it is a document drawing funds on a bank. The check file comprises all the checks drawn on the bank.

Data elements or fields are the most elementary level of information. For example, the check record is composed of several data elements such as the check number, date, payee, amount, and purpose for the check if included. Data elements are one or more characters. The rules for arrangement of characters need to be predetermined. For example, data would be month/day/year. Payee would be first name/middle initial/last name. Amount would be all numeric in one instance and alphabetic in another instance. The data element for date is composed of a variety of numbers and letters. These are called characters. A character by itself, such as the letter *n,* has no meaning. The meaning comes from when a series of characters are put together such as *j, u, n,* and *e,* which put together mean the month June.

Figure 2.1 illustrates the hierarchy of data. A group of characters are put together and acquire meaning when they become data elements. A record comprises a group of data elements with a common relationship (for example, a check's date, payee, amount, and so forth). All the records related to one area

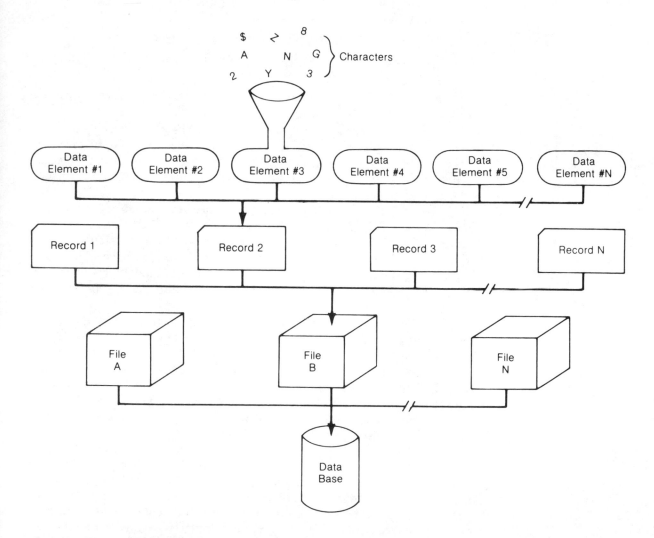

Figure 2.1   Hierarchy of Data

such as checking become a file (such as the check file). When all the files for a particular function (finances, for example) are put together, they are the data base for that function.

As individuals, we have data bases for many functions. We have discussed the cash disbursements data base, but we also have data bases for cash receipts, educational endeavors, hobbies, and investments if we have begun to accumulate a portfolio.

Obviously the data base level is the most meaningful in planning and operating our private lives. For example, we have to consider cash receipts overall as an area of interest and concern. We can't, for example, consider an allowance from our parents as an item separate from all other income. When we think of income planning, we need to include all sources of income in the data base.

As we begin to look at organizations, our thinking should parallel these lines. Because of their size, organizations sometimes consider only one small area at a time. To use data most effectively as information, we need to think of it in the broadest data base terms, rather than at the record or data element level. However, before we get involved in the use of information let's examine how data get into the computer, are processed and are outputted from the computer.

Data Within a Computer System

One of the most confusing aspects about a computer system is how data get into the computer. When we fill out an income tax return, when we complete forms to order products, or when we register for class at college we write information on a form. These forms are called input forms by data processing people. The data we write on the input form go into the computer system. In effect when we complete an input form we are preparing input for the computer, but rarely realize it. The only clue comes when we have to put numbers and letters into boxes.

There are two general premises we must remember when dealing with a computer system. First, a computer system is very detailed, and second, it follows very precise rules. By detailed we mean that the how, where, why, when, and what of doing something is spelled out and must be known in advance. There is no leeway to make guesses and judgments regarding how data are to be entered into the computer. Once data are entered, processing will proceed along a predetermined path for that type of data. By preciseness we mean data must be in the right place, in the right format. For example, if a name is to be written starting in box 1, it must not start in box 2 or 3.

The computer cannot make judgments. It can tell what something is only by knowing first where it is located and second what is to be located in that spot. Let us look at four boxes as they would be viewed by a computer. The boxes must be numbered, or *addressed,* so that the computer can tell them apart. Listed below are four boxes with addresses.

The computer can recognize that there are four boxes and distinguishes them by their individual addresses. The box on the left-most side the computer identifies as box 1. Next is box 2, then box 3, and finally box 4. These numbers are addresses, just as our home or apartment has an address.

Now we must define what type of data will be put in these boxes. Let's assume we will put a number between 0000 and 9999 in the set of four boxes. Each four-box set will represent a unique combination between 0000 and 9999; the position of any individual number in the boxes (its address) will determine its value. We must instruct the computer that what appears in box 1 will represent 0000 through 9000. Whatever number appears in box 2 represents 000 through 900, whatever number appears in box 3 represents 00 through 90, and whatever number appears in box 4 represents 0 through 9. The computer expects a digit in every box. Thus, if we want to put in the number 12, we must add a zero in the thousands box (that is, box 1) and a zero in the hundreds box (that is, box 2). The number 12 in the four boxes will look like this:

1	2	3	4
0	0	1	2

It is extremely important that the numbers appear in the right boxes. When we handwrite a check, an assignment, or a letter, it is not too important where we put the number 12 as long as it is clearly legible and we can recognize it as a 12. Not so with the computer. Let's assume instead of putting the 12 in boxes 3 and 4 we put it in boxes 2 and 3 as follows:

1	2	3	4
	1	2	

Now when the computer looks at the four boxes it recognizes a number and the number is 120. This is because to the computer anything in box 2 represents hundreds, and anything in box 3 represents tens. The fact that you made a slight mistake and were one box off cannot be recognized by the computer. The computer views only what you did and cannot know what you intended to do.

We read occasionally about a check coming out of a computer system for $1,000,000 when it should have been $100. Why? Most likely somebody put a number in a wrong box. As we said, the computer follows rules explicitly. If a number is in the box representing millions, it prints out millions. The computer does what it is told to do. It does it exactly and precisely.

Let's carry our example a little further. We said that our four boxes would represent a number between 0000 and 9999. The computer believes what it is told. Let's assume this amount will be used to prepare weekly paychecks. This works as long as no one earns over $9,999 a week. A good assumption. And it was not until our hypothetical company hired an ex-president of the United States as chief executive officer that a problem occurred. The company agreed to pay the ex-president $12,000 a week.

Now comes a problem that nobody anticipated. How do we get those five numbers into the four boxes? The answer is, we don't. We can write down the five numbers, but the computer will recognize only four. This is why so many input forms use boxes so that the person entering the data will understand that the computer will not accept any more data than there are boxes.

When we try to get the five digits (the 12,000) in, we could enter it as 2000, which eliminates the number on the left, the one representing $10,000. Or we could enter it as 1200, eliminating the zero on the right, which then changes the amount from $12,000 to $1,200. In either situation our new chief executive officer is going to be very unhappy.

There is data processing terminology that describes how data gets placed or misplaced in the boxes. Many of the problems occur because input forms do not use boxes. Before the computer gets the data an individual must transcribe the data from the input form that you will fill out to something the computer can read (for example, a punched card). In the transcribing process, the individual must know where to put the information—into which boxes the data should go. For example, if there are four boxes available and 12,000 is given, a clerk will either send the document back to the originator or make the decision to enter it as 2000 or 1200. Another possibility would be to punch request for two checks, each for 6000.

If the number is to be entered starting in the assigned farthest right box, we say that the field is right justified. This is illustrated in Figure 2.2. Here we are putting a six-digit number into seven boxes; the character 6 goes into box seven.

Left justified means that the farthest left character of the field being entered goes into the farthest left box. In Figure 2.2 we have an example of a left-justified name. An eight-character name composed of seven letters plus a blank are to be put into nine boxes. For left justification, in the example, the letter *J* goes into box one and box nine is left blank.

Numbers are usually right justified, and names are left justified. The empty boxes for numbers may contain blanks or zeros. For mathematical purposes, most computers read blanks as zeros. For names, unused boxes are the spaces between parts of the name.

The last term we need to understand in data entry is *truncated*. Truncated means we lose one or more of the characters from the input data. In our previous example of the chief executive officer's salary, when we tried to put five digits into four boxes we lost one. We have a truncation example in Figure 2.2, which shows six numbers trying to go into five boxes. If we right-justify the number, we truncate the far left character. This means that digit or character at the left end of the field never gets into the computer. If we had left-justified the

Figure 2.2
Data Entry Terminology

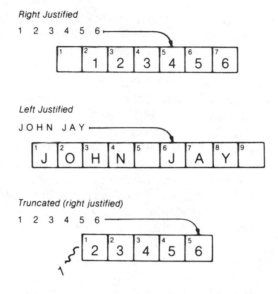

six-digit field, we would have truncated the number 6. If we right-justify the field, as shown in Figure 2.2, we must truncate the number 1.

If you have an extremely long surname, street name, or city name, you will frequently find that name truncated on mailing labels. Magazines allow a fixed number of boxes, or letters, for a name. If your name exceeds that limit, it is truncated. The only alternative to truncation, when there is a fixed number of boxes, is to abbreviate names. You will notice that mailing labels also make extensive use of abbreviations, such as St for street, NY for New York, Wm for William, and so forth.

Let us look at how data are entered, processed, and outputted from a computer. We'll cover this in more detail in later chapters, but it will be helpful to get an overview in order to understand how computers work.

When data are entered into a computer system, the operator knows there is only a fixed number of boxes available for the data being entered. The most familiar example is the punch card. The federal government uses punch cards for savings bonds. Many companies use punch cards for billing purposes.

The punch card is an input record with a fixed number of boxes. The most common punched card has 80 boxes or 80 columns of information. A column, or a box, holds one character of information. A character is any number, letter, or special character such as dollar sign, number sign, or period.

The computer recognizes information in the punched card by the box, or column that that information is punched into. We will study punched cards in more detail in later chapters.

Let us discuss an example of adding two numbers together in a computer.

We enter the two numbers into the computer on a punch card. Next we add them together in the computer, and then print the total on a piece of paper.

Before you can understand how the computer performs this calculation there are two additional pieces of information you need to know. The first is that both computer memory and the output document use the box concept that we previously discussed. Computer memory can be considered to be a series of boxes, each numbered or addressed, and a document printed by a computer is divided into boxes with each box numbered. Computer memory is known by how many boxes it contains. A small computer memory contains 4000 boxes. The boxes will be addressed by the numbers 1 through 4000. If computer memory was five million boxes, the boxes would be addressed by the numbers 1 through 5,000,000. Many people think of computer memory addresses as the equivalent of street addresses. As each house on a street has a unique street address so does each memory box have a unique address. For printing purposes a piece of paper numbers the boxes by line and column. Lines are horizontal on a piece of paper, and columns are vertical. A box on a piece of paper is identified by the coordinates of a line and column. In later chapters we will discuss how to lay out a report on a piece of paper.

The process of adding two numbers together on a computer is illustrated in Figure 2.3. The example will add the number 15 to the number 22. The number 15 is punched onto the card, and the number 22 punched onto the same card. In the first step of the calculation process the computer moves the data from the card into computer memory. Note in Figure 2.3 that the data go from boxes in the card to boxes in computer memory. In the second step of the process the computer adds together the two numbers. The computer locates the numbers to be added by knowing into which boxes it originally put the numbers when they were inputted from the punched card. During the third step the two numbers are added and the total put in other boxes. This step is performed by the instruction *Add*.

During the last step the computer moves the information out of the computer by a process similar to that used in moving data into the computer. The computer knows where in memory the data are located that will be printed on an output document. The computer has been instructed onto which line and column on the printed paper the number is to be placed. If we look at the paper document in Figure 2.3, we see there are nine lines and eight columns. The printer can be instructed to put the total of the calculation, which is the number 37, on line three in columns six and seven. The computer instruction performing this step moves the total from the calculation, from computer memory address seventeen and eighteen to print line three, columns six and seven.

The computer process of adding two numbers together involves moving information from boxes in input, to boxes in computer memory, adding them together in computer memory and then moving the answer to the boxes on the printed report. Prior to the computer process, the two numbers were recorded in boxes on a piece of paper, and then someone transcribed them onto a

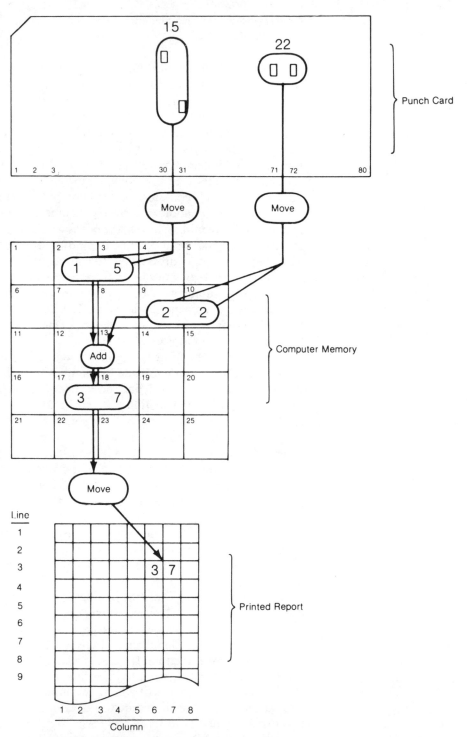

Figure 2.3
Adding Two Numbers on a Computer

punched card. The computer commands that make this process occur are similar to the following English language statements (illustrated in Figure 2.3):

1. Move the data from punch card boxes 31 and 32 to computer memory boxes 2 and 3.
2. Move the data from punch card boxes 71 and 72 to computer memory boxes 9 and 10.
3. Add the data in computer boxes 2 and 3 to the data in computer boxes 9 and 10 and put the results in computer boxes 17 and 18.
4. Move the data from computer boxes 17 and 18 to print line three, columns six and seven.

Computer programmers must learn how to write these statements to instruct the computer.

Information Resource Management (IRM)

Management of the information resource is a developing art. Its primary objective is to meet, with increasingly effective results, the needs of the enterprise for information. This requires identification, review, continual updating of needs, and development of information systems to meet those needs with either internally generated or externally available data. This further requires a framework for the enterprise and thus necessitates the establishment of plans and policies to ensure consistency of information systems with enterprise objectives, plans, priorities, legal constraints (such as data privacy), and security.

Implementation of the IRM concept necessitates the creation of an information system that might be called an information resource management system. This system, in order to be effective, must permeate the enterprise if it is to ensure the integrity of the enterprise's information environment. Such an information system, to be more than a short-lived experiment, must be adequately staffed and funded, and must be supportable with sound cost/benefit analyses. Both short-term and long-range costs and benefits—of all kinds—must be continually projected and monitored. Over time, the enterprise's objectives, priorities, resources, and information requirements, its available technology, the ability of its managers to use information, and the cost/benefit trade-offs associated with information use will change. What will not change is the need for an optimal mix of information system resources, and the need for management at all levels to make certain that the right information is available at the right time to aid in problem solving and decision making for the enterprise.

Before proceeding, it is necessary to understand the meaning of IRM. The principal point in this definition concerns the broad coverage of information and the need for relevance and availability throughout the enterprise.

Information Resource Management (IRM) is whatever policy, action, or procedure concerning information (both automated and nonautomated) that management establishes to serve the overall current and future needs of the enterprise. Such policies, etc., would include considerations of availability, timeliness, accuracy, integrity, privacy, security, auditability, ownership, use, and cost effectiveness.

IRM is currently one of the most significant topics being discussed concerning information systems, and it is debated along a variety of lines. These include business systems planning; information systems analysis, design, and development; database design and implementation; the disciplines of office management, paperwork management, and information sciences management; and the various problems and costs associated with implementing IRM to include each of these areas.

Much of what has been written and spoken about IRM emphasizes two aspects:

- IRM-related technology, both hardware and software
- The implications of IRM on information systems and automated database design

What is too often left unsaid or lost from sight is that IRM's reason for being is to serve the information and decision-making needs of the enterprise. One keynote speaker at a database conference stated: "The essence of management . . . is rational decision-making based on the best available data. Thus, the broad questions of data management lie at the very center of the management process." Extending this more specifically to the topic of IRM we see that related policies and procedures must evolve to serve the total information and decision-making needs of the enterprise.

The Organization and IRM

IRM is an enterprise-wide management program that is global in its objectives and scope. Like all management programs that extend across all organizational components of an enterprise, an IRM program must strive for information consistency, completeness, and compatibility. That is, the information resources of Division A must be defined, described, and noted the same way as are the information resources of Department X.

The goal of consistency has several implications for the information system of which it is a part. Foremost among these is the need to support a "top-down" approach. This top-down approach should reflect the enterprise's organizational structure and, perhaps more importantly, the enterprise plan, enterprise model, or long-range enterprise strategy, and its association with the information systems that support it, as well as the components of each information system. A significant feature of the top-down approach is that it has no inherent limitation of depth, and will thus support the organizational and information components at all levels of the enterprise hierarchy, as well as a global enterprise view.

The needs and realities of large enterprises may require them to implement multiple databases to support the operational aspects of IRM. All that IRM demands with respect to such multiple implementations is consistency of the data contents across the enterprise. This consistency may be best accomplished by treating all data as part of a global, logical definition of data. This definition should be documented in an automated data dictionary.

What is now happening in the IRM environment is an elevation of the data dictionary concept to the enterprise management level. In this arena, the data dictionary is used to manipulate not only data about data, but also data about the information environment—including specific names, places, functions, etc.—by which the enterprise's information holdings are linked to the structure, functions, clientele, etc. of the enterprise itself. Furthermore, if the data dictionary is to be truly enterprise-wide in its scope, it must contain references to both internally generated information and information acquired from external sources.

The data dictionary should provide information about those enterprise information resources required to support management needs at all organizational levels. These needs exist both for those managers directing the business of the enterprise and for those managing its information resources. In addition, the data dictionary must support those people within the enterprise who bridge the gap between the end users of the information and the developers and providers of the information base.

Establishment of a Data Administrator

Information is one of the most valuable resources that an organization has. Once this value is recognized, the need to administer and control that resource becomes obvious. This is resulting in the creation of a new organizational function called data administration. The function is directed by an individual called a data administrator.

The data administrator is to information what the treasurer is to the management of cash. The data administrator should establish data policies, resolve data disputes, and generally ensure that data or information is properly utilized within the organization.

The data administrator function is a relatively new function and has not yet been adopted by many organizations. In most organizations, information is treated as if it is "owned" by the individual user. For example, the payroll manager "owns" the payroll information, the accounts receivable manager "owns" the accounts receivable information, etc. In this type of an environment a data administration function is not possible.

The data administrator is not a data processing technician. A member of senior management should establish management policies regarding data. For example, this individual would establish data policies over security, privacy, definition, consistency, and control.

Segmentation of the Accounting Process

In the past, the cornerstone of accounting control has been segregation of duties. This concept made sense not only for control, but also for good work performance. As an organization grew in size, so the number of different tasks increased.

Next, let's examine the marketing area of an organization in order to see how various tasks became segmented. In a small organization the sales clerk can take the order, distribute the goods, and handle the cash or credit associated with the sale. For example, if you were to hold a garage sale, you could personally handle all aspects of the transactions.

Let's take a giant step to a Fortune 500 organization. In an organization of this size, we may have a sales force of several hundred people, thousands of customers, and millions of transactions in the course of the year. Now it begins to make sense to have specific personnel take orders and establish a distribution center to ship merchandise to the customers. A credit department of many people is needed to determine whether and how much credit will be offered to customers. A special group must prepare invoices and another group is responsible to handle cash receipts. Still another group is charged with the responsibility of maintaining accounts receivable.

This type of organization is common in most major corporations. Since tasks are separated, people in accounts receivable do not fully understand how orders are accepted and processed. One clerk, for example, knows only that sales increase accounts receivable, and credits or cash applied reduce them. If the customer pays on time, little action is necessary other than keeping the accounts up to date. Thus, different departments within an organization handle different segments of accounting associated with the marketing area. Figure 2.4 illustrates this.

A number of accounting entries are associated with the marketing area. In the Fortune 500 company, several different departments are concerned with these entries. In practice, we find one department creating half of an accounting entry, and another department creating the other half of that entry. Table 2.1 illustrates the accounting entries for the marketing area.

As our first entry illustrates, when an order is accepted, inventory is committed to fill that order. The distribution department makes such inventory commitments. In manual systems, it is difficult to execute this type of entry. However, in automated systems, it is very easy to do, because the amount of inventory on hand or on order is in the computerized record.

Once the merchandise has changed hands, the accounting entry to record accounts receivable and sales can be executed. Note that the accounts receivable department is responsible for that half of this accounting entry, while the

**Figure 2.4
Segmentation of the
Accounting Tasks
Associated with
Marketing**

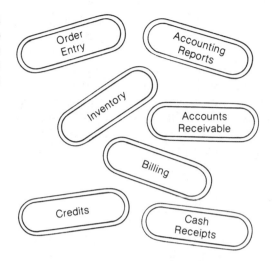

marketing or sales department assumes responsibility for the credit side of the accounting entry.

When goods are shipped to a customer, the cost of the products is transferred from *committed inventory* to *goods sold*. Note again in this case that one department is responsible for half of the accounting entry, and another department is responsible for the other half. Students who leave school to begin work in a large organization may find this concept difficult to comprehend; it is a giant step from a corner store to General Motors.

**Table 2.1
Accounting Entries for
the Marketing Area**

ENTRY OBJECTIVE	ACCOUNTING ENTRY		DEPARTMENT RESPONSIBLE
Order	Inventory: Committed	$xx.xx	Distribution
Entry	Inventory: Open Stock	$xx.xx	Distribution
Accounts Receivable	Accounts Receivable	$xx.xx	Accounts Receivable
Billing	Sales	$xx.xx	Marketing (sales)
Inventory	Cost of Goods Sold	$xx.xx	Accounting
	Inventory: Committed	$xx.xx	Distribution
Credits	Sales: Returns	$xx.xx	Marketing (sales)
	Accounts Receivable	$xx.xx	Accounts Receivable
	Inventory: Returns	$xx.xx	Distribution
	Cost of Goods Sold	$xx.xx	Accounting
Cash	Cash	$xx.xx	Treasurer
Receipts	Accounts Receivable	$xx.xx	Accounts Receivable

For example, handling credits is extremely complex in most organizations. Table 2.1 illustrates but a few of the potential accounting entries. The returned inventory can be sold for scrap, reworked, returned to open stock inventory, sold to employees at reduced rates, and so on.

The cash receipts accounting entry is tightly controlled, because both halves of this entry involve extremely liquid assets. Again, two departments develop this one accounting entry. The treasurer or cashier receives the cash coming into the organization and deposits it in the bank. The accounts receivable department is then notified and adjusts the accounts receivable accordingly.

Changes Occurring in Technology

Over the last thirty years there have been dramatic changes in computing and communications technology. The computer has evolved as a powerful tool, and has been increasing in power more than tenfold each decade. We now have a wide array of computers: large, medium, mini, and minute—even pocket calculators that are more powerful than the large computers of twenty years ago. Communication technology has also grown dramatically. We now have large networks of terminals and computers. We have changes in telephone systems every few years instead of a very stable and stagnant set of systems. Communications and computers have made possible large systems such as CAPS and EQUI-CLAIMS and have provided a basis for regionalizing service while maintaining a common system and centralized data bases.

Where is technology going in the future and how will it change our way of doing business? We expect dramatic changes to continue in the next twenty years. The major changes we will see will occur because systems and services can be larger, more comprehensive, and faster (or more responsive)—and all at lower costs. There are more than enough new ideas around; and as costs come down, new ideas become economic and attractive. What follows are some developments that are expected to become available.

Speech Filing Many simple telephone messages will be automated. Today, people leave messages to call each other back; this causes frustrations and delays. Soon we will have systems with which we will be able to dictate messages to each other and call up on our own telephones to listen to the messages dictated for us. The messages can be stored, and even forwarded to others. Any new message can be automatically sent to a list of people. If you are away from your telephone you can dial in to get your messages.

Electronic Mail and Storage Messages, memos, letters, and contracts that need to be in writing will appear only rarely on paper. They will be prepared on terminals, sent electronically over networks, read from a screen, and indexed and filed electronically.

Managers and staff will be able to use terminals to scan and retrieve documents needed to review history, or to record answers to questions. Paper and copying costs (dollars and wasted time) will be cut (drastically, we hope), mailing delays avoided, and many problems of keeping files up to date and finding things in them should be much simplified.

Image Storage   Some important documents, photographs, signatures, and letters that arrive in nonelectronic form will have to be stored. Today, these are filed because they are too expensive to store in electronic form. With reduced costs we will be able to afford to supplement automated electronic filing systems and keep such documents as "photographic" images in our electronic files, thus eliminating more paper, and saving the problems of transcribing them.

On-Line Reports, Analysis, Graphics   The new systems cannot simply present raw data to executives. Just having all the operating data on line does not mean a manager can just press some buttons and see a useful management report. Actual results that are different from predictions or plans need interpretation. Experts will have to analyze and filter results, look for causes, and separate the effects of each. They will use powerful on-line analytic tools and create management reports using graphics technology to produce diagrams, tables, charts, and graphs to display results. Where models have been developed, new trends can be fed into them to project possible changes and allow management to consider new alternatives.

Retail Data Bases   Today, there are some databases maintained and available for a fee: Stock Exchange prices and volumes; indexed legal rulings; travel and vacation data; industry statistics; and several government statistical publications. More of these services will be available and used by managers. Private exchanges may well develop, and we may also expect in-house databases to be organized so that they are useful to other parts of the organization. For example, both the personnel office and the controller need to look at employee data.

Variety and Convenience of Access   Small terminals will be available for use at home to access business systems. Today, the special communications lines needed are expensive and take time to install. By the year 2000, cable TV systems will allow home terminals to be connected to company systems without having to install special lines, and without being restricted by the limited capacity of telephone lines.

Cable TV Extensions   Sophisticated cable TV, including systems such as "viewdata," will become available. Viewdata is a new type of service that enables suppliers to make statements available about their service and products. Viewers can tune in, scan for products they are interested in, see a telephone number, call up, and conduct business. Many simple functions will be carried out by a simple keyboard, similar to one on a touch-tone phone, and the TV screen will be used for replies. In short, a large variety of devices and services will be developed around the home market.

One-Stop Processing   One-stop processing is a term used to describe a system in which a single person can provide a complete range of services. Thus, a customer can be dealt with by one person without having to go to various desks or counters to be serviced. A good example is an airline reservation system where one clerk can make all the reservations, check credit, issue the ticket, and check baggage. Such systems depend on good on-line databases, relatively cheap terminals, cheap processing, voluminous storage, and, most of all, the ability to design and install such systems even though they require dramatic changes in organizations and in employee attitudes.

General Forces Stimulating Change

Working alongside improvements in technology are consumerism, changes in customers' expectations, and some current frustrations that are stimulating changes in society and business.

First, there is a pervasive attitude emerging today—one expressed by customers, employees, managers, indeed, by all our society. We believe it will also be characteristic of the early twenty-first century. It is expressed in the phrase *I want it now!* A generation of people are growing up in an environment where they write few letters but make extensive use of the telephone. They *expect* to be able to get a response or action right away—buy something with a credit card, make a reservation, arrange an appointment, get a prescription from a doctor.

Second, competitive forces will continue to be a strong driving force, and service orientation may become more important than price (just as has happened with convenience foods). Once service becomes that important, all vendors must adopt the service attitude or face a declining business.

Third, there is the problem of coping with an increasing volume of data. Today, government and business organizations are drowning in data. At the same time, the computing and communications technologies are increasing rapidly in scope and power. Information technology, the techniques by which the tools are used for the interpretation, presentation, and controlled use of data, are in the early stages of development. The current substantial investment in "office of the future" projects by American business, however, reflects a growing interest in this area.

Overall, in the next twenty years we expect that technology, business, and social pressures will accelerate development of systems that respond faster to the needs of business managers, staff, and customers.

The New Manager's World of 2000

There is no single picture of the future, but we can predict a continuance of a general trend that already exists. There will not be one general pattern. Different industries, different organizations, different managers will have different needs and different styles, just as they do today. That is why we can give a general picture with confidence, but specific examples are less reliable.

Much of a manager's time is involved in dealing with messages (telephone calls and memos to be answered), studying data (operating results, status of projects), making decisions (looking at alternatives and weighing possible outcomes), and conducting or attending meetings.

A manager will use on-line systems extensively—some directly for messages, some for looking at reports, and some for following up. His or her staff will use on-line systems to review results, to consider alternatives, and to develop plans. Operating staff will use on-line systems to perform the basic functions of a business.

Good managers will emerge who will operate less "by the seat of their pants" or intuition, and more on evidence. They will set up systems that produce operating data that show what is happening, use models to consider alternatives, and be more analytically oriented than today. It will be possible to make choices much less of a gamble, to expect a faster awareness of, and reaction to, changes. Managers, too, will become impatient. They, too, will "want it now."

A new management philosophy and an increasing tempo of business will require managers to make decisions more rapidly. At the same time, with more information readily available, it will be possible to increase the span of control of an individual manager. There should be fewer people to deal with exceptions or to supplement the automated systems and cover the connecting parts. Most of the processing can be automated. The major outstanding functions will be analysis, decisions, and customer service, as well as planning. Thus, there will be fewer pure administrators and "bean counters," and more managers with the entrepreneurial outlook to take advantage of emerging opportunities. These new managers will have a broader scope of action, will be more "risk" oriented, and will be held more directly accountable for results.

Organizations need to change to support one-stop processing; previous organization structures divided work up so that separate units specialized in specific activities, and a transaction would move through various work units or work stations. In the organization of the future, when we want to deal with a caller on line, whether at a counter or on the phone, we must arrange things so that one person on the organization's staff can deal with all the questions and actions the caller has. We cannot provide service, nor be efficient, if we pass callers from one unit to another.

Employee attitudes need to change because there is an entirely different tempo and interpersonal style required to respond directly to callers rather than processing pieces of paper. The tempo is partially controlled by the caller and work cannot be rearranged into neat piles of similar kind. There is no time to "send for files"—files must be ready at hand. There is no time to refer unusual cases to a supervisor—too many exceptions will stop the system from working. The tempo of both society and business will be affected. It will be a "dynamic society"—willing, able, and wanting to do it now.

Summary

Information management is so pragmatic that it doesn't appeal to management like a new product with high demand and potentially high profit. However, during times of economic stress management is often prompted to take a hard look at effective systems to prevent waste. But also, at such times there is little venture capital to embark on new programs even though logic may dictate it. Unfortunately, until there's a control problem, a fraud, or a successful salesperson with some sophisticated technology prompting special action, information management does not get the attention it deserves as an important asset of an effective ongoing program.

Problems

1. Is the cost of people or equipment the major cost in computer systems?
2. How are organizations affected by the installation of a computer?
3. Name the types of top management decisions that are not being determined by computer systems.
4. State the reasons why organizations are establishing committees of interested personnel to specify computer systems as opposed to letting the data processing department specify the system.
5. Why will managers of the future need to have a better understanding of the computer than today's manager?
6. What effect has the computer had on the manager's control function?
7. How does the computer improve on the manual recording of transactions?
8. What types of tasks performed by people in manual systems can best be accomplished by computer systems?
9. When someone says, "The computer goofed," what really happened?
10. What happens when a computer system receives a condition it has not been programmed to process?
11. How does the computer help top management perform their planning function?
12. Explain the differences between the cost of a manual system and the cost of a computer system.

13. Explain the effect on cost of doubling the number of transactions in both a manual and computer system.

14. Where is the weakest control point in systems that have been computerized?

15. Why is security so important in a data processing department?

16. Could the power of a computer have been used to prevent the failure of the Edsel program at Ford Motor Company? Explain your answer.

17. It was predicted that the computer would replace middle management. Explain why this has not happened.

18. Peter Drucker states that the computer will force managers to make true decisions. What does this statement mean?

19. Do you believe it is a good practice to build the rules into a computer system to authorize transactions? Why?

20. It has been stated that installing a computer system is the equivalent of putting the application processing under a magnifying glass. What do you think is meant by this statement?

21. How will producing fewer hard-copy documents in computer systems affect the organization?

22. Why is privacy of personal information more of an issue in computer systems than it was in manual systems?

23. The ABC College plans to install a computer system to convert their manual registration system to a computer system. The current system calls for two days of registration in the gym. All students are expected at that time. This is a hectic period for college employees with extensive overtime to get all the class lists and schedules prepared. Under the proposed new computer system, computer terminals will be placed in the student lounge. Anyone with a current student number can sit at a terminal any time, day or night, and register for classes during the six weeks prior to the start of class. Class lists can be prepared on a one-hour notice.

    The registrar is concerned his department will not be able to easily adjust to the new system. He has asked you to help prepare his department for the new system. What steps would you recommend?

24. What is the difference between information and information resource management?

25. What role does the data administrator play in the information resource management function?

26. Describe two of the more recent technological advances in automation of information processing.

27. One data processing manager described a major force for technological change as "the demand by people for information accessibility at the point they asked the question." What does this statement mean, and what impact has it had on the use of advanced technology?

EDP AUDIT PROCESS*

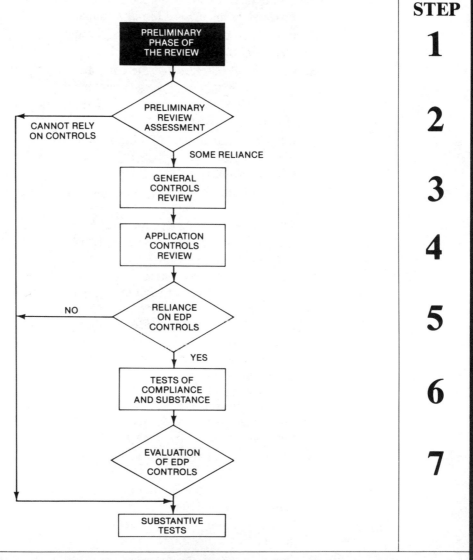

STEP

1

2

3

4

5

6

7

Diagram is adapted from The Auditor's Study and Evaluation of Internal Control in EDP Systems, *pages 21–24. Copyright © 1977 by the American Institute of Certified Public Accountants, Inc. (See Figure 9.1 for a complete explanation of the steps.)*

STEP

1

**ADDRESSED
IN THIS
CHAPTER**

DEFINING AND FLOWCHARTING SYSTEMS

(1) Preliminary Phase of the Review

Purpose: To yield an understanding of the accounting system, including both EDP and non-EDP segments:

- Flow of transactions and significance of output.
- Extent to which EDP is used in significant accounting applications.
- Basic structure of accounting control, including both EDP and user controls.

Method: Inquiry and discussion; observation; review of documentation; tracing of transactions; control questionnaires and checklists.

OBJECTIVE

In order to understand the computer application under review, the auditor frequently flowcharts the application logic. This chapter explains how to flowchart material.

Much audit activity involves the evaluation of a client's system of data processing and accounting controls. To conduct this evaluation, the auditor must document an understanding of the system in working papers. *Flowcharting* is a technique for recording and analyzing the evidence gained from inquiries about a system, observation of data processing activities, and examination of transactions and documents flowing through a system.

Organizations' Purposes and Objectives

Organizations receive their authority to conduct their operations from one of two sources. Corporations have their purposes and objectives stated in articles of incorporation and bylaws. Governmental units receive their authority from legislation. All power, authority, and functions stem from these documents. Articles of incorporation, bylaws, and authorizing legislation are further interpreted through organizational charts, policies and procedures, and other manuals. These documents are translated into systems, which then become the vehicles for accomplishing the purposes and objectives of the organization.

It is important that the objectives of the system are consistent with the purposes and objectives of the organization. Figure 3.1 illustrates the flow from purposes and objectives to systems and also portrays the network of internal controls embracing all systems.

Systems Accomplish Objectives

Systems do not stand alone, but are elements of processing oriented toward meeting the purposes and objectives of the organization. Systems such as accounts receivable, inventory, and cash disbursements are not isolated systems but rather part of an interrelated network of systems. The prime purpose of internal controls is to determine that these interrelated systems function properly.

Data processing is a means of implementing systems. Systems neither begin nor end in the data processing facilities. Systems begin with the origination of a transaction and end with the culmination of the use of the processing results (for example, posting of accounts to the general ledger). Origination of a transaction has associated with it the necessary authorization to originate the transaction. Even in cases where the transaction is entered through an input terminal, it is unusual that preplanning does not occur. This preplanning may be in the form of notes, or throwaway forms, but it does involve some preparatory work.

Organizational barriers prevent most employees from fully appreciating the total system. The auditor is in a unique position to evaluate the total system.

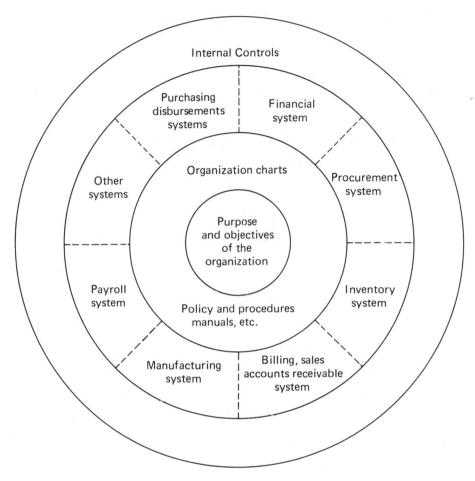

Figure 3.1
Total Systems Concept

Figure 3.2 attempts to put data processing in the proper perspective in the total systems environment.

When analyzing systems, the auditor needs to consider the following:

1. How does the system achieve the purposes and objectives of the organization?

2. What is the interrelationship between the organizational chart and the data processing systems?

3. How does the total systems concept (from transaction initiation through posting to the general ledger) affect the role of data processing in that total systems environment?

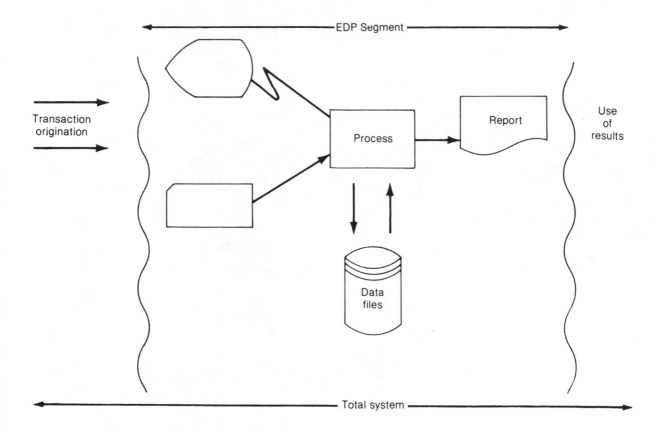

Figure 3.2   EDP Segment of a Total System

Understanding Systems

One of the most difficult tasks an auditor must perform is to comprehend a system. The auditor gains this understanding through evaluation of the systems documentation and inteviews with key individuals in an organization. Because of the complexities of systems in modern organizations, documentation tends to be rather extensive at the detail level and skimpy at the total systems level.

A valuable tool that helps with the explanation of a systems function is flowcharting. Auditors need to understand flowcharting for two reasons:

1. They will be able to comprehend flowcharts developed by systems designers as documentation for that system.
2. They will have a means of auditor documentation to explain the functioning of a system or systems.

Why Flowcharting?

The auditor's initial review of a client's system is concerned with an analysis of the structure and design of the system itself rather than with an intensive examination of the documents and records. To understand the structure and design of the system, the auditor must define the system he or she wishes to evaluate. The flowchart provides the auditor with an accurate and comprehensive method for recording the procedures in the system. The use of a flowchart has several advantages over a narrative description of a system:

- It is much easier to use in describing a system of any size and complexity
- It is much easier to use in recording changes in the system
- It is easier to use in analyzing the system since the charts show the flow of data through the system and provide an easy means of spotting weaknesses or areas where improvements could be made
- Typically it is the method used by the client's EDP personnel to document and represent the system being reviewed by the auditor

Basically, two types of flowcharts are used in EDP systems: a *systems flowchart* and a *program flowchart*. The systems flowchart describes the flow of data through the system without regard to how the computer programs process the data. The program flowchart complements the systems flowchart by describing how the data are processed, the sequence of operations, and the decisions involved in the particular programs in a system.

From an audit standpoint, typically the auditor is more concerned with reviewing a client's systems flowcharts and probably will use systems flowcharting as a method of documenting the client's system in the audit working papers.

Flowcharting Symbols

Flowcharting is applicable for describing manual and electromechanical as well as computer processing, but the complexity of computer systems is the major reason for the widespread use of flowcharting. There is a need both to understand flowcharts drawn by others and to communicate effectively problem solutions that are described in flowchart form. This need is best met if there is agreement on a standard set of flowchart symbols. The symbols used in this text are those published by the American National Standards Institute, Inc. in 1971. Figure 3.3 illustrates the symbols.

The parallelogram is used to indicate an input or output of the system; the

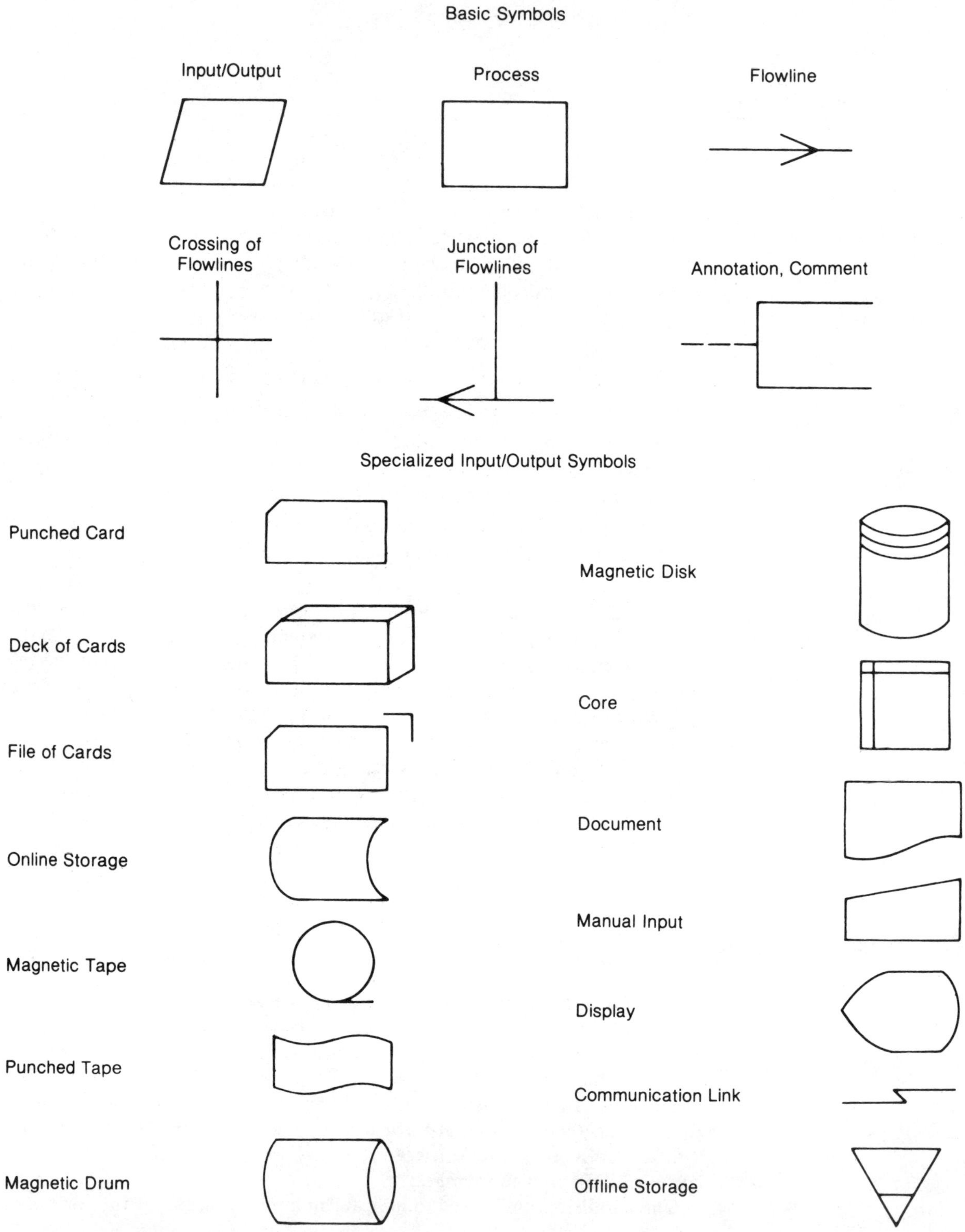

Basic Symbols

Input/Output

Process

Flowline

Crossing of Flowlines

Junction of Flowlines

Annotation, Comment

Specialized Input/Output Symbols

Punched Card

Deck of Cards

File of Cards

Online Storage

Magnetic Tape

Punched Tape

Magnetic Drum

Magnetic Disk

Core

Document

Manual Input

Display

Communication Link

Offline Storage

Figure 3.3   Flowcharting Symbols

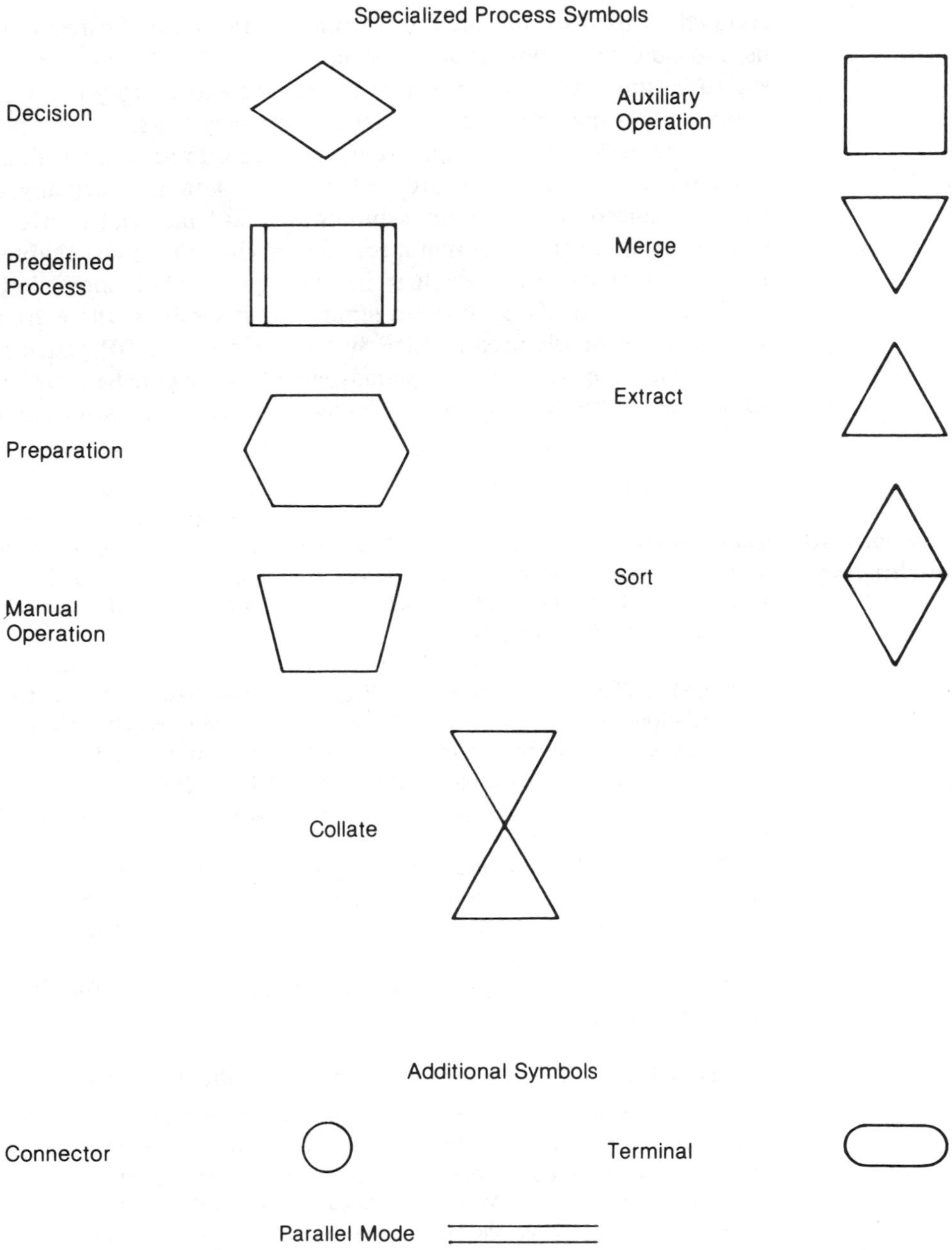

Specialized Process Symbols

Decision

Predefined
Process

Preparation

Manual
Operation

Auxiliary
Operation

Merge

Extract

Sort

Collate

Additional Symbols

Connector

Terminal

Parallel Mode

Figure 3.3   (continued)

rectangle is used to indicate a processing operation; and directional lines are used to indicate the flow of data. The normal flow is from left to right and from top to bottom. Annotation is used for needed explanatory comments. These basic symbols may be used to flowchart simple systems, but typically in EDP systems several types of media are used to record and store data and several types of input–output devices are used to process data. So, normally, the analyst uses specialized input–output symbols that aid materially in describing a system. Using the input–output media summarized in the last chapter, in Table 2.2, we can indicate the specialized input–output symbols shown in Figure 3.3.

In addition to the specialized input–output symbols, there are processing and storage symbols used in EDP systems. Since all EDP systems are really human–machine systems and also may include some punched-card equipment, additional symbols are available to indicate non-EDP operations in the system.

Symbol Use in Flowcharting[1]

Symbol Shape. The actual shapes of the symbols used should conform closely enough to those shown to preserve the characteristics of the symbol. The curvature of the lines and the angles formed by the lines may vary slightly from those shown in this standard so long as the shapes retain their uniqueness.

Symbol Size. Flowchart symbols are distinguished on the basis of shape, proportion, and size in relation to other symbols. Proportion of a given symbol is defined by the rectangle in which that symbol can be inscribed. Dimension and relative size of these rectangles are given with each symbol by a pair of numbers (width : height).

The size of each symbol may vary, but the dimensional ratio of each symbol shall be maintained.

Flowchart symbols are formed by straight and curved line segments. When prepared automatically by machine, they may be formed by patterns of successively printed graphic symbols (asterisks, periods, and so forth) that exhibit the characteristic shapes.

Symbol Orientation. The orientation of each symbol of a flowchart should be the same as shown in Figure 3.3.

Flow Direction. Flow direction is represented by lines drawn between symbols.

FLOWLINE. Normal direction of flow is from left to right and top to bottom. When the flow direction is not left to right or top to bottom, open arrowheads shall be placed on reverse-direction flowlines. When increased clarity is desired, open arrowheads can be placed on normal-direction flowlines. When flowlines are broken due to page limitation, connector symbols shall be used to indicate the break. When flow is bidirectional, it can be shown by either single or double lines, but open arrowheads shall be used to indicate both normal-direction flow and reverse-direction flow.

---

[1] *Flowchart Symbols and Their Usage in Information Processing,* pps. 12–14, © 1971 American National Standards Institute Inc., N.Y., N.Y.

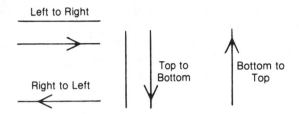

COMMUNICATION LINK. Unless otherwise indicated, the direction of communication link flow is left to right and top to bottom. Open arrowheads are necessary on symbols for which the flow opposes the above convention. An open arrowhead may also be used on any line whenever increased clarity will result.

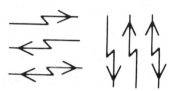

Flowchart Text. Descriptive information with each symbol shall be presented so as to read from left to right and top to bottom regardless of the flow direction.

Symbol Identification. The identifying notation assigned to a symbol, other than a connector, shall be placed above the symbol and to the right of its vertical bisector.

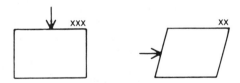

Symbol Cross Reference. Identifying notation(s) of other elements of documentation (including this set of flowcharts) shall be placed above the symbol and to the left of its vertical bisector.

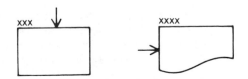

Connector Referencing. Two examples of referencing are listed below.

CONNECTOR COMMON IDENTIFICATION. A common identifier, such as an alphabetic character, number, or mnemonic label, is placed within the outconnector and its associated inconnector.

CROSS REFERENCING CONNECTORS. Additional cross referencing between associated connectors is achieved by placing the chart page(s), coordinates, or other identifier(s) of the associated connectors above and to the left of the vertical bisector of each connector.

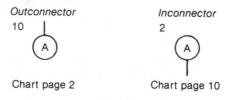

Symbol Striping. Striping is a means of indicating that a more detailed representation of a function is to be found elsewhere in the same set of flowcharts. This representation differs from a predefined process symbol that need not be represented in detail in the same set of flowcharts.

STRIPED SYMBOL. A horizontal line is drawn within, completely across, and near the top of the symbol, and a reference to the detailed representation is placed between that line and the top of the symbol.

FIRST SYMBOL OF DETAILED REPRESENTATION. The terminal symbol shall be used as the first and last symbols of the detailed representation. The first terminal symbol contains an identification that also appears in the striped symbol.

CROSS REFERENCING OF STRIPED SYMBOL AND DETAILED REPRESENTATION. A reference to the location of the detailed representation within the flowchart is placed above and to the left of the vertical bisector of the striped symbol. A reference to the striped symbol is placed above and to the left of the vertical bisector of its associated terminal symbol.

Example: Striped Symbol and Detailed Representation

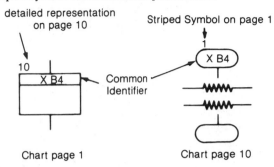

Chart page 1   Chart page 10

Multiple Exits. Multiple exits from a symbol shall be shown by several flowlines from the symbol to other symbols or by a single flowline from the symbol, which branches into the appropriate number of flowlines.

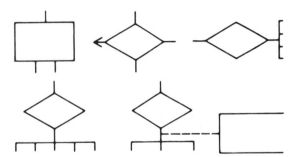

Each exit from a symbol shall be identified to show the logic path that it represents. The logic paths may be represented by a table that indicates their associated conditions and the inconnector references.

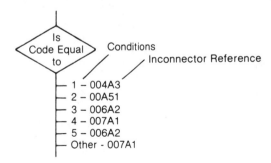

Branching Table. A branching table may be used in lieu of a decision symbol to depict a decision function. The table is composed of a statement of the decision to be made, a list of the conditions that can occur, and the path to be followed for each condition. The terms "Decision Statement" and "Paths" are not part of the standard. The "GO TO" section contains either an inconnector reference or a single flowline exiting to another symbol. Examples of branching table formats are shown below.

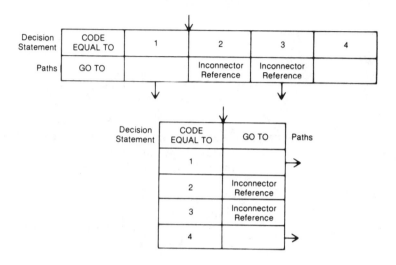

Repetitive Representation of the Same Media. The diagram below is an alternative to a single symbol with appropriate text: the same input/output symbols may be shown in an overlay pattern to illustrate the use or creation of multiple media or files, for example, number of copies, types of printed reports, types of punched card formats, or multiple magnetic tape reels.

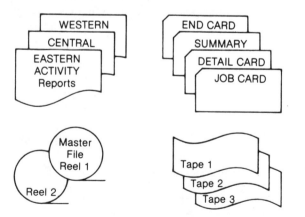

OVERLAY PATTERN. The overlay pattern must be drawn from front to back with the first symbol as the entire I/O symbol. The center line of the second symbol must be offset up or down from the horizontal center line and to the right or left of the vertical center line of the first symbol. Similarly, the third symbol must be offset in the same direction from the second symbol; the fourth from the third and so on for any remaining symbols.

PRIORITY REPRESENTATION. When the multiple symbols represent an ordered set, the ordering shall be from front (first) to back (last).

FLOWLINES WITH REPETITIVE SYMBOLS. Flowlines may enter or leave from any point on the overlay symbols. The priority or sequential order of the multiple symbols is not altered by the point at which the flowline(s) enters or leaves.

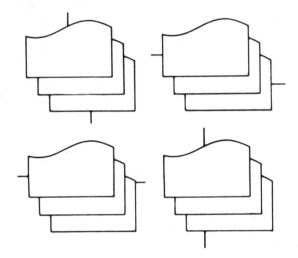

Illustrations of Symbol Use   The use of these symbols can be illustrated for a manual system and for automated processing.

Manual System

The ABC Corporation follows specific procedures in updating its inventory files and in issuing new purchase orders. Following are excerpts taken from the procedures manual of the company as they apply to these procedures.

Entries to stock inventory records are made from four sources:

- Copies of issued purchase orders
- New receipts of stock as indicated by copies of approved receiving reports
- Stores' requisitions as approved by the storekeeper
- Miscellaneous transactions such as returns and adjustments

Incoming documents are posted manually each day to the stock inventory records by a special group of clerks in the accounting department. After posting is completed, the source documents are filed together by date of posting. The ledger cards are analyzed as each posting is made to determine if items on hand plus those on order are below the reorder level. If a "below-minimum" condition exists, a purchase requisition is prepared and forwarded to the purchasing department. Vendors are selected from a master vendor file by employees in the purchasing department. A purchase order is prepared and mailed to the vendor. The master vendor file is updated when an order is placed. Four copies of the purchase order are prepared and routed as follows:

- Original is sent to the vendor
- Copy, with purchase requisition attached, is filed in the purchasing department
- Copy is filed in the receiving department
- Copy is sent to the accounting department to adjust stock inventory records

Figure 3.4 is a systems flowchart for the ABC system using the appropriate symbols already discussed.

Automated Processing

A new computer is to be installed at ABC Corporation and the purchase-order procedures are among the first to be programmed. The following changes will be required in the system.

Input Documents.   Receiving reports and return and adjustment memoranda will be transferred from source documents to punched cards before they enter the system. Stores' requisitions will be prepared originally on mark-sensed cards by the foremen, and these cards will be read and punched by a reproducer as an auxiliary machine operation. Purchase-order information will be entered on the master file records as part of the processing. The system will use sequential batch processing, and so all input cards must be sorted into stock-number order before they can be processed.

Store Ledger and Vendor File.   Store ledger and vendor files will be integrated, and the information on them will be stored on magnetic tape in stock-number order. Each record on the file will contain the following information arranged by fields:

- Stock item number
- Item description
- Detail of current monthly transactions
- Current balance on hand
- Current balance on order
- Total balance on hand and on order

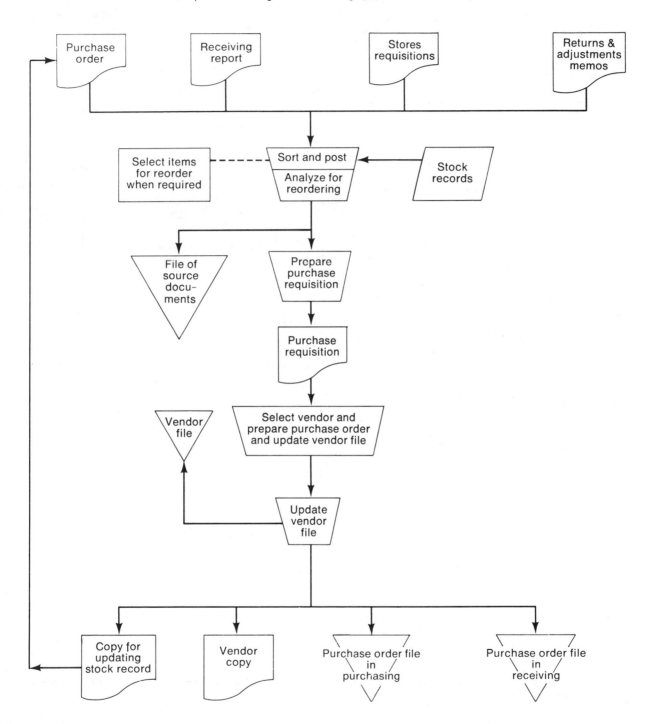

Figure 3.4   Systems Flowchart for the ABC System

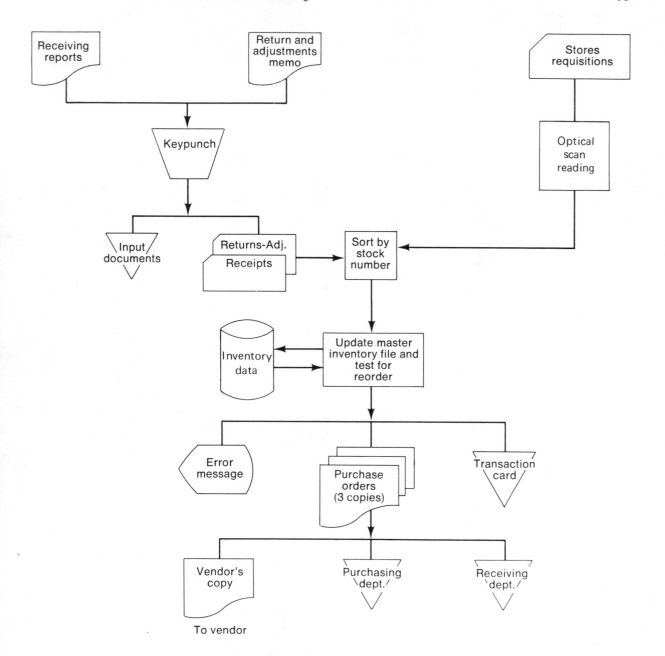

Figure 3.5   Systems Flowchart of Automated Processing of ABC's Purchase-Order Procedures and Store Ledger File Updating

- Reorder point
- Reorder quantity
- Vendor's name and address

Processing.   The master store ledger and vendor file will be updated by the transaction inputs, and a comparison check will be made between the balance on hand and on order and the reorder point. If a new purchase is required, a purchase order is prepared using the vendor's information and the reorder quantity from the master file. If no new order is required, processing of the transaction cards continues. Error messages are printed on the console typewriter if there is any miscoding of stock numbers on the transaction cards.

Figure 3.5 is a systems flowchart depicting the automated processing of ABC's purchase-order procedures and store ledger file updating.

Flowcharting Conventions for Auditors

Up to now we have discussed the standard flowchart symbols and illustrated how they are used. From an auditing viewpoint, several flowcharting conventions are useful in documenting and analyzing a client's system:

- Organization of the flowchart
- Movement of data
    (a) Origin of forms and documents
    (b) Use of arrows to depict flow of data
    (c) Relationship to other documents, forms, and media
    (d) Multiple copies of documents
- Decisions in the processing
- Audit trail

Total Systems Concept and Flowcharting: An Illustration

The total systems concept and flowcharting will be discussed using a series of figures. The figures will depict how the system fits into the organizational chart of the firm and how an auditor might document part of that system through flowcharting. In this series, we shall illustrate the flowcharting conventions by showing on one illustration both the organizational chart and the information flow. This shows the relationship between organizational structure and data.

The system used here for illustrative purposes is a marketing system. The basic financial data cycle associated with the marketing function is shown in three diagrams, Figures 3.6 to 3.8, covering a transaction from the point where an order is received through the point where cash is paid to the firm. The data cycle illustrated by the three figures consists of the following major aspects:

1. Order origination and processing—including credit authorization, pricing, discounts, delivery schedules, commissions.

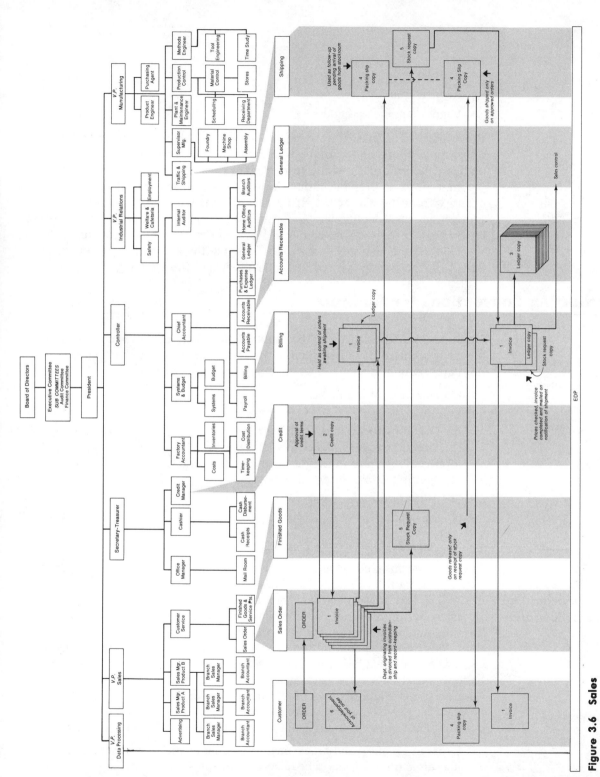

Figure 3.6 Sales

Procedural diagram shown in relation to organization chart to portray the control obtained through segregation of functional responsibility.

SOURCE: From W. T. Porter and J. Burton, *Auditing: A Conceptual Approach*, Wadsworth, 1971.

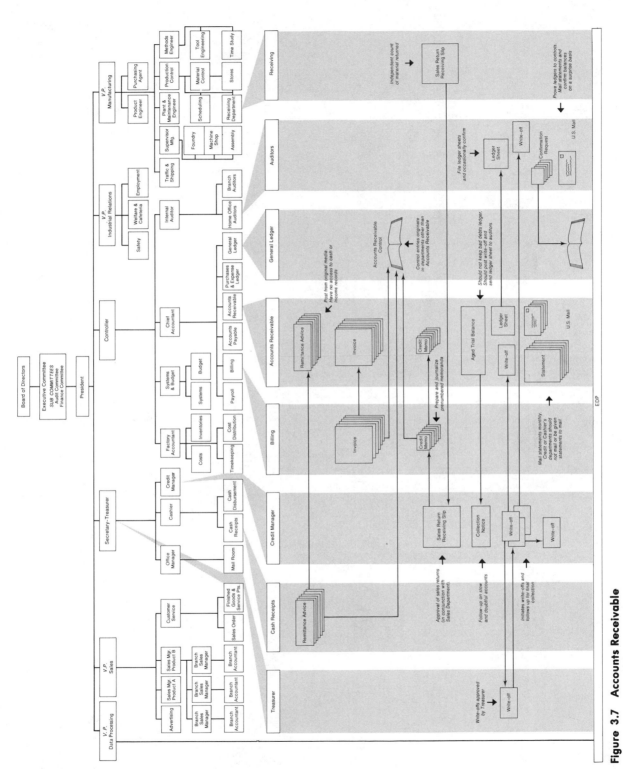

Figure 3.7 Accounts Receivable

Procedural diagram shown in relation to organization chart to portray the control obtained through segregation of functional responsibility.

SOURCE: From W. T. Porter and J. Bruton, *Auditing: A Conceptual Approach*, Wadsworth, 1971.

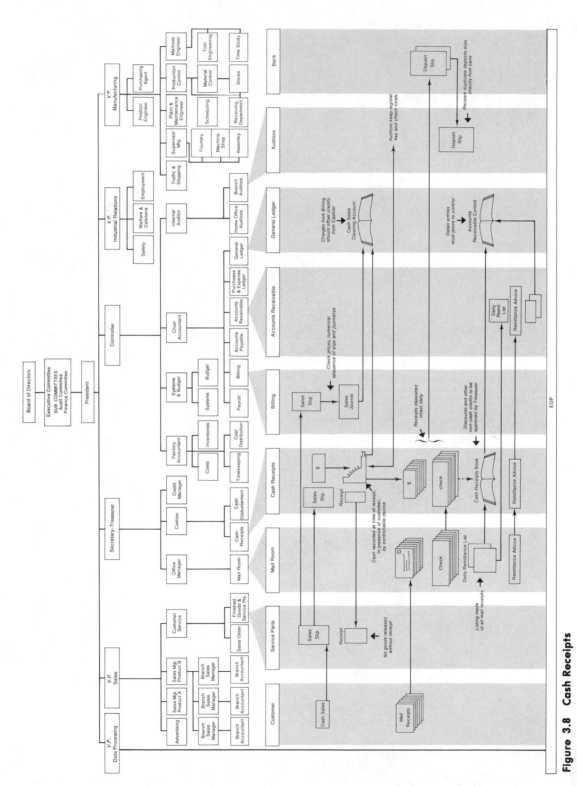

Figure 3.8   Cash Receipts

Procedural diagram shown in relation to organization chart to portray the control obtained through segregation of functional responsibility.

SOURCE: From W. T. Porter and J. Bruton, *Auditing: A Conceptual Approach*, Wadsworth, 1971.

2. Order analysis.

3. Coordination of order entry process with information about inventory availability or production scheduling.

4. Order editing to assure accuracy of order data and propriety of order recording procedures.

5. Order fulfillment, including the assembly, packing, and shipping of the order and the preparation of appropriate documents for invoice preparation.

6. Sales invoice preparation and recording of sales in sales journal, summary, or listing.

7. Accounts receivable posting and preparation of customer statements.

8. Accounts receivable aging and credit collection and control procedures.

9. Handling, recording, balancing, depositing, and summarizing of cash receipts.

10. Sales analysis.

11. Procedures for handling returned goods, price adjustments, invoice errors, writeoffs, etc.

Flowcharting Conventions Illustrated

We shall discuss each of these flowcharting conventions using a series of figures. In this series, we shall illustrate the flowcharting conventions with a manual portion of an order-entry billing process.

Organization

Figure 3.9 presents the organization of a systems flowchart for audit purposes. The organizational units involved in the processing are shown in order to relate the flow of data among the units. Also, the depiction of organizational groupings in the flowchart assists the auditor in analyzing the segregation of functions for internal control purposes. With the flowchart organized as in Figure 3.9, the flow of data is both horizontal and vertical to allow ease of flowcharting and ease of review. Remember, all audit working papers in which flowcharts are included are reviewed by someone!

Movement of Data

Of the next six illustrations (Figures 3.10 to 3.15), Figure 3.10 shows the origin of the form. It is useful to be able to trace all important forms and documents from their origin to their final disposition. The flowchart in Figure 3.10 indicates that the orders are telephoned in and that they are filled out by someone in the office. Note that a copy of the sales order is included somewhere in the working papers (see Figure 3.16 on page 81). It is useful to supplement the

Figure 3.9
Organization of
Flowchart for Audit
Purposes

Customer Branch (Salesman)	A B C Company Present Order Entry System Prepared By: Joe Doe
Sales Order (Office)	
Shipping Warehouse	
Keypunch Computer	

Notes	1.
	
	2.
	
	3. Contains detailed explanations
	explanations of:
	   Operations
	   Forms
	   Files

**Figure 3.10
Origin of Form**

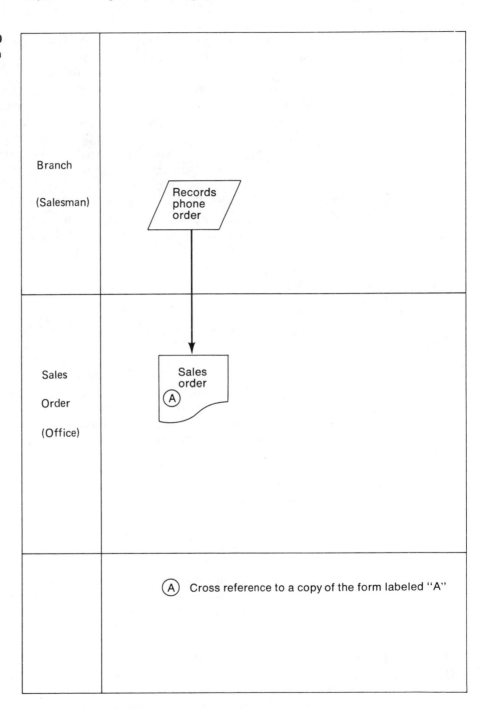

flowchart with copies of all important accounting documents for audit analysis and review and for audit-trail evaluation.

Figure 3.11 shows the movement of the sales order through two manual processing steps. Note how horizontal processing flow and use of directional lines enable the reviewer readily to trace the movement of the sales order through the processing steps to a metric file. Figure 3.12 shows the relationship of the sales order to other forms and documents used in processing. The part and customer numbers that are added to the sales order are taken from the part and customer lists. Note the use of arrows to indicate the flow of data. Figure 3.13 shows how to depict multiple copies of documents involved in processing. In the sales-order illustration, six copies of the invoice are prepared; three are filed numerically and three are sent to the warehouse for order filing. Note again the use of the arrows to indicate the flow of data.

Figure 3.6 depicts the flow by means of an organization chart.

Decisions

Processing data involves operations that require someone to perform an analysis, make a decision, and take action; therefore, flowcharts should clearly indicate what the decisions are and what action is to be taken. Figure 3.14 shows a decision in the sales-order illustration. After the order is filled, the pricing copy of the invoice is checked and the appropriate price is written on the invoice. The final invoice is checked to see if the order is complete. If it is, the invoice is sent to data processing; if not, a backorder in prepared.

Figures 3.6 and 3.15 show how data processing is involved with the various functions of the organization.

Audit Trail

Since the audit trail is valuable for management purposes and is useful to the auditor for testing the system, it is important to highlight it in the flowchart. In this illustration, the audit trail consists of the original sales order, the invoice, and the backorder. Copies of these forms should be included in the working papers as part of the system description, and the labels should be circled in red or highlighted in some other way on the flowchart.

Now that we have discussed flowcharting symbols and conventions for audit purposes, it would be useful to employ them in another illustration.

Illustration of Order-Transmission Phases

We shall flowchart the order-transmission phases of an accounts receivable application. The application is processed on a disk-oriented computer system consisting of four disk storage drives, four magnetic tape units, a card-reader punch, a line printer, and a console typewriter. For transmission of orders, a teletypewriter system is used with orders recorded on punched paper tape. Data

Figure 3.11
Movement of Form

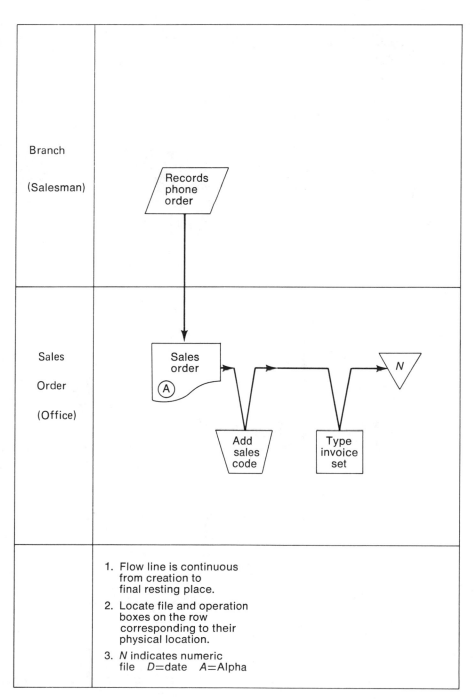

Branch

(Salesman)

Sales

Order

(Office)

1. Flow line is continuous
   from creation to
   final resting place.

2. Locate file and operation
   boxes on the row
   corresponding to their
   physical location.

3. *N* indicates numeric
   file   *D*=date   *A*=Alpha

**Figure 3.12
Relationship to
Other Forms**

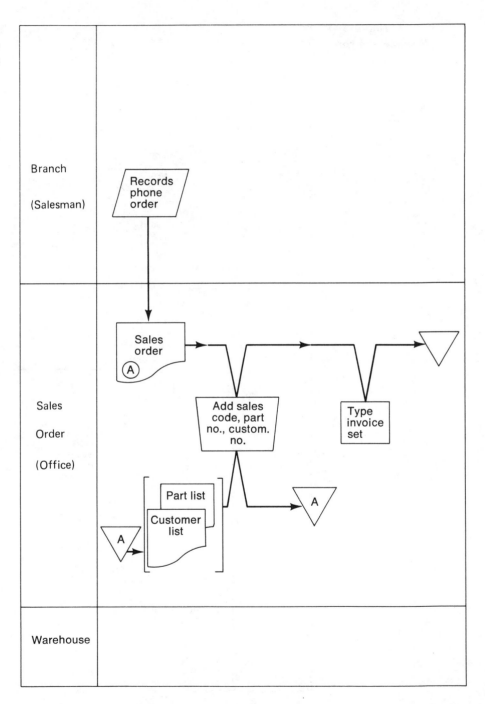

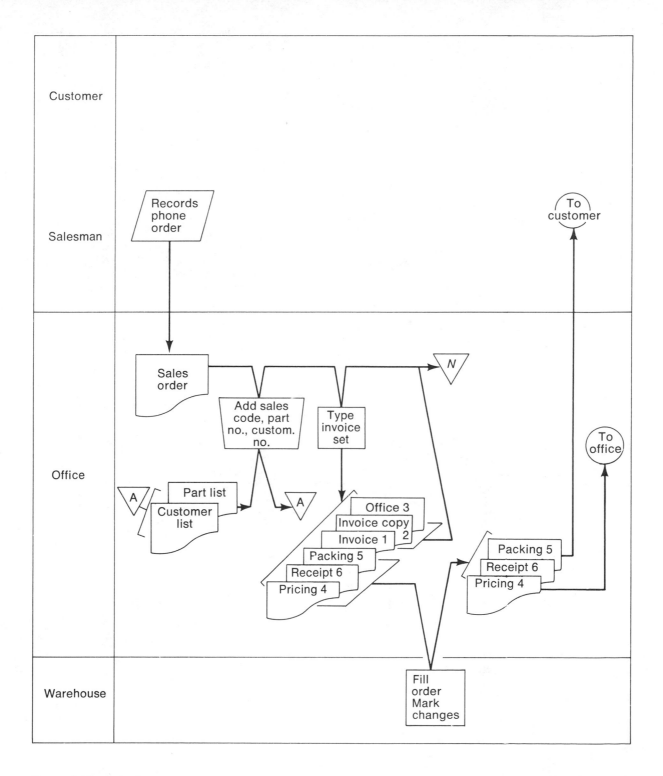

Figure 3.13 Multiple-Copy Forms

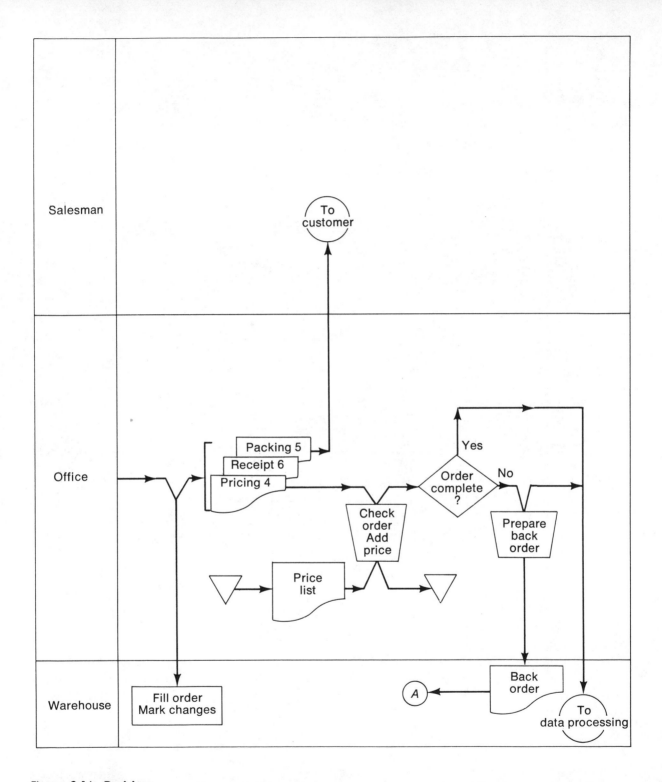

Figure 3.14 Decisions

**Figure 3.15
Organizational Units and
Flow of Data**

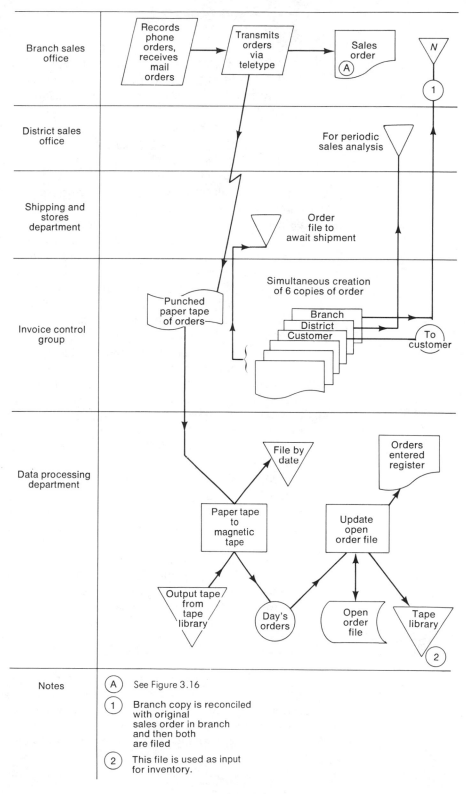

Branch sales office

District sales office

Shipping and stores department

Invoice control group

Data processing department

Notes

Records phone orders, receives mail orders

Transmits orders via teletype

Sales order (A)

N
1

For periodic sales analysis

Order file to await shipment

Punched paper tape of orders

Simultaneous creation of 6 copies of order

Branch
District
Customer

To customer

File by date

Orders entered register

Paper tape to magnetic tape

Update open order file

Output tape from tape library

Day's orders

Open order file

Tape library
2

(A) See Figure 3.16

(1) Branch copy is reconciled with original sales order in branch and then both are filed

(2) This file is used as input for inventory.

on paper tape are converted to magnetic tape with use of a punched-paper-tape reader. Off-line equipment includes keypunching and verifying machines and a card sorter. The narrative description of the order-transmission phase of the system follows.

All orders are transmitted from various sales branches to the home office over the teletypewriter system, and a paper tape is prepared at the home office for the orders received. The original data used to transmit order information are recorded at the sales branches from customer mail orders, phone orders, or the input of salesmen. When orders are transmitted at a sales branch, the data transmitted are recorded at the branch on a sales-order form to be used as a control on the data transmission process.

As data are received at the home office and as the punched paper tape is prepared for orders received, sales orders (see Figure 3.16) are created simultaneously at the home office and distributed by an invoice control group. Six copies of the sales orders are created at the home office. They are distributed to district sales, customers, shipping and stores (three copies, one of which is the packing list copy and another is a delivery receipt), and branches to be compared with copy created at time of order transmission.

The punched paper tape is converted to magnetic tape, and the data on the magnetic tape are then processed as input to update the open order file, which is maintained on a disk pack. During the order-entry run, a daily orders entered transaction register is printed. This register provides a listing of all orders processed with the open order file for the day, together with a financial total of all orders processed. The tape file of the day's orders subsequently is used to update inventory files (reorder analysis) and accounts receivable files (credit analysis).

Now let us approach the flowcharting of this phase of the accounts receivable system outlined above. First, we shall organize the flowchart. To do this, we should determine the organization units involved in the processing activities. They are the sales branches and several departments in the home office: district sales, shipping and stores, the invoice control group, and data processing. Figure 3.15 depicts the organizational units and flow of data in the initial part of the order-transmission phase. The primary audit trail consists of the original sales order, the shipping and stores' copies of the form used for filling the order, and the daily orders entered register.

Program Flowcharts

As mentioned previously, two types of flowcharts are used in automated systems: a systems flowchart and a program flowchart. We have discussed the systems flowchart. The reader has probably noted that this flowchart describes only the flow of data through the system, not how computer programs process the data. For example, Figure 3.15 illustrates two computer programs in the

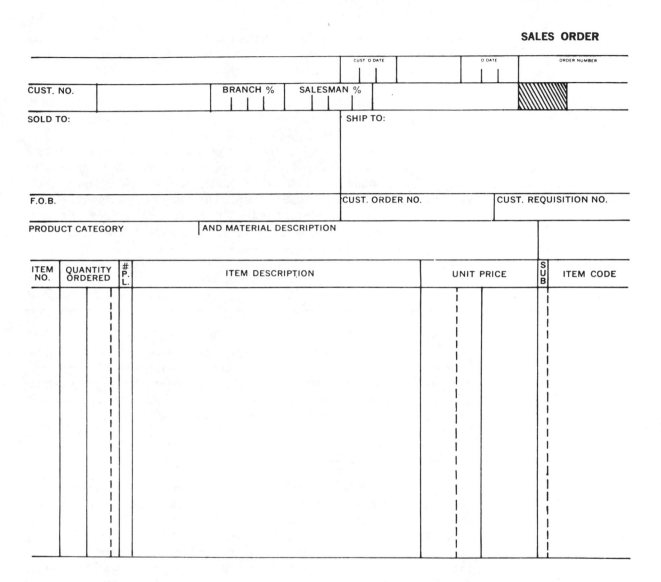

Figure 3.16   Sales Order

systems flowchart: the conversion of paper tape to magnetic tape and the update of the open order file. The systems flowchart for this order-transmission
phase does not indicate how the paper tape is processed or how the open order
file is updated. The sequence of operations and the decisions involved in such
programs are depicted in a program flowchart. Auditors typically do not review

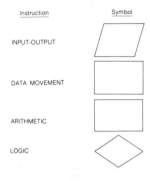

Instruction   Symbol

INPUT-OUTPUT

DATA MOVEMENT

ARITHMETIC

LOGIC

**Figure 3.17
Program Flowcharting
Symbols**

clients' program flowcharts in the analysis of the clients' accounting and data processing system. However, with the increasing use of computer audit programs (to be discussed in Chapter 11), some knowledge of program flowcharts is desirable.

The symbols used in program flowcharting are the same as those used in systems flowcharting and are related to the four basic programming instructions discussed in Chapter 2. (See Figure 3.17 for symbols.)

We shall illustrate the use of these symbols in a program flowchart, by a simple example. Assume that we have card input and each card contains five data fields: part number, old balance (field A), receipts (field B), issues (field C), and flag code (in column 80 of card). The computer process consists of reading the card input, testing the flag field for a 1, computing "new balance = old balance + receipts − issues," and printing the contents of the updated record for those cards with a 1 in the flag field. Figure 3.18 is a program flowchart for this process.

Automatic Flowcharting

Manual flowcharting has the problem of timeliness. There is a tendency to modify the system without updating appropriate flowcharts. Assistance for this problem is provided by automatic flowcharting systems, which use programming source statements as input. From the source-code statement for programming languages (such as COBOL and FORTRAN) it is possible to produce, through other computer programs, logic flowcharts of that program.

HIPO

HIPO, which stands for Hierarchy plus Input-Process-Output is an application function documentation aid. This is a formalized technique designed to assist in the program development process as well as to document the final product. It is a technique designed primarily to trace the flow of data. HIPO has the ability both to document functions and to show a hierarchical interrelationship between those functions. This is valuable because it permits the auditor to locate quickly a particular level of information or a particular function. The hierarchy tells which function initiates actions and which functions react to that action.

Structured Systems Design and Programming

The word structured is used so often in data processing that it has begun to have little meaning. It is used in such terms as structured programming, structured flowcharts, structured walkthroughs, structured design, and structured narratives. The word structured has come to mean an organized approach to various aspects of data processing.

Figure 3.18
Program Flowchart

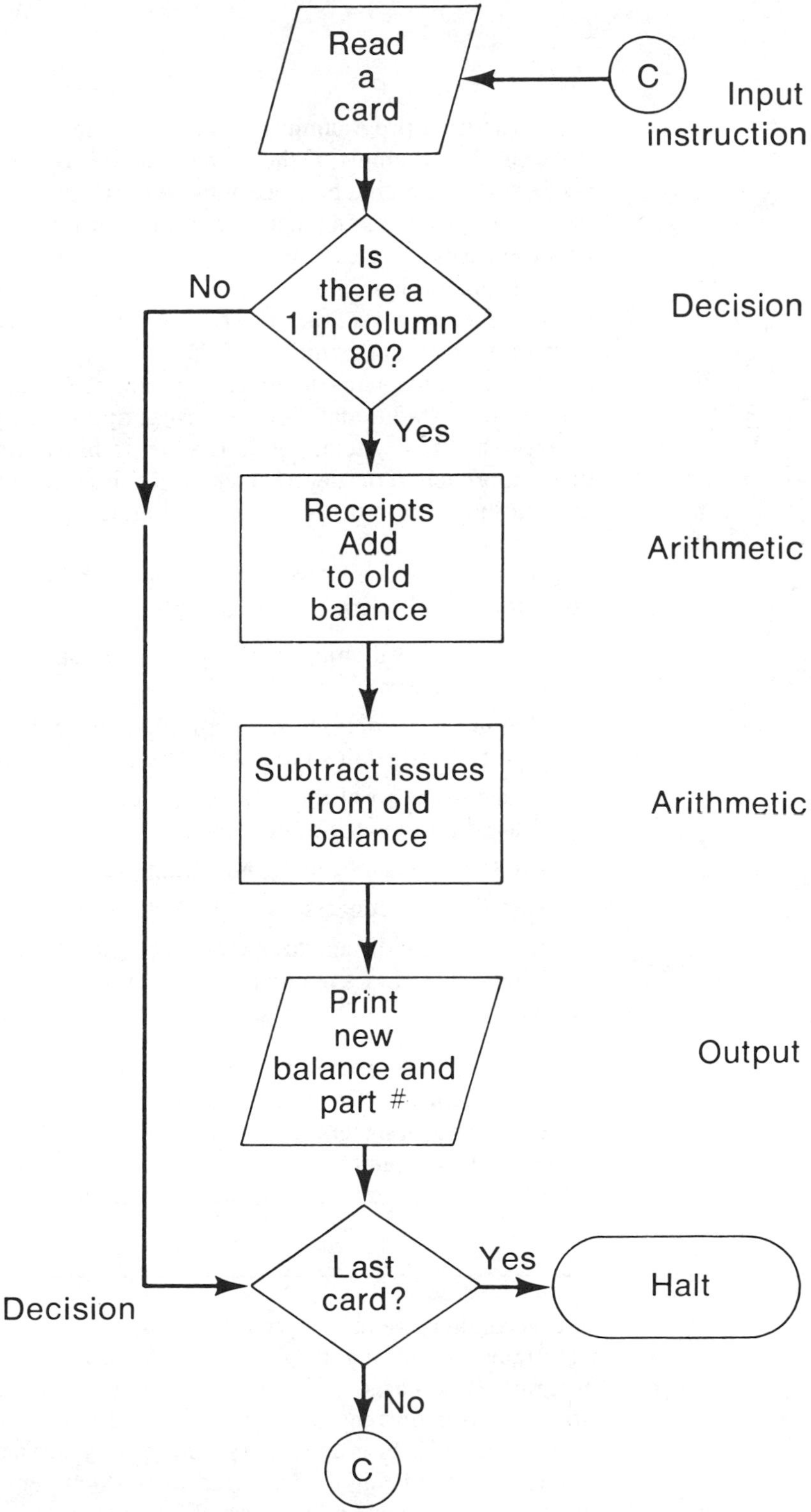

Structured programming is based on the data used to solve the business problem. For example, if the problem is to produce an accounts receivable invoice, then structured programming ties each piece of data used on that invoice back through processing to its source of origin. Structured programming shows how data are generated, and what processing occurred on that data as they progress through the program. If it becomes necessary to change any item on the report it is easy to trace the processing of that item. This makes the maintenance of computer programs much easier.

Structured systems design is a new concept, not just another warmed-over version of a traditional systems design approach. Like structured programming, structured systems design is a hierarchical, modular, and logically organized approach to the development and enhancement of computerized business application. Like structure programming, it is oriented toward output and data structure.

Structured system development approach breaks the systems development task into the following manageable phases:

- Planning—evaluating requests and developing a strategy for satisfying those requests
- Requirements definition—a complete definition of the proposed system in sufficient detail so that it can be properly implemented
- Design—design of the data and procedures needed to produce the desired outputs from those data
- Implementation—the design, coding, and testing of computer programs
- Installation—conversion of the existing system to the new system
- Operations—the actual operation of the new system on the computer. This also includes manual operations and systems maintenance
- Use—the actual use of the outputs from the new system

Systems and programs using the structured approach have proven successful in industry. The major advantage of the structured approach is that it forces systems designers and programmers to think through the problem and solution prior to implementation. Using this process, the probability of the solution solving the need is substantially increased.

Summary

In this chapter, we have discussed an important analytical and documentation technique for auditing: the flowchart. We have illustrated both the systems and program flowcharts, with emphasis on the systems flowchart. The systems flowchart is important to the auditor because it is the primary means by which client companies now describe systems of any size and complexity and because it is more often being used as a means to document, in audit working papers, the auditor's review and analysis of client systems.

Problems

1. *Order processing and billing:* Prepare a systems flowchart for the following order processing and billing system.

   The sales department prepares a six-part sales invoice from customer order and files the order alphabetically by customer. Part 2 is sent to the credit department for credit approval, and the remaining parts are held until credit is approved. Upon arrival, part 2 is returned to sales and filed with the customer's order. Parts 1 (sales invoice) and 3 (posting copy) are sent to the billing department; part 4 is sent to shipping as a packing slip; part 5 is sent to the warehouse as a stock request; and part 6 is sent to the customer.

   The warehouse releases the goods and sends the stock request (part 5) with the goods to shipping. In shipping, the goods are compared with the description on the stock request and units shipped are noted in this request. Shipping takes the packing slip from the files and sends it with the goods to the customer. The stock request (part 5) is sent to billing.

   Billing enters shipped items (marked on the stock request) on the sales invoice (part 1) and on the posting copy (part 3), makes extensions and checks them, compares prices with the price list, and runs a tape of extended amounts shown on the posting copy. The stock request (part 5) is filed numerically; numerical sequence is accounted for at this time. The sales invoice is sent to the customer. The posting copy is sent to general accounting where it is placed in the open invoice file. The tape of extended amounts is also sent to general accounting where it is used to post the total to the sales control account in the general ledger. The open invoice file is balanced monthly to the general ledger sales control.

2. *Cash receipts:* Prepare a systems flowchart for the processing described below. Use the appropriate flowcharting symbols.

   Most cash receipts of the Red, White, and Blue Enterprises are received by mail. All incoming mail is opened and sorted by a mail clerk. After sorting, each check is compared for amount with the remittance advice, which normally accompanies the check, and the remittance advice is stamped "paid." A tape listing of the checks is then prepared by the clerk and is forwarded to the treasurer's office for filing by date and for use in preparing bank reconciliations.

   The checks are forwarded to the cashier, who prepares the deposit slip in duplicate, one for bank deposit purposes to accompany the checks and the other to be filed by deposit date. The remittance advices are sent by the mail clerk to the accounts receivable department. Postings are made in the department to accounts receivable subsidiary ledger records. These records are kept in vertical trays, and entries to them are made with a posting machine. As the receivable records are updated, a *cash received in account* journal is prepared in duplicate: One copy is retained in the accounts receivable department, and the other is forwarded to general ledger accounting. After the accounts receivable records have been updated, the remittance advices are filed alphabetically by date.

3. *Cash disbursements:* Prepare a flowchart from the following information describing a purchasing and cash disbursements system for Environmental Sciences, Inc.

    The purchasing department prepares a four-part purchase order from a written purchase request by the plant superintendent or one of the foremen. Parts 1 and 2 are sent to the vendor; part 3 is filed as a control and follow-up copy for open orders; part 4 is sent to the receiving department for use as a receiving report.

    Goods received are indicated on part 4, which is then sent to purchasing where it is filed with part 3 of the purchase order and held until the vendor's invoice is received. (No perpetual inventory records are maintained.) When the vendor's invoice is received, parts 3 and 4 are taken from the file and checked against the invoice for accuracy of prices and computations. The invoice is assigned a number and recorded in the invoice register. The account distribution code is written on the invoice. Part 3 is then filed numerically. The invoice and part 4 of the purchase order are sent to the accounts payable clerk, who files these two documents by due date.

    When the invoices are due, the clerk pulls the invoices and purchase orders and prepares checks and check copies (the copies show account distribution). From the checks, the clerk prepares an adding-machine tape of the cash amounts and forwards the invoices, purchase orders, checks, check copies, and tape to the general accounting department. A clerk in general accounting posts the amounts on the check copies in the cash disbursements book and totals the postings made from the batch of check copies. The total of the postings is then compared with the total on the tape forwarded from accounts payable. If the totals are not in agreement, the difference is analyzed and reconciled; if they are in agreement, the general accounting clerk forwards the checks with supporting invoices, purchase orders, and check copies to the treasurer for his or her signature.

    The treasurer reviews the supporting data, signs the checks, and returns all items to the general accounting clerk. The general accounting clerk protects the checks and mails them to the vendors, files the check copies by number, stamps the invoices "paid," and forwards the invoices and attached receivers to the purchasing department.

4. Charting, Inc., your new audit client, processes its sales and cash receipts documents in the following manner.

    (a) *Payment on account:* The mail is opened each morning by a mail clerk in the sales department. The mail clerk prepares remittance advices (showing customer and amount paid) if they are not received. The checks and remittance advices are then forwarded to the sales department supervisor, who reviews each check and forwards the checks and remittance advices to the accounting department supervisor.

The accounting department supervisor, who also functions as credit manager in approving new credit and all credit limits, reviews all checks for payments on past due accounts and then forwards the checks and remittance advices to the accounts receivable clerk, who arranges the advices in alphabetical order. The remittance advices are posted directly to the accounts receivable ledger cards. The checks are endorsed by stamp and totaled, and the total is posted in the cash receipts journal. The remittance advices are filed chronologically.

After receiving the cash from the previous day's cash sales, the accounts receivable clerk prepares the daily deposit slip in triplicate. The original and second copy accompany the bank deposit; the third copy of the deposit slip is filed by date.

(b) *Sales:* Sales clerks prepare sales invoices in triplicate. The original and second copy are presented to the cashier; the third copy is retained by the sales clerk in the sales book. When the sale is for cash, the customer pays the sales clerk, who presents the money to the cashier with the invoice copies.

A credit sale is approved by the cashier from an approved credit list after the sales clerk prepares the three-part invoice. After receiving the cash or approving the invoice, the cashier validates the original copy of the sales invoice and gives it to the customer. At the end of each day the cashier recaps the sales and cash received and forwards the cash and the second copy of all sales invoices to the accounts receivable clerk.

The accounts receivable clerk balances the cash received with cash sales invoices and prepares a daily sales summary. The credit sales invoices are posted to the accounts receivable ledger, and all the invoices are sent to the inventory control clerk in the sales department for posting in the inventory control cards. After posting, the inventory control clerk files all invoices numerically. The accounts receivable clerk posts the daily sales summary in the cash receipts and sales journals and files the sales summaries by date. The cash from cash sales is combined with the cash received on account to comprise the daily bank deposit.

(c) *Bank deposits:* The bank validates the deposit slip and returns the second copy to the accounting department where it is filed by date by the accounts receivable clerk. Monthly bank statements are reconciled promptly by the accounting department supervisor and filed by date.

You recognize that there are weaknesses in the existing system and believe a chart of information and document flow would be beneficial in evaluating this client's internal control in preparing for your examination of the financial statements. Complete the flowchart given in Figure 3.19 (pages 88–89) for sales and cash receipts of Charting, Inc., by labeling the appropriate symbols and indicating information flow. (The chart is com-

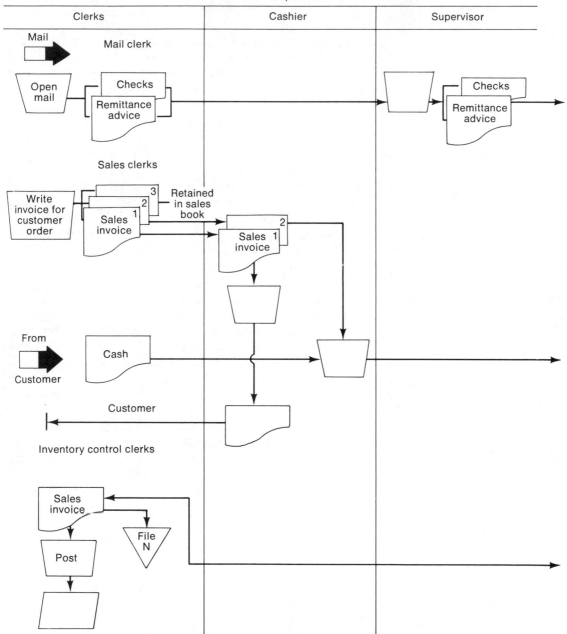

Figure 3.19 Flowchart for Sales and Cash Receipts, Charting, Inc.

SOURCE: Adapted with permission from the Uniform CPA Examination, copyright by the American Institute of Certified Public Accountants, Inc.

Accounting department

Supervisor	Accounts receivable clerk

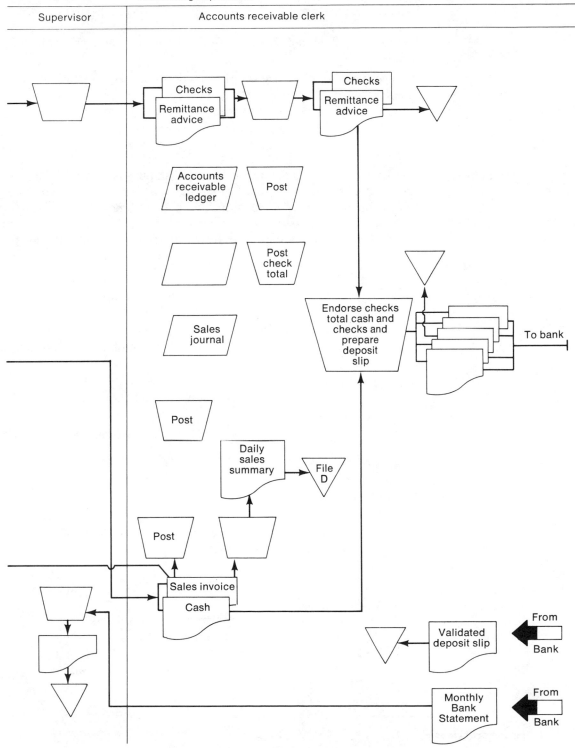

plete as to symbols and document flow. The symbols used are explained in Figure 3.20.)

5. This problem is a continuation of the order-transmission phase of the accounts receivable system described in the chapter. Below is the description of the remaining phases of the system. Prepare a systems flowchart for this system.

Invoicing   The home office does the invoicing for all shipments made. The invoices are prepared by the computer by processing the open order file, which contains data on the order shipped, including the unit price, and transaction data on shipments. The source document creating shipment transactions is the shipping and stores' copy of the order. On this document, shipping per-

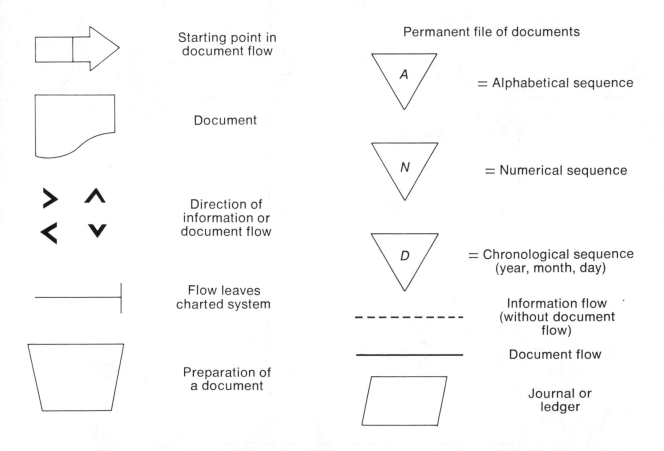

Figure 3.20 Flowchart Symbols

sonnel indicate the quantity shipped, shipping method, freight information, and special charges. This information is in addition to the standard information already printed on this copy of the standard order form (quantity ordered, customer, and branch information). The documents arrive for keypunching. After keypunching and verification, the shipment cards are processed. The data on the cards are converted to data on magnetic tape.

Processing

The shipment transactions on magnetic tape are then processed with the open order file to prepare an invoice. The output from this processing, in addition to invoice, consists of:

- An updated order file
- A tape file of stock items shipped used for sales analysis, production planning, and updating of perpetual inventory files
- A tape file of all the day's billings (invoices) for later updating of accounts receivable files

Six copies of the invoice are prepared (see Figure 3.21) The original and two copies are sent to the customer. The original includes a payment identity coupon, which is torn off and returned by the customer with his or her remittance. The coupon is processed by the cashier, as indicated in the cash receipts section of this system, and is used as a turnaround source document for keypunching cash receipts punched cards to be used in updating the accounts receivable file and in preparing the daily cash receipts–sales register. One copy each of the invoice goes to the invoice control group, salesman, and branch office from which the sale originated.

Accounts Receivable Updating

The accounts receivable records are maintained on portions of two disk files: One file contains the basic accounts receivable records, including data such as account balance, amount on order, credit limit, credit history, delinquency history, and sales history; the other file contains data on the details supporting the account balance such as unpaid invoices.

The accounts receivable files are updated with normal transactions such as cash receipts, billings, credit memos, and new orders. Other types of transactions include new accounts, changes to "permanent" data in customer accounts such as credit limit, and customers' names and addresses.

The cash receipts are initially received in the mailroom, where all company mail is opened. Checks are forwarded to the cashier, who prepares an adding-machine tape of the checks for subsequent comparison with a computer-prepared deposit slip. The payment identity coupon (see Figure 3.21) sent out as part of the customer's invoice is returned with the

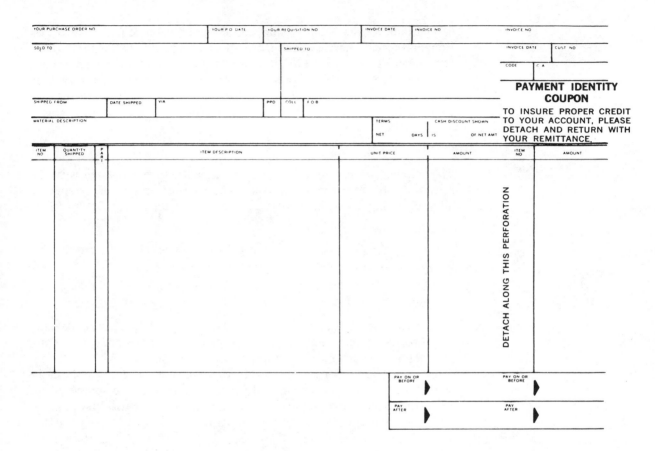

Figure 3.21   Invoice with Payment Identity Coupon

customer's check and is forwarded to the keypunching section where a cash receipts punched card is prepared. (The other primary input transactions are the billings and the day's orders, prepared as a result of previous processing, described earlier in this system.)

All credit memoranda for returned material are initiated by the invoice control group or sales branches upon receipt of a *returned material receiving report*. Branches forward their coupon memoranda, approved by their branch managers, to the home office for approval. All credit memoranda in excess of $1,000 must be approved by the controller before they can be posted in accounts receivable; all other credit memoranda must be approved by the general ledger bookkeeper. Miscellaneous credits also originate in the invoice control group to correct invoicing errors, and they are processed in the same manner as material-returned credits.

After the input transactions are keypunched and verified, they are written on magnetic tape. The input transaction tape and the transaction tapes for billings and orders are then sorted into customer-number sequence for updating the accounts receivable files. The computer processing of the transactions and the accounts receivable files produces the following machine-readable output for subsequent processing and visible output for distribution:

(a) Machine-readable output

    (i)   Updated accounts receivable files.

    (ii) Exception transactions used to prepare a daily exception report for review and follow-up by the input–output control group. (The exceptions are explained later.)

(b) Visible output

    (i)   Daily sales–cash receipts register (see Figure 3.22). This register is prepared in customer-number sequence and, for each customer having transactions that day, shows the cash receipts and/or sales information. Also shown are the balance in the customer's account after the transactions are posted, the grand totals for cash receipts and billings, total sundry cash receipts, the total balance of all accounts receivable, and the number of invoices and cash receipts transactions processed during the day.

    (ii) Cash deposit slip. This slip is actually a part of the daily sales–cash receipts register (see Figure 3.22, right); it lists all cash receipts processed by the computer. This slip is prepared in duplicate and returned to the cashier for agreement with the remittance adding-machine tape and for deposit in the bank.

Preparation of Aged Trial Balance and Monthly Statements

An aged trial balance is prepared at the end of the month by computer processing of the accounts receivable files. The aged trial balance lists, in customer-number sequence, all invoices, credit and debit memos, and *contra* (application of company purchases against a delinquent customer's balance) by data number and amount; the aged trial balance ages the amount according to 30-60-90 and over categories.

As the result of the aged-trial-balance processing program, the computer prepares an *overdue accounts* magnetic tape; this tape is used to prepare an overdue accounts list that shows all overdue accounts for each branch office. Monthly statements are prepared for each customer.

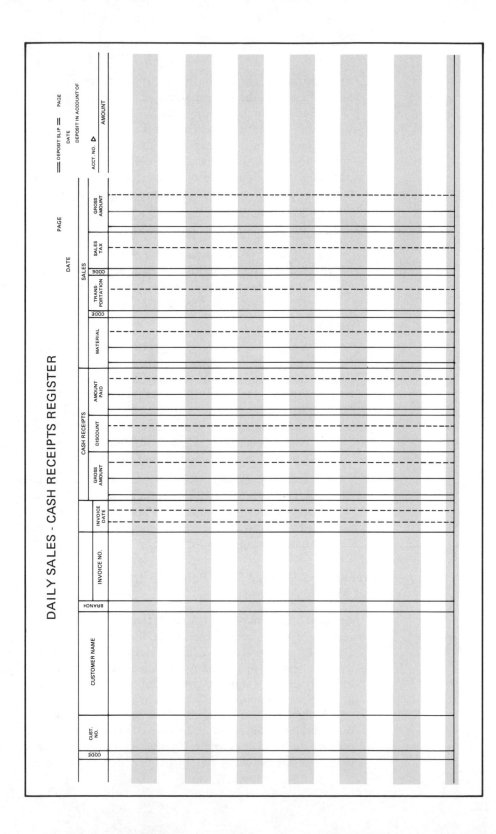

Figure 3.22　Daily Sales–Cash Receipts Register

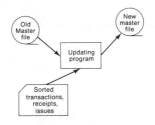

Figure 3.23
Systems Flowchart
Showing the Updating of
an Inventory Master File

6. Prepare a program flowchart for the following updating process.

Figure 3.23 is a systems flowchart showing the updating of an inventory master file, which is compiled in ascending sequence by part number. Each record in the file includes part number and quantity on hand. The file is updated daily by processing changes in stock status (transactions). The transactions are in the form of punched cards, and each card shows part number, transaction code, and quantity. There are two valid transaction codes: code 1 is for the receipt of more stock, and code 2 is for the issue of stock to manufacturing. There can be more than one transaction for each part number in the master file.

Previously the transaction cards were sorted in part-number sequence, and, for each part number, by transaction code. For example, if part number 1,234 had three receipts and one issue during the day, the transaction cards would appear as shown in Figure 3.24. There are no transactions for stock items not found in the master file.

Figure 3.24
Transaction Cards

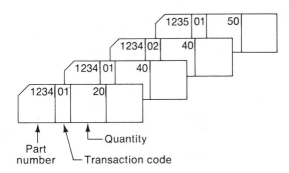

EDP AUDIT PROCESS*

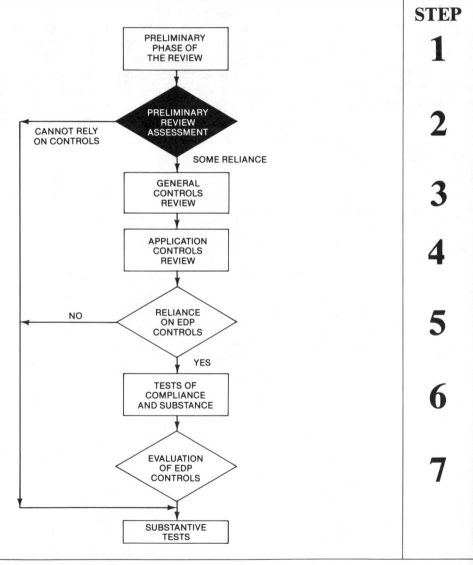

STEP

1

2

3

4

5

6

7

Diagram is adapted from The Auditor's Study and Evaluation of Internal Control in EDP Systems, *pages 21–24. Copyright © 1977 by the American Institute of Certified Public Accountants, Inc. (See Figure 9.1 for a complete explanation of the steps.)*

4

RISKS IN A COMPUTERIZED BUSINESS ENVIRONMENT

(2) Preliminary Phase of the Review—Assessment

Purpose:
- Assess significance of EDP and non-EDP accounting controls.
- Determine extent of additional review within EDP.

Method: Judgment.

OBJECTIVE

The preliminary assessment deals with how well the controls appear to reduce the business risks. This chapter explains how to identify and quantify business risk.

A risk is a condition that can result in loss to an organization. Risks are ever present, although the losses may occur only infrequently. Fire is a risk, but buildings burn down only occasionally. The risk turns into a loss when some event triggers the risk, such as a faulty electrical circuit that causes a fire to occur.

When a computer is introduced into a business organization, the risks change. Some risks may be reduced, while others are increased. In addition, there are new risks associated with a computer that were not present in a manual processing environment. For example, a computer could produce a $1 million weekly payroll check for an hourly employee, an event that is almost impossible in a manual system.

The objective of this chapter is to explain the concept of risk, as well as the new and increased risks occurring within the computer environment. The auditor must understand the new and increased risks in order to evaluate the controls in computer applications. The chapter will also explain how one determines the magnitude of a risk so that it can be determined how many resources can be economically allocated to reduce that risk.

Explanation of Risk

Risk is the potential for loss in an organization. The term *exposure* is frequently used as a synonym for risk. The important concept to remember about risk is that it is ever present and that risks per se cannot be dealt with directly. For example, fire is a risk, and fraud is a risk; but the establishment of policies such as "from this point on, no one will commit a fraud" has little effect on the risk itself.

The risk is turned into a loss by threat. A *threat* is the trigger that causes the risk to become a loss. For example, if fire is a risk, then a can of gasoline in the house, or young children playing with matches, are threats that can cause the fire to occur. While it is difficult to deal with risks, one can deal very specifically with threats.

Threats are reduced or eliminated by controls. Thus, *control* can be identified as anything that tends to cause the reduction of risk. In our fire situation, if we removed the can of gasoline from the home or stopped the young children from playing with matches, we would have eliminated the threat, and thus reduced the probability that the risk of fire would be realized.

If our controls are inadequate to reduce the risk, we have a vulnerability. A *vulnerability,* therefore, can be defined as a flaw in the system of control that will enable a threat to be exploited. For example, if our controls stated that no one should leave gasoline in the home, but did not inform our repair people of the control, they would produce a threat if they brought gasoline into the home. Thus, we would say that we had a vulnerability in our control system.

The process of evaluating risks, threats, controls, and vulnerabilities is frequently called *risk analysis*. This is a task that the auditor performs when he or she approaches the assessment of internal control from a risk perspective. Note that the tendency in auditing today is to go through a formal risk analysis process because of the importance of internal controls in a computerized business environment.

In this chapter, we will explore further the concepts of risk and risk analysis. The objective of this is to understand the importance of risk analysis in the audit process. We will then review many of the new and increased risks associated with the computer. This approach is designed to produce insight into the changing nature of the audit process. As you review these risks, think how many of them might be possible in a manual environment, how many are unique to a computer environment, and which ones might be more severe in a computer environment.

Auditors need to know two things about risk. First, they must identify the risks that are to be addressed in any particular audit process. Second, they must determine the magnitude of those risks. Guidance will be provided later in the chapter on how to determine the magnitude of a risk. (See Exhibit 4.1 for definitions.)

**Exhibit 4.1
Definitions**

RISK

Risk is the potential loss to an organization, as, for example, that resulting from the misuse of its computer. This may involve unauthorized disclosure, unauthorized modification, and/or loss of information resources, as well as the authorized but incorrect use of a computer. Risk can be measured to some extent by performing a risk analysis.

RISK ANALYSIS

Risk analysis is an analysis of an organization's information resources, its existing controls, and its remaining organization and computer system vulnerabilities. It combines the loss potential for each resource or combination of resources with an estimated rate of occurrence to establish a potential level of damage in dollars or other assets.

THREAT

A threat is something capable of exploiting a vulnerability in the security of a computer system or application. Threats include both hazards and events that can trigger flaws.

VULNERABILITY

A vulnerability is a design, implementation, or operations flaw that may be exploited by a threat; the flaw causes the computer system or application to operate in a fashion different from its published specifications and to result in destruction or misuse of equipment or data.

CONTROL

Control is anything that tends to cause the reduction of risk. Control can accomplish this by reducing harmful effects or by reducing the frequency of occurrence.

Risks Generated by Computer Technology

Risk analysis attempts to identify all the risks and then quantify the severity of the risks. A risk is the potential for loss or damage to an organization from materialized threats. Risk can be measured to a large extent by performing a risk analysis process. A threat, as we have seen, is a possible damaging event. If it occurs, it exploits a vulnerability in the security of a computer-based organization.

Risks, which are ever present in a computerized environment, are generated by a variety of threats. Some of these threats are physical—such as fire, water damage, earthquake, hurricane, etc. Other threats are people-oriented—such as errors, omissions, intentional acts of violence, fraud, etc. These risks cannot be eliminated, but controls can reduce the probability of the risk turning into a damaging event. A *damaging event* is the materialization of a risk to an organization's assets.

Auditors should evaluate a computerized environment's vulnerability to materialization of risk. Vulnerability is a weakness that may be exploited by a threat to cause destruction or misuse of its assets or resources. In examining vulnerabilities, the auditor also assesses the strength of the controls that reduce the risk or vulnerability to an acceptable level.

The risks in a computerized environment include both the risks that would be present in manual processing and some risks that are unique or increased in a computerized environment. The auditor must identify these risks, estimate the severity of the risk, and then develop audit tests to substantiate the impact of the risk on the application. For example, if the auditor felt that erroneous processing was a very high risk for a specific application, then the auditor should devise tests to substantiate the correctness or incorrectness of processing. This could be done by the reprocessing of a sample of transactions to determine whether or not the application had processed the transactions correctly.

The use of a computer introduces new and increased risks into the computerized environment. Thus, in addition to the traditional risks, the auditor needs to assess the impact of these new and increased risks. The following discussion reviews these new and increased risks, and provides many of the conditions that cause the risks to occur.

Risks Unique to or Increased in a Computerized Environment

There are risks that are unique to a computerized environment. In addition, some risks found in manual systems are increased in a computerized environment. The auditor should be aware of these special risks because they pose threats not present in a noncomputerized environment.

These risks are problems associated with a computerized environment and include the following:

- Improper use of technology
- Repetition of errors
- Cascading of errors
- Illogical processing
- Inability to translate user needs into technical requirements
- Inability to control technology
- Incorrect entry of data
- Concentration of data
- Inability to react quickly
- Inability to substantiate processing
- Concentration of responsibilities
- Erroneous or falsified input data
- Misuse by authorized end users
- Uncontrolled system access
- Ineffective security practices for the application
- Procedural errors at the EDP facility
- Program errors
- Operating system flaws
- Communications system failure

Each of these risks will be discussed individually.

Improper Use of Technology   Computer technology provides systems analysts and programmers with a variety of processing capabilities. This technology must be matched to the needs of the user to optimize the implementation of those needs. A mismatch of technology and needs can result in an unnecessary expenditure of organizational resources.

One of the more common misuses of technology is the introduction of new technology prior to the clear establishment of its need. For example, many organizations introduce data base technology without clearly establishing the need for that technology. Experience has shown that the early users of a new technology frequently consume large amounts of resources during the process of learning how to use that new technology.

Some of the types of conditions that lead to the improper use of technology are listed on the next page.

- Systems analyst/programmer improperly skilled in the use of technology
- Early user of new hardware technology
- Early user of new software technology
- Minimal planning for the installation of new hardware and software technology

Repetition of Errors

In a manual processing environment, errors are made individually. Thus, a person might process one item correctly, make an error on the next, process the next twenty correctly, and then make another error. In automated systems, the rules are applied consistently. Thus, if the rules are correct, processing is always correct, but if the rules are erroneous, processing will always be erroneous.

Errors can result from application program problems, hardware failures, and failures in vendor-supplied software. For example, a wrong percentage may have been entered for FICA deductions; thus, every employee for that pay period will have the wrong amount deducted for FICA purposes.

The conditions that cause repetition of errors include these:

- Inadequate checks on entry of master information
- Insufficient program testing
- Failure to monitor the results of processing

Cascading of Errors

The cascading of errors is the domino effect of errors throughout an application system. An error in one part of the program or application triggers a second (yet unrelated) error in another part of the application system. This second error may trigger a third error, and so on.

The cascading of error risk is frequently associated with making changes to application systems. A change is made and tested in the program in which the change occurs. However, some condition has been altered as a result of the change, which causes an error to occur in another part of the application system.

Cascading of errors can occur between applications. This risk intensifies as applications become more integrated. For example, a system that is accepting orders may be tied through a series of applications to a system that replenishes inventory based on orders. Thus, an insignificant error in the order-entry program can "cascade" through a series of applications—resulting in a very serious error in the inventory replenishment program.

The types of conditions that lead to cascading of errors include these:

- Inadequately tested applications
- Failure to communicate the type and date of changes being implemented
- Limited testing of program changes

Illogical Processing

Illogical processing is the performance of an automated event that would be highly unlikely in a manual processing environment—for example, producing a payroll check for a clerical individual for over $1 million. This is possible in an automated system as a result of programming or hardware errors, but highly unlikely in a manual system.

Computerized applications do not have human oversight comparable to that incorporated into manual systems. In addition, fewer people have a good understanding of the processing logic of computerized applications. Thus, in some instances illogical processing may not be readily recognizable.

The conditions that can result in illogical processing are these:

- Failure to check for unusually large amounts on output documents
- Fields that are either too small or too large
- Failure to scan output documents

Inability to Translate User Needs into Technical Requirements

One of the major failures of data processing has been a communication failure between users and technical personnel. In many organizations, users cannot adequately express their needs in terms that facilitate the preparation of computerized applications. Likewise, the technical computer people are often unable to appreciate the concerns and requirements of their users.

This needs satisfaction risk is a complex risk. Exposures include failure to implement needs because users were unaware of technical capabilities, improperly implemented needs because the technical personnel did not understand user requirements, users accepting improperly implemented needs because they are unsure how to specify changes, and the building of redundant manual systems to compensate for weaknesses in computerized applications.

The conditions that can lead to the inability to translate user needs into technical requirements include these:

- Users without technical EDP skills
- Technical people without sufficient understanding of user requirements
- Users' inability to specify requirements in sufficient detail
- Multiuser systems with no user "in charge" of the system

Inability to Control Technology

The problems associated with the implementation of new technology have absorbed most of the efforts of data processing personnel. The Systems Auditability and Control (SAC) study by Stanford Research Institute implied that there was too little time left to develop and install technological controls. The result is expenditure of resources to correct technological problems.

Controls are needed over the technological environment. The controls ensure that the proper version of the proper program is in production at the right time; that the proper files are mounted; that operators perform the proper instructions; that adequate procedures are developed to prevent, detect, and correct problems occurring in the operating environment; and that the proper data are maintained and retrievable when needed. The types of conditions that result in uncontrolled technology include these:

- Selection of vendor-offered system control capabilities by systems programmers without considering audit needs
- Too many control tradeoffs for operational efficiency
- Inadequate restart/recovery procedures
- Inadequate control over different versions of programs

Incorrect Entry of Data

In computerized applications, there is a mechanical step required to convert input data into machine-readable format. In the process of conducting this task, errors can occur. Data that were properly prepared and authorized may be entered into computerized applications incorrectly.

Much of the data entered into batch type systems are entered using a keyboard device. Some of these devices are keypunch machines and key-to-disk machines. The data originator manually transcribes the input information onto some type of form, and the form is given to a key operator to enter on computer media. During this keying process, errors are made.

In the newer technology, data can be originated and entered at the same time. For example, order-entry clerks receive orders by telephone and key them directly into computer memory. However, errors can still occur during this process.

Other methods of data entry include optical scanners and process control computers. The latter monitor such items as production machinery, automatic cash dispensers and point-of-sale equipment. These are all mechanical devices and, thus, subject to failure.

The type of conditions that can cause incorrect entry of data include these:

- Human errors in keying data
- Mechanical failure of hardware devices
- Misinterpretation of characters or meaning of manually recorded input
- Misunderstanding of data entry procedures

Concentration of Data

Computerized applications concentrate data in a format that is easy to access. In manual systems, data are voluminous and stored in many places. It is difficult for an unauthorized individual to spend much time undetected browsing through file cabinets or other manual storage areas.

But, using computerized media, unauthorized individuals can browse by using computer programs. This may be difficult to detect without adequate safeguards. In addition, the data can be copied quickly without leaving any visible trail or destroying the original data. Thus, the owners of the data may not be aware that the data have been compromised.

Data base technology increases the risk of data manipulation and compromise. The more data stored in a single place, the greater the value of that information to an unauthorized individual. For example, the information about an individual in the payroll application is restricted to current pay information, but when those data are coupled with personnel history, not only is current pay information available but also pay history, individual skills, years of employment, progression of employment, and perhaps performance evaluation.

The concentration of data increases the problems of greater reliance on a single piece of data and reliance on a single computer file. If the fact entered is erroneous, the more applications that rely on that piece of data, the greater the impact of the error. In addition, the more applications that use the concentrated data, the greater the impact when those data become unavailable because of problems with either the hardware or software used for processing the data.

The conditions that can create problems attributable to the concentration of data in computerized applications include these:

- Inadequate access controls enabling unauthorized access to data
- Erroneous data and their impact on multiple users of the data
- Impact of hardware and software failures that make the data available to multiple users

Inability to React Quickly Much of the value of computerized applications is the ability to satisfy user needs on a timely basis. Some of these needs are predetermined and reports are prepared on a regular basis to meet these needs. Other needs occur periodically, requiring special actions to satisfy them. If the computerized application is unable to satisfy these special needs on a timely basis, redundant systems may be built for that purpose.

One of the measures of success of a computerized application is the speed with which special requests can be satisfied. Some of the newer on-line data base applications with a query language can satisfy some requests within a very short time. On the other hand, some of the older batch-oriented applications may take several days or weeks to satisfy a special request. In some instances, the structuring of the application system is an inhibiting factor in satisfying requests. For example, if an auditor wanted all of the supporting information for a supply requisition in a tape-batched system, the cost and difficulty of satisfying that request may be prohibitive. The reason is that the requisition could be spread over many weeks of processing—owing to back orders, returned shipments, and shipping errors. The evidence supporting the transaction may be spread over many tape files and the cost of processing those files may be exorbitant.

Some of the conditions that can cause computerized applications to be unable to react quickly include these:

- The structure of the computer files is inconsistent with the information requested.
- The general-purpose extract programs are not available to satisfy the desired request.
- Computer time is unavailable to satisfy the request.
- The cost of processing exceeds the value of the information requested.

Inability to Substantiate Processing

Computerized applications should contain the capability to substantiate processing. This substantiation includes both the ability to reconstruct the processing of a single transaction and the ability to reconstruct control totals. Computerized applications should be able to produce all the source transactions that support a control total, and substantiate that any source document is contained in a control total.

Application systems need to substantiate processing for the purposes of correcting errors and proving the correctness of processing. When errors occur, computer personnel need to pinpoint the cause of those errors so they can be corrected. Computerized application customers, other users, and control-oriented personnel, such as auditors, frequently want to verify the correctness of processing.

The conditions that may result in the inability to substantiate processing include these:

- Evidence is not retained long enough.
- The cost of substantiating processing exceeds the benefits derived from the process.
- The evidence from intermediate processing is not retained.

Concentration of Responsibilities

The computerization of an application tends to concentrate the responsibilities of many people into the automated application. Responsibilities that had been segregated for control purposes among many people may be concentrated into a single application system. In addition, a single application system may concentrate responsibilities from many departments within an organization.

The responsibilities in a computerized environment may be concentrated in both the application system and computer-oriented personnel. For example, the data base administrator may absorb data control responsibilities from many areas in the organization. A single computer system project leader may have the processing responsibility for many areas in the organization. New methods of separation of duties must be substituted for the previous segregation of duties among people.

The conditions that cause the concentration of responsibilities in a computerized environment include these:

- The establishment of a data processing programming and systems group to develop computerized applications for an organization
- Centralized processing of computerized applications
- Establishment of a data base administration function

Erroneous or Falsified Input Data

Erroneous or falsified input data is the simplest and most common cause of undesirable performance by an applications system. Vulnerabilities occur wherever data are collected, manually processed, or prepared for entry to the computer:

- Unreasonable or inconsistent source data values may not be detected.
- Keying errors during transcription may not be detected.
- Incomplete or poorly formatted data records may be accepted and treated as if they were complete records.
- Records in one format may be interpreted according to a different format.
- An employee may fraudulently add, delete, or modify data (e.g., payment vouchers, claims) to obtain benefits (e.g., checks, negotiable coupons) for him- or herself.
- Lack of document counts and other controls over source data or input transactions may allow some of the data or transactions to be lost without detection—or allow extra records to be added.
- Records about the data entry personnel (e.g., a record of a personnel action) may be modified during data entry.
- Data that arrive at the last minute (or under some other special or emergency condition) may not be verified prior to processing.
- Records in which errors have been detected may be corrected without verification of the full record.

Misuse by Authorized End Users

End users are the people served by the EDP system. The system is designed for their use, but they can also misuse it for undesirable purposes. It is often very difficult to determine whether their use of the system is in accordance with the legitimate performance of their job:

- An employee may convert information to an unauthorized use; for example, she or he may sell privileged data about an individual to a prospective employer, credit agency, insurance company, or competitor; or may use statistics for stock market transactions before their public release.

- A user whose job requires access to individual records in a file may manage to compile a complete listing of the file and then make unauthorized use of it (e.g., sell a listing of employees' home addresses as a mailing list).
- Unauthorized altering of information may be accomplished for an unauthorized end user (e.g., theft of services).
- An authorized user may use the system for personal benefit (e.g., theft of services).
- A supervisor may manage to approve and enter a fraudulent transaction.
- A disgruntled or terminated employee may destroy or modify records—possibly in such a way that backup records are also corrupted and useless.
- An authorized user may accept a bribe to modify or obtain information.

Uncontrolled System Access   Organizations expose themselves to unnecessary risk if they fail to establish controls over who can enter the EDP area, who can use the EDP system, and who can access the information contained in the system:

- Data or programs may be stolen from the computer room or other storage areas.
- EDP facilities may be destroyed or damaged by either intruders or employees.
- Individuals may not be adequately identified before they are allowed to enter the EDP area.
- Remote terminals may not be adequately protected from use by unauthorized persons.
- An unauthorized user may gain access to the system via a dial-in line and an authorized user's password.
- Passwords may be inadvertently revealed to unauthorized individuals. A user may write his or her password in some convenient place, or the password may be obtained from card decks, discarded printouts, or by observing the user as he or she types it.
- A user may leave a logged-in terminal unattended, allowing an unauthorized person to use it.
- A terminated employee may retain access to an EDP system because his or her name and password are not immediately deleted from authorization tables and control lists.

- An unauthorized individual may gain access to the system for his or her own purposes (e.g., theft of computer services or data or programs, modification of data, alteration of programs, sabotage, denial of services).
- Repeated attempts by the same user or terminal to gain unauthorized access to the system or to a file may go undetected.

Ineffective Security Practices for the Application

Inadequate manual checks and controls to ensure correct processing by the EDP system or negligence by those responsible for carrying out these checks result in many vulnerabilities:

- Poorly defined criteria for authorized access may result in employees not knowing what information they, or others, are permitted to access.
- The person responsible for security may fail to restrict user access to only those processes and data that are needed to accomplish assigned tasks.
- Large funds disbursements, unusual price changes, and unanticipated inventory usage may not be reviewed for correctness.
- Repeated payments to the same party may go unnoticed because there is no review.
- Sensitive data may be carelessly handled by the application staff, by the mail service, or by other personnel within the organization.
- Postprocessing reports analyzing system operations may not be reviewed to detect security violations.
- Inadvertent modification or destruction of files may occur when trainees are allowed to work on live data.
- Appropriate action may not be pursued when a security variance is reported to the system security officer or to the perpetrating individual's supervisor; in fact, procedures covering such occurrences may not exist.

Procedural Errors at the EDP Facility

Both errors and intentional acts committed by the EDP operations staff may result in improper operational procedures and lapsed controls, as well as losses in storage media and output.

Procedures and Controls

- Files may be destroyed during data base reorganization or during release of disk space.
- Operators may ignore operational procedures—for example, by allowing programmers to operate computer equipment.

- Job control language parameters may be erroneous.
- An installation manager may circumvent operational controls to obtain information.
- Careless or incorrect restarting after shutdown may cause the state of a transaction update to be unknown.
- An operator may enter erroneous information at a CPU console (e.g., control switch in wrong position, terminal user allowed full system access, operator cancels wrong job from queue).
- Hardware maintenance may be performed while production data is on-line and the equipment undergoing maintenance is not isolated.
- An operator may perform unauthorized acts for personal gain (e.g., make extra copies of competitive bidding reports, print copies of unemployment checks, delete a record from journal file).
- Operations staff may sabotage the computer (e.g., drop pieces of metal into a terminal).
- The wrong version of a program may be executed.
- A program may be executed twice using the same transactions.
- An operator may bypass required safety controls (e.g., write rings for tape reels).
- Supervision of operations personnel may not be adequate during nonworking-hour shifts.
- Because of incorrectly learned procedures, an operator may alter or erase the master files.
- A console operator may override a label check without recording the action in the security log.

Storage Media Handling

- Critical tape files may be mounted without being write protected.
- Inadvertently or intentionally mislabeled storage media are erased. In a case where they contain backup files, the erasure may not be noticed until it is needed.
- Internal labels on storage media may not be checked for correctness.
- Files with missing or mislabeled expiration dates may be erased.
- Incorrect processing of data or erroneous updating of files may occur when card decks have been dropped, partial input decks are used, write rings mistakenly are placed in tapes, paper tape is incorrectly mounted, or wrong tape is mounted.
- Scratch tapes used for jobs processing sensitive data may not be adequately erased after use.

- Temporary files written during a job step for use in subsequent steps may be erroneously released or modified through inadequate protection of the files or because of an abnormal termination.
- Storage media containing sensitive information may not get adequate protection because the operations staff is not advised of the nature of the information content.
- Tape management procedures may not adequately account for the current status of all tapes.
- Magnetic storage media that have contained very sensitive information may not be degaussed before being released.
- Output may be sent to the wrong individual or terminal.
- Improperly operating output or postprocessing units (e.g., bursters, decollators, or multipart forms) may result in loss of output.
- Surplus output material (e.g., duplicates of output data, used carbon paper) may not be disposed of properly.
- Tapes and programs that label output for distribution may be erroneous or not protected from tampering.

Program Errors Applications programs should be developed in an environment that requires and supports complete, correct, and consistent program design, good programming practices, adequate testing, review, and documentation, and proper maintenance procedures. Although programs developed in such an environment will still contain undetected errors, programs not developed in this manner will probably be rife with errors. Additionally, programmers can deliberately modify programs to produce undesirable side effects, or they can misuse the programs they are in charge of:

- Records may be deleted from sensitive files without a guarantee that the deleted records can be reconstructed.
- Programmers may insert special provisions in programs that manipulate data concerning themselves (e.g., payroll programmer may alter own payroll records).
- Data may not be stored separately from code with the result that program modifications are more difficult and must be made more frequently.
- Program changes may not be tested adequately before being used in a production run.
- Changes to a program may result in new errors because of unanticipated interactions between program modules.

- Program acceptance tests may fail to detect errors that occur for only unusual combinations of input (e.g., a program that is supposed to reject all except a specified range of values actually accepts an additional value).

- Programs, the content of which should be safeguarded, may not be identified and protected.

- A code, or test data with associated output, or documentation for certified programs may not be filed and retained for reference.

- Documentation for vital programs may not be safeguarded.

- Programmers may fail to keep a change log, or to maintain back copies, or to formalize recordkeeping activities.

- An employee may steal programs he or she is maintaining and use them for personal gain (e.g., for sale to a commercial organization, or to hold another organization for extortion).

- Poor program design may result in a critical data value being initialized to zero twice. An error may occur when the program is modified to change the data value but changes it in only one place.

- Production data may be disclosed or destroyed when used during testing.

- Errors may result when the programmer misunderstands requests for changes to the program.

- Errors may be introduced by a programmer who makes changes directly to machine code.

- Programs may contain routines not compatible with their intended purpose, which can disable or bypass security protection mechanisms. For example, a programmer who anticipates being fired inserts a code into a program that will cause vital system files to be deleted as soon as his or her name no longer appears in the payroll file.

- Inadequate documentation or labeling may result in the wrong version of a program being modified.

Operating System Flaws   Design and implementation errors, system generation and maintenance problems, and deliberate penetrations resulting in modifications to the operating system can produce undesirable effects in the application system. Flaws in the operating system are often difficult to prevent and detect:

- User jobs may be permitted to read or write outside assigned storage area.

- Inconsistencies may be introduced into data because of simultaneous processing of the same file by two jobs.

- An operating system design or implementation error may allow a user to disable audit controls or to access all system information.
- An operating system may not protect a copy of information as thoroughly as it protects the original.
- Unauthorized modification to the operating system may allow a data entry clerk to enter programs and thus subvert the system.
- An operating system crash may expose valuable information, such as password lists or authorization tables.
- Maintenance personnel may bypass security controls while performing maintenance work. At such times the system is vulnerable to errors or intentional acts of the maintenance personnel, or anyone else who might also be on the system and discover the opening (e.g., microcoded sections of the operating system may be tampered with or sensitive information from on-line files may be disclosed).
- An operating system may fail to record that multiple copies of output have been made from spooled storage devices.
- An operating system may fail to maintain an unbroken audit trail.
- When restarting after a system crash, the operating system may fail to ascertain that all terminal locations previously occupied are still occupied by the same individuals.
- A user may be able to get into monitor or supervisory mode.
- The operating system may fail to erase all scratch space assigned to a job after the normal or abnormal termination of the job.
- Files may be allowed to be read or written prior to being opened by the operating system.

Communications System Failure

Information being routed from one location to another over communication lines is vulnerable to accidental failures and to intentional interception and modification by unauthorized parties.

Accidental Failures

- Undetected communications errors may result in incorrect or modified data.
- Information may be accidentally misdirected to the wrong terminal.
- Communication nodes may leave unprotected fragments of messages in memory during unanticipated interruptions in processing.
- Communication protocol may fail to positively identify the transmitter or receiver of a message.

Intentional Acts

- Communications lines may be monitored by unauthorized individuals.
- Data or programs may be stolen via telephone circuits from a remote job entry terminal.
- Programs in the network that switches computers may be modified to compromise security.
- Data may be deliberately changed by an individual's tapping the line (requires some sophistication, but is applicable to financial data).
- An unauthorized user may "take over" a computer communication port as an authorized user disconnects from it. Many systems cannot detect the change. This is particularly true in much of the currently available communication protocols.
- If encryption (i.e., use of codes) is used, keys may be stolen.
- A terminal user may be "spoofed" (i.e., tricked) into providing sensitive data.
- False messages may be inserted into the system.
- True messages may be deleted from the system.
- Messages may be recorded and replayed into the system.

Determining the Magnitude of the Risk

Risk analysis is the process used to develop an estimate of the annual loss expectation due to specific threats. The purpose is to pinpoint the significant threats as a guide to identifying areas for more detailed audit analysis and to develop a yardstick for determining the amount of money reasonable to spend on each of the risks. In other words, the cost of a specific audit task should relate to the potential losses in the area being evaluated.

The risk formula is as follows:

Annual Loss Expectation (ALE) = Average Loss per Occurrence × Frequency of Occurrence

The formula can be simplified as ALE = Loss × Frequency. Let's look at how we might use this formula. Assume that the risk we are concerned about is fire. Assume our home is worth $50,000 and further assume that in the event of fire the home would be a total loss. Let us further assume that, for a house of this type, distance from a fire department, construction, etc. the frequency of burning is once every hundred years. In other words, one out of every hundred houses of this type will burn in a year. The annual loss expectation then is $500 (because $50,000 loss times 0.01 frequency equals $500).

This may sound similar to an insurance premium. In fact, it is. Annual loss expectation attempts to estimate what will be the expected loss in any situation in a year.

The annual loss expectation identified the maximum amount of resources that can be expended to exercise economic control over a threat. In our fire example, it would not be worth a $1,000 insurance premium to protect against fire if the ALE is only $500. This same concept can be applied against business losses.

Let us assume that our risk is fraud. Using the annual loss expectation formula, we estimate that if a fraud occurs we would expect to lose $50,000, and in our business we can expect that loss to occur once every hundred years. In other words, the annual loss expectation of the fraud is $500 per year. To spend more than that would be uneconomical. We can apply the same situation to data error entry. If we assume that in entering data into the computer we make 100 errors per week and the average cost to correct an error is $25, then our weekly loss expectation due to data entry errors is $2,500. This tells us the maximum amount we can afford to expend to control those data entry errors. If we can get key verification for less than $2,500 per week it might be a good control—if, in fact, it reduces the number of errors significantly.

Let us assume that with key verification we can reduce the data entry errors from 100 per week to twenty per week. This is a reduction of 80 errors at $25 per error, or a $2,000 loss expectation reduction. This now tells us how much we can afford to spend for key verification. If a key verification operator and a machine cost us $1,200 per month, then we would have a significant return on investment. In other words, for investing $1,200 we would have a return of $2,000 per week.

Annual Loss Expectation Example

To develop the annual loss expectancy, one can construct a matrix of threats and potential losses. At each intersection one asks if the given threat could cause the given loss. For example, one might decide that fire, flood, and sabotage do not cause theft-of-information losses but that in varying degrees all three result in physical destruction losses and losses due to delayed processing. Likewise internal tampering could cause an indirect theft of assets. In each case where there can be significant loss, one multiplies the loss potential by the probability of occurrence of the threat to generate an annual estimate of loss.

As an example of a loss expectancy estimate, consider the simplified case where there are three EDP tasks in which loss could result from delays in completed processing as follows:

| | | DELAY DURATION | | |
TASK	ONE HOUR	FOUR HOURS	EIGHT HOURS	ONE DAY
A	—	—	$10,000	$ 45,000
B	—	$ 5,000	12,000	55,000
C	$3,000	16,000	45,000	160,000
Total	$3,000	$21,000	$67,000	$260,000

Human acts are more difficult to project since there is no easy way to estimate probability of occurrence. However, one can probably estimate potential losses with acceptable accuracy and so pinpoint critical threats. For example, consider fraud via program tampering. An examination of tasks that disburse funds might reveal the following:

TASK	DOLLARS PER CYCLE	EXPECTED PROGRAM CHANGES (NEXT 12 MONTHS)
J	$20,000,000	5
K	200,000	25
L	5,000,000	10

Further assume that the annual probability of each such delay duration resulting from electric power failures has been estimated to be 0.75, 0.31, 0.10 and 0.09, respectively. One could conclude that the annual loss expectancy from electric power failure would be:

$$0.75 \times \$3,000 + 0.31 \times \$21,000 +$$

$$0.10 \times \$67,000 + 0.09 \times \$260,000$$

$$= \$38,860 \ per \ year.$$

The cost of power failures is relatively easy to estimate since both probability of occurrence and effect on operations can be quantified with some precision. Air conditioning and communications failures also fall into this class. Quantifying fire losses is a different matter. One might deal with them by considering several degrees of severity and a number of loss types as shown in Table 4.1. The probabilities of occurrence come from the estimate of inherent fire safety, and the dollar losses are from the estimates of loss potential. A similar technique can be applied to earthquakes, floods, windstorms, and similar natural disasters.

If one assumed that a 1% theft would definitely be detected and also that the embezzler would not attempt to insert a wrongful program change more often than once in ten changes, one could draw these conclusions:

TASK	POTENTIAL THEFT	FRAUD EXPECTATION	ESTIMATED LOSS
J	$200,000	0.5	$100,000
K	2,000	2.5	5,000
L	50,000	1.0	50,000
			$155,000

Such conclusions might appear improbable. Perhaps the assumptions are not valid. The judgment factor plays a large part in arriving at these conclu-

Table 4.1
Estimating Fire Loss

	FIRE DESCRIPTION		
	MINOR FIRE IN EDP AREA	MAJOR FIRE IN BUILDING	TOTAL LOSS FIRE
OCCURRENCE PROBABILITY	0.10	0.05	.0005
Potential Loss Types			
Building Damage	$10,000	$100,000	$3,700,000
EDP Hardware	50,000	10,000	2,100,000
General Equipment	5,000	—	285,000
Supplies, etc.	$10,000	—	130,000
Task D—Delay	—	—	35,000
Task E—Delay	5,000	7,000	100,000
Task F—Delay	12,000	20,000	250,000
File Reconstruct	5,000	—	85,000
Total Potential Loss	97,000	137,000	6,685,000
Annual Loss	$ 9,700	$ 6,850	$ 3,342

sions; repeated attempts may serve to sharpen one's judgment in such matters. As a result of iterative analyses, one might arrive at an annual loss for J of $10,000, or twice that of K, and for task L a loss equal to that for K or $5,000; the revised annual loss potential for the three tasks then would be only $20,000.

The key point is that in attempting the estimate, a clearer picture of the critical exposures and reasonable criteria emerges. It now becomes obvious that task K is just as critical as task J because, even though it disburses only one hundredth as much money per cycle, the program is still in a fluid state and therefore more subject to compromise. Because a quantitative effort has been undertaken, the probability of occurrence of each threat and its effect on the EDP facility have been examined realistically.

Clearly this is not an exact science. Indeed, it is quite likely that one will have to reappraise threats and losses more than once, concentrating on the areas initially identified as most critical, before the loss expectancy estimate reaches a satisfactory level of confidence. In some cases it may not be feasible to generate more than a rough estimate; however, the value of disciplined thinking about risk will be ample reward for the effort to deal with it in a quantitative way.

Selecting Remedial Measures

When the estimate of annual loss has been completed, EDP management will have a clear picture of the significant threats and critical EDP tasks. The response to significant threats can take one or more of the following forms:

> *Alter the environment* to reduce the probability of occurrence. In an extreme case this could lead to relocation of the EDP facility to a less exposed location. Alternatively, a hazardous occupancy adjacent to or inside the EDP facility could be moved elsewhere.

Erect barriers to ward off the threat. These might take the form of changes to strengthen the building against the effects of natural disasters, saboteurs, or vandals. Special equipment can be installed to improve the quality and reliability of electric power. Special door locks, guards, and intrusion detectors can be used to control access to critical areas.

Improve procedures to close gaps in controls. These might include better controls over operations, more rigorous pre-hire screening, or standards for programming and software testing.

Early detection of harmful situations permits more rapid response to minimize damage. Fire or intrusion detectors are both typical examples.

Contingency plans permit satisfactory accomplishment of company missions subsequent to a damaging event. Contingency plans will include immediate response to emergencies to protect life and property and to limit damage, maintenance of plans and materials needed for backup operation off-site, and maintenance of plans for prompt recovery following major damage to or destruction of the EDP facility.

The criteria for selecting specific remedial measures are that the annual cost of the remedial measures shall be less than the reduction in expected annual loss which they bring about and that the mix of remedial measures selected shall be the one having the lowest total cost.

The first criterion simply says that there must be a cost justification for the security program—that it returns more in savings to the EDP facility than it costs. This may seem obvious but it is not uncommon for an EDP manager to call for a security measure without first analyzing the risks. Experience and judgment tell him or her that some particular action is desirable. While this might seem to obviate the need for risk analysis, what it really amounts to is recognition of a possibly serious but unquantified loss potential. It would be more appropriate for the EDP manager to factor his or her judgment into a quantified risk analysis.

The second criterion reflects the fact that a given remedial measure may often be effective against more than one threat. To illustrate, consider this:

REMEDIAL MEASURES			THREATS		
	FIRE	INTERNAL THEFT	EXTERNAL THEFT	HURRI- CANE	SABOTAGE
Fire detection system	X				X
Loss control team	X			X	X
Roving guard patrol	X	X	X		X
Intrusion detectors		X	X		X
Personnel screening		X			X
On-site power generator				X	X
Backup plan	X			X	X

Since a given remedial measure may affect more than one threat, the least cost mix of measures probably will not be immediately obvious. One possible way to make the selection is to begin with the threat having the largest annual loss potential. Consider possible remedial measures and list those for which the annual cost is less than the expected reduction in annual loss. (Precision in estimating cost and loss reduction is not necessary at this point.) If two or more remedial measures would cause a loss reduction in the same area, list them all but note the redundancy. Repeat the process for the next most serious threat and continue until reaching the point where no cost justifiable measure for a threat can be found. When the cost of a remedial measure is increased if it is extended to cover an additional threat, the incremental cost should be noted. At this point one has a matrix of individual threats and remedial measures with estimates of loss reductions and costs and thus an estimate of the net saving, which can also be shown graphically:

REMEDIAL MEASURES				THREATS							
	A			**B**			**C**			**D**	
J	20*	9	11	10	0	10	4	1	3	2	5	−3
K	20*	15	5	12	0	12	6	0	6	4	2	2

* Same effect.

For each threat, the estimated loss reduction, the cost of the remedial measure, and the net loss reduction have been given (in that order). By applying remedial measure J to threat A at a cost of $9,000, a loss reduction of $20,000 can be expected (a net saving of $11,000). Furthermore remedial measure J will reduce the threat B loss by $10,000 at no additional cost and the threat C loss by $4,000 at an added cost of only $1,000. Finally, though, it appears that it would cost more than it would save to apply J to threat D. Therefore J would not be implemented for D. The net loss reduction from J could be expressed as:

$$J (A, B, \& C) = 11 + 10 + 3$$

$$= \$24,000$$

The table indicates that J and K have the same reduction effect on threat A. Since K costs more than J, it might, at first glance, be rejected. However,

$$K (A, B, C, \& D) = 5 + 12 + 6 + 2$$

$$= \$25,000$$

and

$$J (A, B, \& C) + K (A, B, C, \& D) = -4 + 22 + 9 + 2$$

$$= \$29,000.$$

Therefore, while J and K are equally effective on threat A, K appears to be more effective than J on the other threats, but further checking shows that their combined use results in the greatest overall net loss reduction.

By going through the process just described, using preliminary estimates for cost and loss reduction, the EDP security planner can test various combinations of remedial measures. This will enable him or her to identify the subset of remedial measures which appears to be the most effective. At this point the EDP security planner should review the estimates for the candidate subset and refine them as necessary to establish confidence in the tentative choices. In marginal situations this might cause a change of the optimum subset. However, by iterating the process as required, the EDP security planner will finally reach the point where he or she can recommend a given group of remedial measures with considerable confidence. And, almost as important is the ability to defend the rejection of remedial measures that cannot be cost justified.

If all of the above procedures have been followed, the following will have been established and documented:

- Significant threats and probabilities of occurrence
- Critical tasks and the loss of potential related to each threat on an annual basis
- A list of remedial measures that will yield the greatest net reduction in losses, together with their annual cost

With this information at hand EDP management can move ahead with implementation of the physical security program. Since the analysis of remedial measures will have identified those with the greatest impact, relative priorities for implementation can also be established.

Summary

The objective of control is to reduce risk. In an ideal environment, everything would be processed correctly, and there would be no need for control. Unfortunately, that environment does not exist, and risks are present that may introduce damaging events into the processing environment. Controls reduce the number of damaging events to an acceptable level.

In order to evaluate the effectiveness of controls, the auditor must determine the risks present in the computerized environment. Until the risks are understood, the effectiveness of controls in reducing those risks cannot be evaluated. Thus, if the auditor is going to place reliance on controls she or he must both identify the risks and determine the severity of those risks in the operating environment.

The risks described earlier in this chapter can be used to aid in the identification and assessment of the severity of risks in a computerized environment. The auditor may also wish to conduct a risk assessment scenario to identify risks that might not be included in this chapter. A risk assessment scenario normally involves two or more people who have some familiarity with the application under audit. In addition to auditors, this could include user, computer, or management personnel.

The risk scenario is a brainstorming session in which the personnel present attempt to identify conditions (i.e., risks) that may cause application system losses. For example, in a payroll time reporting system, the type of risks could include these:

- Hours worked might be reported twice.
- Individuals might report more hours than they actually worked.
- Reporting documents might be lost.

Problems

1. Define the term *risk*.

2. Explain the term *vulnerability* as it relates to risk, threat, and control.

3. Periodically, the airlines offer coupons to paying passengers, which can be redeemed for flights at a later time. One airline offered a flight anywhere on its system for passengers who flew on that airline during specific months. What type of threats does the airline face from this offer?

4. A computer system in one government agency issued payroll checks to employees in the amount of $1 million. This was for hourly, biweekly employees. What kind of risk caused this to occur?

5. A programmer entered a change into the billing system. The invoices produced by the billing system were correct, but the distribution system began to indicate that items on hand were out of stock. The problem arose because an error made in the billing system was being passed through several other systems to the distribution system. This is called a cascading of errors. What is the most common cause of this risk?

6. If the calculation of risk is determined by multiplying average loss per occurrence times frequency of occurrence—and risk is the sole basis of control, meaning that there is no need for controls when there is no risk—then what are the two implementation objectives of a control?

7. Citibank in New York installed automatic teller machines. Some time after the ATMs were operational, criminals posing as bank employees

stopped people in the middle of transactions and moved them to another terminal, explaining that the terminals were inoperative. When the bank customers left, the criminals then withdrew money from the ATMs that had been opened but not closed by the customers. The bank held that the depositors were at fault because they had failed to follow bank procedures; therefore the bank deducted the fraudulently withdrawn amounts from the customers' accounts. The depositors filed a class action suit against Citibank claiming that the technological controls were inadequate. Citibank settled and reimbursed the depositors for approximately $150,000 of fraudulent withdrawals. How might the bank have averted this type of situation?

8. The ABC Company enters orders into the computer through fifteen data entry terminals. The terminals are in operation fifty weeks a year. The experience of the company has been very good in entering data correctly. On the average, only two errors per week per operator occur. An analysis of the records of the organization show that each error costs the company about $20 to correct. The data processing manager is considering installing a control function to reduce the number of errors occurring. What is the maximum amount the data processing manager could spend on these controls and still have it be cost effective?

Case

**The Daylight
Division of
Universal Industries**

The Daylight Division of Universal Industries manufactures mercury vapor lighting fixtures, which they sell to municipalities and contractors through a five-person sales force. The market for these fixtures is fairly competitive, and industry statistics indicate most manufacturers maintain a 25% to 30% gross margin on sales. Financial information for the most recent 12 months shows the following for Daylight:

Recorded sales	$5,000,000
Cost of sales*	$4,000,000
Units sold*	10,000

Determined by difference between beginning inventory plus production and ending inventory.

Since the lighting fixtures are bulky, they are shipped as single units, with a separate shipping order and invoice for each unit. An evaluation of controls in the revenue and receivables transaction system disclosed that shipping orders are not prenumbered, nor are they matched with invoices. Accordingly, there is a risk that some shipments may not be billed.

Questions

(a) What is your estimate of the maximum exposure arising from this weakness?

(b) What is your estimate of the most likely range of exposure? (Hint: Use loss expectation formula.)

(c) What elements of cost and elements of benefit should a reviewer consider when evaluating improved controls in this case?

EDP AUDIT PROCESS*

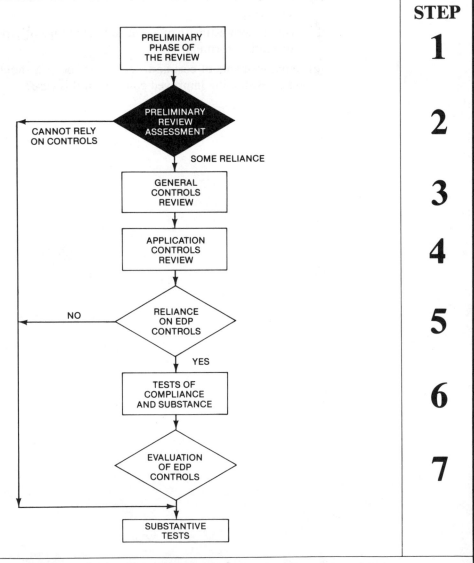

STEP

1

2

3

4

5

6

7

Diagram is adapted from The Auditor's Study and Evaluation of Internal Control in EDP Systems, *pages 21–24. Copyright © 1977 by the American Institute of Certified Public Accountants, Inc. (See Figure 9.1 for a complete explanation of the steps.)*

CONTROLS IN AN EDP ENVIRONMENT

(2) Preliminary Phase of the Review—Assessment

Purpose:
- Assess significance of EDP and non-EDP accounting controls.
- Determine extent of additional review within EDP.

Method: Judgment.

OBJECTIVE

Once the risk has been assessed, the auditor must perform a preliminary assessment of the controls using the data collected in Step 1. This chapter explains the concept of control and how control is related to reliance.

In this chapter we shall discuss the impact of EDP on controls and the types of controls auditors should be familiar with and capable of evaluating. There are several basic reasons why controls are important in automated systems. First, there is a growing reliance by management on computer-generated reports; the accuracy and reliability of such reports are a function of controls in data processing. Second, an increasing amount of resources is being allocated to computerized activities, and a good control process is necessary to make sure that the resources are used effectively. Third, the potential for control problems is great in computerized systems, and indeed, there is much evidence of poor controls in companies today. For example, recent studies indicate program fraud, record destruction, file security problems, and operating inefficiencies due to inadequate controls. Fourth, management has new responsibilities for the effective design and implementation of an internal accounting control system as a result of the passage of the Foreign Corrupt Practices Act in December 1977.

Control Requirements, Objectives, and Responsibilities

The Foreign Corrupt Practices Act (FCPA) requires that all companies, subject to the Securities Exchange Act of 1934, keep in reasonable detail "books, records, and accounts" that accurately and fairly reflect the company's transactions and dispositions of assets. Such companies all must maintain a system of internal accounting controls designed to provide reasonable assurance that

- Transactions are executed in accordance with management's general or specific authorization.
- Transactions are recorded as necessary (a) to permit preparation of financial statements in conformity with generally accepted accounting principles or any other criteria applicable to such statements, and (b) to maintain accountability for assets.
- Access to assets is permitted only in accordance with management's general or specific authorization.
- The recorded accountability for assets is compared with the existing assets at reasonable intervals and appropriate action is taken with respect to any differences.

The two broad, interrelated objectives of internal accounting control are these:

1. Safeguard assets against loss.
2. Produce reliable financial records for internal use and for external reporting purposes.

To make sure these objectives are achieved, four key groups in the company should be involved—the board of directors or its audit committee, operating management, internal auditors, and the company's independent auditors. Assignment of duties and responsibilities will vary among these groups from company to company but will generally follow the approach outlined on pages 127–129.[1]

Role of the Board of Directors

The board should be responsible for approving basic policies and for compliance oversight, not detailed specification and enforcement. Still, the primary responsibility for the sufficiency of a company's measures to comply with the FCPA lies here. The board of directors or its audit committee should

- Understand in broad outline how the recordkeeping and internal accounting control systems function and judge their sufficiency to achieve compliance with the FCPA.
- Broadly monitor compliance, and suggest revisions as needed.
- Review existing policies and consider changes needed to comply with the FCPA; if adequate policies already exist, consider additional communication.
- See that appropriate actions are taken concerning possible violations of the FCPA, if any.

Role of Operating Management

Management's primary responsibility for maintaining adequate and effective recordkeeping and internal accounting control systems and for safeguarding assets is not new. But the FCPA focuses greater attention on these aspects of management's responsibility. In fact, operating management is responsible for detailed implementation to comply with the FCPA.

The board of directors or its audit committee, while exercising its oversight responsibilities, will look to operating management for information and to take any necessary corrective action.

Accordingly, operating management should

- Identify the risks that are inherent in the business and the potential for errors and irregularities.
- Undertake systematically to document and evaluate existing recordkeeping practices and systems of internal accounting controls throughout the company to identify instances of possible nonconformity with a reasonable interpretation of the Act.

[1] *The New Management Imperative—Compliance with the Accounting Requirements of the Foreign Corrupt Practices Act,* Touche Ross, 1975, 1978, pp. 9–10.

- Identify and articulate the factors considered in assessing the practicality and cost/benefit aspects of suggested systems revisions.
- Initiate applicable revisions in corporate policies or directives.

Role of the Internal Auditor

Internal auditors are an important part of internal control. They can, separately or with operating management, accomplish most of the preceding requirements. In addition, they can

- Monitor compliance with existing policies of operating management or the board of directors.
- Assist in special studies for operating management or the board of directors.

Role of the Independent Auditor

The independent auditor is not part of a company's internal accounting control system. He has a unique objective—to form an opinion on the financial statements. This objective causes the independent auditor to plan that examination to search for errors or irregularities that would have a material effect in the financial statements and to use due skill and care in the conduct of the examination.

The adoption of the Act does not change the way an independent auditor goes about determining the scope of his examination. After a preliminary review of a company's internal accounting control systems, the auditor must decide the extent to which he will rely on the systems for his purposes. The auditor may decide that it is both feasible and cost effective to test extensively the internal accounting control systems and place major reliance thereon in formulating an opinion on the amounts in the financial statements. On the other hand, he may decide that it is more effective to perform direct extensive tests of documentation underlying the amounts in the financial statements, rather than relying on the internal accounting control system. In most cases, he will decide on a combination of reliance and direct testing. Accordingly, weaknesses that exist in a company's recordkeeping and internal accounting control systems, or portions thereof, may not be detected during the course of the independent auditor's examination because for valid reasons he has chosen not to rely on such systems.

Currently, if aware of material weakness in internal accounting control, errors or irregularities, or illegal acts, the independent auditor is required to communicate them to management (at least one level above those involved). Depending on the significance of the matters reported, the board or its audit committee may also be advised.

The independent auditor's responsibility for evaluating effectiveness and monitoring compliance of internal accounting control systems parallels the responsibility of the board and its audit committee. The independent auditor is in a unique position in that he can make a "hands on" evaluation of the system, an opportunity not readily available to the board or the audit committee. In addition, the independent auditor brings the experience of similar association with systems of other companies to the evaluation and judgment problem. As a result, the independent auditor has a unique perspective on the company, and the board of directors and audit committee may find the outside auditor especially helpful in fulfilling their policy and oversight duties. In fact, the independent public accountant can assist management in demonstrating compliance with the Act by:

- Recommending plans for the systematic review, documentation, and evaluation of internal controls
- Providing instructional manuals on methods and techniques for describing, testing, and evaluating internal controls
- Conducting training programs for internal auditors and other company personnel selected to review internal controls
- Evaluating the efforts of company personnel reviewing internal controls
- Recommending changes in internal controls to overcome identified deficiencies

Internal Controls—The State of the Art[2]

Internal control deals with the processes and practices by which the management of an organization attempts to ensure that approved and appropriate decisions and activities are made and carried out. It is also aimed at preventing officers and employees from engaging in proscribed and inappropriate activities. The growth in size and complexity of modern corporations, as well as intensified public sensitivity to corporate behavior, have resulted in a great renewal of interest in the subject of internal control.

During 1980, the Financial Executives Institute published the results of an extensive study on internal control. The purposes of this study are twofold. The first is to report on the state of the art of internal control in U.S. corporations. The second is to observe, interpret, and comment on those findings and related issues, like the Foreign Corrupt Practices Act and the state of government–business relations with respect to internal control.

Four of the conclusions of the study have a bearing on the status of control over automated systems:

1. The aspect of internal control that troubles executives most, and which we consider to be most serious, is the increasing dependence of com-

---

[2] *Internal Control in U.S. Corporations: The State of the Art,* Financial Executives Research Foundation, New York, 1980, pp. 7–9. Pages 129–131 are based on this publication, and some of it is quoted directly.

panies on computers for operational effectiveness and for financial reporting. Technological progress in data processing has greatly increased a number of internal control risks, and these are compounded by a substantial shortage in adequately trained data processing and internal audit personnel. Only in rare cases is the control awareness of the data processing management and the technological expertise of the internal audit staff such that they can coordinate their efforts sufficiently to ensure adequate internal control over data processing.

2. Opportunities for the improvement of internal control exist in most companies; opportunities for substantial improvement exist in many companies. The identification of internal control risks, the careful assessment of the potential costs of such risks and of measures to reduce them, and a formal management decision whether to modify present control measures as a result of such assessment—these are anything but common in American industry. As a result of this discrepancy and because of other pressures on management time and energy, internal control weaknesses do exist in many companies.

3. Some executives appear to hold a narrowly defined concept of internal control, while others view it in much broader terms. Frequently, those subscribing to a narrow view see establishment and maintenance of effective internal control as the responsibility of the controller's department, with the internal audit staff playing a monitoring role. Those holding a broader view of the concept typically see internal control as a shared management responsibility, with the controller and internal auditor having a well-defined lead role. But additionally, in these cases, senior management and other executives are seen as playing an important role in being supportive and demonstrating control consciousness. In both cases, executives have often noted that the general shortage of competent internal auditors is made a more serious problem by the fact that, in some companies, the documentation of present controls to show compliance with the FCPA has been assigned to the internal audit staff, thereby reducing the attention internal auditors can give to their expected monitoring function. In other companies, much of the time of internal auditors is devoted to a variety of special assignments for the controller, assignments not related to monitoring internal control.

4. Many company executives have no significant knowledge of internal control practices in other companies, even in their own industry. As we (the authors of this text) interviewed executives, we found that no model of adequate internal control (in the form of some combination of specific measures or practices) was ever cited to the researchers of the Financial Executives Research Foundation report. When asked to identify companies with outstanding systems of internal control, the ex-

ecutives tended to equate good internal control with good management, and to evaluate management on the basis of perceived success in a competitive environment over a long period of time.

The following are key facts from interviews with the internal auditors:

- Of the forty-nine internal audit staffs interviewed, only twenty-one had an EDP auditor.

- Nearly all forty-nine companies recognized the need for devoting more resources to EDP auditing.

- "Resource allocation was not a problem, instead two major reasons were given for the lack of EDP auditors: (1) the difficulty in finding qualified personnel and (2) the difficulty in hiring them. There was general agreement that EDP auditors must have a strong systems background, and they must be trained in accounting and auditing. This was viewed as a difficult combination to hire and/or to train. CPA firms have been a common source of EDP auditors; however, the internal auditors expressed concern that this source has not provided many individuals with a strong systems background. In addition, the career path for the EDP auditor was generally not well specified, which made it difficult to compete in the labor market against companies' systems departments and CPA firms."

"As a result, many companies rely on external auditors for EDP auditing. However, the internal auditors that we interviewed do not believe that an EDP audit by a CPA firm as a part of its regular audit is a total substitute for a comprehensive internal EDP audit."

The following are conclusions from interviews with DP managers:

- "Most managers are uncomfortable about the adequacy of procedures for controlling changes to existing programs. All considered it a significant exposure and most confided that any trusted system programmer could undoubtedly manipulate programs for personal gain. Even more than embezzlement, however, many managers fear the potential in such an uncontrolled situation for rapid and devastating sabotage by a disgruntled or similarly motivated employee."

- About one-third of the data processing managers had a "positive opinion of the effectiveness and quality of the involvement" of the internal auditor in EDP, although they felt the internal auditor's knowledge of EDP was not adequate.

- In some cases, the external auditor was rated highly, but in the majority of cases, both their knowledge of EDP technology and the thoroughness with which they undertake their examinations were seriously questioned.

Control Classifications[3]

There are many ways in which controls have been classified. In the broad sense controls can be classified as accounting and administrative controls.

Accounting Control Accounting control comprises the plan of organization and the procedures and records that are concerned with the safeguarding of assets and the reliability of financial records. Consequently accounting control is designed to provide reasonable assurance of the following:

- Transactions are executed in accordance with management's general or specific authorization.
- Transactions are recorded as necessary to permit preparation of financial statements in conformity with generally accepted accounting principles or any other criteria applicable to such statements and to maintain accountability for assets.
- Access to assets is permitted only in accordance with management's authorization.
- The recorded accountability for assets is compared with the existing assets at reasonable intervals and appropriate action is taken with respect to any differences.[4]

Administrative Control Administrative control includes, but is not limited to, the plan of organization and procedures and records that are concerned with the decision processes leading to management's authorization of transactions.

Such authorization is a management function directly associated with the responsibility for achieving the objectives of the organization and is the starting point for establishing accounting control of transactions.

Other classifications are valuable in communicating the intent of a control. The categorizing of controls as preventive, detective, and corrective can prove most helpful in understanding the objective and intent of a specific control. This is particularly true as we talk about controls directed toward a specific application such as payroll.

Controls are used to reduce adverse effects (exposures) resulting from an event (cause). A *preventive control* is designed to prevent a cause of exposure from happening. A *detective control* is a technique to determine that a cause of an exposure has occurred. A *corrective control* provides the information necessary to assist in the investigation and correction of causes of exposures that

---

[3] Note that different accounting associations use slightly different classifications.

[4] AICPA, Statement on Auditing Standards #1, *p. 20, 1973.*

have been detected. An example of a preventive control is prenumbered checks; a detective control example is a control total; and a corrective control example is an audit trail, which can be used to correct uncovered errors or problems.

These classifications are valuable not only because they show the intent of a control, but also because they show how that control is to be used. For example, a transaction audit trail is used to correct errors detected by the detective control. Too often auditors forget that internal controls serve the purpose of aiding management in directing the actions of the organization. When one understands how controls are used by management the preventive, detective, corrective classifications make more sense. This classification is more in line with the thinking of management than is the traditional accounting control classification.

How Controls Work

The purpose of control is to reduce risk. In Chapter 4 we learned that risk is calculated by multiplying the expected frequency of an undesirable event times the average loss associated with that event. If the risk can be calculated by this formula, and controls are designed to reduce risk, then the same formula can tell us the function of controls.

For the purpose of explaining controls we can redefine control as follows: a *control* is anything that will either reduce the expected frequency of an undesirable event or the average loss associated with that event.

Figure 5.1 is an illustration of how controls work. It shows that the control will either reduce the frequency of, or the loss associated with, an undesirable event. The illustration shows that there are four approaches to reducing a loss associated with risk. Two ways are associated with reducing the frequency and two with the loss.

The frequency of loss occurrence can be reduced by

- Reducing the frequency of error occurrence
- Reducing the opportunity for error occurrence

The loss per occurrence can be reduced by

- Minimizing the amount subject to loss
- Minimizing the impact of loss

As we begin to evaluate how to reduce risk, we should evaluate which of these four alternatives is the best way to reduce a specific risk. For example, in one risk situation we may want to minimize the impact of loss, and in another, reduce the opportunity for error occurrence. Let's examine how each of these four approaches to reduce risk work.

Figure 5.1
How Controls Work

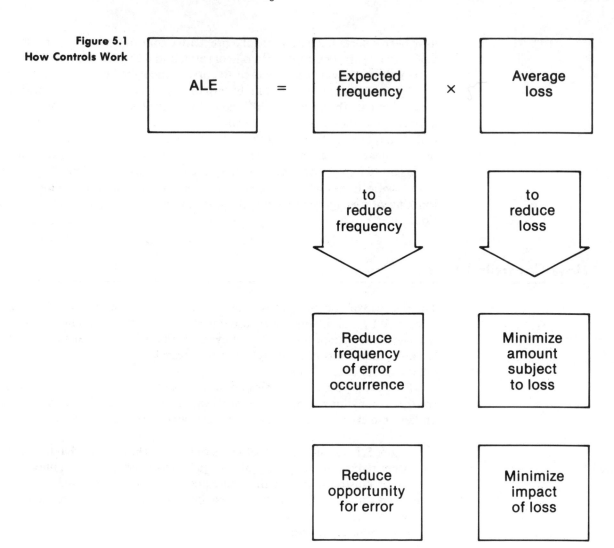

The expected frequency can be reduced by either reducing the number of errors that occur or reducing the opportunity for an error to cause problems. For example, the probability of error in the key entry process is very high. The frequency of error can be reduced by training, good procedures, well-laid-out data entry forms, etc. The opportunity for error can be reduced by key verification, data validation routines in computer programs, and scanning by control personnel.

The average loss per occurrence can be reduced by minimizing the amount subject to loss and minimizing the impact of the loss. If we return to our fire risk example we can easily illustrate these two reduction methods. We can minimize the amount subject to loss by putting in firewalls, building two small locations instead of one big one, or installing sprinkler systems. The impact of the loss can be minimized through insurance, or if it was a computer center, by retaining duplicate copies of the tapes and programs in a remote location.

Control is normally described in the context of accomplishing specific control objectives. Earlier in this chapter, the four basic objectives of internal accounting control were listed. Note that these four control objectives are described both in accounting literature (for example, in the AICPA's SAS 1) and in the Foreign Corrupt Practices Act. When discussing controls, we normally evaluate to ensure that controls are adequate to accomplish those control objectives.

Our previous discussion described controls in the context of reducing risk. Specifically, four approaches were described for reducing risk. These two concepts of control are not inconsistent.

Table 5.1 explains the reduction of risks in both contexts. The four objectives of internal accounting control are cross-referenced to the four approaches to reducing risk in the matrix.

Table 5.1   Reducing Risks Matrix

OBJECTIVES OF INTERNAL ACCOUNTING CONTROL	APPROACH TO REDUCING RISK			
	REDUCE FREQUENCY OF ERROR OCCURRENCE	REDUCE OPPORTUNITY FOR ERROR	MINIMIZE AMOUNT SUBJECT TO LOSS	MINIMIZE IMPACT OF LOSS
1. Transactions are executed in accordance with management's general or specific authorization.		✔		
2. Transactions are recorded as necessary (a) to permit preparation of financial statements in conformity with generally accepted accounting principles or any other criteria applicable to such statements, and (b) to maintain accountability for assets.	✔			
3. Access to assets is permitted only in accordance with management's general or specific authorization.		✔		
4. The recorded accountability for assets is compared with the existing assets at reasonable intervals and appropriate action is taken with respect to any differences.			✔	✔

This matrix shows that if transactions are executed in accordance with management's general and specific authorizations, the opportunity for error should be reduced. If the controls ensure that transactions are processed in accordance with management's intent, intentional and unintentional unfavorable events should be reduced. The proper recording of transactions will reduce the frequency of error occurrence. Experience has shown that most of the problems in automated systems are associated with invalid or improper input. Ensuring that transactions are properly recorded reduces the number of errors.

The opportunity for error can be reduced by controlling access to assets. Adequate access controls restrict processing to individuals authorized. In addition, access controls in an automated application can restrict individuals to those specific transactions for which they are authorized. For example, an accounts receivable file can be divided among several clerks so that each clerk can access only that part of the file he or she is authorized to access.

Recording the accountability for assets will both minimize the amount subject to loss and minimize the impact of loss. Making people accountable for their acts has been shown to improve the quality of work, thereby minimizing the losses. Comparing that accountability at reasonable intervals and taking appropriate action will minimize the impact of loss. Losses will be uncovered sooner so that appropriate corrective action can be taken and if the loss is due to improper acts, restitution can be taken against the responsible individual.

Controls in an EDP Environment

Let's review the problem. The Venetians are said to have developed double-entry bookkeeping in the fifteenth century. That was an important step in the development of the systems that management employs to safeguard valuables. But it was not the first step. Even with single-entry bookkeeping, there were control mechanisms that managers employed. The controls have been gradually refined, over hundreds of years, until we achieved a rather effective system to provide reasonable protection of assets in those organizations that followed the system. Let's just cite a few of the tenets of that system:

- All checks should be signed by two people.
- Those who sign checks should examine invoices and supporting documents to see that the goods were received and the prices correct.
- Those who open mail should prepare lists of checks and deposit them immediately. They should have no access to accounting records; particularly records of receivables.
- The bank statement should be reconciled by someone who cannot write checks or receive cash.

Those are a few. There are dozens more.

Then came the age of the computer. It changed the way transactions and recordkeeping were handled and made many of the controls we accountants cherished obsolete or no longer practical. Let us look at what has happened. What about the good old control of having two people sign checks? Do we still honor that in the federal government? Not exactly. If you have a government check on you, you will note it has only one signature and that is a printed one. Chances are it is signed by Henry Eades, who is the Treasury's disbursing officer. If he tried to sign all the checks that are issued with his signature, he probably could not do it in several lifetimes.

Not only do we not have the checks signed by someone; in the more advanced systems we do not even get the documents together in one place. Transactions in which the order for goods, the invoice from the vendor, and the receiving ticket for the goods are each physically retained in different cities are not uncommon. The match is made by computer.

Assets do not include only cash and inventories either. Many organizations have sensitive information in their computers that they must protect from outsiders. Also, the morality of our times and the computer's ability to assimilate data have made it necessary to protect individuals' privacy. Therefore, the computer has given us a challenge. Those who are concerned with protecting the assets of our organizations—cash, inventories, secret data, private data, and so forth—have to accomplish in a few years what it took hundreds of years to develop before. Moreover, we have to do it in an environment in which we are shooting at a moving target: the capabilities of the equipment are changing so rapidly that what works today may not work tomorrow.

Suitable guidelines for the protection of the integrity of data in data processing systems are identified in ''The Auditor's Study and Evaluation of Internal Control in EDP Systems'' published by the AICPA. In brief, these nineteen control standards are as follows:

1. Functions between the EDP departments and users should be segregated.

2. Persons within the EDP department should not be allowed to originate or authorize transactions, have custody over non-EDP assets, and originate master file changes.

3. Functions within the EDP department must be properly segregated.

4. The procedures for systems design, including the acquisition of software packages, should require active participation by representatives of the users and, when appropriate, the accounting department and internal auditors.

5. Each system should have written specifications that are reviewed and approved by an appropriate level of management and applicable user departments.

6. System testing should be a joint effort of users and EDP personnel and should include both the manual and computerized phases of the system.

7. Final approval should be obtained prior to placing a new system into operation.

8. All master file and transaction file conversions should be controlled to prevent unauthorized changes and to provide accurate and complete results.

9. After a new system has been placed in operation, all program changes should be approved before implementation to determine whether they have been authorized, tested, and documented.

10. Management should require various levels of documentation and formal procedures to define the system at appropriate levels of detail.

11. The control features inherent in the computer hardware, operating system, and other supporting software should be utilized to the maximum extent to provide control over operations and to detect and report hardware malfunctions.

12. Systems software should be subjected to the same control procedures as those applied to the installation of and changes to application programs.

13. Access to program documentation should be limited to those persons who require it to perform their duties.

14. Access to data files and programs should be limited to those individuals authorized to process or maintain particular systems.

15. Access to computer hardware should be limited to authorized individuals.

16. A control function should be responsible for receiving all data to be processed, for ensuring that all data are recorded, for following up on errors detected during processing to see that they are corrected and resubmitted by the proper party, and for verifying the proper distribution of output.

17. A written manual of systems and procedures should be prepared by all computer operations and should provide for management's general or specific authorization to process transactions.

18. Internal auditors or some other independent group within an organization should review and evaluate proposed systems at critical stages of development.

19. On a continuing basis, internal auditors or some other independent group within an organization should review and test computer processing activities.

Areas of Control

Controls are oriented toward three general areas of business operations: the financial data, the business assets of an organization, and the efficiency of their operations. While the introduction of computerized data processing affects the way operations are conducted, it does not affect these three aspects of business operations. The basic objective of control remains the same in either a manual or an EDP environment.

Controls in a data processing environment need to be restructured from those typical of manual systems to those that will complement the characteristics of the computer. Controls can be structured in different ways. We need to examine the different types of controls to fully understand the implications of control in an EDP environment.

Administrative controls in a data processing environment vary only slightly from the controls of manual systems. The underlying authority for administrative control comes from the articles of incorporation in a business organization or from the various constitutions or charters authorizing a governmental unit. Business organizations can vary their operations within the articles of incorporation by action of their boards of directors. Governmental units, through laws or resolutions, can grant authority to perform specific functions. These controls are manifested through organization charts, job descriptions, and organizational policy. Administrative controls provide the framework under which the business of the organization is conducted.

The method of performing a function within an organization is governed by the accounting controls. Accounting controls are subdivided into application and general controls. *Application controls* relate primarily to the accuracy and completeness of data within a specific application in an organization. For example, in a payroll system the application controls affect the computation and preparation of payroll checks and supporting documents and schedules. *General controls* provide the standards and guidelines under which employees function in their work. While aspects of organizational setup are involved in general controls, their main thrust is the procedures and standards involved in performing a function. The standards and procedures in a data processing environment include how systems are documented, the procedures for systems development and changes to systems, and the methods of operating an information processing facility (IPF). IPF includes those functions involving data conversion, storage, control, and the operation of the computer center.

Figure 5.2 illustrates the types of controls and gives examples of the general control classification in an EDP environment. Application control involves accuracy and completeness of transaction data in applications such as payroll, accounts receivable, inventories, etc. It is the only type of control specifically aimed at data. General controls are the procedures and standards governing the functions of developing, maintaining, and operating systems to process data. Aspects of organization structure can become involved in general controls. On the other hand, administrative controls are controls related to the authorization procedures that determine the legitimacy of a function to perform specific acts and the authorization process governing origination of transactions. Administrative controls are implemented through organization structure, each with its authority and organization policy.

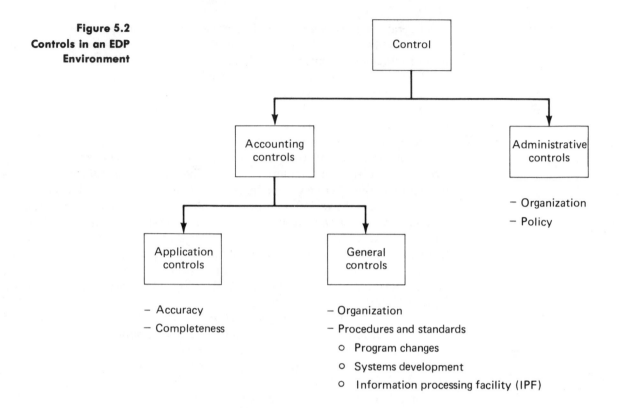

**Figure 5.2
Controls in an EDP
Environment**

Impact of Automation on Control

To examine the impact of the computer on the control process, we shall proceed through a little exercise which, it is hoped, will help develop a control framework for EDP systems. Specifically, we shall examine how controls are achieved in a very basic data processing application: payroll. Figure 5.3 is a flowchart for a payroll process. The flowchart does not represent all the details of an actual payroll system but is used here merely to illustrate the characteristics of a manual process. Take a few minutes to examine this flowchart, paying particular attention to various functions performed by the *people* who process data in this system, namely, the three clerks and the supervisors. As you examine this system, ask yourself what is accomplished by the *division of clerical duties* performed by the people. Also try to see where in the process *visual editing* of the documents is performed and what the editing accomplishes.

In your examination of the payroll system illustrated in Figure 5.3, you should have noted two control characteristics found in manual systems. First,

Area of responsibility

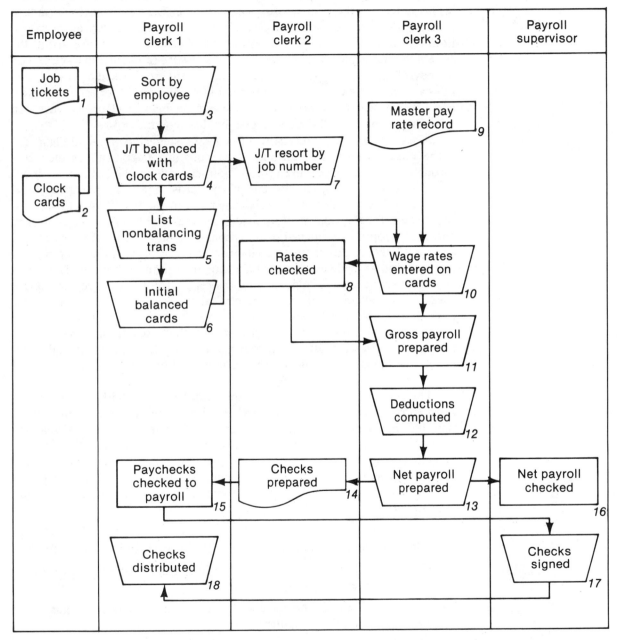

Figure 5.3   Flowchart for Manual Payroll Process

you note a *division of duties* among the three clerks processing the transactions in the systems and the supervisor. Division of clerical duties is important in order to distribute the processing work load, achieve some clerical specialization, and provide a cross-check on important calculations performed in the system. For example, in step 8 we note that the wage rates entered by clerk 3 on the payroll clock cards from the master pay record are checked by clerk 2. Pay rates are obviously very important in computing the payroll for each employee, and checking them is important in achieving a high level of accuracy and reliability in the payroll data generated by this system.

A second control characteristic of manual systems illustrated in Figure 5.3 is the *visual editing* of important transactions and documents as they flow through the system. For example, in our payroll process, the basic input documents are the job tickets and clock cards. Clerk 1, in sorting these documents by employee and by balancing the job tickets with the clock cards, could check for the validity of job codes and reasonableness of hours worked and could stop any abnormal or unreasonable transaction from further processing. Clerk 3 could examine all balance cards to see that they have been properly initialled as evidence that the balancing operation took place. The supervisor examines the payroll listing after the net payroll has been computed as a check on overall reasonableness and clerical accuracy. Clerk 1 compares the payroll listings with the checks prepared to see that they are in agreement. Such visual editing of transactions and documents as they flow through the system is performed to detect invalid transactions, unreasonable amounts, and other improper data. Visual editing is an important control characteristic in manual systems.

The control process in such a system can best be described as a people-oriented control system because people are largely responsible for implementing the control procedures and techniques used to safeguard assets, generate reliable and accurate data, and achieve operational efficiencies. When a computer is introduced into such a system, there is a shift away from a people-oriented system to a computer-oriented control system. To illustrate, let us turn again to the payroll example. If we automated the payroll process, we would need to know:

- What specific payroll processing steps can be performed by a computer?

- How would a computer affect the division of duties among the clerks found in a manual system?

- What checking of arithmetic calculations is necessary when calculations are performed by a computer?

- What steps in the flow can be completely eliminated when a computer is introduced into the system?

- What editing of incoming documents may be performed by a computer to eliminate the need for visual editing during processing?

Take a few minutes to answer these questions.

In your analysis of the impact of the computer on a payroll process, you probably noted that because of the inherent accuracy and speed of the computer, many of the processing steps performed by the three clerks in the manual system can be combined in the stored computer program used to perform the payroll processing. In Figure 5.4, the processing steps that can be performed by a computer are enclosed within a heavy black line. Thus, much of the division of duties found in a manual system can be eliminated.

In a manual system, division of duties is important to perform cross-checking of important arithmetic calculations. Because of the inherent accuracy of computer processing, we can eliminate some of the cross-checking that takes place in manual systems. For example, as shown in Figure 5.4, we can eliminate step 8 in our manual process because entering the wage rates on payroll cards is a computer operation and presumably will not have to be checked again. Because of the computerized processing of many of the steps performed by the clerks, we also find that certain steps are redundant. For example, since the computer balances the job tickets with the clock cards, there is no need to have somebody initial the balance card. Presumably, a computer will generate an exception report listing the nonbalanced transactions for manual follow-up; thus we may eliminate step 6 in the manual process. Also, since both the net payroll listing and checks are prepared by the computer in processing, there is no need for step 15, the checking of the paychecks against the payroll listing.

The manual payroll process involves a great deal of visual editing of the input documents and transactions as they flow through the system. In automated systems, we also need some form of editing to make sure that the data being processed are reasonable, valid, and accurate. In computerized systems, we can incorporate the editing steps into computer programs by the use of *programmed controls*. In the payroll illustration, the computer could edit the job tickets and clock cards for invalid job numbers, invalid employee numbers, and unreasonable hours worked and print out invalid or unreasonable transactions on an exception report for follow-up.

On the basis of the payroll illustration, we can now generalize about the impact of the computer on the control process. First, because of the accuracy and speed of the computer, there is less need for cross-checking of important processing steps, particularly those steps where arithmetic operations are performed by a computer in developing accounting and financial data. Second, there is less need for visual editing since a computer can perform many of the editing steps once performed by people by having programmed controls incor-

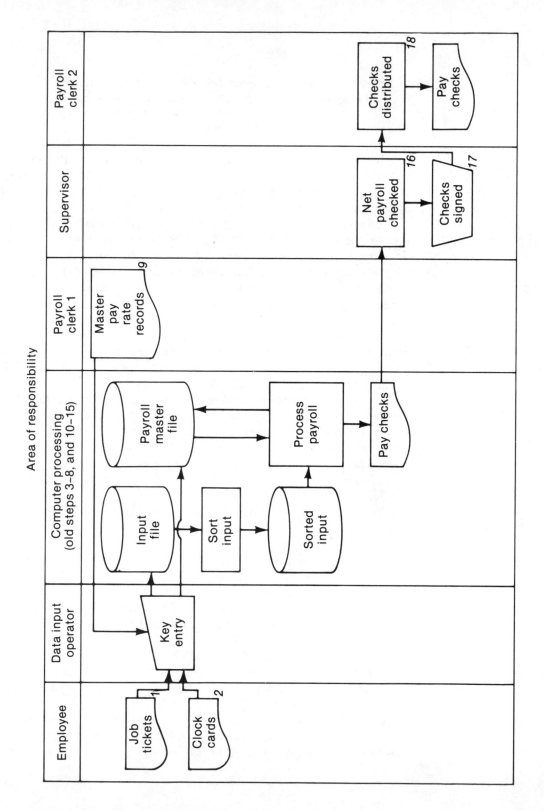

Figure 5.4 Many Manual Processing Steps Can Be Done by the Computer

144

porated into the computer programs. Third, because of the concentration of processing steps in computer programs, there is less need for division of clerical duties in computerized systems. However, this concentration of steps in the computer program suggests that there is much more need to emphasize the control of a data processing center because of the large amount of data and information stored in the computer files and the large amount of processing now embodied in the many computer programs developed by an organization.

Obviously, most computerized systems are designed for more complex operations than simple payroll processing. These include systems designed for other accounting and financial applications and management information–decision systems. Accordingly, computerized systems are complex and difficult to use properly. This complexity suggests the need for systems planning, documentation standards, and adequate operating practices to ensure efficient operation of the data processing system and proper allocation of resources to the computer activity.

Placing Reliance on Control

Unless the auditor can place some reliance on control she or he must do extensive substantive testing. The auditor makes this determination by assessing if there are controls in place directed at reducing each significant business risk. The auditor can do this by identifying the control objectives that address each risk, and looking for specific controls that achieve these control objectives. The material in Chapters 6 to 8 should prove helpful to the auditor in performing the preliminary review as well as the detailed control reviews that follow. The determination of whether or not the auditor can rely on the controls is a matter of judgment based on the identification and documentation of risk and control.

Summary

Because of the concentration and complexity in automated systems, the potential for control problems is great. As one author has suggested[5] there is a need for a control maze to protect an organization from fraud, natural disasters, inadvertent errors, record destruction, and unreasonable transactions. The control maze should consist of various types of controls that complement each other so that a breakdown in one area is detected or compensated for by controls in another area.

In Chapters 6 to 8, we shall discuss each of these major types of controls in detail, with emphasis on control techniques. It is hoped that the discussion will

[5] Joseph J. Wasserman, "Plugging the Leaks in Computer Security," Harvard Business Review, September–October 1969.

develop a control framework that can be used in evaluating controls in EDP systems.

Problems

1. What impact does the Foreign Corrupt Practices Act have on management's responsibility for internal accounting control? What responsibility does the external or independent auditor have for internal accounting control?

2. What are the major objectives of internal accounting control?

3. You meet a friend of your parents at a family function and you discover that he is a member of the board and audit committee of a publicly held company. When he finds out you are interested in accounting and control, he asks you what responsibilities you think the board of a company has for internal accounting control. How do you reply?

4. Discuss the relationship between a risk and a control.

5. Discuss the differences between control in a manual environment and control in an EDP environment.

6. The Turner Corporation periodically ships merchandise to the wrong address, owing to computer master file errors. In the course of a year, about thirty shipments are not returned, at an average loss to the company of $500 per shipment. The data processing manager has suggested a series of controls. Control A would reduce the average loss by 50 percent, Control B would reduce the average frequency of loss by 50 percent, and control C would reduce half of the frequency of loss remaining after Control A is installed. Each of these controls would cost $4,000 per year to implement. Which, if any, or all, of the controls should be installed? (The department wants a return on investment for any installed control.)

7. If the recommendations for installing control(s) in the previous case are adopted, what will be the return on investment to the company from installing that control?

8. In the 1970s, a major aerospace corporation was accused by the SEC of permitting improper business practices in some of the oil-producing countries in the Mideast. The basis of the charge was that the corporation had permitted their marketing people to bribe officials of non-U.S. countries to acquire business. The senior officers of the corporation agreed that the practice may be improper, and that the marketing people had violated the law, but argued that the Securities and Exchange Commission should not prosecute the senior officers because they could not reasonably be expected to oversee all the transactions being processed by

the organization. Do you agree with the contention of the senior officers? If so, state the reasons for your opinion.

9. Accountants and auditors frequently refer to the term "system of internal control." What does this term mean?

10. Most data base systems provide for protecting access to that data base through a security system. Would this security system, which is designed to reduce the risk of unauthorized access, be considered an administrative or an application control, and why?

EDP AUDIT PROCESS*

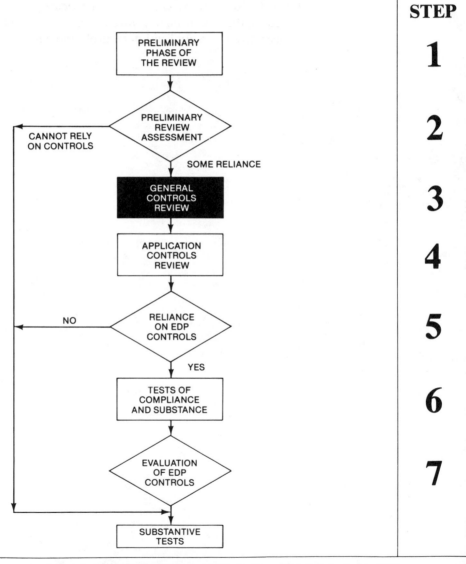

	STEP
PRELIMINARY PHASE OF THE REVIEW	1
PRELIMINARY REVIEW ASSESSMENT	2
GENERAL CONTROLS REVIEW	3
APPLICATION CONTROLS REVIEW	4
RELIANCE ON EDP CONTROLS	5
TESTS OF COMPLIANCE AND SUBSTANCE	6
EVALUATION OF EDP CONTROLS	7

CANNOT RELY ON CONTROLS

SOME RELIANCE

NO

YES

SUBSTANTIVE TESTS

*Diagram is adapted from The Auditor's Study and Evaluation of Internal Control in EDP Systems, pages 21–24. Copyright © 1977 by the American Institute of Certified Public Accountants, Inc. (See Figure 9.1 for a complete explanation of the steps.)

6

GENERAL CONTROLS

(3) Completion of Review—General Controls

Purpose:
- Identify general controls on which reliance is planned and determine how they operate.
- Determine the effect of strengths and weaknesses on application controls.
- Consider tests of compliance that may be performed.

Methods: Detailed examination of documentation; interviewing internal auditors, along with EDP and user department personnel; observing operation of general controls.

OBJECTIVE

An auditor must understand the importance of general controls, particularly in an EDP environment. The types of general EDP controls are explained to aid in the identification and assessment of those controls.

General controls (sometimes called administrative controls) involve policy and procedures. Application controls involve controls over transaction data. The key difference between them is that one (application controls) is data oriented and the other (general controls) is procedure oriented. Thus it is possible for an auditor to evaluate procedures independently from applications.

There are two main reasons why there is merit in an auditor evaluating general controls separately from applications. First, general controls cross application boundaries. Second, the evaluation is strictly a compliance audit of policies and procedures. There is no equivalent of substantive auditing when dealing with general controls. Because these controls cross application boundaries, the individual who can take action on any recommendations is most likely different from the individual who can take action on audit recommendations for a specific application. For example, documentation standards may be decided by the vice president of data processing, but payroll application procedures would be decided by the payroll department manager.

Importance of EDP General Controls [1]

The internal accounting control environment established by management has a significant impact on the selection and effectiveness of a company's accounting control procedures and techniques. In making a preliminary assessment, it is important to recognize that a poor internal accounting control environment would make some control procedures inoperative for all intents and purposes because, for example, individuals would hesitate to challenge a management override of a specific control procedure. However, even a strong control environment cannot provide absolute assurance that control procedures will not be circumvented by employee collusion or management override.

Factors that should be considered in a preliminary assessment would include the degree to which compliance with accounting control procedures is enforced and reinforced through creation of an appropriate organizational structure, use of sound management practices, establishment of accountability for performance, and requirements for adherence to appropriate standards for ethical behavior, including compliance with applicable laws and regulations. Management should also consider the extent to which important corporate and accounting policies and procedures have been formalized, the extent to which internal audits or other supervisory reviews are used, the internal accounting control weaknesses that have been identified in the normal course of business or by audit findings, and the degree to which changes have taken place in the company's organizational structure, accounting system, and personnel.

The method of data processing used by a company may influence its orga-

[1] Pages 150–152 of this text are based on the report of the Special Advisory Committee on Internal Accounting Control, The American Institute of Certified Public Accountants, New York, N.Y., 1978, pages 9–12.

nizational structure and the procedures and techniques used to accomplish the broad objectives of internal accounting control. Accordingly, EDP considerations play an important role in evaluating a company's control environment and its control procedures.

The characteristics of computer systems and computerized controls indicate the need for management to understand the exposures and controls for specific business applications and cycles, and to understand the controls in the computer processes themselves. The degree of reliance that can be placed on controls exercised by the computer system is dependent on the degree of control exercised by management over the development and maintenance of the computer system. For a further discussion of general and application controls over data processing systems that should be considered, see SAS 3, *The Effects of EDP on the Auditor's Study and Evaluation of Internal Control* and certain AICPA guides and guidelines, such as *Management, Control, and Audit of Advanced EDP Systems.*

Physical concentration of data, concentration of different functions within the EDP activity, and the use of common data by multiple users are some of the important characteristics of contemporary computer systems. Accordingly, special consideration should be given to three major threats in an EDP environment: (1) the loss of important information through disaster, (2) the ability of a single individual to make unauthorized changes that negate internal accounting controls or permit improper access to assets, and (3) the possibility of unintentional loss of assets (for example, loss through pricing errors on sales invoices because of errors in the master price file).

Some of the tasks frequently performed in the EDP process itself are listed below.

- Initiation, authorization, execution, and reporting of transactions according to pre-established rules. Examples might include interest and depreciation calculations, orders to purchase or ship merchandise, and automatic preparation of checks for repetitive payments—such as dividends, employee benefits, or freight settlements.

- Preparation or processing of documents that authorize the use or disposition of assets. This indirect access may occur in connection with transactions that are computer initiated.

- Performance of the full range of accounting functions, that is, recording, classifying, summarizing, and reporting transactions.

- Implementation of accounting controls. Those controls may relate to internally generated transactions, internal processing, or internal files, as well as data submitted for processing.

The wide range of tasks that may be performed by the EDP process emphasizes the importance of proper systems development methods and the participation of management in the development process.

Management should also recognize that computer programs are frequently subject to change. If the change process (or program maintenance) is not controlled, an individual can make unauthorized changes or can make incorrect changes that can have an unpredictable effect on the data files. For example, internal transactions may be generated; assets may be indirectly accessed by individuals responsible for accounting for the assets; editing and reporting of errors or exceptions may be subverted. Similarly, to the extent that supervisory programs are changed and the change process itself is not controlled, unauthorized transactions may be initiated and the reporting of those transactions may be suppressed. Finally, to the extent that direct unauthorized access to the computer can occur, data programs can be accidentally or intentionally modified or destroyed.

In considering its organizational structure, management should recognize that the development of contemporary systems consists of identifying the company's business requirements from diverse sources and users and translating them into operational computer instructions. This requires a substantially higher level of coordination among groups within the organization and among technical disciplines than was previously required when systems simply supported individual departments.

Organization and Control

Data processing organizations are logically broken into two separate functions. These are programming and systems, and operations. Because EDP systems are complex and difficult to use properly, the implementation of control in these two areas is important. Control in these areas includes:

1. *Systems and programming*—Control over the implementation of new systems, changes to existing systems, programming standards, and documentation guidelines.

2. *Operations*—The information processing facility requires controls over operating practices, data storage, physical security, record construction procedures, and backup facilities and emergency procedures. The input-output control function is important to ensure that specific tasks are carried out effectively and efficiently. The control function acts as an interface between the data processing department and the user department.

Our discussion of general controls will focus first on organizational structure as a control. Second, a typical middle-sized EDP organization structure will be given and the reasons for the structure discussed. This discussion will state how this organization structure might change in a larger or smaller organization. Third, specific controls will be reviewed for the two main divisions in an EDP organization (i.e., systems, and programming and operations).

Organizational Controls

Although the shape of a company's organizational structure results from a variety of influences, clear lines of authority and responsibility should be apparent. The division of functional responsibilities should provide for a separation among (1) the functions of initiation and authorization of a transaction, (2) the recording of the transaction, and (3) the custody of the resultant asset. Such a division of responsibilities, in addition to safeguarding assets, provides for the efficiencies derived from specialization, makes possible a cross-check that promotes accuracy without duplication or wasted effort, and enhances the effectiveness of a management control system. From a control standpoint, automation has had a great effect on organization structures. The result has been increased centralization of data processing activities and the concentration of data processing functions.

Centralization   Before the advent of EDP systems, most of the individual operating departments—shipping and receiving, production control, inventory control, marketing, budgeting, and accounting—usually did their own clerical paper work. Now a separate functional and organization entity—the data processing center—tightens coordination and helps eliminate duplicate demands by processing data and generating reports that provide operating departments with the bases for carrying on their individual activities.

Other major reasons for the physical centralization of EDP activities are the high fixed cost of both electronic equipment and improved data communications equipment. Data can be transmitted from the source, possibly a remote warehouse or sales branch, to another point for processing; the results of processing are then returned in the desired format to the applicable locations. Such systems are justified when the time and the costs associated with processing data are reduced and, accordingly, management has more timely information on which to control company operations effectively.

Concentration   The centralization of data processing activities has resulted in the concentration of many processing steps into one department and the concentration of traditional accounting data along with operating data. Such concentration is commonly referred to as *integration,* in which related elements of different data processing activities are combined into common and coordinated procedures and a logical work flow. Integration assists in the preparation of desired and necessary managerial reports from a single record of each business transaction, and all transactions are processed in a unified system.

Need for Segregation of Duties

The centralization of data processing into one department emphasizes the importance of proper control of the data processing center itself. As noted, one of the basic principles of internal control is the separation among those people who authorize a transaction, those who have custody of the asset acquired, and those who record the accountability for the asset. This basic separation in accounting, as well as in other functions, must be maintained in order to achieve satisfactory internal control.

To illustrate this basic separation, let us examine segregation of functions in the handling of inventory records of a wholesaler. If the system were a manual one, the accounting department would maintain the inventory records to establish accountability over the goods stored in the warehouse. The people in the warehouse would have custody over the physical inventory, and periodically the physical inventory would be "counted" and reconciled with the "book" inventory found in the inventory records maintained by the accounting department. This periodic reconciliation would reveal any differences that might exist because of ineffective warehousing and/or accounting procedures. The reconciliation would also provide an incentive to the people involved to carry out their work with care. The warehousemen, in turn, would watch the accuracy of receiving room accounts as goods were released for warehousing, for the receiving records of that department would be the basis for charging the warehouse inventory records.

The authorization to replenish inventory by the preparation and transmission of a purchase order to a vendor or supplier would be the responsibility of the purchasing department. The authorization to disburse funds to the supplier for inventory replenishment would be the responsibility of the treasurer after proper reconciliation of information on the purchase order, receiving reports, and vendor's invoice.

Such a division of responsibility helps safeguard inventory assets, provides for efficiency through specialization, and provides cross-checks on the reliability of the purchasing and payable records and warehousing procedures. To confirm your understanding of this basic segregation of functional responsibilities, read through the following illustration as if it were an exercise; it is a narrative discussion of an order processing system. Figure 6.1 is a flowchart of the system.

An Illustration of Organizational Controls

A customer's order is received by a sales department, where a six-part sales invoice is prepared. The original order (part 1) is retained in the sales department and filed alphabetically by customer name; part 2 is sent to the credit department for credit approval; and the remaining parts of the invoice are held until credit is approved. When credit is approved, the remaining five parts of the invoice are then distributed as follows:

- The billing department receives parts 1 (sales invoice) and 3 (posting copy).

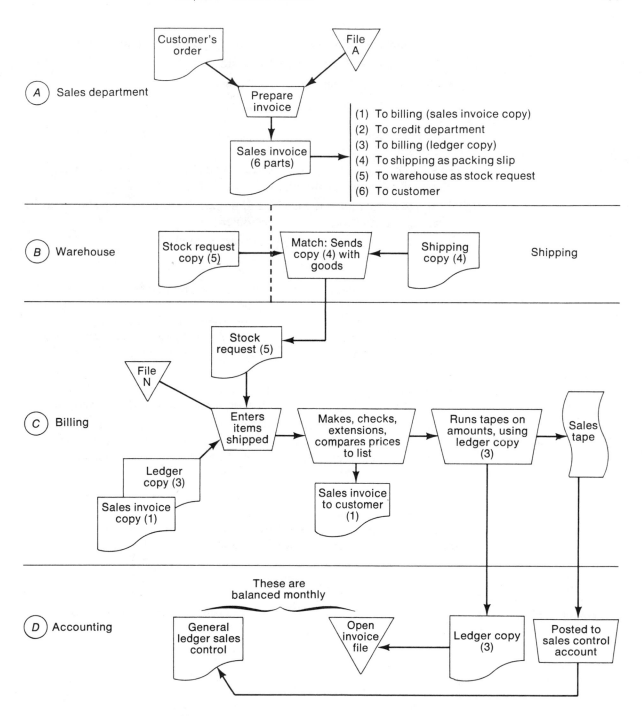

Figure 6.1   Flowchart for Order Processing System

- The shipping department receives part 4 to use as a packing slip.
- The warehouse receives part 5 as a stock request.
- The customer is sent part 6 to acknowledge the order.

The next sequence of events includes:

- The warehouse sends the stock request (part 5) to shipping, along with the ordered goods.
- Shipping checks the goods received against the items ordered. The goods actually shipped are noted on the stock request (part 5).
- Shipping then takes the packing slip (part 4) from the files and sends it, along with the goods, to the customer.
- Shipping sends the stock request (part 5) to billing.

In the last sequence of events:

- The items shipped, as marked on the stock request (part 5), are entered on the sales invoice (part 1) and on the ledger copy (part 3) by clerks in the billing department. At this time, the billing department makes extensions; that is, it determines the amounts to charge the customer, checks the amounts, and runs a tape of the extended amounts shown on the ledger copy.
- The billing department mails the sales invoice (part 1) to the customer, and the stock request (part 5) is filed numerically in the department.
- General accounting receives the ledger copy (part 3), and it is placed in the open invoice file. Also received is the tape of extended amounts, which is used to post the tape's total to the sales control account in the general ledger.

Table 6.1 lists the departments involved in this system and the three basic functions that have been discussed: *authorization, recordkeeping,* and *custody.* Table 6.1 also indicates how the departments in the system can be segregated and what basic functions in the system should be performed by the various

**Table 6.1
Segregation of Functions**

	AUTHORIZATION	RECORDKEEPING	CUSTODY
Order Clerks in Sales Department		X	
Credit Department	X		
Billing Clerks		X	
Warehouse and Shipping Departments			X
General Accounting		X	

departments involved. The purpose of this exercise has been to emphasize the segregation of duties within an organization. You will notice that no single group is responsible for more than one of the three basic functions. Such segregation is extremely important if an organization is to achieve its control objectives.

How Segregation Is Achieved in Automated Systems

In many data processing systems for applications being designed today, programmed decision rules combined with machine-readable files create the impression that the authorization and recordkeeping functions have been merged. For example, let us return to our discussion of the handling of inventory records of a wholesaler. If we had automated the perpetual inventory recordkeeping and maintained the inventory files on some machine-readable form such as magnetic tape or magnetic disk, probably we would have included in the inventory records data such as reorder levels, economic order quantities, and data on the vendors from whom replenishment can be made, in addition to accountability data such as quantity on hand and unit cost. In such a system, of course, we could program some decision rules that would cause a computerized replenishment decision and a printout of a purchase order when the quantity on hand for an inventory item has fallen below the reorder point.

In this kind of system, the authorization function originates with operating personnel. To provide the replenishment decision rules within the stored computer program, the systems designer and programmer would interact with purchasing people who have knowledge of the inventory items, usage history, and vendor history. Thus, the authorization to replenish inventory originates with the operating people and is passed along to systems designers and programmers, who program the parameters to be included in inventory replenishment decisions. Normally the recordkeeping in automated systems is done by computer operations personnel, who handle the inventory files in machine-readable form. Of course, the custody of the assets required through inventory replenishment decisions would still be the responsibility of warehousing personnel.

To maintain the continued integrity of the system where the authorization and recording functions are embodied in the computer program itself, it is necessary to separate (1) the *systems planning and programming function,* (2) the *operations function,* and (3) the *program maintenance and tape library function.* Such separation is important because

- It provides an effective cross-check of the accuracy and propriety of changes introduced into the systems.
- It prevents operating personnel from implementing revisions without prior approval and thorough checking.
- It eliminates access to the equipment by nonoperating personnel and other people who have knowledge of the system.

- It improves efficiency because the capabilities, training, and skills required in carrying out these activities differ greatly.

Inadequate Segregation Segregation of duties is a desired control objective. However, size is frequently the determining factor as to whether or not various duties are segregated. For example, a computer room with one operator cannot have a full-time data librarian.

In situations where desirable segregation of duties does not exist, or is impractical, auditors should look for compensating controls. If an auditor is unable to obtain satisfaction that other controls compensate for the lack of segregation of duties, then additional audit tests should be performed.

Organizational Control: A Checklist Summary

In this chapter we have discussed the basic principles of organizational control in an EDP department. Below is an eight-part checklist based on the organizational control principles that have been discussed.

1. To what executive does the data processing manager report and why?
2. What separation exists between the systems design and programming group and computer operations?
3. What access does the systems design and programming group have to the computer or to any data files and why?
4. What personnel other than operating personnel have access to the computer room and why?
5. How are files in the form of tapes or disks protected from inappropriate use?
6. How are the master copies of computer programs maintained and protected?
7. What functions are performed by the internal control group in the data processing department?
8. What functions are performed by user departments and/or external control groups?

Organization of an EDP Department

Having discussed the basic segregation of functions important in the EDP department, we shall discuss how we group the systems and programming function, the operations function, and the control function to achieve the desired separation of duties and efficiency through specialization.

First, let us examine the medium-sized data processing department shown in Figure 6.2. Normally such a department affords opportunities for specialization and a hierarchy of supervision. The organization is split between systems and programming and those functions relating to the computer operations facility. The operations function is broken into the following groups:

- *Data library*—storage and recordkeeping for all machine-readable media
- *Data conversion*—transcribing from source documents to machine-readable media
- *Technical services*—activities necessary to select and implement computer operating systems and other major vendor-supplied systems (e.g., data base systems, communication systems, etc.)

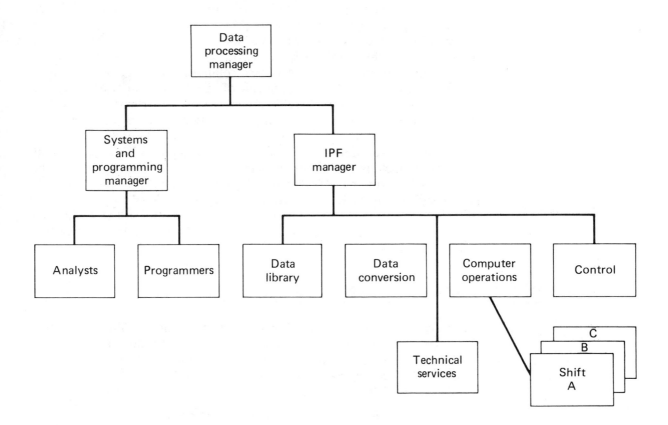

Figure 6.2   Organization Chart for a Medium-Sized Data Processing Department*

* Equipment rental between $5,000 and $15,000 per month.

- *Computer operations*—operation of the computer and related support hardware
- *Control*—control over job flow, completeness and accuracy of data as it moves through the EDP department

With increased size of the department, of course, there are additional opportunities for specialization, with systems analysts separated organizationally from programming. Also, programming may include a separate documentation librarian whose function is to maintain systems and program documentation for all the applications in the system. The systems function may also include data communications specialists because of the technical complexities associated with this area of computerized systems.

The operations function in a large data processing department would also include opportunities for specialization and hierarchies of supervision. Functions such as scheduling of jobs, unit record operations, and security could be established as separate functions.

Small departments can afford only a limited number of people and this fact usually restricts the degree of specialization possible. For example, systems designers may also be programmers, and computer operating personnel may maintain the library. Although segregation of duties is more difficult to achieve in small departments, the basic segregation between the systems and programming function and the computer operating function should be achieved.

Now that we have taken a look at the structure of an EDP department for various sized organizations, let us summarize our findings. We suggested that two distinct functions should be present in the EDP department, namely, (1) the systems and programming function, and (2) the operations function. We suggested further that the EDP department should be restricted from having any direct or indirect control over assets or from having any part in originating transactions. Next we shall consider specific control areas for each of these two distinct functions.

Systems and Programming Controls

The systems and programming group has the responsibility for the implementation of computer systems based on the needs of the organization as established by the user. The user retains the responsibility for the accuracy and completeness of processing by the computer application.

Four general controls will be discussed for this area. These are:

1. The review and approval procedures for new systems.
2. Program testing procedures.
3. Program change procedures.
4. Documentation.

**Review
and Approval
of New Systems**

It is desirable practice to have an EDP-systems-planning steering committee composed of an executive group in an organization. This group

> reviews requests for action, arrives at decisions, resolves conflicts, and monitors the development and implementation of system projects. It also serves to oversee user performance in determining that objectives and benefits agreed to at the inception of a system development project are, in fact, realized.[2]

The committee should establish guidelines for the development and implementation of systems projects and appropriate documentation for management summaries; it should review procedures at important decision points in the development and implementation process. Such control should be exercised to ensure proper review and approval by management of new EDP systems and conversion plans.

**Program Testing
Procedures**

The testing of programs is one of the most critical phases in the development and implementation of systems. Testing is important to make sure that the programs written conform to design specifications and include decision and processing logic to meet user needs. Several steps should be included in program testing procedures:

> The selection of test criteria and the design of the data to carry out the tests should be as comprehensive as possible. The comprehensiveness of the tests may be ensured by participation by user-department personnel, auditors, and technical computer people.

> The test data should include transactions specifically designed to determine if the control features and decision logic in the program work and to give proper responses when "improper" conditions appear. This means the inclusion of invalid, abnormal, incomplete, and illogical transactions. Of course, the tests should also include valid transactions to test all processing steps.

> The programs should be subjected to a series of tests, building up to volume tests. Normally the volume tests should be processed with a group of programs constituting a complete computerized application so that actual operating conditions can be simulated as closely as possible.

> The final testing should evaluate all phases of the system, including manual and computer. The final tests should include the procedures used by the people preparing source data, user departments, the control group, and computer operators as well as the actual computer programs.

[2] J. C. Shaw and W. Atkins, *Managing Computer System Projects,* p. 15, McGraw-Hill, New York, 1970.

The final tests should be performed under actual operating conditions using live data as much as possible.

Finally, the final tests should be done without the direct participation of the programmer(s) to determine if the system can operate independently of programmer assistance. Such a testing procedure will also provide assurance that the documentation and operating instructions are adequate for the operation of the system.[3]

Program Change Procedures

The dynamic nature of most business activities causes program changes. Program changes require well-formulated and well-documented procedures to prevent the manipulation of programs for unauthorized purposes. There are six major procedures necessary for maintaining control over program changes.

1. The nature of the proposed procedure change should be explained in writing, and formal approval for the change should be given by a responsible individual. Major changes should be approved by the systems-planning steering committee in the same manner as for new systems. Minor changes may require only the joint approval of the EDP manager and senior personnel in the user department. The documentation of the proposed procedure change will clear up any initial misunderstandings that may arise when only verbal requests are made. In addition, written proposals will provide a history of changes in a particular system.

2. Changes to the program should be prepared only by the systems group, not by members of the computer operating group. Any change should be supported by adequate systems documentation. If the operator were authorized to make minor changes, it would greatly increase the difficulty of controlling manipulation and of maintaining up-to-date documentation.

3. A change should be tested and given final approval by a person who is separated from and independent of the person designing the change.

4. Once changes are made, the testing of the final revised program should be done by the operations section, and the results should be recorded on program change registers and sent to the EDP manager for approval. The operations section should accept only properly approved changes.

5. Finally, all change sheets or change registers and printouts should be filed in the program run book, thus providing a permanent record of all changes made in the program.

[3] Canadian Institute of Chartered Accountants, *Computer Control Guidelines,* pp. 41–42, 1970.

Documentation   The formulation and documentation of an EDP application can be broken down into three phases: *data systems survey, data systems study,* and *programming.*

The *data systems survey* should outline the scope and objectives of application, the plan and schedule for completion, and estimated costs and benefits. An important part of documentation of a data systems survey, and hence an important control feature, is approval by management before proceeding with the data systems study. Too often, management does not know, much less understand, what EDP is or is not doing for the company; conversely, systems personnel are often not aware of management policies that are important to the design of the system.

The *data systems study* should include a review of present procedures. Such a review should indicate what procedures and controls are necessary and beneficial in the new system and what changes can be made in improving existing procedures. After a review of the present system, the new one should be designed. The design should include adequate definition and documentation for the contents of master files, input and output requirements, methods of processing, and control requirements. In addition, the documentation should include a timetable of data collection, processing, and reporting; estimated execution times; required equipment; and method and timing of conversion. This documentation should be reviewed, approved, and signed by all the department managers concerned in order to ensure that the EDP applications have been thoroughly investigated, documented, and agreed upon before programming begins.

Computer *programming* is the preparation of flowcharts, program listings, and computer operating instructions. During the planning and installation of an EDP system or application, it is desirable to document all aspects of program development as explicitly as possible. Such documentation serves both as an essential tool for understanding and controlling the programs and as a permanent history of all pertinent facts related to each program.

One extremely useful document is the *program run book*. Important run-book requirements on all programs include (1) a description of the purpose of the program, (2) a complete set of flowcharts, (3) a compiled listing of the program, (4) computer operating instructions, (5) program-testing documentation, and (6) a sample of all reports produced by the program. In addition, a *console run book* should be prepared for specific use by computer operating personnel when operating each program. Normally, the console run book includes (1) a flowchart of the portion of the system that the program is part of, (2) identification of input–output units used for input and output files, (3) a list of all program halts and required action, and (4) a description of any exceptions to standard routines and any variable data (dates, constants, and so forth) to be entered in the program.

Efficient program development requires *programming standards*. A programming manual should be set up and maintained and should contain a written record of all policies, procedures, and techniques that are to be standard throughout the organization. The existence of such a manual will facilitate communication and prevent the development of duplicate or conflicting procedures. Many areas of program development lend themselves to standardization, such as program documentation procedures, tape labeling, program testing procedures, and tape retention policies.

To provide an example of the documentation developed in well-controlled EDP systems, we have included in this book a documentation standards manual developed by a medium-sized (employing approximately 40 people) data processing installation. This manual is found in Appendix A. Please take a few minutes to review it, noting specifically how it is organized and the areas with which it deals.

The documentation standards manual in Appendix A provides a good example of what a set of standards must include if it is to be effective. However, there are also other areas where it is essential that sound documentation standards be established: library and file control, data conversion, input–output control, and user department procedures. In the following paragraphs, we shall list in some detail items that must be included as standards in each of these areas. Along with Appendix A, these items may serve as a blueprint or checklist in designing or reviewing a standards manual. (Some of the items that appear in these sections may duplicate, to some degree, material that appears in Appendix A.) It is frequently the case that certain sections of the run manual (particularly those dealing with operating instructions) are reproduced and furnished to the operator or librarian. This is a good practice since fully documented, written instructions for personnel are an important control in preventing errors.

Operations Controls

The information processing facility includes four major areas. These are (1) data conversion operations, (2) computer operations, (3) a media library, and (4) a control function. Our organization chart (Figure 6.2) shows a fifth function, technical services. Technical services include the functions that support the computer operation such as equipment selection, software selection and support, and operating efficiency. Technical services are closely allied with operations and in many organizations are part of computer operations.

Ideally, these five areas should be organizationally independent. However, the first major division should be between operations and control. For this reason, we have segregated the computer operations area into the following two main categories:

- Control function—those practices relating to control
- Operating practices—all other functions

Control Function   The plan of organization and operating procedures for computerized installations should provide for a control function. There are two types of control functions: an *internal* processing control group that is part of the data processing department, and control that is *external* to the data processing department.

In the medium-sized and large data processing installations, there exists a processing control group within the data processing organization. This processing control group should be concerned with ensuring that processing is performed correctly and that no data are lost or mishandled within the department. This *internal control group* should perform the following five functions:

1. Following up on data yet received, and recording the progress of work through the department, thus allowing the computer operators to concentrate on operations.

2. Providing liaison between computer operations and the various user departments.

3. Recording input control totals in a control log to balance with totals generated in the computer processing.

4. Controlling errors rejected by the computer to ensure that all errors are corrected and that corrections are reentered into the system. The monitoring of error frequency is necessary to initiate corrective action in the areas where the errors originate.

5. Ensuring that output reports are available on time, that the final output has been balanced to the control information, and that the output is distributed to authorized personnel.

External control takes several forms, but it is basically concerned with establishing an independent check on the functioning of the data processing department. The check may be performed by user departments or, in large systems, by a special control group set up in the accounting and finance department to form an independent, critical review of performance. Three specific functions of this *external control group* could include the following:

1. Comparison of output with plan to detect unusual or abnormal items and initiate corrective action by the organizational unit responsible.

2. Systematic sampling of individual output to determine whether the systems are functioning as designed.

3. Handling of inquiries, requests, and criticisms of users about output reports and information providing a feedback mechanism to designers and programmers.

Operating Practices   Operating practices are necessary to ensure a high degree of processing reliability of accounting data and provide protection of data files and programs from loss, destruction, or unauthorized alteration or disclosure. Operating practices consist of a broad spectrum of controls directed toward the general operation of EDP operations rather than any one automated application. These practices include the following:

- Access to computer room
- Library and file-control standards
- Data-conversion standards
- Library procedures
- Operational control procedures (related to the scheduling and utilization of files and equipment)
- Physical security of files and equipment
- Record reconstruction procedures
- Backup facilities and emergency procedures
- Passwords
- Privacy of data

Access to Computer Room

Another aspect of EDP organization is the control over access to the machinery and to the operating programs and files. As discussed previously, it is necessary to have a segregation of functions between systems analysts and programmers, on the one hand, and computer operators, on the other. However, separation on an organization chart does little good if the systems analysts and programmers have physical access to the machines and the operating programs and files in the computer room. Ideally, the computer room should be restricted to computer operating personnel; systems analysts and programmers should not be allowed to enter.

There are two basic reasons why access to the computer room should be restricted to computer operators. First, such restriction provides a safeguard on assets by making the manipulation of files and programs difficult by the systems designers and programmers who are involved in developing the systems and programs. For example, let us say that a programmer in a bank has programmed the demand deposit application for the bank. With his knowledge of the program, access to the files in the computer room on which information about the demand depositors is contained may allow him to manipulate the account balances of the bank's depositors (including *his own* balance if he is a depositor).

Second, restricting access to the computer room improves efficiency because tests of new programs and revisions of old ones must be performed according to present schedules; thus the daily processing schedule is not disrupted for these purposes. Suggesting that access to equipment be prohibited to systems analysts and programmers does not preclude the need for testing programs. However, testing should be done without access to the equipment by submitting programs and data at prescribed testing times in the processing schedule and having the results returned to the programmer within a reasonable time period.

Library and File-Control Standards

One valuable section of a standards manual should document procedures to be followed in handling files.

For each file these should specify the following eight elements:

1. File name and number.
2. Authorization for file issue in the case of restricted-access files.
3. Updating cycle.
4. Retention cycle or retention date.
5. File size and block size.
6. In the case of a disk file or any other random-access device, the date and when it is to be copied onto another medium (such as tape, cards, or printed reports).
7. How the files are to be reconstructed in case of damage or destruction.
8. How the files are to be stored (in the library, in a special vault, or in an off-premises storage area).

All files should be controlled by a librarian in a protected area that has restricted access. The librarian should be provided with clear and complete written instructions, covering areas such as these:

- Environmental conditions required in the tape library area
- Fire-protection safeguards required
- Location and use of the off-premises storage area
- Tape, disk, and card file labeling requirements
- Procedures for issuing files to authorized users
- How and when to record tape- or disk-file history data on history card
- Physical retention policies for tapes, disks, etc.
- Tape cleaning and maintenance procedures

Data-Conversion Standards

The persons responsible for data-conversion operations should be provided with written instructions. Data conversion here implies operations necessary to convert data from source documents into machine-readable form, either in a batch or by direct-entry mode. Documentation should include instructions such as those listed on the next page.

- *Source documents*—which data are to be extracted, and in what sequence?
- *Input media*—how are the data to be formatted? What about special codes to be used, use of end-of-field and end-of-record signals, positions to be left blank, method of recording negative amounts, special characters?
- *Control cards*—what method and format are to be used for recording control data?

Input–Output Control Standards Documentation should provide instructions for the internal control group or whoever is responsible for input–output control. These instructions should cover

- Source and description of input
- Sample of output
- Reconciliation and/or balancing of output to control figures
- Anticipated error conditions and actions to be taken
- Disposition of output

Standards for User-Department Procedures Finally, documentation standards must be prepared to cover user department procedures. These should include

- Documents or data to be forwarded for computer processing
- Controls to be established over the documents or data
- Schedules to be observed
- Special codes to be used
- Cutoff procedures to be followed
- Reports and information to be received
- Report schedule
- Steps to be followed in performing a general check of reports or information
- Output review
- Error feedback and correction procedures

Library Procedures

Adequate control procedures are also necessary in the tape and program library function. Access to the library must be controlled to prevent unauthorized individuals from obtaining tapes and thereby circumventing other controls that have been established. Generally, access to the library should be restricted to personnel who require use of the program and other tapes in connection with the normal operation of the system. In very large installations where the tape files are maintained by a tape librarian, access to the files should be restricted to this person.

Apart from a tape-labeling system (both internal and external) and control over access to the tapes, procedures and forms must be set up to maintain the tape and program library effectively. Upon receipt, the reels should be tested to ensure that they are not defective and then given serial numbers. Then they can be assigned to the different applications by these serial numbers, thus permitting efficient scheduling through the data processing system. To achieve efficient use of tapes and to ensure control, a rigorous record system must be maintained on the filing and status of the tapes. Such a system should provide information about the physical location of any given reel, tapes available to be written on, and usage history of each tape.

Operational Control Procedures

Management control over any activity is important to ensure that specific tasks are carried out effectively and efficiently. In an EDP department, operational control procedures are necessary to plan, schedule, and evaluate equipment, personnel, and projects to allow the measurement of the effectiveness of the EDP function.

We have already discussed some operational control procedures such as proper organization, documentation standards, and supervision of operations. In addition to these control procedures, a number of additional controls are desirable. *Proper scheduling* is an important control technique to plan the use of computer resources effectively. The measurement of actual use of resources as compared with the plan may be accomplished with the use of a *utilization record,* which accounts for the computer operation, equipment use, and time involved in processing a job. Such a record should be analyzed and reviewed by responsible operating personnel to determine the time involved in processing each job and the reasons for all lost time.

Another important operational control is *console control.* The operator uses the console of the data processing system to control the system and monitor its operations. The console stops and starts the system and restarts the computer when error conditions cause it to halt. It indicates the instructions being performed and can be used to alter the mode of operation. By using the console, the operator can determine the status of the internal register because it has these data printed out. In addition, the console can be used to enter the data manually into the system. In many cases, the configuration of a computerized system includes a console typewriter that can create a log of console activity.

Several techniques can be employed to provide effective console control:

- Review of the console log by supervisory personnel in the EDP department.

- Rotation of duties among computer operations.
- Accounting for processing time through utilization reports. Time standards can be established for various runs, which can be compared with the actual times recorded on a console printout or in a machine-utilization log.
- Operation of the computer in "nonstop" mode. By use of an operating system that controls the processing and brings into operation the proper programs and data online to the system, and by use of error procedures that do not halt the computer, the EDP system provides that the console operator can make little or no manual intervention during processing.

Physical Security of Files and Equipment

Some control procedures should be designed to ensure the security of programs, files, and data. Obviously, an organization must be concerned with procedures to protect programs, files, and data from fire, theft, and natural disasters such as floods. The best protection against total destruction of important files and programs is their duplication and storage in an area that would be unlikely to be affected by the same disaster affecting the computer room.

In a magnetic tape installation, it is generally practicable to store a duplicate set of important data in an outlying area as a safeguard against fire or water damage to the tape library. The tape library evacuation procedures should also be developed and documented. What specific tapes should be stored off the premises will depend on the particular system. At a minimum, the program tapes and the master file tapes should be filed away from the computer room. In a disk-oriented system, the old master file may not be retained intact after creation of the new master files, and therefore a special run should be made to duplicate the master file for off-premises storage. In both tape- and disk-oriented systems, the transaction data used to update the master file should also be stored at the off-premises location in machine-readable form.

In addition to files and programs, the equipment should be safeguarded. Typically this can be done by restricting access to the computer room to operations personnel only. Also, it may be desirable to place the computer facility in a location that is difficult to find.

Record Reconstruction Procedures

If, despite the presence of control techniques already discussed, the files are updated with incorrect data or inadvertently destroyed, there must be procedures to reconstruct the records. Such procedures, commonly referred to as the *record reconstruction plan,* must permit the recreation of a file with a minimum of effort. Simply stated, the basic operating procedures established under a reconstruction plan prohibit reuse of magnetic tapes until the output from the computer operations—either another magnetic tape or report—is proved correct and usable.

Backup support for magnetic tape files is usually accomplished by use of the *grandfather-father-son* concept. This concept is based on the fact that an organization usually produces an updated master file at each processing by reading the previous period's master file, making changes according to the transactions being processed, and writing the new file. For example, if the inventory master file is updated daily, the following is the backup available for daily processing after processing of Friday's transactions (keep in mind that the processing with tape files creates a new file tape but does not destroy the old one):

- Wednesday's file (grandfather)
- Thursday's file (father)
- Friday's file (son)

If Friday's tape is destroyed during processing on Monday (assuming no weekend activity takes place), Thursday's tape is reprocessed with Friday's transactions in order to recreate Friday's master file. If the the files are to be recreated under the grandfather-father-son concept, the transaction files used to update the son file must also be retained; in such an approach, the grandfather file may be released for other purposes when the son file is deemed correct.

As mentioned previously (in the discussion of direct-access systems), the contents of disk files should be duplicated on another machine-readable medium such as a tape or another disk so that the file can be reconstructed if another file is accidentally damaged or destroyed. The contents of disk files, of course, must be copied frequently enough to provide sufficient computer time to recreate the destroyed master file and to process current transactions. The frequency of the copying process is a function of volume, processing speed, and available computer time.

In very long processing runs, *test point and reprocessing procedures* should be included to permit the computer operator to restart a program at an interim point in the processing rather than having to return to the beginning of the run. Thus when problems occur in certain areas or when problems exist in processing, the operator can reconstruct the computer memory at the last correct interval in the program, thereby permitting processing to restart at that point and saving valuable time.

Backup Facilities and Emergency Procedures

Sometimes events such as fire, floods, and black-outs will cause an organization's computer facilities to be out of operation for an extended period of time. To minimize processing problems during such periods, arrangements should be made for the use of backup facilities and/or alternative power sources. In selecting a computer system for backup, an organization should analyze four characteristics:

1. The availability of the time necessary for reconstruction and for subsequent processing of normal transactions.
2. The hardware configuration of the backup facilities (including memory size), input–output facilities (including memory size), input–output devices, and the model of the computers.
3. The availability of the applicable operating systems and other supporting software used in the original installation.
4. The actual results of processing normal transactions on the backup facilities to determine compatibility with the original installations. Processing should be done periodically on the backup facilities to ensure their continued compatibility with the current system.

In addition to arranging backup facilities, it is desirable to develop procedures to be followed in emergency conditions. Obviously, the time of an emergency is not the time to develop an emergency plan. An emergency plan should include a method to be used to process the current transactions to reconstruct any records that will be destroyed and the priorities to be assigned to various processing jobs. Of course, insurance against fire and business interruptions is also a useful control procedure that provides the organization with protection against financial loss when disasters affect the computer installation.

Passwords

In an on-line system where on-line input devices are used, there should be controls to ensure that specific files are accessed only by authorized personnel. One technique is to restrict access on the basis of hardware control, allowing only authorized people to use specific terminals and setting up specific codes known only to authorized personnel.

Privacy of Data

In 1974, Congress passed a Privacy Act. This limited a federal agency access to personal information held by another federal agency. The large amounts of data being held on individuals by federal agencies, coupled with the ease of getting and combining that information, led to passage of this Act. In addition, some of the information was not correct, and once issued could affect a person's opportunity to gain employment or to get loans or credit approved.

Many of the states followed the federal government's lead in passing privacy laws. These laws govern what state and local governments can and cannot do with information held on individuals. These laws frequently include regulated industries such as banks.

The federal government holds almost four billion records on individuals, most of them stored in thousands of computers. Federally funded projects have substantial additional files. This information is needed to run the social security system, collect taxes, conduct research, measure the economy, and for hundreds of other important purposes. Modern technology, however, makes it possible to turn this storage into a dangerous surveillance system. Reasonable restrictions are needed on the collection and use of this information.

Then-President Carter ordered the following administrative actions:

The practice of comparing computer lists, in so-called "matching programs," designed to detect fraud in various government programs, will be conducted (1) "only after the public has been notified and given the opportunity to identify privacy problems;" (2) "with tight safeguards on access to the data on disclosure of the names of suspects identified by matching;" and (3) "only when there are not cost-effective, alternative means of identifying violators."

The protections incorporated in the Privacy Act of 1974, limiting federal agencies' access to personal information held by other federal agencies, will be extended to include "certain data systems operated by recipients of federal grants." Each federal agency will be required to maintain an office "responsible for privacy issues raised by the agency's activities."

Migration of Control

Internal control is divided into general and administrative controls and application controls. When a control is common to two or more applications, organizations frequently make them general controls. This assures uniformity in the implementation of control throughout the organization, and also eliminates the need for two or more applications areas to "invent" the same controls.

In manual systems, there were many common areas of controls that were difficult to generalize. For example, the security of data needed to be implemented where the data were located, even though the security control objective remained the same for all applications. The payroll department might purchase a locked cabinet in which to store important information, the accounts receivable department might lock up their records in a cabinet located in their department, and so on.

The installation of the first computers did little to change many of these controls. The payroll department converted their records from paper to computer tape, but at the end of computer processing many payroll departments brought their payroll tapes back to the payroll department to lock them in the same cabinet in which they had previously stored their manual payroll records.

As computer systems became more integrated and complex, the need increased to generalize many of the areas previously controlled at the application level. This need is growing because today

- Single applications incorporate functions from many departments.
- The computerization of applications is standardizing the approach used by many applications for solving the same control need.
- Data are being stored and controlled centrally, as opposed to being under the jurisdiction of the application.
- Top management is becoming more involved in information processing.

The transition of control from the application to generalized controls parallels computer technology. For example, when organizations move to data base technology many functions that were controlled at the application level now move to become general controls. Examples include controls over the access and integrity of data in the data base. Access to the entire data base may be controlled by passwords assigned and enforced through administrative procedures, as opposed to controlling access at the application level. Also, data in a data base are used by many. No one single user may have responsibility for the integrity of the entire data base. Thus, administrative controls are necessary to ensure the integrity of the data base.

Segmentation of Application Systems

Applications written on early computers wrote instructions that executed all the tasks needed to be performed. However, it soon became apparent that many of the tasks were common among all applications. The most common task involved getting data in and out of the computer. These tasks were quickly taken over by standardized input–output routines.

As computer hardware developed the capability to process two or more programs concurrently, there was also a need for a system to allocate resources among multiple programs. These functions were standardized for application programs by computer software provided by the manufacturer of the computer, which became known as operating systems.

Next, communication capabilities were added to computers. This necessitated a continual polling of the communication terminals to determine when service was requested. To meet this need, communication systems were added to operating systems. The communication system handled all the complexities of servicing terminal operators and passing that information to the operating system.

Soon, it became apparent that many systems and files contained the same elements of data. This caused problems of timing and consistency; it was impractical to update all common elements simultaneously, therefore, the need to lessen duplication by having all applications use the same elements of data.

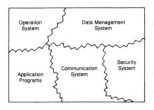

Figure 6.3
Segmentation of an
Application System

This required a new piece of software to manage the data for all application systems. These data management packages were called data base management systems.

The centralization of data and the increased emphasis by the federal government on privacy increased the importance of security over computerized data. The more segmented the application processing, the more difficult it became for each application to develop its own security procedures. Therefore, security systems were developed to fill the gap.

This common segmentation of application systems is illustrated in Figure 6.3. However, there are many other software systems that are performing functions previously written by application programmers. Examples include reports, job accounting packages, recovery utilities, and so forth. In addition, many organizations are buying application systems rather than developing their own applications.

Consequently, organizations are writing less and less computer code, and relying more and more on independent vendors to supply the computer code they need. This is especially true in smaller organizations. In fact, many small organizations have computers, but do not have the capability to program applications on them.

This places an additional burden on the auditor to assess the adequacy of controls when there may be no one in the organization that understands how that system is constructed. In addition, many of these packages are generalized. As such, it is uneconomical for auditors to assess the same package over and over again in each organization.

We will examine each of the four segments whose function has been generalized.

Overview of a Data Base Environment

A file is a collection of related data that has been stored in a manner organized so that it can be retrieved at a later time. A non-data base file normally has only one logical sequence. If one wants to make it possible for both Program A and Program B to access the same file, but in a different logical sequence, the following steps must occur:

- Run 1—Program A is used against the file in its current sequence.
- Run 2—the file is resequenced using a sort program.
- Run 3—Program B is used against the file, which is now in a new sequence.

A data base is a collection of files that can be accessed by a system that manages the data base. Within the data base, relationships are defined for those applications that use the data contained in the data base. Now if both Program A and Program B wish to access the file, it can be performed in the following manner:

- Run 1—Program A is used against the data base, accessing data in one sequence, while Program B is used against the same data base, accessing the same data in a different sequence.

The results produced from Program A and Program B are identical, whether the processing occurs in a non-data base or a data base environment. However, the activities necessary to support the data base environment are different than those used in the conventional environment.

Data have both physical and logical characteristics. The difference between physical and logical characteristics can be explained using a deck of cards as an analogy. A deck of cards contains fifty-two cards, four suits, thirteen cards in each suit. If we look at a deck of cards physically, we can examine each card and see what it is; for example, we can look at the ace of spades, the king of hearts, the three of diamonds, or the eight of clubs. When we do this, we see the *physical* card deck.

The logical perspective of a card deck occurs when we begin playing a game using the cards. For example, if we are to play a game of bridge using cards, we assign a *logical* view to each suit of cards. In this view, the ace is the highest card in the suit and the two is the lowest card. Thus, any time the cards are played the highest card laid down will win. Now the bidding begins and we gain another logical view of the cards. At the end of the bidding, someone will have named one of the four suits trump. We now have a logical view that says that bid suit is higher than any other suit. Thus, following the rules of bridge, a two of the trump suit is higher than the ace of any other suit. We need to apply this same logic to data to see the difference between the physical and logical perspective of data. Consider another example.

We have both a physical and logical view of the organization where we work. The physical view of an organization is the office layout. This is illustrated in Figure 6.4. This figure shows the offices of some of the key personnel in the organization. Looking at it physically, we can see the office and desk where the college president sits, the office and desk where the controller sits, the office and desk where the various deans sit, and so on. This view tells us, for example, how to get from the president's office to the dean of students' office. In a physical perspective of data, we know the physical relationships between the elements of data.

In a data base environment, we call this the physical data base. The illustration represents the physical location of people. Just as a particular office can be located by its physical location, so can a specific piece of data in the data base be located by its physical location. In an office location, we have a representa-

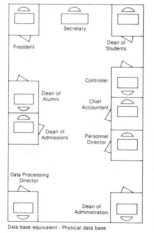

Data base equivalent - Physical data base

**Figure 6.4
Physical View
of an Organization
(Office Layout)**

tion, such as Figure 6.4, which shows us where people are located physically. In a data base, we have the equivalent of a representation, which is called an access method. An access method explains how (by using specific rules) data will be physically stored on a data recording device (for example, a disk pack).

The logical view is the organizational structure. The organizational structure for our office layout is illustrated in Figure 6.5. This organizational chart shows the president as the top officer in the corporation, followed by a second level of two deans, followed by a third level of personnel. From an operating viewpoint, the logical view is more important than the physical view. We need to know the professional relationships as expressed in an organizational chart in order to understand how that organization functions.

In a data base environment, we have the same logical view of data. The equivalent of an organizational chart is called a *schema*. A schema is a view of the entire structure of the data base. In other words, it is the organizational chart showing how the data base is structured. Just as you have only one organizational chart for an organization, so do you have only one schema for a

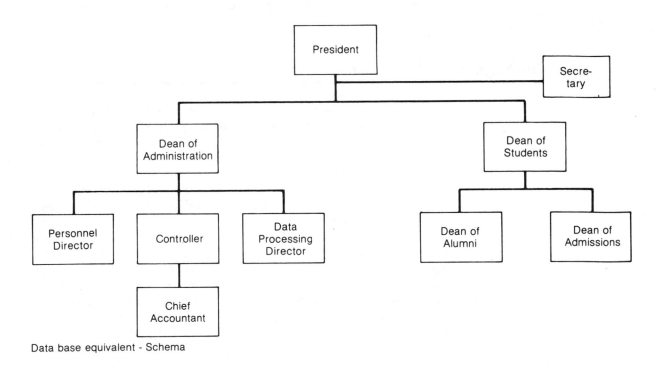

Data base equivalent - Schema

Figure 6.5   Logical View of an Organization (Organization Chart)

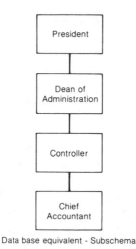

Data base equivalent - Subschema

Figure 6.6
Individual's View
of an Organization
(Chief Accountant's
Chain of Command)

physical data base. A fully detailed schema would show every element of data in the data base, just as a fully detailed organizational chart would show every employee in an organization.

However, everyone does not want to see the full organizational chart, nor does every programmer want to see a full schema. A person's interest is usually concentrated in the area of his or her responsibility. For example, in our organization model, the chief accountant is not particularly concerned about where the personnel director fits in the organization. What the chief accountant is concerned about is his own chain of command; how he fits in the organizational structure, and the relationship between the people that he must work with in order to accomplish his function. This chain of command is illustrated in Figure 6.6. In actual practice the chief accountant would be concerned with people under as well as over his position.

In a data base environment, the equivalent of the chief accountant's chain of command is called a *subschema* (sometimes referred to as an *external schema*). A subschema is the view of data that is envisioned or used by an application programmer. In other words, the subschema is limited to that data which the programmer needs for processing. Just as each individual in an organization has a chain of command from which she or he views the organization, each programmer has a subschema, which is an individual view of the data in the physical data base.

Data Base Management Approach

Every organization does some type of data processing—whether the processing is done manually by a part-time clerk, or whether it is highly automated, using large computer systems and many skilled technicians. Thus, the question is not whether to do data processing, but rather to decide if the current processing is adequate for organizational needs. The question does not yield to a "once-and-forever" type of answer: it is clearly a continuing management concern to ensure that the data processing capability is appropriate to the needs, as those needs undergo continuous change.

Effective management of the organization's data base is founded on two basic principles—establishing control and providing a means for control. In the first step, control is established by the development of the data base administration function, which is discussed in the next section. The second step assumes the first step and deals with the provision of tools for the data base administrator (and the users) for effective processing of the data. For this step, the recommended solution is a data base management system approach.

Data Base
Administration
Function

The first step toward establishing effective control of the data base is a management function—the setting up of the data base administrator. The data base administration function is served by human agent(s) who are responsible for controlling and efficiently utilizing the organization's data resources. Their primary objective is to balance the access to shared data over all users, thereby achieving efficient utilization of data resources despite a diverse and continually changing set of user requirements.

The data base administrator performs a service function within the organization. He is the steward who maintains and manages the data resources for the organization. A key role of the data base administrator is to provide the user community with the necessary data base management tools and to educate users as to their utilization. At the same time he is both a servant of the user community and the agent of the data processing management.

The data base administrator role implies a broad spectrum of responsibilities, which range from informing the users to designing and tuning the data base for optimum performance. Although the role of the data base administrator is closely associated with data base management systems, most of the functions are relevant whether or not such a system is employed. The following subsections discuss several important functions of the data base administrator. Since much has been written on this subject, we highlight only the important functional aspects.

Providing the Proper Tools to the Users   In line with the service role of the data base administrator is his or her responsibility to provide the facilities and tools with which the users can interrogate and update the data base. To meet this need the data base administrator is responsible for acquiring or developing data base management tools suitable to the user's expertise and needs. As a further responsibility, he should augment these tools as the requirements and technology change over time. He should also strive to acquire and develop generalized functions applicable across a diverse spectrum of users.

Data Definition   The data definition process translates data base requirements into a form that can be understood by the end users and processed by the data base management system. There are three important steps in this process. The first step is the establishment of the data dictionary, which compiles data base descriptions. The dictionary provides the means for communicating and establishing common definitions of data.

The second involves the data base management system and is the design of the logical data base. On the basis of user requirements, and constrained by the data structure capabilities of the particular data base management system, the names and relationships of the logical data base are formulated. The second step is specification of the logical data base in a precise manner, using a data definition language. In this step, the names and attributes of every data construct are defined, along with the relationships among the constructs. The primary purpose of the data definition language is to specify formally to the data base management system the important attributes of the data base, such as the data types and relationships. As a result of this processing of a data definition, a printed output is produced to communicate these attributes to the user of the organization. This process establishes a data base, which can be shared by all the users in the organization.

Redefinition Redefinition is similar to data definition in that names, attributes, and relationships of data constructs are defined. It differs in that a set of data constructs has already been specified and modifications in the defined structures are required. The redefinition task implies a conversion task, since the original data definition is changed and the organization of the data must be changed accordingly. This task is also called restructuring and reformatting. Redefinition may necessitate modifications to programs that access the data base.

Creation Once the data have been defined to the data base management system, with all the attributes explicitly described, the source data are translated into a form that is processable under the system. Although at times tedious and laborious, data base creation is usually a one-time-only function. Often the data input functions are accompanied by extensive validation and editing to ensure that raw data are correct for processing. All other additions or changes in the data base are performed by the update function.

Retirement The data retirement function is the migration of elements of data to slower and less costly access storage mechanisms as their demand and utilization decrease over time. Unfortunately this function is not performed regularly in organizations today and is therefore more difficult to control. The key to data retirement is the development of effective policies and the application of procedures to control purging of aged data. The latter requirement implies that data base usage be monitored, which is often not the case in today's systems. One often-used policy is to assume that the older the data, the less value it has to the organization (but its re-creation cost can be high). Under this policy it is desirable to aggregate older data on-line and to store the detail in off-line archival files.

Integrity The goal of data base integrity has a pervasive effect on the data base administration functions. Although integrity protection is never completely achievable (neither the technology nor resources is available), there are several integrity controls that can be invoked by the data base administrator to achieve an effective level of integrity. These controls range from the preventive measures of data definition control through the assurance measures of backup and recovery. Examples of some of the most prominent procedures that a data base administrator uses to achieve data base control include these:

- Control over the data definition ensures that the data conform to the definition and that conformance is maintained through the life of the data.

- Access control protects the data from access by unauthorized persons or for unauthorized purposes. Some form of restricted access is usually required for both privacy and integrity assurance. A regulatory mechanism is required in the data base management system so the data base administrator can manage access control.

- An audit trail should be maintained by the data base administrator to demonstrate that the confidentiality of the data has been maintained. Access is controlled by the same access control mechanism, and its incidence can be controlled by a clear separation of the testing and operational environments of the data base.

- Update control ensures that the user has the appropriate authorization to change data values. There are two levels of concern in update control—data addition, and data modification and deletion. In many situations the need to monitor the modifications and deletions to the data base is greater than the need to monitor the additions.

- Concurrency control provides data base integrity by controlling the concurrent programs that perform the update function. Typically, systems employ some form of lockout mechanisms at the file or record level in the data base to aid the data base administrator in this function.

Quality Control The quality of a data base is measured in terms of its accuracy, completeness, and consistency. The quality control function of the data base administrator endeavors to detect errors in the data to maintain and improve the quality of the data.

One method of achieving quality control is through the application of data validation processes to all states of the data—input, stored, and output. The establishment of validation criteria for these states of data and the execution of the validation routines based on the criteria can ensure a high quality data base. Other quality control measures include consistency checks and completeness criteria.

Performance Monitoring The monitoring function includes such operations as controlling day-to-day operations and maintaining the continuity of data base activity, and keeping a recorded history of data base related events. The monitoring function serves to provide the necessary feedback to the data base administrator for user tuning

(tuning the efficiency of) the data base. Information from monitoring also serves as a basis for the logical and physical reorganization of the data base to serve the current user population.

The system can be monitored to gather volume statistics on interrogation, updates, and individual record activity. Monitoring with respect to the time of successive events yields statistics on response times and update efficiencies. Monitoring the utilization of storage can indicate an imbalance in the overflow areas and wasted space, implying the need to reorganize the data base.

Training of Personnel The introduction of data base technology results in the need to train the user community. Although the vendors of data base management systems often supply courses, this education should be supplemented with in-house education specifically tailored to the operation of the data base. It is the data base administrator's responsibility to identify these areas of need and to develop courses and educational materials to coordinate the necessary training.

Utilization of Data Base Management Systems

In order to provide the data base administrator and the users with an effective set of tools for meeting data base requirements, a data processing system that provides generality, flexibility, adaptability, and control is needed. The state-of-the-art approach to meeting these requirements with reduced cost and complexity is the data base management system. Provided in this section is the definition of and rationale for using a data base management system and the role it plays in the development of a data processing system.

Characteristics of Data Base Management System A data base management system provides a set of common functions that are used to process the data base through a common user interface. Typically the set of common functions includes definition, creation, interrogation, and update. A complete data base management system provides this set of common functions by providing either (a) self-contained capabilities in which high-level languages are used to specify these functions, or (b) host-language facilities, which augment current programming languages with new data handling verbs to facilitate the writing of programs to perform these functions—or both self-contained and host language capabilities.

The user interface is typically either a high-level language in the case of the self-contained capabilities, or a collection of data manipulation procedures in the host-language facilities. The interface between the system and the user has a dual purpose:

- To permit the user to define the relationships among data items; and

- To provide the user with a facility for using meaningful subsets of the data base

Data base management systems provide generalized software tools to support the data processing functions. A number of systems that provide a wide range of capabilities and operating characteristics, with the inevitable design compromises, are readily available. Basically, these systems should be viewed as providing a set of data processing functions from which the organization can develop and tailor a data processing system capability.

Technological Impacts of Data Base

Inherent in the design and implementation of a data base management system are a number of technological tradeoffs that vary from system to system and from one organization to another. These tradeoffs will have to be discussed and understood by users in the organization. Some of the more important tradeoffs are

- *Machine time vs. people time*—probably the most obvious external tradeoff in the use of a data base management system is the substitution of the utilization of hardware resources for the use of analyst/programmer time. These systems generally require more hardware resources and take more hardware execution time. On the other hand, they produce data for a new application more quickly, using less of the analysts' time than conventional methods.

- *User language vs. integrity*—some functions of a user language are at odds with the data base integrity objective and with the provision of an economical checkpoint–restart facility. The command

$$\text{``CHANGE SALARY TO SALARY* 1.05''}$$

can change every salary in the data base, providing a powerful capability for the user. However, the need for integrity of the salary data implies a system logging function in which the expense of logging all the "before" images required by this command is very high.

- *Data independence vs. performance*—data independence at item level is generally at odds with a requirement for high speed, high volume, and sequential processing. Data independence demands that attention be given to each item as it is moved to or from the data base, whereas high volume, sequential processing will normally be expedited by data movement at the group or record level.

- *User interface vs. complexity of data structure*—the need for a simpler user language is in direct opposition to the need for complex data structures. The more powerful the data structure being manipulated, the greater the need for complexities of the user language.

- *Complexity of data structure vs. storage overhead*—the more complex the data structure, the greater the cost for the increase in data storage the user will have to pay. Hence the desire for minimum storage use is in direct opposition to a desire for complex data relationships.
- *Gathering of statistics vs. optimum performance*—the need for accumulation of statistics concerning the use of data will add significant overhead to all the data manipulation processes. The extent of an improvement in performance must be related to the cost of providing the required information.

Overview of an Operating System

The operating system is the "traffic cop" that directs processing in the computer. It is the single piece of software that controls what the computer does and when it does it. This package is normally provided by the vendor of the hardware and run continuously.

Among the functions performed by the operating system are these:

- Initiating the physical read and write command.
- Controlling the channels that control the input–output devices. The channel controllers permit the input–output commands to be executed in conjunction with internal commands. In most larger computers these are performed by microcomputers.
- Initiating jobs (i.e., the programs).
- Allocating memory cycles in a multiprogramming environment. This is usually performed through an interrupt command, which informs the operating system when output transmission has been completed or, on input when the record has been received.
- Communicating with the computer operator.
- Recording operator and operating system actions on an operator log.
- Allocating space for programs and input–output buffer areas. Note that much of the information needed to perform this task is provided to the operating system through the job control language (JCL).
- Diagnosing problems and informing the computer operator of the problems diagnosed.

An operating system is not a single thing but, rather, it is certain capabilities provided by the vendor of the operating system. It is somewhat similar to what the automotive manufacturers provide. If you were to select an automobile you would be offered a variety of options. In determining the car that you want, you select among the options available.

The operating system has a base package that you must accept, plus a series of options like the automobile. An organization selects the options they want, and then the operating system is assembled in much the same manner that a custom-made automobile is assembled. For the operating system, this task of assembling the component parts is called a system generation or SYSGEN.

The individual that puts the operating system together is frequently called a systems programmer. The systems programmer is knowledgeable in how the computer systems actually work. This individual normally understands the computer instructions, the channels, and the way in which the computer physically operates. This does not mean that the individual understands the electronics, but merely how the computer works. The systems programmer is similar to the automobile mechanic. The mechanic may not be able to build an automobile, and may not understand the physics that make it work, but does understand how the component parts work together to make the automobile run.

The operating system is continually improved by the vendor. These improvements correct flaws in the previous version of the operating system and add new enhancements. Many of these enhancements are necessary because the hardware vendor has changed or enhanced the hardware. The new versions of operating systems are frequently called "releases."

Overview of a Communication System

Most computers have a physical limitation on how far they can be located from attached terminals. As long as the terminals are within a specified physical proximity of the central processing unit, the computer can function with its operating system. On the other hand, as the need for remote terminals increases, a communication package must be added to handle the remote units.

Distant communications are normally conducted over common carrier communication lines. The code structure used for data transmission over common carrier communication lines is different from the code characteristics of data within computers. This means that the coding method must be translated from the computer to the communication carrier and then translated back at the next computer site.

The change in code structure, speed of transmission, etc. requires special interface equipment. The types of equipment used are illustrated in Figure 6.7, and the description of each of the units is included in Exhibit 6.1.

From a conceptual viewpoint, the user of computer equipment is unaware of the communication equipment. All the user needs to know is that he or she wants to transmit or access or receive—from a remote site to a central site; from a central site to a remote site; or to and from two remote or two central sites. The communication equipment handles the mechanics of communication.

The communication software involved in the central computer is similar to an operating system. It has a base package and a series of options that can be in-

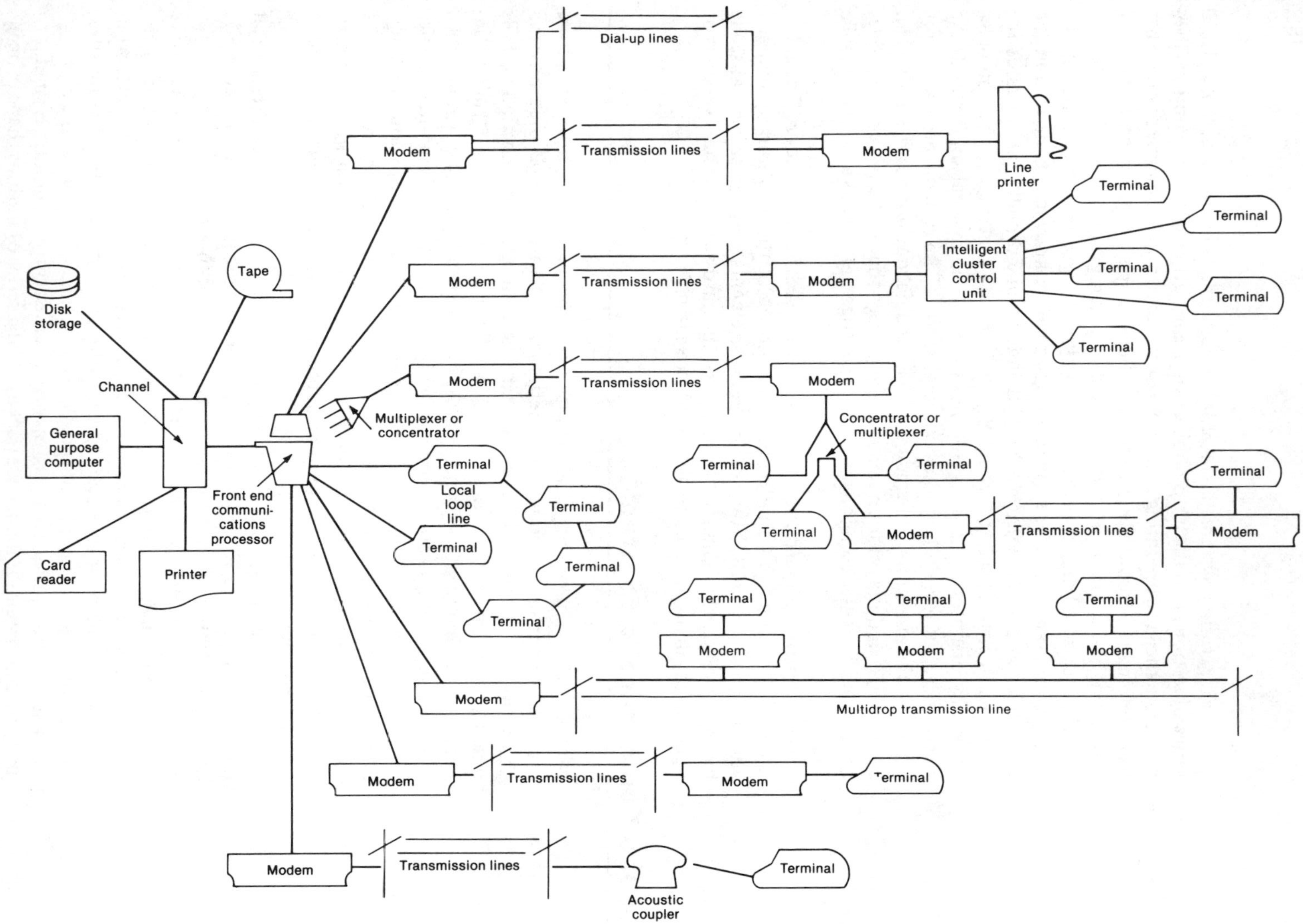

Figure 6.7 Network Configurations

186

cluded. The reason that all the options are not included is one of cost. And, the more options included, the longer it takes to process a transmission.

The individual who coordinates and assembles the communication package is frequently referred to as the communication specialist. This individual may have to interface with a common carrier company as well as generate the communication software. In smaller organizations, or those with limited communication needs, this function may be performed by the systems programmer.

Exhibit 6.1
Definitions of Network
Components in
Figure 6.7

The following list of items enumerates and defines the components of a data communication network. In some cases the item listed may be a characteristic of data transmission rather than an actual component.

1. *Circuits:* A circuit can be a single communication facility or a combination of different types of communication facilities, such as

   • *Satellite:* A facility that uses ultra-high-frequency signaling relayed through a device orbiting the earth.

   • *Microwave:* A facility that uses high-frequency signaling that passes through terrestrial relay points.

   • *Fiberoptics:* A facility that transmits signals through the use of optical media utilizing a fiberglasslike cable.

   • *Wire:* A facility that transmits through a metallic conductor. This facility may utilize long-distance copper wire pairs, coaxial cable, or the copper wire local loop between a user premises and the telephone company's switching office.

2. *Configurations:* These are the methods of connecting communication devices. There are many examples of communication configurations, some of which were shown in Figure 6.6. Examples of these configurations might be as follows:

   • *Dedicated/Private Leased Lines:* These circuits are always available to the customer for transmission and generally are used with on-line real-time systems.

   • *Dial/Switched Circuits:* A circuit connection that is established by dialing a telephone or establishing a physical or logical connection before data can be transmitted.

   • *Point-to-Point Circuits:* This method provides a communication path between two points. It can be a dial-up or a dedicated circuit.

   • *Multidrop Circuits:* This method allows for the sharing of a communication facility. It is similar to a party-line telephone call because several input–output terminals share the same line. Only one terminal can be transmitting on the line at a time.

Exhibit 6.1 (continued)

- *Local Cable:* This method of connecting communication devices consists of a privately owned cable or wire interconnecting many terminals with the computer system.

3. *Multiplexer:* A device that combines several independent data streams into one data stream at a higher signaling speed for transmission to a similar device that separates the high-speed signal into the original independent data streams. Note: Some of the multiplexers are software driven and are similar to concentrators; however, most of them are nonintelligent hard-wired devices.

4. *Concentrator:* A programmable device that will perform the same function as a multiplexer with added functions such as data storage (buffering), message error checking, data flow control, polling, etc.

5. *Front-End Communication Processor:* A programmable device that interfaces a communication network to a host computer. Some of the functions that can be performed by a "front-end" are polling, code and speed conversion, error detection and correction, store and forward functions, format checking, data flow control, network statistics gathering, message authentication, communication routing and control, and the like.

6. *Terminals:* An input–output device that is used to enter messages into the system and/or receive messages from the system.

7. *Modem:* A device that converts from computer code to common carrier code.

Overview of a Security System

Once communication capabilities have been added to a computer, that computer can be accessed over communication lines. This means that the physical security that protected the computer may no longer be effective. In those instances where the computer can be accessed through a dial-up network (i.e., the computer has its own telephone number), then any telephone is a location from which the computer can be accessed.

The on-line computer is protected with a security software package. This is a special piece of software through which interfacing through the computer must pass. For example, if an individual from a remote site wants to access the central computer, that individual's first communication is with the security software package. The objective of this package is to ensure that only authorized individuals use data for which they have a need.

Most software packages use passwords. The two most common password systems today are (1) one in which the user memorizes and enters the password, and (2) one in which the password is magnetically encoded on a card. Frequently, these two systems are used in conjunction. For example, most banks with their automatic teller machines require that an individual enter a card with a magnetically encoded identifier and in addition enter a password. It is only when these two are entered correctly that the transaction is permitted to occur.

The security systems require that the following three steps be taken before they are effective:

1. Individuals needing access to the computer are provided with passwords.
2. The resources protected by the computer are identified.
3. A user profile is prepared, matching users to the protected resources that they have a need to access.

When an individual attempts access, she (or he) is first identified. Then if she requests resources, her request is matched against her profile. If the profile indicates she is authorized to have that resource, processing continues. On the other hand, if either the password is incorrectly entered or the individual asks for a resource that she has not been authorized to use, the access request is denied.

The security of a system is normally under the control of a security officer. This individual is a member of management responsible for protecting the information of the organization. This function encompasses security over both manual and computerized data. The function is widely implemented in banks, and is a growing function in most other industries.

The security officer may be a part-time position in a small organization, and a staff of people in a large organization. The security officer deals with information security as opposed to physical security over the organization. The functions of this office frequently include these:

- Classification of information according to its importance to the organization
- Determination that the privacy rights of individuals are protected
- Establishment of a computerized security system
- Issuance and maintenance of passwords
- Investigation of security violations

Problems

1. How has EDP affected the organization of companies?
2. What factors would you evaluate in organizing the data processing function in a company using EDP?
3. To whom should the head of an EDP department report in the organization and why?

4. Following is a listing of departments and people (i.e., job titles) for a company called the Highrise Gas Company:

```
                     The Highrise Gas Company

           Group A                            Group B

    President                     EDP Manager
    Vice President, Marketing      Systems Development Supervisor
    Vice President, Production     Program Maintenance Supervisor
    Vice President, Finance        Systems Design Department
    Vice President, Administration Control Section
    Controller                    Information Processing Supervisor
    EDP Manager                    Testing Department
                                   Operations Department
                                   Documentation
                                   Programming Department
                                   Program Revisions
```

Design an organizational chart consistent with the idea we have been discussing: segregation of duties to achieve security of assets and operational efficiency. Construct the chart as follows:

(a) The people in Group A should be organized to show an effective relationship and a line of responsibility for the EDP Department within the corporate structure.

(b) The departments in Group B should be organized to show an effective structure within the EDP Department itself.

(Remember: Segregation of duties and efficiency through specialization.)

5. Williams Savings and Loan Association developed its data processing applications using vendor-supplied systems slightly modified for its requirements.[4] The various systems have been operating satisfactorily for the past two years. The department now consists of three keypunch operators, two computer operators, one programmer, and the manager, who assists with systems and programming work. The programmer and the manager also assist the computer operators when required. The general operation of the department is relatively effective, and systems are usually run on a timely basis.

The programmer's prime function is to maintain existing systems, and this requires only 60 percent of his time. He uses his free time to assist the first-shift computer operator during periods of heavy work load. He also assists user departments with file-maintenance coding, and

[4] This problem was adapted from one developed by Peat, Marwick, Mitchell & Co. for use in its internal training program.

he functions as an operator when either the first- or second-shift operator is absent.

Comment on this organizational situation from a control standpoint.

6. What performance reports should the top executive over data processing possess in order to carry out his responsibility?

7. A master accounts receivable file (on magnetic tape) was inadvertently written over in another processing run.
    (a) List some operating control procedures that could have prevented this accident.
    (b) How can the master file be recreated?

8. Discuss the controls that are important for each of the following problems cited in the *Wall Street Journal,* March 22, 1971.
    (a) ". . . five members of an antiwar group broke into (the) . . . computer center and ransacked the place. . . . Someone in the cleanup crew discovered a small, circular magnet about the size of a quarter in the debris. The following Monday, when the computer tapes were checked out, the manager of the center discovered to his horror that the data on 1,000 of the tapes had been erased by such magnets."
    (b) "Sometimes the danger comes from within. A computer employee at one company was given two weeks' notice before he was laid off. The man promptly removed all the labels on 1,500 reels of tape, costing the company thousands of dollars in labor to reidentify the data."
    (c) "A less dramatic but potentially costly security problem is theft or embezzlement by computer personnel. Last summer, for example, [XYZ Company] accused three operators on the night shift of copying nearly three million names from the company's 'most valued' customer list and selling them to a direct-mail advertiser."

9. A recent newspaper article indicated that a Volkswagen dealership burned to the ground. Although the magnetic tapes containing the company records were saved, the entire computer installation was destroyed.
    (a) If you were the auditor of this company and you were called to discuss recovery procedures, what would you suggest to your client?
    (b) What disaster prevention procedures would you suggest to handle future disasters? Comment on procedures for each of the following categories:
    Equipment
    Data
       Master files
       Transactions
    Systems and program

10. Comment on the potential control problems in the following situations.[5]

    (a) Our client, a large city government, processes the payroll for all municipal employees on its own computer. The payroll application is processed on a weekly schedule to allow updating of the master file, including all appropriate changes. The update program produces a printout of the master record before and after each change. The data processing manager reviews the listing to ensure that the changes were properly applied. The listing and change notification are filed by the data processing manager's secretary. The computer room in the basement of City Hall is rather cramped for space. All the tape and disk files are stored on open shelves along the walls of the computer room. Similarly, all the forms used within the data processing, such as tax bills and checks, are stored in the hallway.

    (b) At AM Manufacturing, all computer tapes not being used are stored in a separate room under the control of the tape librarian, who reviews the daily operating schedule each morning and sets up all tapes required for each major application to be run that day. Last Monday, while running the payroll system, an inexperienced operator erased the payroll master file by mounting it as an output tape and overriding the computer error message which indicated that the wrong tape was mounted. The operations manager instructed the operator to recreate the master file by applying the previous week's transactions to the master-file grandfather tape. The previous week's transactions file could not be found, and so the payroll had to be processed manually. The transaction source documents had been returned to the various departmental supervisors and were unavailable because it was the practice of some of the supervisors to discard the source documents after the payroll was issued.

    (c) A client, Accounting Services Inc., is a small data processing service bureau which supplies various computerized accounting services for its customers, including payroll processing. Recently, a computer malfunction was experienced and four days were required for vendor engineers to isolate and correct the problem. During that time, Accounting Services Inc. was unable to locate a compatible equipment configuration on which they could process the six payrolls that were due before the equipment could be repaired. As a result, the six customers were forced to prepare their own checks manually, and the cost was billed to Accounting Services Inc.

11. The Equity Funding Corporation case has been called the greatest fraud since the McKesson & Robbins fraud of the 1930s. Many important

---

[5] The problems in (a) to (c) were adapted from some developed by Peat, Marwick, Mitchell & Co. for use in its internal training program.

issues seem to surface from the published material on the case, which may have an impact on the management control and audit of computerized systems. The following material briefly describes the background of the company, the data processing activities, and audit procedures used. This material should enable the reader to discuss several significant control issues:

(a) What control, security, and audit measures exist to detect fraud when extensive collusion exists?

(b) What operating controls and security measures should be designed into a computerized system to make it difficult for massive fraud to take place?

Background. In the Equity Funding Insurance fraud, management used the corporation's computers to create false insurance policies and to inflate the apparent financial status of the company. By maintaining an artificial picture of healthy corporate revenue, executives at Equity were able to secure loans, continue an aggressive campaign of acquisition, and make their stock the darling of Wall Street.

Some sources believe that the bogus business had its genesis in a questionable deal that Equity Funding Life urged on its employees for a year or so before making up bogus policies. This was "special class" insurance policies offered to employees and their families with free premiums for the first year. The policyholder bought mutual fund shares on an annual basis for 10 years. He then borrowed against the shares to pay the annual premiums of a life insurance policy. After going through this process for 10 years, the policyholder would then cash in enough of his fund shares to pay off his total debt leaving him—it was hoped—with some fund stock remaining and a tidy cash value in it. The idea intrigued Wall Street in the go-go years of the sixties and Equity Funding became a hot company. But this mutual fund–insurance package so attractive to investors also left Equity Funding perennially hungry for cash; the remedy was heavy coinsurance of its new business.

A new life insurance company typically coinsures its business by selling big blocks of the new insurance it writes to another larger well-financed company. Since first-year commissions paid to insurance salesmen are very high in relation to commissions in future years, the buyer of a block of new insurance policies sold by a new life insurance company typically pays $1.80 for every $1 in premiums the seller turns over. The buyer is gambling that not too much of the insurance he has bought will lapse quickly since, in succeeding years, he may get 90 cents of every premium dollar, allowing 10 cents to the seller who is handling all the policy accounts and claims.

With coinsurance in mind, Equity Funding thus "really applied the pressure on us to buy the special class," according to one former executive. A lot of people did, loading up on as much as $50,000 each for themselves and their wives and $25,000 on each of their children, premium-free for the first year. As might be anticipated, in the second year much of this insurance was canceled or sharply reduced. By then, however, Equity Funding Life had sold it to reinsurers, scattering the dubious special class business in among good policies in order to keep the overall lapse rate reasonable.

The major element in the swindle, then, was the falsification of insurance policies that were in turn sold to reinsurers. The chief investigator, Laurence Baker, believes this falsification started in late 1969 or early 1970 and initially involved the running of a computerized simulation program to determine how many insurance policies Equity had to invent in order to generate enough revenue from reinsurance sales to keep the company in good financial position. Next, more than 63,000 of the total 97,000 policies were "created" and recorded in the good old invisible computer files assigned to "Department 99." The "99" designation enabled the computer billing programs used to process the policies to skip the bogus policies when bills were sent to policyholders (the programmed control characteristic again).

The fictitious policies on file were then used in discussions with the reinsurers. At the first meeting, computer printouts of the files containing Department 99 policies were turned over to the reinsurer's auditors. The printouts apparently were accepted (what you see is what you don't get) because Equity's terms of sale were favorable enough to make their policies an exceptionally attractive buy. At later meetings and at year-end audit time, documentation on the policies was requested to support a random selection of the policies in the computer file.

Computers and Simulation. The scandal may be one of the first major cases of fraud significantly assisted by the computer. It appears that the use of simulation models and numerous reruns enabed the bogus policies to be created. In addition, it appears a fictitious department was created.

Computerworld[6] reports four fraudulent uses of the computer:

Reporting the previous year's books and adding new input (such as reinstatements, lapses, death claims, sales, etc.) until the results matched corporate aims.

Accepting falsified, but correct, format input from user departments which created and maintained bogus policies.

Preparing test files at the instructions of the actuarial department, officially for use in insurance-selling simulation studies, but actually used to create falsified input describing bogus policies.

Accepting about 35 sets of falsified input and maintenance documents

[6] *Ibid.*

which resulted in dead policies being revived—accepted as having $3,000 to $5,000 surrender value and cashed in through dummy bank accounts.

All actions except the last one—which was apparently the work of some still untraced independent entrepreneur probably in the insurance company subsidiary—were being handled in order to provide management with data to support its claim as a strong, high-flying conglomerate.

The special department was "Department 99," and systems analysts were told "You don't want to know about that." Evidently, Department 99 contained a list of over 63,000 fictitious policyholders and this file of policyholders was used to inflate the normal policy count very significantly.

Auditors and Auditing. The Equity Funding system was a highly computerized system that required a good deal of planning and deception to conceal the massive fraud that was eventually revealed. First, the phony policies were maintained on the master policy file mixed in with the genuine ones. Printouts do show their existence. By using secret coding numbers to designate fictitious policies, the company set up programs to omit the phony policies when notices were sent out to policyholders.

When the auditors arrived, the company provided printouts, but the lists of accounts given to the auditors had two digits of the five-digit policy number eliminated. This omission made it impossible to readily tell that the list was full of duplicates. The auditors would then select a sample from the list and ask for hard copy of customer statements with loan balances and other data, including addresses. When the auditors asked to see the hard-copy files for audit purposes, they were told that the files were temporarily unavailable and would be turned over the next morning.

Equity Funding would then use the computer early in the evening to reject the duplicates in the sample and see which names had been rejected. Then all-night fraud parties were held, in which employees created hard-copy records to match the rejected duplicates, even submitting addresses of friends who would be asked to cooperate in returning the auditors' confirmation results.

12. The systems development department of the ABC Corporation has developed an on-line payroll application. The system went live six months ago. Since that time the payroll department has requested thirty-three changes to the system. Six changes originated from the new employee section, twelve from the hourly payroll section, ten from the weekly payroll section and five from the payroll control section. Some of the changes from the payroll department were initiated by telephone calls, others were initiated by having a member of the payroll department visit the programmer, and yet others came in the forms of memos

and letters. In addition, the systems development department programming team initiated five changes to improve the operational efficiency of the system, and three to correct errors.

Yesterday the payroll manager called the manager of the systems development department and complained that their program changes were not being installed on an orderly basis. The payroll manager claims that some high priority changes took two months to install, while some low priority changes were done in one day. When the systems development manager asked the system project leader for a status report on changes, the project leader was uncertain as to what changes had been installed, what were in the process of being implemented, and which ones were awaiting action.

The systems development department manager has asked you to develop a system to control program changes. Specifically the manager wants you to develop a form to control payroll changes. Include on the form space for all the information needed to make the program change, plus the information needed to control program changes. Also, document the procedures you recommend to be installed by the project manager to control program changes using this form.

13. Many functions within the ABC University use the accounts receivable file. The billing system of the university is run overnight, using the accounts receivable file as input and produces an updated disk file showing the addition to accounts receivable. The cash receipts system uses the same accounts receivable file at the completion of the billing run to update the accounts receivable file with cash payments received the previous day. During the day, the accounts receivable clerks use the accounts receivable disk file to update via terminal adjustments made to the file based on conversations and correspondence with customers. At the end of the month, the comptroller approves writeoffs and a special run is made to delete from the accounts receivable file the bad accounts. Is this sharing of the accounts receivable file by multiple users a data base application?

14. The accounts receivable data base of the ABC University has the following characteristics:

- The data base is located on tracks 67–126 of disk pack number 1326.
- The data base includes all the accounts receivable customers of the organization.
- The data base includes customers that have a debit or positive balance in their accounts receivable account.

For the above three characteristics, identify which is the schema, subschema, and physical data base description.

15. Listed below are two audit situations. Examine each of these cases and then determine which control objective has been impacted by the audit situation, and how:

Case A—Easy Hospital.   The Easy Hospital recently installed a data base management system. The Easy Hospital is a small hospital and believes that to be competitive against a large hospital they need to be able to provide their customers with immediate answers to their administrative questions. The data base was the method they chose to solve their business problem. Because it was important that data be consistent regardless of who answers the customer's questions, they established a data base administrator function. The data base administrator was given the responsibility for the accuracy, completeness, consistency, and reliability of the company's data in the data base.

Case B—Hard Hospital. The Hard Hospital recently put their accounts receivable records on the data base. The Hard Hospital has 27,000 patient records and 63 accounts receivable clerks maintaining those records by computer terminals. The accounts receivable clerks work two shifts so that they can answer customer inquiries and make adjustments whenever they occur. While the majority of the processing of accounts receivable is done by the automated billing system and automated cash receipts system, the accounts receivable clerks must resolve differences, make minor adjustments, and correct errors uncovered by the automated systems.

16. Users of application systems can be end users, application development analysts, and technical people. For the following three described individuals, indicate which type of interface they need to the data base:

- Individual A—the customer engineer from the computer vendor
- Individual B—an auditor
- Individual C—a systems analyst

Case

Data Base Recovery Case Study

The flowchart in Figure 6.8 represents a payroll application for a student work program. The students are paid on a daily basis for the work performed that day. The payroll system prepares payroll checks for approximately fifty work sites. Each site is connected on-line to the central data bases.

There are three data bases at the central site. These are separate but interrelated data bases. File A includes gross pay, accumulated federal withholding tax, and social security deductions. File B includes accumulated deductions for the benefit programs, such as bond deductions. The transaction file contains

Figure 6.8
Flowchart of a Payroll
Application

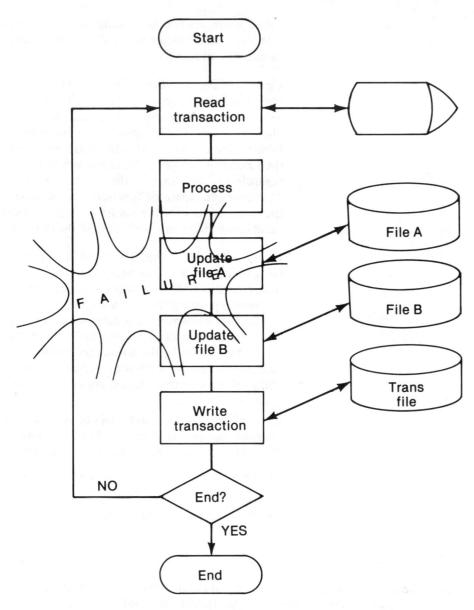

the net pay information. That file is available on-line to the remote site for the preparation of payroll checks.

Each remote site can enter pay information at any time during the day. The payroll information is transmitted to the central processing unit to be processed. The transaction may be processed immediately, or placed into a queue awaiting available computer capacity before processing occurs. Once processing begins, the payroll information is calculated by the process program. It is then sent to a program that updates File A. When this is complete, the data are passed to another program, which updates File B. After File B has been updated, the information is passed to a write transaction program, which places the payroll check net pay image onto the transaction file.

The case disbursing officer at each of the four remote sites can call out these images whenever a student worker wants the check. It is possible for the student to have several check images in the transaction file at any one time. As soon as the check images are transmitted to the disbursing officer, a flag is set in the check image record indicating it has been disbursed.

The system can develop a problem during any part of processing. The flowchart illustrates a problem occurring during the update of File A. However, this problem could have occurred at any point during processing, at one or more remote sites, or at any of the disbursing sites. In addition, problems could develop with any of the three data bases.

You have been assigned to audit the recovery procedures for this payroll data base application. Prior to commencing the audit fieldwork, your supervisor asks you to perform the following task: develop an internal control checklist that would provide you with reasonable assurance as to whether or not recovery controls were adequate.

EDP AUDIT PROCESS*

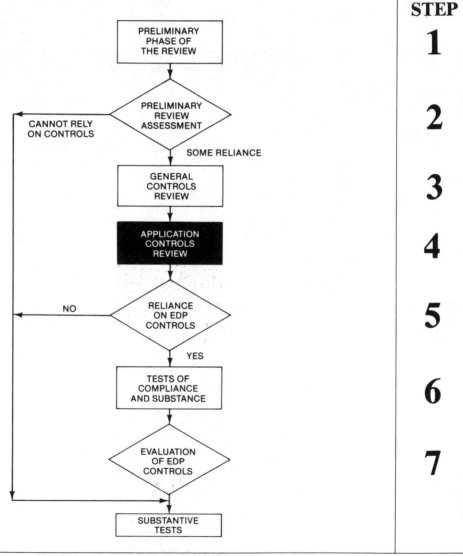

STEP

1

2

3

4

5

6

7

*Diagram is adapted from The Auditor's Study and Evaluation of Internal Control in EDP Systems, pages 21–24. Copyright © 1977 by the American Institute of Certified Public Accountants, Inc. (See Figure 9.1 for a complete explanation of the steps.)

7

STEP

4

**ADDRESSED
IN THIS
CHAPTER**

APPLICATION CONTROL DESIGN

(4) Completion of Review—Application Controls

Purpose:
- Identify application controls on which reliance is planned, and determine how the controls operate.
- Consider tests of compliance that may be performed.
- Consider the potential effect of identified strengths and weaknesses on tests of compliance.

Methods: Detailed examinations of documentation; interviewing internal auditors, EDP, and user department personnel; observing operation of application controls.

OBJECTIVE

This chapter explains how computer systems are designed, and then how controls are designed to reduce the application risks. This background information is helpful in assessing the adequacy of application controls.

Application controls are designed to meet the specific control requirements of each processing application. Application controls contrast with and are complemented by administrative controls and general controls that provide the environment in which the processing takes place. Application controls are designed to ensure that the recording, classifying, and summarizing of authorized transactions and the updating of master files will produce accurate and complete information on a timely basis.

Normally, the processing cycle includes all the procedures in the source and user departments and in the EDP departments to record and prepare source data and ultimately produce useful information during a given unit of time (such as day, week, or month) predetermined by a schedule. In discussing application controls, it is useful to classify them according to whether they are preventive, detective, or corrective controls.

A point to keep in mind when designing controls is that some input errors may be acceptable if they do not cause an interruption in the processing run. A simple example of this would be a misspelled description of an item. In deciding on such tolerance limits, it is necessary to compare the cost of correcting an error to the consequences of accepting it. Such tradeoffs must be determined for each application. Unfortunately there are no universal guidelines available.

The System Development Process

Computer systems are complex processes involving many thousands of instructions. The process begins with a need that must be satisfied. This need is stated as a set of requirements to be met. The system development process must consider those requirements and develop a process that will satisfy the requirements.

The most common methods for developing computerized systems is to divide the developmental tasks into phases. Each phase has certain deliverables to be developed during the phase. The process is similar to that of building a house. In house construction, the first phase is to clear the land; the second phase is to pour the foundation; the third, to create the structure of the home; and the fourth phase is to complete the interior. Another builder might have suggested that there should be a phase denoted for installing the roof, or for putting in the plumbing, etc.

Just as in home building, there is in computer systems development no universally accepted series of phases to be accomplished. The framework used for building computer systems is frequently called the *system life cycle* or *system development life cycle* (SDLC). The SDLC is a methodology used for building a system. The methodology is a tool for documenting, maintaining, and controlling an information system through the process of analyzing requirements, then designing and implementing programs to meet those requirements.

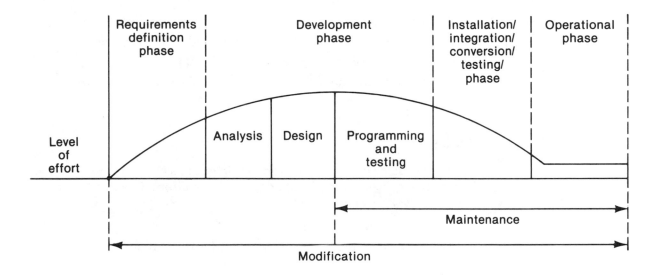

Figure 7.1 Information System Life Cycle

Experience has shown that it is faster and more economical to develop systems using a life cycle or structured methodology than it is to develop it in an unstructured manner. Prior to the implementation of life cycle methodologies, data processing projects were consistently late and over budget. With the new processes, and the controls in those processes, the developmental process is much more a scientific endeavor than an art.

Since there is no standard information system life cycle, the following is presented to define the more common phases within the life cycle. While the name of each phase may be different in different organizations (e.g., requirements are sometimes called needs), the following life cycle discussion is representative of most life cycles. Figure 7.1 provides a pictorial representation of the system development life cycle we will be discussing.

Requirements Definition Phase   This phase occurs as a response to a customer request for an enhancement to an existing production information system or a request for the development of an entirely new information system. The output of this phase would be a preliminary proposal whose key components are these:

- A "rough cut" view of how the system would work
- Hardware/software performance and standards requirements
- Data resources needed
- Staff resources needed

- Impact on other system components
- Computer resource requirements (storage and processing time)
- Benefits (positive and negative; tangible and intangible)
- Summary justification to continue or discontinue the development phase

Development Phase

Analysis

The analysis stage is the formal effort in response to a customer request for an information system enhancement or development effort. This stage is characterized by the following elements:

- Complete analysis of the request
- Interview of customers and other affected users, and documentation of the current information system
- Clarification and acceptance of objectives
- Determination of output, input, and procedures required
- Development and presentation of alternate solutions
- Selection of the best solution
- Information system flowcharting
- Approval and user acceptance of a solution
- Establishment of project schedule and selection of staff
- Final predesign approval and signoff

Design

The design stage is the development of the specifications for the information system, software, and operations. It includes the following:

- Information system that is composed of summary flowcharts and narrative
- Information system composed of midlevel flowcharts and specifications
- Manual and automated procedures, which contain summary flowcharts and specifications
- Program summary: flowcharts and narrative summary
- Program, which contains detailed flowcharts and detailed specifications
- Operations flow, job control, and scheduling, which comprise external balancing and distribution specifications
- Quality assurance approval and signoff

Programming and Testing

Activities during this stage result from the efforts of the programming (coding) personnel. Included are the following:

- Coding in the selected language
- Sorts, merges, and other utilities
- Execution/job control language
- Job stream structures
- Compiles
- Debugging
- Program testing with programmer test data approval and signoff

Installation/ Integration/ Conversion/ Testing Phase

During this phase of the life cycle, the following activities take place:

- Information system testing, including formal test data and parallel testing
- Conversion of affected files and automated/manual procedures
- Integration into the data processing and corporate processing cycles
- Implementation or installation into a distributed and/or centralized location according to an approved implementation schedule
- Quality assurance approval and signoff
- Customer approval and signoff

Operational Phase

The activities during this phase are directed toward the operations assurance effort and include these:

- Review of job schedule, priorities, run times, etc.
- Review of external balance procedures, distribution, etc.
- Review of hardware requirements
- Review of retentions, backup and recovery, disaster recovery
- Review of ownership and trouble call assistance
- Quality assurance signoff that all operations standards are being met

Maintenance and Modification Phase

The activities performed during this phase fall in one of these two categories:

- The continued maintenance of a production information system to keep that system in line with department standards and changing hardware/software configuration, etc.

- The implementation of modification requests to change, add, or delete the processing specifications of an existing production system. A new project life cycle or parts thereof, depending on severity, will be initiated to effect such modification.

The activities described in this and the preceding phases of the system life cycle allow us to begin to understand the relationship of information to systems. Before showing this relationship, it is, however, also necessary to identify and clarify the potential users of the information. Users are those individuals or programs that have a vested interest in the integrity of information. After we know the users, we can examine the relationship between these users and their uses of information during the SDLC.

Users of Information

The potential and actual users of information in the development of information systems can be individuals, but the intent here is to consider them as classes of users or as organizational entities. The following items describe the identity of each user and the functions of these users in the various phases of an information system life cycle:

- The *information resource manager* (i.e., data administrator) is responsible for managing the corporate information resources. These resources include, but are not limited to, manual data and information; automated data and information; voice, text, and image data and information; formal corporate information and its flow; corporate records and information archiving; procedures and forms; and corporate information systems.

- The *systems designer* is responsible for the development of information system design (information flow and processing, man/machine interfaces, etc.) specifications.

- The *programmer* is responsible for developing the computer programs using procedural languages (COBOL, PL/1, etc.), nonprocedural languages (report writers, file management systems, etc.), and program/system generators (input validators, application development tools, etc.).

- The *customer* is a requester or end user of the information system(s) products.

- The *operator* is responsible for the efficient scheduling and operation of the computer-related equipment (computers, printers, COM, etc.).

- The *project manager* is responsible for managing the different information system projects from development analysis through the implementation phases of the life cycle. In some cases, project managers are computer systems analysts; in others, they are lead individuals from the customer areas.

- The *maintainer* is a programmer or analyst responsible for the information system while it is in the maintenance and modification phase of its life cycle.

- The *data base administrator* is the individual responsible for the integrity of the physical data structures and definitions, and for data base performance. This individual is also responsible for the integrity of the logical data structures and definitions.

- The *systems analyst* is responsible for analyzing user needs, information flow and transformation, privacy and security, information processing, and other information system requirements.

- The *auditor* is responsible for analyzing audit and control information during the various phases of the system development life cycle. These individuals may include auditors, quality assurance analysts, and customers.

- *Programs* are automated procedures that may directly access the dictionary for dynamic use of the data.

Uses—Considerations/Processes Used in the Development of Systems

The following is a list of the considerations or processes that occur on or about information throughout the SDLC:

- *Techniques* and *processes* describe algorithms and control processes.

- *Source methodologies* and *justification* describe generic business applications.

- *Networks* describe the relationships between systems components and data, including their dependencies—both implicit and explicit.

- *Data flows* depict the flow of data through the system and identify processes and procedures affected by the flows and processes and procedures affecting the flows.

- *Data structures* depict the characteristics of data and data access techniques.

- *Integrity* describes constraints—business, legal, application, etc.—including security and privacy requirements to ensure correct aspects and consistency of data.

- *Validation criteria* describe legal or illegal domains of values.

- *Data definition generation* describes the information necessary to map data from the business view to the automated view—e.g., skeleton for generating DDL, PL/I declarations, subschemas, etc.
- *Impact analysis* portrays the information necessary to assess the impact of changes to the information system because of modification to the business environment, resource requirements and utilization, system and component interfacing, the user community, etc.
- *Information system design* provides information to assist the definition, design, and integrity of the total system.
- *Backup and recovery* identifies requirements for and constraints to performance of system backup and recovery.
- *Environmental constraints* define the factors that will constrain either the development or the operation of an information system.
- *Monitor application system use* is the use of the data dictionary to maintain information actively on how the information system is being used and who is using it.
- *Conversion* defines those factors to be considered when an information system is being converted from one environment to another.
- *Changes* identify the owner or focal point for information to ensure that change is controlled.
- *Forms design* defines and describes all formats for input and output.
- *Transformations* define codes (or values) with their associated meaning or text.
- *Program code generation* requires the documentation of data definitions, data flow, processing techniques, forms design, algorithms, and networks to create program source for an application development facility.
- *Test data generation* requires the documentation and analysis of data definitions, data flow, processing techniques, forms design, algorithms, and networks to create test data bases, test transactions, test plans, and test reports.
- *Versions* define multiple versions of the same information.

Application Control Objectives

Controls normally are classified according to the location of their implementation: input, process, output. However, the location of controls is not important to their evaluation. The auditor's prime concern should be the objective of a control.

The objectives of application controls are to prevent, detect, or correct the various application causes of exposure. Since the potential for these causes is always assumed to exist, we will summarize the objectives of application controls in five positive statements:

1. Ensure that all authorized transactions are completely processed once and only once.
2. Ensure that transaction data are complete and accurate.
3. Ensure that transaction processing is correct and appropriate to the circumstances.
4. Ensure that processing results are utilized for the intended benefits.
5. Ensure that the application can continue to function.[1]

In most instances controls can be related to multiple exposures. A single control can also fulfill multiple control objectives. For these reasons application controls can be classified according to whether they prevent, detect, or correct causes of exposure.

Preventive Controls

Preventive controls act as a guide to help things happen as they should. This type of control is most desirable because it stops problems from occurring. Computer application systems designers should put their control emphasis on preventive controls. It is more economical and better for human relations to prevent a problem from occurring than to detect and correct the problem after it has occurred.

Preventive controls include standards, training, segregation of duties, authorization, forms design, prenumbered forms, documentation, passwords, consistency of operations, etc.

One question you may raise is, "At what point in the processing flow is it most desirable to exercise computer editing?" The answer to this question is simply, "As soon as possible, in order to uncover problems early and avoid unnecessary computer processing." Some input controls depend on access to master files and so must be timed to coincide with file availability. However, many input validation tests may be performed independently of the master files. Preferably, these tests should be performed in a separate edit run at the beginning of the computer processing. Normally, the input validation tests are included in programs to perform data-conversion operations such as transferring cards to tape. By including the tests in programs performing such operations, the controls may be employed without significantly increasing the computer run time.

Preventive controls are located throughout the entire EDP system. Many of these controls are executed prior to the data entering the computer programs.

[1] From William C. Mair, Donald R. Wood, and Keagle W. Davis, *Computer Control & Audit,* Institute of Internal Auditors, chap. 7, p. 82, 1976. Copyright © 1976 Touche Ross & Co.

Detective Controls   Detective controls alert individuals involved in a process so that they are aware of a problem. Detective controls should bring potential problems to the attention of individuals so that action can be taken. One example of a detective control is a listing of all paychecks for individuals who worked over 80 hours in a week. Such a transaction may be correct, or it may be a systems error, or even fraud.

Detective controls will not prevent problems from occurring, but rather will point out a problem once it has occurred. Examples of detective controls are batch control documents, batch serial numbers, clearing accounts, labeling, and so forth.

Corrective Controls   Corrective controls assist individuals in the investigation and correction of causes of exposures that have been detected. These controls primarily collect evidence that can be utilized in determining why a particular problem has occurred. Corrective action is often a difficult and time-consuming process; however, it is important because it is the prime means of isolating system problems. Many systems improvements are initiated by individuals taking corrective actions on problems.

It should be noted that the corrective process itself is subject to error. Many major problems have occurred in organizations because corrective action was not taken on detected problems. Therefore, detective control should be applied to corrective controls.

Examples of corrective controls are audit trails, discrepancy reports, error statistics, backup and recovery, etc.

Application Control Cycle

The process of designing and assessing application controls follows a predetermined cycle. If the steps within the cycle are not followed, the probability of ineffective application controls increases. On the other hand, when all the control cycle steps are followed, controls are designed through a logical process and the effectiveness tends to increase.

Application controls are generally only effective when they are installed in a strong control environment. Unless the general (administrative) controls are strong, it may not be possible to develop good application controls. It must be remembered that it is the totality of general and application controls that ensures the integrity of processing.

The application control cycle is a four-phased cycle (see Figure 7.2). The cycle begins with the identification of exposures, then moves to designing controls, to building feedback mechanisms to monitor those controls, and then the

Figure 7.2
Application Control Cycle

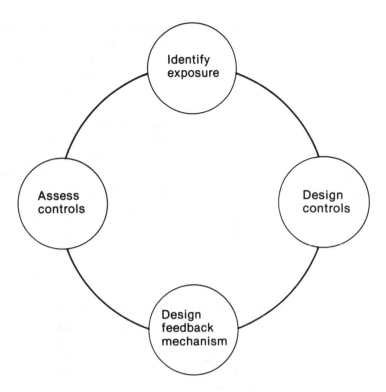

final assessment and adjustment of controls. A more detailed description of each phase follows:

Phase 1—Identify exposure.   The risk or exposure present in an application determines whether or not controls are needed. In designing or assessing controls, the first step is to identify the exposure. The second step is to determine the magnitude of the exposure. Once this has been done, the control requirement can be written. For example, if, in a bank credit card system, the risk of cardholders not paying the amounts charged is assessed at $1 million, both the risk and the magnitude of the risk have been identified. The control requirement then determines the level of loss that is acceptable, which might be $100,000 in the bank credit card example. The control requirement would then be to reduce the loss due to cardholders not paying their charges from $1 million to $100,000.

Phase 2—Design controls.   The objective of the control design process is to install the controls necessary to reduce the risk to the acceptable level. In our control requirement example, we stated that the loss was to be reduced from $1 million to $100,000 per year. This would mean that controls should be installed to reduce the risk to that level. As we know, in most credit card systems the most common controls are credit checks, merchants calling in for credit approval for amounts over X dollars, and issuance of books of bad credit card numbers. Having well-stated control requirements, we also know the amount that can be expended for controls. In our bank credit card example, the maximum amount that can be expended for controls is $900,000 per year. Up to that point, controls are economical, but over that point, assuming that the control requirements are met, control objectives are not economical.

Phase 3—Design feedback mechanisms. Feedback mechanisms are routines that monitor the functioning of controls in order to determine that the controls are meeting the control requirements. Without feedback mechanisms the effectiveness of the controls cannot be monitored. In our bank credit card example, the feedback mechanisms would measure the amount of losses actually incurred because of nonpayment of amounts charged. The feedback mechanism would indicate the amount of losses actually being incurred so that the amount can be assessed to determine whether or not the control requirement is being achieved. In this example, all the feedback mechanism would need to do is record and accumulate losses. These could then be periodically reported to management.

Phase 4—Access controls. Periodically, the information produced by the feedback mechanisms should be analyzed. Again in our credit card example, we would be attempting to determine if the losses on an annualized basis equal, exceed, or are less than the projected $100,000 losses. If the losses closely approximate $100,000, the controls can be considered effective. If the losses exceed $100,000, then the controls need to be tightened. In our bank card example, this may mean that the amount at which merchants call in should be lowered, the books of bad credit cards should be issued more frequently, or the credit checking process should be tightened. On the other hand, if the losses are significantly less then $100,000, then the controls should be loosened. In these instances, the amount at which merchants call in may be increased; credit checking, loosened; or the frequency at which the list of bad credit cards is issued, lengthened. The net effect of lengthening controls is reducing the cost of controls and thus increasing the profitability of the bank.

The effect of the assessment process is to measure both the effectiveness of controls and the magnitude of the exposure. The result of this will be to determine whether or not controls need adjusting, and then make those adjustments.

Control Design Case Study

Exposures are risks or threats to a system or organization. Controls are those means which tend to reduce those risks. For example, if blank payroll checks were stolen, dishonest individuals could fill in those checks and cash them. For that reason, blank payroll checks normally are prenumbered and locked in a secure cabinet. The possibility of the blank checks being stolen is a risk or threat. The amount of funds that could be lost because dishonest people fill in the checks and cash them is an exposure. The system of prenumbering and locking the checks in a secure place is a control utilized to reduce the exposure.

The following list includes the most common exposures that a business organization might encounter:[2]

- *Erroneous recordkeeping*—The recording of financial transactions contrary to established accounting policies. The errors may involve the time of recognition, the value, or the classification.
- *Unacceptable accounting*—The establishment or implementation of accounting policies that are not generally accepted or are inappropriate to the circumstances. This could also lead to further exposures such as statutory sanctions.
- *Business interruption*—This could mean anything from a temporary suspension of operations to a permanent termination of the enterprise. At the extreme, this also affects the accounting principle regarding a "going concern."
- *Erroneous management decisions*—Although objectionable in themselves, they may also lead to other exposures. Such decisions may occur due to misleading information, lack of information, or errors in judgment.
- *Fraud and embezzlement*—This may be perpetrated at different levels—*against* management or *by* management. Direct misappropriation of funds is only one ramification of fraud. Deliberately misinforming management or investors is also fraudulent, even if only to keep one's job.
- *Statutory sanctions*—These are any of the penalties that may be brought by judicial or regulatory authorities having jurisdiction over an organization's operations.
- *Excessive costs*—These are any expenses of the business that could be readily avoided. A related exposure is also a loss of revenues to which the organization is fairly entitled.

[2] Types of exposures and the example have been taken from William C. Mair, Donald R. Wood, and Keagle W. Davis, *Computer Control & Audit,* Institute of Internal Auditors, pp. 11–14, 1976. Copyright © 1976 by Touche Ross & Co.

- *Loss or destruction of assets*—The unintentional loss of physical assets, monies, claims to monies, or information assets.
- *Competitive disadvantage*—Any inability of an organization to effectively remain abreast of the demands of the marketplace or to respond effectively to competitive challenges.

Causes of Exposures

Exposures are normally the result of poor work habits, poorly designed documents, poor timing, incompetence, inadequate supervision, or acts of disgruntled or dishonest employees. Controls tend to diminish the causes of exposure. However, the cause of exposure must occur before an exposure can result. Exposures do not occur simply because there are inadequate controls.

A cause can generate multiple exposures. These exposures may be of different degrees of concern to the organization. It is always good practice in evaluating a condition to rate the conditions by magnitude so that one exposure can be put into the proper perspective in comparison to another exposure.

For example, let us examine an exposure condition in a bank. In this example, the cause of the exposure is the loss of a check after it had been deposited. In a bank, the loss of a deposited check after it had been partially processed would certainly cause erroneous recordkeeping because the depositor would have been given credit for the deposit, but the check could not be charged against the proper account. Excessive costs would also result because an extensive error correction activity would be necessary. If very many items were lost, the bank might have to interrupt normal operations in an attempt to recover. The granting of credit for the deposit, without being able to deduct it from the appropriate account, would constitute the loss of assets. Finally, the depositors' awareness that the bank was losing such transactions could cause them to take their business to a competitor.

The results of the exposure for this loss of a check can be illustrated in tabular form. This table can also depict the magnitude of the exposure. Using this approach, the table that would result from our cause of exposure, "losing a check," would be as illustrated in Table 7.1.

We can also depict the relationship between controls and causes with a table. We can use numbers to signify the strength of the particular control as it affects the particular cause (in this case, the loss of a check). An illustration of such a table is provided in Table 7.2.

This example illustrates that rather than implementing controls against all exposures, it would be better to be selective. The controls listed in Table 7.2 are rated according to their relative strength. An auditor must be aware that cost is an important element in a program of controls. In this example funds for controls would be better spent in a reconciliation procedure rather than for more training for the bank clerks. Reconciliation procedures are given a very reliable strength as a control, while training is rated as useful but not a reliable control against this particular cause.

**Table 7.1
Possible Exposures
Caused by Losing
a Check**

MAGNITUDE OF EXPOSURE*	TYPES OF EXPOSURES
3	Erroneous recordkeeping
	Unacceptable accounting
1	Business interruption
	Erroneous management decisions
	Fraud and embezzlement
	Statutory sanctions
2	Excessive costs
3	Loss or destruction of assets
2	Competitive disadvantage

*Key to magnitude of exposure: 3, virtually certain; 2, probable; 1, possible but unlikely; blank, very unlikely.

From William C. Mair, Donald R. Wood, and Keagle W. Davis, *Computer Control and Audit*, Institute of Internal Auditors, p. 13, 1976. Copyright © 1976 by Touche Ross & Co.

**Table 7.2
Relationship of Controls
To Causes of Exposure**

CONTROLS*	CAUSE OF EXPOSURE: LOSING A CHECK
Training	1
Secure custody	2
Prenumbered form	3
Endorsement	1
Transmittal document	2
Amount control total	3
Document control count	3
Reconciliation	3
Discrepancy reports	2

*Key to strength of controls: 3, very reliable; 2 moderately reliable; 1, useful but not reliable; blank, no significant use.

From William C. Mair, Donald R. Wood, and Keagle W. Davis, *Computer Control and Audit*, Institute of Internal Auditors, page 14, 1976. Copyright © 1976 by Touche Ross & Co.

**Determining
the Effectiveness
and Efficiency
of Controls**

The control design and assessment process attempts to "weigh" the magnitude of the exposure against the strength of controls. A previous process has described how one can determine the magnitude of controls using the Touche Ross & Co. approach. This same approach helps auditors determine the magnitude of controls. (See Tables 7.1 and 7.2.)

The Touche Ross process uses the preventive, detective, and corrective control types. These have been previously described in this chapter. The process also identifies the method of implementation. The two implementation methods are:

- *Discretionary*. The use of the control is left to the option of the user. In other words, these are primarily manual controls in which people are instructed to use the control. On the other hand, there is no guarantee that the control will be used, only that the individual has been instructed to use the control.

- *Nondiscretionary*. These are controls for which the implementation is ensured. Generally, they are automatic controls. In this instance, unless the device fails, the control will be exercised.

The strength of the control can then be assessed by its type and method of implementation. With three types and two methods of implementation, there are six categories in which a control can be placed. Knowing which category the control falls into, the auditor can determine the strength of the control.

The effectiveness and efficiency of controls for the six categories of controls is illustrated in Table 7.3. The strength of the control as illustrated in this figure is shown as the first item in each of the six boxes and is interpreted as follows:

- 3 = very reliable
- 2 = moderately reliable
- 1 = useful but not reliable
- blank = cannot be relied upon

Let's look at a quick example of each of the six categories:

- *Preventive discretionary*—These are manual controls designed to stop an event from occurring. The most common examples are a guard at a door, a supervisor who must sign an order or document before it can be exercised, or having two signatures on a check. This tends to be not a very reliable control, but generally is moderately efficient. The reliability depends on how well the control is exercised.

- *Detective with corresponding corrective discretionary*—This type of control is one designed to detect an event after it has occurred, and take some type of corrective action; but the exercise of this control is at the discretion of an individual. Generally, this is a moderately effective control, but may not be a very efficient control. An example would be a missing invoice number. The control would detect it and at that point an individual would have to begin a search for that missing invoice.

- *Detective without corrective discretionary control*—This is an ineffective control and possibly very dangerous because it may be relied upon. An

**Table 7.3
Effectiveness and
Efficiency of Controls**

METHOD OF IMPLEMENTATION	TYPE OF CONTROL		
		DETECTIVE	
	PREVENTIVE	WITH CORRESPONDING CORRECTIVE	WITHOUT CORRECTIVE
Discretionary	Blank or 1	2	Blank
	Least effective, generally manual controls applied at front end of processing. However, *moderately efficient.*	*Moderately effective* manual controls are probably *least efficient* controls.	*Least effective and possibly dangerous* since users rely improperly on them. *Very inefficient.*
Nondiscretionary	1 or 2	3	Blank
	Moderately effective, generally EDP controls, applied at front end of processing. Probably *most efficient* controls.	*Most effective,* generally controls that are computerized and applied before processing can take place. *Moderately efficient.*	*May have some remote effectiveness* but probably little. *Highly inefficient.*

example would be a warehouse in a deserted area that uses audible fire alarms. In this instance, the fire might start and it would be detected by the audible fire alarm; but because no one is around, no corrective action can be taken. Management relies on the control, but it is ineffective.

- *Preventive nondiscretionary control*—This is a moderately effective control and tends to be very efficient. An example of this type of control would be a password in a security system. The control is always exercised and it prevents individuals without proper authorization from entering the system. The degree of effectiveness depends on how well the passwords are protected and enforced.

- *Detective with corresponding corrective nondiscretionary control*—These tend to be the most effective of all controls and are moderately efficient. The most common control in this category is data validation edits, where corrective action is immediately taken. For example, if a user of a system attempts to enter alphabetic data in a quantity order field, this type of control would detect the fact that invalid data have been entered and if the corrective control is installed, the transaction would be rejected. Because the control is always exercised and because corrective countermeasures are taken, the control is very reliable.

- *Detective without corrective nondiscretionary control*—It matters little whether or not the control is exercised; if no corrective action is taken, the control is unreliable.

Determining If Controls Are Adequate

The assessment of the adequacy of application control can be determined by evaluating at one time the following elements:

- Description of the exposure
- Magnitude of the exposure
- Description of the control
- Strength of the controls

Exhibit 7.1 Control Evaluation

CONTROLS	CAUSE OF EXPOSURE: LOSS OF A CHECK STRENGTH OF CONTROL*
Training	1
Secure custody	2
Prenumbered form	3
Endorsement	1
Transmittal document	2
Amount control total	3
Document control count	3
Reconciliation	3
Discrepancy reports	2

EXPOSURES	MAGNITUDE OF EXPOSURE†
Erroneous recordkeeping	3
Unacceptable accounting	
Business interruption	1
Erroneous management decisions	
Fraud and embezzlement	
Statutory sanctions	
Excessive costs	2
Loss or destruction of assets	3
Competitive disadvantage	2

* Key to strength of controls: 3, very reliable; 2, moderately reliable; 1, useful but not reliable; blank, no significant use.

† Key to magnitude of exposure: 3, virtually certain; 2, probable; 1, possible but unlikely; blank, very unlikely.

If we combine the information developed about a control from Tables 7.2 and 7.3, we can have all the information needed in a single illustration. In our loss of check example, the information developed is combined in Exhibit 7.1 to produce a control evaluation. The magnitude of the exposure is developed by auditor judgment, while the strength of the controls is taken from the control illustration.

Having all this information in one place at one time enables the auditor or the control designer to assess the adequacy of the controls. This is done through judgment.

The judgmental process attempts to determine the actual magnitude of the exposure. In this example, we see that erroneous recordkeeping and loss or destruction of assets is virtually certain, excessive costs and competitive disadvantages are probable, and the business interruption is possible but unlikely. Because there are several virtually certain and probable exposures, a logical assessment would be that the magnitude of the exposure is relatively high. In this instance, we would look for strong controls to reduce that magnitude. In the example, we note that we have four very reliable controls and three moderately reliable controls. Again, the auditor must use judgment. In this example, a logical judgment would be that there are adequate, and perhaps more-than-adequate, controls to reduce this exposure to an acceptable level.

However, it should be noted that just because a single exposure has more than adequate controls does not mean that those controls should be dismantled. The auditor should first determine if there are other exposures also requiring that same control. For example, training may be used as a means of reducing many different exposures.

Application Control Considerations

The control design and assessment process is a complex process. Not only must it take into account the exposures and controls for the application being evaluated, but must also take into consideration:

- Transaction cycles
- Cost versus benefit of controls
- Government regulations

Each of these considerations will be individually discussed.

Transaction Cycles   In automated computerized applications, data flow from one application to another. Thus, transactions flow through cycles of applications rather than being contained in a single application.

The typical transaction cycles are illustrated in Figure 7.3. This shows, for example, that the revenue cycle is composed of the sales of products, the billing

Figure 7.3
Transaction Cycles

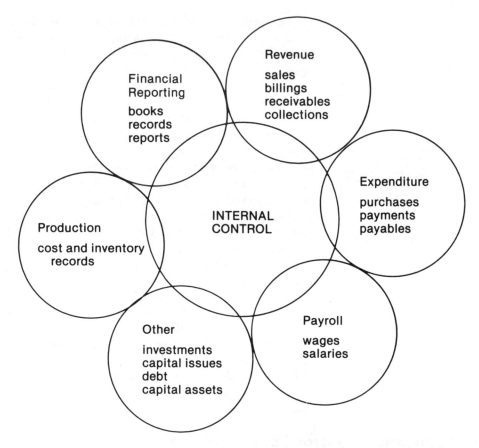

and preparation of invoices to customers, the recording and billing of receivables, and the collection of funds and applications to receivables. A single transaction initiating a sale may flow through all those systems.

When a single transaction flows through multiple systems, there are two effects on the auditor:

- *No need to audit the same transaction in multiple applications*—If an order flows through multiple systems, the auditor would not need to verify that same order in sales, again in billings, again in receivables, and again in collections. Thus, the auditor may be able to rely on the controls in the application systems to reduce the extent of auditing.

- *Cascading effect of errors*—If an error occurs in one system it may cascade and affect other systems. Thus, while a problem may not appear serious in the system in which it occurs, it may cause some serious problems in future systems. Thus, the auditor must take a look at the entire cycle rather than just a single application. In addition, there may even be relations between cycles. Figure 7.3 shows the system of internal control interconnecting through all of the cycles because the results of one cycle frequently affect another cycle.

Cost Versus Benefit of Controls

In information systems there is a cost associated with each control. As we have seen, no control should cost more than the potential errors it is established to detect, prevent, or correct. To the extent that controls are poorly designed or excessive, they become burdensome and may not be used. This failure to use controls is a key element leading to major exposures.

Preventive controls are generally the lowest in cost. Detective controls usually require some moderate operating expense. On the other hand, corrective controls are almost always quite expensive. Prior to installing any control, some cost/benefit analysis should be made.

Controls need to be reviewed continually. This is a prime function of the auditor. The auditor should determine if controls are effective. As the result of such a review an auditor will recommend adding, eliminating, or modifying system controls.

Government Regulations

The auditor should be aware of governmental regulations affecting computerized applications. The regulations are a systems requirement. It is important to incorporate those requirements in the design process. Note that many governmental regulations are industry oriented, such as the Controller of the Currency's regulations for the banking industry.

In rendering assistance in the design of *designing* audit trails, the auditor should also be aware of the requirements of the regulatory authorities. For example, the Internal Revenue Service has issued Revenue Ruling 71-20 dated January 18, 1971, which is reprinted in Exhibit 7.2 (pages 223–225) and which refers to Revenue Procedure 64–12 (also reprinted).

Summary

Application controls are an essential part of a system of internal controls. The auditor must understand how those application controls are developed and how they work. This chapter has described that process as an application control cycle. The specific controls that are used to reduce exposures, plus their location in the application system, will be described in the following chapter.

Problems

1. Review the list of exposures discussed in the chapter. What do you think are the three most significant control exposures of a company? Why?

2. Of the three—preventive, detective, and corrective controls—where would you put the greatest system design effort? Why?

3. What is a means of monitoring a control, and why is it so important to the correct functioning of controls?

4. The auditor's opinion in an audit uses the term "adequacy" of controls. Define the term *adequacy* specifically enough that a layman could understand the meaning of the term as it relates to controls.

5. What is meant by a revenue cycle and what type of applications could one expect to find in a revenue cycle?

6. Why is the cycle concept more important in the computer era than it was in manual systems?

7. The construction of computer systems is frequently compared to the construction of any major product. This is a change from the early days of computer technology when data processing was considered an art. As development of computer systems moved from an art to a science, the concept of a systems development life cycle was introduced. Explain the meaning of this concept and why it was needed.

8. What is the expected documentation produced during the programming and testing phase of the SDLC, and who would want to examine the documentation?

Cases

Data Base Risks: ABC Corporation The ABC Corporation recently installed a data base management system. The corporation selected TOTAL for its payroll application. All the data incorporated in three payroll files have now been put into a single data base. The three payroll files were year-to-date payroll information, employee pay rates and pay history, and employee descriptive information, including deductions specifications. What are the risks (i.e., problems) that would be new or increased as a result of installing the TOTAL data base management system?

Data Base Risks: XYZ Corporation The XYZ Corporation recently introduced a System 2000 data base management system into their corporation. The manager of data processing wanted to eliminate several files with large amounts of redundant data. These were files maintained by the sales department, the accounting department, the credit department, and the distribution center. The data processing manager reasoned that if data only had to be entered once, the savings in data entry cost alone would pay for the installation and operation of the DBMS.

On the basis of the planned use of System 2000, what do you see as the new and increased risks?

Exhibit 7.2

Section 6001.—Notice or Regulations Requiring Records, Statements, and Special Returns

26 CFR 1.6001–1: Records.

Punched cards, magnetic tapes, disks, and other machine-sensible data media used in the automatic data processing of accounting transactions constitute records within the meaning of section 1.6001–1 of the regulations.

Rev. Rul. 71–20 [1]

Advice has been requested whether punched cards, magnetic tapes, disks, and other machine-sensible data media used in the automatic data processing of accounting transactions constitute records within the meaning of section 6001 of the Internal Revenue Code of 1954 and section 1.6001–1 of the Income Tax Regulations.

In the typical situation the taxpayer maintains records within his automatic data processing (ADP) system. Daily transactions are recorded on punched cards and processed by the taxpayer's computer which prints daily listings and accumulates the individual transaction records for a month's business on magnetic tapes. At the month's end the tapes are used to print out monthly journals, registers, and subsidiary ledgers and to prepare account summary totals entered on punched cards. The summary data from these cards is posted to the general ledger and a monthly printout is generated to reflect opening balances, summary total postings, and closing balances. At the year's end several closing ledger runs are made to record adjusting entries. In other situations taxpayers use punched cards, disks, or other machine-sensible data media to store accounting information.

Section 6001 of the Code provides that every person liable for any tax imposed by the Code, or for the collection thereof, shall keep such records

as the Secretary of the Treasury or his delegate may from time to time prescribe.

Section 1.6001–1(a) of the Income Tax Regulations provides that any person subject to income tax shall keep such permanent books of account of records, including inventories, as are sufficient to establish the amount of gross income, deductions, credits, or other matters required to be shown by such person in any return of such tax.

Section 1.6001–1(e) of the regulations provides that the books and records required by this section shall be retained so long as the contents thereof may become material in the administration of any internal revenue law.

It is held that punched cards, magnetic tapes, disks, and other machine-sensible data media used for recording, consolidating, and summarizing accounting transactions and records within a taxpayer's automatic data processing system are records within the meaning of section 6001 of the Code and section 1.6001–1 of the regulations and are required to be retained so long as the contents may become material in the administration of any internal revenue law.

However, where punched cards are used merely as a means of input to the system and the information is duplicated on magnetic tapes, disks, or other machine-sensible records, such punched cards need not be retained.

It is recognized that ADP accounting systems will vary from taxpayer to taxpayer and, usually, will be designed to fit the specific needs of the taxpayer. Accordingly, taxpayers who are in doubt as to which records are to be retained or who desire further information should contact their District Director for assistance.

See Revenue Procedure 64–12, C.B. 1964–1 (Part 1), 672, which sets forth guidelines for keeping records within an ADP system.

---

[1] Also released as Technical Information Release 1062, dated December 31, 1970.

Exhibit 7.2
(continued)

26 CFR 601.105: Examination of returns   Rev. Proc. 64–12
   and claims for refund, credit or abate-
   ment; determination of correct tax
   liability.
(Also Part I, Section 6001; 1.6001–1.)

Guidelines for record requirements to be followed in cases where
part or all of the accounting records are maintained within automatic data processing systems.

SECTION 1. PURPOSE.

.01   The purpose of this Revenue Procedure is to set forth guidelines
specifying the basic record requirements which the Internal Revenue
Service considers to be essential in cases where a taxpayer's records
are maintained within an automatic data processing (ADP) system.
References here to ADP systems include all accounting systems which
process all or part of a taxpayer's transactions, records, or data by
other than manual methods.

.02   The technology of automatic data processing is evolving rapidly; new methods and techniques are constantly being devised and
adopted.   Accordingly, the five points set forth in section 4 of this
Revenue Procedure are not intended to restrict or prevent taxpayers
from obtaining the maximum benefits of ADP provided the appropriate information is present or can be produced by the system.   These
guidelines will be modified and amended as the need indicates to keep
pace with developments in automatic data processing systems.

SEC. 2. BACKGROUND.

The inherent nature of ADP is such that it may not be possible to
trace transactions from source documents to end results or to reconstruct a given account unless the system is designed to provide audit
trails.   Taxpayers already using ADP or contemplating its use have
requested information concerning the types of records that should be
developed and maintained in order to meet the requirements of section
6001 of the Internal Revenue Code of 1954 and the corresponding
regulations.   This section of the Code reads in part as follows:

Every person liable for any tax imposed by this title, or for the collection thereof,
shall keep such records, render such statements, make such returns, and comply
with such rules and regulations as the Secretary or his delegate may from time
to time prescribe   *   *   *

SEC. 3. OBJECTIVES.

Modern machine accounting systems are capable of recording business transactions much more rapidly and with greater accuracy than
manual systems and they are capable of retaining and producing vast
amounts of data.   The ability to produce in legible form the data
necessary to determine at a later date whether or not the correct tax li-
negligible in comparison to the expense that may be incurred at a later
date if the system cannot practically and readily provide the infor-

**Exhibit 7.2
(continued)**

mation needed to support and substantiate the accuracy of the previously reported tax liability.

Sec. 4. ADP Record Guidelines.

.01   ADP accounting systems will vary, just as manual systems vary, from taxpayer to taxpayer. However, the procedures built into a computer's accounting program must include a method of producing from the punched cards or tapes visible and legible records which will provide the necessary information for the verification of the taxpayer's tax liability.

.02   In determining the adequacy of records maintained within an automatic data processing system, the Service will consider as acceptable those systems that comply with the guidelines for record requirements as follows:

(1) *General and Subsidiary Books of Account.*—A general ledger, with source references, should be written out to coincide with financial reports for tax reporting periods. In cases where subsidiary ledgers are used to support the general ledger accounts, the subsidiary ledgers should also be written out periodically.

(2) *Supporting Documents and Audit Trail.*—The audit trail should be designed so that the details underlying the summary accounting data, such as invoices and vouchers, may be identified and made available to the Internal Revenue Service upon request.

(3) *Recorded or Reconstructible Data.*—The records must provide the opportunity to trace any transaction back to the original source or forward to a final total. If printouts are not made of transactions at the time they are processed, then the system must have the ability to reconstruct these transactions.

(4) *Data Storage Media.*—Adequate record retention facilities must be available for storing tapes and printouts as well as all applicable supporting documents. These records must be retained in accordance with the provisions of the Internal Revenue Code of 1954 and the regulations prescribed thereunder.

(5) *Program Documentation.*—A description of the ADP portion of the accounting system should be available. The statements and illustrations as to the scope of operations should be sufficiently detailed to indicate (a) the application being performed, (b) the procedures employed in each application (which, for example, might be supported by flow charts, block diagrams or other satisfactory descriptions of input or output procedures), and (c) the controls used to insure accurate and reliable processing. Important changes, together with their effective dates, should be noted in order to preserve an accurate chronological record.

Sec. 5. Comments or Inquiries.

Comments or inquiries relating to this Revenue Procedure should be addressed to the Assistant Commissioner (Compliance), Attention: CP: A, Washington, D.C., 20224.

EDP AUDIT PROCESS*

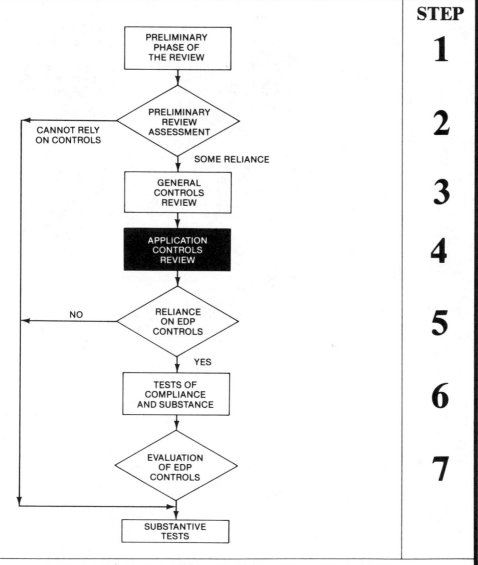

STEP

1

2

3

4

5

6

7

- PRELIMINARY PHASE OF THE REVIEW
- PRELIMINARY REVIEW ASSESSMENT
- CANNOT RELY ON CONTROLS
- SOME RELIANCE
- GENERAL CONTROLS REVIEW
- APPLICATION CONTROLS REVIEW
- RELIANCE ON EDP CONTROLS
- NO
- YES
- TESTS OF COMPLIANCE AND SUBSTANCE
- EVALUATION OF EDP CONTROLS
- SUBSTANTIVE TESTS

Diagram is adapted from The Auditor's Study and Evaluation of Internal Control in EDP Systems, *pages 21–24. Copyright © 1977 by the American Institute of Certified Public Accountants, Inc. (See Figure 9.1 for a complete explanation of the steps.)*

8

APPLICATION CONTROL REVIEW

(4) Completion of Review—Application Controls

Purpose:
- Identify application controls on which reliance is planned, and determine how the controls operate.
- Consider tests of compliance that may be performed.
- Consider the potential effect of identified strengths and weaknesses on tests of compliance.

Methods: Detailed examination of documentation; interviewing internal auditors, EDP, and user department personnel; observing operation of application controls.

> **OBJECTIVE**
>
> This chapter explains many of the controls the auditor may find during an application control review. The objective is to help the auditor identify and assess individual application controls.

Few organizations provide their systems analysts with control design methodologies. Without guidance the designers are left to develop an individualized method for control design. The most common method used by systems analysts is to divide the application system up into pieces and then design controls in those individual pieces.

This book suggests that the proper method for control design is to identify risk and then select controls designed to reduce those risks. In practice, this does not happen. Controls are developed without identifying the risk, and in many instances there are risks, some significant, for which there are no controls.

This chapter explains how controls are actually designed. The chapter explains the six segments of a computerized application, and then identifies the controls used in each of those six segments. The chapter is based on a major study funded by the IBM Corporation, sponsored by The Institute of Internal Auditors, and conducted by Stanford Research Institute; the study is entitled Systems Auditability and Control.

The Process of Designing Controls

Experience is a good teacher in the control design process. As problems occur, they are noted. Controls are then designed to prevent that type of problem from occurring again. As more problems occur, new controls are installed. Over a period of time, the most common problems are detected and controls installed to prevent recurrence.

This same trial-and-error process is used to address automotive risks. We learn that certain types of preventive maintenance, such as changing the oil regularly, reduce problems. We don't identify the risks, but do recognize that taking certain actions has a very positive effect on the operation of the automobile, as well as on the cost of repairs. We learn quickly that the "you can pay me now or pay me later" concept works. Through controls, we decide to pay a little now, rather than a lot later.

The control design process attempts to divide the application system up into its logical components. These components are controllable components. Note that this same concept applies to automobile control. We learn that there are different controls necessary for the various components of the automobile: the engine, transmission, muffler system, tires, and body. Likewise, the computer application can be divided into controllable components. While there is no formal methodology for this, the informal practice was observed and recorded in the $1 million IBM-funded Systems Auditability and Control study.

The components of a computerized application are illustrated in Figure 8.1, which shows the following six parts of an automated application:

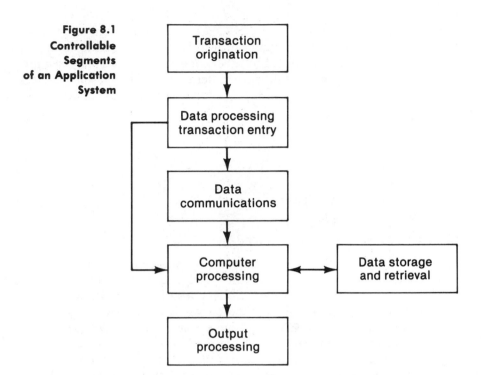

**Figure 8.1
Controllable
Segments
of an Application
System**

1. Transaction origination
2. Data processing transaction entry
3. Data communications
4. Computer processing
5. Data storage and retrieval
6. Output processing

Transaction Origination Controls

An important segment of input processing is the validation of the input itself. This is an extremely important process because it is really the last point in the input preparation where errors can be detected before files are updated. The primary control techniques used to validate the data are associated with the editing capabilities of the computer. Because of the characteristics of the computer, an EDP system has unusual capabilities to examine or edit each element of information processed by it. This editing involves the ability to inspect and accept (or reject) transactions according to validity or reasonableness of quantities, amounts, codes, and other data contained in the input records. The editing ability of the computer can be used to detect errors in input preparation that have not been detected by other control techniques discussed previously.

The editing ability of the computer is achieved by installing checks in the program of instructions, hence the term *program checks*. They include

- Validity tests
- Completeness tests
- Logical tests
- Limit tests
- Self-checking digits
- Control totals
- Error detection and resubmission

Validity tests are used to ensure that transactions contain valid transaction codes, valid characters, and valid field size. For example, in an accounts receivable system, if only input cards coded PB through PL were valid transaction codes, then input with other cards would be rejected by the computer. In a labor data collection system, all time transactions and job transactions could be checked by the computer against the random-access file of active job numbers, and nonmatches would be indicated on a report to the shop foreman.

Completeness checks are made to ensure that the input has the prescribed amount of data in all data fields. For example, a particular payroll application requires that each new employee hired have two input cards in proper sequence and with all necessary information punched. A check may also be included to see that all characters in a field are either numeric or alphabetic.

Logical checks are used in transactions where various portions, or fields, of the record bear some logical relationship to one another. A computer program can check these logical relationships to reject combinations that are erroneous even though the individual values are acceptable. For example, on one system, orders are submitted via teletype and a paper tape is created upon receipt. Data from the paper tape are then transferred to a magnetic tape, creating an open order file. During conversion the orders are edited by a routine that makes a check to determine that the warehouse code, order number, and salesman code are all correct and related to the branch sales office transmitting the order.

Limit tests are used to test record fields to see whether certain predetermined limits have been exceeded. Generally, reasonable time, price, and volume conditions can be associated with a business event. For example, on one payroll application, the computer is programmed to reject all payroll rate changes greater than 15 percent of the old rate. The labor hours field is checked to see if the number of hours worked exceeds 44. In another application, an exception report is generated when a customer's receivable balance plus the total of his unfilled orders exceeds his credit limit.

Self-checking digits are used to ensure the accuracy of identification numbers such as account numbers. A check digit is determined by performing some arithmetic operation on the identification number itself. The arithmetic operation is performed in such a way that typical errors encountered in transcribing a number (such as transposing two digits) will be detected.

Control totals are normally obtained from batches of input data. These control totals are prepared manually, prior to processing, and then are incorporated as input to the computer processing phase. The computer can be programmed to accumulate control totals internally and make a comparison with those provided as input. A message confirming the comparison should be printed out, even if the comparison did not disclose an error. These messages are then reviewed by the internal processing control group.

Error detection and resubmission becomes important when data are entered. Until now we have talked about data control techniques designed to screen the incoming data in order to reject any transactions that do not appear valid, reasonable, complete, etc. Once these errors have been detected, we need to establish specific control techniques to ensure that all corrections are made to the transactions in error and that these corrected transactions are reentered into the system. Such control techniques should include the following:

1. Having the control group enter all data rejected from the processing cycle in an error log by marking off corrections in this log when these transactions are reentered; open items should be investigated periodically.

2. Preparing an error input record or report explaining the reason for each rejected item. This error report should be returned to the source department for correction and resubmission. This means that the personnel in the originating or source department should have instructions on the handling of any errors that might occur.

3. Submitting the corrected transactions through the same error detection and input validation process as the original transaction.

Data Processing Transaction Entry Controls

The following are representative of the types of controls used to ensure that transactions are properly recorded:

- Source-data authorization
- Data conversion
- Source-data preparation
- Turnaround documents
- Prenumbered forms

Source-Data Authorization

Once data have been recorded properly, there should be control techniques to ensure that the source data have been authorized. Typically, authorization should be given for source data such as credit terms, prices, discounts, commission rates, overtime hours, and so forth.

The input documents, where possible, should have evidence of authorization and should be reviewed by the internal control group in data processing. To the extent practical, the computer should be utilized as much as possible to authorize input. This may be done through programmed controls.

Data Conversion

Data conversion is the process of converting data in non-machine-readable form (such as hard-copy source documents) into a machine-readable form (such as punched card, magnetic tape or disk) so that the computer can update files with the transactions. Since the data-conversion process is typically a manual operation, control is needed to ensure that the data conversion has been performed accurately. Data-conversion control techniques include the following:

- Key verification of punched data by verifying either the whole record or important fields in the record or even sampling specific records on a statistical basis to verify that the card-punching process results in an output with errors below an acceptable error level.
- Creation of source documents as a byproduct of the recording operation. For example, when an invoice is typed, a device hooked up to the typewriter automatically produces a punched card or punched paper tape for inventory control and sales analysis purposes.
- Use of turnaround documents that eliminate the need for data conversion.

Source-Data Preparation

In many automated systems, conventional source documents are still used and, therefore, no new control problems are presented prior to the conversion of source documents into machine-readable form. Specially designed forms promote the accuracy of the initial recording of the data. A preaudit of the source documents by knowledgeable personnel to detect misspellings, invalid codes, unreasonable amounts, and other improper data helps to promote the accuracy of input preparation.

In EDP systems where the source document is eliminated or is in a form that does not permit human review, control over source-data preparation should be such that access to, and use of, the recording and transmitting equipment is properly controlled to exclude unauthorized or improper use.

Turnaround Documents   Other control techniques to promote the accuracy of input preparation include the use of turnaround documents designed to eliminate all or part of the data to be recorded at the source. A good example of a turnaround document is the bill you may receive from an oil company. Normally the bill has two parts: one part is torn off and included with the remittance you send back to the oil company as payment for your bill; the other you keep for your records. The part you send back normally includes prepunched data for your account number and the amount billed so that this returned part can be used as the input medium for computer processing of the cash receipts for the oil company.

Prenumbered Forms   Sequential numbering of the input transaction form with full accountability at the point of document origin is another traditional control technique. This can be done by using prenumbered forms or by having the computer issue sequential numbers.

Data Communication Controls

The following communication controls will be discussed here:

- Data transmission
- Control register
- Sequence number checking
- Sending and receiving identification
- Transaction journal
- Positive acknowledgment
- Time and date stamp
- Periodic message reconciliation
- Check sum on message address
- Unlisted phone number (dial-up)
- Error logging

Data Transmission   Once the source data have been prepared, properly authorized, and converted to machine-processable form, the data usually are transmitted from the source department to the data processing center. Data transmission can be made by conventional means (such as messenger and mail) or by data transmission devices that allow data transmission from remote locations on a much more timely basis.

One important control technique in data transmission is *batching,* the grouping of a large number of transactions into small groups. Batching typically is related more to sequential-processing systems where transactions have to be put into the same order as the master files; however, batching may also apply to many direct-access systems where it may be desirable to batch input or control purposes.

Let us examine a payroll example as an illustration of batching. In such an example, the source document may include time cards (source-data preparation) that should have been approved by a foreman (data authorization). For batching, these data time cards could be divided into groups of 25, with a control total for hours worked developed for each batch along with the total for all batches. Each batch transaction and its control totals could then be sent (data transmission) to the internal control group in the EDP department for reconciliation with their batch control totals developed when the same time cards are punched into EDP cards (data conversion). Thus batching and control totals are useful techniques for the control of both data conversion and data transmission. These control totals could also be used during the computer processing phase where the payroll files would be updated. We shall discuss this phase later in the chapter.

Control totals should be developed on important fields of data on each record to ensure that all records have been transmitted properly from the source to the data processing center. Controls might be developed on the number of records in each batch or could be based on some quantitative field of data such as invoice amount or hours worked, etc. Such controls serve as a check on the completeness of the transaction being processed and ensure that all transactions have been received in the data processing center.

Control Register   Another technique to ensure the transmission of data is the recording of control totals in a control log so that the input processing control group can reconcile the input controls with any control totals generated in subsequent computer processing. For example, in a payroll system, we could have batched the time cards and developed control totals on the number of transactions in each batch plus the hours worked shown on the clock cards. These control totals could be used first to ensure that all clock cards generated throughout the company have been received by the data processing center. In addition, the same control totals could be developed during the computer processing used to prepare the payroll listing and reconciled with the control totals established when the data were received in the computer center.

Other Communications Controls   Some of the other data communication controls require little explanation; nonetheless, they make a significant contribution to the integrity of a system.

- *Sequence number checking*—A method in which all messages contain an integral sequence number for each level of the communication system.

Verification techniques must detect duplicate and missing numbers, reject duplicates, and report missing messages.

- *Sending and receiving identification*—A method in which sufficient information is contained in the message to identify uniquely both the sender and the receiver of a message.

- *Transaction journal*—A method of capturing sufficient system and message level data to establish an adequate audit trail or to have an actual copy of every transaction transmitted in the network.

- *Positive acknowledgment*—A method in which the receipt of each message is positively confirmed to the sender.

- *Time and date stamp*—An automatic procedure whereby each message contains time and date information for each major processing node.

- *Periodic message reconciliation*—System facilities to verify completeness of processing by periodically providing summary information to reconcile number of messages, dollar values, control totals, etc., both sent and received.

- *Check sum on message address*—A procedure that verifies the message address, by means of hashing or other summing type of totals.

- *Unlisted phone number (dial-up)*—The acquisition and use of unlisted telephone numbers for the communication system component that can be accessed via dial-up lines.

- *Error logging*—A software program that records error messages, by line and terminal as well as by type and frequency. This recording is to measure the degree of reliability and performance of the communication system. Statistical analysis and management reports are required for evaluation and corrective action to minimize error rates.

Computer Processing Controls

When we discussed input validation, we saw that programmed controls are a very important part of application control. Programmed controls in computer updating of files are also very important since they are designed to detect loss of data, check arithmetic computation, and ensure the proper posting of transactions. Let us examine some of these programmed controls.

Programmed checks to detect *loss or nonprocessing* of data are record counts, control totals, and hash totals. A record count is the number of records processed by the computer. The resulting total can then be compared with a predetermined count. Normally a record count is established when the file is assembled, and the record count is carried as a control total at the end of the file or reel and is adjusted whenever records are added or deleted. For example, a record count may be established for all new hirings or terminations processed. This record count can then be compared internally (if a control card is included with the input transactions) or manually to predetermined totals of new hirings or terminations. Each time the file is processed, the records are recounted and the quantity is balanced to the original or adjusted total. Although the record count is useful as a proof of processing accuracy, it is difficult to determine the cause of error if the counts are out of balance.

A control total is made from amount or quantity fields in a group of records and is used to check against a control established in previous or subsequent manual or computer processing.

A hash total is another form of control total made from data in a nonquantity field (such as vendor number or customer number) in a group of records.

Programmed checks of *arithmetic calculations* include limit checks, cross-footing balance checks, and overflow tests.

Some calculations produce illogical results such as million-dollar payroll checks or negative payroll checks. Such calculations can be highlighted in exception reports with the use of *limit checks,* which test the results of a calculation against predetermined limits. For example, a payroll system may include limit checks to exclude, from machine payroll check preparation, all employees with payroll amounts greater than $500 or less than $0.

Cross-footing balance checks can be programmed so that totals can be printed out and compared manually or totals can be compared internally during processing. For example, the computer-audit program (to be discussed in Chapter 10) is used in testing accounts receivable and in selecting accounts for confirmation. Each account is aged according to the following categories: current, 30, 60, and 90 days. The aged amounts for each account are temporarily stored in accumulators in the central processing unit. When all open items for the account have been aged, the aged totals for the account are compared to the account balance stored elsewhere in the central processing unit. Any difference results in an error indication. The program also includes for all accounts the accumulation and printout of aged amounts for manual comparison with the total accounts receivable balance.

The *overflow test* is a widely used test to determine whether the size of a result of a computation exceeds the registered size allocation to hold it. If so, there must be a means of saving the overflow portion of the results which would otherwise be lost. Overflow control may be programmed or may be available as a hardware or software control provided by the equipment manufacturer.

Accuracy of programming is ensured by proper documentation and extensive program testing procedures. Good documentation will aid in locating programming errors and will facilitate correction even in the absence of the original designer or programmer. Extensive program test procedures under real-life conditions, testing all possible exceptions without actual programmer involvement, will minimize possibilities of hidden program bugs and facilitate smooth running of the system.

In the first- and second-generation computer equipment, a good portion of testing was performed within a program to detect hardware, i.e., mechanical, errors in the equipment itself. Third-generation equipment, however, has elaborate checks built in as an integral part of the equipment and such problems are minimized. These design advances in third generation equipment have minimized the problem of hardware error, and as a result the systems designer or programmer and auditor need not be as concerned about them.

Data Storage and Retrieval Controls

Controls that are effective in ensuring that data are properly stored, updated, and retrieved include these:

- File labeling
- Computer updating of files
- Audit trails
- Data base controls

File Labeling   Programmed checks for *proper postings* may be classified as file checks. Basically, these are controls used to ensure that the correct files and records are processed together. The problem of using the correct file is a significant one in EDP systems because of the absence of visible records and because of the ease with which wrong information can be written on magnetic tapes and disks. The increase in the size and complexity of modern data processing systems has resulted in the growth of large system libraries containing data that can cost thousands of dollars to generate. For the purpose of preserving the integrity of data, various labeling techniques have been devised to provide maximum protection for a file to prevent accidental destruction or erasure and to ensure proper posting, updating, and maintenance. Two types of labels are used, external and internal.

External labels are a physical safeguard that properly falls under the category of documentation and operating practices. They are attached to the exterior of data processing media. For example, the operator places an external label on each tape reel used to store output. An external label should contain information such as job name, job number, date, operator number, reel, file name, type of drive to be used, retention date, etc.

Internal labels are actually written on the data recording media by programmed routines and are in machine-readable form. This type of label properly falls under the category of programmed controls. A *volume label* is a machine-readable record associated with a particular storage medium such as a reel of tape or a disk pack. (*Volume* refers to a physical entity used for storing data and instructions in a data processing system. Examples are reels of tape and disk packs. A file, on the other hand, is a collection of related records.) A *file label* is a machine-readable record associated with a particular file.

Each reel of tape, disk pack, data cell, and so forth, receives a volume label when it is first readied for processing. This volume label is the first record on the volume. It contains a volume serial number that should be checked whenever records are read from or written to any file on the volume, thus providing one safeguard in terms of programmed controls for proper posting of records.

File labels (mentioned briefly in Chapter 2) are of two types: header labels and trailer labels. Generally, header and trailer labels are used with *sequential files*. Since most sequential files in an EDP system are written to and read from magnetic tape, header and trailer labels are used primarily for magnetic tape files. Both labels contain the file name, the date it was created, etc. Header labels are used for most files.

The volume label, typically, is followed by a *volume table of contents* (VTOC). In effect, file labels for all files stored on the device are placed together in the VTOC, rather than scattered at various positions throughout the recording surfaces. A file label in VTOC contains the name, description, and location of each file on the volume. Serial number, sequence number, and creation date are some of the additional information provided.

In many data processing systems, standard formats for volume and file labels are established. An example of direct-access labeling is shown in Figure 8.2.

The trailer label usually contains one or more control totals accumulated during processing. These totals can be checked against totals that will be ac-

**Figure 8.2
Example
of Direct-Access
Labeling**

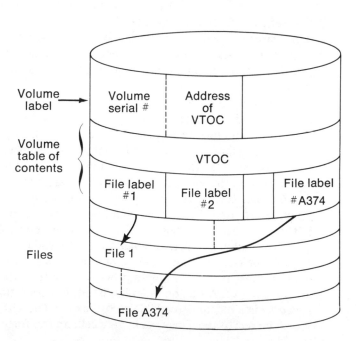

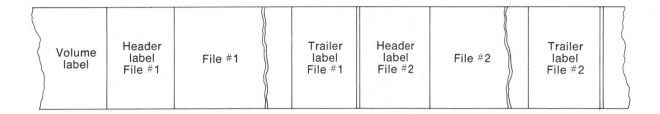

Figure 8.3   Positioning of Labels for One Physical Reel of Tape Containing Two Files

cumulated when the file is read, to guard against "losing" (failing to process) any records in the file. Figure 8.3 shows the positioning of labels for one physical reel of tape containing two files.

The volume label on a direct-access storage device is positioned on the first storage location of the volume. It identifies the volume and also helps prevent the use of the volume by unauthorized persons. This initial volume label may be followed by additional volume labels if supplementary information is needed.

If despite the presence of labels the wrong file is processed or the file is updated with incorrect data or a file is inadvertently destroyed, there must be procedures to restore the data.

Computer Updating of Files

The updating phase of the processing cycle is the computer updating of files with the validated transactions. Normally computer updating involves sequencing transactions, comparing transaction records with master file records, computations, and manipulating and reformatting data, for the purpose of updating master files and producing output data for distribution to user departments or for subsequent computerized processing.

The accuracy of the file updating depends on controls to ensure the programming, hardware checks designed and built into the equipment by the manufacturer, and programmed controls included in the computer programs themselves.

Another control technique for the proper updating of files is *file maintenance*. File maintenance consists of those procedures involved in making changes to the permanent-type information contained in master files, information such as name, address, employee number, and payrate, for example, in a payroll file. Since these data are so important to the proper computerized processing of files, formalized procedures are required to make changes to this type of permanent information. All master file changes should be authorized in writing by the department initiating the change. A notice or register of all changes should be furnished to the initiating department to verify that the changes were made.

Audit Trails Another important aspect of the processing cycle is the *audit trail*. The audit trail consists of documents, journals, ledgers, and work sheets that enable an interested party (e.g., the auditor) to trail an original transaction forward to a summarized total or from a summarized total backward to the original transaction. Only in this way can he determine whether the summary accurately reflects the business's transactions.

The audit trail is essential to the auditor in tracing the systematic flow of data within a company. But management also needs an audit trail in the normal operation of the business in response to inquiries and demands from sources such as customers, employees, vendors, and government agencies.

Because of the capabilities of the computer, significant changes in the audit trail can take place:[1]

1. Source documents, once transcribed onto a machine-readable input medium, are no longer used in the processing cycle. They may be filed in a manner which makes subsequent access difficult.

2. In some systems, traditional source documents may be eliminated by the use of direct input devices.

3. Ledger summaries may be replaced by master files which do not show the amounts leading up to the summarized values.

4. The data processing cycle does not necessarily provide a transaction listing or journal. To provide such a listing may require a specific action at a recognizable cost.

5. It is sometimes unnecessary to prepare frequent printed output of historical records. Files can be maintained on computer media and reports prepared only for exceptions.

6. Files maintained on a magnetic medium cannot be read except by use of the computer and a computer program.

7. The sequence of records and processing activities is difficult to observe because much of the data and many of the activities are contained within the computer system.

The auditor should be aware of the changes that can take place and should provide assistance to his or her client in designing an appropriate audit trail into computerized applications. There are several important guidelines related to the design of proper audit trails:

Because of the need for companies to prepare financial information for both internal and external purposes, there must be a means for establishing the account to which all financial transactions are posted.

---

[1] Gordon B. Davis, *Auditing and EDP,* pp. 119–120, copyright © 1967 by the American Institute of Certified Public Accountants, Inc. Reprinted by permission.

There must be a means for tracing a summarized amount for all accounts back to the individual transactions.

The system should have the capability to supply records necessary for handling inquiries about transactions and accounts. For those transactions and accounts with a large number of inquiries, regular provision should be made. For example, in the banking business, many inquiries are made daily about the status of demand deposit accounts. Listings of the balance of these accounts may be printed each night to provide such a reference; or terminal inquiry may provide on-line inquiry on a current basis.

Data Base Controls   Some of the more effective controls used to ensure the integrity of data in a data base are as follows:

Malfunction reporting is the formalization of the data base error reporting process. Malfunction reporting normally involves a form that identifies problems or malfunctions, identifies the cause of the malfunction, and makes recommendations as to the recommended course of action. In some organizations, this function is performed by a group of specialists who do the error analysis, but not the correction.

A *data dictionary* system (DDS) is a documentation tool for defining data and its use. Many DDSs are software packages available from vendors. The objective of the DDS is to standardize the definition and use of data. The DDS also can be used to define organization, reorganization, access to data, and other operating information needed to implement a data base environment.

An *integrated data dictionary* system connects the DDS to the DBMS in a production environment. A DDS can be off-line and used solely as a documentation tool. However, in an active mode, application systems cannot access or define data unless those data definitions are processed through the DDS. This is one of the strongest controls in a data base environment since it can enforce access rules in addition to enforcing standardized definitions. This concept may not be completely practical with currently available software.

Data element responsibility requires that each data element have one individual or job position accountable for it. The individual has the responsibility for authorizing access to the data element, and assuring the integrity of the data element.

Concurrent data control ensures that data elements will not be misprocessed due to two or more users processing the same data element concurrently. Most data base management systems provide a control that limits change to one program at a time. If a second user wishes to change a data element that is in the process of being changed, that second user is temporarily denied access to the data element.

Deadlock resolution is needed when two users engage in a processing situation in which each is holding a data element wanted by the other and will not release that data element until it receives the data element the other is holding. For example, user A has data element 1 and wants data element 2; while user B has data element 2 and is holding that until user A frees data element 1. Most commercially produced DBMSs have routines to detect and resolve deadlocks.

Output Processing Controls

The output checks consist of procedures and control techniques to do the following:

- Reconcile output data, particularly control totals, with previously established control totals developed in the input phase of the processing cycle
- Review output data for reasonableness and proper format
- Control input data rejected by the computer during processing and distribute the rejected data to appropriate personnel
- Distribute output reports to user departments on a timely basis

Proper input controls and file-updating controls should give a high degree of assurance that the computer output generated by the processing is correct. However, it is still useful to have certain output controls to achieve the control objectives associated with the processing cycle. Basically the function of output controls is to determine that the processing does not include any unauthorized alterations by the computer operations section and that the data are substantially correct and reasonable. The most basic output control is the comparison of control totals on the final output with original input control totals such as record counts or financial totals. Systematic sampling of individual items affords another output control. The testing can be done by the originating group, by the control group, or by an internal audit staff.

One of the biggest controls in any system occurs when the originating group reviews reports and output data and takes corrective action. Review normally consists of a search for unusual or abnormal items. The programmed controls discussed above, coupled with exception reporting, actually enhance the ability of responsible personnel to take necessary corrective action.

Another form of output control in some organizations is the periodic and systematic review of reports and output data by an internal audit staff. This group normally has the responsibility to evaluate operating activities of the company, including computer operations, to determine that internal policies and procedures are being followed.

Two control procedures found effective are output handling and on-time delivery of reports.

Output Handling   To ensure the detection of processing errors in the output and to prevent output from being distributed inappropriately, appropriate policies should be established regarding

- The identification of all printed and other output
- The quality control procedures over output for detection of errors and/or unacceptable conditions
- Standard procedures for the physical handling (decollating, binding, etc.) and delivery of output and the disposal of remnants (e.g., extraneous copies, carbon)
- Standard procedures and assigned accountability for handling of negotiable instruments (e.g., signed checks, purchase orders)

On-Time Delivery of Reports   The delivery of routine reports on a scheduled basis is an important aspect of an effective EDP operation. Late reports can result in substantial losses. Users must schedule their work force on the assumption that routine reports will be delivered on time. Any failure by EDP to meet the schedule can be indicative of problems ranging from minor to very serious. The manager of EDP should routinely receive a "morning report" of those trails where reports were not delivered as per schedule, as well as a weekly or monthly summary of such failures to pinpoint areas where changes must be made.

Exercise 1   The discussion on application controls should have provided you with a good understanding of control techniques useful in the various processing steps. Now it is time to apply these principles and techniques to a practical example. On the following pages, you will find a flowchart (Figure 8.4) for a payroll and job-costing system[2] and record formats (Table 8.1) for the job tickets and time cards that will be processed by this system. The flowchart is only a generalized statement of the process to be performed. The information contained by the job tickets and time cards, along with the flowchart, constitute the system for this exercise.

Controls are required for sections A to C of the system (see the flowchart) to ensure that complete and accurate data are input for the computer processing

---

[2] This exercise and its solution are adapted, with permission, from one developed by Clarkson, Gordon & Co. for use by the Canadian Institute of Chartered Accountants.

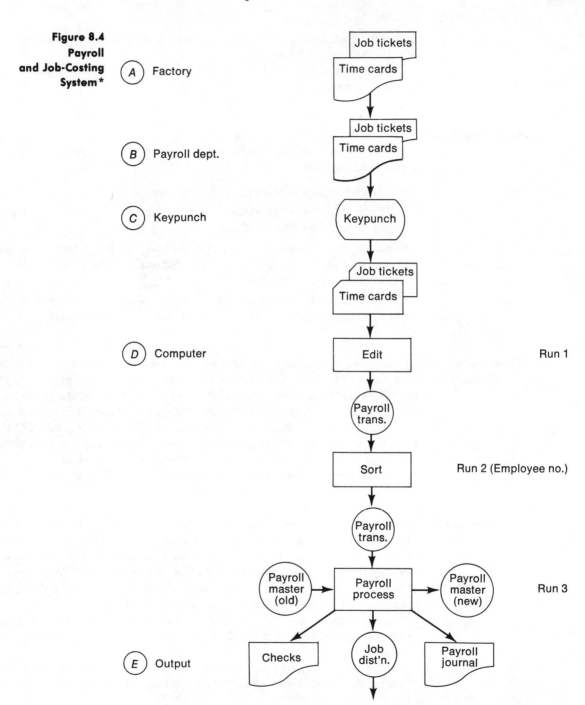

**Figure 8.4
Payroll
and Job-Costing
System***

(A) Factory

(B) Payroll dept.

(C) Keypunch

(D) Computer — Run 1

Run 2 (Employee no.)

Run 3

(E) Output

*Note: Run 3(a) calculates gross and net pay, (b) calculates job costs for labor, (c) updates master record, and (d) prepares payroll.

**Table 8.1
Record Formats,
80-Column Cards**

COLUMN	CONTENT	RANGE
Time card:		
1–3	Blank	
4–5	Department	(01–14)
6–9	Employee number	(0001–9999)
10–27	Employee name	(alphas and blanks)
28–29	Date—month	(01–12)
30–31	Date—week ending	(01–31)
32–34	Regular hours	(00.0–40.0)
35–37	Overtime	(000–595)
38–40	Other (types of authorized absences)	
41–43	Other	(00.0–40.0)
44–80	Blank	
Job ticket:		
1–4	Job number	(0001–9999)
5–10	Part number	(010001–999999)
11–12	Department	(01–14)
13–16	Employee number	(0001–9999)
17–34	Employee name	(alphas and blanks)
35–37	Hours worked	(000–995)
38–80	Blank	

Notes:

[1] Overtime pay is computed on the basis of 1½ times basic rate for hours worked plus authorized absence totaling over 40 hr.

[2] Indirect time is also assigned to job tickets having special overhead job numbers.

of section D. Assume that the functions in sections A to C are performed manually, thus requiring manual controls for the cross-checking and editing of data. Design a set of workable manual controls. (In actual practice, of course, the computer will perform many of these control functions. In exercise 2 you will be required to modify the manual controls you design here so that the machine does them; also, you will be asked to design the edit routines for section D of the flowchart.)

Once you have arrived at a satisfactory solution, check it against the following solution.

Solution

There is no one best or unique solution to this exercise. However, a solution that incorporates most of the control principles discussed so far appears in Figure 8.5. The original flowchart is expanded to show all the control steps to be incorporated in the process. Note that the solution includes controls at all

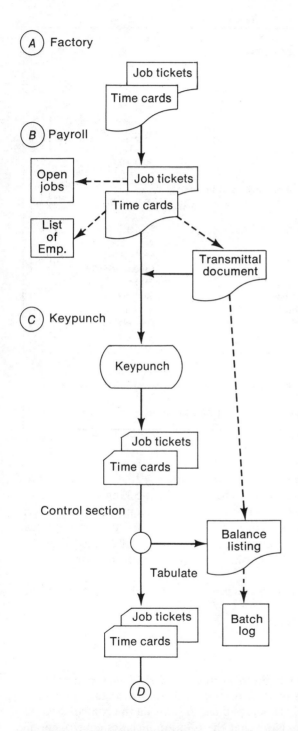

(A) Factory

Job tickets
Time cards

(B) Payroll

Open jobs

Job tickets
Time cards

List of Emp.

Transmittal document

(C) Keypunch

Keypunch

Job tickets
Time cards

Control section

Tabulate

Balance listing

Job tickets
Time cards

Batch log

(D)

1. Foreman approves time cards (TC) and job tickets (JT) for work done. (Data authorization)

2. Add hours per JT and TC and balance. (Cross-checking)

Input Validation:

1. Check foreman's approval.

2. Check to list of open job numbers.

3. Check to list of employees.

4. Ensure total hours per job tickets = hours per time cards.

Data Transmission:

5. Prepare transmittal document with batch number and total hours recorded and approve transmittal document.

6. Check for reasonableness of time charged for individual employee.

Data Conversion:

1. Keypunch and keyverify.

1. Control section balances and records in batch log for subsequent balancing. (Control totals)

1. Tabulate and balance to transmittal document.

Figure 8.5   Expanded Flowchart

Note: Run 3(a) calculated gross and net pay, (b) calculates job costs for labor, (c) = updates master record, and (d) prepares payroll.

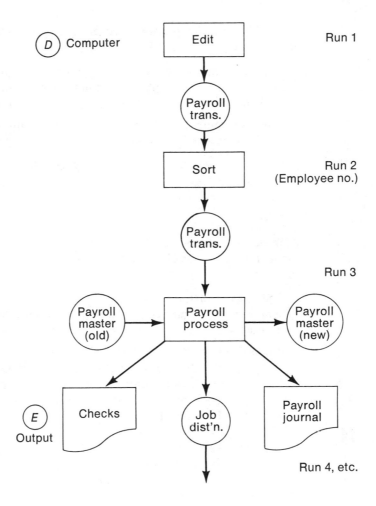

Figure 8.5   (continued)

steps of the input phase, such as source-data preparation, data authorization, data conversion, and input validation.

Exercise 2   In the previous exercise, you analyzed part of a payroll and job-costing system, developing specific manual control procedures to ensure the accuracy, validity, and completeness of input transactions. These control procedures were developed for sections A, B, and C of the flowchart.

In this exercise, continue with your analysis, designing controls for edit run No. 1 of section D. (You will need the record formats in this exercise.) Runs 2 and 3 will be considered after we cover additional material on processing controls.

1. Make a list of controls you feel would be appropriate for run No. 1. (Many of these will replace those manual edits and checks you established for parts A, B, and C in the previous exercise.)

2. Now reexamine the solution to that problem and delete those controls that have become unnecessary on account of adequate computer editing.

Once you have answered the above questions, check them against the following solution.

Solution

Check your solution with the following one. Refer to the flowchart and record formats for job tickets (JT) and time cards (TC) provided in the previous exercise.

1. The programmed controls appropriate for run No. 1 would include character checks and checks of important data field for all individual transactions. The programmed tests could include:

   (*a*) Completeness tests (character check)

       (*i*) Test for blanks; making sure that these fields actually are blank would eliminate any chance of printing unwanted and irrelevant information during the output phase.
   TC: cols. 1–3, 44–80
   JT: cols. 38–80

       (*ii*) Test for numeric
   TC: cols. 4–9, 28–43
   JT: cols. 1–16, 35–40

       (*iii*) Test for alphabetic
   TC: cols. 10–27
   JT: cols. 17–34

   (*b*) Validity tests

       (*i*) Current payroll processing week
       (*ii*) Open job number

   (*c*) Logical test: overtime zero only if "regular hours" + "other" = 40

   (*d*) Limit check: hours over 60 printed out

   (*e*) Self-checking digits: employee number

   Batch checks could include the following:

   (*f*) Hash totals of hours agree to control

   (*g*) Total hours on job tickets less hours on time cards zero balanced (*h*)   Total hours of rejected data established for control and new balance forward calculated

2. Certain input controls developed in the previous exercise can be eliminated. These are:

      (*a*)   Check to list of open job numbers.

      (*b*)   Check to list of employees.

      (*c*)   Ensure total hours per tickets equals total hours per time cards.

      (*d*)   Check for reasonableness of time charged for individual employees.

3. An error report should be made as additional output from the run to report errors detected by the programmed controls included in edit run No. 1.

Exercise 3   Earlier in this chapter, you were asked to analyze a payroll and job-costing system and determine what programmed controls you thought were appropriate for the edit run (run No. 1). Let us now proceed with an analysis of runs 2 and 3 in the computer processing phase.

    As you can see in the flowchart in Figure 8.6, run No. 2 is a *sort* run in which the payroll transactions are sorted by employee number for updating the payroll master file. In run No. 3, that master file is updated, payroll checks are prepared, and a payroll journal is generated. (The first part of the flowchart is included for reference, if needed. Items eliminated by computerization have been crossed out.)

1. Determine the *programmed controls* you feel would be appropriate for runs 2 and 3.

2. In the flowcharts provided, you will notice four primary output reports generated during the processing phase for this payroll application: balance listing, error report, payroll checks, and payroll journal. What different output controls would you incorporate in the payroll system for the above output reports? Specifically, what role will the internal control group and the user department play in this phase?

    When you finish designing these controls, check them against the following solution.

Solution

1. The programmed control to be incorporated in run No. 2 would be that of control totals. In the run, the computer should develop a control total of the number of hours on the payroll transactions and compare them with the totals for the input payroll transactions. There should be a con-

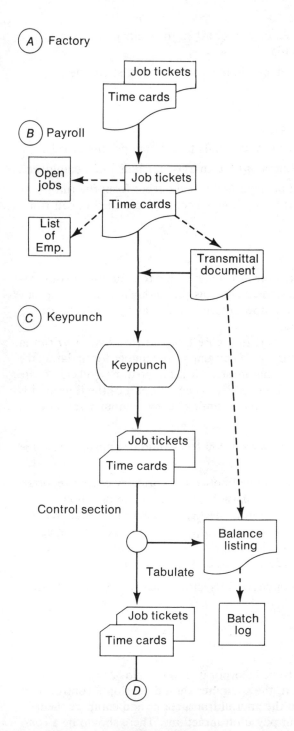

(A) Factory

Job tickets
Time cards

(B) Payroll

Open jobs

Job tickets
Time cards

List of Emp.

Transmittal document

(C) Keypunch

Keypunch

Job tickets
Time cards

Control section

Tabulate

Job tickets
Time cards

Balance listing

Batch log

(D)

1. Foreman approves time cards (TC) and job tickets (JT) for work done. (Data authorization)
2. Add hours per JT and TC and balance. (Cross-checking)

Input Validation:

1. Check foreman's approval.
2. ~~Check to list of open job numbers.~~
3. ~~Check to list of employees.~~
4. ~~Ensure total hours per job ticks - hours per time cards.~~

Data Transmission:

5. Prepare transmittal document with batch number and total hours recorded and approve transmittal document.
6. ~~Check for reasonableness of time charged for individual employee.~~

Data Conversion:

1. Keypunch and keyverify.

1. Control section balances and records in batch log for subsequent balancing. (Control totals)

1. Tabulate and balance to transmittal document.

Figure 8.6   Expanded Flowchart

Note: Run 3(a) calculated gross and net pay, (b) calculated job costs for labor, (c) = updates master record, and (d) prepares payroll.

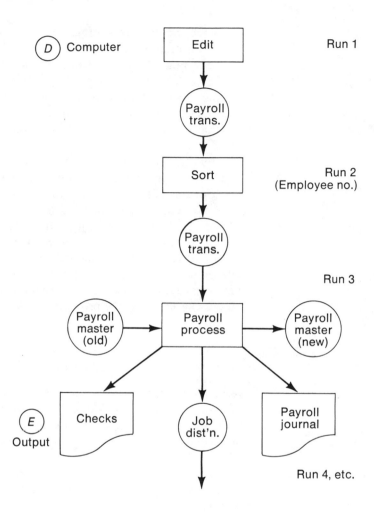

Figure 8.6 (continued)

sole printout if the totals do not agree. A record count total would also be useful.

In run No. 3, the update run, the programmed tests could perform:

(a) Check header labels on all files and write new labels for files created.

(b) Test the gross pay calculation for each employee against the predetermined limit. (The amount of the limit should be determined by discussions with the personnel department in the system design phase.) Any calculations exceeding that limit should be processed, but before distributing the checks, they should be reported on an exception basis, which is reviewed by the payroll department.

(c) Print out on an error report NO MASTER and NO TIME REPORTED conditions.

(d) Compare each number and name on transactions file records against the name and number on master file records. This will ensure that transaction data are being "posted" to the proper master record.

(e) Accumulate a total on gross pay for all employees, which must agree with accumulated total costs distributed to open jobs.

(f) Develop control totals for each file processed and check against totals recorded on the trailer labels on all input files, and write new totals on trailer labels for output files. The control totals in this case could be a total of the number of records processed and the number of records added and deleted.

(g) Balance the number of checks written with the number of blank checks issued. Any discrepancy should be reconciled, and any misprinted checks should be properly destroyed by the internal control group.

2. Following are some of the output controls that could be implemented by the internal control group and the user department:

(a) Reconcile totals recorded on the balance listing with those totals listed on the control log, adjusting the former in terms of rejected items shown on the error report generated during edit run No. 1.

(b) Balance totals on the balance listing to totals on the payroll journal.

(c) Review all computer printouts for printer malfunctions: garbled characters and blanks, errors, reasonableness, and completeness of output.

(d) Make certain that output was distributed only to authorized users.

(e) Maintain a copy of error reports for their records and follow-up.

(f) The user department also has responsibilities with respect to reviewing output for reasonableness, accuracy, and validity. In our payroll application, these responsibilities include reviewing the payroll journal to determine overall reasonableness and completeness, and to check agreement of journal control totals with any control totals developed independently by the user department. (These totals may be number of employees, gross pay, hours invoiced, or the like.) Further, the user department should provide the data processing department with complete feedback on any errors they find. Specific procedures should be established for this feedback.

Exercise 4   To illustrate the audit-trail notion, let us use the payroll and job-costing system discussed previously in this chapter.

Suppose an employee receives his paycheck and politely suggests that his check did not reflect all the time he worked during that period. Furthermore, he does not understand all the deductions. An audit trail in the payroll system provides the means by which his questions may be answered.

You will note on the flowchart (Figure 8.6) that an audit trail, in this system, will consist of the following documents: source documents (time cards and job tickets), balance listing, error reports, and payroll journal. In addition, the payroll and personnel departments should have documents supporting "permanent" data contained in the master records for each employee. The documents would cover such items as wage rate, FICA taxes, health insurance, payroll savings, and so forth.

In this exercise, determine how you would use the audit trail in the system to answer the employee's questions. Take a few minutes to jot down your answers before reading on.

Solution

Perhaps your first inclination would be to take the employee's request and shove it off on the personnel department, but that may not be the best approach, and the personnel department will have to use the audit trail anyhow.

In all likelihood, you would start with the payroll journal, which should show, for each employee, the gross pay, amount of each deduction, and net pay. The journal may even provide data on his wage rate and hours worked. You have to work back from the payroll journal to the time card for this employee to support the hours used in the payroll calculations. The time card should be examined for approval by the foreman and the actual hours should be shown to the employee. If he disagrees with the hours shown on the approved time card, it should be suggested that he take the matter up with his foreman. As to the propriety and reasonableness of the deductions, perhaps someone in the payroll department should *first* determine what deductions have been authorized by the employee and what deductions are necessary to satisfy the taxing authorities. These should then be explained to the individual employee. It may be that he does not fully understand the nature of some deductions, that errors in calculations were made, or that deductions were made for which there has been no authorization.

Summary

In this chapter we discussed application controls from the viewpoint of preventing, detecting, and correcting problems or exposures. We emphasized the need for programmed control to edit the input data and to check on the accuracy of the computerized updating of machine-readable files. We also discussed the reasons for an audit trail and some guidelines to be used in audit-trail design.

The auditor needs to make a distinction between preventive, detective, and corrective controls. However, since the auditor looks at systems, the analysis may be made according to data processing function. Below is a checklist that can be used in evaluating the application controls in client systems according to data processing function:

1. Control over Input and Output for the Application

   (*a*) What controls exist over the creation of data and their conversion to machine-readable form?

   (*b*) What controls exist over the transmittal and input of data to detect the loss or nonprocessing of data (i.e., financial control totals, hash control totals, record counts, sequential numbering of input documents)?

   (*c*) How are those input control totals and control totals developed during computer processing runs for this application checked and reconciled? Who does the checking and reconciliation?

   (*d*) If data transmission is used, what controls are used to determine that transmission is correct and no messages are lost?

   (*e*) How are the input data tested for validity, correctness, and sequence? (In answering this question, you may wish to comment on how each important data field of the input is validated.)

   (*f*) How is the distribution of output controlled?

   (*g*) What control function does the internal processing control group or user department exercise in evaluating the quality of output?

2. Program Control over Computer Processing for the Application

   (*a*) What control totals are used to check the completeness of processing?

   (*b*) Are tape label checks used, and if not, what controls are exercised to make sure that the proper files are being processed?

   (*c*) How are limit tests used to check the reasonableness of significant items in the transactions being processed?

   (*d*) What controls are used to ensure that all important arithmetic calculations are performed correctly?

3. Control over Handling of Errors

   (*a*) How does the application provide for adequate console printout of control information, such as switch settings, control violations, operator intervention, etc.?

(b)   What restart provisions are provided when a program is interrupted?

(c)   What controls exist for identifying, correcting, and reprocessing data rejected by the program as a result of program control?

(d)   How are unmatched transactions handled (where there is no master record corresponding to the transaction record)?

4. Control over Program and Data Files

(a)   What documentation exists for the application?

(b)   How are the test data documented and kept up to date?

(c)   What controls exist over master-file changes?

(d)   How are the contents of master files periodically checked to ensure that thc data are properly authorized?

(e)   What backup and reconstruction provisions exist for the application?

5. Audit Trail

(a)   What records or references exist to allow tracing any transaction forward to a final total, or any summary total or account balance back to the original source document or input?

(b)   How does the system provide historical information of the activity in financial accounts and a periodic trial balance or listing of the financial accounts?

(c)   How are the source documents retained, and for what time period, to allow easy accessibility and identification with related output records and documents?

Problems

1. The following multiple-choice questions have been adapted from recent CPA examinations. They cover controls discussed in this chapter and in the previous one.

(a)   Daylight Corporation's organization chart provides for a controller and an EDP manager, both of whom report to the financial vice president. Internal control would not be strengthened by

(i)   Assigning the programming and operating of the computer to an independent control group, which reports to the controller

(ii)   Providing for maintenance of input data controls by an independent control group, which reports to the controller

        (*iii*)   Rotating periodically among machine operators the assignments of individual application runs

        (*iv*)   Providing for review and distribution of computer output by an independent control group, which reports to the controller

(*b*)   Minimum requirements for effective documentation of the data processing system should include

        (*i*)   Hash totals

        (*ii*)   Source documents

        (*iii*)   Batch control tickets

        (*iv*)   Program flowcharts

(*c*)   A technique for controlling identification numbers (part number, man number, etc.) is

        (*i*)   Self-checking digits

        (*ii*)   Echo checks

        (*iii*)   Parity control

        (*iv*)   File protection

(*d*)   In a batch processing system, control over the punching into cards of hours worked could be most efficiently established by use of

        (*i*)   Dual punching

        (*ii*)   Batch verification

        (*iii*)   Hash totals

        (*iv*)   Sight checking

(*e*)   A situation that would represent a serious internal control problem is

        (*i*)   Maintenance of controls by machine operators

        (*ii*)   A disk-to-cards dump performed monthly

        (*iii*)   Key verification of selected fields in punched cards

        (*iv*)   Backup files stored in off-premises facilities

(*f*)   The primary documentation upon which a company should rely for an explanation of how a particular program operates is the

        (*i*)   Run manual

        (*ii*)   Periodic memory dump

        (*iii*)   Maintenance of three generations of master files

        (*iv*)   Echo-check printout

(*g*)   The basic form of backup used in magnetic tape operations is called

        (*i*)   Odd parity check

        (*ii*)   Dual-head processing

        (*iii*)   File-protection rings

        (*iv*)   The son–father–grandfather concept

(*h*)   In designing a payroll system, it is known that no individual's paycheck can amount to more than $300 for a single week. As a result, the payroll program has been written to bypass writing a

check and will print out an error message if any payroll calculation results in more than $300. This type of control is called
- (*i*)   A limit or reasonableness test
- (*ii*) Error review
- (*iii*) Data validity test
- (*iv*) Logic sequence test

(*i*)   The night operator understood more about programming than anyone realized. Working through the console, he made a change in a payroll program to alter the rate of pay for an accomplice in an operating department. The fraud was discovered accidentally after it had been going on for several months. The best control procedure would be
- (*i*)   Review of console log for unauthorized intervention
- (*ii*) Payroll review and distribution controls outside of data processing
- (*iii*) Audit trail use of payroll journal output
- (*iv*) Control total review

(*j*)   A customer payment recorded legibly on the remittance advice as $13.01 was entered into the computer from punched cards as $1,301.00. The best control procedure would be
- (*i*)   A limit test
- (*ii*) A valid field test
- (*iii*) Keypunch verification
- (*iv*) A check digit

(*k*)   A program for the analysis of sales provided questionable results, and data processing personnel were unable to explain how the program operated. The programmer who wrote the program no longer works for the company. The best control procedure would be
- (*i*)   A run manual
- (*ii*) Operator instructions
- (*iii*) Layouts
- (*iv*) Assembly-run checking

(*l*)   Due to an unusual program error that had never happened before, the accounts receivable updating run did not process three transactions. The error was not noted by the operator because he was busy working on a card-punch malfunction. There were control totals for the file that were printed out. An examination of the console printout would have disclosed the error. The best control procedure would be
- (*i*)   An error message requiring operator response before processing continues
- (*ii*) Reconciliation of control totals by control clerk

     (*iii*) Internal audit review of console log

     (*iv*) Label checking by next computer program

  (*m*) A new computer program to process accounts payable was unreliable and would not handle the most common exceptions. The best control procedure would be

     (*i*) Test data

     (*ii*) Documentation

     (*iii*) An error report

     (*iv*) Assembly-run error printouts

  (*n*) A batch of cards was next to the computer waiting for processing. The personnel manager, showing some visitors through the installation, pulled a card from the batch to show the visitors what it looked like. He absentmindedly put the card into his pocket rather than back into the batch. The missing card was not detected when the batch was processed. The best control procedure would be a

     (*i*) Trailer label

     (*ii*) Transmittal control log

     (*iii*) Control total

     (*iv*) Missing-data check

  (*o*) An apparent error in input data describing an inventory item received was referred back to the originating department for correction. A week later the department complained that the inventory in question was incorrect. Data processing could not easily determine whether or not the item had been processed by the computer. The best control procedure would be

     (*i*) Input edit checks

     (*ii*) Missing-data validity check

     (*iii*) Transmittal control

     (*iv*) An error log

  (*p*) A weekly payroll check was issued to an hourly employee based on 98 hours worked instead of 38 hours. The time card was slightly illegible and the number looked somewhat like 98. The best control procedure would be

     (*i*) A hash total

     (*ii*) A code check

     (*iii*) Desk checking

     (*iv*) A limit test

  (*q*) A sales transaction document was coded with an invalid customer account code (seven digits rather than eight). The error was not detected until the updating run when it was found that there was no such account to which the transactions could be posted. The best control procedure would be

     (*i*) Parity checks

     (*ii*) Keypunch verification

        (*iii*)   A hash total check

        (*iv*)   A check digit

(*r*)   An expense report was prepared by the cost center. One executive questioned one of the amounts and asked for the source documents that support the total. Data processing was not able to routinely do so. The best control procedure would be

        (*i*)   An error listing

        (*ii*)   An audit trail

        (*iii*)   Transmittal control

        (*iv*)   Documentation

2.   For the following problem, describe weaknesses in internal control over information and data flows and the procedures for processing shipping notices and customer invoices and recommended improvements in the controls and processing procedures. Organize your answer sheets as follows:

Weakness	Recommended Improvement

George Beemster, CPA, is examining the financial statements of the Louisville Sales Corporation, which recently installed an off-line electronic computer. The following comments have been extracted from Mr. Beemster's notes on computer operations and the processing and control of shipping notices and customer invoices:

To minimize inconvenience Louisville converted without change its existing data processing system, which utilized tabulating equipment. The computer company supervised the conversion and has provided training to all computer department employees (except keypunch operators) in systems design, operations, and programming.

Each computer run is assigned to a specific employee, who is responsible for making program changes, running the program, and answering questions. This procedure has the advantage of eliminating the need for records of computer operations because each employee is responsible for his own computer runs.

At least one computer department employee remains in the computer room during office hours, and only computer department employees have keys to the computer room.

System documentation consists of those materials furnished by the computer company: a set of record formats and program listings. These and the tape library are kept in a corner of the computer department.

The company considered the desirability of programmed controls but decided to retain the manual controls from its existing system.

Company products are shipped directly from public warehouses, which forward shipping notices to general accounting. There a billing clerk enters the price of the item and accounts for the numerical sequence of shipping notices from each warehouse. The billing clerk also prepares daily adding machine tapes ("control tapes") of the units shipped and the unit prices.

Shipping notices and control tapes are forwarded to the computer department for keypunching and processing. Extensions are made on the computer. Output consists of invoices (in six copies) and a daily sales register. The daily sales register shows the aggregate totals of units shipped and unit prices, which the computer operator compares to the control tapes.

All copies of the invoice are returned to the billing clerk. The clerk mails three copies to the customer, forwards one copy to the warehouse, maintains one copy in a numerical file, and retains one copy in an open invoice file that serves as a detail accounts receivable record.

3. Which of the control techniques would you suggest using for data conversion and transmission in the following situations? (You may use more than one control technique.)

   (*a*) Sales orders, where data are initially recorded on sales order forms and then punched into cards. Typically, these sales orders would show the customer's name and number, quantity sold, and salesman's name and number.

   (*b*) Cash receipts, which show customer number and the amount received from customers.

   (*c*) Changes to wage-rate field in payroll master records.

4. What is the basic purpose of programmed controls and how do programmed controls operate?

5. In each of the following situations, explain how the reasonableness check will be performed by a computer editing process, and indicate what information would be necessary to accomplish the editing.

   (*a*) A manufacturer wants the amount on each incoming customer order to be checked against predetermined credit limits.

   (*b*) A medical insurance company wants each claim to be checked to report any maternity benefits claimed by anyone except married females.

   (*c*) A wholesaler wants all payrates checked against pay scales established by union contract.

   (*d*) A hospital pharmacy wants all drug requests from patient floors to be compared with predetermined normal dosages.

   (*e*) A research company wants all time cards showing direct time charges to research contracts to be checked as to the validity of those contracts.

6. Bill Goatly, CPA, has examined the financial statements of the Frey Manufacturing Company for several years and is making preliminary plans for the audit for the year ended June 30. During this examination, Goatly plans to use a set of generalized audit programs. Frey's EDP manager has agreed to prepare special tapes of data from company records for the CPA's use with the GAPs.

The following information is applicable to Goatly's examination of Frey's accounts payable and related procedures:

(*a*)   The formats of pertinent tapes are given below.

(*b*)   The following monthly runs are prepared:

  (*i*)   Cash disbursements by check number

  (*ii*)   Outstanding payables

  (*iii*) Purchase journals arranged (1) by account charged and (2) by vendor

(*c*)   Vouchers and supporting invoices, receiving reports, and purchase order copies are filed by vendor code. Purchase orders and checks are filed numerically.

(*d*)   Company records are maintained on magnetic tapes. All tapes are stored in a restricted area within the computer room. A grandfather–father–son policy is followed for retaining and safeguarding tape files.

The questions in Problems 2 and 6 have been adapted by permission from recent CPA examinations.

7. The Perry and Porter Corporation seems to have been having inventory shortages during the past few months. However, they have had difficulty in determining the exact shortage because they do not want to spend the money to take a physical inventory. Their regular physical inventory is not scheduled for another six months. You have been asked to help with this control problem.

The Perry and Porter Corporation maintains perpetual inventory records. When orders are received, they are entered into the computer through a terminal. The terminal records the ordered product number and ordered quantity. Then a shipping document is transmitted to the distribution center. While the order is usually shipped the same day, it may be two to three days before confirmation is received in the computer system that the order was actually shipped. The perpetual-inventory-on-hand balance is not reduced until the shipping confirmation is received. Sometimes there are shortages of inventory on the floor and part of a shipment ordered cannot be sent. In those cases a document is prepared showing the actual quantity shipped. Again, it takes two to three days for this information to reach the computer.

Ordered inventory is received in the distribution area. If the inventory is acceptable, it is moved into the storage area, but the paperwork takes two to three days for processing. Until processing is complete, the perpetual inventory record in the computer system does not include the inventory recently received in the distribution center.

What the controller wants is a procedure that will enable the corporation to take a physical inventory for only one or two products, and then get a record from the perpetual inventory system of the amount of inventory that should have been on hand at the time the physical inventory was taken. This encompasses reconciling inventory received in the distribution center but not recorded on the perpetual inventory record, and inventory removed from the distribution center and shipped to customers but not recorded in the perpetual inventory quantities. What type of procedures would you recommend to enable a computer-generated inventory amount to be developed that can be reconciled to a spot inventory count in the distribution center?

Cases

Collateral Deposit

Dan Matt, a junior auditor for Kramp and Co., was assigned the responsibility of conducting a preliminary application review of a client bank's loan department operations.

Dan had completed his flowchart and explanation of the loan process and turned it over to his senior. He was writing up his assessment of the process from his notes when his senior interrupted and asked what happened to the collateral received on loans. Dan recognized the significance of this omission and agreed to check it out right away.

Collateral can be anything of value acceptable to the bank, but is typically some type of security. Dan found that customers turn over any collateral to their loan officer, who prepares a prenumbered four-part form that describes the collateral and serves as a receipt. Each copy of the form is a different color to facilitate identification. The customer receives the original of the collateral receipt form, which is pink. The second (white) copy of the form is sent directly to the collateral records clerk. The loan officer takes the third (blue) copy to the vault custodian along with the collateral. The final (yellow) copy is filed for reference purposes. In the loan officer's presence, the vault custodian compares the blue copy of the receipt with the collateral. If they are in agreement, the vault custodian signs the blue copy. He then attaches a tag to the collateral, and carries it and the blue copy of the collateral receipt to the vault attendant. The vault attendant also compares the description on the blue copy with the tagged collateral. If they match, the vault attendant opens the vault and jointly with the vault custodian deposits the collateral within. The vault attendant notes the location on the blue copy and signs it. The completed blue copy is then sent by the vault attendant to the collateral clerk. Until the blue copy is received, the collateral clerk keeps the unmatched white copy filed numerically.

Upon receipt of the blue copy from the vault attendant, the collateral clerk compares it to the white copy previously received directly from the loan officer. If the blue and white copy are in agreement, the collateral clerk makes an entry in the collateral register in numerical order. The white copy is then destroyed and the blue copy of the collateral receipt is placed in a permanent file by name. Any differences are resolved with the loan officer's assistance.

Questions

1. Prepare a flowchart of the collateral receipt process.
2. Indicate any apparent weaknesses pointed out in the description of the collateral receipt process.

Collateral Withdrawal

Dan Matt drew up a flowchart for the depositing of collateral (Case 1) and turned it over to his senior. The senior inquired if collateral were only deposited and never withdrawn. Dan realized that he had not followed the collateral process through to its completion. He still had to investigate the withdrawal of collateral, which resulted when the loan was paid.

Dan found that the customer initiates the withdrawal of collateral by presenting the pink receipt copy to the loan officer. The loan officer forwards the customer's request for return of his collateral to the collateral clerk who prepares a prenumbered, four-part withdrawal form. Each copy of the form is a different color to facilitate its distribution. The original (pink) of the request is sent back to the loan officer, the second (blue) copy is sent to the vault custodian, and the third (white) copy is filed by the collateral clerk with the deposit form. Again, the yellow (fourth) copy is filed for future reference. The vault custodian takes the blue copy of the request to the vault attendant, and together they remove the collateral and match it against the request. If they match, both the vault custodian and the vault attendant sign the blue copy of the request. If they are not in agreement, the vault custodian contacts the loan officer to iron out the discrepancy. The signed blue copy is sent back to the loan officer, accompanied by the collateral. The loan officer verifies that everything is proper and then signs the blue copy and turns the collateral over to the customer. The customer, after verifying that the collateral is correct, signs the pink copy of the request, which had been on file with the loan officer. Then both the blue and the pink copies are returned to the collateral clerk. The collateral clerk matches the two copies of the request to the white copy in his file. If they are all in agreement, he records the return of the collateral in his log, staples the copies together, and files them in the completed file by number.

Questions

1. Prepare a flowchart of the collateral withdrawal process using the description given in the case.

2. Indicate any apparent weaknesses in the collateral withdrawal process as described.

Manual Versus Computerized Systems   Two versions of the same transactions follow: one is a manual version, one is computerized. Determine how controls change when the system is computerized and what control weaknesses exist in each system. Compare the weaknesses and relate them to the use or absence of use of a computer.

Manual System

MIDWEST ATHLETIC SUPPLIES, INC.
COMPANY PROCEDURES
SALES AND ACCOUNTS RECEIVABLE
12–31–DD

Sales   Midwest Athletic Supplies, Inc. is a wholesale distributor of athletic and sporting equipment and sells to a wide range of customers—including retail stores, schools, clubs, and professional athletic organizations. Credit limits and credit terms vary widely among the company's customers.

The company employs no salesmen of its own. All sales are made from the company's catalog, which is reprinted every six months. Several independent jobbers buy from the company at catalog prices and resell at whatever markup they can get.

There are two order clerks in the sales department. Approximately 60 percent of all orders are received in the mail and the remainder are received by telephone. The order clerks prepare a two-part prenumbered sales order form for each order received. The order form shows the customer name and address and the catalog numbers, quantity, unit price, and extended price for all items ordered. The copy of the order form is retained in the sales department in numerical order and the original is sent to Marvin Betts, the credit manager.

A separate accounts receivable card is maintained for each customer. In addition to the current balance, the accounts receivable card shows the established credit limit and credit terms. Mr. Betts compares each sales order form with the customer's accounts receivable card to ensure that the order will not exceed the credit limit. He then notes the terms of sales on the order form and signs it before sending it to the warehouse. Mr. Betts is responsible for establishing credit limits for new customers and for reviewing all credit limits at least semi-annually. In addition, his approval must be obtained before an account is written off. He reviews the monthly accounts receivable aging. During the ten years

Mr. Betts has been with the company, Midwest has had very few uncollectible accounts. Mr. Betts takes great pride in the fact that his company has a much better collection experience than most of its competitors.

When the approved sales order form is received in the warehouse, the merchandise is removed from stock and packed, but not sealed. The order number is written on the packing carton, stock-out items are lined out on the order form, and the order form is signed and sent to the billing clerk.

The billing clerk prepares a four-part prenumbered sales invoice, which lists only the items packed (as opposed to the items ordered, which would include stock-out items). The billing clerk checks the unit prices used on the order form to the current catalog. The invoice also shows the sales order number. The billing clerk enters the invoice number and amount on the daily sales listing. The daily sales listing is totaled at the end of the day and is used to prepare the daily entry in the sales journal, which is, in turn, posted to the ledger at the end of the month. The daily sales listings are filed in chronological order.

The original of the sales invoice is mailed to the customer after it has been posted to the accounts receivable cards. The first copy is filed in numeric order. The second copy is sent to the warehouse as authorization to ship the order and is packed with the shipment. The third copy, together with the original sales order form, is returned to the sales department where it is matched with the sales department's copy of the order form. The order clerks check the accuracy of the invoice and then file it, and both copies of the order form, numerically in a filled-order file. Stock-outs are reported to the purchasing agent and unfilled orders over one week old are followed up by the head of the sales department.

Cash Receipts   Substantially all cash receipts are received by mail. All payments are by check; the receipt of cash in the mail is extremely rare. All mail is opened by the receptionist. All sales orders are sent to the sales department. The receptionist prepares an adding machine tape of cash receipts that she gives to Bob Murphy, the controller. She then sends the receipts to the billing clerk for posting to the accounts receivable cards. After posting the receivable cards, the billing clerk prepares a tape of the cash receipts and a cash journal entry. The receipts, tape, and cash journal entry are sent to Bob Murphy who compares the totals to the tape prepared by the receptionist. Bob's secretary makes the deposit each day and returns the authenticated deposit slip to Bob. Bob approves the cash journal entry and gives it to the general ledger clerk for posting.

End-of-Month Procedures   The general ledger clerk posts the cash journal (which includes receipts and disbursements) to the general ledger.

The general ledger clerk totals the sales journal and posts the totals to the general ledger.

The billing clerk prepares an aged trial balance of receivables, from the receivable cards, and gives it to Mr. Betts who reviews it and compares the total to the balance in the general ledger control account.

Computerized System

MIDWEST ATHLETIC SUPPLIES, INC.
COMPANY PROCEDURES
SALES AND ACCOUNTS RECEIVABLE
12–31–EE

Sales   Midwest Athletic Supplies, Inc. is a wholesale distributor of athletic and sporting equipment and sells to a wide range of customers—including retail stores, schools, clubs, and professional athletic organizations. Credit limits and credit terms vary widely among the company's customers.

The company employs no salesmen of its own. All sales are made from the company's catalog (which is reprinted every six months) or through independent jobbers who buy from the company at catalog prices and resell at whatever markup they can get.

There are two order clerks in the sales department. Approximately 60 percent of all orders are received in the mail and the remainder are received by telephone. The order clerks prepare a single copy of a prenumbered sales order form for each order received. The order form shows the customer name and number and the catalog numbers and quantities for all items ordered.

Each afternoon, at four o'clock, all the sales orders written since four o'clock on the previous afternoon are batched. The control clerks prepare a two-copy batch-header form, which shows the following:

- The name of the document (sales orders forms)
- The date of the batch
- A control total of quantities on all of the order forms
- A hash total of catalog numbers on the order forms
- A hash total of customer numbers
- A record count

The copy of the batch-header is retained in the sales department. The original is sent to the EDP department with the batched sales orders.

Since the EDP department is quite small, the controller, Bob Murphy, performs the functions that would be performed by an EDP manager and system analyst in a large installation. In the latter capacity, as systems analyst, Bob relies heavily on the computer manufacturer's representatives and confines himself primarily to establishing requirements for information. The following are the other client personnel involved in EDP:

- *Agnes Fowler (programmer)*—Agnes has written all the programs currently being used in the revenue cycle application. The programs are all written in the COBOL language because, at present, the company has only a COBOL compiler. Agnes is familiar with the FORTRAN, RPG, and PL/1 languages as well. Bob Murphy has issued strict instructions that Agnes is never to operate the computer during the actual processing of live data.

- *Beatrice Koot (computer operator)*—Beatrice was formerly the billing clerk. In 19EE the company sent her to the computer manufacturer's operators' school.

- *Cynthia Bell and Margaret Heck (keypunch operators)*—Cynthia is in charge of the keypunch operation and Margaret reports to her. The company has two keypunch machines and one key verifier machine. In addition to keypunching, Cynthia has the following duties.

> She maintains a log of computer operations showing date, application (program used), operator name, time started, time finished, and a description of problems encountered.
>
> She maintains control over batch-headers and compares control totals, hash totals, and record counts to the amount shown on the printed output.
>
> She maintains a copy of all error listings and checks errors off as they are subsequently corrected and reprocessed by the user department. She is responsible for follow-up with the user department on all uncorrected errors after four days.

When the daily batch of sales orders is received in keypunching by Cynthia, she checks the accuracy of the record count shown on the batch-header. She (or Margaret) then punches a separate IBM card for each item on each sales order—showing sales order number, customer number, catalog number, and quantity. All these fields are then key verified before the cards are sent into the computer room. At this time, the sales orders and batch-header are sent back to the sales department where they are held awaiting the printed output.

Beatrice runs the punched cards against a card-to-tape conversion program, which converts the sales order data on the punched cards to magnetic tape. The tape of transactions can then be conveniently stored and the cards destroyed. During this card-to-tape routine several edit checks of the input data are made:

- Because the company's customer numbers all range between 1000 and 4890, although there are some gaps in this sequence, a validity check on the customer number is performed.

- Because the catalog numbers range from 30700 to 98500, a validity check on the catalog number is performed.

- The company's experience has shown that, although quantities ordered vary widely between products and customers, an order for a quantity in excess of 200 or any item is rare. Therefore a limit check on quantities is performed.

The company's detailed accounts receivable file is now maintained on a magnetic tape file ("accounts receivable master file"). This file contains a record for each customer showing the same information that was previously shown on the receivable cards. The records are arranged on the tape file in customer number order.

The company maintains an inventory-catalog file on magnetic disks. The records within the inventory-catalog file are arranged in catalog number order and include the following items of information for each catalog number:

ITEM	EXAMPLE
Catalog number	71433
Description	Shuttlecock
Unit of measure	3.0
Unit cost	0.70
Unit selling price	0.85
Quantity on hand	240.0

Since the accounts receivable master file is maintained on tape in customer order number and since the transaction file of the day's sales orders is in sales order number order, the transaction file is run through the computer against a sorting program, which produces a new transaction tape sorted into customer order number.

The client has four tape drives plus the disk pack equipment. The inventory-catalog file is loaded on the disk pack. The sorted transaction file and the accounts receivable master file are loaded onto tape drives #1 and #2, respectively, and blank tapes are loaded onto the other two tape drives. Then the processing run is started.

The first record on the transaction file is matched, by customer number, with the appropriate record on the accounts receivable master file. Then the quantity ordered is compared to the quantity on hand as shown on the inventory-catalog file. If the quantity on hand is less than the quantity ordered, or if the catalog number cannot be found in the inventory-catalog file, then the transaction is printed out on an error listing at the console typewriter and the computer reads the next transaction record. Otherwise, the quantity ordered is subtracted from the quantity on hand and the new quantity on hand is recorded in working storage until all items on that order have been successfully processed, (i.e., all part numbers correct, sufficient quantity on hand and invoice as a whole does not exceed credit limit). Next, the quantity ordered is multiplied by the unit selling price to obtain the extended amount. The extended amount is added to the receivable balance, as shown in the accounts receivable master file, and this sum is compared to the credit limit, which is also included in the accounts receivable master file. If the credit limit is exceeded, the transaction is listed on the error listing and the master record for that customer is not updated. The inventory file is also not updated. Otherwise, the master record is updated and the sales order number and amount is added to the master record and the new balance is computed. At this time also, the on-hand inventory is updated for completed transactions. The updated customer record is written on tape drive #3 and the record on tape drive #2 (yesterday's updated master file) is not changed. (It should be noted that whenever there is a customer record for which there are no transactions, the customer record is written on tape drive #3. At the end of processing, tape drive #2 will contain the old master file and tape drive #3 will contain the new master file.)

Before proceeding to read the next transaction record, the computer writes (on tape drive #4) all of the information necessary to complete the invoice: customer name and address, catalog number, quantity, unit price, extended amount, terms, and sales order number. This file is called the daily invoice file. At the end of the daily invoice file the computer writes (1) the total number of transactions processed, (2) the total quantities processed, and (3) hash totals of customer numbers and catalog numbers for the transaction processed.

In addition, at the end of the updated accounts receivable master file, the computer writes: (1) a reconciliation of the total of accounts receivable before processing to the total after processing and (2) a hash total of customer numbers in the file.

The old receivable master file is retained for one week, as are all the transaction files.

Each day the daily invoice file is used to print the sales invoices (four copies) and the daily sales register (two copies). The first copy of the sales register is used to post the sales journal manually. The second copy is sent to the sales department, together with the error listings, where the order clerks reconcile the totals shown on the register to their pre-established batch totals. All errors are corrected and reprocessed with the next day's batch of sales orders. The sales register is filed by date with the batch-header.

The sales invoices are numbered by the computer to correspond with the sales order numbers. The second copy of the sales invoice is filed numerically in the sales department with the sales order form. The third and fourth copies are sent to the warehouse. The warehouseman pulls the merchandise from stock and packs it. He then prepares a two-part bill of lading: the original accompanies the shipment together with the third copy of the invoice; the other copy is attached to the fourth copy of the invoice and is sent to the sales department where it is matched and filed with the second copy of the invoice.

When the sales department receives the bill of lading and the fourth copy of the invoice from the warehouse, the original of the sales invoice is mailed to the customer. All documentation is filed numerically, by sales order number, in the completed order file. The head of the sales department follows up on all unfilled orders over one week old.

Cash Receipts   All mail is opened by the receptionist. She prepares a two-copy cash receipts listing which shows customer number, amount, and the number of invoice being paid (if the customer has included that information). The first copy of the listing is sent to Cynthia Bell for keypunching and the second copy, together with the receipts, is sent to Bob Murphy. Bob's secretary makes the bank deposit daily and returns the authenticated deposit slip to Bob for filing.

The receipts list is keypunched onto cards and the cards are converted to tape. Then the tape of cash transactions is sorted into customer number order and the transaction file matched with the accounts receivable master file and an updated master file is produced. A daily cash report is printed showing the transactions processed and errors are corrected and reprocessed the next day. The cash journal is posted (manually) each day from the totals on the receipts list.

EDP AUDIT PROCESS*

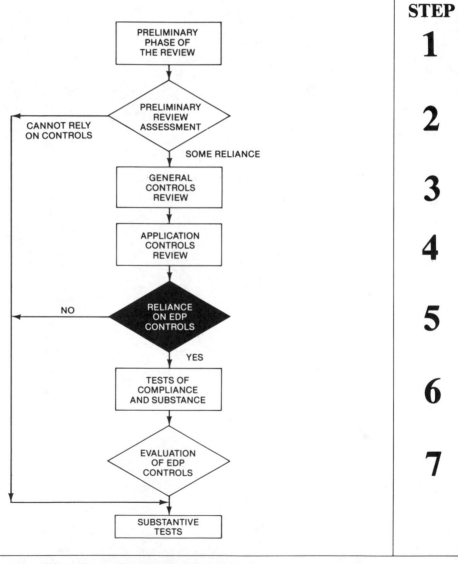

STEP

1

2

3

4

5

6

7

Diagram is adapted from The Auditor's Study and Evaluation of Internal Control in EDP Systems, *pages 21–24. Copyright © 1977 by the American Institute of Certified Public Accountants, Inc. (See Figure 9.1 for a complete explanation of the steps.)*

9

STEP

5

ADDRESSED IN THIS CHAPTER

EDP AUDIT PROCESS

(5) Completion of Review—Assessment

Purpose: For each significant accounting application

- Consider the types of errors or irregularities that could occur.
- Determine the accounting control procedures that prevent or detect such errors and irregularities.
- Assess effectiveness of EDP and non-EDP accounting controls.

Method: Judgment.

OBJECTIVE

The assessment of the adequacy of control is done by auditor judgment. In order to put judgment in perspective, the entire audit process is repeated in this chapter, with emphasis on this step of assessment.

In the preceding chapters we discussed EDP concepts and controls in order to provide a technical background to the auditor for approaching the audit examination of a client using a computer for accounting and financial applications. Now, we want to talk about auditing procedures to be used in EDP systems.

In describing these procedures, it is useful to structure the discussion in terms of the major phases of an audit examination: the evaluation of the system and the evaluation of the records produced by the data processing system.

In this chapter we shall cover the review and evaluation of the system of internal control. In Chapter 10 we shall discuss the evaluation of the records produced by the system.

The Effect of EDP
on the Audit Process

On all audits, auditing objectives remain the same whether EDP is employed or not. Auditing procedures required to accomplish these audit objectives, however, may be changed by the method of data processing used and may require the auditor to employ specialized EDP expertise.

Products of any information system, whether computerized or not, can be inaccurate or incomplete. There has been a tendency for some auditors to accept computer products as reliable simply because they are deceptively neat, which suggests accuracy, and also because there is a perception that computers never make mistakes. Auditors should not accept computer products at face value for a number of reasons. First, alterations made to data in computer files are not readily apparent when reviewing a computer product. Second, computer product reliability is affected by data processing controls, which are seldom consistently used in an organization's systems. Third, these products are produced by a technology in which continuous changes in equipment and techniques hinder long-term credibility of a system.

The reliability of computer-based products must, therefore, be evaluated so that we can determine the risks in using such products. It should be remembered that EDP controls review helps determine only the potential for error; the actual dollar value of errors, as well as the quantity of errors, must still be determined through regular audit tests.

As a general rule, the use of EDP by an organization will affect the audit process under the following circumstances:

When EDP is an important integral part of an organization's operations, the audit should include an appropriate examination of the functioning of the EDP system.

Further, if computer products or output are to be used in a report or in support of a finding, an appropriate examination should be made to provide reasonable assurance that the information is reliably consistent with its intended use.

In determining the extent of examination, the auditor should consider the importance of the computer-processed information in relation to the audit objectives and the degree of risk in using information that may contain inaccuracies.

On each assignment, the auditor must determine whether there would be a serious adverse effect on the accomplishment of the audit objectives if the information being used were incomplete or inaccurate in any material respect. The auditor is responsible for performing sufficient evaluation work to provide reasonable assurance that information, whether processed by computer or otherwise, is relevant, accurate, and complete.

Auditing EDP Applications

The audit of an EDP application can be accomplished by performing the following seven steps (see Figure 9.1 for an overview of the EDP audit process):

- Step 1—Preliminary phase of the review
- Step 2—Preliminary review assessment
- Step 3—Completion of review of general controls
- Step 4—Completion of review of application controls
- Step 5—Completion and assessment of review
- Step 6—Tests of compliance
- Step 7—Evaluation of accounting controls

The performance of each step is discussed individually.

Step 1—Preliminary Phase of the Review

"The preliminary phase of the auditor's review should be designed to provide an understanding of (a) the flow of transactions through the accounting system, (b) the extent to which EDP is used in each significant accounting application, and (c) the basic structure of accounting control." (SAS No. 3, paragraph 25.) Using this knowledge, the auditor can assess the significance of accounting control within EDP, in relation to the entire system of control, and can then determine the extent of additional review required. The depth of the preliminary phase of the review necessary to develop an understanding of each significant accounting application and its controls varies according to the nature and complexity of the system.

**Figure 9.1
Study and Evaluation
of EDP-Based
Applications***

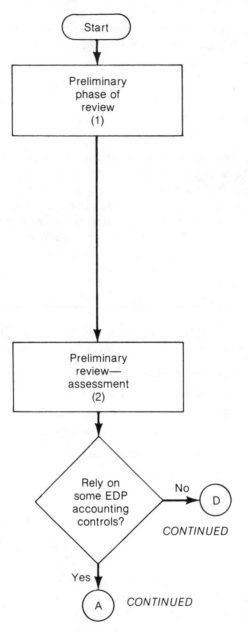

(1) Preliminary Phase of the
Review

Purpose
Understand accounting system
including both EDP and non-
EDP segments:
- Flow of transactions and
  significance of output.
- Extent to which EDP is used
  in significant accounting applications.
- Basic structure of accounting
  control, including both EDP
  and user controls.

Methods
Inquiry and discussion; observation; review of documentation;
tracing of transactions; control
questionnaires and checklists.

(2) Preliminary Phase of the
Review—Assessment

Purpose
- Assess significance of EDP and
  non-EDP accounting controls.
- Determine extent of additional
  review within EDP.

Method
Judgment.

* This chart is a simplified illustration and does not portray all possible decision paths. Note that at any
point after the preliminary phase of the review, the auditor may decide not to rely on EDP accounting controls
for all or some applications (see Statement on Auditing Standards No. 3, paragraph 26). The auditor would
then complete the design of the substantive audit tests. According to SAS No. 1, Section 320.70, substantive

**Figure 9.1
(continued)**

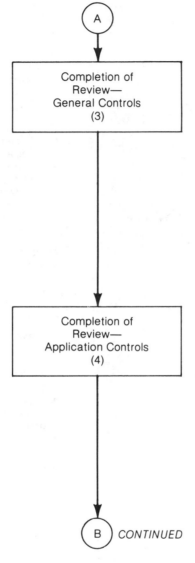

(3) Completion of Review—
    General Controls

Purpose
- Identify general controls on
  which reliance is planned and
  determine how they operate.
- Determine the effect of
  strengths and weaknesses on
  application controls.
- Consider tests of compliance
  that may be performed.

Methods
Detailed examination of documentation; interviewing internal
auditors, EDP and user department personnel; observing
operation of general controls.

(4) Completion of Review—
    Application Controls

Purpose
- Identify application controls on
  which reliance is planned, and
  determine how the controls
  operate.
- Consider tests of compliance
  that may be performed.
- Consider the potential effect of
  identified strengths and weaknesses on tests of compliance.

Methods
Detailed examination of documentation; interviewing internal
auditors, EDP, and user department personnel, observing
operation of application controls.

---

tests consist of the following classes of audit procedures: (1) tests of details of transactions and balances and
(2) analytical review of significant ratios and trends and resulting investigation of unusual fluctuations and
questionable items.

**Figure 9.1
(continued)**

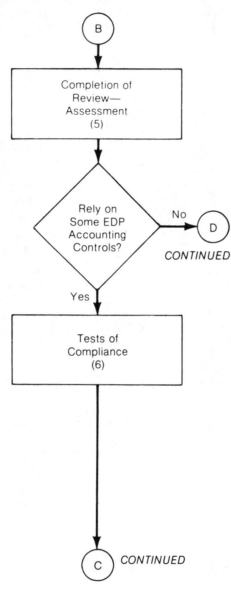

(5) Completion of Review—
Assessment

Purpose
For each significant accounting
application
- Consider the types of errors or
  irregularities that could occur.
- Determine the accounting
  control procedures that prevent
  or detect such errors and
  irregularities.
- Assess effectiveness of EDP and
  non-EDP accounting controls.

Method
Judgment.

(6) Tests of Compliance

Purpose
- Determine whether the necessary control procedures are prescribed and followed satisfactorily.
- Provide reasonable assurance
  that controls are functioning
  properly.
- Consider and, to the extent
  appropriate, document when,
  how, and by whom controls are
  provided.

Methods
Examination of records; test of
control procedures; inquiry;
observation.

**Figure 9.1
(continued)**

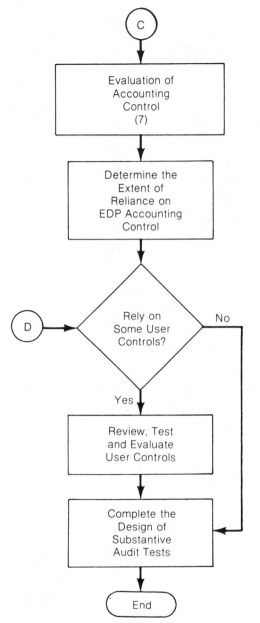

(7) Evaluation of Accounting
Control

Purpose
For each significant accounting
application
- Consider the types of errors or
irregularities that could occur.
- Determine the accounting control procedures that prevent or
detect such errors and irregularities.
- Determine whether the necessary control procedures are
prescribed and followed satisfactorily.
- Evaluate weaknesses and assess
their effect on the nature,
timing, and extent of auditing
procedures to be applied.

Method
Judgment.

During the preliminary phase of the review, the auditor should obtain an understanding of how the computer system generates the data—from preparation of source documents through final distribution and use of output. While learning how the system works, the auditor should identify potential areas for testing, using familiar audit techniques, such as these:

- Reviewing documentation—including system documentation files, input preparation instructions, and users' manuals
- Interviewing personnel—including users, systems analysts, and programmers
- Inspecting, comparing, and analyzing records

To understand document flow, certain background information must be obtained through discussions with management, from previous audits or evaluations, or from system documentation files. Because this information may not be current or complete, it should be verified with the responsible programmer or analyst. The auditor will need to obtain all this information:

- Name (title) of the computer application
- Purpose of the application
- System name and identification number
- Date the system was implemented
- Type of computer used (manufacturer's model) and location
- Frequency of processing and type of processing (batch, on-line)
- Person(s) responsible for the computer application and the data base that generates the computer product

An agency user or other person in the computer center may already have a document flow diagram showing the origin of data and how it flows to and from the computer. (This diagram should not be confused with either a system flowchart, which shows detailed computer processing of data, or a program flowchart, which describes a computer program.) More often than not, the auditor will have to develop document flow in a familiar format, whether it is a narrative description, a block diagram using simple symbols, a flowchart using standard symbols, or some combination. The document flow diagram or narrative description should show all the following data:

- Each source document by title and ID number (copies should be attached)
- The point of origin for all source documents
- Each operating unit or office through which data pass
- The destination of each copy of the source document and action taken (i.e., document filed, audited, keypunched)

- Actions taken by each unit or office through which the data pass (i.e., items recorded in a ledger, unit prices added and extensions computed, control numbers recorded and checked)
- Controls over the transfer of source documents between units or offices to ensure none are lost, added, or changed (i.e., record counts, control totals, arithmetic totals of important data, etc.)
- Recipients of computer outputs

Document flow should not describe the actual computer processing inside the "black box"; this is beyond the scope of the preliminary review. If computer output is the product of more than one input, this condition should be clearly noted in the document flow description.

Document flow in a typical payroll system is shown in Figure 9.2, which is a block diagram with rectangular symbols; Exhibit 9.1 shows the same document flow in narrative form.

The auditor must clearly understand what is being recorded by the information system; therefore, the individual elements of data must be defined. Titles can be deceptive. For example, is a cost amount for the current period or a cumulative cost? Is the cost accrued or incurred? What are the components of the cost amount? Has the composition of cost changed during the fiscal periods covered by the reviews?

The organization's data element dictionary is a good source for these definitions; however, if one is not available, a record layout may contain the needed definitions. Table 9.1 illustrates a simple record layout.

In many instances there is no one-to-one relationship between data elements and the data in a computer-processed report or file. Some common differences are shown in Table 9.2.

Step 2—Preliminary Review Assessment

After completing the preliminary phase of the review, the auditor should be in a position to assess for each significant accounting application the significance of accounting control within EDP in relation to the entire system of accounting control. Thus the auditor should be able to determine the extent of her or his review of EDP accounting control. Let's break down this assessment a little further.

The auditor may conclude that accounting control procedures within the EDP portions of the application or applications appear to provide a basis for reliance thereon and for restricting the extent of the substantive tests.

The auditor may conclude that there are weaknesses in accounting control procedures in the EDP portions of the application or applications sufficient to preclude his or her reliance on such procedures. In that event, the auditor would discontinue the review of those EDP accounting control procedures and forego performing compliance tests related to those procedures; *he or she*

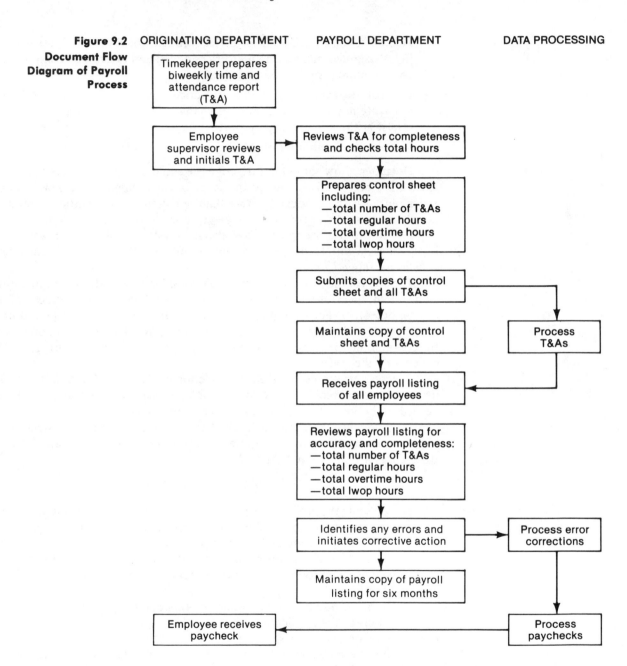

Figure 9.2 Document Flow Diagram of Payroll Process

Exhibit 9.1
Narrative Document
Flow of Payroll Process

The following procedures are used to process a biweekly employee payroll:

- At the end of the pay period, a timekeeper completes a time and attendance (T&A) report.

- The employee's supervisor reviews and initials the T&A and submits it to Payroll Department.

- Payroll clerk reviews T&A for completeness and checks total hours reported.

- When all the T&A reports are received, the payroll clerk prepares a control sheet that shows totals for number of T&A reports, number of regular hours, overtime hours, and LWOP hours.

- Payroll clerk keeps the originals and sends a copy of the control sheet and all T&A reports to Data Processing.

- Data Processing enters the payroll data on the terminal.

- At the completion of payroll processing, a listing of all employees paid is sent to the payroll clerk.

- The payroll clerk reviews the listing for completeness and accuracy—which includes a comparison of the number of T&A reports, regular hours, overtime hours, and LWOP hours with the control sheet totals.

- Any discrepancies are researched and resolved. Errors affecting pay are corrected and resubmitted to Data Processing for immediate action. Errors in leave are corrected in the subsequent pay period.

- The payroll clerk keeps the payroll listing for 6 months.

- The payroll process also prints the paycheck and mails it directly to the employee.

would not be able to rely on those EDP accounting control procedures. The auditor would assess the potential impact on the financial statements of such weaknesses as have come to her or his attention, and would accomplish the audit objectives by other means.

The auditor may decide not to extend the preliminary review and not to perform tests on compliance related to accounting control procedures (either in general or as to certain procedures) within the EDP portions of the application or applications, even though he or she concludes that the controls appear adequate. In that event, *the auditor would not be able to rely* on those EDP ac-

**Table 9.1
Record Layout:
Description of Payroll
Data File**

DATA ELEMENT	POSITION IN DATA FILE	DATA ELEMENT DESCRIPTION
SSN	1–9	Social security number
Name	10–29	Name—last, first, middle initial
Grade	30–31	Payee's grade
Salary	32–37	Yearly salary
Taxes	38–43	Weekly tax deduction
Insurance	44–49	Weekly insurance deduction
Bond code	50	Bond deduction code

BOND CODE	BOND AMOUNT	WEEKLY DEDUCTION
1	$ 100	$ 2
2	200	4
3	500	10
4	1,000	20

Hours	51–52	Hours worked during current pay period.

counting control procedures. Situations of this type could be those in which either of the following situations occurs:

1. The auditor concludes that the audit effort required to complete the review and test compliance would exceed the reduction in effort that could be achieved by reliance upon the EDP accounting controls.

**Table 9.2
Examples of Differences
Between Computer
Output and Data
Elements**

DIFFERENCES	EXPLANATION
Total deductions on a payroll report might represent an addition of several data elements (taxes + health insurance + bonds + . . .).	The computer program used to produce the report adds the individual deductions and prints the total.
Bond deductions might be represented by a 1-character code on the data file.	The computer program converts the 1-character code to a dollar amount (e.g., 1 = $100 bond, 2 = $200 bond, etc.).
Weekly salary appears on the report; only annual salary is found in the data file.	The computer program converts the yearly salary into a weekly amount through division by weeks.
Average annual salary appears as an individual statistic while annual salaries are recorded in the data file.	The computer program totals all annual salaries in the file and divides the total by the number of records.
A report might show details and summary statistics for GS–12s while the data base contains payroll information for all grade levels.	The computer program selects only GS–12 records for printing and summarization.

2. The auditor concludes that certain EDP accounting control procedures are redundant because other accounting control procedures are in existence.

Step 3—Completion of Review of General Controls

The auditor's review and evaluation of internal control provides assurance to the auditor that errors and irregularities in the system may be discovered with reasonable promptness, thus ensuring also the integrity of the financial records. The auditor's review of the processing system and its control aspects assists in determining additional auditing procedures appropriate to the formulation of an opinion on the outputs produced by that system whether they be financial statements or management reports. In determining that a company's data processing system and control procedures will provide reliable and accurate financial information, the auditor must review and evaluate the system in sufficient detail to provide reasonable certainty of the following points:

- The input data are correctly recorded and transcribed.
- All authorized transactions are processed without additions or omissions.
- The processing steps performed, such as arithmetic computations, accumulations, and comparisons, are correct.
- The output is distributed to proper individuals and on a timely basis.

Basically, the auditor evaluates the elements of an internal control system designed to provide reliable and accurate records, safeguard assets, and promote operational efficiencies in the conduct of company activities. The auditor is concerned with two primary areas of internal accounting control, namely administrative and accounting controls. Accounting controls are further broken down into general and application controls.

The approach to the review of these controls can be divided into two parts: a general review and a detailed review of specific accounting applications. The discussion in this chapter will be limited to the review and evaluation of controls in the EDP portion of the system. Non-EDP aspects of computer-based systems generally will not include procedures and controls different from those encountered by auditors in non-EDP systems today. Of course, auditors must consider the total system of internal control, not just the EDP portion.

The *general review* of the EDP system should be designed to help the auditor evaluate the administrative and general controls within the EDP system and determine the extent of the more detailed review of specific processing applications in which he or she is interested. Typically the auditor's principal sources of data for making the review are organization charts, documentation standards, and interviews with responsible data processing personnel. The manner in which the auditor retains the necessary information for her or his working papers is largely a matter of individual or firm preference. Many firms have designed EDP controls questionnaires that are useful for obtaining information on specific controls in EDP systems. Appendix B, part I, is a questionnaire used by one major public accounting firm. This accounting firm has given us permission to reproduce the questionnaire in its entirety in the book. Please refer to the questionnaire at this point so that we can discuss the types of questions that are raised and the types of controls that the questionnaire suggests the auditor should evelute.

Administrative and General Controls

As the structure of the questionnaire suggests, the review of the organization of the data processing department should begin by obtaining an organization chart, if available, or by completing a chart such as the one shown in part I, B of the questionnaire. The organization of the EDP department should be such that there is a division of functional responsibilities and duties between systems designers, programmers, and computer operators and that the staffing of these functions is made with competent personnel.

Segregation of Duties Questions 1a, 2, 3, and 4 in part I, D of the questionnaire relate to the segregation of duties within the EDP department. As was discussed in Chapter 5, it is necessary to separate the systems planning and programming function, machine-operating function, and the control function in order to maintain the continued integrity of the system where the authorization and recording function are embodied in the program itself.

Rotation of Personnel Questions 5 and 6 in part I, D of the questionnaire relate to a general plan of rotation of the various processing jobs among operators and to policies for vacation. Periodic rotation is desirable to check on the effectiveness of a person who normally processes the same application; it also ensures that more than one person will be familiar with a particular application. Periodic or annual vacations are desirable for the same reason.

Limited Access Another important aspect of organizational control is limiting access to the computer room to only authorized personnel. Typically, only computer operating personnel should have access to the machine room. Such restrictions enhance operational efficiency by minimizing interruptions to processing schedules. By preventing systems designers and programming personnel from having access to the computer or any data files, the company can prevent or make difficult any fraudulent tampering with the information contained in the files of the company.

Operating Practices

The management of the data processing resource encompasses many activities and operating practices: planning of future applications; development of documentation standards to promote adequate documentation of existing applications; development of control procedures over input and output; implementation of program testing and program change procedures; protection of files from hazards such as fire, theft, and inadvertent destruction; development of equipment maintenance and file-reconstruction procedures, and backup support to minimize interruptions in processing; and provision of adequate insurance to provide financial protection against interruptions in processing and loss of equipment, software, and data files.

Future Applications   Part I, C of the questionnaire suggests that the auditor determine existing applications and those planned in the future. Planning of new applications and the scheduling and control of resources committed to new applications is an important part of the management of the data processing department. Normally, an EDP steering committee, made up of executives throughout the company involved in data processing, is responsible for developing and approving an overall plan for future applications—including a timetable of implementation, equipment and personnel resources to be committed to new applications, and yardsticks to be used to measure actual progress compared to plan.

The auditor should review existing applications to help plan the current audit examination. He or she should review planned applications to determine what process the company uses to plan and control systems efforts and to determine what future applications will significantly affect the audit examinations in the future.

Documentation   Questions 10 to 14 and 23 of the questionnaire (part I, D) relate to documentation standards. Documentation is essential for management's understanding of applications, for a review of existing systems by analysts and programmers, and for making changes to existing applications. The auditor's review of documentation standards provides information about the operating efficiency of the systems and programming activities. Documentation also provides the auditor with information about the existence of the particular accounting and financial system under review. However, inadequate documentation does not necessarily affect the auditor's procedures in determining the existence and reliability of a system if transaction registers, error listings, and output reports are available for review and testing.

Question 23 of the questionnaire relates documentation to organization control. We noted in the discussion of organization control the need to restrict analysts and programmers, who have knowledge of program details, from access to data files. Question 23 suggests that, conversely, the operators who have access to the equipment and data files do not have documentation that provides program details. Normally, operators are given documentation that provides information on how to "run" the jobs; hence, the operating instructions provided are called *run books* and contain information set forth in question 14.

Machine Operations   Questions 15 to 19 (part I, D) relate to control over operations in the machine room, including procedures to promote adherence to operating instructions, scheduling and utilization of equipment and applications, and review and appropriate distribution of output reports. A review of such procedures again provides the auditor with information about operating efficiency. However, in the review of specific detailed financial and accounting applications, the auditor should be concerned with procedures for controlling distribution of output and for handling errors found in processing.

Vendor-Supplied Software   Most organizations develop only part of their computerized business applications. The other parts are purchased or obtained from vendors. Some of this software is used to handle the common processing functions on computers, such as inputting and outputting data, while in other instances the entire application is purchased from a software vendor.

Many of the controls necessary to ensure the accuracy and completeness of processing are incorporated within vendor-produced software. For example, operating systems have controls to ensure that records written to a computer file are not lost. Some of these controls are mandatory, while others are optional.

Vendors usually supply a piece of software that can be modified to meet specific needs of an organization. Many of these options are controls. For example, communication systems normally come with an option to include or exclude the use of passwords.

The individuals that create or generate the version of the software to be used by an organization are usually called systems programmers. The systems programmers frequently exercise great authority over what controls are included or excluded from these vendor-produced software systems. The reason that responsibility falls to the systems programmer is usually because no one else in the organization has the technical knowledge or interest to assess the value of the optional controls supplied by the vendor.

Many organizations purchase entire applications. For example, an organization may purchase a payroll system, a general ledger system, a billing accounts receivable system, etc. When these applications are used, the organization is totally dependent on the controls included by the vendor. If there are weaknesses in those controls, there may not be employees skilled enough to recognize them. Thus, the responsibility may fall on the organization's auditors, either internal or external.

Because of the growing dependence of organizations, especially smaller ones, on vendor-produced software, the need for auditor involvement in assessing controls in those systems is increasing. However, to evaluate the controls in these vendor-supplied systems usually requires more extensive data processing skills than are necessary for assessing in-house-produced applications. The reason is that with in-house-produced applications employees are available to explain the system structure and system controls. In vendor-supplied software, much of this investigation may have to be conducted by the auditor using documentation supplied by the vendor. This process is frequently hampered by the vendor's desire not to disclose the internal workings of the application. The copyright laws over computer programs are still very weak, and if the software vendor releases the computer code for examination, it could be copied and used by competitors without compensation.

Program Testing   Questions 20 to 22 (part I, D) relate to program testing and program change procedures. The auditor's review of program testing procedures provides information about the extent of the client's testing of existing programs. The client's tests provide a useful starting point for the auditor in preparing test data for his direct testing of programs, an approach to be discussed subsequently.

Program Changes   Authorization of program changes is as important, in computerized systems, as authorization of input data since the programs contain the procedures for processing input and generating output. Program changes require well-formulated and well-documented procedures to prevent the manipulation of programs for unauthorized purposes. Several procedures necessary for maintaining control of program changes were outlined previously in Chapter 5.

The auditor normally is concerned with the nature and extent of changes to programs involved in processing accounting and financial transactions. Substantial changes to such programs during the period under examination will probably require the auditor to revise his audit tests of the system. If the format of the master files has been changed and if the auditor is using computer audit programs to validate data in the files, some revisions of the computer audit programs are usually necessary.

File Protection and Retention   Questions 24 and 28 (part I, D) relate to file protection and retention. The client's practices for protection of files are important. If protection procedures are inadequate, the client may have costly interruptions in processing and reconstruction activities. Inadequate protection procedures may cause problems for the auditor since the audit trail may not be available. Inadequate retention procedures may mean the unavailability of data for audit purposes and may result in a tax liability to the client in the event records are not available for examinations by government agencies such as the Internal Revenue Service.

Knowledge of the client's retention procedures is important if the auditor wants to use the computer to validate or test the files. Without knowledge of the retention cycle, the auditor may plan to use files that no longer exist. The auditor should specify, in writing, in advance of the audit examination the files that should be retained for audit purposes.

Backup Procedures   Questions 25 to 27, 29, and 30 (part I, D) relate to procedures to minimize equipment failures, to provide backup facilities in the event of failure, and to analyze the adequacy of insurance to cover loss of data and programs and payments for use of alternative facilities. Again, the auditor should be concerned with these procedures to determine the existence and effectiveness of management practices to provide continuous operation of the data processing facilities.

Communication Procedures   These procedures involve control over access to use of computer resources as well as message control. These procedures will be discussed in more detail in Chapter 11.

At this point, you should have a pretty good idea about what is involved in the *general review* of organizational control and operating practices. Now let us turn to a discussion of the detailed review of specific accounting applications having audit significance.

Step 4—Completion of Review of Application Controls

After reviewing organization charts, documentation standards, organizational controls, and operating practices with the use of a questionnaire as shown in Appendix B, part I, the auditor should have an overall understanding of the client's system including the scope and objectives of all major applications. After this initial review, the auditor's work sheets should contain a general description of the system supported by system flowcharts and narratives (prepared by the client when available) and the completed questionnaire with notes to indicate:

- The audit significance of the EDP system to the client's operations
- The audit significance of specific applications within the system, indicating those applications to be reviewed in detail
- Any weaknesses in organizational control and operating practices and the impact of these weaknesses on auditing procedures

A detailed review and evaluation of procedural controls in an EDP system is required when the EDP system in general or certain applications in particular have audit significance. For example, the external auditor would make a detailed review when an application involves the processing of accounting and financial data that builds up account balances in financial statements.

To evaluate the procedural controls, the auditor requires:

(1) Knowledge and understanding of the procedures and methods prescribed; and (2) a reasonable degree of assurance that they are in use and are operating as planned.[1]

---

[1] AICPA, *Statement on Auditing Standards,* #1, p. 27, 1973.

These two steps in evaluation will be referred to hereafter as *review of the system* and *tests of compliance.* An AICPA task force flowcharted the steps an auditor could perform in conducting a study and evaluation of EDP-based applications (see Figure 9.1). Steps 1 to 5 involve the review of the system, and steps 6 and 7 are the tests of compliance.

Review of System

A detailed review of the system should encompass an understanding of both the details of the processing and the major controls over the major phases of the organization—input, processing, and output. A useful starting point to enable the auditor to determine the details of processing is the review of the client's documentation such as systems flowcharts, narrative description, and record layouts of transactions being processed and the master files being updated. The auditor's review of the client's documentation should be followed by inquiries of accounting and data processing personnel about the specific control aspects of the accounting and financial application. Part II of the questionnaire in Appendix B provides questions that should be asked by the auditor in reviewing a specific application. As you can note by reviewing this part of the questionnaire, the auditor should be involved in reviewing documentation for the specific application to determine the nature of the input controls, processing controls, output controls, and file controls.

Input Controls   Input controls are designed to determine that (1) all transactions have been properly recorded at the source, (2) the data are properly authorized, (3) all data have been transmitted from the recording point to the computer processing point, (4) all transactions are converted into machine-readable form, (5) all input data are validated through an editing process, and (6) all errors detected are corrected.

The questionnaire in Appendix B, part II, provides questions on the preceding steps that are primarily associated with computerized processing—namely, data transmission, data conversion, input validation, and error detection and correction. For example, questions B-1, B-4, and C-1 relate to data transmission; B-2 and B-3 relate to data conversion; C-2 relates to input validation; and B-5 relates to error correction.

Of course, the auditor should be concerned with evaluating all aspects of the client's control procedures, and must evaluate the manual portion of the system including preparation of source documents and the authorization of input data. Authorization of input data, particularly changes to master file data such as payrates and number of dependents in payroll processing, and unit costs and economic order levels in inventory processing, is extremely important in computerized systems because of the significance of such data in the calculating of financial results and in generating output. Because of the importance of these changes, normally a change record is prepared. This record may show the data contained in the file record, both before and after the changes, together with a description of the file change transaction. The change record should then be given to the departments initiating and authorizing the change.

Computer Processing Phase   The computer processing phase involves (1) sequencing or sorting transactions for updating master files; (2) comparing transaction files and master files to determine that the proper files are being procured; (3) performing arithmetic computations with certain fields of data to arrive at new totals such as inventory on hand, customer accounts-receivable balance, gross and net pay for a pay period and year to date; (4) updating the master files with the transaction data; and (5) generating updated master files in machine-readable form such as tapes or disks and generating printed reports for accounting and operational purposes.

The auditor should be concerned with reviewing the control techniques associated with each of these steps in computer processing and specific questions in Appendix B, part II, can be related to each of the steps. For example, question C-3 relates to sequencing checks; C-4 relates to file identification; and D-1 relates to file updating and the creation of output files.

Programmed controls in the computer processing phase are generally important to determine and detect loss or nonprocessing of data, to determine whether arithmetic functions have been performed correctly, and to determine that all transactions are posted to the proper records.

To detect loss or nonprocessing of data, record counts, control totals, and hash totals are developed and written on the trailer label on each file created. The resulting total can then be compared with a predetermined count or the control total established the last time the file was processed. Questions D-2, D-3, and E-1 relate to the auditor's review of procedures for establishing control totals during computer processing and reconciling these control totals to totals developed previously.

Programmed controls are also useful to check arithmetic calculations and should include checks such as limit checks, cross-footing balance checks, and overflow tests. Such checks are useful after arithmetic computations have been performed during the computer processing phase and before output is generated in order to determine the reasonableness and accuracy of the calculations processed. Such programmed checks should preclude the possibility of a "million dollar" paycheck being generated or the "$899,000 billing for two railroad tickets."

Output Controls   If a client has good input controls and good controls during computer processing, the computer output generated usually is correct. However, output controls can be used to achieve the objectives associated with the overall processing cycle. The function of output controls is to ensure that processed data do not include unauthorized alterations by the computer operations section and that output is substantially correct and reasonable. Output controls should be designed to ensure that only authorized personnel receive the output produced. The auditor should be concerned in reviewing some basic output controls (such as the comparison of control totals of data processed with totals independently obtained from prior processing) and making sure that output reports are reviewed and distributed to appropriate personnel.

File Control   Section E of part II of the questionnaire includes questions on the control of files containing accounting and financial data. File control is a very important aspect of data processing management since machine-readable records and files have replaced traditional ledgers and registers found in manual accounting systems. File control is perhaps more important in computerized systems than in manual systems because computer-readable files are more easily destroyed than manually prepared records and are more subject to misuse because the contents are not recognizable without the use of the computer. A recent newspaper article reported that a year-end ticker-tape celebration in Los Angeles resulted in the throwing out of a confidential punched-card file of shareholders and their holdings used by a firm specializing in proxy solicitations.

The auditor should review the client's file control procedures related to these concerns:

- Protection against fire and theft or other accidental damage (E-1)
- Record retention and reconstruction in the event files are destroyed (E-2)
- Periodic checking of contents of master files by printout and review (E-4)

Transaction Flow Auditing

A method used to document application controls in computerized applications is transaction flow auditing. This control review method requires the auditor to identify the following:

- The organization's cycles of business activities (such as those identified in Figure 7.3)
- The types of transactions that flow through each cycle (for example, in the payroll cycle these are new employee transactions, employee rate increase transactions, hours worked transactions, absences transactions, etc.)
- The functions performed within each cycle to recognize, authorize, process, classify, and report transactions (these are the activities performed within each cycle; for example, in a payroll system activities include authorizing a change to pay rates, the classification of absences by type, and the preparation of output such as payroll checks)
- Specific internal control objectives for each cycle
- The internal control techniques used to achieve each stated objective

Transaction flow auditing requires the auditor to develop a flowchart showing what transactions flow through the business activity being audited. As the auditor traces the transaction flow, the auditor would indicate the various functions performed on that transaction in the order in which they occur. The control objective at each point is identified, as well as the technique used to achieve that objective.

Using this flowchart of transaction processing, documented in accordance with the transaction flow auditing methodology, provides the auditor with the type of information needed to assess the adequacy of internal control.

Arthur Andersen & Co. has published a book explaining the control objectives they use in transaction flow auditing and their method of classifying those control objectives. A complete set of the objectives of internal accounting controls makes transaction flow auditing practical.

Objectives of Internal Accounting Controls

Objectives of internal control for an entity's cycles and its financial planning and control function can be developed using a step-down analysis. As shown in Figure 9.3 the analysis begins with the broad objectives of internal control contained in authoritative U.S. professional literature.

From such an analysis, two levels of objectives can be identified:

- Systems control, and financial planning and control objectives
- Cycle control objectives

The systems control and financial planning and control objectives are more specific than the broadly stated objectives of internal control contained in the authoritative literature. Cycle control objectives can be developed from the systems control objectives by refining them for the different categories of transactions found within a cycle.[2]

Systems Control Objectives   There are ten systems control objectives that apply to all accounting systems in all industries.

For convenience in reference, the systems control objectives are identified as A through J. The first four (A through D) are pervasive and deal with authorization, classification, substantiation and evaluation, and physical safeguards. The final six (E through J) address the flow of transactions through a system (Figure 9.4).

---

[2] *A Guide for Studying and Evaluating Internal Accounting Controls,* pp. 45–49, Copyright 1978, Arthur Andersen & Co.

INTERNAL CONTROL OBJECTIVES

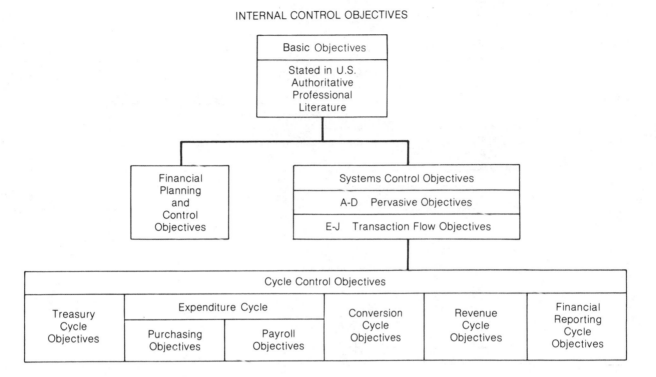

Figure 9.3   Internal Control Objectives

The systems control objectives are:

A. Authorizations should be in accordance with criteria established by the appropriate level of management.

B. Transactions should be classified in a manner that permits the preparation of financial statements in conformity with generally accepted accounting principles and management's plan.

C. Report and data base contents should be periodically substantiated and evaluated.

D. Access to assets should be permitted only in accordance with management's authorization.

E. Economic events should be recognized and submitted for acceptance on a timely basis.

F. All, and only, economic events meeting management's criteria should be accurately converted to transactions and accepted for processing on a timely basis.

RELATION OF SYSTEMS CONTROL OBJECTIVES TO TRANSACTION FLOW

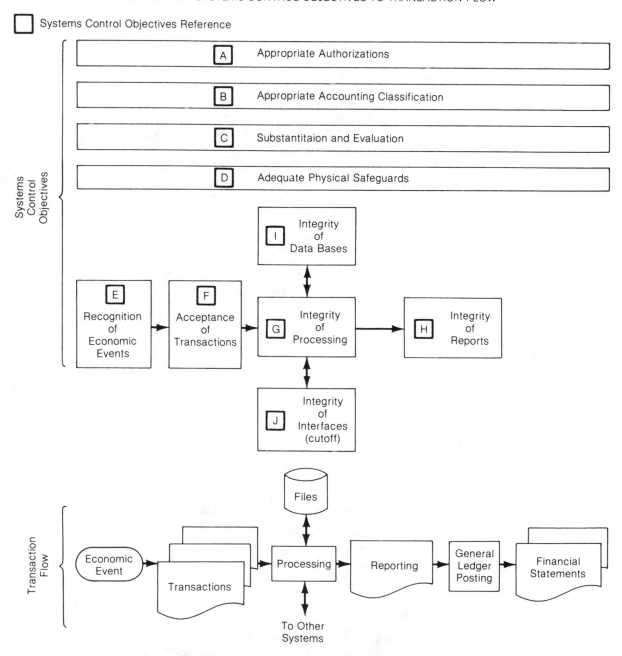

Figure 9.4   Systems Control Objectives and Transaction Flow

G. All accepted transactions should be processed accurately, in accordance with management's policies, and on a timely basis.

H. The results of processing should be reported accurately.

I. Data base elements should accurately reflect the results of processing.

J. Events affecting more than one system should result in transactions that are reflected by each system in the same accounting period.

Systems control objectives apply to all cycles. They are not intended, however, to be used directly in evaluating an entity's internal control techniques. Rather, they represent a base from which specific cycle control objectives applicable to an individual entity can be developed.

Financial Planning and Control Objectives   In addition to the ten systems control objectives, there are four financial planning and control objectives that may be used to evaluate the techniques management uses to define and communicate the objectives and business of the entity. The financial planning and control objectives also help in the assessment of long- and short-range plans for the entity and of the framework for reporting to the designated representatives of stockholders, owners, or members.

The relationship of these matters to internal accounting controls may seem remote, particularly since the management planning process extends beyond accounting and financial disciplines and embraces marketing, production, public relations, and legal and legislative considerations. A financial plan is, however, a quantification of an entity's total planning process. A well-developed, properly communicated, and effectively administered financial plan is a powerful tool for controlling economic events.

The four financial planning and control objectives are these

1. The objectives of the entity and the nature of its business activities should be defined and communicated.

2. A strategic (long-range) plan should be maintained and communicated.

3. A short-range plan should be developed and communicated.

4. Management's plans and the performance of the entity should be regularly reported to the designated representatives of the shareholders, owners, or members.

Cycle Control Objectives   Specific internal control objectives can be derived for each of an entity's recognized cycles from the systems control objectives. Cycle control objectives should address authorization, transaction processing, classification, substantiation and evaluation, and access to assets within each cycle:

- *Authorization objectives* derived from systems control objective A. These objectives address controls for securing compliance with policies and criteria established by management as part of the financial planning and control function.

- *Transaction processing objectives* derived from systems control objectives E through J. These objectives address the controls over recognition, processing, and reporting of transactions and adjustments.
- *Classification objectives* derived from systems control objective B. These objectives address controls over the source, timeliness, and propriety of journal entries.
- *Substantiation and evaluation objectives* derived from systems control objective C. These objectives address periodic substantiation and evaluation of reported balances and the integrity of processing systems.
- *Physical safeguard objectives* derived from systems control objective D. These objectives address access to assets, records, critical forms, processing areas, and processing procedures.

The illustrative cycle control objectives are oriented toward a manufacturing entity in which the following cycles are recognized:

- Treasury
- Expenditure (purchasing)
- Expenditure (payroll)
- Conversion
- Revenue
- Financial reporting

The illustrative objectives make certain assumptions about the entity. For example, the functions that are assumed to be part of the expenditure (purchasing) cycle are purchasing, receiving, accounts payable, and cash disbursements. In the conversion cycle, as another example, it is assumed that the entity has a cost accounting system.

While the illustrative cycle control objectives have a particular industry orientation and are based on a number of assumptions, they probably are usable, with only minor modifications, by many entities in a wide variety of industries.

Such modifications as are required should be made to recognize the nature of economic activity in an entity's industry and the terminology and transaction processing methods that are unique to the industry. For example, objectives identified for a particular retail company that makes only cash sales may address controls over cash registers (which are not much of a problem to most manufacturers) while ignoring customer accounts receivable. Similarly, the objectives for a utility might recognize that services delivered are billed on the basis of meter readings rather than delivery tickets. Whatever modifications are made, however, the internal control objectives for a cycle should be derived from the ten systems control objectives to assure coverage of each major control within each significant flow of activity.

**Step 5—
Completion
and Assessment
of Review**

During its final stages, or at the end of the review, the auditor may determine that (1) due to weaknesses, the controls do not provide a basis for reliance, or (2) tests of compliance of specific controls would not be cost effective. Under these circumstances, the auditor might change earlier, tentative decisions to rely on these controls and decide to terminate the review. The auditor would then assess the potential impact on the financial statements of any weaknesses that have come to his attention and may decide to accomplish the audit objectives by other means. (SAS No. 3, paragraph 26b.)

The auditor's decision to terminate a review may be made at one of two levels: (1) reliance will not be placed on EDP controls for any accounting application so that the entire review would be terminated, or (2) reliance will not be placed on the controls over one or more significant accounting applications so that review of the application controls would be terminated for them but would continue for the remaining applications.

**Step 6—Tests
of Compliance**

Once the auditor has reviewed the client's documentation for the specific application with which he is concerned and has made inquiries of responsible data processing and accounting personnel with the use of the questionnaire such as found in Appendix B, he should have a pretty good understanding of the nature of the specific application and the types of controls included. The information obtained through the auditor's initial review of the system should then be supplemented by tracing different types of transactions through the system. The tracing of transactions is designed to establish the existence of system procedures and to confirm the auditor's understanding of the system obtained through discussions with responsible executives and management and through the review of systems documentation.

The auditor may be able to test the system without the use of the computer in some processing situations; in other situations, he may find it desirable, if not necessary, to test with the use of the computer.

If the processing application being evaluated is well documented and a visible audit trail exists, the auditor may test the existence and effectiveness of the client's controls and processing procedures by checking source data, control reports, error listings, transaction registers, and management reports. The auditor, in effect, views the computer program as a black box and makes an inference about what goes on in the program by looking at known input (source documents) and known output (i.e., error listings or transaction registers). Testing without using the computer or by using conventional source documents and printed outputs is a process quite familiar to auditors and need not be discussed any further.

In testing the data processing system, the computer is used primarily to obtain information about the operation of a set of programs in an application and the programmed controls. Basically, there are three methods of testing a system with the computer: the test-data approach, the minicompany approach, and the controlled reprocessing of actual transactions using audit software.

Test-Data Approach

The test-data approach is one of the methods available to the auditor in evaluating computer-based systems. This approach is primarily used to obtain information about the operation of the computer program or set of programs in an application and about the program controls. Because of theoretical limitations and practical difficulties in the implementation of this approach, this method has not been widely used in auditing, but its use in certain systems suggests that the auditor should be aware of such an approach.

The test-data method is probably most applicable when any of three situations exists:

1. A significant part of the system of internal control is embodied in the computer program.
2. There are gaps in the audit trail making it difficult or impractical to trace input to output or to verify calculations.
3. The volume of records is so large that it may be more economical and more effective to use test-data methods instead of manual-testing methods.

Since most accounting and financial processing systems involve the updating of records, the use of test data usually involves the use of master records. So, as Figure 9.5 suggests, the sample transactions processed with master records determine how the client's computer program and programmed controls update the master files and generate output.

As the diagram indicates, the auditor, on the basis of his understanding of how the client's computer program (including the programmed controls) should operate, develops predetermined processing results, which he compares to the actual results from his testing process. On the basis of the comparison of actual results to predetermined results, he makes some conclusions about the effectiveness and existence of the system and the programmed controls.

Although the diagram of Figure 9.5 shows the transactions in the form of punched cards, test data do not necessarily take the form of a deck of punched cards. Transactions may be introduced into the system in the form of hard-copy source documents, on machine-readable form such as punched cards or prepunched badges used to activate source-recording devices, or through remote inquiry terminals in on-line real-time systems. Of course, the test data must be in machine-readable form to be processed with the client's computer programs.

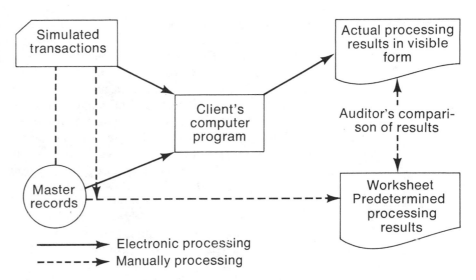

Figure 9.5
Why Sample Transactions
Are Processed

The inherent advantage of creating test transactions over selecting actual transactions is that the auditor may include representative types of transactions in his tests with relative ease. Conventionally, to test the system, the auditor selects actual accounting transactions previously processed by the client. Typically, this approach calls for tracing several transactions from the recording of the source documents, through whatever intermediate records might exist, to the output reports or records produced. Often this approach is incomplete and inexact and the transactions do not include the ones requiring exception handling. By creating transactions, the auditor can process data that are truly representative and that can include any type of transaction he wishes.

By several methods, the auditor can determine the types of transactions to be included in his test data. One approach is to analyze the client's data used to test the client's computer programs. Many of the client's test data test processing steps and controls that the auditor is interested in testing. Such a method is the most expedient since many transactions can be devised by mere duplication or slight modification of the client's test data. This method has the added advantage of reviewing the client's procedures in testing his programs. Such a review may be highly informative and beneficial to EDP operating people by uncovering outdated tests and areas in the program not being tested at all. Another and more time-consuming method of determining types of transactions to include in the test data involves analyzing the client's input records and creating simulated transactions in accordance with the auditor's test objectives. Normally, a combination of the two approaches is necessary to include all the transactions the auditor is interested in processing.

Regardless of the approach used to determine the types of transactions to be processed, several observations should be made. All possible combinations within all data fields need not be set out as separate transactions. Distinction should be made between data fields that merely represent identification data (that is, account numbers, social security numbers) and those that involve variable data. In the case of the former, only a limited number of possibilities need be included to test the identification routines in the program. For example, to test sequence checking and identification comparison routines, a transaction with a valid transaction code and employee number and containing valid information could be placed out of sequence in the test deck. Additional tests for sequence checking and identification comparison would not be necessary. Not all combinations within variable data fields need testing either.

To illustrate, let us look at Table 9.3, which shows the fields and their description for a rate-change input card in a payroll system. The transaction will change an employee's hourly rate and pay code. The transaction is program edited for validity of dates, alpha name, old pay code and rate, and whether the new rate is equal to the old rate. In addition, any new rate greater than $10 is excepted. The tests developed for this transaction were (1) valid rate change with all other fields valid, (2) rate change greater than $10 (3) valid rate change, old rate wrong, (4) valid rate change, old rate equal to new rate, and (5) valid rate change, alpha name wrong.

It is necessary to include in the test data at least two of each type of variable requiring alternative handling in order to test the complete processing of a normal transaction and to test the existence and effectiveness of programmed controls. For example, in the above illustration, all rates equal to or less than $10 are handled by the normal processing routine; all rates greater than $10 are handled by an exception routine.

The tests should include transactions that determine the processing and handling of the following general conditions:

- Valid conditions

- Out-of-sequence conditions

Table 9.3
Rate-Change
Card Format

CARD FIELD	DESCRIPTION
4–12	Social security number
13–14	Transaction code (03)
16	Division
18–22	New hourly rate
24–29	Rate change date
30	New payroll code
31–34	First four characters of last name (alpha name)
48–52	Old hourly rate
75	Old payroll code

- Out-of-limits conditions
- Routines arising from a major decision point where alternative processing takes place as a result of comparing transaction records with master records, that is, where the transaction identification number can be greater than, equal to, or less than the identification number on the master record
- Units of measure differences (for example, tons instead of pounds)
- Incomplete, invalid, or missing input information
- Wrong master and/or transaction files
- Numeric characters in fields where alphabetic characters belong and vice versa
- Characters in certain fields that exceed prescribed length (an overflow condition)
- Illogical conditions in data fields where programmed consistency checks test the logical relationship between the fields
- Conditions where transaction codes or amounts do not match the codes or amounts established in tables stored in internal memory

Obviously, all these conditions cannot be tested with each type of transaction, but the majority of them may be tested in processing all transactions included in the test deck.

Obtaining Master Records The auditor must obtain master records in machine-readable form with which to process the test transactions. The contents of the master records must also be available in visible form to compute the predetermined results for comparison with output resulting from the processing of test data. There are several methods of obtaining master records. One is to obtain actual master records. With sequential processing, obtaining the actual master records in machine-readable form is usually not much of a problem since the master file is not written over or destroyed in processing the test transactions. Random processing presents a problem since the master records maintained on random-access equipment are written over or destroyed by processing transactions. To protect the client's master records, the test data can be run immediately after the content of the random-access file has been transferred to cards or tape. After this transfer, the master records are on both the random-access master files and on magnetic tape, or punched cards if tape units are not available. The test data can then be processed against the tape or card files as discussed above. In such a situation, the client's computer program would have to be altered slightly to have the computer read and write tape or card files, rather than read and write random-access files. Where the auditor must run his test transactions between the transfer cycles, the random-access files may be protected by physically locking the files to prevent writing on them and altering the program, so that the WRITE RANDOM ACCESS FILE instruction becomes WRITE TAPE OR CARD FILE.

In some installations, simulated master records are used, against which the test data are processed by the company's programmers in testing the system. These master records, although comparatively few in number, represent actual master records. The advantage of these simulated master records is the ease with which they can be used and changed to reflect certain conditions necessary for testing and the ease with which they can be printed out for visible review. For example, one company uses 24 simulated master records in punched-card form as a test model payroll master file. These 24 records are used instead of the 20,000-employee master record file to avoid time in selecting, processing, and printing actual master records. The use of simulated masters is based on the premise that the computer cannot tell the difference between the processing of a test master record and an actual master record. The auditor also can create simulated master records for testing the system. These records, of course, must be recorded in appropriate machine-readable form and organized according to file specifications required for processing with the client's computer programs being tested.

Creation of simulated master records may be the only method of obtaining master records with which to process the auditor's test data in on-line real-time systems. The auditor's use of actual master records in such systems is hard to justify since it would seriously disrupt the client's opeations. In on-line real-time systems, transactions are generated randomly at remote terminals and require immediate processing; the transactions are posted to master file records unpredictably. To introduce test data for processing with actual master records would require control and necessary interruption of the client's processing; without such control, it would be difficult to discern the results of test-data processing and to leave a trail of the records updated in the test processing. Creation of simulated master records would enable the auditor to generate, at random and from the desired terminals, those transactions necessary to test the client's processing system.

Although actual master records may be readily obtained in machine-readable form in many systems, getting the same records in printed form without advance planning is difficult. One method is to time the tests so they are processed with the output master file used to prepare a printed report, such as the accounts receivable aged trial balance or an inventory report. Another method is to have an inquiry program prepared that will print out selected master records from the master file to be used in processing the test transactions. Most installations have the ability to inquire into any file, and the auditor may, with little planning, have his file-searching needs met by a routine procedure.

Effect of Tests on System   Obviously, the auditor does not want to have his test data affect the results produced under normal operating conditions. Accordingly, he must carefully consider what effects the processing of the test data will have on the results of the system. For example, the output tape resulting from the processing of test data should be clearly labeled so as to prevent improper use and subsequent incorrect processing of operating data. The protection of random-access files, discussed earlier, is another important consideration in the use of test decks.

Any tests processed along with actual transactions or actual master records must be carefully controlled to preclude undesired results. For example, in an audit test to determine that the open order file was reviewed periodically for unusual items, a valid order was transmitted by the auditor from a sales-branch location and the shipping copy was destroyed. This order had to be controlled by the auditor to prevent shipping of the order and to ensure subsequent removal from the open order file.

Control of Client's Program One of the important procedures for testing a company's EDP system is to make sure that the program being tested is the one the company actually uses to process data. Basically, there are two ways this can be achieved.

First, if the data processing organizational and administrative controls are adequate, the program can be requested on a surprise basis from the EDP librarian and duplicated for the auditor's control and use in processing test data. The auditor may also request test data, previously processed with the auditor's of the program, to be processed with the client's operating program; the auditor can then compare the results. This method has the added advantage of checking any computer operator intervention.

Second, the auditor may request on a surprise basis that the operating program be left in the computer after operating data have been completely processed so that he may process his test data with it. This method has an advantage over the first method in that it usually ensures a current version of the program. In many installations, and particularly in earlier stages of conversion, program changes are frequent and may make it quite difficult for the auditor to review and check all significant changes in order to be satisfied with the operations performed by the program.

Once the auditor has obtained the client's processing program, he should duplicate the program, retain the copy for his own use, and then observe the processing of his test data with this controlled copy.

Preparation and Processing of Test Data In addition to determining the types of transactions and obtaining master records and the client's regular processing program, the auditor must carefully design test data, obtain the necessary equipment and/or personnel, and obtain computer time from authorized personnel to prepare and process the test data and to get the output in the desired form. Most of these arrangements involve advance planning with systems and computer operations people.

Essentially, the test data should be designed to limit the work required of the auditor in reviewing the results of the test. The auditor's interpretation and evaluation of the test results can be simplified and made less time consuming with special codings or distinctive names that allow invalid test transactions to be identified easily, sorted out of valid tests, and listed on separate output listings.

The case study in Appendix C illustrates many of the points discussed above in the use of test data to evaluate internal control in EDP systems. The reader may wish to read the case study before proceeding with the remainder of this chapter.

Minicompany Approach

We indicated that the test-data approach is one of three methods of testing a system with the use of the computer. Another approach is the minicompany approach. This approach is in a somewhat experimental state. It appears to have great potential for fast-response (on-line real-time) systems. This approach overcomes some of the limitations of the test-data approach and makes possible the remote entry of test data, on-line testing, and surprise testing of systems.

The *minicompany* can be defined as

a means of passing fictitious test transactions through a computer system simultaneously with live data, without adversely affecting the live files or outputs. In other words, it is a small sub-system of the regular system. A separate set of outputs, including statistics and reports, are produced for the minicompany.[3]

Let us see how the minicompany could be used in the system described in the payroll case study in Appendix C. In the labor recording system, a fictitious department could be set up and records for fictitious employees included as part of the live master file. The test transactions or minicompany transactions could be entered into the system through the terminals used for time recording and run with normal transactions of the actual departments. Exception reports on clock-in transactions and job transactions could be prepared for the minicompany for unusual or error-type transactions entered. The valid transactions for the minicompany recorded on the daily transactions tape could be separated from the actual data and then processed in a normal manner, generating daily labor reports and providing input for payroll processing and preparation of payroll reports including payroll checks. The results of the minicompany's input could be compared with results predetermined to indicate any irregularities in controls or processing.

[3] From Joseph J. Wasserman, "Plugging the Leaks in Computer Security," *Harvard Business Review,* September–October 1969, pp. 119–129.

Controlled Reprocessing

The third method of testing the operation of computer programs in an EDP system calls for the preparation of separate programs, independent of those used for the client's day-to-day application processing. These independent programs accept the same input as the client's programs, use the same files, and attempt to produce the same results. The results are then matched with the results from the client's processing. After the same files and transactions have been reprocessed, the results should be identical and directly comparable to the financial results produced by the client's processing.

The important characteristic of controlled reprocessing is that independent processing of client data takes place. The use of audit software, which we shall discuss in the next chapter, makes it possible to create the independent programs with a minimum of effort by audit personnel.

The method of controlled reprocessing involves a substantial use of the computer in performing audit procedures and is a method best suited for situations that justify use of the computer rather than the use of manual procedures based on visible audit-trail printouts. Such a method, like the test-data approach, should be considered when there is a volume of data to be processed and tested and/or when the processing to be verified is complex or otherwise difficult to follow by means of visible printout.

There are many valuable new auditing techniques for computerized applications. Some of these are not well known. Descriptions of the most used advanced auditing techniques are contained in Chapter 13. That chapter also includes a discussion of the situations in which these techniques are most effective.

Step 7—Evaluation of Accounting Controls

When evaluating EDP accounting controls and the other elements of accounting control, the auditor should again:

- Consider the types of errors and irregularities that could occur.
- Determine the accounting control procedures that should prevent or detect such errors and irregularities.
- Determine whether the necessary procedures are prescribed and are being followed satisfactorily.

After doing these tasks, the auditor should evaluate any weaknesses. That is, the auditor needs to consider the type of potential errors and irregularities not covered by existing control procedures—to determine their effect on (1) the nature, timing, or extent of auditing procedures to be applied and (2) any suggestions to be made to the client. (SAS No. 1, Sec. 320.65.)

Evaluation of System: A Summary

In this chapter, we have discussed the first major phase of an audit examination: the review and evaluation of the data processing system. We have recommended that the auditor complete the following three steps in his review:

1. Obtain an understanding of the system.

2. Obtain information to evaluate the client's control over the data processed in the specific applications with which he is concerned.

3. Perform tests to determine if the controls function as designed.

The understanding and testing of the system should be achieved through an analysis of the client's entire system of internal control including the processing performed by the computer. This analysis should be made, in most cases, by a review of systems documentation and discussions with client personnel with the use of EDP-controls questionnaires.

Once the auditor has reviewed and tested the system, he is in a position to make an evaluation of the adequacy of the client's control system and to determine what additional audit procedures are required and what recommendations for improving the system should be made. The additional audit procedures may take the form of additional tests of the system and/or tests of the accounts and records produced from the system.

Problems

1. (a) Define test data.
   (b) Flowchart the test-data process.
   (c) What is the auditor's purpose in using test data?

2. (a) Are test data only in the form of punched cards?
   (b) Explain some EDP applications where tests would be in some machine-readable form other than punched cards.

3. (a) Why is it important that the auditor determine where test data are to be entered into the system?
   (b) Why would the auditor wish to enter tests at a point other than the source document origination point?

4. (a) Why is it difficult for the auditor to select actual transactions representative of all types of transactions?
   (b) Why can test data include representative tests with relative ease?

5. (a) Why is there a problem of processing test data with actual master records in a direct-access EDP system?
   (b) What measures can be taken in such systems to obtain master records to process with test data?

6. (a) Why is it important that the auditor be assured that the program he is testing is the one his client actually uses to process data?

   (b) Describe audit procedures you would use to obtain the actual processing programs.

   (c) How can the auditor ensure that his test data are being processed with the client's actual processing programs?

The questions in Problems 7 and 8 have been adapted by permission from the CPA examinations:

7. You have been engaged by Central Savings and Loan Association to examine its financial statements for the year ended December 31.

   In January of the current year the association installed an on-line real-time computer system. Each teller in the association's main office and seven branch offices has an on-line input–output terminal. Customers' mortgage payments and savings account deposits and withdrawals are recorded in the accounts by the computer from data input by the teller at the time of the transaction. The teller keys the proper account by account number and enters the information in the terminal keyboard to record the transaction. The accounting department at the main office has both punched card and typewriter input–output devices. The computer is housed at the main office.

   In addition to servicing its own mortgage loans, the association acts as a mortgage servicing agency for three life insurance companies. In this latter activity the association maintains mortgage records and serves as the collection and escrow agent for the mortgagors (the insurance companies), who pay a fee to the association for these services.

   You would expect the association to have certain internal controls in effect because an on-line real-time computer system is employed. List the internal controls that should be in effect solely because this system is employed, classifying them as

   (a) Those controls pertaining to input of information.

   (b) All other types of computer controls.

8. The Meyers Pharmaceutical Company has the following system for billing and recording accounts receivable:

   (a) An incoming customer's purchase order is received in the order department by a clerk who prepares a prenumbered company sales order form in which is inserted the pertinent information, such as the customer's name and address, customer's account number, and quantity and items ordered. After the sales order form has been prepared, the customer's purchase order is stapled to it.

   (b) The sales order form is then passed to the credit department for credit approval. Rough approximations of the billing values of the orders are made in the credit department for those accounts on which credit limitations are imposed. After investigation, approval of credit is noted on the form.

(c) Next the sales order form is passed to the billing department where a clerk types the customer's invoice on a billing machine that cross-multiplies the number of items and the unit price, then adds the automatically extended amounts for the total amount of the invoice. The billing clerk determines the unit prices for the items from a list of billing prices.

The billing machine has registers that automatically accumulate daily totals of customer account numbers and invoice amounts to provide "hash" totals and control amounts. These totals, which are inserted in a daily record book, serve as predetermined batch totals for verification of computer inputs. The billing is done on prenumbered, continuous, carbon-interleaved forms having the following designations:

(i) "Customer's copy"

(ii) "Sales department copy" for information purposes

(iii) "File copy"

(iv) "Shipping department copy," which serves as a shipping order

Bills of lading are also prepared as carbon copy by-products of the invoicing procedure.

(d) The shipping department copy of the invoice and the bills of lading are then sent to the shipping department. After the order has been shipped, copies of the bill of lading are returned to the billing department. The shipping department copy of the invoice is filed in the shipping department.

(e) In the billing department one copy of the bill of lading is attached to the customer's copy of the invoice and both are mailed to the customer. The other copy of the bill of lading, together with the sales order form is then stapled to the invoice file copy and filed in invoice numerical order.

(f) A keypunch machine is connected to the billing machine so that punched cards are created during the preparation of the invoices. The punched cards then become the means by which the sales data are transmitted to a computer. The punched cards are fed to the computer in batches. One day's accumulation of cards makes up a batch. After the punched cards have been processed by the computer, they are placed in files and held for about two years.

List the procedures that a CPA would employ in his examination of his selected audit samples of the company's

(a) Typed invoices, including the source documents

(b) Punched cards

(*Note:* The listed procedures should be limited to the verification of the sales data being fed into the computer. Do not carry the procedures beyond the point at which the cards are ready to be fed to the computer.)

Cases

Olympia Manufacturing Company*

In connection with his examination of the financial statements of the Olympia Manufacturing Company, a CPA is reviewing procedures for accumulating direct labor hours. He learns that all production is by job order and that all employees are paid hourly wages, with time and a half for overtime hours.

Olympia's direct labor hour input process for payroll and job-cost determination is summarized in the flowchart shown in Figure 9.6.

Steps A and C are performed in timekeeping, step B in the factory-operating departments, step D in payroll audit and control, step E in data preparation (keypunch), and step F in computer operations.

For each input-processing step A through F:

(a) List the possible errors or discrepancies that may occur.
(b) Cite the corresponding control procedure that should be in effect for each error or discrepancy.

Your discussion of Olympia's procedures should be limited to the input process for direct labor hours, as shown in steps A through F in the flowchart. *Do not discuss* personnel procedures for hiring, promotion, termination, and pay rate authorization. *In step F do not discuss* equipment, computer program, and general computer operational controls. Organize your answer for each input-processing step as follows:

Possible Errors
Step   or Discrepancies   Procedures

(a) Develop your thoughts about the testing of the following system. In this regard:
   (i) Determine the objectives of your audit tests. For example, you probably want to have some evidence that controls exist to make sure the orders transmitted by the branches are recorded on the open order file.
   (ii) For each objective, determine the specific tests you would perform and the records and documents (audit trail) you would use in performing the tests.
   In completing this requirement, do not try to perform your tests with the use of the computer but try to use the existing audit trail.
(b) Develop test data to use the computer to evaluate the processing and controls in the system.

*This case has been adapted by permission from a recent CPA examination.

Figure 9.6
Direct Labor Hour Input
Process for Payroll
and Job-Cost
Determination

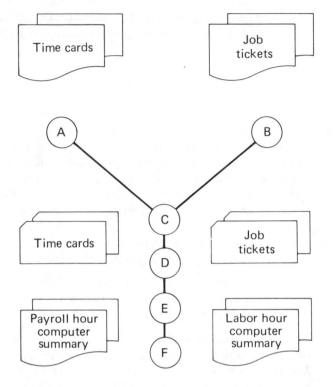

This is a description of an accounts receivable system in a medium-sized manufacturing company. Trade accounts average about $2 million. Approximately 300 accounts (about 5 percent of the accounts) make up about 80 percent of the total dollar value.

The application is processed on a disk-oriented computer system consisting of four disk storage drives, four magnetic tape units, a card-reader punch, a line printer, and a console typewriter. For transmission of orders, a teletypewriter system is used with orders recorded on punched paper tape. Data on paper tape are converted to magnetic tape with use of a punched-paper-tape reader. Off-line equipment includes keypunch and verifying machines and a card sorter.

Order Transmission

All orders are transmitted from various sales branches to the home office over the teletypewriter system, and a paper tape is prepared at the home office for the orders received. The original data used to transmist order information are recorded at the branch from customer mail orders, phone orders, or salesmen inputs.

When the order is transmitted at the branch, the data transmitted are recorded at the branch on a sales order form to be used as a control on the data transmission process.

As the data are received at the home office and as the punched paper tape is prepared for orders received, sales orders (see Figure 9.7) are simultaneously created at the home office. Six copies of the sales order are created at the home office with distribution to district sales; customer; shipping and stores (three copies, one of which is the packing list copy and another is a delivery receipt); and branch, to be compared with copy created at time-of-order transmission.

As the orders are transmitted, they are checked for character validity, parity, and completeness. Error messages are printed out and transmitted back to the branch for correction of incoming orders.

The punched paper tape is next converted to magnetic tape at which time a record count is established on orders received from each branch. During this run, the orders are also checked for completeness and for illogical conditions such as incorrect salesmen code for a particular branch. Once the data are edited, the valid orders (now on magnetic tape) are processed as input to update the open order file, maintained on a disk pack. During the order-entry run, a daily orders entered transaction register is printed. This register provides a listing of all orders processed with the open order file for the day and provides a dollar total of all orders processed. The tape file of the day's orders is used subsequently to update the inventory files (reorder analysis) and to update the accounts receivable files (credit analysis).

Invoicing

The home office does the invoicing for all shipments made. The invoices are prepared by the computer by processing the open order file which contains data on the order shipped including the unit price and transaction data on shipments. The source document creating shipment transactions is the shipping and stores copy of the order. On this document, shipping personnel indicate the quantity shipped, shipping method, freight information, and special charges (see Figure 9.7). This information is in addition to the standard information already printed on this copy of the standard order form (quantity ordered, customer, and branch information).

The documents arrive for keypunching in the input–output control section of data processing from the various shipping points of the company. The I/O control section edits the shipping documents for accuracy and reasonableness and prepares batch totals on the documents that are acceptable. Batch totals include a record count of the shipping documents in each batch and quantity shipped. After editing, the shipping documents are sent to keypunching. After keypunching and verification, the shipment cards are processed by the opera-

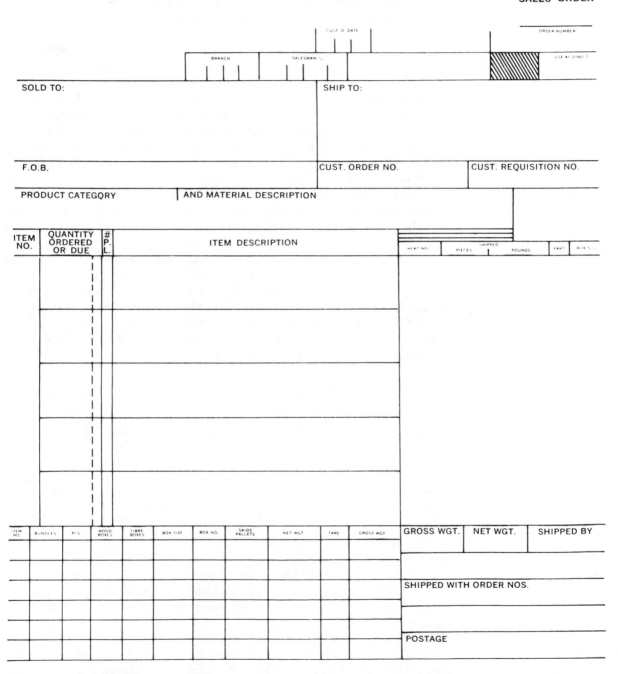

Figure 9.7 Sales Order

tions section of data processing. The data on the cards are converted to data on magnetic tape.

Batch Control and Edit Tests   All batches of shipments are approximately for 150 to 200 cards each. As the shipment cards are processed by the computer, the data contents of all cards are edited for completeness and validity to ensure that all relevant fields are validly punched. A record count and quantity total for each batch of shipments is accumulated by the computer. Also, a total is accumulated on the quantity field in each shipment transaction. Identified by batch number, these control totals (record counts and quantity totals) together with the original control totals and the revised totals (as explained below) are printed by the high-speed printer. Code numbers indicate whether or not the batch is in balance. The batch-balancing logic is as set forth in the following five steps:

1. The computer stores the data contained in the batch control card (a card that precedes each batch of shipment cards) and verifies that this card precedes the detail cards for any given batch.

2. For each detail card, the computer matches the batch number with the number of the batch control card and accumulates the appropriate data (quantity shipped, the number of records, etc.). All shipments for which the batch number does not match are completely rejected. The card goes into the reject pack, the contents are printed, and no control total accumulation is made.

3. At the same time, the computer performs validity tests on selected data from each detailed card. If they result in rejected transactions, the rejected shipment cards are routed into the reject pack; the data are printed, and a control total accumulation, separate from that for excepted cards, is made.

4. When the computer, by reading in the batch control card for the next batch, detects the end of the batch, it compares the sum of its internally generated control totals, valid items, and rejected items to the control total on the control card. If the figures agree, the batch is in balance. The batch number and all control figures are then printed on the console typewriter, along with a code indicating "in balance." If the batch is *not* in balance, the batch number and all control figures are printed with the code indicating "out of balance." In addition the computer writes on the output tape a trailer control record for the batch with identification.

5. These batch totals are all added together by the computer to one set of grand totals as follows: total number of shipment records, and total quantity shipped for all the shipments in the card file.

    These composite control figures are printed on the console typewriter and also written on the output magnetic tape, now containing the shipments, as a final trailer control record.

Every time the shipment transactions tape is processed, a record count and quantity control total are accumulated during the process. These control totals must agree with the totals on the trailer count record on the input transaction file.

Processing   The shipment transactions on magnetic tape are then processed with the open order file to prepare an invoice. The output from this processing, in addition to the invoice, consists of

- An updated order file
- A tape file of stock items shipped (used for sales analysis, production planning, and updating of perpetual inventory files)
- A tape file of all the day's billings (invoices) for subsequent preparation of a daily status report and for subsequent updating of the accounts receivable files

Six copies of the invoice are prepared (see Figure 3.21 in Chapter 3). Three copies are sent to the customer. The original includes a payment identity coupon. This coupon is torn off and returned by the customer with his remittance. The coupon is processed by the cashier as indicated in the cash receipts section of this system and is used as a turnaround source document for keypunching cash receipts punched cards to be used in updating the accounts receivable file and in preparing the daily cash receipts–sales register.

One copy each of the invoice goes to the input–output control group, salesman, and branch office from which the sale originated.

In addition to the batch controls described above, addition control data are printed out at the end of the processing on the console typewriter. These data are distributed to the input–output control group for review and follow-up. The control data include all the following:

- Number of shipment transactions processed by the computer
- Total number of invoices prepared
- Total number of shipment cards processed but not invoiced because there was no order in the open order file
- Total number of invoices for partial shipments
- Total dollar amount of invoices written
- Total dollar amount of open orders on the open order disk files

At periodic intervals, the open order file is printed so that visible review can be made by the input–output control group for unusual delays in shipping and invoicing and for back orders.

Daily Status Report   The daily status report is prepared by processing the file of the day's billings (invoices) and the file of the day's orders. The daily status report indicates, by product, orders entered for the day, month to date, and last month to date; backlog today, and backlog a month ago (see Figure 9.8). The report also shows total orders, total billings, and total backlog. The total orders can be compared to the total orders on the daily orders entered register resulting from the initial processing of orders (described in the first part of this system). The total billings for the day can be compared with total billings shown on the daily cash receipts-sales register, the output of subsequent processing in this system.

DAILY STATUS REPORT

PRODUCT	ORDERS ENTERED — TODAY	MONTH TO DATE	LAST MONTH TO DATE	NET MONTH TO DATE	NET BILLINGS — TODAY	MONTH TO DATE	LAST MONTH TO DATE	BACKLOG — TODAY	LAST MONTH SAME DATE
CARBON & ALLOY GRADES	35,285	106,623		103,552	2,082	61,979		179,555	
HIGH SPEED GRADES	564	18,610		17,877	2,103	22,548		75,487	
AIR MELT HI TEMP ALLOYS		12,633		12,633		79,353		384,236	
TOTAL HOT MILL PRODUCTS $	35,850 $	137,867 $	$	134,063 $	4,185 $	163,881 $	$	639,279 $	
CARBON & ALLOY GRADES		4,970		4,961	397	11,945		32,158	
HIGH SPEED GRADES	9,947	36,424		35,126	1,455	26,056		209,869	
36 COMMODITY DRILL ROD	1,401	10,789		9,998	1,236	15,188		13,216	
AIR MELT HI TEMP ALLOYS	14,045	18,348		19,452	37	6,820		46,786	
TOTAL GLOBE PRODUCTS $	25,395	70,533 $	$	69,539 $	3,127 $	60,011 $	$	302,032 $	
FLAT GROUND STOCK	751	10,105		9,929	1,056	9,228		4,977	
HIGH SPEED TOOL BITS	15,350	32,238		32,158	446	14,868		53,952	
TOTAL BIT PRODUCTS $	16,101 $	42,344 $	$	42,087 $	1,503 $	24,097 $	$	58,929 $	
STERCON HI TEMP ALLOYS		100,300		100,772		105,014		270,455	
STERCON STAINLESS								2,394	
STERCON T&D & HS STEELS		739		191		1,986		3,430	
STERCON ENGR ALLOYS		81		81		193		12,711	
TOTAL STERCON PRODUCTS $		101,121 $	$	100,661 $	$	107,193 $	$	288,992 $	
MISCELLANEOUS		6,662		3,315				3,315	
CONVERSION ORDERS	198	573		541		68		14,606	
TOTAL STEEL DIVISION $	77,346 $	351,866 $	$	346,352 $	8,816 $	355,184 $		$ 1,289,233 $	
CARBIDE POWDERS		4,846		4,846		5,363		10,843	
UNGROUND TIPS & BLANKS	4,126	64,166		64,333	4,858	36,804		116,852	
UNGROUND INSERTS	390	9,262		9,262	317	4,340		36,115	
ROUNDS, RINGS & ROLLS	2,479	8,021		9,570	1,699	9,634		14,699	
PERCUSSION INSERTS		185		185		6,200		11,466	
GROUND TIPS & BLANKS	506	9,977		9,664	533	4,927		20,567	
MECHLY HELD INSERTS	6,001	29,206		29,228	1,025	23,158		93,102	
MECHANICAL TOOLHOLDERS	391	3,296		3,296	315	5,127		7,229	
BRAZED TOOLS	2,684	24,749		24,929	1,967	21,582		37,360	
DIES, NIBS & DIECARB	3,828	29,548		30,297	1,254	24,479		60,724	
MINING TOOLS & TIPS	311	14,098		14,743	1,555	8,831		46,768	
WEARCARB	4,087	7,532		7,532	12,349	12,631		21,876	
MISC & ODD LOT	30	3,210		3,210	125	2,294		16,052	
TOTAL REGULAR PRODUCTS $	25,036 $	215,336 $	$	214,956 $	26,003 $	165,443 $	$	511,579 $	
HEAVY METAL	193	51,001		51,001	541	1,731		50,995	
SILTUNG								22,557	
SPEC PRODUCTS-OTHER		2,980		3,205		1,996		1,871	
TOTAL TRAFFORD PRODUCTS $	193 $	53,981 $	$	54,206 $	541 $	3,728 $	$	75,425 $	
HOUSTON PRODUCTS	134	18,919		18,919	23	21,774		207,940	
PROJECTILES & BARTER									
TOTAL TUNGSTEN DIVISION $	25,363 $	288,237 $	$	288,083 $	26,567 $	190,945 $		$ 794,946 $	
SUNDRY & R & D SALES		7,065		7,065				12,645	
COMPANY TOTALS $	102,710 $	647,169 $	$	641,500 $	35,383 $	546,129 $		$ 2,096,824 $	
LESS CREDITS									
NET BILLINGS				$	35,383 $	546,129 $			
-STEEL STORE PRODUCTS-	24,499	138,369		134,896	4,841	121,090		131,977	
-TUNGSTEN STORE PRODUCTS	8,745	80,725		79,327	5,616	73,345		175,125	

Figure 9.8   Daily Status Report

Accounts Receivable Updating

The accounts receivable records are maintained on portions of two disk files. One file contains the *basic* accounts receivable records containing data such as account balance, amount on order, credit limit, credit history, delinquency history, and sales history (see Table 9.4). The other file contains data on the details supporting the account balance such as unpaid invoices and "suspense"

DATA FIELD	NUMBER OF CHARACTERS	DATA FIELD	NUMBER OF CHARACTERS
Customer number	7	Sales history (material amount only; by product line—steel, tungsten, sundry):	
Current A/R balance	9		
Amount on order:			
Steel	9	Third prior year	9
Tungsten	9	Second prior year	9
Sundry	9	First prior year	9
Credit limit:		This year to date	9
Amount	7	This month	9
Date limit established	6	Potential	9
Credit history:		Profit at standard—year to date	9
Date account opened	6	Payment history:	
Highest credit extended	9	Payment ratings (company	
Date highest credit extended	6	establishes payment ratings	
Original credit limit	9	0–9 based on payments for	
Date original credit limit		each quarter):	
established	6	Third prior year, by quarter	4
Previous credit limit	9	Second prior year, by quarter	4
Date previous credit limit		First prior year, by quarter	4
established	4	This year, by quarter	4
Number of months of previous		Dollars paid this quarter:	
credit limit	2	By discount	9
Number of items currently		By due date	9
delinquent	3	Customer name and address	136
Amount currently delinquent	9		
Delinquency history:		ACCOUNTS RECEIVABLE ITEM RECORD FOR UNPAID INVOICES	
Months reporting	2		
Months delinquent	2	Item record code	1
Consecutive months		Customer number	7
delinquent	2	Date	5
Last month delinquent	4	Invoice number	12
Highest delinquency:		Gross amount of invoice	9
Number of items	3	Net amount of invoice	9
Amount	9	Cash discount	7
Date	4		
Date last sale	6		

Table 9.4 Accounts Receivable Basic Record Description

items such as customer payments for which a specific invoice is not initially identifiable and credit memorandums unassigned to a specific unpaid invoice.

The accounts receivable files are updated with normal transactions such as cash receipts, billings, credit memos, and new orders. Other types of transactions include new accounts and changes to permanent data in customer accounts, such as credit limit, customer names and address, etc.

The cash receipts are initially received in the mail room where all company mail is opened. Checks are forwarded to the cashier who prepares an adding-machine tape of the checks for subsequent comparison with a computer-prepared deposit slip. The payment identity coupons (see Figure 3.21 in Chapter 3) returned with the customer checks are forwarded to the keypunching section and cash receipts punched cards are prepared. For customer payments for which no coupons are returned, the input–output control group prepares appropriate source documents for keypunching.

The other primary input transactions are the billings and the day's orders prepared as a result of previous processing described earlier in this system.

All credit memorandums for returned mail are initiated by the input–output control group or the branches upon receipt of a returned-material receiving report. Branches forward their coupon memorandums, approved by the branch manager, to the home office for approval. All credit memorandums in excess of $1,000 must be approved by the controller before they can be posted to accounts receivable. All other credit memorandums must be approved by the general ledger bookkeeper. Miscellaneous credits also originate in the input–output control group to correct invoicing errors. These are processed the same as material-returned credits.

The source documents for keypunching credits issued and sundry cash receipts (very minor in amount) originate with the general ledger bookkeeper. The source documents for new accounts, changes in "permanent" data, and other adjustments originate in the branch or by the input–output control group.

Batch totals are developed on these input transactions as follows:

Input	Batch Totals
Cash receipts	Total dollar amount
Credit memos	Total dollar amount
New accounts and changes in "permanent" data	Record counts

All batches are approximately 150 to 200 cards each, and the batching process and checking is performed in a fashion similar to that described previously. After the input transactions are keypunched and verified, they are converted to magnetic tape. During this conversion process, the data contents of the input cards are edited to ensure the validity of transaction codes and to assume completeness. Batch totals are checked and control totals are developed and written out on the trailer record of this transactions output tape. This transactions tape

and the transaction tapes for billings and order are then sorted into customer-number sequence for updating the accounts receivable files.

The computer processing of the transactions and the accounts receivable files produces the following machine-readable output for subsequent processing and visible output for distribution:

1. Machine-readable output

    (a) Updated accounts receivable files.

    (b) Exception transactions used to prepare a daily exception report for review and follow-up by the input–output control group. The exceptions are explained later.

2. Visible output

    (a) Daily sales–cash receipts register (see Figure 3.22 in Chapter 3). This register is prepared in customer-number sequence and shows, for each customer having transactions that day, the cash receipts and/or sales information. Also shown are the balance in the customer's account after the transactions are posted; the grand totals for cash receipts and billings; total sundry cash receipts; the total balance of all accounts receivable; and the number of invoices and cash receipts transactions processed during the day. The input–output control group compares the total billings printed on the daily sales–cash receipts register to the total billings shown on the daily status report. The group also compares the total cash receipts processed with the input batch totals prepared on cash receipts.

    (b) Cash deposit slip. This slip is actually a part of the daily sales–cash receipts (see Figure 3.22, right side) and lists all cash receipts processed by the computer. This slip is prepared in duplicate and returned to the cashier for agreement with the remittance adding-machine tape and for deposit in the bank.

Preparation of Daily Exception Report   An exception report is prepared daily by processing the exception transactions resulting from the accounts receivable update run. These transactions were produced as the result of programmed controls in the computer programs that cause the accounts receivable transactions to be posted to the accounts receivable magnetic tape files.

Exception report cards may be classified as exceptions to operational policies, or as information only, or as errors in input data.

The exception codes and an explanation of the codes are as follows:

A. Order received today over credit limit. A credit limit check is not made until the order is received, processed for shipment, and posted to the accounts receivable files. The computer program then compares the total of the customer balance and orders entered with the amount of the credit limit on the customer record.

B. Order received today, from new customer.

C. Order received today, no credit limit in basic record.

D. Order received today, from delinquent account.

E. Account opened today.

F. Inactive account (no sales last three years).

G. Account closed today.

H. Account with credit balance.

 I. Item delinquent today.

 J. Delinquent item, paid today.

K. 01 (Subcode): Cash discount not taken but allowable because it is within 5-day grace period. 02: Cash discount taken but should be disallowed. 03: Cash discount allowable but not taken because the discount is less than $1.00.

L. Unassigned payment in item record. Customer remits payment without identity coupon and the payment cannot be identified by some other means.

M. Unassigned credit in item record. All credits except those for the same amount as in invoice or group of invoices are processed unassigned until payment is received for the remaining amount due in the invoice(s) for which the credit(s) apply.

N. Difference in amount between accounts receivable balance and total of open items in item record file.

O. Confirmation of change. Change is printed out (that is, name, address, credit limit).

P. Answer to query. Exception report shows what is in a customer's record.

Q. Error card. Card shows, by code, the type of error in the punched card input and information on the card that is not processed because of the error. Several of these errors relate to program checks for proper date, proper sequence of customer number, and valid transaction codes.

Preparation of Aged Trial Balance and Monthly Statements   An aged trial balance (see Figure 9.9) is prepared at the end of the month by computer processing of the accounts receivable files. The aged trial balance lists, in customer-number sequence, all invoices, credit and debit memos, and contra (application of company purchases against a delinquent customer's balance) by data number and amount; the aged trial balance ages the amount according to 30-60-90 days and over categories.

As the result of the aged trial balance processing program, the computer prepares an *overdue accounts* magnetic tape used to prepare an overdue accounts list that shows all overdue accounts for each branch office. Monthly statements are prepared for all customers who request them.

```
                    OPEN ITEM - AGED TRIAL BALANCE                          SEP 20, 19X3

                        ACCOUNTS   RECEIVABLE

  INVOICE  INVOICE OR C/M                                                        UNSHIPPED
    DATE   OR PAYMENT NO. C    TOTAL GROSS    30 TO 59 DAYS  60 TO 89 DAYS  90 OR MORE    ORDERS VALUE

   9/10/63  T601940-S -01 4         6.30
                                    6.30

   8/30/63  T801564-S -01 4        40.04
                                   40.04

   8/22/63  G101291-S -01 4        14.33
   9/17/63  G101864-S -01 4        27.44
                                   41.77

   9/19/63  G602473-S -01 4        31.58
                                   31.58

   8/30/63  T601761-S -01 4        39.00
                                   39.00

   9/17/63  S602348-S -01 4        58.00
                                   58.00

   8/22/63  G701588-S -01 4        74.52
                                   74.52

   8/27/63  B801401-SD-01 4        35.30
   8/27/63  G801693-SD-01 4         5.83
   8/28/63  G801796-SD-01 4         1.74
   9/10/63  G801810-SD-01 4        12.49
   9/10/63  G802032-SD-01 4        69.25
   9/11/63  B802103-SD-01 4        52.95
                                  177.56

   8/27/63  B801699-S -01 4        19.21
                                   19.21

   9/13/63  T802156-L -01 4        88.84
   9/12/63  T802157-S -01 4        35.75
                                  124.59
```

Figure 9.9   Aged Trial Balance

Briand Kitchen Aids   Briand Kitchen Aids has just implemented a massive decentralization plan in an attempt to improve its financial condition and control over operations. Each operating function is now organized as a responsibility center and is held accountable for its use of resources. Management hopes this reorganization will help reverse Briand's recent decline in sales and profits. The company had its peak sales year nine years ago with $510 million, but last year sales were only $325 million.

Briand Kitchen Aids is a diversified manufacturer of high quality cooking utensils and appliances, ranging from pots to stoves. Its main office and manufacturing plant is located in Detroit, Michigan, with wholesale distribution warehouses throughout the Midwest and eastern United States.

Briand's worsening financial position has been caused primarily by three factors: First, the cost of steel, a major element in all of Briand's products, has risen rapidly. Second, a sharp wage increase has made Briand's labor-intensive products more costly to produce. Third, and by far the most significant, the appliance business has just not been that good in recent years. When people have to stretch their budgets, one way is to retain their old kitchen appliances a bit longer. The company has faced other difficulties since its organization in 1913, and management is confident it will weather this one as well.

Under the decentralized system, computer operations has been made a profit center. An organizational chart of the newly reorganized data processing department is shown in Figure 9.10. Briand management feels that by treating computer operations as a profit center, and billing user departments for services received, computer users will request only information that will at least pay for itself.

For the time being, top management has decided that the central headquarters will bear the costs of the systems development area. New projects will continue to be justified as capital investments—and reviewed and monitored on that basis. Management felt that to do otherwise, at this stage, might discourage some desirable projects.

Philip Conrad, of Briand's internal audit department, has been assigned

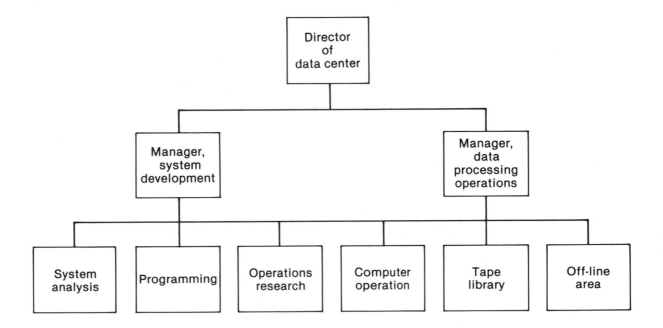

Figure 9.10   Organizational Chart of the Data Processing Center

the task of reviewing the initial determination of costs involved in the operation of the data processing center. His responsibility also includes validating the reasonableness of the allocation of these costs to the specific operating areas within the data center. Philip hopes to develop rates on a per unit usage basis that are equitable yet facilitate costing. His first step in analyzing costs was to appraise the basic units proposed to measure computer usage and that of related equipment. Philip found that the computer center management had decided on the following:

"Kilobyte second" will be used as the basic chargeable measure for the central processing unit. A kilobyte second is defined as 1000 bytes of primary storage space (core memory) used for one second. The kilobyte second defines computer usage as a function of two factors, time and space. A billing rate using the kilobyte second could be computed by the following formula:

$$Cost\ per\ Kilobyte\ Second = \frac{Total\ CPU\ Cost\ per\ Year}{Total\ Billable\ Kilobyte\ Seconds\ per\ Year}$$

The average number of kilobyte seconds per year is 1,820,000,000.

The billed cost of data storage on disk will be determined by both the space used and the number of reads from, and writes to, the disk (DREW). The cost of space usage would use the formula:

$$\frac{Disk\ Pack\ Cost\ Per\ Year}{Number\ of\ Tracks\ Available}$$

Number of tracks available = number of disk drives x number of tracks per surface x number of read/write surfaces (for 3330 IBM disk drive).

$$(28)\ (404)\ (19) = 215,000$$

Number of disk drives, obviously, is 28. To compute the cost per DREW the following formula is used:

$$\frac{Disk\ Drive\ Controller\ Cost\ per\ Year}{Average\ Number\ of\ DREWs\ Used}$$

Average number of DREWs per year = 1,125,000,000.

Tape drives will be billed at one usage rate, which is based on only the number of reads from, and writes to, the tape (TREW):

$$\frac{Cost\ of\ Tape\ Drives}{Average\ Number\ of\ TREWs\ Used}$$

Average number of TREWs per period = 9,100,000,000.

Time-sharing option (TSO) would be billed using three different rates: TSO connect charges, CPU usage, and the number of reads and writes from disk. CPU usage would be billed to the user on the basis of kilobyte seconds and at the same rate as other computer usage. The reads and writes from disks are billed at the regular cost of DREW (as determined earlier). TSO connect charges will be billed to the user based on a set cost per hour of use, determined as follows:

TSO Connect Costs per Period

*(Number of Hours Available)	**(Number of users)	***(Percent utilization)

*Hours available = 3,000
**12 users presently
***Utilization = 60%

Off-line printer cost will be charged out by cost per hour (approximately 6,600 hours). All bursting and deleaving costs will also be allocated to the off-line printer. The off-line printer is used only for larger jobs, which are usually the ones that require bursting and decollating. The on-line printer is used only for small printouts and its cost is included in the CPU time.

Card reader average usage is 15,000,000 cards per year. Its cost will be applied on a charge per card read.

Philip, after tentatively accepting those units for billing the users, assigned his assistant to gather cost data on data center operations. During the gathering of the cost data, the assistant reported that not all the essential cost elements were available; therefore, she produced the cost schedule (shown in Exhibit 9.2) by categorizing information from the general ledger.

Philip, after reviewing the cost schedules, found that a substantial percentage of the costs were chargeable to the management of the data center. There was no basic unit in which these administrative costs could be charged to the various data processing operations. To resolve the problem he sent a note to the manager of data processing operations explaining the difficulty he was having. The manager sent back a memo (shown in Exhibit 9.3).

Sam Fead, the manager of the stove division of Briand, was worried when he heard that all computer usage would be billed out to the users. Sam was preparing his budget for the next fiscal year and wondered how much his division would be charged for computer operations. He was especially concerned

Exhibit 9.2
Cost Schedule

PAYROLL COSTS (including salaries, taxes, and benefits)

PERSONNEL LOCATION	PER YEAR
Computer Room	$205,000
Tape Library	44,000
Administrative:	
Management	156,000
Staff	66,000
Xerox Copier	19,000
I/O Control	59,000
Printer (off-line)	33,000
Bursting and Deleaving	5,000

RENTAL EXPENSE

IBM 370/158	$325,000
Software Programs	12,500
Disk Drives and Controller	93,000
Tape Drives and Control Units	171,000
TSO Teleprocessing Unit	20,000
Card Readers and Card Punch	15,600
On-Line Printer	46,000
Xerox Copier	65,500*
Off-Line Printer and Control Unit	55,000
Tape Cleaner Rental	7,800

EQUIPMENT DEPRECIATION

Owned Disk Drives and Controller	$140,000
Disk Packs	4,400
Bursting and Deleaving Equipment	1,800

MAINTENANCE

CPU	$ 37,000
Disk Drive	47,000
TSO	300
On-Line Printer	300
Off-Line Printer	2,600
Bursting and Deleaving	190

UTILITY EXPENSE

Administrative	$ 25,000
Computer Room	36,000
TSO	15,000

MATERIAL AND SUPPLIES

PERSONNEL LOCATION	PER YEAR
On-Line Printer	$ 23,500
Xerox Copier	26,500
Off-line Printer	9,000

MISCELLANEOUS

Administrative	$ 25,000
Computer Room	26,000
Tape Library	15,000

  * For every copy over 5,200,000 (per year) there is an additional $.004 charge per copy.

Exhibit 9.3
Management's Memo
to Auditor

To: Philip Conrad
From: Manager of Data Processing Operations
Subject: Administrative Cost Allocation

In a meeting with the managers involved in the administration of the data processing activities, we decided the management cost of the data center should be allocated in the following manner:

13%—off-line area
17%—tape library
70%—computer operations

All costs for input/output control should be allocated in the same manner as administrative costs.

Philip, I wish you continued luck in your endeavor to make computer operations into a cost center. Feel free to contact me at any time if you need further assistance.

---

about a new simulation project, which would provide him with a weekly forecast of manufacturing requirements. It had taken three years to develop and he was afraid this had been a wasted effort because the project would be too costly to run on the computer under his limited budget. He called Philip and explained his uneasiness about the new chargeout policy. Philip assured Sam that the usage cost would not be extraordinary, but this did little to relax him. Sam wanted to know exactly how much the simulation would cost him—a specific amount that could be included in his budget. Philip explained to Sam that only an estimate of the cost of his simulation project could be provided now. This would be obtained by letting an analyst review the simulation program and speculate on the computer usage requirements. Once the computer center's costing system is operational, however, all billing will be performed by a software program that will keep track of all usage by user application.

The analyst, after reviewing the simulation program, decided that it would require the following amounts of data center resources each year:

- Kilobyte seconds used: 20,000,000.
- Number of disk tracks used: 7,600.
- DREWs performed: 17,000,000.
- TREWs performed: 135,000,000.
- 25 hours of the TSO.
- 10 hours of off-line printer time.

- 85,000 cards.
- Due to confidential material in the simulation report, no copies will be reproduced at the data center.

The analyst reminded Sam that these figures were only approximations of the actual resources needed to process the simulation program. The actual requirements of the program should be within $\pm$ 10 percent of this estimate, however.

Requirements

Prepare an estimated cost of running the simulation for a year. (One approach may be as follows.)

(a) Allocate the administrative costs to computer operations, the tape library, and the off-line area.

(b) Calculate total CPU cost and cost per kilobyte second.

(c) Find the total cost of CPU time for the simulation program.

(d) Calculate total DREW cost, cost per DREW, and projected cost for the simulation project.

(e) Calculate space usage cost per unit and total disk cost for the simulation project. (Remember administrative cost allocations.)

(f) Calculate cost per TREW and projected cost for the simulation program.

(g) Calculate TSO cost per hour and projected cost for the simulation program.

(h) Find total cost for TSO for the simulation project. (Remember to allocate administrative costs.)

(i) Find off-line printer cost per hour and projected cost for the simulation program.

(j) Find the cost per card and the projected cost for the simulation program. Calculate the amount of administrative costs allocated to the card reader and punch those which are allocated to the simulation program.

(k) Calculate the estimated total cost of the simulation program for the coming year.

EDP AUDIT PROCESS*

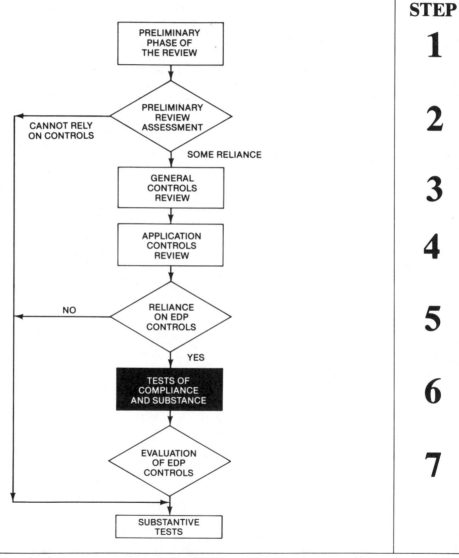

	STEP
PRELIMINARY PHASE OF THE REVIEW	1
PRELIMINARY REVIEW ASSESSMENT	2
GENERAL CONTROLS REVIEW	3
APPLICATION CONTROLS REVIEW	4
RELIANCE ON EDP CONTROLS	5
TESTS OF COMPLIANCE AND SUBSTANCE	6
EVALUATION OF EDP CONTROLS	7

*Diagram is adapted from The Auditor's Study and Evaluation of Internal Control in EDP Systems, pages 21–24. Copyright © 1977 by the American Institute of Certified Public Accountants, Inc. (See Figure 9.1 for a complete explanation of the steps.)

EVALUATION OF RECORDS PRODUCED BY EDP SYSTEMS

(6) Tests of Compliance

Purpose:
- Determine whether the necessary control procedures are prescribed and followed satisfactorily.
- Provide reasonable assurance that controls are functioning properly.
- Consider and, to the extent appropriate, document when, how, and by whom controls are provided.

Methods: Examination of records; test of control procedures; inquiry; observation.

OBJECTIVE

The auditor may need to write computer programs to evaluate evidence in electronic format. This chapter explains what audit software does and how to use it.

As discussed in Chapter 9, the audit examination consists of two major phases: the evaluation of the system of control and the evaluation of records produced by the data processing system. In this chapter we shall examine the second phase, the evaluation of the records produced by the system.

Much of the output from the data processing system may take the form of visible records such as trial balances for accounts receivable, inventory listings, sales and cash receipts registers, and payroll registers. Such records may be evaluated using traditional auditing methods—such as performing arithmetic calculations and tests, selecting samples from printed listings, tracing selected items to reporting records to supporting records and authoritative documents, and/or confirming directly with outsiders.

Normally, the visible output is printed from machine-readable output such as magnetic tape and magnetic disk. Hence, the auditor may use the computer for evaluating records by developing or obtaining computer-audit programs and processing the machine-readable records with such programs.

Uses of Computer Programs in Auditing

A computer program can be used for any computational or comparison task for which quantitative criteria can be established. The following seven applications are only a few examples of these types of tasks in auditing:

1. Testing extensions and footings.
2. Summarizing data and performing analyses useful to the auditor.
3. Examining records for quality: completeness, consistency, invalid conditions, etc.
4. Selecting and printing confirmations.
5. Selecting and printing audit samples.
6. Comparing the same data maintained in separate files for correctness and consistency.
7. Comparing audit data with company records.

A common characteristic of these applications is the fact that the auditor can define clearly and precisely what is to be computed, compared, summarized, printed, etc.

Testing Extensions and Footings The computer can be used to perform the simple summations and other computations in order to test the correctness of extensions and footings. The speed and low cost per computation of the computer means that it takes only a small amount of extra time and expense to perform the test in all records rather than in a sample.

Summarizing Data and Performing Analyses

The auditor frequently needs to have the client's data summarized in different ways for analysis. Examples are aging of accounts receivable, preparation of annual usage, requirements of parts and inventory, listing all credit balances in accounts receivable and all debit balances in accounts payable, and so forth.

Examining Records for Quality

The quality in visible records is readily apparent as the auditor makes use of them in his examination. Sloppy recordkeeping, lack of completeness, and other conditions affecting the quality of the records are observed by the auditor in the normal course of the audit. If the records are in machine-readable form, the auditor has the option of using the computer to examine the records. In using the computer, a program is written to examine the records for completeness. For example, the customer file records might be examined to determine the number of records in which there is no credit limit specified. The records can also be tested for consistency between different items in valid conditions, e.g., account balances exceeding credit limit in unreasonable amounts or more than ten dependents for payroll deduction purposes on a person's payroll record.

Selecting and Printing Confirmations

Using quantifiable selection criteria, the computer can select and print out the confirmation requests. As an example, one auditing firm has designed a multi-part form that is prepared on a computer. A single printing prepares a first request, a mailing envelope, a return envelope, a control copy, and a second request should it be needed. The form is designed so that the first request is stuffed in the mailing envelope, which contains the return envelope. The savings in audit time when preparing large numbers of confirmations are substantial. A computer program can be written to select the accounts according to any criteria desired and using any sampling plan.

Selecting and Printing Audit Samples

A computer can be programmed to select audit samples through either the use of random numbers or systematic selection techniques. The sample selection may be programmed to use multiple criteria, such as random samples of items under a certain dollar amount plus all items having a certain characteristic such as high dollar values. The samples selected in this way can be used for audit tests such as confirmation and price tests of inventory items.

Comparing the Same Data Maintained in Separate Files

Where there are two or more separate records having data fields that should be the same, the computer can be used to test correctness and consistency. For example, the pay rates on the payroll master tape may be compared with the pay rates used in computing the payroll as shown on a transaction tape.

Comparing Audit Data with Company Records

Audit data such as inventory test counts can be compared to the inventory records by using computer programs. This requires that the audit data be converted to machine-readable records. Other examples of this use are tracing cash receipts to accounts receivable records or comparing inventory costs with the master file cost data.

Obtaining a Computer-Audit Program

Three approaches have been used in obtaining suitable computer programs for use in evaluating and testing records: programs written by the client, programs written by or under supervision of the auditor, and generalized audit programs.

Programs Written by the Client

Frequently, analysis desired by the auditor is also useful to the client. Therefore, the client may write computer programs for his own use or prepare the program if the auditor requests the analysis and there is also internal use for it. Examples are programs to age accounts receivable, analyze inventory turnover and obsolescence, and review open order files. Obviously, before using such programs, the auditor will need to test the client's programs. The extent of testing would depend, of course, on how much the auditor can rely on the controls over programs and operations installed with the system. As a general rule, the auditor should, at minimum, obtain and review the program documentation and run book, and should perform tests that demonstrate that the program correctly performs the required functions. These tests might only require manual recalculation of the functions performed for a sample of records. However, if the program includes exception reporting or complex processing, the tests might require the review of test runs using records from the actual client file or records from an auditor-prepared test file. In certain circumstances, a review of the program code might be necessary.

Writing an Audit Program

Since a computer-audit program is written in the same way as any other computer program and since the programming process is explained very well in other literature, we shall not discuss in detail the steps involved in preparing a computer program to perform audit activities.

In general, there are five aspects of developing computer-audit programs:

1. Determining the required audit objectives and procedures, and preparing a document that defines, in detail, the required processing.
2. Developing a systems flowchart that includes all inputs, outputs, and major processing steps.
3. Developing program specifications using flowcharts, decision tables, and/or narratives that describe program logic and processing steps.

4. Coding, debugging, and testing.

5. Processing and review of results.

The extent to which the auditor can perform each of these tasks depends upon many factors, such as the auditor's knowledge of data processing, the auditor's competence in developing computer programs, the complexity of the programs being developed, the source language being used, and the availability of client programming assistance.

Generalized Audit Programs

It has been apparent to auditors for many years that there are many audit functions that fundamentally change very little from client to client. This is not really a very novel observation. Indeed, public accounting firms issue guides that suggest an outline of procedures to be employed in audit examinations and specific procedures that may be included in individual client audit programs.

The idea of generalized computer programs is also not a novel one. Computer manufacturers and other organizations have been involved in developing generalized programs or software for a number of years. These programs perform activities related to both the operation of the computer system (systems programs) and the manipulation and processing of data used in the management of the business (applications programs).

Generalized programs that perform a wide range of computer-audit functions are also available and may be used with a minimum of user training and preparation. One approach is the use of a program applicable to all clients in an industry. For example, there could be a brokerage audit program, in which the generalized audit programs are developed to perform standard audit procedures having to do with confirmation, margin computations, and so forth. The client's files are converted to a standard format on magnetic tape and this data file is processed by a program used for all clients. The conversion program is unique for each client and the client's computer is used only if it fits the model and configuration specification for which the brokerage audit program is written. It should be noted that even though two computer systems are not program-compatible, they may be data-compatible if records are put on magnetic tapes.

Another approach, using programs known as *audit software packages,* has experienced widespread development and use. Audit software packages provide the capability of an easy-to-use programming language designed especially for auditors. These packages, intended for use by nonprogrammers, can perform a wide range of general data processing functions—such as reading files, selecting certain records and fields for processing, sorting and summarizing records, performing user-specified calculations, and printing user-specified reports.

There are many audit software packages available. Appendix D includes a list of these software packages. Although the packages differ in design and in the technical and information requirements necessary to use them, they are similar in the audit functions they can perform.

In the remainder of this chapter, we shall discuss audit software packages and how they can be used to help the auditor evaluate client records.

Using Audit Software Packages

Several distinct phases, each with one or more major steps, are involved in using audit software packages. These include

1. Audit objectives, feasibility, and planning phase

   (a) Define audit objectives.
   (b) Prepare a preliminary audit program.
   (c) Obtain information from client about computer and file characteristics, record layouts, and file availability.
   (d) Determine that the computer and files are compatible with the audit software package.
   (e) Finalize audit procedures and establish a work plan for subsequent phases.

2. Application design phase

   (a) Define audit software application requirements including logic, calculations, format of reports, and how the application will be controlled.
   (b) Develop an overall flowchart of the planned audit software application.

3. Coding and testing phase

   (a) Code the audit software specification forms.
   (b) Keypunch the specification forms.
   (c) Test the application using a test file or a portion of an actual client file.

4. Processing phase

   (a) Process the application using the actual client file that is to be audited.
   (b) Review results to ensure that the results meet audit and control objectives.

It is essential that audit objectives be defined clearly. This normally involves planning a preliminary audit program that includes as much detail as the available information allows. Normally, the individual in charge of the audit approves such a plan.

Once the audit objectives have been formulated, the auditor should obtain information from the client about computer and file characteristics. This information might include the following items:

- Computer manufacturer and model number
- Types of tape and disk units
- Input–output devices available for use with audit software
- Addresses of all input–output units to be used in processing
- Type and release number of the operating system
- Type of file used: card, tape, disk
- Type of data records: fixed or variable length
- Length of data records
- Blocking factor, if the file is blocked
- Number of reels or packs in a file
- Number of channels on tape: 7 or 9
- Tape density
- Approximate number of records in file
- Header label information on input files

The auditor also obtains the record layouts for the client files to be analyzed. Record layout information may be verified by obtaining and analyzing a dump of several blocks of records. In addition, the auditor must obtain information about the availability of the client's files including identification of the processing and retention cycles. If the required files will not be retained during the period in which the auditor wishes to process the files, the auditor should revise the audit schedule or request that the client retain the files specifically for the audit.

The auditor may require some technical assistance to obtain information on computer and file characteristics and to determine that the computer and files are compatible with the audit software package to be used. Most software packages have been designed for specific computer systems. However, a package designed for one system usually can be used to process files created on another manufacturer's equipment. For example, tape files created on other equipment can usually be translated and used on an IBM system. In addition, most disk files can be copied to an IBM-compatible tape through the use of standard manufacturer-supplied software.

Case Study Using Audit Software   In discussing the steps involved in the use of audit software packages, it is best to introduce a case that illustrates an actual package performing specific audit tasks. The case involves the audit of accounts receivable, and assumes that a client processes his accounts receivable records by computer. A detailed accounts receivable record, on tape, is established for every customer invoice processed. Each detailed record is retained until the entire invoice amount is paid. In addition, an accounts receivable master record, on disk, is maintained for every active customer. If feasible, an audit software package will be used to perform certain procedures related to the audit of these records.

This case will illustrate the use of an audit software package called STRATA. The use of STRATA in our example does not imply that STRATA is the only audit software package recommended for use. The selection of an audit software package should be made after consideration of the many available packages.

Also, the case study does not include all possible audit procedures that might be performed by audit software in an accounts receivable audit. Rather, the case is intended to demonstrate typical audit functions that might be accomplished with such a package.[1]

Capabilities of Computer-Audit Software

Before an auditor begins the tasks required to develop an audit software application, he would be trained in the general functions of the software and in the specific coding rules used to specify processing requirements. The major functions that may be performed using STRATA are as follows:

1. *Create* a work file. This is accomplished by reading records from the file being audited and creating a new file comprised of "work" records in an auditor-specified format.

2. *Update* the work file using data contained in records from a second client file.

3. *Summarize* work records, producing a summary record that contains totals of data contained in detailed record fields.

4. *Sort* records into a new sequence required for calculations, report printing, or other processing.

5. *Calculate* additional values to be included in work records or to test existing file values.

6. *Generate* new files in auditor-specified formats.

7. *Print* reports in auditor-specified formats.

8. *Select* certain records for special processing, randomly or based upon a test of values contained in the client or work records.

After the *create* function, one or more of the other STRATA functions may be combined in any sequence and used as often as required. Other capabilities include table look-up, temporary storage for accumulation of

---

[1] This case has been adapted, by permission, from a case copyrighted by Touche Ross & Co.

values, and the printing of confirmations. In addition, the job control statements (JCL) used by the computer operating system to control processing are produced automatically.

Major functions are described in greater detail in the following paragraphs.

The *create* function allows generalized audit software to read a wide variety of computer record formats. This variety of formats occurs in records used by different companies for similar applications and in different applications within the same company. For example, sales records used in Company A are almost certain to differ in length and format from sales records in Company B. Similarly, inventory records will differ in size and format from those used in payroll. In the absence of a generalized create function, a separate program would be required for each unique record format. In an auditor-specified format, the create function creates work records that correspond to records on the client file.

The *update* function compares auditor-designated control fields in records on the work file to designated control fields in records on a second client file. If the control fields are identical, auditor-specified values from the second client file are inserted into fields of the work record.

The *summarize* function compares auditor-designated control fields in individual work records. If the control fields of two or more work file records are identical, a single new summary work record is created. Numeric fields in the new summary record contain a total of the values contained in the summarized records. Nonnumeric fields of the summary record contain the values present in the first record used to create the summary record.

The *sort* function may be used to resequence the work file into an ascending or descending sequence based on the values of auditor-specified sort control fields. STRATA automatically sorts, as required, to resequence files for the update, summarize, and print functions.

The *calculate* function includes a full set of mathematical, move, and conditional operations that can be used by the auditor to duplicate procedures performed by fairly complex computer programs. The auditor can calculate values to include on work records, to test existing record values, or to accumulate in temporary storage.

The *generate* file function creates a new file of card, tape, or disk records in an auditor-specified format. A generated record may include one or more fields from a work record.

The *print* function is used to print one or more reports, each with unique, auditor-specified columns, headings, totals, and subtotals. The reports may include a detail line for every work record, or they may print only auditor-specified totals and subtotals.

The *select* function can be used in conjunction with the create, update, calculate, and print functions. Auditor-specified fields are tested and the results of the tests determine if the record will be selected for further processing. For example, during the create phase, clients' records could be tested for the value of a department number field, and only records with a specified department number would be used to create work records. Similarly, an amount field in a work record could be tested and only records with a value greater than a specified amount would be printed on a report.

Use of Computer-Audit Software

As previously indicated, the phases in developing an audit software application are as follows:

1. Audit objectives, feasibility, and planning
2. Application design
3. Coding and testing
4. Processing

The tasks performed in our case study and the end products of each phase are described in the following paragraphs.

Phase 1: Objectives, Feasibility, and Planning Developing an audit software application includes defining audit objectives and obtaining information on computer file and record characteristics. If the application appears feasible, a plan of action for all subsequent phases is prepared.

For this case study, the auditor decided to use audit software to:

- Foot the accounts receivable detail file
- Prepare an aged trial balance of open items on the accounts receivable detail file
- Prepare a list of customer balances with the customer with the largest balance first, followed by other customers in descending balance order

The aging of the file will be based on invoice date. The report will include subtotals for each customer of all open items invoiced in the past 30 days, the past 31 to 60 days, the past 61 to 90 days, and all items open over 90 days. In addition, a final total of these four categories will be developed for all customers. The aging report will be used to verify the client's aged trial balance.

The second report, the list of customer balances in high-to-low sequence, will be used to determine which accounts should be selected for confirmation. It is the auditor's expectation that large accounts will be confirmed on a 100 percent basis and the remaining accounts will be confirmed on a sample basis. The second report will be used to judgmentally determine the cutoff point for 100 percent confirmations.

After the second report is analyzed, the auditor tentatively plans to develop a subsequent audit software application to select accounts for confirmation and to print the confirmation requests.

Having determined audit objectives and the tentative procedures necessary to achieve these objectives, the auditor meets with representatives of the client's EDP staff to obtain information about the client's computer configuration. In our case study the computer information obtained was as follows:

- The computer has 524,288 bytes of main storage.
- The computer operating system is OS/VS1.
- The input–output devices available include magnetic disk units; magnetic tape units, 9 track, 1,600 BPI density; card reader; and printer.

In addition, the following information was obtained about the accounts receivable files:

The accounts receivable detail file is on a single reel of magnetic tape; the record length is 60 bytes with 10 records to a block; the file label is ARDETAIL; and the file contains approximately 15,000 records.

The detail file is updated daily, and unless the auditor requests special retention, the old file is retained for 5 days.

The accounts receivable master file is a disk file; the record length is 100 bytes with 6 records to a block; the file label is ARMAST; the file is organized sequentially and contains approximately 1,500 records.

The master file is updated on an as-required basis, approximately once per week; a copy of the old file is not retained.

The record layouts of the detail and master records are as illustrated in Table 10.1.

The auditor would now analyze the information to determine that STRATA is compatible with the client's computer and files, and that the data contained in the client records are adequate to achieve defined audit objectives. In our case, STRATA is compatible and there is adequate data to achieve specified audit objectives. The auditor will, however, have to make special arrangements to ensure that copies of the required files are retained beyond their normal retention date.

Phase 2: Application Design   The auditor can now proceed to the design phase of the audit software application. This includes the definition of detailed processing requirements and the preparation of an overall flowchart of the planned application.

In our case study, items that define the detailed processing requirements include these:

- Layouts of required reports, as illustrated in Exhibit 10.1
- A narrative description of the formula to be used to test the date field and to assign the balance amount values to one of the four aging categories

ACCOUNTS RECEIVABLE DETAIL RECORD LAYOUT

FIELD NAME	LOCATION	FORMAT
Batch number	1 to 5	Character
Record code	6 to 8	Character
Division	9 to 11	Character
Customer number	12 to 19	Character
Invoice number	20 to 25	Character
Invoice date (month/day/year)	26 to 31	Character
Original invoice amount	32 to 37	Packed, 2 decimal
Current open amount	38 to 43	Packed, 2 decimal
Date of last payment	44 to 48	Character
Amount of last payment	49 to 54	Packed, 2 decimal
Filler	55 to 60	Character (blanks)

ACCOUNTS RECEIVABLE MASTER RECORD LAYOUT

FIELD NAME	LOCATION	FORMAT
Customer number	1 to 8	Character
Customer name	9 to 23	Character
Address 1	24 to 38	Character
Address 2	39 to 53	Character
Address 3	54 to 68	Character
Zip code	69 to 73	Character
Credit limit	74 to 78	Packed, zero decimal
Filler	79 to 100	Character (blanks)

- A brief statement as to how the application will be controlled
- A flowchart of the application, as illustrated in Figure 10.1

In this application, control could be established by comparing the final report totals to the client's book value of open accounts receivable and by manually aging several customer accounts and comparing the results.

The application design phase serves two objectives. First, it expands the conceptual ideas developed during planning into the detailed descriptions of application features necessary for specification coding. Second, it provides nontechnical end products that may be reviewed by audit engagement managers and other members of the audit team.

Phase 3: Coding and Testing With the audit objectives finalized and the end products of the design phase completed, the auditor can begin to code the audit software specification sheets. The specification sheets for STRATA, and other software packages, are the means by which the auditor adapts the generalized software to his specific application requirements and to the unique format of the client's files. The specification coding for audit software is analogous to coding source code for a conventional programming language such as COBOL

Receivables Aging Report — Report 1					
Customer Number	Customer Name	Under 30	30 to 59	60 to 89	90 and over	Customer Balance
XXXXXXXX	X-(15)-X	XX,XXX.XX	XX,XXX.XX	XX,XXX.XX	XX,XXX.XX	XX,XXX.XX
(*Note*: One line per customer, customer number sequence.)						
Final totals		XXX,XXX.XX	XXX,XXX.XX	XXX,XXX.XX	XXX,XXX.XX	XXX,XXX.XX

High-to-Low Balances — Report 2			
Customer Number	Customer Name	Customer Balance	Cumulative Balance
XXXXXXXX	X-(15)-X	XX,XXX.XX	XXX,XXX.XX
(*Note*: One line per customer, customer balance sequence.)			
Final totals		XXX,XXX.XX	XXX,XXX.XX

Exhibit 10.1 Layouts of Planned Reports

or FORTRAN. As will be illustrated later, audit software requires only a small fraction of the coding required to accomplish similar tasks using conventional programming languages. After coding, the specification sheets are used as the source document from which specification cards are keypunched. As the first step in processing, the specification cards are read into computer memory where they are used to sequence and condition the routines performed by the audit software package. Using STRATA the auditor would code specification sheets that define the following:

- General characteristics of the computer and input–output devices
- The format of the work record
- Characteristics of the client's file (label, tape or disk, etc.)
- Characteristics of the client's records (block size, record length, location and length of fields, etc.)
- Required functions (sort, summarize, etc.)
- Required calculations
- Characteristics of required reports

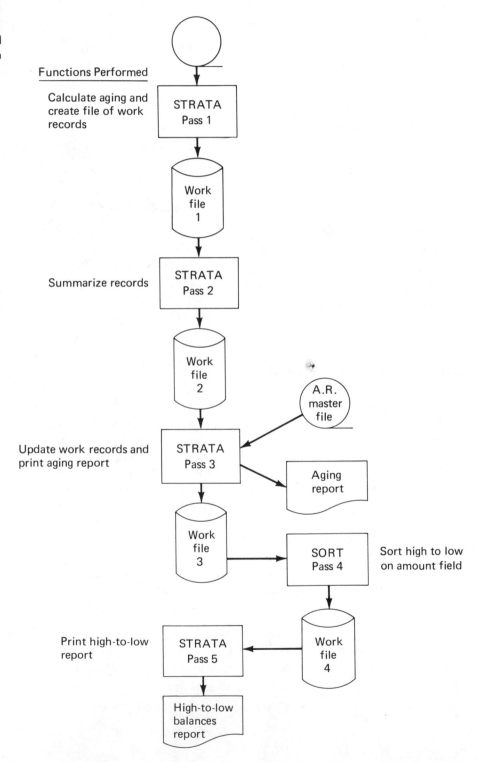

**Figure 10.1
Flowchart of Planned
Application**

Functions Performed

Calculate aging and create file of work records

Summarize records

Update work records and print aging report

Sort high to low on amount field

Print high-to-low report

Since each audit software package has its own specification forms and coding rules, we shall not consider in detail how the auditor codes the specification sheets. Figures 10.2 and 10.3 are, however, included as examples of the STRATA specification coding. Figure 10.2 is the code that defines the format of work file records, and Figure 10.3 is the code that defines the print requirements of the aging report.

When specification cards have been coded and keypunched, the application is ready to be tested. If the testing is done using the client's computer and files, the test will demonstrate conclusively that the software package is compatible and that the auditor understands the format of the records. Testing may also indicate that errors are present in the auditor's specification coding, such as violations of the specification coding rules and conventions. In addition, the test may demonstrate errors in the way the auditor sequenced functions or specified logic and calculations. Finally, testing provides an opportunity to review the actual reports produced by the application. STRATA, and most audit software, includes a test option that permits an actual run of the application but limits the number of records processed. For example, in our case application, the detail file has approximately 15,000 records. The test option could be used to run a test that only processes 100 records.

Phase 4: Processing   Usually testing is completed in advance of the required audit date. When testing is completed, the auditor makes final arrangements to ensure the availability of the client's files as of the required audit date. When the files to be audited become available, they are processed using the audit software application. These files are frequently retained for a period after processing in case reprocessing is required. Reprocessing might be required because an

WORK FIELD NO.		WORK FIELD NAME	STORAGE FORMAT			REDEFINITION			Do Not Punch
			ALPHA-NUMERIC	NUMERIC		STARTING WORK FIELD	STARTING LOCATION		LEFT-MOST BYTE LOCATION
			LENGTH	Decimal Places	Indicative Y Yes				
5	6 8	9 22	23 25	26	27	28 30	31 33		Memo Only
2	W 0 1	C U S T O M E R N O	8						
2	W 0 2	U N D E R 3 0		2					
2	W 0 3	3 0 T O 5 9		2					
2	W 0 4	6 0 T O 8 9		2					
2	W 0 5	9 0 A N D O V E R		2					
2	W 0 6	C U S T O M E R B A L		2					
2	W 0 7	C U S T O M E R N A M E	1 5						
2	W 8							DO NOT PUNCH	
2	W 9								
2	W 0								

Figure 10.2   Work Record Specification Coding

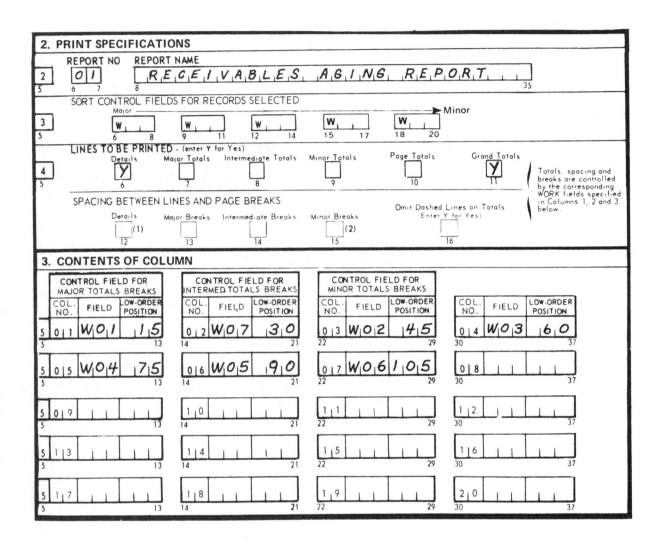

Figure 10.3   Aging Report Print Specification Coding

error was not detected during testing or because analysis of the resulting reports indicates the need for expanded audit procedures.

Finally, results are reviewed and appropriate documentation is filed in the audit work papers. The review of results must ensure that the application satisfied the audit objectives and that adequate control over the application was achieved. The first page of both case study reports are included in Figures 10.4 and 10.5. Analysis of these two reports indicates that our objectives were achieved. The final total of the aging report (not shown in Figure 10.4) is a

```
STRATA-OS 360/370              RECEIVABLES AGING REPORT                    04/05/77
                                                                          REPORT 1 PAGE 1

CUSTOMER NO    CUSTOMER NAME      UNDER 30    30 TO 50    60 TO 80    90 AND OVER    CUSTOMER BAL
-----------------------------------------------------------------------------------------------------
   04609631    NEW HAVEN STEEL        .00      120.95       42.75           .00          163.70
   04610705    AMERICAN STAMP      125.00        5.50         .00           .00          130.50
   04611279    MOROW CASTING        36.30       43.88         .00           .00           80.18
   04718493    SWIFT-CRAFT          57.98       54.67         .00         38.80          151.45
   04719386    ROBBINS & WHITE      54.14       14.11         .00           .00           68.25
   04722877    ACME PRODUCTS          .00         .00         .00        215.92          215.92
   04738490    SEERO INC.           15.99         .00         .00           .00           15.99
   04763028    NAICCO LEASING         .00       73.80         .00           .00           73.80
   04769480    ST. PAUL LABS       124.48       48.80         .00           .00          173.28
   04791873    GEO-TECH RESEARCH    48.28       57.60         .00           .00          105.88
   04800365    S & S TESTING         6.70         .00         .00           .00            6.70
   04837173    WINSTON REED INC.    71.90      129.05         .00           .00          200.95
   04842671    BIC INDUSTRIES      108.31       97.11         .00           .00          205.42
   04866843    ALLEN PRODUCTS       66.73       90.19       87.46           .00          244.38
   04888688    JACK BENEDICT CO.    12.11      204.98         .00           .00          217.09
   04891700    PARAGON GLASS        21.61       39.82      152.18           .00          213.61
   04900924    WELLER LTD.            .00         .00         .00         93.83           93.83
   04912967    GELLMORE FABRICS     55.27      118.12         .00           .00          173.39
   04928394    EWING FREIGHT       117.53       93.16         .00           .00          210.69
   04931111    KPC COMPANY          11.00       39.90         .00           .00           50.90
```

Figure 10.4 STRATA-Produced Aging Report*

  *Note: Only top of first page is presented.

```
STRATA-OS 360/370                HIGH TO LOW BALANCES REPORT             04/05/77
VERSION 6.21 RUN 0251                                                    REPORT 02-PAGE 1

CUSTOMER NO.    CUSTOMER NAME       CUSTOMER BAL.     CUMULATIVE
-----------------------------------------------------------------------------------------
  12012321      CLARKSON-HAMILTON     33,164.47       33,164.47
  12012036      FW QUINN & CO         19,946.08       53,110.55
  12012474      BELL HAGER LAB        17,416.01       70,526.56
  09999217      MARITIME WINCH         6,959.24       77,485.80
  04999911      LANDIS ELECTRIC        3,853.73       81,339.53
  04296736      JK BROSKIN             3,547.83       84,887.36
  12015313      DATA RESEARCH INC      3,151.70       88,039.06
  12012612      JCD CORP               3,087.44       91,126.50
  12012043      OAKLAND SUPPLY         2,888.10       94,014.60
  12012110      RACON PLASTICS         1,838.21       95,852.81
  12012035      HOUSTON PRODUCTS       1,287.70       97,140.51
  12008560      ROBERT LEWIS INC         775.48       97,915.99
  10416516      SMITHTON PRESS           688.96       98,604.95
  09999001      PIID INC                 569.41       99,174.36
  04999541      TEKDATA                  560.61       99,734.97
  04772158      RAFFCO                   414.00      100,148.97
  04999711      METTLER & KEEFE          330.02      100,478.99
  09999123      DAK APPLIANCES           328.01      100,807.00
  12013036      WESTERN MOTORS           259.27      101,066.27
  12012819      LISS & CROSS             251.67      101,317.94
```

Figure 10.5 STRATA-Produced High-to-Low Balance Report*

  *Note: Only top of first page is presented.

footing of the file that can be compared to the client's accounts receivable book value. Similarly, the aging totals may be used to test the accuracy of the client's aged trial balance of receivables. In addition, the aging report can be reviewed to identify possible doubtful accounts. The high-to-low customer balances report also meets our audit objectives. The report indicates that 15 customers with balances greater than $500 account for over $99,000 of receivables. All other customers have relatively low balances. On the basis of this report, the auditor might decide to confirm all accounts with a balance greater than $500 and confirm all other accounts on a sample basis.

How STRATA Performed the Application

Having completed our discussion of the steps involved in an audit software application, we will now consider how STRATA actually processed the application. Audit software packages have different operating characteristics and, depending on the auditor's specifications, the same package will operate differently for each unique application. Conceptually, however, most packages operate in a similar fashion and understanding one package facilitates the learning of most other packages.

To describe application processing, we will again refer to Figure 10.1, the flowchart of the planned application. In our sample application, actual and planned processing were identical. The application began with the client's accounts receivable detail file and later used the client's accounts receivable master file. In addition, four disk work files are used by the *summarize, update, and sort* functions. To explain the effect of processing on individual records, Figure 10.6 illustrates the processing of a detail file that contains only four records. This small file includes three records for customer 1002 and one record for customer 1001. The client file is in customer-number sequence, and the fields in the records are those previously identified in Table 10.1, the record layouts. Blank fields indicate the absence of data; for example, no payments have been made against three of the detail records; therefore, their Last Pay Date field is blank. (An actual dump of records would indicate that alphanumeric fields without data contain blanks; numeric fields without data contain zeros.)

In our case study, the first auditor-specified functions aged the Open Amount value and created work records. The aging uses the *calculate* function to test the value of the Invoice Date field. Depending upon the date present, the Open Amount value is moved to one of the four aging fields of a work record. Values in the Open Amount and Customer Number fields would also be moved to their respective fields in the work record. As illustrated in Figure 10.6, after the aging and creation of work records, Work File 1 would contain a work record that corresponds to each client detail file record. The work records are in a revised, auditor-specified format. Each record contains data from a detail client record and also includes a blank Customer Name field required for the

EFFECT OF PROCESSING UPON RECORDS

A. R. DETAIL FILE RECORDS BEFORE S T R A T A PROCESSING

BATCH	CODE	DIV.	CUSTOMER NO.	INVOICE NO.	INVOICE DATE	ORIGINAL AMOUNT	OPEN AMOUNT	LAST PAY DATE
1 1 4 0	D	1 0 1	1 0 0 2	A 2 0 1 1	1 1 5 7 7	5 6	6	3 0 6 7 7
1 3 1 7	D	1 0 1	1 0 0 2	A 3 4 0 4	3 1 1 7 7	4	4	
2 1 1 9	D	1 0 1	1 0 0 2	A 3 9 1 8	3 2 3 7 7	1 4 0	1 4 0	
9 1 1	D	1 0 1	1 0 0 1	A 2 7 7 3	2 0 7 7 7	1 1 0	1 1 0	

WORK FILE 1 — AFTER AGING AND WORK RECORD CREATE

WO1 CUSTOMER NO.	WO2 <30 DAYS	WO3 30-59 DAYS	WO4 60-89 DAYS	WO5 >90 DAYS	WO6 OPEN AMOUNT	WO7 CUSTOMER NAME
1 0 0 2			6		6	
1 0 0 2	4				4	
1 0 0 2	1 4 0				1 4 0	
1 0 0 1		1 1 0			1 1 0	

WORK FILE 2 — AFTER SUMMARIZE

WO1	WO2	WO3	WO4	WO5	WO6	WO7
1 0 0 2	1 4 4		6		1 5 0	
1 0 0 1		1 1 0			1 1 0	

WORK FILE 3 — AFTER UPDATE

WO1	WO2	WO3	WO4	WO5	WO6	WO7
1 0 0 2	1 4 4		6		1 5 0	N E W Y O R K G & E
1 0 0 1		1 1 0			1 1 0	E T C C O R P

WORK FILE 4 — AFTER SORT

WO1	WO2	WO3	WO4	WO5	WO6	WO7
1 0 0 1		1 1 0			110	E T C C O R P
1 0 0 2	1 4 4		6		150	N E W Y O R K G & E

Figure 10.6   Effect of Processing on Records

subsequent update processing. Work records are created only as physical records on a work file if a work file is required for subsequent processing. If, for example, the user decided that his audit objectives could be met by an aging report *without* customer name, STRATA could produce this report in a single pass and a Work File 1 would not be created.

Continuing with our example, Work File 1 containing four records was created. This file was then processed by the summarize function to produce

Work File 2, which contains only two records. On Work File 2, the aging fields of the customer 1002 summary record contain the total of the amounts originally contained in the three customer 1002 records. In our case study, the detail file contained 15,000 records for 1,500 active customers. Therefore, the summarize function would have reduced the work file from 15,000 to 1,500 records. This reduction would substantially reduce the computer processing time required for the application.

After the update, Work File 3 records contain values in the Customer Name fields. These values were obtained from accounts receivable master file records.

Following the update, Work File 3 is resequenced by the sort function to produce Work File 4. The sort, performed in descending sequence on the Open Amount field, causes the record for customer 1002 to move to the front of the file, as required, for the high-to-low printing of customer balances.

The final pass in our application uses the print function to read the resequenced work file and print the list of customer balances in high-to-low sequence.

Testing Data for Reliability

The procedures described in Chapters 8 and 9, and in this chapter, provide the auditor with a systematic approach for testing the data's reliability. Although the suggested procedures are presented in logical sequence, there is no requirement that all work steps be completed. The auditor should do only what is necessary to satisfy data validation requirements.

Some suggested tests for data reliability are listed below. The auditor may use any or all of these tests or develop some other means to test the computer data. The key is to perform enough tests to support an opinion on the data's reliability.

On operational audits (a major function for internal auditing), the internal controls evaluation may follow confirmation tests (i.e., tests to confirm the reasonableness of data). Since the auditor must select elements of data to be confirmed without knowing internal control strengths and weaknesses, emphasis should be placed on selecting data which, if found to be incomplete or inaccurate, would affect audit conclusions. Confirmation sources include the following six categories of information.

Regular Users of Computer Data

The auditor should begin confirmation tests with principal users because they use the information often and are directly affected by inaccuracies in the information.

Typically, users of computer products have varying knowledge about the product's quality. To obtain confidence in confirmation responses, the auditor should interview enough users to develop a general idea about the computer output's usefulness.

When there are a large number of principal users or several users at different locations, it may be impractical to interview each one personally. In these cases the auditor may (1) select a sample of users based on number, location, or some other suitable criterion, (2) interview users by telephone, or (3) distribute the questionnaire for users to complete. If users complete questionnaires, the auditor must maintain control over the questionnaires and conduct some follow-up to ensure accurate responses.

When conducting interviews, it is especially important to obtain evidence of incomplete or inaccurate data mentioned by users. The auditor should do the following:

- Identify the nature of the problem. Look for overstated or understated amounts, incorrect totals, incomplete data fields, and negative balances that should be positive.
- Determine the frequency of errors. They may be isolated instances or recurring.
- Determine if users can explain why errors are occurring. Since data errors affect users, they may have conducted studies to show the magnitude and cause of errors.
- Determine if users keep manual records for use in lieu of computer reports or other output. Manually maintained records in a computer environment can mean poor quality of computer output and unnecessary expenditures for duplicate recordkeeping. The auditor may also find that manual records better satisfy the need for reliable audit evidence.

Third Parties   Confirming data with third parties is beneficial because a third party is often independent of the information system that generated the data. Some examples include the following sources and types of data:

- *Banks*—cash balances on hand, numbers or amounts of loans
- *Warehouses*—assets stored, volume of transfers
- *Training institutions*—number of students serviced, dollar volume of contracts
- *Common carriers*—rates for freight shipments, volume of passengers between selected locations
- *Medical facilities*—daily rates for patient care, types of outpatient services available
- *Private business concerns*—billings for utility services, wholesale prices of generic drugs

Suppliers of Input Data   Persons or organizations supplying input to the computer system were identified earlier in the document flow diagram. If they are not the same as regular users of the system output, they may be contacted to confirm the accuracy and completeness of the data they prepared for system processing.

EDP Department Personnel The auditor should contact EDP department personnel to determine the history and number of errors associated with a specific application or product of a system.

Computers are almost always programmed to edit data that are entered for processing. These edits help determine whether the data are acceptable. If any item of the data contains errors or fails to meet established edit criteria, it is rejected. A computer record of rejected transactions should be available from the control group responsible for reviewing output. Errors shown on this record can be related directly to the application being processed.

The auditor should exercise care in reaching conclusions about edit tests because a system with many rejected transactions may actually produce reliable information. For example, a system with insufficient computer edits may routinely accept erroneous data and print out few rejected transactions, while a system with extensive edits may reject many transactions but actually produce a far more accurate final product.

The point is that the auditor can use these edit reports to identify (1) problems that users are having with the system and (2) the length of time users are taking to correct these errors.

Common Sense Tests Through discussions with systems designers and data users, the auditor should have developed criteria to judge the data's reasonableness. For instance, the following kinds of questions help:

- Are amounts too small? (cost per mile to operate a one-ton truck = $.004; three universities in the state of New York)
- Are amounts too large? (accrued annual leave balance for 1 employee = 3,000 hours; a single student loan for $150,000)
- Are data fields complete? (social security payments listed for only 46 states; all 9 federal census regions listed but no program enrollment data shown for 2 of them; checks listed in numerical order but one group of checks within the series not accounted for)
- Are calculations correct? (columns of data include 4-digit items but the column total includes only 3 digits; unit cost extension for 1,200 items which should be for only 120 items)

These common sense tests can be done quickly and can alert the auditor to data reliability problems.

Comparison Tests GAO audits are usually "first-time" investigations. Certain comparisons, other than comparing current period data with previous data, can be useful. This is especially true if the data being compared come from independent sources. Some of the more typical sources of information against which the auditor may compare data include the following:

- *Source documents*—Any time information in a computer-processed report, listing, or file can be compared with data on the original source documents, the auditor should consider doing so. However, because of computation, summarization, and other data manipulation that may occur as the data pass through the system, the end product may not readily be compared with the raw data that entered the system. One example is salary check. Source data for a salary check will usually consist of (1) a time and attendance record for hours worked, (2) a W-4 form for tax exemptions, (3) other forms authorizing various payroll deductions, and (4) personnel forms showing employment grade, promotion actions, etc. Obviously, the net amount of a salary check cannot be directly compared to any one of these source documents.

- *Physical counts and inspections*—A physical count can be made to verify information concerning the quantities, types, or conditions of any tangible assets. When this techniue is used, the comparison should be made both ways—from the record to the physical count and from the physical count to the record.

- *Computed amounts*—This test requires an independent calculation of an amount, which can then be compared with the amount shown in the computer report or file. Examples include computations of benefit payments for selected categorical grant recipients, investment repayment balances on government construction projects, loan balances and delinquent amounts, and resale prices of foreclosed and repossessed properties.

- *Records, files, and reports from other sources*—The validity of recorded data may also be checked by comparing the data with the same type of information obtained from another independent source. Reports on company programs and activities issued by outside contractors, universities, internal audit groups, privately funded foundations, and others may contain useful information.

If these third-party reviewers, however, obtained information from activities they are evaluating, it may be the same information the auditor has chosen to review for reliability. This precludes its use for data comparison purposes unless the third-party organization has itself evaluated the reliability of the information. Experience has shown that this type of reliability testing is seldom done, and the auditor should never assume it has been done.

Summary

Audit software is a powerful tool that allows the auditor to develop his own automated audit procedures, directly access automated client records, and examine large amounts of audit evidence at computer speeds. Computer programs can be used by the auditor to examine the quality of a client's automated records and to perform a wide range of other auditing tasks. Programs designed to read unique client records and perform a specific audit procedure may be written by the client or by the auditor. If a program is written by the client, the auditor must take certain steps to make certain that the program actually performs the required audit procedure. The auditor may also use generalized audit software to read client records and perform a wide variety of data processing functions—including calculations, file updates, record summarization, sorts, and report printing. Generalized software is tailored to unique record formats and required audit procedures by the use of auditor-coded specifications. The successful use of generalized audit software involves an application development process with four distinct phases: defining objectives, determining feasibility, and planning; design of the application; coding and testing; and application processing.

Problems

1. (a) Flowchart the processing of data with computer-audit programs.
   (b) Differentiate between test data and computer-audit programs.

2. Describe how computer-audit programs could be used in performing audit procedures in
   (a) Accounts receivable
   (b) Inventory
   (c) Fixed assets
   (d) Liabilities
   (e) Payroll

3. Flowchart the tasks involved in developing a computer-audit program.

4. Below are the data fields in a payroll master record for salaried employees. You decide to develop a computer-audit program to perform some of the audit procedures in salary payroll.
   (a) List the audit procedures you would include in such a program and the auditing objective of each procedure.
   (b) Prepare a program flowchart to show the detailed processing steps in your program.

Data Fields:
Salary Payroll Master Records

Plant code	Retirement rate	Year-to-date salary
Salary grade	Federal withholding tax	Bond balance
First initial	Bond deduction	Bond issue
Middle initial	Federal tax exemption	Year-to-date social security
Last name	Social security tax	Year-to-date state tax
Social security number	State tax exemption	Year-to-date federal tax
Annual salary	State withholding tax	Title
Biweekly gross pay	Pay period	

5. The Wheelox Company has a large general mail-order business with annual sales of about $100 million. Most of the sales are made on a monthly payment plan basis. On December 31, there were approximately 10,000 open accounts with total receivables of approximately $4,500,000. Very few customers' balances exceed $1,000. The company's general office maintains the accounts receivable records. The large volume of transactions processed by the company has necessitated extensive segregation of duties and frequent balancing of data during processing. Accordingly, the company's internal accounting controls are considered to be very good.

(a) List the audit procedures you would perform in your year-end audit work of accounts receivable for this company.

(b) Indicate, on the basis of your knowledge of audit software, how such software could be used to perform the procedures you list.

(c) Assuming you do the accounts receivable confirmation work at some date prior to year end, indicate how a computer-audit program could be used to review activity from the confirmation date to year end.

A complete record of each customer's account is stored on magnetic tape and includes the following.

Description	Positions Required on Tape Record
Type of account	1
Customer account number	9
Customer name and address	60
Credit limit	1
Status code	1
Number of transactions this month	2
Current month's charges	6
Current month's payments	6
Current month's credits	6
Balance	6
Aged balance over 30 days	6
Aged balance over 60 days	6
Aged balance over 90 days	6
Aged balance over 120 days	6
Year account opened	2
Year last active	2
Total purchases this year to date	6
Total returns this year to date	6
Number of months active	2
Number of months over 90-day category	2
Total purchases last year	6
Total returns last year	6
Number of months active last year	2
Number of months over 90-day category last year	2
Highest balance owed	6

All source documents are in the form of cards or are converted to cards. Daily, all the transactions in account sequence are read into the computer and processed against the customer master tape. Each account is updated and analyzed to determine whether the transactions just processed have created a condition that should be brought to the attention of the authorization or collection sections. Exception reports are automatically printed and forwarded to these groups to alert them to such conditions as accounts over credit limits, unusual buildups, and payments by delinquent accounts.

During the order filling, collection, and credit processes, totals are generated to control all input transactions entering the data processing system. The computer operation accumulates totals of all input that must agree with the predetermined totals developed outside the system.

A control record is kept on tape for each cycle. As the accounts are updated, the day's transactions are accumulated and added to the starting control figure for each cycle. The new control figures are balanced with the sum of all the individial accounts in the cycle (accumulated as each account is processed). In addition, a detailed transaction and cycle control report is prepared, providing an audit trail in customer account number sequence.

6. For the case described in problem 10 in Chapter 9, determine the audit *objectives* and audit *procedures* that you would use to evaluate the accounts receivable files of the company. The record layout of the information contained in the accounts receivable files is shown in Table 9.4 of the case.

   After you have determined your audit procedures, indicate which procedures could be performed with the use of the computer.

7.* In the audit of Greenline Manufacturing Company for the year ended 12-31-X8, Roberta Bond, CPA, concluded that the lack of an audit trail for the property, plant, and equipment accounts precluded auditing that area in the traditional manner. As a result, the decision was made to use a generalized audit program in the verification of certain aspects of the accounts. The generalized audit program includes the following specific objectives:

   • Foot the file and print totals by major property category for cost of all assets, cost of current additions, and accumulated and current depreciation for both book and tax purposes.

   • Prepare a listing of all additions over $5,000 for vouching and inspection.

   • Prepare a listing of all disposals for detailed verification.

* Problem 7 has been adapted by permission from the CPA examination.

- Verify the calculations of depreciation expenses for both book and tax purposes.

The permanent asset master files for 12-31-X7 were saved by the client and include the same information as the 12-31-X8 files. Their contents are as follows:

ELEMENT NUMBER	DESCRIPTION OF CONTENTS
1	Asset number
2	Description
3	Type code
4	Location code
5	Year of acquisition
6	Cost
7	Accum. Deprec.—beginning book
8	Depreciation—YTD book
9	Useful life
10	Tax depreciation method
11	Accum. Deprec.—beginning tax
12	Depreciation—YTD tax

(*Note:* All fixed assets use the straight-line method for book depreciation. Tax depreciation may be straight-line, double-declining balance, or sum-of-the-years' digits.)

(*a*) Explain in detail how the information on the 12-31-X7 and 12-31-X8 master files should be used to fulfill the four audit objectives.

(*b*) List the reports that will be generated by the Generalized Audit Program (GAP).

(*c*) Explain what additional verification is necessary on each of these reports to satisfy the auditor that property, plant, and equipment is fairly stated.

EDP AUDIT PROCESS*

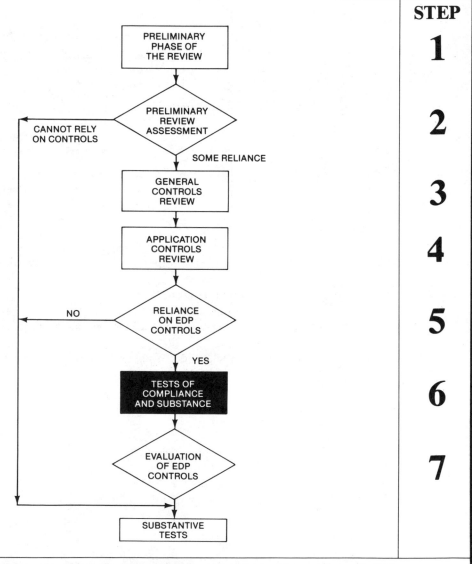

STEP

1

2

3

4

5

6

7

PRELIMINARY
PHASE OF
THE REVIEW

PRELIMINARY
REVIEW
ASSESSMENT

CANNOT RELY
ON CONTROLS

SOME RELIANCE

GENERAL
CONTROLS
REVIEW

APPLICATION
CONTROLS
REVIEW

NO

RELIANCE
ON EDP
CONTROLS

YES

TESTS OF
COMPLIANCE
AND SUBSTANCE

EVALUATION
OF EDP
CONTROLS

SUBSTANTIVE
TESTS

*Diagram is adapted from The Auditor's Study and Evaluation of Internal Control in EDP Systems, pages 21–24. Copyright © 1977 by the American Institute of Certified Public Accountants, Inc. (See Figure 9.1 for a complete explanation of the steps.)

AUDITING RECORDS PRODUCED BY SERVICE CENTERS

(6) Tests of Compliance

Purpose:
- Determine whether the necessary control procedures are prescribed and followed satisfactorily.
- Provide reasonable assurance that controls are functioning properly.
- Consider and, to the extent appropriate, document when, how, and by whom controls are provided.

Methods: Examination of records; test of control procedures; inquiry; observation.

OBJECTIVE

Many organizations have their records processed by an outside service center. This chapter explains the audit implications of, and how to audit, records processed by a service center.

In all the preceding chapters, we have been concerned primarily with auditing a client's systems and records where an in-house computer has been involved. Many organizations are now using outside service centers to process accounting and financial data. The auditor with a client using a service center may be faced with problems that are both new and unique. For the first time, the auditor may be dealing with the problem of auditing financial data processed by a computer. In addition to the usual auditing problems of EDP systems, the service center adds the complicated aspect of a distinct and separate outside entity, which may nevertheless be an integral part of the client's data processing and internal control system.

This chapter discusses the nature of service centers and the audit approach when a client uses a service center for processing accounting data.

Nature of Service Centers

A service center is any organization that provides data processing functions for other organizations, including the actual processing function itself.[1] Service centers usually offer the following services: equipment-time rental, information processing, and systems and programming assistance. These services generally require skilled personnel and expensive equipment, both of which are available to customers on an as-needed basis.

Such services are now provided by many types of organizations, including those formed exclusively to provide data processing services as well as equipment manufacturers, banks, CPA firms, and others. Accordingly, the industry's typical firm defies description. Some organizations employ few people and provide services limited to information processing or equipment-time rental. Other organizations, offering more sophisticated services, maintain large staffs consisting of systems designers, programmers, mathematicians, statisticians, and engineers, in addition to equipment operators.

Service centers also differ in that some operate tabulating equipment while others operate electronic computers only, or a combination of both. Capabilities will vary, especially among those service centers operating electronic computers. Their effectiveness depends on the computer's design, age, peripheral equipment available, and particularly upon qualifications of their personnel.

Organization of Service Centers   A service center is usually organized along functional lines. Certain functions such as sales, systems and programming, and operations must be performed by all service centers to achieve satisfactory operating results.[2]

---

[1] J. L. Roy, "The Changing Role of the Service Bureau," *Datamation,* March 1970, p. 52.

[2] For a more detailed discussion of the organization and operation of service bureaus, see *Audits of Service Center Produced Records,* AICPA, 1974, Chap. 1.

Figure 11.1 represents the organization of a service center with revenues slightly in excess of $5 million. Smaller service centers may combine the systems analysis and programming functions; in fact, they may be performed by the same individuals. In smaller service centers, sales and customer service may be handled by the chief executive or incorporated in another function. Some ser-

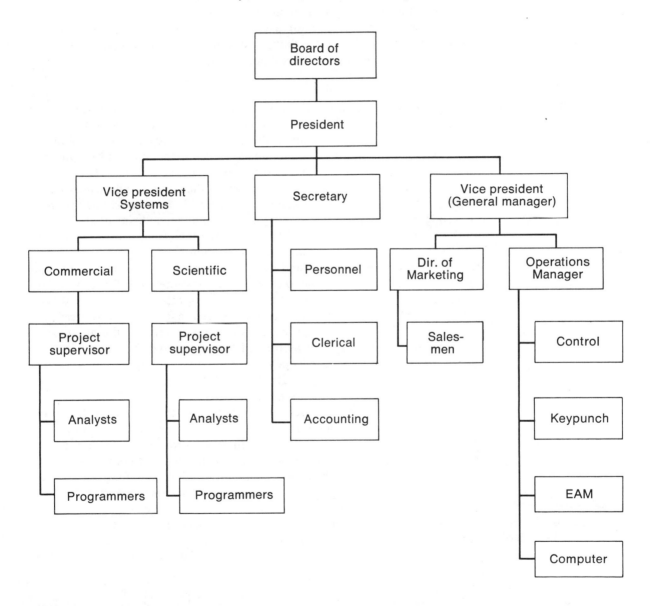

Figure 11.1 Service Center Organization

vice centers also use the account executive approach, where each client is assigned to an account executive who is responsible for developing a system for the client and maintaining a working relationship with her or him.

The functions and duties of systems design and programming are usually separate from computer operations. In such cases programmers are not allowed to operate the computer for regular processing.

The operations manager of a control group is usually responsible for receiving and controlling input data, reconciling control information, and correcting and reprocessing incorrect data.

Operations[3]

The operations cycle starts with the user delivering input data to the service center for processing. The input data may be either in the form of hard-copy documents or in a machine-readable form (e.g., punched cards prepared by the user). Although usually delivered to the service center manually or by mail, they may also be forwarded by a telcommunication system.

The permanent (master) files against which the input is to be processed are usually retained by the service center. A master file may be retained in tape, disk, or card form depending on the system and equipment being used. Changes in the master file data are often submitted as file-mainenance adjustments and processed before the processing of the transactions.

Most service center processing is designed to provide the user with the final output document (invoice, payroll check, etc.) together with the appropriate listings or registers. Occasionally, the end product of the processing consists of punched cards or other machine-readable records that must be processed further or printed at the user's office. Most service centers require an advance schedule of all processing to be performed and reports to be prepared. Upon request, service centers can usually provide special purpose reports, but these are generally supplied on a delayed basis. The data stored in the master files are not commonly reproduced except on special request.

The responsibility for record retention usually rests with the user. Therefore, the reports obtained from the service center must contain all necessary historical data, and the user must arrange for them to be stored. The service center usually retains only those records that are necessary for the reconstruction of files in the event of loss, destruction, or significant error.

Responsibilities and Controls

The role of the service center may vary from simply operating a program prepared by the user to providing full data processing service. The trend is toward the latter arrangement because it requires fewer EDP skills of the user. In this

---

[3] This section and the next two sections are reprinted by permission, with changes, from a previous AICPA study by Gordon B. Davis, *Auditing and EDP,* copyright 1968 by the American Institute of Certified Public Accountants, Inc.

case, the service center participates (and often takes the initiative) in the design of the system and accepts full responsibility for the programming and program testing as well as for the operation of the system. The user's participation is limited to establishing the requirements of the system and contributing toward its design. The user should acquire a sufficient knowledge of the system to enable him or her to provide the necessary input, react to exceptions and differences reported, and understand the output records.

In keeping with the service concept, the service center usually assumes full responsibility for hiring, training, and supervising the personnel who program and operate the system. The user seldom has any voice in these matters; in fact, she or he is often uninformed about the qualifications of the personnel at the service center and has contact only with the account executive or other liaison personnel.

The user of a service center should be concerned about the security measures taken to protect the information held at the center. A few users are so sensitive in this regard that they furnish the service center with code numbers instead of names for customers or employees and retain the responsibility for inserting the names on the output.

Another important aspect of security concerns the service center's provision for master file reconstruction in the event of loss or destruction. Methods used for in-house installations (fireproof vaults, off-premises storage, etc.) apply equally well in service centers. The user should also be concerned about these provisions and about the arrangements the center has made for backup facilities. The question of backup may be critical in cases where the service center obtains its computer time by off-shift rental of computers belonging to other organizations.

The printouts and other data retained by the user should always be sufficient for the reconstruction of processing in the event of a service center failure and should provide an adequate audit trail.

User Controls   The controls that ensure the orderly and supervised processing of data are the responsibility of the service center's management. To check the completeness and accuracy of the service center's processing, the user generally establishes some overall input data controls (e.g., control totals, document counts, number of accounts, etc). He or she may also review the output documents and records completely or on a sampling basis, depending on the nature and volume of the processing. The user may also undertake to test-check manually some of the processing performed by the service center.

The user should make provisions to protect against loss of source documents in transit to and from the service center. For example, if a bank's paid but unposted checks are transported to a service center for processing, a microfilm copy should be kept at the sending bank. Another approach is to use a copy of the source documents for data processing input purposes.

To ensure the timely and complete processing of all transactions, both the user and service center usually review and screen the input data. The user corrects any errors or omissions he detects before the data are sent. Any erroneous data items detected by the service center's review or computer-input validation (editing) routines are left unprocessed; they are listed and returned to the user.

The user may correct the data items and resubmit them with the next batch, or, as in the case of payroll, she or he may have to process them manually if it is not practicable to wait until the next cycle of processing. If processing is performed manually, an adjustment must be prepared to update the master records at the next processing.

Audit Approach

The auditor whose client uses a service center should determine the extent to which the service center is used in processing the client's accounting and financial data. Service center processing can be divided into two categories:

1. The processing of a client's statistical data.
2. The processing of a client's financial data.

Service Center Processing of Statistical Data

In those cases where only statistical data are processed, the auditor would not be directly concerned with the processing if such processing had little or no effect on his examination of the financial statements. For example, after developing a sales control total, a client may send copies of sales invoices to a service center that prepares sales summaries by customer, salesmen, and product groupings. Such statistical data may sometimes influence the way the client plans and conducts business operations. The sales summaries in the preceding illustration might be used in developing marketing plans, profit plans within product groups, and inventory control models. Consequently, the auditor may wish to make a periodic review of the validity and accuracy of the data being processed and make some use of the data in the audit.

Service Center Processing of Financial Data

When a service center processes client financial data, the auditor's first step is to evaluate the significance of the application(s) processed. Where significant, the auditor must then determine the nature and extent of the system of internal control maintained by the client organization over the application(s). The auditor may then determine whether or not a review at the service center is required for any application, basing the decision on

- Materiality of the application
- Nature of controls maintained by the client organization

- Nature of the controls at the service center and their bearing on the reliability of the financial records
- Degree of reliance the auditor places on the elements of internal control provided by the service center

The results of this review and evaluation process will be used in determining the nature and extent of audit procedures to be applied.

Consider the example of a bank processing payroll applications for many customers and also performing on-line accounting for several savings and loan associations in the area. In the auditor's judgment, the nature of the payroll processing for his or her client did not require a review of the service center's controls but rather an evaluation of the client's input and output controls and test of data in the payroll records. However, in the auditor's judgment the nature and extent of controls maintained at both the client savings and loan association location and the service center for the savings and loan application were significant in determining the reliability of the financial records, and therefore required review.

System Evaluation

To evaluate the controls, the auditor requires

> . . . (1) knowledge and understanding of the procedures and methods prescribed and (2) a reasonable degree of assurance that they are in use and are operating as planned[4]

These two phases of evaluation are referred to hereafter as *review of the system* and *tests of compliance with the system*. Once the auditor had decided to evaluate the controls at the service center, she or he might consider using an approach similar to the one outlined in the following paragraphs.

Review of the System

As discussed in Chapter 9, the review of the system can be divided into two parts: a general review and a detailed review of specific accounting applications processed by the service center. The general review would consist of an evaluation of organizational control, documentations practices, and security provisions. Many of the specific control techniques associated with each of these areas have been covered in previous chapters since they are similar to techniques used in in-house computer centers. However, several unique differences exist in a service center environment that should be discussed.

---

[4] AICPA, *Statement on Auditing Standards* #1, p. 27, 1973.

Organizational Control

One of the most significant elements introduced when a client uses a service center is the presence of a processing system that is external—physically, operationally, and legally—to the client organization. Since a service center takes the place of the client's own data processing center, the auditor should be concerned with a proper division of duties among all persons involved. The auditor should therefore review the plan of organization and assignment of functional responsibilities in regard to both service center and client personnel involved in data processing.

The service center facilities may provide a better division of duties than may be found in many in-house operations. Even so, the auditor should determine specifically the access that programmers have to critical files and computer equipment. The auditor should also determine whether any of the service center's personnel involved in data processing operations have access to the client's assets.

Documentation

Documentation reviews generally involve information provided both by user and service center. Thus a coordinated review of documentation at both locations is often necessary. Coordination of review procedures is required because changes in personnel, in duties, in authorized program instructions, etc., may not be fully documented at either location, whether by design or through lack of specific reporting criteria. The coordinated review may also disclose that certain controls may either be redundant—maintained at both locations—or absent. The mere absence of documentation, while it may expose the service center and/or the client to operating problems, may not necessitate additional audit steps when other controls are adequate.

The auditor will have several purposes in reviewing the different elements of documentation. As an example, the auditor could review sufficient documentation to build an understanding of both management objectives (problem statement) and the manner in which these objectives will be attained (systems flowcharts, narratives, program listings). The computer file and record and report layouts describing the organization of computer-readable data may also serve these objectives. In addition, documentation could provide the auditor with the information necessary for the use of computer-assisted audit techniques.

Security

The auditor should be concerned with the control techniques used to ensure the security of client programs, files, and data. When processing client data, the service center usually maintains the client files and records; this makes possible either deliberate or accidental manipulation of the programs, files, and records by service center or other unauthorized personnel. Locations of the files and records may also limit the auditor's access to the records and cause problems with regard to the timing of the evaluation of the records produced by the service center.

To ensure adequate security of client programs, data, records, and reports, the following control techniques can be used:

- Access to the service center should be limited to authorized personnel.

- To discourage misuse of the client's data, codes may be used instead of detailed descriptions in dealing with confidential information. Confidential data may include payroll information, prices, and customer account balances.

- Client employees should be in attendance for confidential processing operations to ensure the protection of such data.

- Documents, reports, and files should be placed in secure storage facilities when not in use.

The auditor should also identify the procedures and documentation for controlling program revisions involved in processing client data. The auditor should evaluate the process of authorizing program revisions and the persons responsible for authorizing and approving the changes. He or she should also assess the documentation of program changes that should provide an accurate chronological record of the system. In addition the procedures used to test the program changes should be reviewed as well.

When the processing at the service center has been completed, reports and original documents should be returned to the client without delay. Confidential reports should be packaged as soon as they are released and stored in locked containers while awaiting pickup. Master files should be returned to the service center library.

The auditor should determine the adequacy of the client's control over *master file changes*. Lack of control over these changes may lead to operating problems and serious control inadequacies. The service center should provide the client with control totals of master file records processed in each run so that the client can check for loss or nonprocessing of master records. The center should also provide the client with a transaction list of all master file changes so that he or she can determine that these changes have been authorized and made properly.

The service center should have adequate procedures to provide security against accidental destruction of records and to ensure continuity of processing. Such provisions as backup files, off-premises storage, operating instructions, and fire protection procedures should be reviewed. The client should also have adequate insurance to cover loss of data and file-reconstruction costs. It is advisable for the client to consider such insurance even though the service center may carry its own, since the client has no direct control over the amount or nature of the center's coverage. The reliability, dependability, and financial stability of a service center can also be important factors in the center's ability to ensure continuity of processing.

Procedural Controls

Once the auditor has gained an understanding of the general controls at the service center, the next step is to obtain information on the details of the procedural controls in the applications having audit significance.

Procedural controls consist of techniques encompassing input, processing, and output controls to ensure the complete and accurate processing of data. The auditor's review of the client's system of internal control should be concerned with the ability of the data processing system to generate accurate, complete, and authorized financial and accounting data. The control procedures established at the service center are mainly to ensure accurate processing of data received from the client. It is normally the client's responsibility to establish the necessary input–output controls for the data submitted for processing and to ensure that the output received from the service center agrees with the input submitted.

Input Controls The service center is responsible for the orderly, supervised, accurate, and reliable processing of data transmitted from the client. To ensure this, service centers usually perform editing functions on the incoming client data. The editing function of the computer examines each element of information and accepts or rejects transactions according to the validity or reasonableness of quantities, amounts, codes, and other data contained in the input record. Computer editing can detect errors in input preparation that have not been detected by human review and inspection.

Input control may also be established by keeping copies of all source documents sent to the service center; by developing control totals—document counts, dollar total, etc.—on data sent for processing; and by reconciling these input control totals with control totals furnished by the service center upon the completion of the processing. The auditor may review these controls by examining the procedures over the preparation and coding of input, the input forms, and other means employed by the client to establish control over data sent to the service center for processing.

Processing Controls The auditor may review the types of controls used to detect and correct errors in processing. The client might be able to provide such information since he or she should be aware of what types of errors can occur, and of the responsibilities for preventing and detecting errors, and of what types of errors will be detected by the computerized portion of the processing. The auditor most likely will need to interview service center personnel to understand the controls built into the service center's computer program to detect input errors and errors in processing. The auditor also will want to check the adequacy of procedures for recording errors and controlling corrections and resubmissions.

Computerized editing as a processing control is achieved by installing checks in the service center's program of instructions or editing routines for detecting errors; hence the term *programmed controls*. Types of programmed controls (as discussed in Chapter 8) include valid code tests, incomplete data tests, sequence tests, and tests of reasonableness.

Output Controls   The auditor should review the adequacy of output controls to determine that the processed data are correct and do not include any unauthorized alterations. The most basic output control is the client's comparison of control totals established on input data with the control totals developed by the service center during the processing of the data. Periodic sampling of individual items processed affords another output control. And the reports, obviously, should be reviewed by the client for reasonableness.

Audit Trail   The auditor should determine if the records maintained by the client and at the service center provide an audit trail. The audit trail may be traced by the service center's listing of all input data processed, by periodic printouts of ledger balances and contents of master files, or by retaining comparable machine-readable data.

Tests of Compliance   A second step in the evaluation consists of tests of compliance to see if the system described does exist and operate effectively. The nature and extent of testing for compliance will depend on (1) the initial evaluation of internal control, (2) the nature of the application, and (3) the availability of data. If the application being evaluated is documented and a visible audit trail exists, the auditor may test the client's compliance in performing prescribed controls and procedures by checking source data, control reports, error listings, transaction listings, and management reports.

Most service center processing consists of batch-processing systems or batch-controlled systems having detailed audit trails. This type of processing is characterized by three features:

1. The recording of transactions manually, followed by conversion to machine-readable form.

2. The collection of transactions in batches, to be sorted and processed sequentially against a master file. This process normally involves the development of batch totals to control the movement of data within the system.

3. The production of reports, often at each processing run.[5]

[5] See Davis, *Auditing and EDP,* p. 134.

In most batch-oriented systems, the auditor may perform tests on available source documents, transaction listings, and output records in essentially the same manner as he or she would do for a noncomputer system, or, in other words, without the use of the computer. Another method of testing compliance is to use the computer by introducing test data through the service center processing system. Such data normally consist of transactions illustrating valid and invalid conditions that the auditor wishes to test, e.g., wrong pay rate, abnormal number of hours worked, and an employee for whom there is no master payroll record. Appendix E contains a case study on the use of the computer in testing an on-line processing system for savings and loan associations. At this point, you may wish to read the case study and then return for the conclusion of this chapter.

Evaluation of Controls

Up to this point, we have discussed the auditor's approach to the completion of the following steps:

- Gaining an understanding of the system, including processing and controls performed by the service center
- Performing compliance tests to ascertain that the controls function as designed
- Obtaining the information needed to evaluate the client's control over the data processed at the service center

The evaluation of the system is achieved through an understanding and testing of the client's system of internal control, including the processing performed by the service center. This evaluation will have to be made, in most cases, by discussions with client and service center personnel and may include testing at the service center.

Once these steps have been completed, the auditor is in a position to make an evaluation of the adequacy of the client's internal control system and to determine what additional audit procedures are required. The additional audit procedures may take the form of additional tests of the system and/or tests of the account balances resulting from the system.

Use of Computer Audit Programs

Much of the output from the service center processing may take the form of visible records—such as aged trial balances for accounts receivable, inventory listings, sales and cash receipts registers, and payroll registers. Such records may be evaluated by using traditional auditing methods (e.g., performing arithmetical calculations and tests, selecting samples from printed listings, tracing selected items to supporting records and authoritative documents, and/or confirming directly with outsiders).

Normally, the client's printed output is prepared from machine-readable output such as magnetic tapes and magnetic disks. Hence the auditor may use the computer for evaluating records by developing or obtaining computer audit programs and processing with them the machine-readable records. For example, a CPA firm might request the client's service center to provide magnetic tape files or copies containing the client's accounts receivable records. The CPA firm could then process these tape files with computer-audit programs to select accounts for confirmation purposes and perform clerical accuracy tests. In the payroll case study, the auditor might use computer-audit programs to select samples from the payroll master file for tracing to support personnel records, as well as for other audit tests of payroll records.

The steps involved in obtaining and using computer audit programs were discussed in Chapter 10.

Problems

1. Why would organizations use service centers?

2. How would the organization of a service center differ from the organization of an EDP center in a company using its own computer? Why the differences, if any?

3. What controls would you expect the user of a service center to maintain in the following applications processed by a service center: payroll, accounts receivable, inventory?

4. What circumstances have to prevail for the auditor to review the service center controls for applications processed for her or his client organization?

5. Why is the security over files and programs so important when service centers process client data? Why should the auditor be concerned?

Case

Payroll for Grocery Stores   This case study presents a payroll application using service center processing. The payroll process described is one used by a group of grocery stores (part of a national chain) located in a metropolitan area. The system is primarily described in terms of computer runs once the data are received at the service center.

The processes described are performed weekly. A systems flowchart of these processes is shown in Figure 11.2.

Because this is a case study of service center processing of a payroll application, we need to determine the following:

• Evaluate the processing controls in the system.

• What audit trail exists for evaluating the processing system?

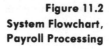

Figure 11.2
System Flowchart,
Payroll Processing

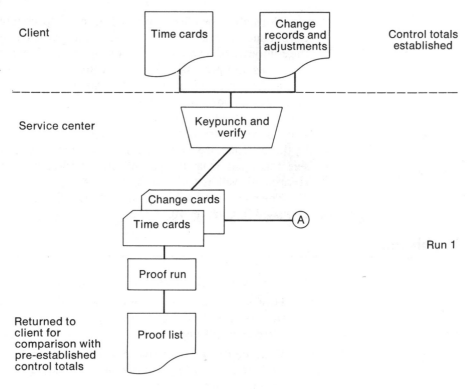

- What tests could be performed with the use of the audit trail?
- How could the computer be used to test the system? To validate the data in the payroll files?

Conventional source documents, such as time cards and payroll record changes, are prepared initially by client personnel. The time cards show employee numbers, number of hours worked, job number, and so forth. The payroll record changes are prepared to change data in the payroll master records. Change records would be prepared for a change in payroll rate, deductions, employee's name, employee's address, number of dependents, adjustments to year-to-date totals, terminations, and additions of new employees.

These source records are sent to the service center for a series of processing operations. The first operation is the keypunching and verification of the information on the source documents into punched cards.

The client's control objectives over input are to determine that all transactions recorded are transmitted to and received by the service center. Internal control is achieved by the client's grouping the time cards and record changes into batches and preparing control totals, such as hours worked, for each batch. The punched cards prepared at the service center could then be run

**Figure 11.2
(continued)**

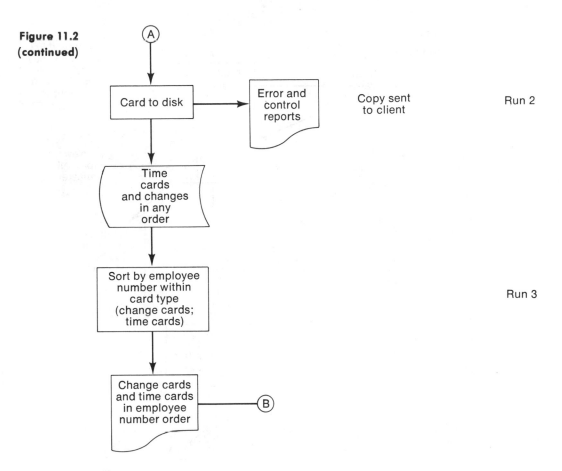

through proof runs and totals could be accumulated by batch and compared with the client's preestablished amounts. A proof transaction listing could be prepared and returned to the client. Out-of-balance batches could be printed for clerical review, correction, and reentry.

Processing

After the proof runs, the punched cards are converted to magnetic disk and sorted by employee number. In this conversion run, the control objectives would be attained if the data received are complete, accurate, and reasonable and if the control totals agree with preestablished totals. Internal control is achieved by installing checks in the computer programs to detect errors (programmed checks). These include checks to detect invalid transaction codes, incomplete transactions, unreasonable pay rates, and number of hours worked. Program instructions also accumulate batch totals and compare them against

Figure 11.2 (continued)

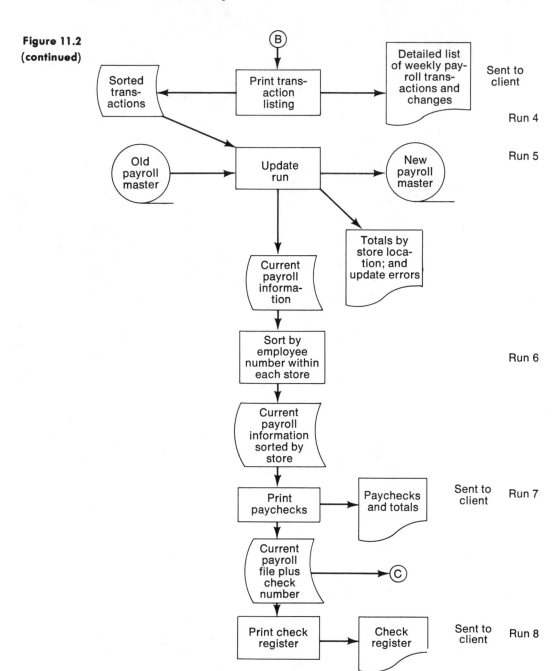

Figure 11.2 (continued)

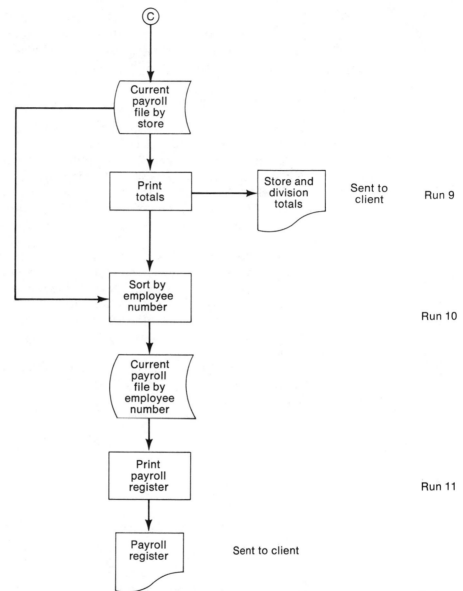

previously established totals. Invalid data and control discrepancies are printed on error listings that are sent to the client. The sorted payroll transactions are listed showing the weekly payroll transactions for each employee. A copy of the list is sent to the client.

Updating Payroll Files

The payroll master files, maintained on magnetic tape, are then updated with the valid transactions for any changes and payroll computations. Gross and net are calculated; year-to-date and period-to-date payroll data are accumulated and written on the new payroll master file. Current payroll information such as name, employee number, store number, hours worked, deductions, and gross and net pay is written on magnetic disk. Payroll totals by store location are printed along with update errors (for example, a missing master record for an employee).

The current payroll data are then sorted by employee number for each store and paychecks are printed. The next run results in the printing of the check register which together with the payroll checks is sent to the client. Store and division payroll totals are printed for the client.

The current payroll information on magnetic disk is then sorted into employee-number order, and a payroll register is printed for distribution to the client.

The service center prepares, on client request, a current list of all employees in the payroll master file. Payroll tax returns are prepared quarterly and W–2 forms are prepared annually.

EDP AUDIT PROCESS*

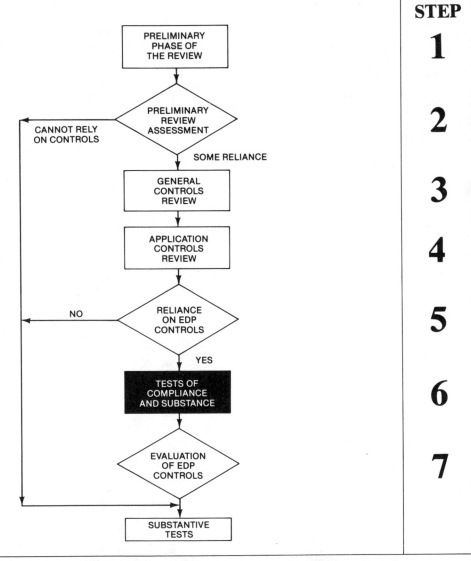

STEP

1

2

3

4

5

6

7

*Diagram is adapted from The Auditor's Study and Evaluation of Internal Control in EDP Systems, pages 21–24. Copyright © 1977 by the American Institute of Certified Public Accountants, Inc. (See Figure 9.1 for a complete explanation of the steps.)

AUDITING
DATA SYSTEMS

(6) Tests of Compliance

Purpose:
- Determine whether the necessary control procedures are prescribed and followed satisfactorily.
- Provide reasonable assurance that controls are functioning properly.
- Consider and, to the extent appropriate, document when, how, and by whom controls are provided.

Methods: Examination of records; test of control procedures; inquiry; observation.

OBJECTIVE

Hard-copy evidence tends to be replaced by electronic evidence in data base/data communication systems. This chapter explains the audit implications, and methods used, in auditing advanced EDP technology.

Data systems are computerized applications that use both data communication and data base technology. These systems have been called on-line real-time (OLRT) systems. These systems are receiving increased attention in the plans for corporate data systems, and auditors must be aware of the distinctive features of such systems and the means of evaluating the controls and audit trail in these systems. Although such systems have been referred to in previous chapters, a more detailed discussion of the nature of data systems, the potential control problems, and the means of evaluating the controls would be useful to the reader.

Data Systems

Data systems are those in which transactions are processed as soon as they occur and any necessary responses are made immediately. Typically they involve remote terminals under the control of the central processing units, and information reflecting current activity is introduced into the computer processing as it occurs.

The most readily apparent example in our mobile world is the airline reservations system in which many terminals located in ticket agent offices and airports are linked to a large-scale computer through a data transmission network. These terminals enable reservations agents to inquire of the seat availability on scheduled flights as soon as the customer inquiry is made, to respond to the customer within seconds as to the seat availability, to influence the customer's decision, and, in fact, to bring about a customer's decision in most cases.

Such systems have been made economically feasible for organizations much smaller than airline companies by several computer hardware and software developments:

- Simple electromechanical detection devices that make it possible to capture many data inputs cheaply, unobtrusively, and with no extra human intervention at their point of origin. Since capturing data and getting them into the system for processing has typically been a costly and error-prone process, the development of such devices may make it feasible to broaden and increase the detail of the data on which an accounting system is based. Examples of such devices currently in use are photoelectric counters to record production output or cash registers automatically producing either machine-recognizable signals or machine-readable tapes.

- Data communications systems and multiplexors that make it possible to transmit data over regular telephone lines when and from where it originates directly into a computer system. The data communications equipment takes care of transmitting and receiving the data; the multiplexor works like an automatic switchboard for the computer, accepting signals from all the input–output stations whenever they arrive and making sure that each signal gets into the computer properly. These developments could help to broaden geographically the reach and use of an accounting system and could significantly reduce the time lags in updating information and answering management inquiries.

- Recognition of optical and audio patterns that promise the ability to capture a wide variety of written, spoken, and graphic data in computer-readable form. Currently, some limited forms of written, spoken, and graphic data may be input directly to a computer. Although such devices are still in their infancy, their development and appearance in the future promise to make it feasible to collect accurately data that in the past have been either too costly, too cumbersome, or even impossible to capture.

- Cathode-ray-tube displays and audio-response units that make it possible to output information quickly and directly to the user in a form that he can understand easily and absorb rapidly. These devices should help to speed up the information dissemination process, eliminate a lot of paper flow when a hard copy is not needed, and enable a wider group of people (e.g., customers or salesmen) to interact directly with the system.

- Direct-access bulk storage devices (e.g., disk file, data cells, virtual memory) and in-file organization and retrieval techniques that permit the storage of literally billions of characters of information on-line, each accessible by a computer in less than 1 second. In addition, most of these bulk storage devices have interchangeable storage media (e.g., removable disk packs) so that an unlimited amount of data can be stored off-line but available to be put on-line for direct access by the computer after a short setup time. These devices may make it possible to broaden, yet still manipulate efficiently, the files of data on which an accounting system is based.

- Time-sharing systems (coupled with some of the developments above) that permit the power of a single computer to be distributed to several users in different locations simultaneously. Operating in a time-shared mode, a computer works for a short time (measured in microseconds) exclusively for one user, then works for another and another, finally getting back to the first user to start the process again. However, owing to the high speed of the computer, it appears to each user that his requests for information or computation are processed immediately even though the computer has processed the requests of several other users in the meantime.

- User-oriented programming languages, control languages, and compilers that extend computer and information retrieval power to users who have no computer experience. The inexperienced user can express what he wants done in a near-English language, and the computer, under control of a *translator* program, translates what he says into the machine instructions necessary to do the processing he requested.

- Data analysis, model building, and quantitative techniques that provide the user with tools to investigate and understand more fully the environment in which he operates, and, based on that understanding, permit him to predict with greater confidence the future effects of alternative strategies under several possible environment situations. Although we shall probably never be able to "see" the future clearly, these techniques can help us to guess more confidently about what might happen.

- Distributive processing, the physical linking together of two or more computers with a communication network that permits any one computer in the network to utilize the resources available within the network. This would permit a small computer at one site to use the power of a larger computer in the network at another site. Thus, the work to be performed by the system can be distributed over two or more computers.

New and Increased Risks

The use of data systems introduces new and increased risks to an organization. These risks are primarily attributable to the sharing of information and processing resources among diverse users. Data systems imply immediate response to processing requests. This not only requires new and complex technology, but requires that most of the controls be automated because of the need to apply these controls concurrently with processing.

The areas of increased risk and a discussion of each follow.

Assignment of Responsibilities

Using a data base normally involves the transition of responsibilities from the application environment to a centralized data base environment. In any shifting of responsibilities, there is new concern of concentration of functions in one area. Functions previously segregated by application area are now concentrated in the data base administration function. These duties include the documentation of data, the organization of data, the access to data, the edit and validation of data, and the architecture and maintenance of the data base.

Multiple Users Using a Data Base

When many users depend on the same source of information, there is more reliance upon that information. Data systems are integrated into the day-to-day business operations. No longer is data processing an independent function. Without the proper functioning of the data system, the organization may not be able to function.

Concurrent Update of a Single Data Element

In a data base environment, it is possible for two users to have the same piece of data at the same time. Theoretically, each can update that data, and then return it to the data base for storage. Without proper controls, one of these updates will be lost, or cause the other user of the data to make erroneous decisions.

Balancing Data in a Data Base

In a non-data systems environment, the detailed records are often balanced to the total each time processing occurs. In a data systems environment, the details are reconciled to the control totals as specified by individual applications. With concurrent processing, and the complexity of data base technology, it is possible for the detail records to get out of balance with the totals, and that condition not be known for a lengthy period of time.

Maintaining an Adequate Audit Trail

In a data systems environment, the data may be maintained independently of the processing programs. This means that there may not be a single audit trail for any application system. Some of the processing occurs in the data base segment, and other processing occurs in the application segment. For example, the data base environment may control access, edit and validation of data, and include some processing to verify the integrity of the data base. The results of this processing will be retained in the data base segment audit trail. In addition, each application may have an audit trail for its processing. Thus, not only is processing separate from data but the audit trail may likewise be separated.

Accessibility of Data

The data systems concept means greater availability of and accessibility to data. In an application where the processed data are contained by the application, the data can be physically safeguarded. Without data communications, organizations can turn their computer room into a vault. The computer center becomes an impenetrable area. As such, the data are available and accessible only to people who could physically enter the computer room. This not possible in a data system.

Communications Technology

The new technology required for a data base carries with it the concern that it will not be properly managed. Developing and implementing new technology in an organization is a complex process. It can also be a costly process if not performed properly.

Accounting Cutoff Cutoff is a business-related function, but it is more complex in a data systems environment. The major risk is that the data in a data base may not be able to be easily reconciled to outside controls. For example, in a batch system, cutoff is inherent in the design of the system (that is, the last run is the cutoff), but in a data base environment, the appropriate cutoff point is not built in.

Control Requirements

Data systems are characterized by the entry of data from remote devices directly to a central computer via communication lines. After processing, data are returned to remote devices via communication lines. Thus controls for such systems must be concerned with controlling data at both the remote location and the central location and with the accuracy of transmission between the locations.

One author has outlined five general types of system and software controls that are important in data systems:[1]

1. General environmental controls for the entire system.
2. Recovery controls for recovering from emergencies and contingencies.
3. Message and terminal controls over data transmissions, terminal usage requirements, accessibility, and terminal and line problems.
4. Data base controls.
5. Processing controls.

Environmental Controls One of the basic environmental controls in a data system is the *console log*. Such a log is used to record an audit trail of internal activities, to provide operating instructions, and to allow the operator to communicate with the computer.

Because of the importance of data communications in data systems, the console log should be supplemented by a control terminal—an in-house terminal devoted solely to monitoring the system to determine transmission line and terminal problems and messages regarding the status of communication queues and alternate routing of messages.

Because backup and recovery capability is so important in a data system, a data system should have a *history log*. This log should be maintained on a low-cost machine-readable medium to provide an audit trail and a basis for

---

[1] Carol P. Eastin, "System and Software Controls for On-Line Systems," *Management Controls,* June 1972, pp. 141–145. Excerpts reprinted by permission of PMM & Co.

analysis of system effectiveness. If the history log contains all input and output communication messages, hardware failure messages, beginning and end of program indications, and communication startup and shutdown detail, the log can be used to identify sporadic line, terminal, or peripheral device problems before a complete breakdown occurs, to detect attempts to break security, and to perform volume analysis.

Another aspect of environmental control is *memory protection.* In data systems, there usually is multiprogramming where two or more programs are handled simultaneously by overlapping or interweaving their execution. If two or more programs are in storage at the same time, an incorrect modification by one program may cause it to store data in the set of locations occupied by another program, thereby destroying an instruction or data in the second program. To prevent this from happening, there must be some method of memory protection. The typical approach is for each block of data to have a storage key. Each program segment trying to use this block of storage would have an instruction that sets an identical storage key. If, after modification, one of the instructions attempted to store outside the boundaries assigned to it, the program key and the data block key would not agree; the instruction would not be executed; and an error condition would be signaled.[2]

Since communications are important in data systems, it is essential to maintain *control* over commands to the *communication software system.* Shutdown and startup of the system should be thoroughly documented on the console and control terminal, including time, operator, and any unusual conditions. Also, any status changes to the communications software system while it is operational should be well controlled. Requests for status changes should be edited, the new status documented in detail, and a regular reminder of status changes sent to the control terminal. Thus there can be control over authorized or accidental status changes.

Most telecommunication operating systems have passwords controlling access to the system. Individuals wishing to use the system must identify themselves via a system of passwords. Failure to enter the correct password after a set number of tries can result in a terminal being shut down. After shutdown, only a supervisor can reopen the terminal. Once an individual has been identified properly by means of a password, the system can restrict that individual to those resources of the system that are available for her or his use.

Recovery Controls   Basically recovery controls are necessary to prevent the loss of data from a failure of a data system, and to keep the system operational if possible or restore operations as soon as possible.

If a central computer failure occurs, backup facilities must be available. For such switching, the software system must be able to accommodate different

---

[2] Gordon B. Davis, *Computer Data Processing,* p. 284, McGraw-Hill, New York, 1969.

hardware environments, especially if the two hardware systems are not identical. When restart is successfully initiated, all remote locations should be notified automatically of the difficulties and informed of the last message number received and queued from the location and the last computer message sent to them.

Sometimes failure occurs when unexpected peak volumes overload the communication software capacity. To handle such situations, the software should be capable of warning the control terminal operator so that action can be taken to temporarily shut down the lines. In addition, it is desirable to have an overflow capability within the system.

Failure of a peripheral device requires a switch of devices to handle key software files and application files. If an application file is involved, it should be reestablished through standard file-recovery procedures and the application restarted from the checkpoint or beginning.

Sometimes problems are created by line or terminal failures. Such failures are solved by waiting or by sending messages through an alternative route.

Message and Terminal Controls

To ensure complete and accurate transmission of data, proper terminal usage, and general system security, message and terminal controls are necessary. When transmission is taking place, there must be some indication that the transmission is accurate and complete. Normally, messages are transmitted in the following format: a beginning-of-message indicator, data, and an end-of-message indicator. If there is more than one message being transmitted, an end-of-transmission indicator is also used. Hardware character parity checking should also be used to check on the accuracy of the transmission. In addition, the communications software should automatically retransmit to the sender any messages that are in error. To ensure the receipt of all messages, sequence numbers should be contained in the message data and the sequence should be checked by the software.

Several techniques should be used to maintain system security and to prevent unauthorized access to data files and programs in the system. Special passwords and authority lists can be supplied by the sender of messages. The software should be able to determine that the proper sender location and proper authority are involved in transmitting certain types of transactions. For high-security or sensitive transactions, the amount of testing should be greater. For example, the passwords used should not be retained in printable format or for any extended period of time.

When the use of terminal hardware is restricted for a given application, the system's programs must confirm the restrictions. For example, banks often require that passbooks be inserted in the terminal before certain transactions are submitted. Some systems use a different template for each transactions type. Overrides may be allowed with the use of templates or supervisor keys, but basic editing should not be bypassed. Supervisors are quite often less adept than clerks with terminal equipment.

It is important to log all messages on the history log and selected messages on the control terminal, as indicated previously. All messages should be time-stamped before they are placed on any log or queue. The control terminal log contains messages in error and is used to detect problems requiring immediate action. The history log is used for message backup and contains all messages, valid or invalid. It can be analyzed for potential terminal problems and header inconsistencies.

Each application system should also make extensive security checks and perform the actual validation of message content. This validates the input, as in any system, and is a double-check on the software.

Finally, the software should be able to recap the day's activities for each terminal. The recap should show the sequence numbers of messages received and sent, any out-of-sequence messages received and, any unusual occurrences. This recap is used to veryify manual logs at the remote location.[3]

Data Base Controls

One of the potential control problems in data systems is unauthorized access to data files. First, there must be control over data access from remote terminals through passwords. In their most basic form they ensure that an authorized terminal and user are requesting access to the system. In dial-up systems this requires entry of a terminal and user code. In directly connected terminals only the user code may be necessary. The problem of access, however, is complicated by the necessity of being more selective than simply the granting or refusing of access. For example, files containing sensitive information cannot be available to all persons having general access to the system. Thus a comprehensive password system may contain several levels of access information such as terminal identifiers and user codes, which identify the individual and his access classification. The access classification code may, in turn, simply delineate the data files available to that individual and/or terminal or may be much more complex: restricting read–write access on each file or making individual fields or groups of fields on a data file inaccessible.

The determination of the type of access restrictions is based on several factors. Among them are these three:

1. The nature of the data: Obviously, access to sensitive data such as marketing planning information, stockholder lists, customer information, and the like must be more strictly controlled than the inventory of office furniture.

2. The structure of the data files: For example, a file containing data of a single level of security classification is normally less costly to secure than a file imbedded with varying levels of sensitivity. The former allows record level control while the latter may preclude it.

3. The cost of security: Generally, as the level of control becomes more discreet, i.e., moves toward the field level, the cost of security goes up rapidly—the cost being measured in terms of computer storage required;

[3] Eastin, op. cit., pp. 143–144.

processing time for security measures; implementation costs; and often overlooked, the cost of maintaining, utilizing, and verifying the security measures.

If a program, software, or hardware failure occurs, the data files must be brought to status at the appropriate restart point. The use of the history log is important in reaching appropriate restart points.

When interruptions are more serious, it may be necessary to rebuild an entire file. To do so requires a process of copying or duplicating application files on a low-cost medium on a regular basis. The frequency of duplication depends on the nature of the applications. For inquiry files, perhaps a daily backup for files is enough. For files that are being updated by transactions during the day, perhaps the updated records should be duplicated concurrently with the update cycle. In this way, if the master file is destroyed, the backup file (which can be physically protected), in conjunction with the backup master with which processing began, can be used to quickly recreate the master up through the last transaction processed. The question again is one of cost weighed against the nature of the business and the structure and criticality of the application(s).

Processing Controls   Most of the processing controls we discussed in Chapter 8 for batch-oriented systems apply as well in data systems. Validity, completeness, and limit tests, self-checking digits, sequence checks, and batch controls are very important since transactions in data systems appear very much the same to the processing or application program as they appear in traditional batch systems.

Another important aspect of processing control is the need for an audit trail. In data systems, we can eliminate the need for printed audit trails but a complete audit trail should be maintained in the form of a transaction history on a low-cost, mechanized medium. The system should be designed to supply full or partial printed audit trails when requested.

How to Audit a Data System

A data communication audit should be conducted as a transaction flow analysis. *Transaction flow analysis* is a technique of tracing a transaction or group of transactions from the point of original entry (the terminal), through the data communication network, to the computer. Using this technique, the auditor is able to evaluate the flow of transactions, the hardware and software, the transmission media, and, in some cases, the manual interface controls that involve the people who run the network. It is wise for the auditor to trace the flow of transactions starting at both ends of the network (terminal and computer) and to reconcile the findings. The audit should include the operating software system, the communications software, and data base management systems, as well as each sensitive application using the data communications network.

To assist with the audit, this chapter depicts a matrix that matches the various resources (e.g., terminals) with the exposures (e.g., errors and omissions) so the auditor can determine which resources may be subject to what type of exposure. The data system resources are listed below and are defined later in this chapter:

- Terminals
- Distributed intelligence
- Modems
- Local loop
- Lines: dial-up, point-to-point, multipoint, and loop
- Multiplexor, concentrator, switch
- Front end
- Computer
- Software
- People

The safeguard matrix (Table 12.1) lists resources down the left column, and the exposures across the top row. Within each of the cells of the matrix, various safeguards are listed for the auditor to consider when reviewing the security of the network. The seventeen safeguards are listed below and are defined later in this chapter:

1. Physical security controls
2. Audit trails
3. Backup
4. Recovery procedures
5. Error detection/correction
6. Authentication
7. Encryption
8. Operational procedures
9. Preventive maintenance
10. Format checking
11. Insurance
12. Legal contract
13. Fault isolation/diagnostics
14. Training/education

RESOURCES	EXPOSURES					
	ERRORS AND OMISSIONS	DISASTERS AND DISRUPTIONS	LOSS OF INTEGRITY	DISCLOSURE	DEFALCATION	THEFT OF RESOURCES
Terminals	2, 3, 5, 9, 13	1, 3, 4, 8, 11	1, 2, 5, 6, 8, 13	1, 2, 6, 11, 13, 17	1, 2, 6, 8	1, 2, 6, 17
Distributed Intelligence	2, 3, 5, 6, 9, 10, 13, 16	1, 3, 4, 8, 11	1, 2, 5, 6, 8, 13, 16	1, 11, 13, 16	1, 2, 8	1
Modems	3, 5, 9, 13	1, 3, 8, 11	1, 13	1, 11, 13	1	1
Local Loop	3, 5, 9, 13	1, 3, 8	1, 5, 6, 7, 13	1, 7, 11, 13		
Lines: Dial-up, Point-to-point, Multipoint, and Loop	3, 5, 9, 13	3, 4, 8, 17	5, 6, 7, 13	1, 7, 11, 13		
MUX/CONC/Switch	3, 5, 9, 13, 16	1, 3, 8, 11	1, 2, 3, 4, 5, 6, 7, 8, 13, 16	1, 7, 11, 13	1, 2, 6, 8	1, 2, 6
Front-End Processor	2, 3, 4, 5, 9, 10, 13, 16, 17	1, 3, 8, 11	1, 2, 3, 4, 5, 6, 8, 10, 13, 16	1, 7, 13, 16	1, 2, 6, 8	1, 2, 6
Computer	2, 3, 4, 5, 8, 9, 10, 13, 14, 15, 16, 17	1, 3, 4, 8, 11	1, 2, 3, 4, 5, 6, 8, 10, 13, 16	1, 7, 13, 16	1, 2, 6, 8	1, 2, 6, 17
Software	3, 4, 5, 8, 13, 15, 16, 17	1, 3, 4, 11, 15	1, 2, 3, 4, 5, 6, 8, 10, 13, 16	1, 7, 13, 16	6, 8, 12, 15, 16, 17	1, 2, 6, 12, 17
People	1, 2, 3, 4, 6, 8, 10, 11, 13, 14, 15, 17	1, 3, 8, 11, 12, 15	1, 2, 5, 6, 8, 11, 12, 14, 15, 16, 17	1, 2, 6, 8, 12, 13, 14, 17	1, 2, 6, 8, 11, 12, 17	2, 14, 15, 17

Table 12.1   Matrix of Safeguards to Audit a Data Communications Network

15. Documentation
16. Testing
17. Reporting and statistics

In conducting an audit, any resource subject to an exposure should have some type of safeguard that the auditor must consider. In making this evaluation, the auditor should "walk through" the data communications network, weighing the safeguards listed for each specific resource against its exposure in the specific application system. This is an important point: the auditor should use the matrix to review the communication security in light of each of the specific applications utilizing the data communications network.

The user of the matrix is advised that there are some basic limitations that must be recognized:

- The safeguards listed in the matrix are intended only as guidelines, not as standards, and should not be considered all inclusive with regard to a specific application system.

- The safeguards listed will assist in making a data system secure; it must be emphasized that security is relative, not absolute.

- Safeguards listed may not apply in all application situations, and therefore, a general knowledge of data communications and data base is assumed.

Resources   The following ten resources are those resources that constitute an end-to-end data communications network. This section defines each of the resources that are listed on the matrix of Table 12.1:

- Terminals—the devices used for input or output of computer-recognizable information.

- Distributed intelligence—The provision of capabilities for error detection or correction, authentication, message formatting, data validation and check sums, protocol, and any other logical and arithmetic function for validating the integrity of the data transmitted from the terminal.

- Modems—Modem is an acronym for MOdulator/DEModulator. The function performed is conversion of the data signals from a terminal to electrical forms acceptable for transmission on the particular communication links employed and vice versa.

- Local loop—The communications facility between the customer's premises and the communications carrier central office. The local loop is assumed to be metallic pairs of wire.

- Lines—The common carrier facilities used as links in the communications network between central offices. These include terrestrial and satellite facilities.

dial-up: the switched telecommunication network and the various services provided therein, e.g., Toll, WATS, CCSA (Common Control Switching Arrangements).

point-to-point private lines: dedicated leased facilities between two end points.

multipoint or loop configured private line: dedicated leased facilities shared among several (greater than two) end points.

- Multiplexor, concentrator, and switch—

multiplexor: a device that combines, in one data stream, several data signals from independent end points.

concentrator: an intelligent multiplexor.

switch: a device that allows interconnection between any two lines connected to the switch.

- Front-end processor—A device that interconnects the communications lines to the computer and performs a subset of the following functions: code and speed conversion, protocol, error detection and correction, format checking, authentication, data validation, and statistical data gathering.

- Computer—An electronic data processing device referred to here only for its communications processing capability.

- Software—The instructions in the computer that cause the communications application processing functions to be performed.

- People—The individuals responsible for inputting data, operating and maintaining the equipment, writing the software, and managing the data communications environment.

Exposures The following six items depict the basic areas of exposure that are listed across the top of the matrix. This section defines the basic exposures to which a data communication network is subjected:

- Errors and omissions—Inadvertent or naturally occurring problems excluding those resulting from deliberate or malicious actions. They include but are not limited to inaccurate data; incomplete data; and malfunctioning devices, lines, or software.

- Disasters and disruptions (natural and manmade)—The destruction or temporary breakdown of the personnel or facilities required for the communication system to function. This results from natural and manmade disasters, such as common carrier breakdown, public utility breakdown, hardware/software breakdown, and the occurrence of a series of events each with low probability of causing catastrophic loss.

- Loss of integrity—The condition that exists when the system (including its hardware, software, data, and configuration) is not in one of its intended states—i.e., it has been subjected to accidental, fraudulent, or malicious action or destruction. Mere disclosure is not included in this definition. (Errors and omissions were treated separately in this matrix.)

- Disclosure—The unauthorized exposure of information.

- Defalcation—The intentional breach of the integrity of a system or its data by an individual or a group of individuals in a position of trust or performing their assigned tasks.

- Theft of resources—The use of the facilities or services of a system for other than the intended purposes.

Safeguards   The following seventeen safeguards are the major categories of safeguards that an auditor should consider when reviewing the security of a data communication network. This section defines each safeguard. It should be noted that security measures applied to data communication networks can be costly. It is of great importance that a realistic and pragmatic evaluation be made of the potential threat as well as the possible safeguards for countering the threat to ensure a cost-effective application of these safeguards. The auditor should conduct a threat assessment with regard to a potential loss of the application involved, the probability of that loss, and the cost of providing an adequate safeguard:

- Physical security controls—The use of locks, guards, badges, sensors, alarms, and administrative measures to protect the physical facilities, computer, data communications, and related equipment. These safeguards are required for access monitoring and control for and the physical protection of the computer and to protect data communications equipment from damage by accident, fire, and environmental hazard, both intentional and unintentional in nature. These safeguards are employed to detect, deter, prevent, and report security exposures. Audit consists of determination of existence of specific physical security measures, effectiveness of their functioning, and testing of reliability.

- Audit trails—A chronological record of system activities that is sufficient to permit the reconstruction, review, and examination of the sequence of environments and activities surrounding or leading to each event. Selected journals or reports include computer log-on/log-off, physical access log-in/log-out, resource allocation and use, reconciliation of inputs to outputs, frequency of specific events, forward and backward tracing, and network utilization. This safeguard is employed to detect, recover, correct, or report security exposures. Audit consists of determination of reasonableness, completeness, and scope.

- Backup—The availability and protection of resources to be used to replace or duplicate those used in normal operation. This includes operational and written procedures for regular review, update, and testing of backup resources. This safeguard is employed to prevent loss, and to correct or to help recover from errors. Audit should determine appropriateness of backup techniques for risk involved.

- Recovery procedures—The actions, procedures, or systems used to restore resources to normal operational capability in a timely, cost-effective manner. Audit should determine workability or feasibility of recovery procedures.

- Error detection/correction—The techniques, procedures, or systems used to detect and correct errors by methods such as echoing, forward error correction, and automatic detection and retransmission methodologies. This may involve validation through selective algorithms, parity checks, check sum, etc. This safeguard is used to detect and correct errors. The auditor should determine limitations of techniques, procedures, or systems.

- Authentication—The act of identifying or verifying the identity, authenticity, and eligibility of a terminal, message, user, or computer. Authentication devices are used to detect, prevent, and deter exposures. These include but are not limited to user passwords, keys, badges, message sequencing, terminal/computer callback, network protocol, and encryption. The auditor should determine existence and completeness of the safeguards.

- Encryption—Transformation of data to hide original contents or prevent undetected modification. The considerations are these:

    Data should be specified precisely to meet some standard, e.g., the NBS Data Encryption Standard.

    There must be a match between vulnerabilities and characteristics of the communication system and the data involved.

    There should be various ways to encrypt, e.g., link-by-link or end-to-end means.

    Administrative procedures must exist to select keys to be used, dictate when to change them, and control their distribution.

    Encryption should be integrated into system design in future applications when justified by the appropriate cost/risk analysis.

    Communications overhead needs to be added to distribute keys, initialize and synchronize devices, and recover from communications errors.

    The auditor should first evaluate vulnerabilities of system and data, review the objectives of the encryption system, and then measure the effectiveness of the physical and administrative procedures supporting encryption.

- Operational procedures—The administrative regulations, policies, and day-to-day activities supporting the security safeguards of a data communication system, such as these:

    Specification of the objectives of ADP security for an organization, especially as they relate to data communications.

    Planning for contingencies of security "events," including recording of all exception conditions and activities.

    Assurance to management that other safeguards are implemented, maintained, and audited, including background checks, security clearances and hiring of people with adequate security-oriented characteristics; separation of duties; mandatory vacations.

    Development of effective safeguards for deterring, detecting, preventing, and correcting undesirable security events.

    Cost effectiveness, often resulting in related benefits such as better efficiency, improved reliability, and economy.
    The auditor should look for the existence of current administrative regulations, security plans, contingency plans, risk analysis, personnel understanding of management objectives, and then review the adequacy and timeliness of the specified procedures in satisfying these.

- Preventive maintenance—Scheduled diagnostic testing should be supplemented by cleaning, replacement, and inspection of equipment to evaluate its accuracy, reliability, and integrity. This maintenance program should do the following:

    Develop schedules for testing and repair.

    Ensure that maintenance personnel are given the time and resources to deter or prevent failure of equipment.

    Keep inventory of replacement parts, based on failure statistics, such as Mean Time Between Failure (MTBF) for each device.

    Keep maintenance records and analyze them for recurring problems or statistically unexpected security exposures.

    Perform unscheduled replacement or testing for specific devices to detect unauthorized modification ("bugging," etc.). This reduces the likelihood of failures during critical periods and, as a by-product, detects unauthorized modification of resources.
    The auditor should review maintenance schedules, records, inventory of parts, "downtime," cost-to-repair-or-replace charts, and compare these with those of similar systems.

- Format checking—A method of verifying data as being reasonable through checks and balances. There should be an automated verification system to detect data entry errors using methods such as range checking (numerical fields), record counts, alphabetic characters in numeric fields, field separators, etc.

    The auditor should evaluate areas where format checking can be used and verify that adequate checks are made.

- Insurance—Financial protection against major losses. Insurance is used to share a potential or actual loss and to protect against or recover from major disasters by budgeting resources over the long term.

    The auditor should evaluate (1) whether protection may be more easily obtained from alternative safeguards, and (2) whether major catastrophies could expose the organization to unacceptable risks.

- Legal contract—An agreement for performing a specific service on a specific costing basis, generally incurring specific liability. Examples include bonding, conflict of interest agreements, clearances, nondisclosure agreements, and the like. Other examples include agreements establishing liability for specific security events; and agreements not to perform certain acts (failure to honor the prohibition means that a penalty will be incurred). The auditor should review the legal document for adequacy and protection afforded.

- Fault isolation/diagnostics—The techniques used to ascertain the integrity of the various hardware/software components comprising the total data communications entity. These techniques are used to audit the total environment and to isolate the offending elements either on a periodic basis or upon detection of a failure. These techniques include diagnostic software routines, electrical loopback, test message generation, and administrative and personnel procedures. The auditor should review the adequacy of the techniques used for fault isolation.

- Training/education—Training and education of employees aids in preventing problems and in correcting them when they have occurred. It serves to define responsibility clearly and to familiarize employees with accepted procedures. The auditor should review ongoing educational policies. Education also includes training in the whys, including why security and controls are important to the organization. The potential repercussions of a failure and the need to follow procedures or observe controls should also be addressed. The auditor should ensure that management is aware of the need and advantages of education and that training is used on a continuing basis.

- Documentation—Documentation is a precise description of programs, hardware, system configuration, and procedures intended to assist in prevention of problems, identifying the causes of problems, and recovering from the problems. It should be sufficiently detailed to assist in reconstructing the system from its parts. The auditor should determine that documentation exists to the extent required to meet reasonable anticipated needs.

- Testing—The techniques used to validate the hardware and software operation to ensure integrity. Testing, including that of personnel, should uncover departures from specified operation. The auditor should determine that testing exists to the extent required.

- Reporting and statistics—The gathering and reporting of information defining the usage of all facets of the data communications entity. This category also includes the generation of exception reports for management: traffic statistics, maintenance statistics, error performance, and terminal usage by time and activity. The auditor should determine that reporting and statistics exist to the extent required to meet future planning needs.

Evaluation of Controls

Controls in a communications system involve both general and application controls. Most of the controls relating to the transmission of data are general controls. These controls apply to all computer applications using communication facilities. The application controls are structured to meet the needs of a specific application.

The approach to the review and evaluation of controls in data systems is similar to the approach used in batch-oriented systems. The auditor must first make a review of the EDP system to determine the administrative and general controls and the operating practices within the system. The auditor will review organization charts and documentation standards, and will interview the responsible data processing personnel as outlined in Chapter 9. In this general review, the auditor will be concerned with evaluating the client's controls for recovery from emergencies and failures, access to data files, backup file procedures, and controls over data transmission, terminal usage, and accessibility.

The addition of remote terminals and complex operating programs to handle data communications will make the general review of systems a more complicated task. Because of the increased complexity and increase of potential for security problems, the auditor will need to be more knowledgeable of EDP systems than in the past and will have to review control functions more closely. The auditor, of course, will still have to evaluate the application controls used by the client. A review of specific system documentation supplemented by tests of the processing will still be required. In the area of testing, it appears that major changes in the audit process will be required in data systems.

Present testing techniques will not be feasible in an on-line system, and it may be necessary for the auditor to alter his concept of testing. As in traditional systems, the auditor's main objectives will be to determine whether the system is working properly and whether system controls are functioning to preserve system integrity, but he will not be able to trace individual transactions through the system or to utilize statistical testing as it is presently understood.

For those portions of the system that lie entirely outside the computer system, it should be possible for the auditor to test the system using traditional methods; however, testing at the input and output points and testing within the computer cannot be done directly. In a batch system, testing is done by devising test transactions, processing them through the computer system, and comparing the output with predetermined results. In order to test an on-line system, it will be necessary to devise transactions that will not alter the data base or the records. This is important because, if the tests do alter the data base, then the auditor is introducing errors into the system. It might be possible to devise tests that reverse the errors introduced, but it is doubtful that the client would allow such tampering with the records. The rate at which data are introduced into the system and the complexity of the processing programs would make it almost impossible to guarantee data integrity.[4]

There appear to be two trends emerging for auditing data systems. The first is that audits will occur on a more frequent basis. Because data systems are closely integrated into the method of conducting business and because there is increased reliance on programmed controls, the computer system plays a more important role in the functioning of the organization than did the manual systems. This, coupled with the lack of a hard-copy audit trail, necessitates more frequent evaluation of the controls in data systems. The second trend concerns the area of testing. The use of test data with fictitious master records and the minicompany approach outlined in Chapter 9 are becoming more important to the auditor in evaluating data systems. Because these systems function continuously, it is difficult to stop the system at a specific point to perform an extensive test. Therefore, testing by auditors is occurring concurrently with the processing of data through the data system. Appendix E is a case study of the evaluation and testing of an on-line system.

Summary

Data systems will most likely change the nature of the audit process, particularly in the area of testing. More emphasis will have to be placed on the evaluation of controls in such systems. Because of the increased complexity of data systems, computer audit specialists will be required with knowledge and training in data communications operating systems and systems testing techniques, as well as in computer-audit programs.

Problems

1. What is an on-line real-time system? How does it differ from a batch-oriented system?

2. What unique control problems exist in a data system?

3. Recently, a newspaper article revealed theft by time sharing. The alleged theft was a plotting program proprietary to the firm, Information Systems Design (ISD). The person charged with the theft was a programmer employed by an ISD competitor, University Computing Co.

[4] William F. Lewis, "Auditing On-Line Computer Systems," *The Journal of Accountancy,* October 1971, p. 51.

(UCC). It was ISD's claim that the programmer used the identification number of a mutual client to access ISD's system illegally to take the plotting program.

In the same article two other cases were cited. In Chicago, a policeman was indicted by a federal grand jury for tapping the FBI's National Crime Information Center computer to get information for private use. The dossier of a financier was allegedly accessed by a policeman who in turn passed the information on to his brother-in-law, a lawyer who was considering taking on the financier as a client.

Another case was the theft of 217 Penn Central Railroad boxcars. The cars were discovered on the tracks and yards of a tiny Illinois railroad. According to attorneys, someone had to tamper with Penn Central's computers to shuttle the boxcars to the small railroad and to "make them disappear."

Comment on these aspects:

(a) The controls that appeared to be absent or ineffective to allow such "thefts" to occur.

(b) The auditor's responsibility to evaluate controls in such systems to prevent theft by time sharing.

4.* You have been engaged by Central Savings and Loan Association to examine its financial statements for the year ended December 31, 19X1. The CPA who examined the financial statements at December 31, 19X0, rendered an unqualified opinion.

In January 19X1 the association installed an on-line real-time computer system. Each teller in the association's main office and seven branch offices has an on-line input–output terminal. Customers' mortgage payments and savings account deposits and withdrawals are recorded in the accounts by the computer from data input by the teller at the time of the transaction. The teller keys the proper account by account number and enters the information in the terminal keyboard to record the transaction. The accounting department at the main office has both punched card and typewriter input–output devices. The computer is housed at the main office.

In addition to servicing its own mortgage loans the association acts as a mortgage servicing agency for three life insurance companies. In this latter activity the association maintains mortgage records and serves as the collection and escrow agent for the mortgagors (the insurance companies) who pay a fee to the association for these services.

(a) Assume you determine that an adequate system of internal control is in effect. Prepare an audit program for the examination of the mortgage accounts for which the association acts as the mortgage

*Problem 4 has been adapted from a CPA examination.

servicing agency. (Do not consider computer processing of the mortgage accounts in your audit program.)

(b) You would expect the association to have certain internal controls in effect because an on-line real-time computer system is employed. List the internal controls that should be in effect solely because this system is employed, classifying them thus: (1) those controls pertaining to input of information; (2) all other types of computer controls.

Cases

Establishing the Data Base Administration Function

The Teaching Hospital has a data processing department comprising a system section, programming section, and operations section. The department was established approximately fifteen years ago. During that time, the Teaching Hospital has designed and implemented over fifty-five applications.

Three months ago, the Teaching Hospital installed IBM's data base management system. Since that time, they have converted the entire revenue cycle to the data base. This includes all the applications dealing with order entry, billing, accounts receivable, customer credit, customer information, sales, inventory, inventory replenishment, shipping inventory, merchandise returns, and credits. The new system encompasses the application of eight different departments in the corporation.

The data base management system was put into production by a systems programmer in the operation department. The systems programmer worked in conjunction with six different project leaders to convert their individual application files to the revenue data base. In reality, this is two data bases—one for customer information, which includes sales, cash receipts, etc.; the second for inventory, shipments, and automatic replenishment information.

The task of maintaining the data base is becoming too much for the one systems programmer to accomplish. The systems programmer has sent a request to the operations manager for a second person. However, the operations manager is beginning to become concerned about the method of data base operation. The operations manager has asked the data processing manager to study the situation and make some recommendations.

The data processing manager felt that it would be good to conduct an audit of the area before making any organizational changes. You have been asked to review the organizational structure of the data base from a control perspective, and to make recommendations to the data processing manager as to how the area should be organized.

Reviewing Controls in the Data Base

You have been assigned to review the controls in the Medicaid claims data base for the X Region. You have identified the problems that can occur in the claims data base management system and are primarily concerned about the concurrent update problem. From your previous work, you know that the controls over the concurrent update should be in the data base management system software. What type of controls do you expect to find in the data base management system software to reduce the concurrent update problem?

Data Integrity Testing   You have been assigned to an audit of the billing procedures of the St. Louis Medical Center Inc. This hospital has approximately $250 million per year in billings. They have consolidated all their sales information into a revenue data base. This data base is the only means the hospital has for accumulating all their sales amounts.

The data base management system is one developed by the St. Louis Medical Center data processing personnel. They felt that if they designed their own data base management system, the conversion from their existing tape systems would be much easier. The conversion is now complete and operating successfully.

Associated with the data base management system is a data dictionary, which they also designed. In preparation for the audit, they have prepared for you an output listing showing all the data in their billing history data base.

What type of audits would you perform on this data base to ensure the integrity of the data base?

EDP AUDIT PROCESS*

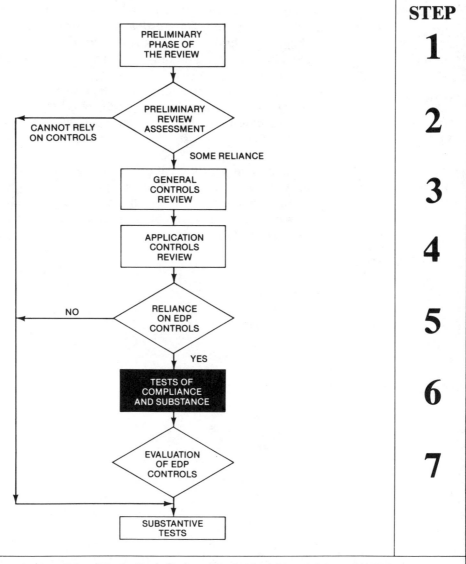

STEP

1

2

3

4

5

6

7

13

STEP

6

**ADDRESSED
IN THIS
CHAPTER**

ADVANCED AUDITING TECHNIQUES

(6) Tests of Compliance

Purpose:
- Determine whether the necessary control procedures are prescribed and followed satisfactorily.
- Provide reasonable assurance that controls are functioning properly.
- Consider and, to the extent appropriate, document when, how, and by whom controls are provided.

Methods: Examination of records; test of control procedures; inquiry; observation.

OBJECTIVE

The chapter describes the techniques used by EDP auditors, and explains how and when to use these new EDP audit techniques.

Business and government are continually increasing their dependence on computerized data processing systems. The systems are growing in complexity and size. Therefore, it is becoming increasingly important that adequate control and audit considerations be designed into these systems. Just as methods of business are being restructured because of the capabilities of the computer, so must audit and control concepts be restructured to complement the characteristics of computerized data processing systems.

Traditional auditing has implied evaluation of historical data. Many of the advanced EDP auditing techniques in use today still analyze historical data. Auditing in a data processing environment is moving toward auditing transactions in conjunction with normal processing. Some of the advanced EDP audit techniques are designed to audit transactions during the normal processing cycle. Other advanced EDP auditing techniques use dummy data to check compliance of application systems with organization policy. Auditors are also becoming involved in analyzing computer application programs. This provides the organization with assurance that controls built into the application systems are functioning.

Advanced EDP Systems Characteristics

Most data processing systems in operation today are based on the manual systems that preceded the computer. Many systems evolved by moving from a manual system to the logic of the manual system converted to unit record equipment; then the logic of the unit record equipment was transposed to a computer system. This resulted in computerized systems with many of the characteristics and controls that existed in the manual system. The value of the computer in this type of converted system is the increased speed, increased accuracy, and the stabilization of the manual effort necessary to handle an increase in volume.

As systems designers and programmers became more proficient in the use of the computer, the application systems evolved into more complex and integrated systems. Instead of the computer being a support tool for the user, it has become an integral part of the operation. In such integrated systems it is no longer possible to run these operations without interfacing with the computer during the transactions cycle.

These advanced systems can be defined as those systems that possess one or more of the following characteristics:

- Telecommunication
- Data integration
- Automatic transaction initiation
- Temporary audit trail

Telecommunications   Telecommunications is the facility of linking two or more pieces of terminal and computer hardware together. It provides the processing linkages for features described as on-line real-time processing, remote job entry processing, and distributive processing systems.

Many telecommunications systems are described as transaction-driven systems because as transactions are entered into the system, they are processed. In many cases, this is interactive processing with an individual "conversing" with the computer to process the transaction. For example, in an airline reservation system, the airline clerk communicates with the computer to determine availability of space prior to making a reservation; the airline clerk can then obtain costs and actually book the seat while the customer waits on the telephone or in person.

Data Integration   Data integration is placing all data involving one processing entity (e.g., customer, employee, vendor, etc.) into one data processing record. Early data processing systems were designed to handle a specific function. For example, a billing system had the function of preparing computer-generated invoices. Accounts receivable systems were charged with the function of recording receivables and applying cash against those receivables. Inventory systems received and released inventory. Credit systems established approved customers with authorized credit limits. Each of these systems operated independently of the other systems and had its own series of controls.

As data processing technology advanced, these systems became more integrated. The results of one system were recorded on tape. The tape was then fed into the next system, which utilized that tape as input. This has led some organizations to maintain all data regarding one customer on one record. This means that all data relating to one accounting entity (e.g., customer, employee, etc.) is integrated into one data base. All related functions are then processed against that data. The advantage is that data need be recorded only once. The disadvantages are that some of the normal checks and balances that existed because data were recorded two or more times no longer exist. Thus, if data were recorded wrong initially, many uses of that data would be affected by the inaccurate recording.

Automatic Transaction Initiation   In manual systems and early computerized systems, transactions had to be authorized by clerks or supervisors prior to being processed. This meant that before orders were shipped or cash transferred, an individual authorized that transaction. As computer systems become more integrated and complex, the length of time between the entrance of a transaction into a computer system and the recording of any output is increasing.

During the increased processing cycle of transactions, the computerized system itself initiates transactions. For example, in a computerized billing system, the computer can tally a running balance on the inventory levels of items in stock. When a particular item reaches the order level quantity, the computer system automatically initiates a replenishment order for that product.

Certain department stores are now tied electronically to banks. The entering of a transaction in the department store triggers a transaction that is electronically transferred to the bank, then at the bank a computer-generated transaction charges the customer's bank account with the amount of the purchase.

As computer systems continue to grow in size and complexity, the number of these automatically initiated transactions will increase. The checks and balances that are present in manual systems, or in manual segments of computer systems to verify the authenticity of a transaction, are not present when the computerized application initiates that transaction. Manipulation and the potential for repetitive errors exist in these cases unless there are adequate controls.

Temporary Audit Trail Manual systems and early computer systems retained complete audit trails. At many points during the process cycle hard-copy documents either existed or were produced from the computer system. The advent of telecommunications, data integration, and automatic transaction initiation has changed the character and scope of an audit trail.

Advanced computer systems do not have the extensive paper audit trail that existed in earlier systems. In addition, the vast number of transactions occurring (e.g., an interactive order-entry system may involve 15 or 20 interactions between the clerk and the computer) makes it impractical to save all the different aspects of a transition.

This change in the traditional audit trail will affect the way the auditor audits a computerized system. It may no longer be possible to audit systems on an annual or periodic basis. Auditing may be forced to move back much closer to the point when transactions are processed or shortly thereafter.

Implications of Advanced EDP Systems

The impact of data processing on business operations is just beginning. The characteristics of the advanced EDP systems just described indicate the need for restructuring control and audit concepts. Management must be prepared to fund the cost of these controls and audit processes at the same time they fund the cost for new computer systems.

The approaches and techniques currently being used by many auditors are no longer effective in an advanced EDP environment. Auditing is undergoing a transition from manual approaches to using the computer as a tool. The remainder of this chapter will describe some of the newer approaches to auditing.

Many of the techniques described are not being practiced by many auditors in the field on a regular basis. Effective use of these techniques requires auditors with heavy data processing knowledge.

Characteristics of EDP Auditing

Prior to describing specific audit techniques, it is necessary to discuss different aspects of those techniques. Auditors need to consider the following in selecting a technique to meet a specific audit objective:

- Purpose of technique
- Type of data on which technique operates
- Who supplies the audit technique

Because of the power of advanced auditing techniques, they may be used by internal auditors, external auditors, both groups of auditors, managers, or control personnel.

Purpose of Technique   Listed below are six general purposes for advanced EDP audit techniques. These purposes are not of equal importance to the audit function. Purposes 3 through 6 tend to be performed primarily by internal auditors.

1. Compliance testing: to determine whether or not the system performs in accordance with organization policy and procedure

2. Substantive testing: to determine whether the account balances adequately reflect the amounts on the accounts of the organization

3. Review performance of a system: to determine that the system is making the most effective use of the computer resources

4. Extend the audit trail: to provide additional data not readily available in the system audit trail

5. Verify correct program being utilized: techniques to determine that the system in use is the one to be in use, and only contains authorized routines

6. Audit planning and control: to provide data for audit planning or to control the audit process.

Data Used   There are three types of data that can be used with an advanced EDP auditing technique: live data, historical data, and test data. Figure 13.1 illustrates the uses of these data approaches. The use of live data implies that the audit is occurring as a transition is being processed. The audit of historical data is analyzing transactions at any time after they have been processed. Test data are used to verify compliance to policies and procedures by running tests on the computer applications system.

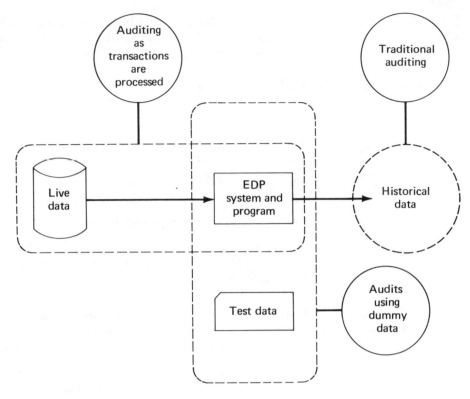

**Figure 13.1
Audit Approaches
for Advanced
EDP Systems**

Capability Supplied

While some advanced techniques are auditor supplied (i.e., obtained exclusively for use by auditors), others come from other sources. In many instances, computer vendors supply techniques valuable for audit purposes as part of their operating system software. In other cases, software vendors supply them or software programmers in the auditor's organization develop routines for control purposes which can then be used by auditors for audit purposes.

Advanced Audit Techniques

Auditors are using and continue to develop new techniques for auditing computer systems. These techniques are designed to complement the characteristics of the computer systems. The techniques described in this chapter are not exhaustive, but do represent the more commonly used techniques.

The techniques that will be discussed here are listed in Table 13.1 together with the purpose(s) for which each technique is best suited. A matrix providing a brief description and the advantages and disadvantages of each technique is given in Table 13.2.

TECHNIQUES	PURPOSE					
	COMPLIANCE TESTING	SUBSTANTIVE TESTING	REVIEW PERFORMANCE OF A SYSTEM	EXTEND THE AUDIT TRAIL	VERIFY CORRECT PROGRAM BEING UTILIZED	AUDIT PLANNING AND CONTROL
AUDIT PLANNING AND MANAGEMENT						
Audit Area Selection						✔
Simulation/Modeling						✔
Scoring						✔
Multisite Audit Software						✔
Competency Center						✔
TESTING COMPUTER APPLICATION PROGRAM CONTROLS						
Test-Data Method	✔					
Base Case System Evaluation		✔				
Parallel Operation		✔				
Integrated Test Facility	✔					
Parallel Simulation		✔				
SELECTION AND MONITORING OF DATA PROCESSING TRANSACTIONS						
Transaction Selection						✔
Embedded Audit Data Collection						✔
Extended Records				✔		
VERIFICATION						
Generalized Audit Software	✔	✔				
Terminal Audit Software	✔	✔				
Special-Purpose Audit Programs	✔	✔				
ANALYSIS OF COMPUTER PROGRAMS						
Snapshot	✔					
Manual Tracing and Mapping	✔					
Computer-Aided Tracing and Mapping	✔					
Control Flowcharting	✔					
COMPUTER SERVICE CENTER						
Job Accounting Data Analysis						✔
Audit Guide						✔
Disaster Testing			✔			
APPLICATION SYSTEMS DEVELOPMENT						
Postinstallation Audit	✔	✔	✔			
Control Guidelines for Use During System Development						✔
System Development Life Cycle			✔			✔
System Acceptance and Control Group			✔			✔
Code Comparison					✔	

Table 13.1   Purpose of Advanced EDP Audit Techniques

EDP AUDIT PRACTICES	DESCRIPTION OF PRACTICE	ADVANTAGES	DISADVANTAGES
Techniques for audit planning and management			
Audit area selection	Key indicator information for location or areas to assist the internal auditor in determining which locations to audit.	Improves efficiency of auditing.	Requires similar operations.
Simulation/modeling	A procedure to compare estimates of expected values to actual values to identify potentially important differences.	Uses live data for analysis.	Costly to operate.
Scoring	Assigns a numeric value to a computer application system to classify computer application systems in order of their auditability needs.	Sets audit priorities.	Requires careful evaluation.
Multisite audit software	Audit programs are developed at a central location and are installed at the outlying data centers.	Minimizes lack of EDP experience.	Requires similar remote operations.
Competency center	A computer center, established at a central location, that is responsible for the execution of audit software programs.	More competent audit extracts.	Transmittal cost of data.
Techniques for testing computer application program controls			
Test-data method	Verifies processing accuracy of computer application systems by executing these systems using specially prepared sets of input data that produce pre-established results.	Verifies processing logic and controls.	Time consuming if extensive tests performed.
Base case system evaluation	Utilizes sufficient transaction data processed by a computer application system to ensure that all programs are functioning correctly.	Comprehensive test.	Extensive user involvement needed.
Parallel operation	Processing production data and files using both the existing and the newly developed procedures, and comparing processing results to identify unexpected differences.	Runs data twice, normally through old and new systems.	Two systems may have differences.
Integrated test facility	Uses auditor-developed fictitious or dummy entity within the framework of the regular application processing cycle.	Evaluates system in normal operating environment.	Difficult to back out test transaction.
Parallel simulation	Use of one or more special computer programs to process "live" data through test programs.	Uses the same data as the production run.	Time and cost to develop.

Table 13.2   EDP Audit Practices

EDP AUDIT PRACTICES	DESCRIPTION OF PRACTICE	ADVANTAGES	DISADVANTAGES
Techniques to select and monitor data processing transactions			
Transaction selection	Uses software specified or developed by the internal auditor to screen and select transactions that have been input to the production computer application system.	Screens all transactions.	Cost to develop and run.
Embedded audit data collection	Uses one or more specially programmed data collection modules embedded in the computer application system to select and record data for subsequent analysis and evaluation.	Continual monitoring of application activity.	Data retained for analysis may be voluminous.
Extended records	Gathers together by means of a special program or programs all the significant data of an individual transaction.	Provides comprehensive audit trail for transactions.	Cost of building and maintaining.
Techniques for verification			
Generalized audit software	A set of computer programs that have the capability to process computer data files under the control of input parameters supplied by the internal auditor.	Extract languages designed for auditors.	Operational inefficiencies.
Terminal audit software	Accesses, extracts, manipulates and displays data from on-line data bases using remote terminal inquiry commands.	Terminal operation.	Same as any on-line system.
Special-purpose audit programs	Specially tailored programs to extract and present data from a specific application system's files, usually in an invariable format.	Auditors learn intricacies of EDP operations.	High level of EDP experience required.
Techniques to analyze computer application programs			
Snapshot	Takes a picture of the parts of computer memory that contain the data elements involved in a computerized decision-making process at the time the decision is made.	Provides selected core dumps during processing.	EDP personnel needed to implement.
Manual tracing and mapping	Procedures to identify the flow of transactions and associated application controls.	Emphasis on manual processing.	Not automated.

Table 13.2   (continued)

EDP AUDIT PRACTICES	DESCRIPTION OF PRACTICE	ADVANTAGES	DISADVANTAGES
Computer-aided tracing	Shows the trail of instructions executed through an application.	Shows trail of executed instructions.	Uses extensive computer time.
Computer-aided mapping	A technique to assess the extent of system testing and to identify specific program logic that has not been tested.	Lists unexecuted program instructions.	Requires special processor.
Computer-aided flowcharting	Technique provides the documentation necessary to explain the system of control.	Flowcharts system of controls.	Cost to develop and maintaim.
Techniques to audit the computer service center			
Job accounting data analysis	A feature of the computer operating system software that provides the means for gathering and recording information to be used for evaluating systems usage.	Provides data on the use of EDP resources.	Vast amounts of data to analyze.
Audit guide	A series of questions to provide assistance to the auditor in performing an audit.	Extensive checklist based on experience.	Auditors may place too much reliance on the guide.
Disaster test	The auditor, on an unannounced basis, will simulate a disaster in the computer service center to test the adequacy of the data center contingency plans.	Test plans that are normally not tested.	Disruption of computer center schedule.
Application systems development techniques			
Postinstallation audit procedures	The formal, standardized procedures to be followed by auditors in examining computer application systems after they are placed in a production environment.	Organized audit of both manual and computerized segments.	Auditors may overrely on approach.
Controls guidelines for use during systems development	Control guidelines are designed to provide a general framework for the satisfaction of the organization's control objectives.	Help ensure proper controls.	Auditor loses objectivity.
Systems development life cycle	Divides the systems development process into phases and identifies quality control checkpoints at the end of critical tasks in the phases.	A quality control technique.	Requires highly skilled EDP auditor.
Systems acceptance and control group	Group performs systematic review of computer applications during systems development to maintain effective computer application systems standards.	Assures the quality of controls.	Function is part of EDP development.
Code comparison	Comparison of two copies of a program made at different times to verify that program change and maintenance procedures and program library procedures are being followed correctly.	Ascertains correct program is operational.	Does not address legitimacy of the application.

Table 13.2 (continued)

The advanced auditing techniques listed are those identified by a two-year study sponsored by The Institute of Internal Auditors and funded by the International Business Machines Corporation. The Systems Auditability and Control study attempted to identify what practices were being used by auditors to assess computerized business applications. The identified techniques were divided into the following categories:

- Techniques for audit planning and management—This category includes two kinds of internal audit tools and techniques: first, techniques used to evaluate application systems for inclusion in current internal audit plans; and second, techniques to provide internal audit staffs with specialized EDP audit capabilities.

- Techniques to test computer application program controls—This category of EDP audit tools and techniques is used to test computational routines, programs, or whole applications in order to evaluate controls or verify processing accuracy and continued compliance with specified processing procedures. Such techniques are used for both the evaluation of application systems controls and for compliance testing.

- Techniques to select and monitor data processing transactions—Data processing audit tools and techniques used to select and capture production data for subsequent manual audit and verification are included in this classification. These techniques are typically used to monitor production activity and select samples as part of a continuous auditing activity within the normal production process. Selection criteria are usually parameter controlled and use range tests, sampling techniques, or error conditions to trigger the selection of records for subsequent evaluation by internal auditors. Such techniques are used in compliance testing to monitor transaction processing and to select data for verification. This category includes input transaction selection programs, which are independent of application system programs, audit modules embedded within application systems, and the extended record technique.

- Techniques for data verification—Data processing audit tools and techniques, such as generalized audit software, are included in this category. These techniques are used subsequent to production processing to select data from files based on logical or statistical sampling requirements, to foot and balance files or logical sections of files, such as divisional organizations or classes of accounts, to screen files for exception values, missing data, or duplicate entries, or to format reports for audit use. Also included is a modeling technique used to evaluate account balances.

- Techniques to analyze computer application programs—Data processing audit tools and techniques used to evaluate processing logic and procedures internal to application programs, system of programs, and JCL

(Job Control Language) are included in this section. These techniques are used during application systems development as well as during periodic postimplementation compliance testing. Included are snapshot, tracing, mapping, and flowcharting aids.

- Techniques to audit the computer service center—During field interviews, the study documented the internal audit techniques that are used to evaluate and verify general controls in the computer service center.
- Techniques to audit application system development—In this category, five audit techniques are presented that are useful to internal auditors reviewing the controls governing application system development.

The following are the criteria that an auditor should consider in selecting a technique:

A. Choose a technique that will meet the audit objective.
B. Select a technique for which the auditor has the necessary training and background.
C. Consider only techniques for which appropriate time is available.
D. Utilize a technique for which the capability exists within the organization.

We will briefly describe the twenty-eight advanced auditing techniques.

Auditing Planning and Management Techniques

Audit Area Selection

There are five of these advanced auditing techniques. Audit area selection is a technique used to identify high-risk areas among like processing units such as sales districts. For example, a corporation may wish to audit high-risk sales districts more frequently than those of low risk. To do this, the organization would select a number of key indicators—such as number of products returned, number of errors made in entering data, number of products damaged, number of customer complaints, and so forth. All the sales districts would then be compared using this common data. The ones indicating the most serious problems, such as the most units returned per units sold, would be subjected to more audits than like districts having fewer problems.

Simulation and Modeling

This is another technique used to select high-risk areas and is effective for a single area. An area of processing is simulated through a model, again using key indicators. For example, a bank may develop a model of branch activities. This model includes key indicators such as the number of checks cashed, number of deposits, number of mortgage installments paid, etc. These characteristics are fed into the model to produce a simulation of the day's processing. If actual processing deviates significantly from this model, then auditors investigate to determine the cause of the difference.

Scoring

Scoring is a technique that helps the auditor select high-risk areas among unlike systems or activities. While audit area selection requires like activities, such as sales units, distribution centers, etc., scoring can compare unlike units. Scoring uses external measurement characteristics. For example, an insurance company uses a similar system to determine if people are acceptable for insurance. They will score an individual's risk based on characteristics such as age, occupation, weight, whether the individual smokes, etc. Without ever seeing the individuals, the life insurance company can assess the risk of any person. It is a generalized assessment process that requires using general characteristics that apply universally to the activities or systems being evaluated. The same concept can be applied to audit area selection using characteristics such as dollar value of transactions processed, number of customer complaints, skill of users and systems personnel, etc.

Multisite Audit Software

This technique standardizes the audit process for like locations. It requires activities or locations with similar functions, such as branch banks, distribution centers, etc., which use common computer systems. The audit staff prepares computer programs and packages that can be run on the common functions computer systems. This permits predeveloped automated techniques to be used by auditors with minimal computer skills.

Competency Center

The competency center is a centralized body of highly skilled computer people to aid financial auditors in the execution of audits of computerized applications. Tasks performed by the people in the competency center include writing programs to perform data analyses, review of controls in computerized applications, and evaluating the work papers of financial auditors.

Testing Computer Application Program Controls Techniques

Test-Data Method

There are three of these advanced auditing techniques. Test data is a simulated transaction that can be processed through a computer system to determine whether live transactions of the same type will be processed accurately and improper ones identified and rejected. This technique determines whether the computer program rules (i.e., computer instructions) process data accurately and whether the controls in the system can prevent improper results, such as an exorbitant payroll check. However, using test data cannot be regarded as a complete audit of a computer system. For example, test data will not disclose (1) invalid but properly prepared input data or (2) some changes in computer programs that might be made to produce fraudulent results. Test data must be supplemented with other procedures to provide satisfactory audit coverage. However, when used correctly test data provides a great deal of information about the way computer programs work.

Base Case System Evaluation

Base case is an exhaustive set of test data. Test data verifies a single transaction. As such, it tests only a limited number of conditions. For example, a single test data transaction for a payroll system may test the normal calculation of pay for an individual working forty hours a week. On the other hand, base case will test every possible condition in the payroll application. That is, it will test overtime conditions, absence conditions, pay subject or not subject to FICA deductions, excused and unexcused absences, employees on and not on the payroll, invalid input as well as valid input, and all other conditions. Development of a set of base case transactions is a time-consuming and extensive process. One organization estimated it took 20 percent of the total system development effort to create a set of base case conditions. However, once established it provides very good assurance that the system will function properly.

Parallel Operation

Parallel operation is used to test a computer application that has been recently changed. The application is run using both the old and new system and the results are compared. It is used primarily to provide assurance that the new system is functioning properly. A major drawback to parallel operation is that, when the number of changes is extensive, comparing the old and the new system will cost more than value received from this technique.

Integrated Test Facility

The integrated test facility is the sole advanced auditing technique that enables the auditor to enter test data into a live computer run for the purpose of verifying correct processing. The data are introduced into the systems as if they were part of a live transaction and then processed through the system according to the rules of the system. The results of that transaction must be removed from the accounting records of the organization before they are incorporated into the organization's books of account.

For example, an organization could establish a dummy customer account. Once that has been done, the auditor can purchase items from the organization against that account. At a pre-established address the auditor can receive merchandise from the organization, be invoiced, pay or not pay the invoices, return goods, and perform any other activity that might be undertaken by a customer of the organization.

In payroll systems a special department could be established, time cards turned in for its dummy employees, and checks drawn for those employees as part of the payroll system. Obviously discretion has to be used depending on the cost of product consumed and the risk of having negotiable instruments produced for test purposes.

The integrated test facility can be likened to the quality control function in a product environment. In quality control it is not unusual for products of the organization to be consumed in a test function. Thus, it should come as no surprise for the auditors to consume company products in testing the data processing environment.

The important and difficult aspect of the integrated test facility is backing out test transactions at some point during the process. Some organizations have done this by inserting special routines into the application programs to pull out the test transactions. Other organizations have done it by letting the transactions flow completely through the system and then having the internal auditors make adjusting journal entries. In either case, it is necessary for the results of the integrated test facility processing to be accumulated in a special account. This may be a customer number account, a special department established for the integrated test facility usage, or any other unique accounting entity. It is essential that the transactions be consolidated into one account for ease of backing them out of the books of account of the organization.

Appendix C is a case study example of how an auditor could use the integrated test facility audit technique.

Parallel Simulation   Most advanced data processing techniques are best suited for compliance testing because of the consistency with which computers can apply systems rules. It is logical to assume that once the auditor has determined that a specific rule is being applied correctly, the computer will continue to apply that rule correctly, assuming programs are unchanged.

Simulation is an audit technique aimed at substantive testing. It is the only advanced auditing technique under which simulation operates to reprocess all or part of a specific computer application and then compare the results from the simulation with those generated by the organization's normal processing. However, because of the cost of simulating full applications, the auditor normally simulates only specific segments of an application. For example, in a payroll audit the auditor may wish to simulate the FICA deduction segment of the application.

To implement the technique, the auditor learns the processing rules and then writes a program to perform according to those rules. This simulated program is often written in an audit software language. The example of the recalculation of the FICA deduction is one in which the auditor independently wrote that processing logic. The same input records that were fed into the payroll application system are then fed into the auditor's simulation program. The simulation program in this example only calculates and accumulates the FICA deduction. The accumulated FICA deduction then is compared to that of the actual computer application payroll programs. If they are the same, the auditor can assume the actual organization programming is operating correctly.

Selecting and Monitoring of Data Processing Transactions Techniques

Transaction Selection

There are three of these advanced auditing techniques. Transaction selection provides the auditor with transactions from operational systems selected by predetermined criteria and delivered on a real-time basis. Real-time notification implies the auditor is aware of questionable transactions shortly after they have occurred. Traditionally, auditors will examine a group of transactions and in that examination process look for questionable or unusual transactions. This is a hit or miss process. Real-time notification enables the auditor to concentrate his effort on these questionable or unusual transactions.

Auditors develop the criteria for selecting these questionable transactions. For example, they may decide to question credits of over $1,000, price overrides of plus or minus 15 percent from regular selling prices, or employees who have worked more than 70 hours in 1 week. The criteria for selection can be as complex as the auditor's experience permits. Normally, the criteria initially are quite simple and grow more complex over a period of time.

The criteria for selecting transactions for audit pruposes then are coded and inserted into the application system. These selection routines should operate independently of the application systems programs. The real-time notification programs will be connected to the application system by operating system interaction. The auditors are provided with a list of questionable transactions immediately after the application system has run or, in the case of on-line systems, on a periodic basis. Upon receiving this listing, the auditors can follow up on the questionable transactions or can direct control groups to make the examination and provide the auditor with the results of those examinations.

Embedded Audit Data Collection

The computer provides the auditor with a vehicle to monitor the operation on a continual basis. The audit log is the mechanism of recording the results of those observations. Real-time notification is an application system-oriented technique, while audit log is a technique for analyzing the entire data processing operation.

The audit log would be a special tape or disk used for recording transactions. This log or disk is available to the auditor for analysis purposes. At selected times the auditor would either list or perform a computerized analysis of the data on this log for further investigation purposes.

The types of data that might be collected on an audit log are these:

- Attempts to override a password
- Unauthorized access to a data file
- Utilization of systems override features
- Use of hardware override features
- Attempts to access the audit log file

This technique is most useful as a compliance test, but it can be used for substantive testing in certain situations. For example, audit logs could be used to select all credit transactions on a specific application system. Currently, audit logs must be designed by an organization, and thus can be costly to develop and operate.

Extended Records

The audit trail in most organizations' computer system applications is incomplete. This incompleteness is caused by an unwillingness to expend the funds to maintain all the audit-trail data or by not thinking through what is needed for audit-trail purposes. The latter is often the true case. The extended records technique appends to the historic records from a computer application those data elements necessary to complete the audit trail.

In most computer applications, a series of decisions are made based on rules. Unfortunately, there are always more conditions occurring than rules can be developed to handle. For these uncovered cases, decisions are made by default. It is for these transactions that it is most difficult to provide an adequate audit trail. Auditors should be involved in the audit trail thought process during the development stage of a computer application system.

Examples of some of the types of information that are not normally retained are

- Individuals authorizing price overrides
- Name of supervisor authorizing excused absences of employees
- Input data rejected for manual correction

Appending this type of information to the historical records of an application system would complete the audit trail. It is an advisable practice to have the auditor work with the systems people on a periodic basis to determine the completeness of the audit trail.

Verification   There are three of these advanced auditing techniques.

Generalized Audit Software

Audit languages are computer programming languages oriented toward the vocabulary and the needs of the auditor. They are oriented to extract data from files and put that data in report format. The computational part of the language performs the traditional audit functions of selection, stratification, footing, cross-footing, and most mathematical operations. These languages also offer the capability of drawing statistical samples from a data file.

Audit languages are the most widely used audit technique for EDP systems in existence today. They are offered by most of the major CPA firms, as well as several independent vendors specializing in EDP auditing (see Appendix D). Efforts are under way by the AICPA to develop a common audit software language that would be implemented by computer vendors. This language would then be available to all auditors for use on most computer hardware systems. One drawback to many of the audit software languages today is that they are implemented only for IBM equipment.

See Chapter 10 for a detailed description of how audit software can be used.

Terminal Audit Software

Terminal audit software is generalized audit software executed using a computer terminal. While generalized audit software requires the auditor to compile programs using an iterative process, terminal audit software substantially reduces that time. The difference is that in terminal audit software the auditor can substantially reduce both the compile and execution time of a program by using a computer terminal.

Special-Purpose Audit Programs

Generalized audit software is a computer language oriented toward the vocabulary and needs of an auditor. The more common computer languages are generalized in nature and not designed for any specific background or discipline. When auditors write programs in these generalized languages, such as COBOL, RPG, BASIC, or FORTRAN, they are writing special-purpose audit programs to achieve an audit objective. Sometimes these special-purpose audit programs are written because the objectives cannot be achieved using a generalized audit software language, while in other instances the auditors do not have a generalized audit software package available. In addition, a few organizations believe that their auditors should write in the same languages that the data processing people use.

Analysis of Computer Programs Techniques

There are four of these advanced auditing techniques.

Snapshot

An auditor's test of operations involves following the processing of a transaction through an organization. This both familiarizes the auditor with the organization's procedures and enables the auditor to determine if the organization's policies and procedures are being adhered to. These objectives are accomplished by following and observing the different processing steps in a transaction cycle. However, in a computerized environment, this must be done electronically and not manually.

Tagging is a technique of affixing an identifier to a transaction. This identifier or "tag" then indicates that this is a special transaction. At predetermined points throughout the computer systems application, an audit trail is provided of the flow that this "tagged" transaction took during the processing cycle. Then the auditor is provided with a report showing the trail of the tagged transaction as it flowed through one or more programs in the application system. For example, an auditor could tag all credits of over $1,000, or all employees of a specific department, or questionable input transactions. Tagging can be done by actually affixing a special code to an input transaction (e.g., an asterisk in card column 80 of input) or it can be done logically so that the computer analyzes and looks for such things as credit transactions over $1,000.

The tagging technique is useful for compliance testing purposes. The auditors see which parts of the programs are executed and, thus, are enabled to determine which procedures were executed during the processing cycle. The auditor must analyze the trail provided by the tagging technique to determine whether or not organization policy and procedure are being followed. This technique works on live transactions as they are being processed through the application system.

Manual Tracing and Mapping

Manual tracing and mapping provides the same capabilities as computer-aided tracing and mapping. The reason many auditors do not manually trace transactions, or manually map programs, is because it is a time-consuming task. As such, the benefits may not justify the cost. However, when done on the computer the cost of performing the technique is usually substantially reduced.

Computer-Aided Tracing and Mapping

Computer-aided tracing uses a special programming option to permit a printout of the path through a computer program taken to process a specific transaction. When a trace option is executed, the individual using that technique receives a listing of each statement or program executed, together with all the points where the logic was transferred from one statement or instruction to another. It is a costly technique to use because of the computer time and auditor time required to accomplish the necessary analysis. Thus, it should be used only when it is necessary to review detailed code and detailed execution.

Computer-aided mapping shows what parts of a program can be entered during the execution of that program. It in effect maps those parts of the computer program that are functional, and shows which parts of the program are nonexecutable. This is helpful in isolating computer code that is not used and in isolating potential segments of code that may be activated for unauthorized purposes. For example, one programmer in the payroll system had a routine in the system that would only be activated when his employee number no longer appeared on the payroll master. Mapping would isolate these types of conditions.

Control Flowcharting

Control flowcharting is a technique that shows what controls govern transaction processing. The technique traces the flow of transactions through computerized business applications (both manual and computerized parts) indicating at which point those transactions are subject to control. For example, in flowcharting a transaction to add an employee to the payroll master, control flowcharting would show where and how that additional employee was authorized, where it was determined that that employee had not already been added to the payroll, where the new employee was added to the control totals, etc. The auditor then uses this control flowchart as an aid in assessing the adequacy of control over transactions.

Computer Service Center Techniques

There are three of these advanced auditing techniques.

Job Accounting Data Analysis

Monitoring is the utilization of hardware and/or software to review the functioning of a computer system. Monitoring is used primarily by data processing systems personnel in an effort to improve the efficiency of their computer operations. However, the auditor may also wish to use these data to review systems activity.

Hardware and software monitors provide systems activity in the following areas:

- Use of internal CPU time
- Use of hardware features

- Access to data files
- Communication activities
- Use of computer resources and who uses those resources

The hardware and software monitors provide data about the functioning of the computer system. The auditors can use hardware and/or software monitors to conduct performance audits. Auditors can also use those monitors to look for unauthorized access to data and unauthorized use of computer resources. The objective of monitors is to answer questions regarding who is using the resources and how efficiently they are being utilized. The results are used to bill users for the portion of the computer resources utilized and can be used to analyze the efficiency of specific programs or applications. Monitors also can show unauthorized attempts to break password protection mechanisms.

Audit Guide

Audit guides are standardized approaches to audits. In a computerized application, audit guides are used to assess the adequacy of control in a computerized application, to evaluate the controls in the computer center, data library, and other support areas, and to assess the adequacy of general controls over the computer environment. Many published audit guides are general in nature and need to be adapted to a particular audit situation. Auditors are cautioned to use them as a *guide* and not as the sole basis for performing a complete audit. The advantages of an audit guide are that it aids the auditor in reviewing all pertinent areas and it provides a consistency of reviews. It also can be used by audit management in assessing the adequacy of an audit. The disadvantages are that there can be a misinterpretation as to the importance and meaning of questions and procedures in the audit guide, and that auditors may rely on it too heavily and not use sufficient judgment in conducting the audit.

Disaster Testing

As computerized applications become more integrated into the day-to-day processing of an organization, the organization's reliance on those systems increases. Because of this, organizations have developed elaborate procedures to restart and recover operations after a disaster. Unfortunately, few organizations ever test these procedures. Some of the reasons for not testing them include the unavailability of adequate computer time, or the feeling that the procedures were properly thought through and did not require testing. Disaster testing is a means of determining whether or not the disaster procedures work. To use the technique, an auditor enters the computer room unannounced and informs the data processing manager that a simulated disaster has occurred. Normally the auditor will pick a single application such as a payroll and asks the data processing department to reconstruct processing for that application without using any information or facilities in the computer room. While this procedure can be time consuming and costly, it is the only sure method for determining whether, in fact, the disaster procedures work.

Application System Development Techniques

There are five of these advanced auditing techniques.

Postinstallation Audit

During the development of a new application, systems are built to user specifications. A postinstallation audit assesses whether or not the operational application has met those specifications. This requires that the control specification be documented and measurable. For example, an auditor cannot audit a specification such as "adequately controlled." However, the auditor can assess that an error message will be produced if an item is sold for less than 90 percent of normal selling price. Postinstallation audits are normally conducted within three months after a computer system becomes operational.

Control Guidelines for Use During Systems Development

One of the major difficulties organizations face in control assessments is the variety of methods for implementing controls. Without guidelines, systems designers can design and implement those controls they believe are needed, and in a manner that they feel is either easiest to implement or most beneficial to the user. This results in a diversity of approaches that are difficult to both maintain and assess. Control guidelines specify the types of controls needed and many times include the method of implementation. For example, control guidelines usually cover file labels, control totals, audits, and edits of input data, file integrity controls, use of passwords, etc.

System Development Life Cycle

The system development life cycle is an orderly approach to the development of a computerized application. The life cycle breaks up the system development process into manageable and controllable segments. Most life cycles include:

- Feasibility—A determination as to whether or not the implementation of a new system is beneficial and cost effective.
- Design—The development of the system blueprints for the construction of the system. Includes design of data and specification of processing.
- Programming—Involves the coding, compiling, assembling, and testing of the various programs within the system.
- Testing—The assessment as to whether or not the implemented system meets the specifications.
- Operations—The actual operation of the new system on the computer. This phase includes manual operations, computer operations, and systems maintenance.

There are many variations of the system development life cycle. Some organizations have as many as fifteen phases, others as few as four. The underlying concept is to specify and control the methods by which the computer systems are developed.

System Acceptance and Control Group

A system acceptance and control group has the responsibility to review computer applications during the development process. This group is similar to a quality control function in a factory. Their responsibility is to determine that the organization's guidelines and standards are followed, that the system is developed according to the development procedures, and that the needs and requirements of the user are satisfied. Normally senior systems analysts staff this function, which is also called a quality assurance or systems assurance group.

Code Comparison

A difficult problem for the auditor is to verify that the correct version of a program is operating in the production environment. Recompiling and comparing is a technique that enables the auditor to perform this function. The auditor retains or has available the source code of the correct version of the program. The auditor then has that recompiled into object code and compared against the object code version in production. If these two versions compare equally, then the auditor can be assured that the correct version is running in production. Any discrepancies warrant further audit investigation.

Although twenty-eight EDP audit tools and techniques have been identified, only a few are used extensively. The most commonly used EDP audit tools and techniques are these:

- Generalized audit software
- Manual tracing and mapping
- Test-data method
- Parallel operation
- Transaction selection

Summary

The rapid rate at which the computer technology is accelerating indicates that even newer EDP auditing techniques are needed. The techniques described in this chapter necessitate a major retraining effort for many thousands of auditors now in the field. These techniques are also indicative of the caliber of individual who is necessary as the auditor of the future.

Problems

1. Name the four characteristics that make advanced EDP systems different from tape-batch systems.

2. What are the three types of data that can be used with an advanced EDP auditing technique? State the advantages and disadvantages of each.

3. State the advantages to internal auditing management from using advanced EDP audit techniques for audit planning and management.

4. One of the most commonly used advanced EDP audit techniques is generalized audit software. What are the advantages and disadvantages of generalized audit software?

5. What are the criteria that an auditor should consider in selecting an advanced EDP audit technique?

6. What type of characteristics are used by the scoring audit technique to measure an area for risk? How does this technique help improve audit efficiency?

7. Explain how the integrated test facility can be used for testing compliance.

8. Explain the difference between the transaction selection audit technique and the embedded audit data collection technique. Under what circumstances would you recommend that embedded audit data collection be used over transaction selection?

9. What is the main advantage of audit software over special-purpose audit programs?

10. How does control flowcharting differ from systems and programming flowcharting?

11. What advanced EDP audit technique can the auditor use to verify that the correct version of a program is operating in the production environment?

Case

Automatic Inventory Replenishment

The Longwood Corporation recently installed an automatic inventory replenishment system. The system is designed to automatically create a purchase order when the on-hand inventory drops below the reorder quantity. For example, if product X's reorder point is 100, then whenever the on-hand quantity for product X falls below 100 a purchase order will be issued. The reorder quantity and supplier have already been determined and are included in the computer data base.

Each inventory record in the inventory file contains the following data elements:

Name of Data Element	Length of Data Element
Inventory stock number	6
Inventory stock name	25
On-hand inventory quantity	7
Reorder point quantity	6
Reorder quantity	6
Vendor name	20
Vendor address	30
Inventory committed for future orders	6
Inventory on demonstration	6
Average amount sold per month for the last twelve months	6

You have been assigned to audit the automatic inventory replenishment system. The auditor in charge has given you two assignments. These are:

Assignment #1

You are to write an audit software program to extract data from inventory file to evaluate the effectiveness of the automatic inventory replenishment system. What fields do you believe should be extracted from the inventory file in order to determine whether or not the automatic inventory replenishment system is functioning properly? For this assignment you are asked to list the fields you want and why. You are to limit your extracted data to 100 characters per record. Then prepare a report line showing how you want those 100 characters displayed.

Assignment #2

The auditor in charge would like you to establish an integrated test facility for the purpose of verifying the automatic replenishment rules. Indicate what type of integrated test facility you would set up for this purpose, how you would operate it, and how you would control it.

EDP AUDIT PROCESS*

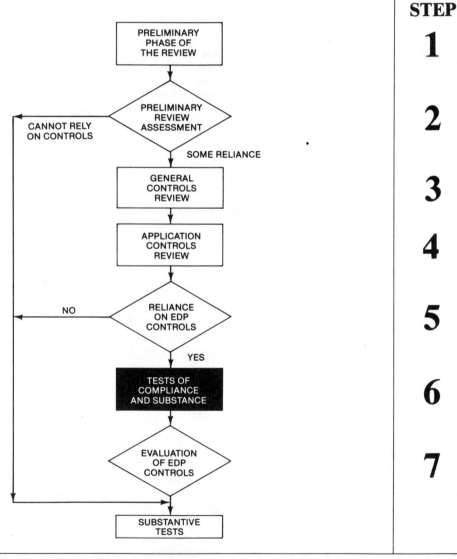

STEP

1

2

3

4

5

6

7

PRELIMINARY
PHASE OF
THE REVIEW

PRELIMINARY
REVIEW
ASSESSMENT

CANNOT RELY
ON CONTROLS

SOME RELIANCE

GENERAL
CONTROLS
REVIEW

APPLICATION
CONTROLS
REVIEW

RELIANCE
ON EDP
CONTROLS

NO

YES

TESTS OF
COMPLIANCE
AND SUBSTANCE

EVALUATION
OF EDP
CONTROLS

SUBSTANTIVE
TESTS

Diagram is adapted from The Auditor's Study and Evaluation of Internal Control in EDP Systems, *pages 21–24. Copyright © 1977 by the American Institute of Certified Public Accountants, Inc. (See Figure 9.1 for a complete explanation of the steps.)*

14

STEP

6

ADDRESSED IN THIS CHAPTER

AUDIT AND CONTROL OF COMPUTER CRIME

(6) Tests of Compliance

Purpose: • Determine whether the necessary control procedures are prescribed and followed satisfactorily.

• Provide reasonable assurance that controls are functioning properly.

• Consider and, to the extent appropriate, document when, how, and by whom controls are provided.

Methods: Examination of records; test of control procedures; inquiry; observation.

OBJECTIVE

Criminals frequently abuse new technology before auditors learn how to detect those abuses. This chapter explains the methods used to abuse computer systems and how to prevent and detect them.

The effective control of computer-related crime is an interdisciplinary matter involving computer technology, law, crime investigation, audit, and crime prosecution. Business, economic, and white-collar crimes are changing rapidly as computers proliferate within the activities and environments in which these crimes occur. Computers, it is safe to say, are creating a new kind of crime.

The introduction of new occupations has extended the traditional occupations of criminals to include computer programmers, computer operators, tape librarians, and other computer specialists. Although crimes have traditionally occurred in environments of manual human activities, some new crime is now perpetrated inside computers—in the specialized environment of rooms with raised flooring, lowered ceilings, large grey boxes, flashing lights, moving tapes and disks, and the hum of air conditioning motors.

This chapter explores the new methods of committing crime when it is associated with a computer. The chapter will discuss the new jargon that is developing to identify automated criminal methods, such as "data diddling." The chapter also suggests who might perpetrate computer crimes using the different techniques, and it provides some suggested methods for detection as well as the audit evidence to examine.

The material in this chapter is taken from a study conducted by Donn B. Parker, SRI International, for the law enforcement assistance administration section of the U.S. Department of Justice. The authors are indebted to the U.S. Department of Justice for the use of this material.

Definition of Computer-Related Crime

Computers have been involved in most types of crime, including fraud, theft, larceny, embezzlement, bribery, burglary, sabotage, espionage, conspiracy, extortion, and kidnapping. Criminal justice agencies having limited experience with computer-related crime have generally thought of it as crime that occurs inside computers. This narrow definition has recently broadened as the proliferation of computers into most societal functions proceeds at an increasing pace. The public media have added to the confusion through sensationalized, distorted, often incorrect reporting by journalists and their sources who do not sufficiently understand the technology.

The timing of some crimes is also different. Traditionally, the time of criminal acts is measured in minutes, hours, days, weeks, months, and years. Today some crimes are being perpetrated in less than 0.003 of a second (3 milliseconds). Thus, automated crime must be considered in terms of a new time scale because of the speed of the execution of instructions in computers.

Geographic constraints do not inhibit perpetration of this new crime. A telephone with a computer terminal attached to it in one part of the world could be used to engage in a crime in an on-line computer system in any other part of the world.

Computer-related crime is not well understood in the criminal justice and business communities, and no consensus on its definition exists. One definition is that it is a form of white-collar crime committed inside a computer system. An example is the making of unauthorized changes to a computer program to transfer funds from inactive accounts into a favored account, and then "legitimately" withdrawing the funds. Another definition is that it is the use of a computer as the instrument of a business crime. An example would be gaining access to a computer over communication lines by using one's own computer.

The definition of computer-related crime should be based on the problem that needs to be solved. The problem addressed is twofold: (1) how to reduce the incidence of any type of crime in which a knowledge of computer technology is needed to understand the intentional acts that result in losses, and (2) how to successfully prosecute the perpetrators. Whereas this is now predominantly a white-collar crime, it is the criminal justice and business communities who must be prepared to deal with any illegal acts that are based on an understanding of computer technology. A study of 669 reported cases of computer abuse over the past eight years has revealed that computers are involved in an increasing number of crimes of all types except murder and person-to-person street crimes. The proliferation and use of personal small computers make even the latter crimes subject at least to the indirect involvement of computer technology.

The broadest definition of computer crime is called for. The term "crime" is used here (as is usual) as a convenience to mean "alleged crime" because no harmful or antisocial act is a crime until a court declares it so by convicting a party for violating a law. Three terms have been used to describe the subject: *computer abuse, computer crime,* and *computer-related crime. Computer abuse* is any intentional act involving a computer in which one or more perpetrators made or could have made a gain and one or more victims suffered or could have suffered a loss.

Computer crime is a common term used to identify illegal computer abuse; however, it implies direct involvement of computers in committing a crime. Therefore, we adopt the term *computer-related crime* to convey the broader meaning of *any illegal act for which knowledge of computer technology is essential for successful prosecution.* This definition is based on the scope and nature of the particular problem being addressed. The crimes and alleged crimes may involve computers not only actively but also passively when usable evidence of the acts reside in computer-stored form. The victims and potential victims include all organizations and persons who use or are affected by computer and data communication systems. People about whom data are stored and processed in computers also are included.

Computer-related crime goes far beyond business, white-collar, or economic crime. It could include violent crime that destroys computers or their content or jeopardizes human life and well-being because they are dependent on the correct functioning of computers controlling sensitive processes.

Computers can play any of four roles in crime:

- Object—Cases include destruction of computers or of data or programs contained in them or supportive facilities and resources, such as air conditioning equipment and electrical power, that allow them to function.
- Subject—A computer can be the site or environment of a crime or the source of or reason for unique forms and kinds of assets.
- Instrument—Some types and methods of crime are complex enough to require the use of a computer as a tool or instrument. A computer can be used actively—as in automatically scanning telephone codes to make unauthorized use of a telephone system. It could also be used passively —as in the simulation of a general ledger in the planning and control of a continuing financial embezzlement.
- Symbol—A computer can be used as a symbol for intimidation or deception. This could involve the false advertising of nonexistent services—as in a dating bureau.

All known and reported cases of computer-related crime involve one or more of these four roles.

The dimensions of the definition of computer-related crime become a problem in some cases. If a computer is stolen in a simple theft, one in which, based on all circumstances, it could have been a washing machine or milling machine and made no difference, then a knowledge of computer technology is not necessary; and it would not be a computer-related crime. However, if knowledge of computer technology is necessary to determine the value of the article taken, the nature of possible damage done in the taking, or the intended use by the thief is at issue, then it would be a computer-related crime. To illustrate, if an individual makes a telephone call to a bank funds transfer department and fraudulently requests a transfer of $10 million to his account in a bank in Zurich, two possibilities occur. If the clerk who received the call was deceived and keyed the transfer into the computer terminal, the funds transfer would not be a computer-related crime. No fraudulent act was related directly to a computer, and no special knowledge of computer technology would be required. However, if the clerk was in collusion with the caller, the fraudulent act would include the entry of data at the terminal and would be a computer-related crime. Knowledge of computer technology would be necessary to understand the terminal usage and protocol. These examples indicate the possibilities of rational conclusions in defining computer-related crime.

Classification of Computer-Related Crime

A classification of computer-related crime is based on a variety of lists and models from several sources to produce standards for categorization. The classification goes beyond white-collar crimes because, as we have seen, computers have been found to be involved in robbery, larceny, extortion, espionage, and sabotage.

Senator Abraham Ribicoff's 1980 Senate Bill (S240) to amend Title 18 of the U.S. Criminal Code is an omnibus crime bill making crimes of unauthorized acts in, around, and with computer and telecommunication systems. He identifies four main categories of computer-related crime:

1. The introduction of fraudulent records or data into a computer system.

2. Unauthorized use of computer-related facilities.

3. The alteration or destruction of information or files.

4. The stealing, whether by electronic means or otherwise, of money, financial instruments, property, services, or valuable data.

A computer abuse study has identified categories in several dimensions:

- By type of loss—Physical damage and destruction from vandalism, loss of intellectual property, direct financial gain, and use of services.

- By the role played by computers—As object of attack, on account of its unique environment and forms of assets produced, as instrument, and as symbol.

- By type of act relative to data, computer programs, and services—Modification, destruction, disclosure, and use of services.

- By type of crime—Fraud, theft, robbery, larceny, arson, embezzlement, extortion, conspiracy, sabotage, and espionage.

- By modi operandi—Physical attacks, false data entry, superzapping, impersonation, wire tapping, piggybacking, social engineering, scavenging, Trojan horse attacks, trap door use, asynchronous attacks, salami techniques, data leakage, logic bombs, and simulation.

These classifications can be developed into a set of complete, detailed descriptions and models of computer-related crime. They can be useful for a variety of research and practical purposes in investigation and in the prosecution of computer-related crime.

History of Computer-Related Crime

Computer abuse started with the emergence of computer technology in the late 1940s. As the number of people in the computer field began to increase, the facet of human nature of doing harm to society for personal gain took hold as it does with any segment of the human population; the problem of crime became especially acute as computer technology proliferated into sensitive areas in society. This occurred first in military systems and then in engineering, science, and finally in business applications.

The first recorded computer abuse occurred in 1958. The first federally

Table 14.1
Computer Abuse Cases:
Incidence and Loss
by Type of Crime
(Yearly)

CASES: Total known cases
of this type in year, whether or
not loss is known.
KNOWN LOSSES: In thousands
of dollars.
AVERAGE LOSS: Average for
cases where loss is known.

YEAR	TYPE 1 PHYSICAL DESTRUCTION			TYPE 2 INTELLECTUAL PROPERTY DECEPTION AND TAKING		
	NUMBER OF CASES; PERCENT OF TOTAL	KNOWN LOSSES FOR TYPE 1	AVERAGE LOSS PER CASE, TYPE 1	NUMBER OF CASES; PERCENT OF TOTAL	KNOWN LOSSES FOR TYPE 2	AVERAGE LOSS PER CASE, TYPE 2
1958	— —	—	—	— —	—	—
1959	— —	—	—	— —	—	—
1962	2 0%	—	—	— —	—	—
1963	1 50%	2,000	2,000	— —	—	—
1964	1 17%	—	—	2 33%	2,500	2,500
1965	— —	—	—	1 13%	—	—
1966	1 33%	‹1	‹1	— —	—	—
1967	2 50%	‹1	‹1	— —	—	—
1968	1 8%	—	—	3 25%	7,203	3,602
1969	4 20%	2,000	2,000	8 40%	1,003	334
1970	8 21%	3,600	900	6 16%	6,843	1,369
1971	7 12%	—	—	20 34%	9,844	1,641
1972	17 23%	11,148	2,230	19 26%	180	30
1973	10 13%	4	2	26 35%	26,782	2,435
1974	7 10%	2,010	1,005	20 27%	2,197	439
1975	5 6%	115	58	21 25%	91,670	13,096
1976	5 8%	1,110	370	19 32%	49,465	7,066
1977	14 16%	2,252	322	16 18%	17,946	2,991
1978	10 24%	2,523	841	13 31%	300	50
1979	2 10%	—	—	11 55%	—	—
TOTAL	97 14%	26,761	836	185 28%	215,932	3,322

prosecuted computer-related crime, identified as such, was the alteration of bank records by computer in Minneapolis in 1966. Table 14.1 is a computer-produced index of collected cases of computer abuse. Some fraction of the 669 cases can be considered to be computer-related crimes (where illegal activities have been proved).

Pursuit of the study of computer-related crime and computer abuse has been controversial. In 1970, a number of researchers concluded that the problem was merely a small part of the effect of technology on society and was not worthy of specific, explicit research. The increase in substantial losses associated with intentional acts involving computers proved the fallacy of this view. The explicit identification of computer-related crime as a subject for research and development of preventive measures in criminal justice suffered a similar fate in the mid-1970s. Researchers argued that computers should not be the focus in a study of various types of crime. They believed the involvement of computers should be subordinate to the study of each specific type of crime, both manual and automated. The uniqueness of characteristics of computer-

TYPE 3 FINANCIAL DECEPTION AND TAKING			TYPE 4 UNAUTHORIZED USE OF SERVICES			ALL TYPES		
NUMBER OF CASES; PERCENT OF TOTAL	KNOWN LOSSES FOR TYPE 3	AVERAGE LOSS PER CASE, TYPE 3	NUMBER OF CASES; PERCENT OF TOTAL	KNOWN LOSSES FOR TYPE 4	AVERAGE LOSS PER CASE, TYPE 4	TOTAL CASES	TOTAL KNOWN LOSSES	AVERAGE LOSS
1 0%	<1	<1	— —	—	—	1		
1 0%	278	278	— —	—	—	1	278	277
— —	—	—	— —	—	—	2	—	—
1 50%	81	81	— —	—	—	2	2,081	1,040
3 50%	100	100	— —	—	—	6	2,600	1,300
4 50%	126	63	3 38%	—	—	8	126	63
2 67%	28	14	— —	—	—	3	28	9
— —	—	—	2 50%	10	10	4	10	5
6 50%	5,251	1,313	2 17%	—	—	12	12,454	2,075
4 20%	6	2	4 20%	2	2	20	3,011	376
13 34%	8,910	810	11 29%	—	—	38	19,353	967
24 41%	5,943	540	8 14%	351	175	59	16,137	849
19 26%	3,090	257	18 25%	107	21	73	14,524	518
28 37%	206,274	11,460	11 15%	7	1	75	233,066	6,474
34 47%	3,952	158	12 16%	3	3	73	8,162	247
49 58%	6,513	176	9 11%	14	5	84	98,312	2,006
30 51%	2,026	78	5 8%	—	—	59	52,601	1,461
44 51%	47,501	1,319	13 15%	154	77	87	67,853	1,330
17 40%	12,384	826	2 5%	—	—	42	15,207	633
4 20%	200	200	3 15%	—	—	20	200	200
284 42%	302,661	1,462	103 15%	646	32	669	546,001	1,685

related crime across all the different types of crime was not considered sufficient to warrant explicit research.

Computer-Related Crime Methods and Detection

Auditors should deal with computer-related crime as much as possible in the context of their experience with other, more traditional, crime. However, when computer technology plays a key role that cannot be avoided, a thorough understanding of criminal methods involving computers is essential. In addition, an awareness of the types of people who have the skills and knowledge to use these methods along with knowledge of what is likely evidence of their use and of detection methods can all be most helpful to the auditor.

This section describes twelve computer-related crime methods in which computers play a key role. Although several of the methods are far more complex than the nonexpert will understand in detail, these brief descriptions will aid investigators and prosecutors to comprehend sufficiently to interact with technologists who can provide the necessary expertise to deal with them. Most technologically sophisticated computer-related crimes will use one or more of these methods.

The results of computer-related crimes are modification, disclosure (taking), destruction, and use or denial of use of services, computer equipment, computer programs, or data in computer systems. Depending on the meaning of the data, kinds of services, or purpose of the programs, the acts range over many known types of crime. The methods, possible types of perpetrators, likely evidence of their use, and detection are described in the following twelve sections. Like most aspects of computer technology, a jargon describing the now-classical methods of computer-related crime has developed.

Data Diddling   This is the simplest, safest, and most common method used in computer-related crime. It involves changing data before or during their input to computers. The changing can be done by anybody associated with or having access to the processes of creating, recording, transporting, encoding, examining, checking, converting, and transforming data that ultimately enter a computer. Examples are forging or counterfeiting documents; exchanging valid computer tapes, cards, or disks with prepared replacements; source entry violations; punching extra holes or plugging holes in cards; and neutralizing or avoiding manual controls.

Data are normally protected by manual methods, and once data are in the computer, they can be automatically validated and verified. Manual controls include maker–checker–signer roles for trusted people with separation of responsibilities or dual responsibilities that force collusion to perpetrate fraudulent acts. Batch-control totals can be manually calculated and compared in the computer with matching computer-produced batch-control totals. In this method, data are batched into small groups, and data are added together to produce a sum that is the control total. Another common control is the use of check digits or characters imbedded in the data based on various characteristics of each field of data (e.g., odd or even number indicators or hash totals). Sequence numbers and time of arrival can be associated with data and checked to ensure that data have not been removed or reordered. Large volumes of data can be checked by using utility or special-purpose programs in a computer. Evidence of data diddling is discovered data that do not correctly represent data as found at sources, lack equality with redundant or duplicate data, do not match earlier forms of data (determined by reversing the manual processes that have been carried out), control totals or check digits that do not check or meet validation and verification tests in the computer.

A typical example is the case of a timekeeping clerk who filled out data forms of hours worked by 300 employees in a department of a railroad company. He noticed that all data on the forms that were entered into the timekeeping and payroll system on the computer included both the name and the employee number of each worker. However, the computer used only employee numbers for processing and even for looking up employee names and addresses to print on payroll checks. He also noticed that outside the computer all manual processing and control was based only on employee names because nobody identified people by their numbers. He took advantage of this dichotomy of controls by filling out forms for overtime hours worked and using names of employees who frequently worked overtime but entering his own employee number. This was never discovered, and his income was increased by several thousand dollars every year until by chance an auditor examining W–2 federal income forms noticed the unusually high annual income of the clerk. An examination of the timekeeping computer files and recent timekeeping data forms and a discussion with the clerk's supervisor revealed the source of the increased income. The clerk was confronted with the evidence and admitted his fraudulent activities. The clerk's activities were not sophisticated but surely represent a data-diddling computer-related crime. Well-designed timekeeping and payroll systems use the first few letters of employees' names appended to their identification numbers to reduce the likelihood of this type of crime.

Potential data-diddling perpetrators are employed in different kinds of occupations. Table 14.2 summarizes these potential perpetrations, the methods of detecting data diddling, and the sources of evidence.

Table 14.2 Detection of Data Diddling

POTENTIAL PERPETRATORS	METHODS OF DETECTION	EVIDENCE
Transaction participants	Data comparison	Data documents Source
Data preparers	Document validation	Transactions Computer-readable
Source data suppliers	Manual controls and instrumentation analysis	Computer data media Tapes Cards
Nonparticipants with access		Disks Storage modules
	Computer validation and verification exception	Manual logs, journals, and exception reports
	Reports analysis	Incorrect computer output
	Computer output	
	Integrity tests	

Trojan Horse

The Trojan horse method is the covert placement of computer instructions in a program so that the computer will perform unauthorized functions but usually still will allow the program to perform its intended purposes. This is the most common method in computer program-based frauds and sabotage. Instructions may be placed in production computer programs so that they will be executed in the protected or restricted domain of the program and have access to all the data files that are assigned for exclusive use of the program. Programs are usually constructed loosely enough to allow space to be found or created for inserting the instructions.

There are no practical methods of preventing and detecting Trojan horse methods if the perpetrator is sufficiently clever. A typical business application program can consist of over 100,000 computer instructions and data. The Trojan horse can also be concealed among up to 5 or 6 millions of instructions in the operating system and commonly used utility programs, where it waits for execution of the target application program, inserts extra instructions in it for a few milliseconds of execution time, and removes them with no remaining evidence. Even if it is discovered, there is no indication of who may have done it except to narrow the search to those programmers who have the necessary skills, knowledge, and access. Such programmers include employees, former employees, contract programmers, consultants, or employees of the computer or software suppliers. The perpetrator usually attempts to benefit from his acts by converting them to economic gain directly or through accomplices. If the conversion to assets can be determined and traced, there is a chance of apprehension.

A suspected Trojan horse might be discovered by comparing a copy of the operational program under suspicion with a master or other copy known to be free of unauthorized changes. Backup copies of production programs are routinely kept in safe storage, but smart perpetrators will make duplicate changes in them. Also programs are frequently changed without changing the backup copies, thereby making comparison difficult. Utility programs are usually available to perform comparisons of large programs, but their integrity and the computer system on which they are executed must be assured. This should be done only by qualified and trusted experts.

A Trojan horse might also be detected by testing the suspect program with data and under conditions that might cause the exposure of the purpose of the Trojan horse. However, the probability of success is low unless exact conditions for discovery are known. This may prove the existence of the Trojan horse, but usually will not determine its location. A Trojan horse may also reside in the source language version or only in the object form and may be inserted in the object form each time it is assembled or compiled—e.g., as the result of another Trojan horse in the assembler or compiler.

The methods for detecting Trojan horse frauds are summarized in Table 14.3. The table also lists the occupations of potential perpetrators and the sources of evidence of Trojan horse crime.

**Table 14.3
Detection of Trojan
Horse Crimes**

POTENTIAL PERPETRATORS	METHODS OF DETECTION	EVIDENCE
Programmers having detailed knowledge of a suspected part of a program and its purpose and access to it	Program code comparison	Unexpected results of program execution
	Testing of suspect program	Foreign code found in a suspect program
	Tracing of possible gain from the act	
Employees Contract programmers Vendor's programmers Users of the computer		

Salami Techniques

An automated form of crime involving the theft of small amounts of assets from a large number of sources is identified as a salami technique (taking small slices without noticeably reducing the whole). For example, in a banking system the demand deposit accounting system for checking accounts could be changed (using the Trojan horse method) to randomly reduce a few hundred accounts by 10 cents or 15 cents by transferring the money to a favored account where it can be legitimately withdrawn through normal methods. No controls are violated because the money is not removed from the system of accounts. Instead, a small fraction of it is merely rearranged. The success of the fraud is based on the idea that each checking account customer loses so little that it is of little consequence. Many variations are possible. The assets may be an inventory of products or services as well as money.

One salami method in a financial system is known as the "round down" fraud. The round down fraud requires a computer system application where large numbers of financial accounts are processed. The processing must involve the multiplication of dollar amounts by numbers—such as in interest rate calculations. This arithmetic results in products that contain fractions of the smallest denomination of currency, such as the cent in the United States. For example, a savings account in a bank may have a balance of $15.86. Applying the 2.6 percent quarterly interest rate results in adding $0.41236 ($15.86 × .026) to the balance for a new balance of $16.27236. However, because the balance is to be retained only to the nearest cent, it is rounded down to $16.27, leaving $0.00236. What is to be done with this remainder? The interest calculation for the next account in the program sequence might be the following $425.34 × 0.026 = $11.05884. This would result in a new balance of $436.39884 that must be rounded up to $436.40, leaving a deficit or negative remainder of $0.00116, usually place in parenthesis to show its negative value ($0.00116).

The net effect of rounding in both these accounts, rounding down to the calculated cent in the first and adding 1 cent in the second, leaves both accounts accurate to the nearest cent and a remainder of $0.0012 ($0.00236 − $0.00116). This remainder is then carried to the next account calculation, and so on. As the calculations continue, if the running or accumulating remainder goes above 1 cent, positive or negative, the last account is adjusted to return the remainder to an amount less than 1 cent. This results in a few accounts receiving 1 cent more or less than the correct rounded values, but the totals for all accounts remain in balance.

This is where the creative computer programmer can engage in some trickery to accumulate for himself a fancy bit of change and still show a balanced set of accounts that defies discovery by the auditor. He merely changes the rules slightly in the program by accumulating the rounded down remainders in his own account rather than distributing them to the other accounts as they build up.

A look at a larger number of accounts shows how this is done. First, if rounded down correctly, the accounts would be as shown in Table 14.4. The interest rate applied to the total of all accounts ($3,294.26) results in a new total balance of $3,379.91 ($3,294.26 × 1.026) and a remainder of $0.00076 when the new total balance is rounded. This is calculated by the program as verification that the arithmetic performed account by account is correct. However, note that several accounts (those marked with an asterisk) have 1 cent more or less than they should have.

Now suppose the programmer writes the program to accumulate the round amounts into his own account, the last account in the list. The calculations will be as shown in Table 14.5. The totals are the same as before and the verification shows no tinkering. However, now the new balances of some accounts are 1 cent less, but none are 1 cent more as in the previous example. Those extra cents have been accumulated and all added to the programmer's account (the last account in the list) rather than to the accounts where the adjusted remainder exceeded 1 cent.

Clearly, if there were 180,000 accounts instead of the 18 accounts in this example, the programmer could have made a tidy profit of $300 ($0.03 × 10,000). This could result in a significant fraud over several years.

There are only two ways that the auditor might discover this fraud. She or he could check the instructions in the program, or could recalculate the interest for the programmer's account after the program had been executed by the computer. A clever programmer could easily disguise the instructions that produce the fraudulent calculations in the program in a number of ways. However, this would probably be unnecessary because an auditor or anybody else would probably not wade step by step through a program so long as use of the program showed no irregularities.

This program method would show no irregularities unless the programmer's account were audited. It is unlikely that his account—one account among 180,000—would be audited. Besides, the programmer could have opened the account using a fictitious name or the name of an accomplice. He could also oc-

OLD BALANCE	NEW BALANCE	ROUNDED NEW BALANCE	REMAINDER	ACCUMULATING REMAINDER
$ 15.86	$ 16.27236	$ 16.27	$ 0.00236	$ 0.00236
425.34	436.39884	436.40	(0.00116)	0.00120
221.75	227.51550	227.52	(0.00450)	(0.00330)
18.68	19.16568	19.17	(0.00432)	(0.00762)
* 564.44	579.11544	579.12	(0.00456)	(0.01218)
		579.11		(0.00218)
61.31	62.90406	62.90	0.00406	0.00188
101.32	103.95432	103.95	0.00432	0.00620
* 77.11	79.11486	79.11	0.00486	0.01106
		79.12		0.00106
457.12	469.00512	469.01	(0.00488)	(0.00382)
111.35	114.24510	114.25	(0.00490)	(0.00872)
* 446.36	457.96536	457.97	(0.00464)	(0.01336)
		457.96		(0.00336)
88.68	90.98568	90.99	(0.00432)	(0.00768)
* 14.44	14.81544	14.82	(0.00456)	(0.01224)
		14.81		(0.00224)
83.27	85.43502	85.44	(0.00498)	(0.00722)
127.49	130.80474	130.80	0.00474	(0.00248)
331.32	339.93432	339.93	0.00432	0.00184
37.11	38.07486	38.07	0.00486	0.00670
* 111.31	114.20406	114.20	0.00406	0.01076
		114.21		0.00076
$3294.26	Total	$3379.91		

Table 14.4   Example of Rounded Down Accounts

casionally change to other accounts to reduce further the possibility of detection.

Experienced accountants and auditors indicate that the round down fraud has been known for many years, even before the use of computers. They say that a good auditor will look for this type of fraud by checking for deviations from the standard accounting method for rounding calculations.

Salami acts are usually not fully discoverable within obtainable expenditures for investigation. Victims have usually lost so little individually that they are unwilling to expend much effort to solve the case. Specialized detection routines can be built into the suspect program, or snapshot storage dump listings could be obtained at crucial times in suspect program production runs. If the salami acts are taking identifiable amounts, these can be traced, but a smart perpetrator will randomly vary the amounts of accounts debited and credited.

The actions and life styles of the few people and their associates who have

OLD BALANCE	NEW BALANCE	ROUNDED NEW BALANCE	REMAINDER	ACCUMULATING REMAINDER	PROGRAMMER'S REMAINDER
$ 15.86	$ 16.27236	$ 16.27	$ 0.00236	$ 0.00000	$0.00236
425.34	436.39884	436.40	(0.00116)	(0.00116)	0.00236
221.75	227.51550	227.52	(0.00450)	(0.00566)	0.00236
18.68	19.16568	19.17	(0.00998)	(0.00998)	0.00236
* 564.44	579.11544	579.12	(0.00456)	(0.01454)	0.00236
		579.11		(0.00454)	
61.31	62.90406	62.90	0.00406	(0.00454)	0.00642
101.32	103.95432	103.95	0.00432	(0.00454)	0.01074
77.11	79.11486	79.11	0.00486	(0.00454)	0.01560
457.12	469.00512	469.01	(0.00488)	(0.00942)	0.01560
* 111.35	114.24510	114.25	(0.00490)	(0.01432)	0.01560
		114.24		(0.00432)	
446.36	457.96536	457.97	(0.00464)	(0.00896)	0.01560
* 88.68	90.98568	90.99	(0.00432)	(0.01328)	0.01560
		90.98		(0.00328)	
14.44	14.81544	14.82	(0.00456)	(0.00784)	0.01560
* 83.27	85.43502	85.44	(0.00498)	(0.01282)	0.01560
		85.43		(0.00282)	
127.49	130.80474	130.80	0.00474	(0.00282)	0.02034
331.32	339.93432	339.93	0.00432	(0.00282)	0.02466
37.11	38.07486	38.07	0.00486	(0.00282)	0.02952
* 111.31	114.20406	114.20	0.00406	(0.00282)	0.03358
		114.23		0.00076	0.00000
$3294.26	Total	$3379.91			

Table 14.5   Example of Rounded Down Accounts Converted to Programmer's Account

the skills, knowledge, and access to perform salami acts can be closely watched for aberrations or deviations from normal. This could be successful because real-time actions are usually required to convert the results to obtainable gain. The perpetrator or his accomplice will usually withdraw the money from the accounts in which it accumulates in legitimate ways. Records will show an imbalance between the deposit and withdrawal transactions, but all accounts would have to be balanced relative to all transactions over a significant period of time. This is a monumental and expensive task.

Many financial institutions require employees to use their financial services and make it attractive for them to do so. Employees' accounts are more completely and carefully audited than others. This usually forces the salami perpetrators to open accounts under assumed names or arrange for accomplices to do it. Investigation of suspected salami frauds might be more successful through concentrating on the actions of possible suspects rather than through reliance on technical methods of discovery.

**Table 14.6
Detection of Salami
Techniques**

POTENTIAL PERPETRATORS	METHODS OF DETECTION	EVIDENCE
Financial system programmers	Detail data analysis	Many small financial losses
	Program comparison	
Employees		Unsupported account buildups
Former employees	Transaction audits	
Contract programmers		
Vendor's programmers	Observation of financial activities of possible suspects	Trojan horse code changed or unusual personal financial practices of possible suspects

Table 14.6 lists the methods of detecting the use of salami techniques. The table also lists potential perpetrators and source of evidence of the use of the technique.

Superzapping

Superzapping derives its name from superzap, a macro/utility program used in most IBM computer centers as a systems tool. Any computer center that has a secure computer operating mode needs a "break glass in case of emergency" computer program that will bypass all controls to modify or disclose any of the contents of the computer. Computers sometimes stop, malfunction, or enter a state that cannot be overcome by normal recovery or restart procedures. Computers also perform unexpectedly and need attention that normal access methods do not allow. In such cases, a universal access program is needed. This is similar in one way to a master key to be used if all other keys are lost or locked in the enclosure they were meant to open.

Utility programs such as superzap are powerful and dangerous tools in the wrong hands. They are normally used only by systems programmers and computer operators who maintain computer operating systems. They should be kept secure from unauthorized use. However, they are often placed in program libraries where they can be used by any programmer or operator who knows of their presence and how to use them.

A classic example of superzapping, resulting in a $128,000 loss, occurred in a bank in New Jersey. The manager of computer operations was using a superzap program to make changes to account balances to correct errors—as directed by management. The regular error-correction process was not working correctly because the demand-deposit accounting system had become obsolete and full of errors as a result of inattention in a computer changeover. The operations manager discovered how easy it was to make changes without the usual controls or journal records; and he made changes transferring money to three friends' accounts. They engaged in the fraud long enough for a customer to find a shortage: quick action in response to the customer's complaint resulted in indictment and conviction of the perpetrators. The use of the super-zap program leaves no evidence of changes to the data files; it made discovery of the fraud through technical means highly unlikely.

Unauthorized use of superzap programs can result in changes to data files that are normally updated only by production programs. There usually are few if any controls that would detect changes in the data files from previous runs. Application programmers do not anticipate this type of fraud; their universe of concern is limited to the application program and its interaction with data files. Therefore, the detection of fraud will result only when the recipients of regular computer output reports from the production program notify management that a discrepancy seems to have occurred. Computer managers will often conclude that the evidence indicates data entry errors, because it would not be a characteristic computer or program error. Considerable time can be wasted from searching in the wrong areas. When it is concluded that unauthorized file changes have occurred independent of the application program associated with the file, a search of all computer usage journals might reveal the use of a super-zap program, but this is unlikely if the perpetrator anticipates this. Occasionally, there may be a record of a request to have the file placed on-line in the computer system if it is not normally in that mode. Otherwise, the changes would have to occur when the production program using the file is being run or just before or after it is run. This is the most likely time of the act.

Detection of the superzap acts may be possible by comparing the current file with father and grandfather copies of the file where no updates exist to account for suspicious changes. Table 14.7 summarizes the potential perpetrators, methods of detection, and sources of evidence in superzapping crime.

Trap Doors In the development of large application and computer operating systems, it is the practice of programmers to insert debugging aids that provide breaks in the code for insertion of additional code and intermediate output capabilities. The design of computer operating systems attempts to prevent both access to them and insertion of code or modification of code. Consequently, system programmers will sometimes insert code that allows compromise of these requirements during the debugging phases of program development and later when the system is being maintained and improved. These facilities are referred to as trap doors. Normally, trap doors are eliminated in the final editing but sometimes they are overlooked or purposely left in to facilitate ease of making future access and modification. In addition, some unscrupulous programmers may purposely introduce trap doors for later compromising of computer programs. Designers of large complex programs may also introduce trap doors inadvertently through weaknesses in design logic.

POTENTIAL PERPETRATORS	METHODS OF DETECTION	EVIDENCE
Programmers with access to superzap programs and computer access to use them	Comparison of files with historical copies	Output report discrepancies
	Discrepancies noted by recipients of output reports	Undocumented transactions
Computer operations staff with applications knowledge	Examination of computer usage journals	Computer usage or file request journals

Trap doors may also be introduced in the electronic circuitry of computers. For example, not all the combinations of codes may be assigned to instructions found in the computer and documented in the programming manuals. When these unspecified commands are used, the circuitry may cause the execution of unanticipated combinations of functions that allow compromise of the computer system.

During the use and maintenance of computer programs and computer circuitry, ingenious programmers invariably discover some of these weaknesses and take advantage of them for useful and innocuous purposes. However, the trap doors may also be used for unauthorized, malicious purposes as well. Functions that can be performed by computer programs and computers that are not in the specifications are often referred to as negative specifications. It is difficult enough for designers and implementers to make programs and computers function according to specifications and to prove that they perform according to specifications. It is currently not possible to prove that a computer system does not perform functions that it is not specified to perform.

Research is continuing on a high-priority basis to develop methods of proving the correctness of computer programs and computers according to complete and consistent specifications. However, it is anticipated that it will be many years before commercially available computers and computer programs can be proved correct. Therefore, trap doors continue to exist, and there is never any guarantee that they have all been found and corrected.

In one computer-related crime, a systems programmer discovered a trap door in a FORTRAN programming language compiler. The trap door allowed the programmer writing in the FORTRAN (FORmula TRANslation) language to transfer control from his FORTRAN program into a region of storage used for data. This caused the computer to execute computer instructions formed by the data and provided a means of executing program code secretly by inputting data in the form of computer instructions each time the FORTRAN progam was run. This occurred in a commercial time-sharing computer service. The systems programmer in collusion with a user of the time-sharing service was able to use large amounts of computer time free of charge and obtain data and programs of other time-sharing users. In another case, several automative engineers in Detroit discovered a trap door in a commercial time-sharing service in Florida that allowed them to search uninhibitedly for privileged passwords. They discovered the password of the president of the time-sharing company and were able to obtain copies of trade-secret computer programs that they proceeded to use free of charge. In both of these cases the perpetrators were discovered accidentally. It was never determined how many other users were taking advantage of the trap doors.

There is no direct technical method for the discovery of trap doors. However, when the nature of a suspected trap door is sufficiently determined, tests of varying degrees of complexity can be performed to discover hidden functions used for malicious purposes. This requires the expertise of systems programmers and knowledgeable application programmers. Large amounts of computer services and time could be wasted if persons without sufficient expertise attempted to discover trap door usage. Investigators should always seek out the most highly qualified experts for the particular computer system or computer application under suspicion.

It is wise for the investigator always to assume that the computer system and computer programs are never sufficiently secure from intentional, technical compromise. However, these intentional acts usually require the expertise of only the very few technologists who have the skills, knowledge, and access to perpetrate them. Table 14.8 lists the potential perpetrators, methods of detection, and sources of evidence of the use of the trap door techniques.

Logic Bombs   A logic bomb is a computer program executed at appropriate or periodic times in a computer system to determine conditions of the computer that facilitate the perpetration of an unauthorized, malicious act. For example, in one case, secret computer instructions were inserted (a Trojan horse) in the computer operating system and were executed periodically. The instructions were to test the year, date, and time of day clock in the computer so that on a specified day two years later, at 3:00 P.M., the time bomb, a type of logic bomb, would go off and trig-

Table 14.8
Detection
of Trap Door Crimes

POTENTIAL PERPETRATORS	METHODS OF DETECTION	EVIDENCE
Systems programmers	Exhaustive testing	Computer output reports that indicate that a computer system performs outside of its specifications
Expert application programmers	Comparison of specification to performance	
	Specific testing based on evidence	

ger the printout of a confession of a crime on all the 300 computer terminals on-line at that time and then would cause the system to crash. This was timed so that the perpetrator would be geographically a long distance from the computer and its users. In another case, a payroll system programmer put a logic bomb in the personnel system so that if his name were ever removed from the personnel file (indicating termination of employment), a secret code would cause the entire personnel file to be erased.

A logic bomb can be programmed to trigger an act based on any specified condition or data that may occur or be introduced. Logic bombs are usually placed in the computer system using the Trojan horse technique. Methods to discover logic bombs in a computer system would be the same as for Trojan horses. Table 14.9 summarizes the potential perpetrators, methods of detection, and kinds of evidence of logic bombs.

Asynchronous Attacks

Asynchronous attack techniques take advantage of the asynchronous functioning of a computer operating system: most computer operating systems function asynchronously because the services that must be performed for the various computer programs make conflicting demands simultaneously on the computer. For example, several jobs may simultaneously call for output reports to be produced. The operating system stores these requests and, as resources become available, performs them in the order in which resources are available to fit the request—or according to an overriding priority indication. Therefore, rather than executing requests in the order they are received, the system performs them asynchronously, on the basis of resources available.

There are highly sophisticated methods of confusing the operating system to allow it to violate the isolation of one job from another. For example, in a large application program that runs for a long period of time, it is customary for it to have checkpoint restarts. These allow the computer operator to set a switch manually to stop the program at a specified intermediate stopping point

Table 14.9 Detection of Logic Bombs

POTENTIAL PERPETRATORS	METHODS OF DETECTION	EVIDENCE
Programmers having detailed knowledge of a suspected part of a program and its purpose and access to it	Program code comparisons	Unexpected results of program execution
	Testing of suspect program	
		Foreign code found in a suspect program
Employees Contract programmers Vendor's programmers Users of the computer	Tracing of possible gain from the act	

from which it may be restarted at a later time in an orderly manner without losing data. This requires the operating system to save the copy of the computer program and data in their current state at the checkpoint. The operating system must also save a number of system parameters that describe the mode and security level of the program at the time of the stop. It might be possible for a programmer or computer operator to gain access to the checkpoint restart copy of the program, data, and system parameters. He could change the system parameters in such a way that, on restart, the program would function at a higher priority security level or privileged level in the computer and thereby give the program unauthorized access to data, other programs, or the operating system. Note that checkpoint restart actions are usually well documented in the computer console log.

Even more complex methods of attack could be used besides the one described in this simple example. However, the technology is too complex to present here. The investigator should be aware of the possibilities of asynchronous attacks and seek adequate technical assistance if there are suspicious circumstances resulting from the activities of highly sophisticated and trained technologists. Evidence of such attacks would be discernible only in unexplainable deviations from application and system specifications in computer output or characteristics of system performance. Table 14.10 lists the potential perpetrators and methods of detecting asynchronous attacks.

Scavenging   Scavenging is a method of obtaining information that may be left in or around a computer system after the execution of a job. Simple physical scavenging could be the searching of trash barrels for copies of discarded computer listings or carbon paper from multiple-part forms. More technical and sophisticated methods of scavenging can be done by searching for residual data left in a computer after job execution.

For example, a computer operating system may not properly erase buffer storage areas used for the temporary storage of input or output data. Some

Table 14.10 Detection of Asynchronous Attacks		
POTENTIAL PERPETRATORS	**METHODS OF DETECTION**	**EVIDENCE**
Sophisticated and advanced system programmers	System testing of suspected attack methods	Output that deviates from normally expected output or logs containing characteristics of computer operation
Sophisticated and advanced computer operators	Repeat execution of a job under normal and safe circumstances	

operating systems do not erase magnetic disk or magnetic tape storage media because of the excessive computer time required to do this. Therefore, new data are written over the old data. It may be possible for the next job to be executed to read the old data before they are replaced by new data. This might happen in the following way. If storage was reserved and used by a previous job and then assigned to the next job, the next job would gain access to the same storage, write only a small amount of data into that storage, but then read the entire storage area back out for its own purposes, thus capturing—scavenging—data that were stored by the previous job.

In one case, a time-sharing service in Texas had a number of oil companies as customers. The computer operator noticed that every time one particular customer used computer services his job always requested that a scratch tape (temporary storage tape) be mounted on a tape drive. When the operator mounted the tape, he noticed that the read-tape light always came on before the write-tape light came on, indicating that the user was reading data from a temporary storage tape before he had written anything on it. After numerous incidents of this, the computer operator became curious and reported it to management. Simple investigation revealed that the customer was engaged in industrial espionage, obtaining seismic data stored by various oil companies on the temporary tapes and selling this highly proprietary, valuable data to other oil companies.

The detection of scavenging usually occurs as a result of discovering suspected crimes involving proprietary information that may have come from a computer system and computer media. The information may be traced back to its source and that involves computer usage. It is probably more likely that the act was a manual scavenging of information in human-readable form or the theft of magnetic tapes or disks rather than electronic scavenging.

In one case, valuable data were found on continous forms from a computer output printer. Each page of the output had a preprinted sequence number and the name of the paper company. An FBI agent was able to trace the paper back to the paper company. On the basis of the type of forms and sequence numbers, he traced it from there to the computer center where the paper had been used. The sequence numbers were traceable to a specific printer and time at which the forms were printed. Discovery of the job that produced the reports at that time and the programmer who submitted the job from the computer console log and usage accounting data was straightforward. Table 14.11 lists the potential perpetrators. The table also summarizes the methods of detection and the kinds of evidence typical with scavenging techniques.

Data Leakage   A wide range of computer-related crime involves the removal of data or copies of data from a computer system or computer facility. This possibility can offer the most dangerous exposure to the perpetrator. His technical act may be well hidden in the computer; however, to convert it to economic gain, he must get

Table 14.11
Detection
of Scavenging Crimes

POTENTIAL PERPETRATORS	METHODS OF DETECTION	EVIDENCE
Users of the computer system	Tracing of discovered proprietary information back to its source	Computer output media
Persons having access to computer facilities and adjacent areas		Type font characteristics
	Testing of an operating system to discover residual data after execution of a job	Similar information produced in suspected ways in the same form

the data from the computer system. Output is subject to examination by computer operators and other data processing personnel.

Several techniques can be used to leak data from a computer system. The perpetrator may be able to hide the sensitive data in otherwise innocuous looking output reports. This could be done by adding to blocks of data. In more sophisticated ways the data could be interspersed with otherwise innocuous data. An even more sophisticated method might be to encode data to look like something different from what they are. For example, a computer listing may be formatted so that the secret data are in the form of different lengths of printer lines, number of words or numbers per line, locations of punctuation, and use of code words that can be interspersed and converted into meaningful data. Another method is by controlling and observing the movement of equipment parts, such as the reading and writing of a magnetic tape, which causes the tape reels to move clockwise and counterclockwise in a pattern representing binary digits 0 and 1. Observation of the movement of the tape reels results in obtaining the data. Similar kinds of output might be accomplished by causing a printer to print and skip lines in a pattern where the noise of the printer, recorded with a cassette tape recorder, might be played back at slow speed to again produce a pattern translatable into binary information.

These are rather exotic methods of data leakage that might be necessary only in high-security, high-risk environments. Otherwise, much simpler manual methods might be used. It has been reported that hidden in the central processors of many computers used by the U.S. Army in the Vietnam War were miniature radio transmitters capable of broadcasting the contents of the computers to a remote receiver. These were discovered when the computers were returned to the United States from Vietnam.

Investigation of data leakage would probably best be conducted by interrogating data processing personnel who might have observed the movement of sensitive data. It might also be possible to examine computer operating system usage journals to determine if and when data files may have been accessed.

Table 14.12
Detection
of Crimes
from Data Leakage

POTENTIAL PERPETRATORS	METHODS OF DETECTION	EVIDENCE
Computer programmers	Discovery of stolen information	Computer storage media
Employees		
Former employees	Tracing computer storage media back to the computer facility	Computer output forms
Contract workers		
Vendor's employees		Type font
		Trojan horse or scavenging evidence

Data leakage might be conducted through the use of Trojan horse, logic bomb, and scavenger methods. Possible use of these methods should be investigated when data leakage is suspected. Evidence will most likely be in the same form as evidence of scavenging activities described above. Table 14.12 summarizes the detection of crimes resulting from data leakage.

Piggybacking and Impersonation

Piggybacking and impersonation can be done physically or electronically. Physical piggybacking is a method for gaining access to controlled access areas when control is accomplished by electronically or mechanically locked doors. Typically an individual with his or her hands full of computer-related objects (such as tape reels) stands by the locked door looking "helpless." When an authorized individual arrives and opens the door, the piggybacker goes in after or along with him. Turnstiles, mantraps, or a stationed guard are the usual methods of preventing this type of unauthorized access. The turnstile allows passage of only one individual with a metal key, an electronic or magnetic card key, or combination lock activation. A mantrap is a double-doored closet through which only one person can move with one key action. Success of this method of piggybacking is dependent on the quality of the access control mechanism and the alertness of authorized persons in resisting cooperation with the perpetrator.

Electronic piggybacking can take place in an on-line computer system where individuals are using terminals, and identification is verified automatically by the computer system. When a terminal has been activated, the computer authorizes access, usually on the basis of a key, secret password, or other passing of required information (protocol). Compromise of the computer can take place when a hidden computer terminal is connected to the same line through the telephone switching equipment and used when the legitimate user is not using his terminal. The computer will not be able to differentiate or recognize the two terminals, but senses only one terminal and one authorized user. Piggybacking can also be accomplished when the user signs off improperly, leaving the terminal in an active state or leaving the computer in a state where it assumes the user is still active.

Impersonation is the process of one person assuming the identity of another. Physical access to computers or computer terminals and electronic access through terminals to a computer require positive identification of an authorized user. The verification of identification is based on some combination of (1) something the user knows, such as a secret password; (2) something the user is—i.e., a physiological characteristic, such as finger print, hand geometry, or voice; and (3) something the user possesses, such as a magnetic stripe card or metal key. Anybody with the correct combination of identification characteristics can impersonate another individual.

An example of a clever impersonation occurred when a young man posed as a magazine writer and called upon a telephone company, indicating that he was writing an article on the computer system in use by the telephone company. He was invited in and given a full and detailed briefing on all the computer facilities and application systems. As a result of this information, he was able to steal over $1 million worth of telephone equipment from the company. In another case, an individual stole magnetic stripe credit cards that required secret personal identification numbers (PIN) associated with each card for use. He would call the owners of the cards by telephone, indicating that he was a bank official, had discovered the theft of the card, and needed to know the secret PIN number to protect the victim and issue a new card. Victims invariably gave out their secret PINs and the impersonator then used the PINs to withdraw the maximum amount allowed through automatic teller machines that required the cards and numbers for identification.

Electronic door access control systems frequently are run by a minicomputer that produces a log showing accesses and time of accesses for each individual gaining access. Human guards frequently do equivalent journaling through the keeping of logs. Detection of unauthorized access can be accomplished by studying journals and logs and by interviewing people who may have witnessed the unauthorized access. Table 14.13 summarizes the methods of detecting computer crime committed by impersonation methods.

Wire Tapping   There is no verified experience of data communications wire tapping. The potential for wire tapping grows rapidly, however, as more computers are connected to communication facilities and increasing amounts of electronically stored assets are transported from computer to computer over communication circuits. Wire tapping has not become popular, as far as is known, because of the many easier ways to obtain or modify data.

Wire tapping requires equipment worth at least $200 (available at any Radio Shack store) and a method of recording and printing the information. Recording and printing can usually be done more directly and easily through

Table 14.13
Detection
of Impersonation Acts

POTENTIAL PERPETRATORS	METHODS OF DETECTION	EVIDENCE
Employees, former employees, vendor's employees	Access observations	Logs, journals, equipment usage meters
	Interviewing witnesses	
Contracted persons	Examination of journals and logs	Other physical evidence
Outsiders		
	Specialized computer programs that analyze characteristics of on-line computer user accesses	

the computer system or by impersonation through terminals. The perpetrator usually will not know when the particular data he is interested in will be sent. Therefore, he must collect relatively large amounts of data and search for the specific items of interest. Identification and isolation of the communications circuit can also pose a problem for the perpetrator. Interception of microwave and satellite communications represents even greater difficulty because of the complexity and cost of the equipment to perform the operation. In addition, the perpetrator must determine whether there are active detection facilities built into the communication system.

The best method of protecting data is encryption (secret coding of the data) using an encryption key. New, powerful products are now on the market to provide encryption. It is anticipated that most valuable data will be routinely encrypted within the next several years. This probably will greatly reduce the threat of wire tapping.

Wire tapping should be assumed to be the least likely method used in the theft or modification of data. Detection methods and possible evidence will be the same as in the investigation of voice communication wire tapping. Table 14.14 summarizes the potential perpetrators, detection, and evidence in wire-tapping acts.

Table 14.14
Detection
of Wire Tapping

POTENTIAL PERPETRATORS	METHODS OF DETECTION	EVIDENCE
Communications technicians and engineers	Voice wire-tapping methods	Voice wire-tapping evidence
Communications employees		

Simulation and Modeling   A computer can be used as a tool or instrument of a crime for planning or control. Complex white-collar crime often requires the use of a computer because of its sophisticated capabilities. An existing process can be simulated on a computer or a planned method for carrying out a crime could be modeled to determine its possible success.

In one case involving a million dollar manual embezzlement, an accountant owned his own service bureau and simulated his company's accounting and general ledger system on his computer. He was able to input correct data and modified data to determine the effects of the embezzlement on the general ledger. He also had the capability to run the simulation in the reverse direction by inputting to the computer the general ledger data he wished to have. He then ran the system in reverse to determine the false entries in accounts payable and accounts receivable that would result in the required general ledger output.

In one phase of an insurance fraud in Los Angeles in 1973, a computer was used to model the company and determine the effects of the sale of large numbers of insurance policies. The modeling resulted in the creation of 64,000 fake insurance policies in computer-readable form that were then introduced into the real system and subsequently resold as valid policies to reinsuring companies.

The use of a computer for simulation and modeling normally requires extensive amounts of computer time and computer program development. Investigation should include a search for significant amounts of computer services used by the suspects in complex fraud. This can be done by determining recent business activities of suspects and investigating the customer lists of locally available commercial time-sharing and service bureau companies. If use of the victim's computer is suspected, usage logs may show unexplained amounts of computer time used by the suspects.

Usually a programmer with expertise in simulation and modeling would be required to develop the application needed. In some cases, it was found that the computer programmers had no knowledge that their work was being used for fraudulent purposes. Evidence in the form of computer programs, input data, and output reports would require the attention of a computer programmer expert or systems analyst to determine the nature of the modeling or simulation. Table 14.15 lists the potential perpetrators, methods of detection, and kinds of evidence in simulation and modeling techniques.

Summary

Computer crime has frequently been referred to as a Bonnie and Clyde type of technological abuse: Bonnie and Clyde were bank robbers who were robbing banks using automobiles when police were still on horseback. Thus, they benefitted from an advanced technology while the law enforcement agencies were still using an older technology.

**Table 14.15
Detection
of Simulation
and Modeling
Techniques**

POTENTIAL PERPETRATORS	METHODS OF DETECTION	EVIDENCE
Computer application programmers	Investigation of possible computer usage by suspects	Computer programs
Simulation and modeling experts		Computer program documentation
		Computer input
Managers in positions to engage in large, complex embezzlement		Computer-produced reports
		Computer usage logs and journals

Statistics show that the criminal element of society is taking advantage of computer technology to defraud, embezzle, and abuse organizational resources. On the other hand, auditors, law enforcement agencies, and prosecutors are still reluctant to invest the resources necessary to train their people in computer technology. Unfortunately, while the auditors are still playing catch-up, criminals are studying the newer types of technology to learn how to abuse that as well. The solution to computer crime is an abundant supply of auditors and enforcement officials knowledgeable in computer crime and computer technology.

Problems

1. A computer programmer incorporated a routine into his program to search for his employee number on the payroll master tape. The employee assumed that if his employee number were not on the payroll master, he would be no longer working for the corporation. On discovery of the number's absence, the computer was then to scramble all the pay amounts for the pay period. What type of computer crime is this, and how could it have been detected before it occurred?

2. The Equity Funding Insurance Company case was described in an earlier chapter. In this case, the company committed a massive fraud by creating fictitious insurance policies and claims against those policies. Some argue that this is a computer crime, and others argue that it is not. Which argument would you support and why?

3. One of the major concerns of corporations is the loss of their data maintained on computer media. They fear that the data will be compromised

through copy to another computer medium. How might such a computer crime be detected?

4. The average loss in a computer crime is significantly greater than that in a noncomputer crime. Why do you believe this occurs?

5. A major telephone company was defrauded many years ago by a college student. The student recognized through examining computer listings thrown out in the trash that the telephone company had installed an automatic ordering system for installers. Understanding the codes, the college student was able to telephone the company's computer over touch-tone telephone and order parts to be delivered at authorized sites. After delivery, the student would pick up the orders and sell them on the black market. When the student was turned in by a fellow student to the police, the telephone company was asked to determine how much the student had defrauded. The telephone company was unable to determine the size of the fraud, or even the fact that a fraud had occurred. What are the characteristics of the telephone company's computer system that make fraud detection impossible?

EDP AUDIT PROCESS*

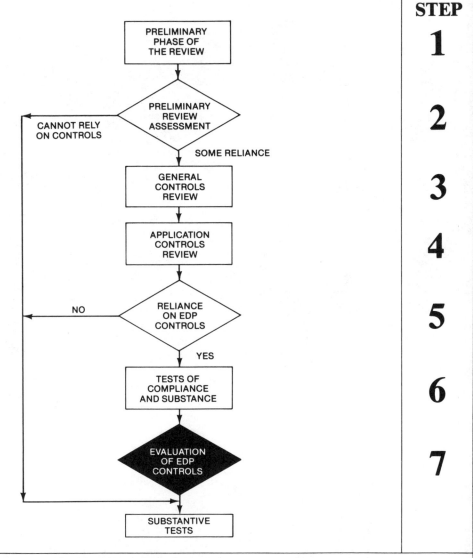

STEP

1

2

3

4

5

6

7

PRELIMINARY
PHASE OF
THE REVIEW

PRELIMINARY
REVIEW
ASSESSMENT

CANNOT RELY
ON CONTROLS

SOME RELIANCE

GENERAL
CONTROLS
REVIEW

APPLICATION
CONTROLS
REVIEW

RELIANCE
ON EDP
CONTROLS

NO

YES

TESTS OF
COMPLIANCE
AND SUBSTANCE

EVALUATION
OF EDP
CONTROLS

SUBSTANTIVE
TESTS

Diagram is adapted from The Auditor's Study and Evaluation of Internal Control in EDP Systems, *pages 21–24. Copyright © 1977 by the American Institute of Certified Public Accountants, Inc. (See Figure 9.1 for a complete explanation of the steps.)*

15

CASE STUDY

(7) Evaluation of Accounting Control

Purpose: For each significant accounting application

- Consider the types of errors or irregularities that could occur.
- Determine the accounting control procedures that prevent or detect such errors and irregularities.
- Determine whether the necessary control procedures are prescribed and followed satisfactorily.
- Evaluate weaknesses and assess their effect on the nature, timing, and extent of auditing procedures to be applied.

Method: Judgment.

OBJECTIVE

The final evaluation of the adequacy of control is made by auditor judgment. As a means of explaining judgment in an EDP audit, a case study is examined in detail.

The purpose of this chapter is to illustrate, through the use of a brief case study, several useful points about evaluation of EDP controls:

- The auditor's evaluation of controls for a typical accounting system that involves EDP.
- The relationship of the auditor's evaluation of a client's system and the specific audit procedures performed with transactions and accounts processed by the system.
- The use of the computer in performing selected audit procedures.

After each major phase of the case study audit engagement, we will inject "Case Study Commentary" to summarize the significance of the audit steps performed.

Background Information

The XYZ Company manufactures pumps and hydraulic equipment used by the military and by the mining industry. They have been an audit client for many years.[1]

The client has two operating divisions, manufacturing different product lines that are reported separately in the company's financial statements.

The total payables for last year were $96,000,000. These payments represent the following types of transactions:

	DIVISION A	DIVISION B
	(in millions of $)	
Purchases of inventory	$36	$51
Additions to fixed assets	3	2
Maintenance supplies	1	3

Daily payments range from $200,000 to $500,000; they average $350,000. Individual payments average $1,000 but can be as high as $100,000. The company buys from approximately 500 vendors; the 20 largest vendors account for approximately 10 percent of all purchases.

In past audits, the audit approach has involved primarily substantive audit procedures, and most work was done near year's end. Company management is interested in opportunities for increased reliance on controls. In addition, the client has indicated some concern about the adequacy of controls over EDP.

Initial audit activities determined that purchases of materials and related payments are significant types of transactions processed by the client's formal accounting system.

---

[1] This case is adapted, by permission, from a current one used by Touche Ross & Co. for internal training purposes.

Understanding the System

To develop an initial understanding of the purchasing and payment system, the following audit tasks were performed by members of the audit team:

- Interviews with supervisors and key employees in the purchasing, payables, and accounting departments
- Interviews with the EDP department supervisors and staff responsible for the related EDP system
- Review of the client's documentation that describes the EDP phase of the system

After performing these tasks, the audit team members prepared an integrated flowchart of EDP and manual processing (Figure 15.1), plus a narrative description of significant processing activity (Exhibit 15.1), and a narrative description of controls (Exhibit 15.2). The auditors traced several transactions through the system to verify the accuracy of the system description.

This initial audit work was reviewed by engagement management. The objectives of this review of the initial audit tasks were to determine the major processing and control features of the purchasing and payment systems, and to identify potential errors in the system.

Major Processing and Control Features

The initial review determined that the major features of the purchasing and payment system were as follows:

- All purchasing activity is handled on a manual basis.
- Both operating divisions use a common system that produces separate payments and related reports for each division.
- Purchase orders are used for all purchases and, in anticipation of vendor shipments, copies of related orders are sent to the receiving department and to the accounts payable department.
- When shipments are received, a receiving report is completed and attached to the related purchase order. These documents are forwarded to the payables department and retained on file until related vendor invoices are received.
- The receipt of a vendor invoice initiates the flow of transactions through the EDP phase of the accounting system. When vendor invoices are received, they are manually matched to corresponding purchase orders and receiving reports, and only approved vendor invoices are forwarded to EDP. The EDP system holds the approved payment until a designated payment date and then produces checks payable to vendors.

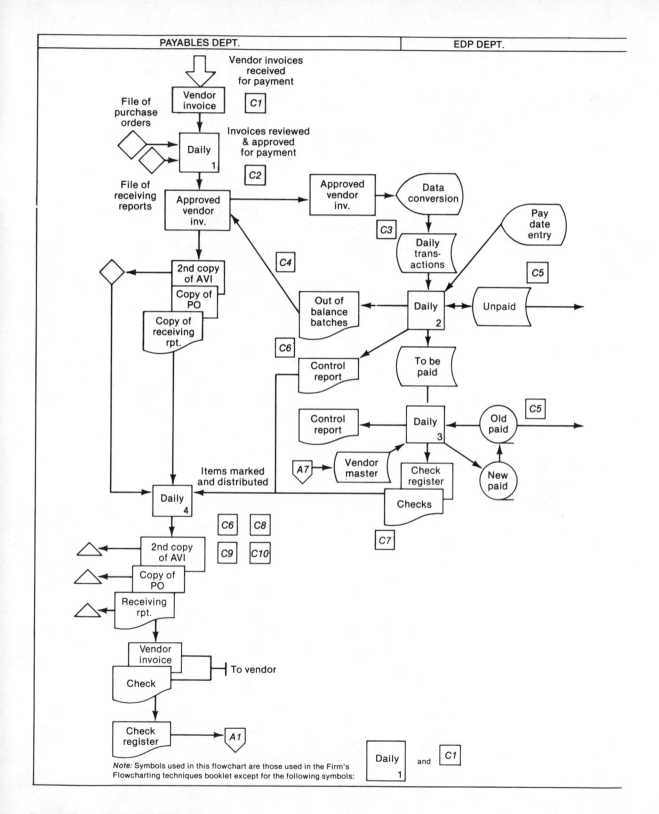

Figure 15.1 Integrated Flowchart

Monthly 5 → Unpaid / Unpaid → QTR 6 — Source accounts payable due entries

→ 7A — To purchasing dept.

C11

C17   C17

C13

All payments for month

Paid → C5

Paid — Files of all payments for a month   C5   C15

Monthly 7

QTR 8 → YTD payments by division type → QTR 9 — Source of expense postings

C15   C17

(2nd copy)

Payments by division type → 3A — Copy to divisional managers

C14

C16

KEY

Symbol	Meaning	Symbol	Meaning	Symbol	Meaning
□	Manually prepared document	Daily 1	A major manual or EDP processing step	△ ◇	Manual files
⬡	Computer prepared document	C1	A control	○	EDP tape file
⬭	Entry via video display terminal	⬠	Off-Page connector	⬯	EDP disk file

463

Exhibit 15.1
Narrative Description
of Significant Processing
Activity

1. Vendor invoices received for payment are matched to supporting purchase orders and receiving reports; pay date and expense classification are coded on each invoice; approved invoices are then forwarded to EDP.
2. Approved invoices are converted to records on a disk file; once a day this file is used to update the unpaid invoice file; the unpaid invoice file is used to produce the to-be-paid file, based on transaction pay dates.
3. Lists of checks from vendors and a check register are prepared daily; the file of invoices paid this month is updated.
4. Checks, the check register, receiving reports, purchase orders, and approved vendor invoices are filed and distributed.
5. Monthly, all unpaid invoices on the unpaid file are listed on a report that includes totals by division and type of purchase.
6. Quarterly, accounts payable due are posted from the last monthly unpaid invoice report.
7. Monthly, the paid invoice file is used to produce a report of this month's payments by division and type of payment.
8. Quarterly, the monthly paid invoice files are merged and summarized to produce a year-to-date report of payments by division and type of payment.
9. Quarterly, expenses are posted from the year-to-date report of payments.

Exhibit 15.2
Narrative Description
of Controls

1. Vendor invoices, purchase orders, and receiving reports are matched and reviewed.
2. Approved vendor invoices are batched, and a batch total is established for the total amount to be paid; a batch control log is used to account for all batches.
3. Amount fields are verified by dual entry.
4. Out-of-balance batches are returned to the payables department for correction.
5. Internal tape labels are used to ensure the use of the correct file.
6. A total representing all input plus the total of the old unpaid file less the total of the to-be-paid file is manually compared to the total of the new unpaid file. (Note that this same control is performed by the EDP and payables departments.) The reconciliation documents are retained.
7. Totals of all checks printed and of the check register are compared to control totals from the program that produced the to-be-paid file.
8. An adding machine tape of checks is run and the total is compared to the check register total.
9. Checks are matched to related purchase orders, receiving reports, and vendor invoices; and then checks are signed using a check signer controlled by a department supervisor.

10. Prenumbered check stock is used; a review for missing checks is performed daily.
11. Unpaid invoice report total is manually compared to the unpaid file total on the last control report.
12. Unpaid invoice report total is manually compared to unpaid control total maintained by the payables department (see control number 6).
13. The report of unpaid vendor invoices is reviewed for resonableness.
14. The payments report total is compared to a total of all monthly payments (as indicated by the daily check register reports).
15. The quarterly payments report is reviewed for reasonableness and payments by division and type are compared to budgeted expenses.
16. Division managers review payment reports for reasonableness and investigate significant discrepancies.
17. General ledger postings are reviewed for completeness and accuracy by the controller.

- The EDP system produces a variety of reports—including a daily check register, a monthly report of approved payments not yet paid, and payments by division and expense classification.

Potential Errors   The audit team identified the following eleven potential errors:

1. Liabilities incurred but not recorded
2. Purchase amounts recorded incorrectly
3. Purchases not authorized
4. Purchases recorded but goods not received
5. Purchases charged to wrong accounts
6. Purchases recorded in the wrong period
7. Payments recorded but not made
8. Payments made but not recorded
9. Payment amounts recorded incorrectly
10. Payments recorded in wrong period
11. Unauthorized payments made

Case Study Commentary   Up to this point in the case, the auditors have performed steps to gain sufficient understanding of the client's existing system to determine its major processing and control features and to identify potential errors that they should evaluate.

Evaluation of System Controls

The next phase of the audit is to evaluate system controls and to prepare audit documentation of the evaluation. One useful technique used by some auditors is the control evaluation work sheet. This work sheet contains the following elements:

- Potential errors and related causes of error
- The assessed magnitude of inherent risk for each cause of error (i.e., the likelihood, before considering the effect of internal controls, that material errors in the financial statements might result)
- Controls
- The apparent reliability of controls
- Key controls that might be tested and relied upon

Table 15.1 shows the completed control evaluation work sheet for this audit engagement for the first five of the eleven identified potential errors. To fill in the column "Potential Causes of Potential Errors," the auditors must consider the transactions being processed with regard to various things that could go wrong in their processing.

**Table 15.1
Control Evaluation
Work Sheet**

POTENTIAL ERROR	POSSIBLE CAUSES OF POTENTIAL ERRORS	INHERENT RISK	RELATED CONTROLS	APPARENT CONTROL RELIABILITY
1. Liabilities incurred but not recorded	A. Individual invoices lost or not converted	LOW	C2, (C6)	HIGH
	B. Batches of invoices lost or not converted	LOW	C2, (C6)	HIGH
	C. One or more days of input lost due to wrong file used	HIGH	C5, (C6)	HIGH
	D. "Unpaid" report does not include all transactions on "unpaid" file	HIGH	(C11), (C12), C13	HIGH
	E. Not posted to G/L	HIGH	(C17)	MOD

2. Purchase amounts recorded incorrectly	A. Input documents include incorrect values	LOW	(C1)		HIGH
	B. Amount values not accurately converted	MOD.	C2, (C6)	C3,	HIGH
3. Purchases not authorized	A. Unauthorized payment transactions are introduced within the EDP portion of the system	LOW	C1, (C9,)	C8, C10	HIGH
	B. Unauthorized payment transactions are introduced within the accounts payable department.	LOW	(C1)		HIGH
4. Purchases recorded but goods not received	A. Invoices processed for goods not received	MOD	(C1)		HIGH
	B. Transactions duplicated in conversion or processing	LOW	C2, (C6)		HIGH
	C. One or more days of processing duplicated	HIGH	C5, (C6)		HIGH
5. Purchases charged to wrong accounts	A. Input documents not correctly coded	MOD.	C1,	C15,	MOD
	B. Division or account codes not accurately converted	HIGH	C15,	C16	LOW
	C. Incorrect posting to G/L	HIGH	(C17)		MOD

Note: Circled controls are controls that might be relied upon.

To fill in the column "Inherent Risk," the auditors must eliminate error rates and determine the probable magnitude of errors. For example, there might be a high error rate during data conversion, but the magnitude of each error would be relatively small; whereas, the use of the wrong file only once during the year could result in significant errors.

The entries recorded in the "Related Controls" column refer to the controls listed on the Narrative Description of Controls (Exhibit 15.2), which the auditors prepared during the initial phase of the audit. The controls circled are those that the audit team decided they rely on.

The work sheet assessment of apparent control reliability uses the high, moderate, and low definitions included in the audit process (i.e., when reliability is high, no monetary errors are expected to remain in the records of transactions; when moderate, errors are expected but are not expected to be material; when low, the resulting errors may cause a material error in the financial statements). The assessment of apparent control reliability was based on the inherent risk of errors and the ability of related controls to prevent or detect such errors. For example, an assessment of high control reliability may be appropriate in either of two circumstances, if the risk of errors is low and controls are reasonably effective, or if the risk of errors is high and controls are very effective. A "low" assessment would be given if there were no controls or if there were weak controls.

The evaluation documented in Table 15.1 includes only causes of error in the EDP phase, but considers controls in both the EDP and manual phases of the accounting system. The complete evaluation of internal controls would also consider risks in the manual phases of the system.

As illustrated in Table 15.1, most of the potential EDP causes of error in this system are controlled by more than one control; therefore, only certain controls were identified for possible reliance. These controls were selected because they apparently controlled many causes of errors, and they produced testable audit evidence that could be subjected to compliance tests.

Summary of Controls

The next step in the evaluation of controls is to prepare a summary controls work sheet, which is used to move from the detailed analysis of many controls to a summary presentation of controls that might be relied upon. Table 15.2 shows such a summary prepared for the case study example. The controls in the client's system that might be relied on are listed on the left side of the work sheet; the potential errors are listed across the top. The auditors checked the controls that might be relied on for each potential error and made a judgment at the bottom of the work sheet about the reliability—high to low—of the controls.

Tests of Controls   The next audit step was to prepare and perform tests of controls to get audit evidence that the control procedure did what it was supposed to do. Normally, an auditor prepares a list of tests for each control procedure to be tested and then documents the results of the tests in the working papers. Table 15.3 shows the tests that the auditors performed for the first two control procedures listed in the summary control work sheet (Table 15.2).

Case Study   In this phase of the audit examination, the choice of procedures, the auditors
Commentary   have performed steps to determine what degree of reliability could be assigned to the client control procedures. The starting point was a list of the client's apparent control procedures prepared from the auditor's initial review of the client's system. Next, the auditors assessed the potential errors that could occur and determined the reliability of the controls in detecting such errors. In determining the reliability of controls, tests of controls were used.

All of this phase was designed to determine the likelihood of errors in the financial statements and what substantive audit procedures should be performed.

Substantive Audit Procedures

The last phase of the audit examination involves audit procedures designed to support the auditor's conclusion on the financial statements and to form an opinion thereon. The nature and extent of the audit procedures in this phase depends, to a large extent, on the auditor's assessment of the likelihood of errors in the financial statements.

In determining the audit procedures to be used, it is useful to begin with potential errors that could occur and the substantive procedures that could be used to deal with each potential error. Table 15.4 is a substantive procedures work sheet which the auditor prepared before selecting the actual tests to be performed. This work sheet shows what procedures are most cost effective, in that they deal with multiple potential errors. For example, the procedure of confirming account payable balances relates to all but two of the eleven potential errors.

Once the general audit procedure was selected, the specific procedures were developed to provide an ''audit program'' to be followed. Exhibit 15.3 shows the specific procedures used in the last phase of the audit.

CONTROLS THAT MIGHT BE RELIED UPON	LIABILITIES INCURRED BUT NOT RECORDED	PURCHASE AMOUNTS RECORDED INCORRECTLY	PURCHASES NOT AUTHORIZED	PURCHASES RECORDED BUT GOODS NOT RECEIVED
1. Vendor invoices, purchase orders, and receiving reports are matched and reviewed		✔		✔
2. Approved vendor invoices are batched, and a batch total is established for the total amount to be paid; a batch control log is used to account for all batches				
6. A total representing all input plus the total of the old unpaid file less the total of the to-be-paid file is compared to the total of the new unpaid file	✔	✔		✔
8. Tape of checks is run and compared to check register total				
9. Checks are matched to related purchase orders, receivers, vendor invoices; and then checks are signed using a check signer controlled by a department supervisor			✔	
10. Prenumbered check stock is used; a review for missing checks is performed daily				
11. Unpaid invoice report total is compared to the unpaid file total on the last control report	✔			
12. Unpaid invoice report total is compared to unpaid control total maintained by the payables department	✔			
14. Payments report total is compared to a total of all monthly payments				
15. Quarterly payment report reviewed for reasonableness, compared to budgets				
17. Controller reviews general ledger postings for accuracy and completeness				
Apparent reliability of controls	HIGH	HIGH	HIGH	HIGH

Table 15.2 Summary Controls Work Sheet

PURCHASE CHARGED TO WRONG ACCOUNT	PURCHASES RECORDED IN WRONG PERIOD	PAYMENTS RECORDED BUT NOT MADE	PAYMENTS MADE BUT NOT RECORDED	PAYMENT AMOUNTS RECORDED INCORRECTLY	PAYMENTS RECORDED IN WRONG PERIOD	UNAUTHORIZED PAYMENTS MADE
						✔
						✔
		✔				
		✔				✔
						✔
	✔					
			✔	✔	✔	
			✔		✔	
			✔	✔	✔	
LOW	LOW	HIGH	HIGH	HIGH	LOW	HIGH

**Table 15.3
Tests of Controls
Work Sheet**

CONTROL NUMBER AND DESCRIPTION	TEST NUMBER AND DESCRIPTION

1. Vendor invoices, purchase orders, and receiving reports are matched and reviewed.	1. Select a sample of purchase orders from the "payment by division and and type report." Obtain the purchase orders and related invoices, receivers, checks, and batch control tapes.
	  • Note that the invoices are properly matched with these purchase orders.
	  • Note that receivers are properly matched with <u>new</u> purchase orders.
	  • Note evidence (initials, stamp, etc.) of review.
	2. Observe that purchase orders are issued in sequence. Account for a sample of purchase orders issued to be sure that all purchase orders issued are properly processed.

2. Approved vendor invoices are batched, and a batch total is established for the total amount to be paid; a batch control log is used to account for all batches.	3. Use the same sample used for control test 1.
	  • Note that invoices are on the batch control tape.
	  • Note that the control tape agrees with the batch control log.
	4. Select a sample of entries from the batch control log and agree them to batch control sheets.

6. Total representing all input plus the total of old unpaid file less the total of the to-be-paid file is compared to the total of the new unpaid file.	5. Select a sample of daily reconciliations of the old unpaid file to the new unpaid file. Note that these reconciliations appear complete and inquire about any unusual items. Reperform some of these reconciliations.

8. Tape of checks is run and compared to the check register total.	6. Use the same sample used for test 1.
	  • Note that checks are included on the tape of checks run daily.
	  • Note that the tape of checks agrees with the comparable check register total.

9. Checks are matched to related purchase orders, receivers, and vendor invoices; and then checks are signed using a check signer controlled by a department supervisor.

10. Prenumbered check stock is used; a review for missing checks is performed daily.

11. Unpaid invoice report total is compared to the unpaid file total on the last control report.

12. Unpaid invoice total is compared to unpaid control total maintained by the payables department.

14. Payments report total is compared to a total of all monthly payments.

15. The quarterly payments report is reviewed for reasonableness and payments by division and type are compared to budgeted expenses.

17. General ledger postings are reviewed for completeness and accuracy by the controller.

7. Observe the matching process.
   - Note that checks are compared to the supporting documents.
   - Note that checks are signed with the mechanical check signer.

8. Observe the client's review for missing checks on several occasions Select a sample of checks issued and account for their disposition.

9. For all months, obtain the reconciliation documents for Control 11.
   - Review the documents, inquiring about unusual or incomplete items.
   - Reperform at least one month.

10. For all months, obtain the reconciliation documents for Control 12.
   - Review the documents, ✔ inquiring about unusual or incomplete items. ✔
   - Reperform at least one month. ✔

11. For all months, obtain the reconciliation documents for Control 13.
   - Review the documents, inquiring about unusual or incomplete items.
   - Reperform at least one month.

12. For all four quarters, obtain the reconciliation documents for Control 15.
   - Review the documents inquiring about unusual or incomplete items.
   - Reperform control for all quarters.

13. Observe the review process.

14. Observe attributes of the review (e.g., the check marks).

SCHEDULE	
PREPARED BY	DATE
REVIEWED BY	

WORK SHEET D-1	LIABILITIES INCURRED BUT NOT RECORDED	PURCHASE AMOUNTS RECORDED INCORRECTLY	PURCHASES NOT AUTHORIZED	PURCHASES RECORDED BUT GOODS NOT RECEIVED
PHASE II SUBSTANTIVE PROCEDURES (CONTROL TESTING)				
1. Agree monthly payment reports to general ledger	✔	✔		✔
2. Confirm purchases/payments with vendors		✔✔		✔
3. Agree output to invoices		✔✔	✔	
4. Agree invoices to receivers			✔✔	✔✔
5. Verify accuracy of coding				
6. Compare payment report total to monthly disbursements				
7. Agree payment reports to checks				
8. Agree purchase orders to unpaid reports	✔✔			
PHASE III SUBSTANTIVE PROCEDURES (VERIFIES ACCOUNT BALANCES)				
1. Confirm account payable balances	✔✔	✔✔		✔✔
2. Review payments after year end				
3. Analyze purchase and payment activity	✔	✔	✔	✔
4. Foot the purchase and payment reports	✔✔	✔✔		

✔✔ Indicates a frequently used procedure, ✔ indicates a sometimes used procedure.

Table 15.4 Substantive Procedures Work Sheet

PURCHASE CHARGED TO WRONG ACCOUNT	PURCHASES RECORDED IN WRONG PERIOD	PAYMENTS RECORDED BUT NOT MADE	PAYMENTS MADE BUT NOT RECORDED	PAYMENT AMOUNTS RECORDED INCORRECTLY	PAYMENTS RECORDED IN WRONG PERIOD	UNAUTHORIZED PAYMENTS MADE
✔✔	✔	✔	✔	✔	✔	
✔✔	✔	✔		✔	✔	
✔	✔✔					
✔✔						
		✔✔	✔✔	✔✔	✔✔	✔✔
		✔	✔	✔	✔	✔
✔	✔	✔✔	✔✔	✔✔	✔	
	✔✔				✔✔	
✔	✔	✔	✔	✔	✔	✔
		✔✔	✔✔	✔✔		

Exhibit 15.3
Description
of the Substantive
Procedures

1. Agree monthly payments to general ledger entries.
   Description
   - Obtain all monthly unpaid reports and agree the total to entries in the general ledger accounts payable account.
   - Obtain all monthly payments reports by division and type, agree the totals to entries in the general ledger expense accounts and to debits to accounts payable.
2. Confirm purchases and payments with vendor.
   Description
   - Select a sample of transactions from the payments by division and type report.
   - Confirm purchase and payment transactions with vendors.
3. Agree output to invoices.
   Description
   - Select a sample of transaction from the report of payments by division and type.
   - Agree information to invoices.
4. Agree invoices to receiver.
   Description
   - Use the same sample as in test 3.
   - Agree information to receivers and purchase orders.
5. Verify accuracy of coding.
   Description
   - Use the same sample as in test 3.
   - Agree information to receivers and purchase orders.
6. Compare payment report total to monthly disbursements.
   Description
   - Compare the total of the payment report by month to the total of monthly disbursements shown on bank records.
   - *Note:* This would likely be incorporated with a "proof of cash" procedure. This procedure also applies to error types in the sales and collections cycle.
7. Agree payment report to checks.
   Description
   - Use the same sample as in test 3.
   - Agree information to checks.
   - Note any errors in division identified, expense class, type of expenditure, amount, vendor identified, and date received.
8. Agree purchase orders to output.
   Description
   - Select a sample of purchase orders.
   - Agree purchase orders to the report of payments by division and type, or the unpaid report if not yet paid.
9. Confirm accounts payable balances.
   Description
   - Select the most active vendors and request statements of amounts due. (The statements are usually requested as of year's end, but in-

terim balances can also be confirmed. If interim balances are confirmed the period between the interim date and year end should be tested in some manner to ensure that no errors have occurred during this time.

10. Review payments after year's end.
    Description
    - Review payments made after year's end.
    - Review the open invoice and purchase order files as of the end of field work.

11. Analyze purchase and payment activity.
    Description
    - Review purchases and payments by division and type specifically:
      Compare the level of activity each month for fluctuations.
      Compare actual activity with budgets and note significant variances.
      Compare purchases by type with changes in the corresponding asset and expense accounts.
      Compare purchases and payment data with information obtained in other parts of the audit.

12. Foot the purchase and payment reports.
    Description
    - Foot the payment report by division and type for the year.
    - Foot the unpaid invoice report as of the end of the year.

Use of Computer: A Summary

The audit tests and procedures identified for this case study situation include both those procedures that normally would be performed without the use of the computer and those that could be performed with the use of the computer.

For example, computer audit software would be very helpful to confirm purchases and payments with vendors, agree purchase orders to output, confirm accounts payable balances, analyze purchase and payment activity, and foot the purchase and payment reports. These additional audit tests can be easily performed by audit software as other audit objectives are being accomplished. These and similar tests might be accomplished by adding one to three additional audit software commands.

16

CPA EXAMINATION QUESTIONS ON EDP AUDITING (1977–1982)*

To assist you in preparing for the CPA examination, we have reproduced, word for word, the following questions from the exam. What follows is representative of the questions that the CPA examination covers.

Technical Questions

1. Auditors often make use of computer programs that perform routine processing functions such as sorting and merging. These programs are made available by electronic data processing companies and others and are specifically referred to as
   a. Compiler programs.
   b. Supervisory programs.
   c. Utility programs.
   d. User programs.

2. In a computerized system, procedure or problem-oriented language is converted to machine language through a (an)
   a. Interpreter.
   b. Verifier.
   c. Compiler.
   d. Converter.

*Material from Uniform CPA Examination Questions and Unofficial Answers, copyright © 1982 by the American Institute of Certified Public Accountants, Inc., is adapted with permission.

3. Where disk files are used, the grandfather–father–son updating backup concept is relatively difficult to implement because the
   a. Location of information points on disks is an extremely time-consuming task.
   b. Magnetic fields and other environmental factors cause off-site storage to be impractical.
   c. Information must be dumped in the form of hard copy if it is to be reviewed before being used in updating.
   d. Process of updating old records is destructive.

4. The use of a header label in conjunction with magnetic tape is **most** likely to prevent errors by the
   a. Computer operator.
   b. Keypunch operator.
   c. Computer programmer.
   d. Maintenance technician.

5. To replace the human element of error detection associated with manual processing, a well-designed automated system will introduce
   a. Dual circuitry.
   b. Programmed limits.
   c. Echo checks.
   d. Read after write.

6. An auditor should be familiar with a client's electronic data processing hardware and software. An important element of the client's software is the program. Another element of software is the
   a. Cathode ray tube (CRT).
   b. Central processing unit (CPU).
   c. Magnetic tape drive.
   d. Compiler.

7. The computer system **most** likely to be used by a large savings bank for customers' accounts would be
   a. An on-line, real-time system.
   b. A batch processing system.
   c. A generalized utility system.
   d. A direct access data base system.

8. The program flowcharting symbol representing a decision is a
   a. Triangle.
   b. Circle.
   c. Rectangle.
   d. Diamond.

9. Which of the following is a computer test made to ascertain whether a given characteristic belongs to the group?
   a. Parity check.
   b. Validity check.

    c. Echo check.

    d. Limit check.

10. The most efficient and **least** costly method of dumping information for purposes of maintaining a backup file is from disk to

    a. Dump.

    b. Printout.

    c. Cards.

    d. Tape.

11. An auditor should be familiar with a client's electronic data processing hardware and software. An important element of the client's software is the program. Another element of software is the

    a. Cathode ray tube (CRT).

    b. Central processing unit (CPU).

    c. Magnetic tape drive.

    d. Compiler.

12. Accounting functions that are normally considered incompatible in a manual system are often combined in an electronic data processing system by using an electronic data processing program, or a series of programs. This necessitates an accounting control that prevents unapproved

    a. Access to the magnetic tape library.

    b. Revisions to existing computer programs.

    c. Usage of computer program tapes.

    d. Testing of modified computer programs.

13. Parity checks, read-after-write checks, and duplicate circuitry are electronic data processing controls that are designed to detect

    a. Erroneous internal handling of data.

    b. Lack of sufficient documentation for computer processes.

    c. Illogical programming commands.

    d. Illogical uses of hardware.

14. The machine-language program that results when a symbolic-language program is translated is called a (an)

    a. Processor program.

    b. Object program.

    c. Source program.

    d. Wired program.

Control-Oriented Questions

1. A procedural control used in the management of a computer center to minimize the possibility of data or program file destruction through operator error includes

    a. Control figures.

    b. Crossfooting tests.

   c. Limit checks.

   d. External labels.

2. Which of the following is likely to be **least** important to an auditor who is reviewing the internal controls surrounding the automated data processing function?

   a. Ancillary program functions.

   b. Disposition of source documents.

   c. Operator competence.

   d. Bit storage capacity.

3. Assume that an auditor estimates that 10,000 checks were issued during the accounting period. If an EDP application control which performs a limit check for each check request is to be subjected to the auditor's test-data approach, the sample should include

   a. Approximately 1,000 test items.

   b. A number of test items determined by the auditor to be sufficient under the circumstances.

   c. A number of test items determined by the auditor's reference to the appropriate sampling tables.

   d. One transaction.

4. During the review of an EDP internal control system an auditor may review decision tables prepared by the client. A decision table is usually prepared by a client to supplement or replace the preparation of

   a. An internal control questionnaire when the number of alternative responses is large.

   b. A narrative description of a system where transactions are not processed in batches.

   c. Flowcharts when the number of alternatives is large.

   d. An internal control questionnaire not specifically designed for an EDP installation.

5. When erroneous data are detected by computer program controls, such data may be excluded from processing and printed on an error report. The error report should most probably be reviewed and followed up by the

   a. EDP control group.

   b. System analyst.

   c. Supervisor of computer operations.

   d. Computer programmer.

6. In the study and review of a client's EDP internal control system, the auditor will encounter general controls and application controls. Which of the following is an application control?

   a. Dual read.

   b. Hash total.

   c. Systems flowchart.

   d. Control over program changes.

7. In updating a computerized accounts receivable file, which one of the following would be used as a batch control to verify the accuracy of the posting of cash receipts remittances?
   a. The sum of the cash deposits plus the discounts less the sales returns.
   b. The sum of the cash deposits.
   c. The sum of the cash deposits less the discounts taken by customers.
   d. The sum of the cash deposits plus the discounts taken by customers.

8. In a daily computer run to update checking account balances and print out basic details on any customer's account that was overdrawn, the overdrawn account of the computer programmer was never printed. Which of the following control procedures would have been **most** effective in detecting this irregularity?
   a. Use of the test-deck approach by the auditor in testing the client's program and verification of the subsidiary file.
   b. Use of a running control total for the master file of checking account balances and comparison with the printout.
   c. A program check for valid customer code.
   d. Periodic recompiling of programs from documented source decks, and comparison with programs currently in use.

9. Accounting control procedures within the EDP activity may leave **no** visible evidence indicating that the procedures were performed. In such instances, the auditor should test these accounting controls by
   a. Making corroborative inquiries.
   b. Observing the separation of duties of personnel.
   c. Reviewing transactions submitted for processing and comparing them to related output.
   d. Reviewing the run manual.

10. Which of the following would **lessen** internal control in an electronic data processing system?
    a. The computer librarian maintains custody of computer program instructions and detailed listings.
    b. Compuer operators have access to operator instructions and detailed program listings.
    c. The control group is solely responsible for the distribution of all computer output.
    d. Computer programmers write and debug programs which perform routines designed by the systems analyst.

11. In an electronic data processing system, automated equipment controls or hardware controls are designed to
    a. Arrange data in a logical sequential manner for processing purposes.
    b. Correct errors in the computer programs.
    c. Monitor and detect errors in source documents.
    d. Detect and control errors arising from use of equipment.

12. When preparing a record of a client's system of internal accounting control, the independent auditor sometimes uses a systems flowchart, which can **best** be described as a
   a. Pictorial presentation of the flow of instructions in a client's internal computer system.
   b. Diagram which clearly indicates an organization's internal reporting structure.
   c. Graphic illustration of the flow of operations which is used to replace the auditor's internal control questionnaire.
   d. Symbolic representation of a system or series of sequential processes.

13. Which of the following is an effective internal accounting control used to prove that production department employees are properly validating payroll timecards at a time-recording station?
   a. Timecards should be carefully inspected by those persons who distribute pay envelopes to the employees.
   b. One person should be responsible for maintaining records of employee time for which salary payment is **not** to be made.
   c. Daily reports showing time charged to jobs should be approved by the foreman and compared to the total hours worked on the employee time cards.
   d. Internal auditors should make observations of distribution of paychecks on a surprise basis.

14. Automated equipment controls in an electronic data processing system are designed to detect errors arising from
   a. Operation of the electronic data processing equipment.
   b. Lack of human alertness.
   c. Incorrect input and output data.
   d. Poor management of the electronic data processing installation.

15. A control feature in an electronic data processing system requires the central processing unit (CPU) to send signals to the printer to activate the print mechanism for each character. The print mechanism, just prior to printing, sends a signal back to the CPU verifying that the proper print position has been activated. This type of hardware control is referred to as
   a. Echo control.
   b. Validity control.
   c. Signal control.
   d. Check digit control.

16. Where computers are used, the effectiveness of internal accounting control depends, in part, upon whether the organizational structure includes any incompatible combinations. Such a combination would exist when there is **no** separation of the duties between
   a. Documentation librarian and manager of programming.

b. Programmer and console operator.

c. Systems analyst and programmer.

d. Processing control clerk and keypunch supervisor.

17. Which of the following is **not** a medium that can normally be used by an auditor to record information concerning a client's system of internal accounting control?

a. Narrative memorandum.

b. Procedures manual.

c. Flowchart.

d. Decision table.

EDP Auditing Methods Questions

1. An auditor's flowchart of a client's internal control system is a diagrammatic representation which depicts the auditor's

a. Understanding of the system.

b. Program for compliance tests.

c. Documentation of the study and evaluation of the system.

d. Understanding of the types of irregularities which are probable, given the present system.

2. The auditor's preliminary understanding of the client's EDP system is primarily obtained by

a. Inspection.

b. Observation.

c. Inquiry.

d. Evaluation.

3. An auditor will use the EDP test data method in order to gain certain assurances with respect to the

a. Input data.

b. Machine capacity.

c. Procedures contained within the program.

d. Degree of keypunching accuracy.

4. A decision table is most closely associated with which of the following auditor functions?

a. Preparation of a generalized EDP computer audit program.

b. Preliminary review of the client's system of internal control.

c. Performance of tests of balances and transactions.

d. Preparation of an audit program.

5. Compliance testing of an advanced EDP system

a. Can be performed using only actual transactions since testing of simulated transactions is of **no** consequence.

b. Can be performed using actual transactions or simulated transactions.

c. Is impractical since many procedures within the EDP activity leave **no** visible evidence of having been performed.

d. Is inadvisable because it may distort the evidence in master files.

6. After a preliminary phase of the review of a client's EDP controls, an auditor may decide not to perform compliance tests related to the control procedures within the EDP portion of the client's internal control system. Which of the following would **not** be a valid reason for choosing to omit compliance tests?

a. The controls appear adequate.

b. The controls duplicate operative controls existing elsewhere in the system.

c. There appear to be major weaknesses that would preclude reliance on the stated procedure.

d. The time and dollar costs of testing exceed the time and dollar savings in substantive testing if the compliance tests show the controls to be operative.

7. Which of the following is an advantage of generalized computer audit packages?

a. They are all written in one identical computer language.

b. They can be used for audits of clients that use differing EDP equipment and file formats.

c. They have reduced the need for the auditor to study input controls for EDP-related procedures.

d. Their use can be substituted for a relatively large part of the required compliance testing.

8. Which of the following is necessary to audit balances in an on-line EDP system in an environment of destructive updating?

a. Periodic dumping of transaction files.

b. Year-end utilization of audit hooks.

c. An integrated test facility.

d. A well-documented audit trail.

9. Which of the following client electronic data processing (EDP) systems generally can be audited without examining or directly testing the EDP computer programs of the system?

a. A system that performs relatively uncomplicated processes and produces detailed output.

b. A system that affects a number of essential master files and produces a limited output.

c. A system that updates a few essential master files and produces **no** printed output other than final balances.

d. A system that performs relatively complicated processing and produces very little detailed output.

10. A primary advantage of using generalized audit packages in the audit of an advanced EDP system is that it enables the auditor to
    a. Substantiate the accuracy of data through self-checking digits and hash totals.
    b. Utilize the speed and accuracy of the computer.
    c. Verify the performance of machine operations which leave visible evidence of occurrence.
    d. Gather and store large quantities of supportive evidential matter in machine-readable form.

11. Which of the following **best** describes the primary reason for the auditor's use of flowcharts during an audit engagement?
    a. To comply with the requirements of generally accepted auditing standards.
    b. To classify the client's documents and transactions by major operating functions, e.g., cash receipts, cash disbursements, etc.
    c. To record the auditor's understanding of the client's system of internal accounting control.
    d. To interpret the operational effectiveness of the client's existing organizational structure.

12. One reason why an auditor uses a flowchart is to aid in the
    a. Evaluation of a series of sequential processes.
    b. Study of the system of responsibility accounting.
    c. Performance of important, required, dual-purpose tests.
    d. Understanding of a client's organizational structure.

13. An auditor can use a generalized computer audit program to verify the accuracy of
    a. Data processing controls.
    b. Accounting estimates.
    c. Totals and sub-totals.
    d. Account classifications.

14. During which phase of an audit examination is the preparation of flowcharts **most** appropriate?
    a. Review of the system of internal accounting control.
    b. Tests of compliance with internal accounting control procedures.
    c. Evaluation of the system of internal administrative control.
    d. Analytic review of operations.

15. The purpose of using generalized computer programs is to test and analyze a client's computer
    a. Systems.
    b. Equipment.
    c. Records.
    d. Processing logic.

16. A computer service center processes, for an auditor's client, financial data that has a material effect on that client's financial statements. The independent auditor need **not** consider a review of the service center controls **if**
    a. The service center controls have already been reviewed by the internal audit team of the client.
    b. The service center processes data exclusively for the audit client and its subsidiaries.
    c. The user controls relied upon, which are external to the service center, are adequate to provide assurance that errors and irregularities may be discovered with reasonable promptness.
    d. The service center is a partially owned subsidiary of the client company, whose financial statements are examined by another CPA.

17. One important reason why a CPA, during the course of an audit engagement, prepares systems flowcharts is to
    a. Reduce the need for inquiries of client personnel concerning the operations of the system of internal accounting control.
    b. Depict the organizational structure and document flow in a single chart for review and reference purposes.
    c. Assemble the internal control findings into a comprehensible format suitable for analysis.
    d. Prepare documentation that would be useful in the event of a future consulting engagement.

18. An independent auditor studies and evaluates a client's electronic data processing system. The auditor's study portion includes two phases: (1) a review or investigation of the system and (2) tests of compliance. The latter phase might include which of the following?
    a. Examination of systems flowcharts to determine whether they reflect the current status of the system.
    b. Examination of the systems manuals to determine whether existing procedures are satisfactory.
    c. Examination of the machine room log book to determine whether control information is properly recorded.
    d. Examination of organization charts to determine whether electronic data processing department responsibilities are properly separated to afford effective control.

19. The primary purpose of a generalized computer audit program is to allow the auditor to
    a. Use the client's employees to perform routine audit checks of the electronic data processing records that otherwise would be done by the auditor's staff accountants.
    b. Test the logic of computer programs used in the client's electronic data processing systems.

    c. Select larger samples from the client's electronic data processing records than would otherwise be selected without the generalized program.

    d. Independently process client electronic data processing records.

20. Auditors often make use of computer programs that perform routine processing functions such as sorting and merging. These programs are made available by electronic data processing companies and others and are specifically referred to as

    a. User programs.

    b. Compiler programs.

    c. Supervisory programs.

    d. Utility programs.

EDP-Oriented Questions

1. If a control total were to be computed on each of the following data items, which would **best** be identified as a hash total for a payroll EDP application?

    a. Gross pay.

    b. Hours worked.

    c. Department number.

    d. Number of employees.

2. A management information system is designed to ensure that management possesses the information it needs to carry out its functions through the integrated actions of

    a. Data-gathering, analysis and reporting functions.

    b. A computerized information retrieval and decision-making system.

    c. Statistical and analytical review functions.

    d. Production-budgeting and sales-forecasting activities.

3. The client's EDP exception reporting system helps an auditor to conduct a more efficient audit because it

    a. Condenses data significantly.

    b. Highlights abnormal conditions.

    c. Decreases the EDP compliance testing.

    d. Is an efficient EDP input control.

4. Totals of amounts in computer-record data fields which are **not** usually added but are used only for data processing control purposes are called

    a. Record totals.

    b. Hash totals.

    c. Processing data totals.

    d. Field totals.

5. What is the computer process called when data processing is performed concurrently with a particular activity and the results are available soon enough to influence the particular course of action being taken or the decision being made?
   a. Batch processing.
   b. Real-time processing.
   c. Integrated data processing.
   d. Random access processing.

6. Which of the following employees normally would be assigned the operating responsibility for designing an electronic data processing installation, including flowcharts of data processing routines?
   a. Computer programmer.
   b. Data processing manager.
   c. Systems analyst.
   d. Internal auditor.

7. When erroneous data are detected by computer program controls, such data may be excluded from processing and printed on an error report. The error report should most probably be reviewed and followed up by the
   a. Supervisor of computer operations.
   b. Systems analyst.
   c. EDP control group.
   d. Computer programmer.

8. Which of the following employees in a company's electronic data processing department should be responsible for designing new or improved data processing procedures?
   a. Flowchart editor.
   b. Programmer.
   c. Systems analyst.
   d. Control-group supervisor.

9. An electronic data processing technique, which collects data into groups to permit convenient and efficient processing, is known as
   a. Document-count processing.
   b. Multi-programming.
   c. Batch processing.
   d. Generalized-audit processing.

10. Which of the following is a characteristic of an integrated system for data processing?
   a. An integrated system is a real-time system where files for different functions with similar information are separated.
   b. A single input record describing a transaction initiates the updating of all files associated with the transaction.
   c. Parallel operations strengthen internal control over the computer processing function.

    d. Files are maintained according to organizational functions such as purchasing, accounts payable, sales, etc.

EDP Audit Problems

1. **(Estimated time—15 to 25 minutes)**
   The following five topics are part of the relevant body of knowledge for CPAs having field work or immediate supervisory responsibility in audits involving a computer:

   1. Electronic data processing (EDP) equipment and its capabilities.
   2. Organization and management of the data processing function.
   3. Characteristics of computer based systems.
   4. Fundamentals of computer programming.
   5. Computer center operations.

   CPAs who are responsible for computer audits should possess certain general knowledge with respect to each of these five topics. For example, on the subject of EDP equipment and its capabilities, the auditor should have a general understanding of computer equipment and should be familiar with the uses and capabilities of the central processor and the peripheral equipment.

   Required:
   For each of the topics numbered 2 through 5 above, describe the general knowledge that should be possessed by those CPAs who are responsible for computer audits.

2. **(Estimated time—15 to 25 minutes)**
   An auditor is conducting an examination of the financial statements of a wholesale cosmetics distributor with an inventory consisting of thousands of individual items. The distributor keeps its inventory in its own distribution center and in two public warehouses. An inventory computer file is maintained on a computer disk and at the end of each business day the file is updated. Each record of the inventory file contains the following data:

   - Item number
   - Location of item
   - Description of item
   - Quantity on hand
   - Cost per item
   - Date of last purchase
   - Date of last sale
   - Quantity sold during year

The auditor is planning to observe the distributor's physical count of inventories as of a given date. The auditor will have available a computer tape of the data on the inventory file on the date of the physical count and a general purpose computer software package.

Required:

The auditor is planning to perform basic inventory auditing procedures. Identify the basic inventory auditing procedures and describe how the use of the general purpose software package and the tape of the inventory file data might be helpful to the auditor in performing such auditing procedures.

Organize your answer as follows:

Basic inventory auditing procedure	How general purpose computer software package and tape of the inventory file data might be helpful
1. Observe the physical count, making and recording test counts where applicable.	*Determining which items are to be test counted by selecting a random sample of a representative number of items from the inventory file as of the date of the physical count.*

3. **(Estimated time—15 to 25 minutes)**

When auditing an electronic data processing (EDP) accounting system, the independent auditor should have a general familiarity with the effects of the use of EDP on the various characteristics of accounting control and on the auditor's study and evaluation of such control. The independent auditor must be aware of those control procedures that are commonly referred to as "general" controls and those that are commonly referred to as "application" controls. General controls relate to all EDP activities and application controls relate to specific accounting tasks.

Required:

a. What are the general controls that should exist in EDP-based accounting systems?

b. What are the purposes of each of the following categories of application controls?
   1. Input controls
   2. Processing controls
   3. Output controls

4. **(Estimated time—15 to 25 minutes)**

During an audit engagement Harper, CPA, has satisfactorily completed an examination of accounts payable and other liabilities and now plans to determine whether there are any loss contingencies arising from litigation, claims, or assessments.

Required:

What are the audit procedures that Harper should follow with respect to the existence of loss contingencies arising from litigation, claims, and assessments? Do not discuss reporting requirements.

5. **(Estimated time—15 to 25 minutes)**

A partially completed charge sales systems flowchart is shown in Figure 16.1. The flowchart depicts the charge sales activities of the Bottom Manufacturing Corporation.

A customer's purchase order is received and a six-part sales order is prepared, therefrom. The six copies are initially distributed as follows:

- Copy no. 1—Billing copy—to billing department.
- Copy no. 2—Shipping copy—to shipping department.
- Copy no. 3—Credit copy—to credit department.
- Copy no. 4—Stock request copy—to credit department.
- Copy no. 5—Customer copy—to customer.
- Copy no. 6—Sales order copy—file in sales order department.

When each copy of the sales order reaches the applicable department or destination it calls for specific internal control procedures and related documents. Some of the procedures and related documents are indicated on the flowchart. Other procedures and documents are labeled letters *a* to *r*.

Required:

List the procedures or the internal documents that are labeled letters *c* to *r* in the flowchart of Bottom Manufacturing Corporation's charge sales system.

Organize your answer as follows (note that an explanation of the letters *a* and *b* which appear in the flowchart are entered as examples):

Flowchart Symbol Letter	Procedures or Internal Document
a.	Prepare six-part sales order.
b.	File by order number.

6. **(Estimated time—15 to 25 minutes)**

After determining that computer controls are valid, Hastings is reviewing the sales system of Rosco Corporation in order to determine how a computerized audit program may be used to assist in performing tests of Rosco's sales records.

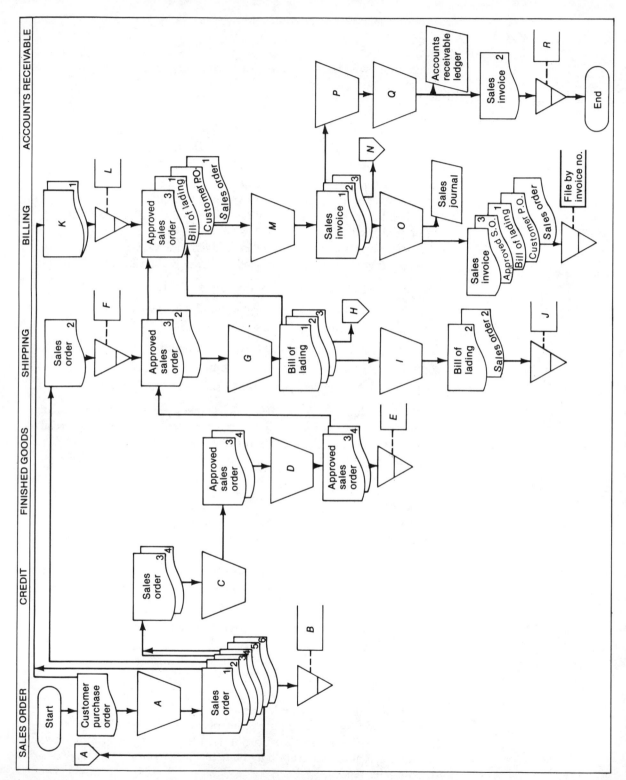

Figure 16.1 Bottom Manufacturing Corporation: Flowchart of Credit Sales Activities

494

Rosco sells crude oil from one central location. All orders are received by mail and indicate the pre-assigned customer identification number, desired quantity, proposed delivery date, method of payment and shipping terms. Since price fluctuates daily, orders do not indicate a price. Price sheets are printed daily and details are stored in a permanent disk file. The details of orders are also maintained in a permanent disk file.

Each morning the shipping clerk receives a computer printout which indicates details of customers' orders to be shipped that day. After the orders have been shipped, the shipping details are inputted in the computer which simultaneously updates the sales journal, perpetual inventory records, accounts receivable, and sales accounts.

The details of all transactions, as well as daily updates, are maintained on disks which are available for use by Hastings in the performance of the audit.

Required:
a. How may a computerized audit program be used by Hastings to perform substantive tests of Rosco's sales records in their machine-readable form? **Do not discuss accounts receivable and inventory.**
b. After having performed these tests with the assistance of the computer, what other auditing procedures should Hastings perform in order to complete the examination of Rosco's sales records?

7. **(Estimated time—15 to 25 minutes)**
In the past, the records to be evaluated in an audit have been printed reports, listings, documents and written papers, all of which are visible output. However, in fully computerized systems which employ daily updating of transaction files, output and files are frequently in machine-readable forms such as cards, tapes, or disks. Thus, they often present the auditor with an opportunity to use the computer in performing an audit.

Required:
Discuss how the computer can be used to aid the auditor in examining accounts receivable in such a fully computerized system.

8. **(Estimated time—15 to 25 minutes)**
Internal control comprises the plan of organization and all of the coordinate methods and measures adopted within a business to safeguard its assets, check the accuracy and reliability of its accounting data, promote operational efficiency, and encourage adherence to prescribed managerial policies.

Required:
a. What is the purpose of the auditor's study and evaluation of internal control?

b. What are the objectives of a preliminary evaluation of internal control?

c. How is the auditor's understanding of the system of internal control documented?

d. What is the purpose of tests of compliance?

9. **(Estimated time—15 to 25 minutes)**

Johnson, CPA, was engaged to examine the financial statements of Horizon Incorporated which has its own computer installation. During the preliminary review, Johnson found that Horizon lacked proper segregation of the programming and operating functions. As a result, Johnson intensified the study and evaluation of the system of internal control surrounding the computer and concluded that the existing compensating general controls provided reasonable assurance that the objectives of the system of internal control were being met.

Required:

a. In a properly functioning EDP environment, how is the separation of the programming and operating functions achieved?

b. What are the compensating general controls that Johnson most likely found? **Do not discuss hardware and application controls.**

10. **(Estimated time—15 to 25 minutes)**

A CPA's audit working papers contain a narrative description of a **segment** of the Croyden Factory, Inc., payroll system and an accompanying flowchart (see Figure 16.2).

Narrative. The internal control system with respect to the personnel department is well-functioning and is **not** included in the accompanying flowchart.

At the beginning of each work week payroll clerk No. 1 reviews the payroll department files to determine the employment status of factory employees and then prepares time cards and distributes them as each individual arrives at work. This payroll clerk, who is also responsible for custody of the signature stamp machine, verifies the identity of each payee before delivering signed checks to the foreman.

At the end of each work week the foreman distributes payroll checks for the preceding work week. Concurrent with this activity, the foreman reviews the current week's employee time cards, notes the regular and overtime hours worked on a summary form, and initials the aforementioned time cards. The foreman then delivers all time cards and unclaimed payroll checks to payroll clerk No. 2.

Required:

a. Based upon the narrative and accompanying flowchart, what are the weaknesses in the system of internal control?

b. Based upon the narrative and accompanying flowchart, what inquiries should be made with respect to clarifying the existence of **possible additional weaknesses** in the system of internal control?

Note: Do not discuss the internal control system of the personnel department.

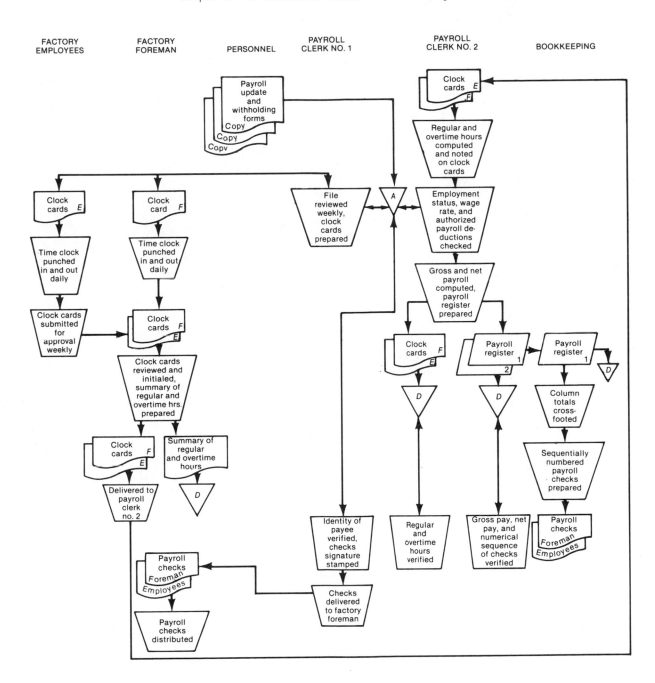

Figure 16.2   Croyden Inc., Factory Payroll System: Flowchart

Documentation Standards Manual for a Medium-Sized Installation

This documentation standards manual is prepared in three sections:

1. Systems documentation
2. Program documentation
3. Run book documentation

This manual was prepared for use in a medium-sized computer installation serving many user departments within the company and some companies outside the organization. The manual has been abridged and modified for illustrative purposes.

Systems Documentation

This section of the manual describes guidelines to be used in preparing good systems documentation; included in this procedure are a checklist of suggested documentation and descriptions of each item included in the checklist.

Purpose and Preparation The purpose of systems documentation is to provide a systems analyst with the information he or she needs for engineering changes to the system.

Parts of this documentation are to be prepared as a segment of the original system specifications that result from a system survey or feasibility study, prior to installation.

The documentation should be prepared by the project leader and her or his assistants during the development of the project. After the system is installed, the project leader is responsible for bringing this documentation into its final form.

Checklist of Contents

Items to be included in systems documentation are these:

- Title page and table of contents
- System introduction
- Systems flowchart
- System input
- System output
- System files
- Processing narrative
- Operations considerations
- Testing procedures
- System change authorization

The checklist and the following descriptions of each major item should be regarded as the minimum guidelines for system documentation. Other information may be included at the discretion of the project leader.

Title Page

The title page is on 8 ½ x 11 paper and is the first page of the documentation package. It should include the following:

1. User department name is the first entry on the title page.
2. The system title must appear next on the page. It must clearly state the particular system; for example, accounts receivable.
3. Date of installation of the original system should appear next. Following this date should be the installation dates of each system change authorization and its associated modification number. Every time there is a new system change authorization, an addition must be made to the title page.
4. "Prepared by" entry must contain the name of the preparer of the documentation book. This may be the systems analyst or another person who has taken the responsibility for documentation.
5. The name of the systems analyst should appear as the next entry.
6. The "reviewed by" entry must have the name of the project leader and systems coordinator typed. The preparer is not released from his

documentation responsibility until the documentation is initiated by the parties mentioned.

A table of contents should follow the title page.

System Introduction

An introduction to the system should be in a narrative form. The narrative should be organized as follows:

- Situation—A brief description of the company situation in which the system functions should be written. This should include such items as company size and its products.
- Statement of problem—A brief paragraph or two should be written describing the basic problems for which the system is a solution.
- Recommended solution—This portion should be an overall statement of the system which resolves the problem. Included in this statement should be a concise outline of the system's functions, purposes, and methods of operation.
- Work performed—A statement or list of specific items to be performed should be included here.
- Results—The last portion of the introduction should be a discussion dealing with benefits and accomplishments of the new system.

Systems Flowchart

A systems flowchart illustrating the complete flow of information through the system should be included in the documentation package.

If a computer system is a component of the overall system, a computer run-to-run chart should also be included in this section.

System Input

The system input category of systems documentation should be organized into two parts—source documents and computer input.

Source Document   The source document part should be organized with a section for each source document as follows:

- Introduction—The introduction should include the scope, function, and responsibility for origination.
- Contents—A brief description of each entry as to number of characters and type of entry (numeric, etc.). In this portion, a complete description of any codes should be included, such as deduction codes, shift, type of work, etc.

- Preparation procedure—A detailed description of any steps to be taken in editing, batching, or audit controlling should be included so as to ensure proper preparation of the source document.
- Form—The form itself should be displayed.

Computer Input   All computer inputs should be prepared on standard forms. All input should have the individual fields labeled and described using the COBOL picture reference code.

All instructions needed to prepare the input for the computer should be spelled out. This section would include keypunch instructions, batching instructions, control total instructions, and other related instructions.

System Output

The system output category of systems documentation should be organized by each individual output.

- Introduction—This introduction should include a statement describing the scope, function, and responsibility for its use.
- Contents—A brief description of each field as to the number of characters and type of entry (numeric, etc.) should be written. If the output is from a computerized system, the standard forms should be used to illustrate the extents of each field and punctuation required for body lines, headers, and totals. If the output is from a manual system, a narrative should be used to describe the contents.
- Form report—Either the form or a sample of the computer report should be displayed. Show all pertinent totals (minor, intermediate, major, and grand).
- Distribution and control procedures—A procedure should be included that details, in a step-by-step manner, the distribution of output indicating number of copies, routing, and retention periods. Also included in this procedure should be all necessary control instructions to ensure proper handling through the system.

System Files

The system files category of systems documentation should include only permanent files to be maintained regardless of the media used, tape, card, disk, etc. This portion should be organized by each file.

- Introduction—The introduction to the file should include the scope and function of the file.

- Contents—There should be a brief description of each item on the file. Included in this description should be the type of item (numeric, etc.), number of characters, and origination.
- Layout—All file layouts should be prepared using a standard form. In the record name and remarks area, the blocking factor, number of characters per record, as well as the file name, should be stated. All items of the file should be laid out according to standard procedures.
- Backup and retention procedures—A procedure covering the methods to be used for file backup and the retention cycles for the file should be included.

Processing Narrative

The system specifications for processing should be described in a narrative form and organized by type. There should be two types, manual and computer.

A manual-processing narrative should be organized as a procedure giving a detailed step-by-step instruction of processing the input to obtain the desired output.

For computer function or program specifications, the computer-processing narrative should be organized following the narrative description guidelines given in the program documentation section of the user's manual. If the narrative is included in the documentation, it need only be referenced.

Operations Considerations

If the system requires machinery, a description of equipment and its selection criteria should be stated. Also, timing estimates for processing should be made and included.

An important procedure that must be included is a statement on machine, program, and data backup. Under this category should be included any machine rental or service contracts that the analyst deems necessary.

Testing Procedures

The analyst or project leader must prepare a test procedure for the entire system. This procedure should be designed and prepared in such a way as to allow use of the procedure to check out any later system changes.

System Change Authorization

All system change authorizations should be filed in this section. Included in this section should be a description of the change and all supporting documentation (card layouts, etc.).

Program Documentation

Scope This subject describes the contents of good program documentation for individual computer programs. Included in the procedure is a checklist of documentation content, a description of each item included, and some helpful exhibits.

Checklist Items to be included in program documentation are these:

- Title page
- Run flowchart
- Narrative description
- Card input and output
- Report output
- File layouts
- Testing
- Program change authorization
- Program listing
- Run instructions
- Miscellaneous

Title Page

The title page is on an 8½ x 11 sheet of paper and should include the following elements:

- Program identification number is used in identifying the program on program listings, job control cards, and other documentation.
- User name must be placed on the next line on the page.
- A system title must appear next on the page. It must clearly state the particular system; for example, accounts receivable, accounts payable, production control.
- The program title is the name given to the particular program; i.e., update, aged analysis, statement.
- Date of installation of the original program. Following this date should be the dates of installation of each program, change authorization, and also the modification number. Every time there is a new program change authorization, an addition must be made to the title page.

- "Prepared by" entry must contain the name of the preparer of the documentation. This may be the programmer who wrote the system or another person who has taken the responsibility for documentation.
- "Reviewed by" entry must have the initials of both the project leader and program coordinator before the preparer is released from his documentation responsibility.

Run Flowchart

The run flowchart is on a sheet of 8½ x 11 paper and is the second page of the documentation package. The description that follows explains what must be included in the flowchart.

The flowchart guide and template should be used for symbol and convention standards.

The center box should be large enough to contain any comments about the program. The comments should, in general terms, describe the function of the program. The program identification number and title should appear at the top of the box.

Punched-card input should appear to the left of the box and above any magnetic tape symbols. An identification of each card should appear within the symbol including a card type and a general descriptive name, that is, ER09 Cash Receipts. Also, a "sys" number should be included on the first card.

If a parameter card is used, it should appear separate and above other input punched cards. Fields used and their respective card columns should be shown in a footnote.

Punched-card output should appear to the right of the box above any magnetic tapes. The descriptive information should be the same as for punched-card input.

All printer output should appear above the box. The identification of each report should be written within each symbol as well as the logical unit-"sys" number. A footnote should contain the following: form name, number of copies, notation of special printer loop, characters of print line, disposition, and decollating or bursting instructions.

Magnetic tape input should appear on the left-hand side of the box. Included inside of the tape, if possible, should be the name of the file as expressed within the program, the "sys" number or logical unit assigned, and finally the hardware unit given in the machine nomenclature, that is, 180, 092, OOE. A footnote should contain the following information: sequence of the file, blocking factor, and number of characters per record. (Use range for variable records.)

Magnetic tape output should appear to the right side of the box. If the output tape is a new master (grandfather–father–son), the symbol should be horizontal to the old master. The rest of the information should be the same as tape input.

Disk files should appear below the box. The file name should appear inside the disk symbol. Also, the logical "sys" number and the hardware drive number should appear inside the symbol. A footnote should contain the following: file organization (sequential, index sequential, or direct); access method (sequential or random); record key; blocking factor; and number of characters per record.

Narrative Description

The program specifications should be described in a narrative form. This narrative should be organized into five sections: introduction, housekeeping, file handling, controls, and end of job.

1. Introduction section should give a description of purpose and general objectives of the program.
2. Housekeeping section should set forth all specifications dealing with the program setup, such as parameter cards, file totals to be cleared or rolled, and other miscellaneous operations.
3. File-handling section should be organized by each output master file. Within each file update, all specifications should be grouped by transaction type. Within each tape output report file, all specifications should be grouped by output transaction type. Print specifications should be specified by body line and control breaks.
4. Controls section should specify what audit trails, record counts, grand totals, or other controls should be included.
5. End-of-job section should specify what totals are to be shown and on what device, which tapes are not rewound, and other exceptions to the normal end of job.

Card Input and Output

All card input should be shown on standard forms. The format is constructed as follows:

*   Identify the card type and describe its use as it relates to the system.
*   Identify each field descriptively, the columns in which the field lies, and the COBOL picture reference.
*   Write a brief description of the particular field to follow the field description.

Report Output

All printer output should be shown on standard forms. Also, if possible, a sample printout of the report should be included as documentation as well as samples of any total pages.

File Layouts

All file layouts for magnetic tape and disk should use the standard forms. The file name and record names should appear in the record name and remarks area.

All fields should be identified with a name, packed or unpacked, and the COBOL picture reference: S9 (8).

Testing

All testing materials should be documented as to their use, mode of operation, etc. If possible, all test data should be documented and maintained for later program change debugging.

Program Change Authorization

All program change authorizations should be filed in this section. Included in this section should be

- The change descriptions
- Program flowcharts describing changes
- Any other miscellaneous documentation

Program Listing

The program listing should be the original copy. (The second copy is maintained in the run book.)

Run Instructions

This section should have the same documentation as the run book.

Miscellaneous

This section should house all additional notes or other documentation used in programming that might be useful in program maintenance.

Run Book Documentation

Scope   A run book must be prepared for each computer system currently in operation. Operator instructions for several related programs can be grouped together to form a run book for a system such as payroll, production control, or accounts payable. This procedure includes a checklist of documentation content, a description of each item included, and relevant exhibits.

Checklist Run book documentation should include the following elements:

1. Title page
2. Computer system run-to-run chart
3. Individual computer runs
    (a) Run layout forms
    (b) Run script
    (c) Card layouts
    (d) Sample reports
    (e) 80–80 listing of control cards

The third section must be repeated for each individual program in the system.

Title Page

The title page is on 8½ x 11 paper and is the first page of the documentation package.

- The user name must be placed at the top of the page.
- A system title must appear on the next line. It must clearly state the particular system, e.g., accounts receivable, accounts payable. Just below the system title, the client account charge number should appear.
- Following the charge number must be an index of each program using a descriptive name (such as master update), the program ID number, and the date of installation of the program.
- "Prepared by" entry must contain the name of the person who prepared, edited, or compiled the majority of the information.
- The project leader's name must appear next in line.
- "Reviewed by" entry must have the initials of the project leader and the operations coordinator before the preparer is released from his documentation responsibility.

Computer System Run-to-Run Chart

The run-to-run flowchart should follow the title page. It serves the function of an introduction to the overall operations problem.

Individual Computer Runs

There must be an individual section for each functional program composed of the following:

- Run layout forms
- Run script

- Card layouts
- Sample reports
- 80–80 listing of control cards

This program constitutes the total documentation required per program.

Run Layout Forms   The run layout forms are prepared by the programmer. They are used as the primary reference guide for operations.

If there is not sufficient room on these forms to describe a function completely, place a brief description on the form along with a cross-reference to a more complete description in the run script.

Run Script   The primary function of the narrative script is to supply the operation's personnel with a detailed explanation of an individual program run.

- Setup and labels—The script should include setup instructions per specific device in a step-by-step manner. If label conventions are used, the correct label identification should be shown.
- Input—If input is on cards, there should be a detailed explanation of deck structure including a sample 80–80 listing. If batch-control cards are required, there should be a layout of the cards as well as an explanation for reconciling batch totals to source documents. Included in the above explanation should be the name and telephone number of the responsible individual at the client's office as well as the assigned analyst.
- Programmed halts and displays—Any program-originated halts should be explained in depth relating the cause and the action to take. The same explanation should be given to program-originated displays.
- Output—The script should detail output form disposition as well as bursting and decollating instructions. Also, responsibilities of output delivery should be stated.
- Balancing control totals—Control total checks should be described as follows: $A + B + C + D = E$. If E is not equal to the sum, an appropriate action should be stated.
- Backup—Backup procedure should be detailed for all input files, master files, and output files. Any retention periods should be described in this section.
- Restart—Restart procedures should be detailed including all prerequisites to rerunning the program.
- Other—The run script should contain a detailed description of any other items that would be useful to the operator.

Card Layouts A copy of all card layouts found in program documentation should be added to the run book.

Sample Reports A copy of all sample reports found in program documentation should be added to the run book.

80–80 Listing of Control Cards An 80–80 listing of controls should be the last entry for each program. The listing should not include any object decks, but should include all control cards, such as these:

- Job cards
- Extent cards
- Label cards
- Assign cards

EDP Controls Questionnaire*

An EDP controls questionnaire follows on pages 512–528.

*Adapted by permission from material developed by Peat, Marwick, Mitchell & Co.

PART I – SYSTEM AND CONTROL QUESTIONNAIRE

Accountant _____

Date _____

Company _____ Period ended _____

Branch, division, or subsidiary_____

SYSTEM AND CONTROL QUESTIONNAIRE

INSTRUCTIONS

This questionnaire is to be prepared for clients who have a data processing system and should be considered as a supplement to the questionnaire on internal control. Part I asks general questions about the overall operation of the system. Part II deals with specific details of a particular application. Separate Part I's should be prepared for each data processing system when the client operates multi-systems and separate Part II's should be prepared for each major accounting application. The selection of major applications may present a problem; however, the importance of an application should be measured in terms of the financial impact of the items which will be processed.

This questionnaire provides a basis for verifying that, in general, minimum control is being exercised over the system. In some cases the particular requirements of an individual system may create the need for lines of inquiry and investigation which exceed the scope of this questionnaire. In these cases, the auditor must use his own judgment in formulating an evaluation of the system. The questions in Part I are designed to aid in evaluating the management controls within the data processing system. Thus, a "no" answer may not have a direct effect on the audit procedures to be followed. However, a large number of "no's" would indicate a potentially weak control system and should cause the auditor to extend the scope of his detail testing of the system and its records. Basically, a "no" answer should result in a comment in our letter to management.

Completion of this questionnaire is only the first phase in evaluating the system of internal control. Having learned how the system is supposed to operate, the auditor must now test the system to determine that it functions as it was described. The nature and extent of this testing is a matter for the auditor's individual judgment.

To validate the operation of the system, one of the following methods should be employed:

(a) Tracing selected transactions from input data to final results. This approach involves "auditing around the computer." In some cases economic factors or considerations of practicality may indicate this is the best approach to be employed.

(b) Tracing selected transactions from input data to summary transaction listings (i.e., a daily transaction list) and then tracing summary totals into final totals (i.e., a monthly recap list).

(c) If listings are not normally prepared, arrange to have current work listed and select current input data for tracing as outlined in (a) or (b) above.

(d) Reprocessing of client data using programs validated and controlled by PMM&Co. and comparing the output to the client's output. This may be done using client programs which have been reviewed by PMM&Co., by using manufacturer supplied utility programs, by using available computer audit program packages, by writing special programs for audit purposes, or by reviewing and modifying client programs to perform audit functions.

(e) If the client has a test deck which was used to validate his program when it was written, review the test deck to determine if it is reasonably complete and then process the deck using the client's program. The output should be checked for accuracy.

(f) If no test deck is available, prepare one and then process the deck using the client's program. The output should be checked for accuracy.

PART I – SYSTEM AND CONTROL QUESTIONNAIRE

Accountant _____

Date _____

Company _____ Period ended _____

Branch, division, or subsidiary_____

INSTRUCTIONS

This part of the questionnaire is designed to assist in evaluating the general management techniques and controls employed within the data processing operation. The following questions are general in nature and are designed to establish the basic frame of reference for the review of the internal control.

A.   Equipment & Programming Languages – (Obtain client's listing if available or complete the following).

    1.   Equipment

        Quantity   Description

        _____   _____

        _____   _____

        _____   _____

        _____   _____

        _____   _____

        _____   _____

        _____   _____

        _____   _____

        _____   _____

        _____   _____

Equipment on Order

        _____   _____

        _____   _____

        _____   _____

Note: For tape drives (magnetic tape) indicate whether 7 – channel or 9 – channel and recording density (200 bits per inch, 556 BPI, 800 BPI, or 1600 BPI).

    2.   Programming Languages Used

        _____

        _____

        _____

        _____

        _____

PART I – SYSTEM AND CONTROL QUESTIONNAIRE

Accountant _____

Date _____

Company _____ Period ended _____

Branch, division, or subsidiary _____

B.   Organization Chart

Obtain a detailed chart, if available, or complete the following chart. Use interconnecting lines to show lines of authority and responsibility. If a position shown below does not exist, mark X through it. If positions exist that are not shown below, make additions as necessary.

SENIOR EXECUTIVE

Name _____

Title _____

EDP MANAGER

Name _____

PROGRAMMING SUPERVISOR	SYSTEMS SUPERVISOR	CONTROL SUPERVISOR	OPERATIONS SUPERVISOR
Name _____	Name _____	Name _____	Name _____
PROGRAMMERS	**ANALYSTS**	**CONTROL CLERKS**	**KEYPUNCH OPERATORS**
Number _____	Number _____	Number _____	Number _____
		LIBRARIANS	**OPERATORS**
		Number _____	Number _____

PART I – SYSTEM AND CONTROL QUESTIONNAIRE

Accountant _____

Date _____

Company _____ Period ended _____

Branch, division, or subsidiary_____

C. Applications

    1. General Applications (Complete C-2 for applications of specialized industries.)

Description	Check One Yes	No	Comments
Cash receipts			
Cash disbursements			
Accounts receivable			
Inventory:			
Perpetual			
Cost accounting data			
Year-end physical counts			
Management (automatic reorder, economic order quantity)			
Fixed assets			
Accounts payable			
Payroll			
General ledger			
Sales			
Budgets			
Other:			
List proposed applications:			

Note: See Part II for specific questions about evaluating the internal control for each application.

PART I – SYSTEM AND CONTROL QUESTIONNAIRE

Accountant
Date

Company _____ Period ended _____

Branch, division, or subsidiary _____

C.   **Applications**

2. Specific Industry Applications.

Description	Comments
List proposed applications:	

PART I – SYSTEM AND CONTROL QUESTIONNAIRE

Accountant

Date _____

Company _____ Period ended _____

Branch, division, or subsidiary_____

Question	Answer		
	Yes	No	Remarks *
D. Organization and Operating Controls - (When applicable, all operating shifts are to be considered.)			
1. Does the internal auditor's program include a review of: a. The arrangement of duties and responsibilities in the data processing department? b. Programs supplied by the data processing department which are used to prepare audit data? c. The controls of the serviced departments over the processing performed by the data processing department?			
2. Have procedures been established by which the qualifications of the Data Processing employees to perform their functions can be determined?			
3. Are all proof and control functions performed by personnel other than machine operators and programmers?			
4. Are the functions and duties of computer operators and programmers separate and distinct?			
5. Are the operators assigned to particular jobs or applications subject to periodic rotation?			
6. Are operators required to take vacations?			
7. Are the employees in data processing separated from all duties relating to the initiation of transactions and master file changes?			
8. Are departments that initiate changes in master file data or program data factors furnished with notices or a register showing changes actually made? (Examples of such changes are revisions in pay rates, selling prices, credit limits, and tax tables.)			
9. Are blank checks and other negotiable paper which are used by the data processing department controlled by someone independent of the machine operators?			
10. Have documentation procedures and standards been established?			
11. Is there supervisory review of documentation for adequacy, completeness and current status?			
12. Have standardized programming techniques and procedures (i.e., program formats, flowcharts, initialization routines, tape labeling, coding, etc.) been compiled in a programming manual and is the manual current?			
13. Are standardized operator instructions and run descriptions prepared and made available to the computer operators? Note: These instructions are generally incorporated into "run books."			

*NOTE — In the case of a "No" answer, the "Remarks" column should (1) cross-reference either to the audit program step (or steps) which recognizes the weakness or to the supporting permanent file memorandum on accounting procedures which explains the mitigating circumstances or lack of importance of the item, and (2) indicate whether the item is to be included in the draft of the letter to management on internal control.

PART I – SYSTEM AND CONTROL QUESTIONNAIRE

Accountant _____

Date _____

Company _____ Period ended _____

Branch, division, or subsidiary_____

Question	Yes	No	Answer Remarks *
14. Do these run books contain the following information:			
a. Explanation of the purpose and character of each run?			
b. Identification of all machine system components used and the purpose thereof?			
c. Identification of all input and output forms and media?			
d. Detailed set-up and end-of-run operator instructions, including all manual switch settings required?			
e. Identification of all possible programmed and machine halts (before end of job), and specifically prescribed restart instructions for each?			
15. Is control being effectively exercised to verify operator's adherence to prescribed operating procedures?			
(This is normally accomplished by a combination of periodic observation of operator performance and the daily examination of formal operating "logs" where significant events and actions are entered by the machine and/or the operators.)			
16. Are adequate machine operation logs being maintained?			
(As a minimum, a formal entry of each machine operation exception [such as machine and programmed halts and the operator action taken] should be made. In order to exercise maximum control and to maintain information essential to analyzing the effectiveness and nature of machine utilization, the client should enforce maintainance of a running, accurate log of run sequence and operator identification, run start and stop times, all exceptions, and rerun actions taken.)			
17. Is a schedule maintained of the reports and documents to be produced by the EDP system?			
18. Are output reports and documents reviewed before distribution to ascertain the reasonableness of the output?			
19. Are there adequate procedures for control over the distribution of reports?			
20. Have formal program testing procedures been established to check the functioning of new applications and revisions to existing programs?			
21. Is a file of test data prepared and maintained for each new or revised program?			
22. Are there adequate procedures for the authorization, approval and testing of program revisions? (Indicate the person(s) or level of authority who may approve program revisions.)			
23. Are reasonable precautions in force to prevent access of operators and unauthorized personnel to program details that are not necessary to their functions and which would assist them in perpetrating deliberate irregularities?			
(This is a difficult condition to assess. However, not infrequently, a complete disregard of control will be encountered. General and detail logic charts, program coding sheets, card program decks, and program tapes may be stored in unlocked desks and file cabinets. If these conditions exist, the potential for irregularities and accidental destruction of vital records must be brought to the client's attention.)			

*NOTE – In the case of a "No" answer, the "Remarks" column should (1) cross-reference either to the audit program step (or steps) which recognizes the weakness or to the supporting permanent file memorandum on accounting procedures which explains the mitigating circumstances or lack of importance of the item, and (2) indicate whether the item is to be included in the draft of the letter to management on internal control.

PART I – SYSTEM AND CONTROL QUESTIONNAIRE

Accountant _____

Date _____

Company _____ Period ended _____

Branch, division, or subsidiary_____

Question	Yes	No	Answer Remarks *
24. Are procedures for issuing and storing magnetic tape, disk packs, and program documentation formally defined and are such responsibilities assigned to a librarian, either as a full-time or part-time duty?			
25. Have arrangements been made for alternate processing at some other location in the event of breakdown?			
26. Is there a written procedure for utilizing the backup facilities?			
27. Have the backup facilities been used or tested?			
28. Are copies of all important master files and programs stored in a fireproof off-premise storage location?			
29. Does insurance coverage include the cost of recreating lost files, rewriting destroyed programs, and payments for the use of alternate equipment?			
30. Are preventive maintenance procedures in effect to minimize potential equipment failure?			
31. Are security provisions in effect at all times to restrict unauthorized access to the data processing department?			

*NOTE — In the case of a "No" answer, the "Remarks" column should (1) cross-reference either to the audit program step (or steps) which recognizes the weakness or to the supporting permanent file memorandum on accounting procedures which explains the mitigating circumstances or lack of importance of the item, and (2) indicate whether the item is to be included in the draft of the letter to management on internal control.

| PART II – SPECIFIC APPLICATION QUESTIONNAIRE | Accountant _____ |
| | Date _____ |

Company _____ Period ended _____

Branch, division, or subsidiary_____

SYSTEMS QUESTIONNAIRE

GENERAL

This questionnaire must be completed for each major accounting application where a computer is used to process financial data. This intensive review should be planned so that all the client's major accounting applications will be covered over a period of years and that the audit papers will contain a reasonably current description of all the clients major computerized accounting applications. Completed questionnaires not revised in a particular year should be reviewed to determine if they basically reflect the client's current systems and procedures. If they do not, changes should be recorded on the questionnaire.

The answers to the questions are designed so that:

1. A "no" answer indicates less than the minimum control required. The reason for the "no" must be explained. As a "no" answer may have an impact on the audit, the audit program should be revised where applicable. The attached audit program guide lists audit steps to be considered when "no" answers are received to selected questions.

2. A "N/A" answer (not applicable) means a particular question is not a factor in the client's system. All "N/A's" must be accompanied by a brief explanation.

INSTRUCTIONS

Review the list of applications prepared in Part I, Section C. Determine those applications which have an audit impact and decide which are major applications from an audit standpoint. For the applications selected, perform the following:

1. Ask the client to provide system flowcharts. If the client does not have system flowcharts, it may be necessary to prepare them in order to complete the review of internal control. Since this may involve a large amount of time, consult with the partner or manager on the engagement before undertaking any large flowcharting effort. Lack of such documentation is a weakness in management control and should be an item in our letter to management.

2. Complete the specific application questionnaire.

3. Review the flowcharts and the questionnaire and verify their accuracy by testing them against the documentation, output, and other hard copy which can be used to determine that the controls operate as described. These tests *do not* have to be extensive since they are only concerned with systems verification.

4. Obtain a set of control reports for a test period. Review for evidence that controls are being utilized and enforced in accordance with the system design.

5. Examine controls over error correction procedures, paying particular attention to those controlling corrections to master file records.

6. Analyze the completed questionnaire(s):

    a. Evaluate the effect of internal control deficiencies and prepare a list of comments with recommendations for improvement. Wherever possible, an explanation of the possible consequences resulting from inadequate controls should be included.

    b. Review your findings and conclusions with the audit management on the engagement.

    c. Prepare comments to be included in a letter to management.

PART II – SPECIFIC APPLICATION QUESTIONNAIRE

Accountant

Date

Company _____ Period ended _____

Branch, division, or subsidiary_____

At the completion of the review of a particular application, the following information should be considered for inclusion in the workpapers as deemed necessary to adequately describe the system and the work performed.

1. System flowchart.

2. Written description of the system with copies of input and output layouts and sample printouts.

3. A brief description of the file control procedures.

4. Notes regarding the procedural tests performed to verify the existence and satisfactory operation of controls.

5. Application questionnaire.

6. Notes concerning control weaknesses, if any, in the system.

Note: Identify any gaps which exist in the audit trail associated with this system and consider possible solutions such as a special printout of the file used, a special computer program for audit purposes, alternative audit procedures, etc. Discuss your conclusions with the audit management on the engagement.

PART II – SPECIFIC APPLICATION QUESTIONNAIRE

Company _____ Period ended _____

Branch, division, or subsidiary _____

The following audit steps are to be used as a guide in response to "no" answers to selected questions on the Data Processing Internal Control Questionnaire Part II - Specific Applications. These suggested audit steps relate only to the more significant questions and are to be used as a guide in developing an audit program for a specific engagement. Additional or alternative auditing procedures, considered necessary or desirable should be adopted. For "yes" answers, the related audit step should be marked "N/A" (not applicable).

B.   Input Controls

Question 1

1.   Transactions may be lost before they enter the system and are recorded for data processing. Make a reasonably comprehensive test of current or historical records to insure that basic source transactions are being entered in the system. Determine the initial document which triggers an entry to the system and trace a test group to insure they were recorded.

Question 2

2.   Transactions may be improperly entered in the system. Follow the basic procedure outlined in Item 1 to verify if data is being correctly recorded.

Question 3

3.   Data may be lost during the conversion process. Obtain, for a current date, a printout of the original data and the data after conversion. On a test basis, verify that the conversion is complete and correct. This can be done by tracing items from one file to another in both directions.

Question 4

4.   As in Question 1, transactions may be lost. On a test basis, communicate directly with other locations and obtain copies of the data they submitted as input to the system. Trace this input to the related files.

Question 5

5.   Obtain several examples of errors and trace through to correct processing.

C.   Program and Processing Controls

Question 2

6.   Improper or erroneous data may be entering the system. Obtain, on a test basis, a printout of the input data and manually perform the tests outlined in the Questionnaire.

D.   Output Control

Questions 2 and 3

7.   Control totals may not be correctly verified. On a test basis, review the reconciliation and vertification of control totals.

Questions 4 and 5

8.   Error corrections may be improperly entered. On a test basis, review error listings and trace corrections into the related files.

E.   File Control

Question 4

9.   Errors may have gotten into master file records. On a test basis, obtain a printout of the master file and trace selected items to their underlying support.

PART II – SPECIFIC APPLICATION QUESTIONNAIRE

Accountant _____

Date _____

Company _____ Period ended _____

Branch, division, or subsidiary _____

Question	Answer		
	Yes	No	Remarks *

A.   Documentation

General

Documentation consists of workpapers and records which describe the system and procedures for performing a data processing task. It is the basic means of communicating the essential elements of the data processing system and the logic followed by the computer programs. Preparing adequate documentation is a necessary, though frequently neglected, phase of computer data processing. A lack of documentation is an indication of a serious weakness within the management control over a data processing installation.

Is the program or programs supported by an adequate documentation file?

A minimum acceptable level of documentation should include:

1.   Problem statement
2.   System Flowchart
3.   Transaction and activity codes
4.   Record layouts
5.   Operator's instructions
6.   Program flowchart
7.   Program listing
8.   Approval and change sheet
9.   Description of input and output forms

B.   Input Controls

General

Input controls are designed to authenticate the contents of source documents and to check the conversion of this information into machine readable formats or media. Normally these controls will not be designed to detect 100% of all input errors since such an effort would be either too costly or physically impractical. Therefore, an economic balance must be maintained between the cost of error detection and the economic impact of an undetected error. This should be considered when evaluating input control. Judgment must be used when identifying "essential information," the accuracy of which *must* be verified. The following questions can also be used to evaluate internal control practices used in master file conversions.

1.   Are procedures adequate to verify that all transactions are being received for processing?

(To accomplish this, there must be some systematic procedure to insure all batches that enter the machine room for processing or conversion are returned from the machine room. Basic control requirements are being met if the answer to *one* of the following questions is "yes.")

a.   Are batch controls (at least an item count) being established *before* source documents are sent to the machine room for keypunching or processing?

*NOTE –   In the case of a "No" answer, the "Remarks" column should (1) cross-reference either to the audit program step (or steps) which recognizes the weakness or to the supporting permanent file memorandum on accounting procedures which explains the mitigating circumstances or lack of importance of the item, and (2) indicate whether the item is to be included in the draft of the letter to management on internal control.

PART II – SPECIFIC APPLICATION QUESTIONNAIRE

Accountant _____

Date _____

Company _____ Period ended _____

Branch, division, or subsidiary _____

Question	Answer		
	Yes	No	Remarks *
b. If batch controls are established *in* the machine room, is there some other form of effective control (such as prenumbered documents) which provides assurance that all documents have been received?			
c. If no batch control is used, is there some other means of checking the receipt of all transactions? If yes, describe. (For example, in a payroll operation, the computer may match attendance time cards and corresponding job tickets for each employee as the master file is updated.)			
2. Are procedures adequate to verify the recording of input data on cards, magnetic tape or disk?			
(Control is being maintained if the answer to *one* of the following questions is "yes.")			
a. Are important data fields subject to machine verification?			
b. If only some (or none) of the important data fields are verified, is an alternate checking technique employed?			
Some acceptable alternate techiniques are:			
1) Self checking digits 2) Control totals 3) Hash totals 4) Editing for reasonableness			
3. If input data is converted from one form to another (card to tape, cards to disk) prior to processing on the computer system, are controls adequate to verify the conversion?			
Normal conversion controls include:			
a. Record Counts b. Hash totals c. Control totals			
4. If data transmission is used to move data between geographic locations, are controls adequate to determine transmission is correct and no messages are lost? Controls would normally include one or more of the following:			
a. Message counts b. Character counts c. Dual transmission			
5. Is the error correction process and the re-entry of the corrected data subject to the same control as is applied to original data?			
(If control over corrections is lax, the correction process may be the largest source of error in the system.)			
6. Are source documents retained for an adequate period of time in a manner which allows identification with related output records and documents?			
(Failure to maintain documents may make it impossible to recreate files in the event they are damaged or destroyed.)			

*NOTE — In the case of a "No" answer, the "Remarks" column should (1) cross-reference either to the audit program step (or steps) which recognizes the weakness or to the supporting permanent file memorandum on accounting procedures which explains the mitigating circumstances or lack of importance of the item, and (2) indicate whether the item is to be included in the draft of the letter to management on internal control.

Co.	PART II – SPECIFIC APPLICATION QUESTIONNAIRE	Accountant		

Company _____ Period ended _____

Branch, division, or subsidiary_____

Question	Answer		
	Yes	No	Remarks *

C. Program and Processing Controls

General

Programs should be written to take the maximum advantage of the computer's ability to perform logical testing operations. In many cases, tests which could be employed are not used because the programmer does not know the logical limits of the data to be processed. Since the auditor will usually have a good knowledge of the proper limits of the data, he is in a position to detect weakness in program controls.

1. Is adequate control exercised to insure that all transactions received are processed by the computer?

(Note: The answer to one of the following two questions should be "yes.")

a. If predetermined batch control techniques are being used, does the computer accumulate matching batch totals in each run wherein the corresponding transactions are processed, and is there adequate provision for systematic comparison of computer totals with predetermined totals?

(Note: Having the computer internally match totals is more accurate than external visual matching. In addition, it should be noted that very often original batch totals are internally combined into pyramid summary totals as different types of input transactions are merged during progressive stages. This is acceptable if it does not create a serious problem in attempting to locate errors when the overall totals are compared.)

b. If no batch total process is in use, is there an effective substitute method to verify that all transactions are processed? (Example: Any application where source documents are serially numbered and the computer system checks for missing numbers.)

2. Is adequate use being made of the computer's ability to make logical data validity tests on important fields of information?

These tests may include:

a. Checking code or account numbers against a master file or table.

b. Use of self-checking numbers.

c. Specific amount or account tests.

d. Limit tests.

e. Testing for alpha or blanks in a numeric field.

f. Comparison of different fields within a record to see if they represent a valid combination of data.

g. Check for missing data.

*NOTE –   In the case of a "No" answer, the "Remarks" column should (1) cross-reference either to the audit program step (or steps) which recognizes the weakness or to the supporting permanent file memorandum on accounting procedures which explains the mitigating circumstances or lack of importance of the item, and (2) indicate whether the item is to be included in the draft of the letter to management on internal control.

PART II – SPECIFIC APPLICATION QUESTIONNAIRE

Accountant _____

Date _____

Company _____ Period ended _____

Branch, division, or subsidiary_____

Question	Yes	No	Answer Remarks *
3. Is sequence checking employed to verify sorting accuracy of *each* of the following:			
a. Transactions which were presorted before entry into the computer (sequence check on first input run)?			
b. Sequenced files (sequence check incorporated within processing logic that detects out–of–sequence condition when files are updated or otherwise processed)?			
4. Are internal header and trailer labels on magnetic media files (i.e., tape, disk, data cell) tested by the program?			
Such tests should include:			

a. Input
     1) Correct file identification
     2) Proper date
     3) Correct sequence of files
     4) Record count check
     5) Control and hash total check			

b. Output Retention date has passed.			
5. If processing requires more than 30 minutes of computer time for any one program, are there adequate provisions for restarting the program if processing is interrupted?			
D. Output Control			
General			
Output control is generally a process of checking if the operation of input control and program and processing controls has produced the proper result. The following controls should be in effect in most data processing operations:			
1. Are internal header and trailer labels written on all magnetic media files created as output?			
Header labels consist of an identification record which is written as the first record on each file. The labels normally contain:			

a. File identification (usually a code number)
   b. Date created
   c. File sequence number (for multiple reel or volume files)
   d. Retention date or period (used to determine the earliest date on which a file may be released for reuse)			

Trailer labels consist of a control record which is written as the last record on each file. These labels normally contain:			

a. Record count
   b. Control or hash totals for one or more fields
   c. End-of-file or end-of-reel code			

*NOTE – In the case of a "No" answer, the "Remarks" column should (1) cross-reference either to the audit program step (or steps) which recognizes the weakness or to the supporting permanent file memorandum on accounting procedures which explains the mitigating circumstances or lack of importance of the item, and (2) indicate whether the item is to be included in the draft of the letter to management on internal control.

PART II – SPECIFIC APPLICATION QUESTIONNAIRE

Accountant

Date

Company _____ Period ended _____

Branch, division, or subsidiary_____

Question	Answer		
	Yes	No	Remarks *
2. Are all control totals produced by the computer reconciled with predetermined totals? (Basically, control totals on input plus control totals on files to be updated should equal the control totals generated by the output.)			
3. Are control total reconciliations performed by persons independent of the department originating the information and the data processing department?			
4. Are error corrections and adjustments to the master file: a. Prepared by the serviced departments' personnel and b. Reviewed and approved by a responsible official who is independent of the data processing department?			
5. Are procedures adequate to insure that all authorized corrections are promptly and properly processed and that the corrections result in a file that matches the control totals?			
E. **File Control** **General** As data processing files (cards, tape, disk) can be destroyed by careless handling or improper processing, proper file control is vital in all data processing installations.			
1. Are control totals maintained on all files and are such totals verified each time the file is processed?			
2. Are all files supported by enough backup to permit the file to be recreated if it is destroyed during processing? (The kind of support required depends upon the type of the file. The most common types of backup are outlined below. In each case minimum control is being maintained if any of the support described is being provided. a. Card files Since each card in the file is an independent physical unit, processing damage will usually only effect a few cards which can be repunched. However, one safeguard should be employed. The retention period on source documents should be adequate to permit repunching of card files. b. Tape files Are all tape files subject to a minimum of son, father, grandfather support? (For example, if an updated accounts receivable tape is written every day, today's tape (son) should be supported by yesterday's tape (father), the day–before–yesterday's tape (grandfather), and all the transaction records which were used to update the files. Should today's tape be destroyed, the father tape and the transactions could be processed to recreate today's tape.)			

*NOTE – In the case of a "No" answer, the "Remarks" column should (1) cross-reference either to the audit program step (or steps) which recognizes the weakness or to the supporting permanent file memorandum on accounting procedures which explains the mitigating circumstances or lack of importance of the item, and (2) indicate whether the item is to be included in the draft of the letter to management on internal control.

PART II – SPECIFIC APPLICATION QUESTIONNAIRE

	Accountant
	Date

Company _____ Period ended _____

Branch, division, or subsidiary_____

Question	Answer		
	Yes	No	Remarks *

c. Disk files and mass storage files

File support can take many different forms. The following are typical of controls employed:

1) Is the file periodically dumped to magnetic tape and are all transaction records retained between dumps so files may be reconstructed?

2) If disk packs are used, are the disks supported on a son, father basis?

3) Is the file periodically dumped to cards or to the printer and are all transaction records retained between dumps so files may be reconstructed?

4) Are two copies of the file maintained on the disk with only one file being updated until the processing has been verified?

3. Are all files physically protected against damage by fire or other accidental damage?

This question may be answered "yes" if the following provisions have been made:

a. All files, supporting transaction files and programs should be stored in temperature and humidity controlled fireproof storage areas.

b. All important master files should be reproduced periodically and the duplicate copy should be stored off-premises. If this technique is not employed, some alternate form of master file protection should be employed.

4. Are there adequate provisions for periodic checking of the contents of master files by printout and review, checking against physical counts, comparison to underlying data, or other procedures?

*NOTE – In the case of a "No" answer, the "Remarks" column should (1) cross-reference either to the audit program step (or steps) which recognizes the weakness or to the supporting permanent file memorandum on accounting procedures which explains the mitigating circumstances or lack of importance of the item, and (2) indicate whether the item is to be included in the draft of the letter to management on internal control.

Test-Data Case Study

The EDP system reviewed and tested by auditors in this case study consists of an automated system that records labor transactions and processes the payroll in a major plant for a large manufacturer. This case study illustrates many of the points already discussed in the review and testing of internal control in an EDP system.

Summary of Labor-Recording System

Automatic time-recording devices are located throughout the shop areas. For the thousands of employees covered by this system, these devices completely replaced the human timekeepers and manually prepared time cards. Data from the system flows through to the company's payroll and job-order cost accounting and control records. Basic timekeeping tools are (1) the plastic employee badge, prepunched with identifying information, and (2) the job card, prepunched with the charge number and other information about a particular job.

The badge is permanently assigned to each employee. The job cards follow the parts or assemblies to be worked on. Exceptions are indirect labor and other special cards, which are located in racks adjacent to the input devices. Clock-in on reporting for work requires only insertion of the badge into the input devices and depression of certain keys. Check-in on a job requires insertion of the badge and one or more job cards, and depression of other keys.

All input devices are linked electrically to a central control box, a master clock, and an inline key punch that creates a punched card for each entry. The cards are converted to magnetic tape for passing through computer processes. The first of these, a match against an employee identification master tape, begins one-half hour after the beginning of each shift.

Within an hour after shift start, an exception report has been prepared for distribution to shop foremen. This report indicates absences, tardy clock-in, preshift overtime, and failure to check in on a job. Each exception must be approved by the shop foreman. Transactions accepted in this first processing routine plus transactions accepted for the remainder of the shift are "posted" to a direct-access file arranged by employee. Transactions rejected must be analyzed and corrected for reentry into the processing cycle.

All labor transactions for the day are read out into another magnetic tape that goes through a series of further computer processes:

- Preparation of final report to shop foremen. Again prepared for exceptions only, this shows overtime, early clock-out, and other items for approval by foremen.

- Daily report that balances job time by employee with time between clock-in and clock-out.

- Daily labor tape prepared after step 2.

- Matching a job transaction against a direct-access file of job numbers. This processing involves application of labor standards on certain jobs, accumulation of time by classification, and preparation of output tapes for numerous reports. These reports include daily reports of actual and budgeted time to certain shops, summary management reports by type of labor, and job status reports.

- Entry of the daily labor tape from step 3 above in another computer run for the payroll process.

Audit Approach

In pre-EDP days, an auditor was able to begin with either a payroll report or a labor distribution report and to trace individual time charges back through the system to underlying time cards or other source documents. This is obviously impossible when the labor transaction is initiated mechanically.

To evaluate this labor-recording and payroll system, the auditors decided upon a two-phase review:

1. Testing of actual transactions from their initiation through to final reports; the transactions were selected according to the normal testing of labor charges and employees' payroll records and paychecks.

2. Testing of the labor-recording and payroll system in normal operations by use of simulated, but realistic, transactions designed to test not only routine processing but also the various exception procedures.

Emphasis was placed on the second phase because it enabled many facets of the operation to be tested with only a small number of transactions. In designing the simulated transactions, the auditors made a thorough review of the client's system flowcharts and documentation describing the programmed controls. Also, inquiries were made of responsible persons about the various control points designed in the system.

Tests of Labor Recording

In testing the labor-recording system, 42 simulated transactions were developed, including these 13 that are especially significant:

1. Employee clocks in on time, works normally for full shift.
2. Employee checks in on job without clocking in.
3. Employee clocks in but fails to record a job transaction.
4. Employee is absent.
5. Employee is tardy.
6. Employee is tardy but within 3-minute "grace period" allowed.
7. Employee leaves before shift ends.
8. Employee leaves early but returns.
9. Night shift employee clocks in on day shift.
10. Employee works overtime into next shift.
11. Employee is loaned to a different shop.
12. Employee charges jobs improperly (for example, direct time charged as indirect time).
13. Employee uses transactor keys improperly when checking in on job.

Since the auditors desired to perform the test under normal operating conditions, using actual shop locations and job cards, the only simulated items necessary were a group of employee badges. The employee information was entered in the master records to agree with the badges.

Using the transactions outlined above, the test was carried out in two shops during normal working hours. Both day and night shifts were used. Data processing supervisors were made aware of the general nature of the test but not of the specific types of transactions being tested. Shop foremen were not informed until after they had questioned the simulated transactions that appeared as exceptions on attendance reports.

All transactions were traced through to reports that emerged from the data processing system on the same day and the following day. These included preliminary and final attendance exception reports, exception reports of erroneous job transactions, and the daily balance report of proper job and attendance transactions.

The auditors identified, with two exceptions, every simulated transaction as being processed properly and concluded that the system was functioning as it had been described to them. The two exceptions were system discrepancies.

The auditors made extended tests on a subsequent day to determine the reasons for these discrepancies. The first discrepancy resulted in the rejection of certain apparently proper transactions as exceptions. This happened because the client had previously made a change in "leave early" cards but had failed to collect all the superseded cards from the rack in the shop.

The second discrepancy was the result of a programming error. The program instructions said, in effect, "If the next-to-last employee in the processing cycle is an exception, do not process the last employee." Since the simulated employee master records used by the auditor were the last on the master file and since the simulated transaction for the next-to-last employee was an exception, the transactions for the last employee were not processed.

Tests of Payroll Processing

To test payroll processing, the auditors again designed simulated transactions to be processed with simulated employee payroll master records by the client's computer payroll programs. Payroll is processed by applying pay rates, included in the permanent portion of the employees' master payroll records, to the labor-hour transactions accumulated in the variable portion of the employees' master records. The labor is accumulated by employee for biweekly payroll processing and by job for weekly accounting distribution reports. The fixed portion of the master record includes, in addition to the pay rate, data such as name, social security number, number of tax exemptions, budget section, year-to-date amounts, vacation, and sick-leave hours. The variable portion contains earnings and deduction data resulting from payroll transactions processed. The variable section, of course, is cleared at the end of each payroll period.

In developing the transactions, the auditors first reviewed the client's flowcharts and other documentation that described the input formats, programmed controls, output, and exception reporting for all transactions processed by the computer payroll programs. They then reviewed the tests designed by the company's programmers to test the payroll programs. Many of the company's tests were selected by the auditors for inclusion in their tests. The auditors also formulated additional tests. All test transactions to be processed were then keypunched and listed in transaction number sequence. The nature and objective of each test was described on this transaction listing as an aid in reviewing and in subsequent debugging of the test processing. The listing was, of course, included in the work papers; 196 transactions were included in the test data, among them the following:

- Employee is hired on same day as terminated.
- Employee has rate change greater than programmed limit.
- Employee charges labor hours while on vacation.

- Employee is not entitled to bonus, charges bonus hours.
- Employee requests vacation hours exceeding vacation hours balance in master record.
- Employee charges labor hours exceeding the programmed limit.
- Terminated employee charges labor hours.
- Terminated employee requests cash advance.
- Employee has accumulated year-to-date earnings and FICA tax at taxable limit prior to processing of valid labor hours.
- Employee requests tax exemptions exceeding programmed limit.
- Valid employee charges normal labor hours.

The auditors requested, on a surprise basis, the client's computer programs from the EDP librarian. The reel serial numbers of the program tapes were then traced to the proper documentation in the EDP library. The auditors had previously reviewed the client's organization controls and EDP library procedures (physically and organizationally, the EDP library and programming activity were segregated). Based on this review, the auditors were assured that the client's regular computer programs were being obtained. The auditors then controlled the programs and the test data, observed the processing of the test data, and obtained the processing results.

Again, the results of processing proved highly satisfactory and enabled the auditor to evaluate properly the adequacy of the system of data processing and internal controls. The processing of the test data did disclose a few areas where programming changes would result in strengthened internal control. These program changes were largely concerned with input validity checks and reasonableness tests on incoming data. The tests also indicated that some documentation and some of the client's test data were no longer current.

As mentioned previously, the audit program also included some conventional tests of labor charges and employees' payroll records. The procedures included (1) reconciling payrolls paid with distributed labor, (2) tracing labor distribution from accounting entries to weekly and daily reports, and (3) tracing information from actual employee master records selected randomly to evidence supporting pay rates, exemptions, and all deductions.

Audit Software

The major audit software packages that have been developed are listed here.

FIRM	SOFTWARE	FIRM	SOFTWARE
Alexander Grant & Co. One First National Plaza Chicago, Ill. 60670	AUDASSIST	Dylakor Software Systems, Inc. 16255 Ventura Boulevard Encino, Calif. 91436	{ DYL–250 { DYL–260
Arthur Andersen & Co. 69 West Washingon Street Chicago, Ill. 60602	{ AUDEX { AUDEX 100	Cullinane Corporation Wellesley Office Park 20 William Street Wellesley, Mass. 02181	EDP–Auditor
U.S. Department of Commerce Springfield, Va. 22151	AUDIT	Department of Health, Education and Welfare Audit Agency Office of the Assistant Secretary, Comptroller 330 Independence Avenue, S.W. Washington, D.C. 20201	HEWCAS
Deloitte, Haskins & Sells 1114 Avenue of the Americas New York, N.Y. 10036	AUDITAPE		
Dataskil Reading Bridge House Reading, England	AUDITFIND	Informatics, Inc. 21050 Vanowen Street Canoga Park, Calif. 91303	MARK IV AUDIT
Coopers & Lybrand 1251 Avenue of the Americas New York, N.Y. 10020	AUDITPAK II	Computer Resources Corp. 23 Leroy Avenue Darien, Conn. 06820	PROBE
Program Products, Inc. 95 Chestnut Ridge Road Montvale, N.J. 07645	AUDIT ANALYZER	Programming Methods, Inc. 1301 Avenue of the Americas New York, N.Y. 10019	SCORE–AUDIT
Ernst & Whinney 1300 Union Commerce Building Cleveland, Ohio 44115	{ AUTRONIC–16 { AUTRONIC–32	Touche Ross & Co. 1633 Broadway New York, N.Y. 10019	STRATA
John Cullinane Corporation 20 William Street Wellesley, Mass. 02181	{ CARS { EDP AUDITOR	Peat, Marwick, Mitchell & Co. 345 Park Avenue New York, N.Y. 10022	S/2170

Savings and Loan Association Case Study

This case illustrates the problems and procedures of conducting a review of a service center that processes with standardized programs financial data for many savings and loan associations. The case study will describe the nature of the data processing service provided and the audit procedures performed in the review of the service center. The procedures described are those performed to review and evaluate the service center processing and internal control; additional audit procedures are necessary (and indeed performed) to validate data of the individual user organizations.

Description of the Data Processing System

The service center provides on-line processing and inquiry service for approximately thirty savings and loan associations in the region. The applications include the processing of all savings accounts as well as mortgage, collection, and passbook loan accounts. The processing results in the following reports by the association branch office and/or in summary for the association.

Savings Account Processing Reports

- A daily transaction listing in account number sequence or by sequence of entry for each teller, summary control balances, and exception listings including new and closed accounts, hold data, and transferred accounts.
- Weekly listings of name and address file changes.

- Monthly trial balance in account number sequence including anticipated dividends.
- Quarterly trial balance and printouts of account histories and dividends paid.
- Semiannual listings of employee accounts and of accounts over $15,000.
- Confirmation notices for outside audits.
- Annual proxy listings and 1,099 reports.

Mortgage Loan, Collection Loan, and Passbook Loan Processing Reports

- Daily transaction listing in account number sequence or by sequence of entry for each teller, summary control balances, and exception reports including payments other than contractual amounts, prepaid and paid-off loans, additions, and assumptions.
- Weekly listing of name and address file changes.
- Semimonthly delinquency reports and notices.
- Monthly reporting as follows: notices of contract collections; participation or serviced loan reports; borrowers' statements or bills and receipts; account trial balance; new loans; scheduled items; statistical analysis including average portfolio yield, dwelling types, geographic areas, and loan class.
- Quarterly trial balance and account history listing.
- Semiannual listings of employee accounts and confirmation notices (not to exceed 10 percent of accounts).
- Annual borrowers' summary statements, 1,099 reports, and escrow analyses.

The cost of the preceding services is levied according to the number of accounts involved and based on an annual charge specified in the contract.

Planning and Conducting the Audit

Development of auditing standards for the examination of financial statements of savings and loan associations, particularly those insured by the Federal Savings and Loan Insurance Corporation, has been a specialized endeavor. The earliest efforts to develop these standards were made in 1940 by a special committee of the American Institute of CPAs. The published industry audit guide *Audits of Savings and Loan Associations,* prepared and revised by that committee, has been reviewed and approved by the United States Savings and Loan League, the American Savings and Loan Institute, and the governmental regulatory agency, the Division of Examinations of the Federal Home Loan Bank Board. In addition, the FHLBB has issued its own set of auditing requirements specifying certain procedures as mandatory for acceptance of independent audits by the regulatory agency. Certain state regulatory agencies likewise have published guidelines for independent audits.

The following audit procedures are of importance when a savings and loan association is being serviced by a computer service center:

1. Count and reconciliation with the association's records of all cash on hand, teller cash, vault cash, and other cash items.

2. Trial balancing and proof to control accounts of subsidiary accounts covering loans, savings, and related reserves.

3. Direct mail confirmation of selected loan and savings accounts with the borrowers and savers. Initially, the regulatory agency required a minimum confirmation sample of 10 percent in number and amount of loan and savings accounts. This requirement has subsequently been changed so that the determination of confirmation sample size is left to the judgment of the auditor—a judgment based on his evaluation of internal control and other factors.

The three types of procedures discussed above are frequently performed on an unannounced basis at an interim date which may be different from the date of preparation of audited financial statements. It normally is not necessary that the performance date of these procedures coincide with the end of a month or accounting period of the association. All the above procedures have to be performed using the data of the individual savings and loan associations even though the data were processed by a centralized service center using standardized computer programs. The above procedures must be performed by the auditor of the individual association.

In addition, the examination must include a review of the association's system of internal control. The review should satisfy the auditor that there is a plan of organization providing appropriate segregation of functional responsibilities, along with a system of authorization and record procedures adequate to provide reasonable accounting control. The auditor must, of course, make sufficient tests of the system to determine that it was functioning effectively throughout the audit period.

The review of the association's system of internal control requires that the auditor be familiar with the features of the computer system utilized in the service center. The auditor should consider, as part of his internal control review of the association, a review of the elements of control that the service center maintains over subsidiary accounting records. Such a review is especially important in an on-line system where the initial recording of transactions is normally not fully documented.

The service center processed work for ten savings and loans that had the same auditing firm performing their annual examinations. Rather than visit the center ten times, each time reviewing one client's records, the auditors decided to conduct an overall system review that would cover all ten clients. Because processing was standardized, this approach was considered logical and effective. In addition, it seemed likely that auditors who handled the other savings and loans processed at the center could make use of the review conducted by the first firm in evaluating their clients' internal control system. Indeed, the audit firm that conducted the review made the working papers available to the auditors of the other savings and loans using the system. Of course, even after the review of the audit working papers on the system, the other auditors would, and did, perform additional procedures to evaluate the controls and validate the data of their client.

The audit objectives in the review of the service center were to (1) accomplish the internal control review requirements of savings and loan association audit engagements, (2) maximize the use of automation in performing other audit procedures, and (3) generally appraise the quality and reliability of computing service being received by savings and loan associations.

The auditors involved in performing a review of the service center developed and performed the following audit program:

1. Review of the overall controls of the service center—including organizational controls, processing controls, documentation practices, program change procedures, and file protection and security procedures. This review was conducted by using a questionnaire similar to the one included as Appendix B.

2. Detailed review of the savings and mortgage loan applications. This detailed review included preparation of systems flowcharts and analysis of programmed controls.

3. Processing of test data to determine the existence and effectiveness of the programmed controls.

4. Preparation of a report for other CPAs describing the internal control existing within the service center's on-line system over individual associations' programs and data.

Testing Approach

Step 3 above indicated that the auditors tested the system to determine that it was operating as it was represented to operate. Several methods exist for testing an on-line system, as is the case with most other mechanized systems. The auditors decided in favor of a test-data approach as opposed to selecting sample transactions and tracing them through the system or analyzing the processing afforded by transactions selected by a special program prepared for that purpose. The auditors made three observations:

1. Conventional manual testing methods of tracing selected sample transactions through the system could have been utilized. Normally, however,

the auditor uses a sample he considers representative. Because the system allows many types of transactions to be processed, and about 10 percent of the transaction types make up about 90 percent of the volume, it appeared probable that a very large sample would be required if it were to include all or most of the transaction types.

2. The number of transactions in the sample could be greatly reduced by using a computer program to scan the history files and select test transactions. However, this method could not be economically justified because definition of the sample selection program specifications would have included nearly all the elements of test-data preparation.

3. The test-data approach appeared economically justified, if considered over a period of years. The auditors realize the computer program is, within reasonable time limits, fixed. They also know the equipment is sufficiently reliable so that tests ascertaining that the program performs in a certain manner can be used as evidence that the program has consistently performed in the same way.

After deciding to test the system using the test-data approach, the auditors determined the scope of their testing and the methods of entering the tests into the system. The scope of the test transactions reflected the auditors' assessment of the system as represented to them and their experience in testing EDP systems. Because of the lack of complete documentation in the service center, the auditors prepared and processed transactions designed to test the system in considerable detail.

The alternatives regarding method of input were entry through the teller terminal of the service center and entry through teller terminals in one or more associations.

Using the service center's terminal would have required modification of association programs to allow access by this foreign terminal. Thus the auditors would have been testing the system logic but not the actual programs used by the associations. Furthermore, testing during normal operating hours could not have been accomplished.

The auditors decided to process selected transactions through the associations' terminals and examine the results. They felt that there were several positive attributes achieved by testing through association terminals, including these:

- Ability to test actual association programs
- No additional computer time requirements
- Ability to test the central system at sporadic intervals without service center awareness
- No necessity to prepare, modify, or control programs

So that the test would not affect the client's files and normal operating reports, the auditors processed the test transactions with simulated master records located in an unused portion of the service center's files.[1]

Report on Service Center

The auditors prepared a report, for use by other CPAs, describing the internal control review in the service center and controls in existence over the individual association's programs and data. The auditors making the review made the report and their work papers available to other CPA firms handling other savings and loan associations using the service center. These documents included the audit procedures and tests performed and the results thereof. The other auditors could, of course, use the report and work papers to evaluate their clients' internal control system, including the service center processing.

---

[1] For a detailed explanation of test data and the use of simulated master records, see Gordon B. Davis, *Auditing and EDP,* chap. 11, American Institute of Certified Public Accountants, 1968.

APPENDIX

Glossary

This glossary contains selected terms used in this book. Almost 85 percent of the entries in this glossary are taken or adapted from, with permission, the glossary contained in *AUERBACH Computer Technology Reports* published by AUERBACH Publishers, Inc. The AUERBACH glossary is one of the most readable glossaries available. The definitions of data base, dump, emulator, high order, OCR, record layout, RPG, storage protection, throughput, and utility program are taken from, with permission, William C. Mair, Donald R. Wood, and Keagle W. Davis, *Computer Control & Audit* (Institute of Internal Auditors, 1976, copyright © 1976 by Touche Ross & Co.).

Several different types of cross references are used. Their meanings are as follows:

- Same as—The referenced term has the same meaning as the term containing the reference and the referenced term is the preferred one.

- Synonymous with—The referenced term has the same meaning as the term containing the reference and the term containing the reference is the preferred one.

- Contrast with—The referenced term is a related term that has a meaning significantly different from that of the term containing the reference.

- See also—The referenced term is a related term whose definition provides additional background or clarification.

- See—The referenced term is an alternative or qualified form of the term containing the reference.

Access Time   The time interval between the instant when a computer or control unit calls for a transfer of data to or from a storage device and the instant when this operation is completed. Thus, access time is the sum of the waiting time and transfer time. Note: In some types of storage, such as disk and drum storage, the access time depends on the location specified and/or on preceding events; in other types, such as core storage, the access time is essentially constant.

Accounting Control   The plan of organization and the procedures and records that are concerned with the safeguarding of assets and the reliability of financial records. See also *control*.

Address   A name, numeral, or other reference that designates a particular location in a *store* or some other data source or destination. Note: Numerous types of addresses are employed in computer programming.

Address Modification   The process of changing the address part of a machine instruction.

Alphabet   An ordered set of *characters* used for the representation of sounds in a spoken language; in English, the twenty-six letters *A* through *Z*.

Alphameric   Same as *alphanumeric*.

Alphanumeric   Pertaining to a *character set* that includes both alphabetic characters (letters) and numeric characters (digits). Note: Most alphanumeric character sets also contain special characters.

Analysis, Systems   The examination of an activity, procedure, method, technique, or business to determine what must be accomplished and how the necessary operations may best be accomplished.

Arithmetic Unit   A section of a *computer* in which arithmetic, logical, and/or shift operations are performed.

Array   The use of computer elements to show relationships in one or more dimensions. In assembler programming, an array is a series of one or more values represented by a SET symbol.

Assembler Program   The assembler is an assembly program that accepts a symbolic-coding language. It is composed of simple, brief expressions that provide rapid translation from symbolic to machine-language relocatable-object coding for the computer. The assembly language includes a wide and sophisticated variety of operations that allow the fabrication of desired fields based on information generated at assembly time. The instruction-operation codes are assigned mnemonics that describe the hardware function of each instruction. Assembler-directive commands provide the programmer with the ability to generate data words and values based on specific conditions at assembly time.

Audio-Response Unit   Same as *voice-response unit*.

Audit Software   A collection of programs and routines associated with a computer that facilitates the programming and operation of the computer and the evaluation of machine-readable records for audit purposes. See also *computer-audit program*.

Audit Trail A means for systematically tracing the progress of specific items of data through the steps of a process (particularly from a machine-generated report or other output back to the original source document) in order to verify the validity and accuracy of the process.

Auditape An audit software package developed by Haskins & Sells. Probably the first one developed for audit purposes. Most of the major accounting firms have now developed audit software packages, some of which are available to interested parties. In addition, several commercial software companies have developed audit software packages.

Auditing The examination of information by a third party other than the preparer or the user with the intent of establishing its reliability and the reporting of the results of this examination with the expectation of increasing the usefulness of the information to the user. Specific purpose audits are conducted by specific types of auditors. See also *external auditor, internal auditor*.

Auxiliary Storage *Storage* that supplements a computer's *working storage*. Note: In general, the auxiliary storage has a much larger capacity but a longer *access time* than the working storage. Usually, the computer cannot access auxiliary storage directly for instructions or instruction operands.

Backup Pertaining to equipment or procedures that are available for use in the event of failure or overloading of the normally used equipment or procedures. Note: The provision of adequate backup facilities is an important factor in the design of every data processing system and is especially vital in the design of *real-time* systems, where a system failure may bring the total operations of a business to a virtual standstill.

Batch Processing A technique in which items to be processed are collected into groups (i.e., batched) to permit convenient and efficient processing. Note: Most business applications are of the batch-processing type; the records of all transactions affecting a particular master file are accumulated over a period of time (e.g., 1 day), then they are arranged in sequence and processed against the master file.

Batch Total A sum of a set of items that is used to check the accuracy of operations on a particular batch of records.

Batching The process of grouping a large number of transactions into small groups usually for control purposes. See also *batch total*.

BCD (Binary Coded Decimal) Pertaining to a method of representing each of the *decimal* digits 0 through 9 by a distinct group of *binary* digits. For example, in the 8–4–2–1 BCD notation, which is used in numerous digital computers, the decimal number 39 is represented as 0011 1001 (whereas in pure binary notation it would be represented as 100111).

Binary   Pertaining to the number system with a radix of 2, or to a characteristic or property involving a choice or condition in which there are two possibilities. Note: The binary number system is widely used in digital computers because most computer components (e.g., vacuum tubes, transistors, flip-flops, and magnetic cores) are essentially binary in that they have two stable states. Example: The binary numeral 1101 means: $(1 \times 2^3) + (1 \times 2^2) + (0 \times 2^1) + (1 \times 2^0)$, which is equivalent to decimal 13.

Binary Coded Decimal   See *BCD*.

Bit   A binary digit; a digit (0 or 1) in the representation of a number in *binary* notation.

Bits per Inch   See *BPI*.

Block   A group of words, characters, or digits that are held in one section of an input–output medium or store and handled as a unit, e.g., the data recorded on a punched card or the data recorded between two *interblock gaps* on a magnetic tape.

Block Diagram   A diagram of a system, instrument, computer, or *program* in which selected portions are represented by annotated boxes and interconnecting lines. Note: A *flowchart* is a special type of block diagram that shows the structure and general sequence of operations of a program or process.

Blocking   Combining two or more *records* into one *block*. Note: The principal purpose of blocking is to increase the efficiency of computer input and output operations. For example, the effective data-transfer rates of most magnetic tape units can be greatly increased by reducing the need for frequent tape stops and starts through combining multiple short records into blocks that are several thousand characters in length.

BPI (Bits per Inch)   A unit of measure used in discussing recording density. See also *recording density*.

Branch   (1) Same as *conditional transfer*. (2) A set of instructions that are executed between two successive conditional transfer instructions.

Buffer   A *storage* device used to compensate for differences in the rates of flow of data or in the times of occurrence of events when transmitting data from one device to another. For example, a buffer holding one line is associated with most *line printers* to compensate for the large difference between the high speed at which the computer can transmit data to the printer and the relatively low speed of the printing operation itself.

Card   Usually same as punched card; see also *edge-notched card, edge-punched card, magnetic card*.

Card Field   In a punched card, a group of columns (or parts of columns) whose punchings represent one item. For example, a three-column field might hold an item representing order quantity, whose value ranges from 000 to 999.

Central Processor   The unit of a *computer* system that includes the circuits which control the interpretation and execution of *instructions*. Synonymous with *CPU* (central processing unit) and *main frame*.

Change Register   Printout of the results of testing changes to a program. This register acts as a document for management review and approval of the change and as a permanent record of all changes to a program.

Channel   A path or group of parallel paths for carrying signals between a source and a destination. See also *input–output channel*.

Character   A member of a set of mutually distinct marks or signals used to represent *data*.

Character Set   A unique representation of characters established by a professional group or vendor to describe the characters represented or displayed by a computer system.

Check   A method or process for determining the accuracy of some aspect of processing, such as a hardware check or arithmetic check.

Check Bit   A binary *check digit*. Note: A *parity check* usually involves appending a check bit of the appropriate value to an array of bits.

Check Digit   A *digit* associated with a *word* or part of a word for the purpose of checking for the absence of certain classes of *errors*.

COBOL (COmmon Business Oriented Language)   A *process-oriented language* developed to facilitate the preparation and interchange of programs to perform business *data processing* functions. Every COBOL *source program* has four divisions, whose names and functions are as follows: (1) identification division identifies the source program and the output of a compilation; (2) environment division specifies those aspects of a data processing problem that are dependent upon the physical characteristics of a particular computer; (3) data division describes the data that the object program is to accept as input, manipulate, create, or produce as output; (4) procedure division specifies the procedures to be performed by the object program, by means of English-like statements such as SUBTRACT TAX FROM GROSS-PAY GIVING NET-PAY. PERFORM PROC-A THRU PROC-B UNTIL X IS GREATER THAN Y.

Code   A predefined method for specifying the way data is represented in a computer system.

Code Translation   The conversion of code from one format to another. For example, the conversion of code translated over a common carrier line to a code used by a computer.

Coder   An individual whose function is writing a computer program.

Coding   An ordered list or lists of the successive *instructions* that will cause a computer to perform a particular *process.*

Collator   A hardware device that can merge, match, or collate punched cards or other computer media.

Communication   The transfer of information from one person, place, or device to another. See also *data communications.*

Compiler   (1) A program that converts programmer statements into machine language. (2) A computer program that *compiles.* Note: Compilers are an important part of the basic *software* for most computers; they permit the use of *process-oriented languages* which can greatly reduce the human effort required to prepare computer programs. However, the computer time required to perform the compilation process may be excessive, and the object programs produced by the compiler usually require more execution time and more storage space than programs written in *machine language* or *symbolic coding.*

Compiles   The process of converting programmer statements into machine language.

Completeness Tests   A type of *program check* designed to test input for the prescribed amount of data in the input fields.

Computer   A device capable of solving problems by accepting *data,* performing prescribed *operations* on the data, and supplying the results of these operations, all without intervention by a human operator.

Computer-Audit Program   A computer program written for a specific audit purpose or procedure. A computer-audit program can be written by or under the supervision of the auditor for a specialized audit application (i.e., brokerage house auditing) or can be developed by adapting *audit software* routines for specific audit purposes.

Computer Operations   A function within an EDP department primarily concerned with the production of computer-processed information. With the computer at the hub, computer operations are primarily concerned with bringing data into the computer center, getting it to the computer, and delivering results to users at minimum costs.

Computer Operator Instructions   A set of instructions prepared by a programmer, as part of program *documentation,* for specific use by computer operators when operating programs. Synonymous with *console run book.* See also *operating system.*

Conditional Transfer   An instruction that may or may not cause a departure from the normal sequence of executing instructions depending upon the result of some *operation,* the contents of some register, or the setting of some indicator.

Configuration   A specific set of equipment units which are interconnected and (in the case of a computer) programmed to operate as a system. Thus, a computer configuration consists of one or more storage devices and one or more *input–output* devices. Synonymous with *system configuration*.

Console   A portion of a *computer* that is used for communication between operators or maintenance engineers and the computer, usually by means of displays and manual controls.

Console Log   See *log*.

Console Run Book   A book containing computer operator instructions for a run. Same as *computer operator instructions*.

Console Switch   See *switch*.

Control   The plan of organization and all the coordinate methods and procedures adopted within a business to safeguard its assets, check the accuracy and reliability of its accounting data, promote operational efficiency, and encourage adherence to prescribed managerial policies (AICPA definition). See also *accounting control*.

Control Log   A record of *control totals* used by the control function in an *EDP department* to enable the reconciliation of control totals generated in related computer processing runs.

Control Totals   Totals developed on important data fields in input records and on number of records processed to ensure that data have been transmitted, converted, and processed correctly. See also *batch total, hash total, record count*.

Control Unit   (1) A section of a *computer* that effects the retrieval of instructions in the proper sequence, interprets each instruction, and stimulates the proper circuits to execute each instruction. (2) A device that controls the operation of one or more units of peripheral equipment under the overall direction of the *central processor*.

CPU   Same as *central processor*.

Cross-Footing Check   A *program check* in computer processing in which individual items used in arriving at result items are totaled and the total is compared to an independently derived result total; for example, a total net pay figure reached by subtracting a deduction item total from a gross pay total can be compared with a total net pay figure developed by other program steps.

Cylinder   A collective term for the group of locations that can be accessed without physical movement of the read/write heads in a *random-access* storage device. Note: In a storage device in which all the heads move in unison, there will normally be one cylinder corresponding to each discrete position of the head mechanism.

Data   Any representation of a fact or idea in a form capable of being communicated or manipulated by some *process*. The representation may be more suitable for interpretation either by human beings (e.g., printed text) or by equipment (e.g., punched cards or electrical signals). Note: *Information,* a closely related term, is the meaning that human beings assign to data by means of the known conventions used in its representation.

Data Base   An integrated file containing multiple record types or segments that may be accessed in a nonsequential manner.

Data Communications   The transmission of data from one point to another.

Data Conversion   See *data transcription.*

Data Field   See *field.*

Data Movement   See *data transfer.*

Data Processing   A systematic sequence of *operations* performed upon *data* (e.g., handling, computing, merging, sorting, or any other transformation or rearrangement whose object is to extract information, revise the data, or alter their representation).

Data Structure   The manner in which *data* are represented and stored in a computer system or program.

Data Transcription   Conversion of *data* from one *medium* to another without alteration of their information content. Note: The conversion may be performed by a manual keystroke operation, by a computer system, or by a specialized converter, and may or may not involve changes in the format of the data.

Data Transfer   The movement of *data* from a source to a destination (e.g., from one storage location or device to another).

Data Transmission   See *data communications.*

Decimal   Pertaining to the number representation system within a radix of ten.

Decimal Digits   The characters zero through nine.

Decision Table   A table that lists all the contingencies to be considered in the description of a problem, together with the corresponding actions to be taken. Note: Decision tables permit complex decision-making criteria to be expressed in a concise and logical format. They are sometimes used in place of *flowcharts* for problem definition and documentation. Moreover, *compilers* have been written to convert decision tables into programs that can be executed by computers.

Deck   A grouping of computer media, such as a collection of punched cards.

Density   See *recording density.*

Detail File   A *file* containing information that is relatively transient, such as records of individual transactions that occurred during a particular period of time. Synonymous with *transaction file.* Contrast with *master file.*

Digit   A single character of information, usually synonymous with numerical characters zero through nine.

Direct Access   Same as *random access*.

Disk Storage   A type of *magnetic storage* that uses one or more rotating flat circular plates with a magnetic surface on which data can be stored by selective magnetization of portions of the surface.

Document   (1) A *medium* and the *data* recorded on it for use (e.g., a check, report sheet, or book). (2) By extension, any record that has permanence and can be read by man and/or machine.

Documentation   The collecting, organizing, storing, citing, and disseminating of *documents* or the *information* recorded in documents. Note: Complete, up-to-date documentation of all *programs* and their associated operating procedures is a necessity for efficient operation of a computer installation and maintenance of its programs.

Drum Storage   A type of *magnetic storage* that uses a rotating cylinder with a magnetic surface on which data can be stored by selective magnetization of portions of the surface.

Dump   A printed record of the contents of computer storage usually produced for diagnostic purposes.

Dynamic Relocation   The movement of part or all of an active (i.e., currently operating) program from one region of storage to another, with all necessary *address* references being adjusted to enable proper execution of the program to continue in its new location. Note: Dynamic relocation helps to ensure effective utilization of *working storage* in a *multiprogramming* environment.

EAM (Electrical Accounting Machine)   Pertaining to *data processing* equipment that is predominantly electromechanical such as *keypunches, collators,* mechanical *sorters,* and *tabulators.* Note: EAM equipment is still widely used in lieu of, or in support of, electronic digital computers. (The computers themselves are classified as *EDP* equipment rather than EAM equipment.)

EBCDIC (Extended Binary Coded Decimal Interchange Code)   An 8-bit *code* that represents an extension of a 6-bit BCD code that was widely used in computers of the first and second generations. Note: EBCDIC can represent up to 256 distinct characters and is the principal code used in many of the current computers.

Edge-Notched Card   A card of any size provided with a series of holes near one or more of its edges for use in coding information for a simple mechanical search technique. By notching away the edge of the card into a particular hole, the card can be coded to represent a particular item. Cards containing desired information can be selected from a deck by inserting a long needle into the appropriate hole position and lifting the deck, allowing notched cards to fall from the deck while un-notched cards remain.

Edge-Punched Card A card on which data can be recorded by punching holes, in patterns and codes similar to those used for *punched tape,* near one edge. Note: Many punched-tape readers and punches can be equipped to utilize edge-punched cards as well. *Unit records* can be stored and selectively retrieved more conveniently on edge-punched cards than on punched tape.

Edit (1) To modify the form or *format* of data. Editing may involve the rearrangement of data, the addition of data (e.g., insertion of dollar signs and decimal points), the deletion of data (e.g., suppression of leading zeros), *code translation,* and the control of layouts for printing (e.g., provision of headings and page numbers). (2) An input control technique used to detect input data that are incomplete, invalid, unreasonable, etc. Editing can be performed manually or by computer. See also *edit run.*

Edit Run A separate computer process to edit input data before regular processing of *detail files* and *master files* takes place.

EDP (Electronic Data Processing) *Data processing* performed largely by electronic equipment, such as electronic digital *computers.*

EDP Department This department is responsible for *systems analysis,* program development, and *computer operations.*

Electrical Accounting Machine See *EAM.*

Emulator A hardware device that enables a computer to execute object language programs written for a different computer design.

Error A discrepancy between a computed, measured, or observed quantity and the true, specified, or theoretically correct value or condition. Note: An error may result from an equipment fault or a human misake, but errors also arise from insufficient precision, which is foreseen and accepted.

Error Listing *Hard copy* of errors detected in the processing of data by *program checks* in *edit runs* or in regular processing.

Execute To carry out an *instruction* or an *operation,* or to run a *program.*

External Auditor Usually a CPA; typically involved in rendering an independent opinion on the reasonableness of an organization's financial representations.

External Label A specialized record used to identify an assorted collection of data, such as a paper label attached to a reel of magnetic tape to identify its contents. Contrast with *internal label.*

External Storage Data storage other than main storage; for example, storage on magnetic tape or direct access devices. Synonymous with auxiliary storage and secondary storage.

Field   (1) In a *punched card,* a group of columns whose punchings represent one *item.* (2) A subdivision of a computer *word* or *instruction,* (e.g., a group of bit positions within an instruction that hold an *address*). (3) A subdivision of a *record.*

File   A collection of related records, usually (but not necessarily) arranged in sequence according to a *key* contained in each record. Note: A *record,* in turn, is a collection of related items, while an *item* is an arbitrary quantity of data that are treated as a unit. Thus, in payroll processing, an employee's pay rate forms an item, all the items relating to one employee form a record, and the complete set of employee records forms a file.

File Maintenance   The updating of a *file* to reflect the effects of nonperiodic changes by adding, altering, or deleting *data* (e.g., the addition of new programs to a *program library* on magnetic tape).

File Processing   The periodic updating of a *master file* to reflect the effects of current data, often transaction data contained in a *detail file* (e.g., a weekly payroll run).

File-Protection Ring   A removable plastic or metal ring the presence or absence of which prevents an employee from writing on a magnetic tape and thereby prevents the accidental destruction of a magnetic tape file. Note: The most common method involves the insertion of the ring to allow writing and the removal of the ring to prevent writing.

Fixed-Length Record   A *record* that always contains the same number of characters. The restriction to a fixed length may be deliberate, in order to simplify and speed processing, or it may be dictated by the characteristics of the equipment used. Contrast with *variable-length record.*

Flowchart   A diagram that shows the structure and general sequence of operations of a *program* or *process* by means of symbols and interconnecting lines which represent operations, data, flow, and equipment.

Format   A predetermined arrangement of *data* (e.g., characters, items, lines), usually on a form or in a file.

FORTRAN (FORmula TRANslating System)   A *process-oriented language* designed to facilitate the preparation of computer programs to perform mathematical computations. The essential element of the FORTRAN language is the assignment statement; for example, $Z = X + Y$ causes the current values of the variables X and Y to be added together and causes their sum to replace the previous value of the variable Z.

Hard Copy   Pertaining to *documents* containing data printed by data processing equipment in a form suitable for permanent retention (e.g., printed reports, listings, and logs), as contrasted with "volatile" output such as data displayed on the screen of a cathode-ray tube.

Hardware   Physical equipment, such as mechanical, magnetic, electrical and electronic devices. Contrast with *software.*

Hash Total   A *control total* that can be used to establish the accuracy of processing whereby a total of data is made by adding values that would not normally be added together (e.g., the sum of a list of customer numbers).

Head   A hardware device that is used to read or write information to and from a storage medium.

Header Label   A machine-readable record at the beginning of a file containing data identifying the file and data used in file control.

High Order   The left-most digital within a number representing the highest order of magnitude in the number.

IDP (Integrated Data Processing)   Data processing by a system that coordinates a number of previously unconnected processes in order to improve overall efficiency by reducing or eliminating redundant data entry or processing operations. An example of IDP is a system in which data describing orders, production, and purchases are entered into a single processing scheme that combines the functions of scheduling, invoicing, inventory control, etc.

Index   (1) An ordered list of the contents of a *document, file,* or *storage* device, together with keys that can be used to locate or identify those contents. (2) To modify an *address* by adding or subtracting the contents of an *index register.*

Index Register   A *register* whose contents can be added to or subtracted from an *address* prior to or during the execution of an *instruction.* Note: Indexing (i.e., the use of index registers) is the most common form of *address modification* used in stored-program computers. Indexing can greatly simplify programming by facilitating the handling of *loops, arrays,* and other repetitive processes. Some computers have many index registers, some have only one, and others have none.

Information   The interpretation or meaning assigned to data by humans or the meaning of information through conventions.

Input   (1) The process of transferring *data* from *external storage* or *peripheral equipment* to *internal storage* (e.g., from punched cards or magnetic tape to core storage). (2) Data that are transferred to an input process. (3) Pertaining to an input process (e.g., input *channel,* input *medium*). (4) To perform an input process. (5) A signal received by a device or component. Note: As the above definitions indicate, *input* is the general term applied to any technique, device, or medium used to enter data into data processing equipment, and also to the data so entered.

Input–Output   A general term for the techniques, devices, and media used to communicate with data processing equipment and for the data involved in these communications. Depending upon the context, the term may mean either input *and* output or input *or* output. Synonymous with *I/O.*

Input–Output Channel A *channel* that transmits *input* data to, or *output* data from, a *computer*. Note: Usually a given channel can transmit data to or from only one peripheral device at a time. However, some current computers have *multiplexor channels,* each of which can service a number of simultaneously operating peripheral devices.

Instructions A specific command or task that will be performed by a specific statement or operation.

Integrated Data Processing See *IDP*.

Interblock Gap The distance between the end of one *block* and the beginning of the next block on a *magnetic tape*. The tape can be stopped and brought up to normal speed again in this distance, and no reading or writing is permitted in the interblock gap because the tape speed may be changing. Synonymous with *interrecord gap* and *record gap* (but use of these two terms is not recommended because of the important distinction between *blocks* and *records*).

Internal Auditor An auditor who is typically involved in appraising the accounting, financial, and operating controls within an organization in which he is employed and who renders the results of his appraisal to management.

Internal Label A record magnetically recorded on tape to identify its contents as an integral part of the program function. Contrast with *external label*. See also *header label*.

Internal Storage Storage controlled by the central processing unit of a computer, which is directly addressable by the computer programmer.

Interrecord Gap Same as *interblock gap*.

I/O Same as *input–output*.

Key Part of a grouping of information that is used to identify that group or record of information.

Keypunch A keyboard-actuated card punch. The punching in each column is determined by the key depressed by the operator.

Language A set of commands or rules that are used to represent actions or information to another individual or machine.

Library An organized collection of information for study and reference purposes. See also *program library*.

Line Printer A hardware device that can print a group of characters as a single unit, or at a single time.

Log A record of the operations of data processing equipment, which lists each job or run, the time it required, operator actions, and other pertinent data.

Loop A sequence of *instructions* that can be executed repetitively, usually with modified addresses or modified data values. Each repetition is called a cycle.

Machine Language A *language* that is used directly by a computer. Thus, a machine-language program is a set of instructions which a computer can directly recognize and execute, and which will cause it to perform a particular process.

Machine-Readable Pertaining to *data* represented in a form that can be sensed by a data processing machine (e.g., by a card reader, magnetic tape unit, or optical character reader).

Magnetic Card A thin, flexible card with a magnetic surface upon which *data* can be stored. Note: Some large-capacity *auxiliary storage* devices use a large number of magnetic cards, contained in interchangeable cartridges. One card at a time is extracted from the cartridge, transported to a read/write station where data are read and/or recorded and then returned to the cartridge.

Magnetic-Core Storage (1) A storage device consisting of magnetically permeable binary cells arrayed in a two-dimensional matrix. (A large storage unit contains many such matrices.) Each cell (core) is wire wound and may be polarized in either of two directions for the storage of one binary digit. The direction of polarization can be sensed by a wire running through the core. (2) The use of planes of magnetic cores; data and information are determined and represented by the positive or negative magnetic state of the core.

Magnetic Storage A device or medium that can store data by utilizing the magnetic properties of the storage medium or device.

Magnetic Tape A tape with a magnetic surface on off-line devices cannot be controlled by a computer except through human intervention.

Main Storage The addressable storage under the direct control of the central processing unit. This is normally the storage in which the program is located.

Master File A grouping of data that is relatively permanent or is considered to be the official authoritative records of an organization such as the customer master file or price master file.

Medium The material on which data is recorded, such as punched cards, magnetic tape, or diskette.

Multiplexor Channel A channel designated to operate with a number of I/O devices simultaneously. Such I/O devices can transfer records at the same time by interleaving items of data.

Multiprocessor A computer that is able to execute two or more computer programs simultaneously.

Multiprogramming A computer system that can process two or more computer programs concurrently by interleaving their execution.

Object Language The language or code into which a language is translated. For example, source code languages, such as COBOL, must be translated into object code languages, such as machine language, before they can be executed.

Off-Line Equipment not under the control of the central processing unit, for example, a printer.

On-Line Pertaining to equipment or devices that are in direct communication with the *central processor* of a computer system. Contrast with *off-line*. Note: On-line devices are usually under the direct control of the computer with which they are in communication.

Operating System An organized collection of routines and procedures for operating a computer. These routines and procedures will normally perform some or all of the following functions: (1) Scheduling, loading, initiating, and supervising the execution of *programs*. (2) Allocating storage, input–output units, and other facilities of the computer system. (3) Initiating and controlling input–output operations. (4) Handling errors and *restarts*. (5) Coordinating communications between the human operator and the computer system. (6) Maintaining a log of system operations. (7) Controlling operations in a *multiprogramming, multiprocessing,* or *time-sharing* mode.

Operation (1) A general term for *any* well-defined action. (2) The derivation of a unit of *data* (the "result") from one or more given units of data (the "operands") according to rules that completely specify the result for any permissible combination of values of the operands. (3) A *program* step undertaken or executed by a *computer* (e.g., addition, multiplication, comparison, shift, transfer).

Operation Code A code that is used to represent a specific operating command, normally means a machine language code.

Output (1) The process of transferring *data* from internal storage to external storage or to peripheral equipment (e.g., from core storage to magnetic tape or a printer). (2) Data that are transferred by an output process. (3) Pertaining to an output process (e.g., output *channel,* output *medium*). (4) To perform an output process. (5) A signal transmitted from a device or component. Note: As the above definitions indicate, *output* is the general term applied to any device or medium used to take data out of data processing equipment, and also to the data so transferred.

Overflow In an arithmetic operation, the generation of a quantity beyond the capacity of the register or storage location that is to receive the result.

Pack To store several short units of data in a single storage cell in such a way that the individual units can later be recovered (e.g., to store two 4-bit BCD digits in one 8-bit storage location or one magnetic tape row).

Parallel Processing Same as *multiprocessing*.

Table F.1

	Even Parity			Odd Parity		
Data bits	0	1	1	0	1	1
	0	1	0	0	1	0
	0	1	0	0	1	0
	0	1	1	0	1	1
	0	1	1	0	1	1
	1	1	0	1	1	0
Parity bit	1	0	1	0	1	0

Parity Bit   A *bit* (binary digit) that is appended to an array of bits to make the sum of all the 1-bits in the array either always even (even parity) or always odd (odd parity). For example, see Table F.1.

Parity Check   A *check* that tests whether the number of 1-bits in an array is either even (even parity check) or odd (odd parity check).

Peripheral Equipment   All the *input–output* units and *auxiliary storage* units of a computer system. Note: The *central processor* and its associated *working storage* and *control units* are the only parts of a computer system that are not considered peripheral equipment.

Process   A system of *operations* designed to solve a problem or lead to a particular result.

Process-Oriented Language   A *language* designed to permit convenient specification, in terms of procedural or algorithmic steps, or data processing or computational *processes.* Examples include ALGOL, *COBOL,* and *FORTRAN.*

Program   (1) A plan for solving a problem. (2) To devise a plan for solving a problem. (3) A computer routine, i.e., a set of *instructions* arranged in proper sequence to cause a *computer* to perform a particular *process.* (4) To write a computer routine.

Program Check   Tests in the program to determine the absence of certain classes of errors in input or for the correct performance of processing steps. The tests are carried out by a series of *instructions* in a *program.*

Program Department   The individuals, group, or department responsible for developing and implementing programs within an organization.

Program Flowchart   A *flowchart* diagramming the processing steps and logic of a computer program; contrast with *systems flowchart.*

Program Library   An organized collection of tested *programs,* together with sufficient *documentation* to permit their use by users other than their authors.

Program Run Manual   See *run manual*.

Program Segment   See *segment*.

Programmer   A person who devises *programs*. Note: The term *programmer* is most suitably applied to a person who is mainly involved in formulating programs, particularly at the level of *flowchart* preparation. A person mainly involved in the definition of problems is called an *analyst*, while a person mainly involved in converting programs into coding suitable for entry into a computer system is called a *coder*. In many organizations, all three of these functions are performed by programmers.

Programming Language   An unambiguous language used to express *programs* for a computer.

Punched Card   A card used for representing information by punching a pattern of holes in the card.

Punched Tape   A continuous stream of tape, usually paper, used to represent data through a pattern of punched holes in the tape.

Random Access   Pertaining to a *storage* device in which the *access time* is not significantly affected by the location of the data to be accessed; thus, any item of data that is stored on-line can be accessed within a relatively short time (usually less than 1 sec). Synonymous with *direct access*. Contrast with *serial access*.

Read/Write Head   A device used to read or write data on a storage medium.

Real-Time   (1) Pertaining to the actual time during which a physical process takes place. (2) Pertaining to a mode of operation in which the instance of occurrence of certain events in the system must satisfy restrictions determined by the occurrence of events in some other independent system. For example, real-time operation is essential in computers associated with process control systems, message switching systems, and reservation systems.

Record   A collection of related items of data. Note: A *file*, in turn, is a collection of related records. Thus, in payroll processing, an employee's pay rate forms an item, all the items relating to one employee form a record, and the complete set of employee records forms a file. See also *fixed-length record* and *variable-length record*.

Record Count   A count of the number of records in a file or the number of records processed by a program.

Record Gap   Same as *interblock gap*.

Record Layout   A diagram showing the nature, location, size, and format of fields within a record.

Record Mark   A *special character* used in some computers either to limit the number of characters in a data *transfer* operation or to separate blocked *records* on tape.

Recording Density   The number of useful *storage cells* per unit of length or area (e.g., the number of *rows* [or characters] per inch on a magnetic tape or punched tape, or the number of bits per inch on a single *track* of a tape or drum).

Recording Track   See *track*.

Register   A storage device used to contain a specific amount of data. Registers are frequently used to assist in the processing of computer instructions, such as for mathematics or movement of data.

Reproducer   A *punched-card* machine that has two separate card-feed paths, one equipped with a sensing station and the other with a punching station. Its basic function is to *copy* data from one *deck* of cards into another deck of cards in card-by-card fashion.

Rerun   To make another attempt to complete a job by executing all or part of the process again with the same or corrected inputs.

Rerun Point   A place in a *program* where its execution can be reestablished after an equipment failure or some other interruption. Note: At a rerun point, sufficient data have been recorded to permit a *restart* from that point in the event of a subsequent interruption. Thus the provision of rerun points at reasonable intervals can save computer time by making it unnecessary to rerun a program from the beginning whenever a run is interrupted.

Restart   To reestablish the execution of a *program* whose execution has been interrupted, using the data recorded at a *rerun point*.

RPG   Abbreviation for Report Program Generator. A high-level-source computer language designed particularly to facilitate the rapid preparation of reports.

Run   A performance of a specific *process* by a *computer* on a given set of *data,* i.e., the execution of one routine or of several routines which are linked to form one operating unit, during which little or no human intervention is required.

Run Book   The instructions provided the computer operator on how to execute a computer program or series of programs.

Run Manual   A manual documenting the processing system, program logic, controls, program changes, and operating instructions associated with a computer run.

Segment   One of the parts into which a program is divided by a *segmentation* process.

Segmentation   The division of a *program* into parts so that each part can be stored within a computer's *working storage* and contains the necessary linkages to other parts.

Each part thus formed is called a *segment*. Note: Segmentation makes it possible to execute programs that exceed the capacity of a computer's working storage; it is performed automatically by some *compilers*.

Self-Checking Number A numeral that contains redundant information (such as an appended check digit), which permits the numeral to be checked for accuracy after it has been transferred from one medium or device to another.

Sequence To arrange items so that they are in the order defined by some criterion of their keys. Note: Often the keys are groups of numbers or letters, and the items are arranged so that the keys of successive items are in numeric or alphabetic order.

Sequential Processing Same as *batch processing*.

Serial Access Pertaining to a *storage device* in which there is a sequential relationship between the *access times* to successive locations, as in the case of *magnetic tape*. Contrast with *random access*.

Software The collection of *programs* and routines associated with a *computer* (*compilers* and *operating systems*) which facilitate the programming and operation of the computer. Contrast with *hardware*.

Sorter A device used to resequence the order in which data is stored.

Source Document A document from which data are extracted, e.g., a document that contains typed or handwritten data to be keypunched.

Source Language A *language* that is an input to a *translation* process. Contrast with *object language*.

Source Program A *program* written in a *source language* (e.g., written in COBOL, FORTRAN, or symbolic coding for input to a compiler or assembler).

Special Character A character that is not a letter, numerical character, or a space indicator; for example, a dollar sign.

Storage A device in which data can be held. See *internal* and *external storage* for types cf storage devices.

Storage Protection A provision by the software to protect against unauthorized reading or writing between portions of storage.

Store (1) A device into which *data* can be inserted and retained, and from which the data can be obtained at a later time. (2) To insert or retain data in a storage device.

Stored-Program Computer A *computer* that, under control of *instructions* held in an internal *store*, can synthesize, alter, and store instructions as if they were data and can subsequently execute these new instructions. Thus a stored-program computer is capable of modifying its own *programs*, a feature that permits great flexibility and responsiveness to changing problem conditions.

Switch   (1) In a *program,* an *instruction* or parameter that causes selection of one or two or more alternative paths (i.e., sequences of instructions). The selection once made, persists until it is altered. (2) In *hardware,* a device that can be placed in one of two or more distinct settings by a human operator or an instruction.

Symbolic Address   A computer location of information that is represented in symbols rather than actual storage addresses.

Symbolic Coding   *Coding* that uses *machine instructions* with *symbolic addresses.* Note: The input to most assemblers is expressed in symbolic coding. Mnemonic *operation codes* are usually employed along with the symbolic addresses to further simplify the coding process. For example, a two-address instruction that subtracts an employee's taxes from his gross pay might be written SUB TAX GPAY.

System Configuration   (1) Same as *configuration.* (2) The rules for interconnecting the available equipment units that collectively define the range of possible configurations for a particular computer system.

Systems Analysis   The examination of an activity, procedure, method, technique, or business to determine what needs to be done and how it can best be accomplished.

Systems Flowchart   A flowchart diagramming the flow of work, documents, and operations in a data processing application.

Tabulator   A device used to process and total data. It uses primarily punched cards as the storage medium.

Telecommunications   The transmission of signals over long distances, such as by radio or telegraph. See also *data communications.*

Temporary Storage   Storage locations used by a *program* to store intermediate results that are generated and must be temporarily retained.

Terminal   A point or device in a system or communications network at which data can either enter or leave.

Test   Predetermined data used to run a complete system or program to establish its adequacy and reliability.

Test Data   See *tests.*

Throughput   Useful work performed by a computer system during a period of time.

Time Sharing   (1) The use of a given device by a number of other devices, programs, or human users, one at a time and in rapid succession. (2) A technique or system for furnishing computing services to multiple users simultaneously, while providing rapid responses to each of the users. Note: Time-sharing computer systems usually employ *multiprogramming* and/or *multiprocessing* techniques, and they are often capable of serving users at remote locations via a *data communications* network.

Track   That part of a data storage *medium* that is influenced by (or influences) one head (e.g., the ring-shaped portion of the surface of a drum associated with one nonmovable head, or one of several divisions, most commonly 7 or 9, running parallel to the edges of a magnetic tape).

Trailer Record   A *record* that follows another record or group of records and contains pertinent data related to that record or group of records.

Transaction File   Same as *detail file*.

Transfer   Changes the sequence in which computer instructions are performed. The point at which processing changes is frequently referred to as a *branch,* jump, or transfer.

Unit Records   A record that contains one complete grouping of information; commonly used with punched-card technology, with the punched card being the unit record.

Utility Program   A standard routine that performs a process required frequently such as sorting, merging, data transcription, printing, etc.

Variable-Length Record   A *record* that may contain a variable number of characters. Contrast with *fixed-length record*.

Voice-Response Unit   A device that accepts digitally coded input (usually from a computer) and converts it into machine-generated human-voice messages which can be transmitted over telephone lines. Usually the human-voice messages are replies to digital inquiries entered via push-button telephones.

Word   A grouping or character string of information considered to be a self-contained entity of information.

Working Storage   The storage locations in a computer that can be accessed directly for instructions used in arithmetic and logical operations. Synonymous with *main storage*.

APPENDIX

Bibliography

American Institute of Certified Public Accountants, *Statement of Auditing Standards No. 3, The Effects of EDP on the Auditor's Study and Evaluation of Internal Control,* New York, 1974.

——, *The Auditor's Study and Evaluation of Internal Control in EDP Systems,* New York, 1977.

——, *Audit Considerations in Electronic Fund Transfer Systems,* New York, 1978.

——, *Guidelines to Assess Computerized General Ledger and Financial Reporting Systems for Use in CPA Firms,* New York, 1979.

——, *Audit Approaches for a Computerized Inventory System,* New York, 1980.

Authur Andersen & Co., *A Guide for Studying and Evaluating Internal Accounting Controls,* Chicago, 1978.

AUERBACH Publishers, Inc., *EDP Auditing,* Pennsauken, NJ, 1978.

Burrill, Claude W., and Ellsworth, Leon W., *Modern Project Management: Foundations for Quality and Productivity,* Burrill-Ellsworth, Tenafly, NJ, 1980.

Canadian Institute of Chartered Accountants, *Computer Control Guidelines,* Toronto, Ontario, Canada, 1971.

——, *Computer Audit Guidelines,* Toronto, Ontario, Canada, 1975.

Davis, Gordon B.; Schaller, Carol A.; and Adams, Donald L., *Auditing & EDP,* 2d ed., American Institute of Certified Public Accountants, New York, 1981.

Davis, Keagle, and Perry, William E., *Auditing Computer Applications: A Basic Systematic Approach,* Ronald Press, New York, 1982.

EDP Auditors Foundation, *Control Objectives—1980,* Streamwood, IL, 1980.

FTP, Inc., *Auditing Computer Systems,* Port Jefferson Station, NY, 1977.

The Institute of Internal Auditors, *Hatching the EDP Audit Function,* Altamonte Springs, FL, 1975.

———, *Systems Auditability and Control—Audit Practices,* Altamonte Springs, FL, 1977.

———, *Systems Auditability and Control—Control Practices,* Altamonte Springs, FL, 1977.

———, *Systems Auditability and Control—Executive Report,* Altamonte Springs, FL, 1977.

———, *How to Acquire and Use Generalized Audit Software,* Altamonte Springs, FL, 1979.

Lott, Richard W., *Auditing the Data Processing Function,* American Management, New York, 1980.

Macchiverna, Paul R., *Auditing Corporate Data Processing Activities,* The Conference Board, New York, 1980.

Mair, William C.; Davis, Keagle; and Wood, Donald, *Computer Control and Audit,* The Institute of Internal Auditors, Altamonte Springs, FL, 1976.

Martin, James, *Principles of Data Base Management,* Prentice-Hall, Englewood Cliffs, NJ, 1976.

National Bureau of Standards, *Performance Assurance and Data Integrity Practices,* Washington, DC, 1978.

———, *Audit and Evaluation of Computer Security II: Systems Vulnerabilities and Controls,* Publication 500–57, Washington, DC, 1980.

The National Computing Centre, Ltd., *Where Next for Computer Security?,* Manchester, England, 1974.

Perry, William E., *Selecting EDP Audit Areas,* EDP Auditors Foundation, Carol Stream, IL, 1980.

———, *Auditing Data Systems,* EDP Auditors Foundation, Carol Stream, IL, 1981.

———, *EDP Audit Workpapers,* EDP Auditors Foundation, Carol Stream, IL, 1981.

———, *Planning EDP Audits,* EDP Auditors Foundation, Carol Stream, IL, 1981.

Sardinas, Joseph, and Burch, John G., *EDP Auditing: A Primer,* John Wiley & Sons, New York, 1981.

Sawyer, Lawrence B., *The Practice of Modern Internal Auditing,* 2d rev. ed., The Institute of Internal Auditors, Altamonte Springs, FL, 1981.

Thomas, A. J., and Douglas, I. J., *Audit of Computer Systems,* International Publications Service, 1981.

Weber, Robert A. G., *EDP Auditing: Conceptual Foundations and Practice,* McGraw-Hill, New York, 1981.

Wilkins, Barry J., *The Internal Auditor's Information Security Handbook,* The Institute of Internal Auditors, Altamonte Springs, FL, 1979.

INDEX